Communicating
About Health

Communicating About Health

Current Issues and Perspectives

FOURTH EDITION

Athena du Pré
University of West Florida

New York   Oxford
Oxford University Press

Oxford University Press is a department of the University of Oxford.
It furthers the University's objective of excellence in research,
scholarship, and education by publishing worldwide.

Oxford   New York
Auckland   Cape Town   Dar es Salaam   Hong Kong   Karachi
Kuala Lumpur   Madrid   Melbourne   Mexico City   Nairobi
New Delhi   Shanghai   Taipei   Toronto

With offices in
Argentina   Austria   Brazil   Chile   Czech Republic   France   Greece
Guatemala   Hungary   Italy   Japan   Poland   Portugal   Singapore
South Korea   Switzerland   Thailand   Turkey   Ukraine   Vietnam

For titles covered by Section 112 of the US Higher Education Opportunity
Act, please visit www.oup.com/us/he for the latest information about
pricing and alternate formats.

Published by Oxford University Press
198 Madison Avenue, New York, NY 10016
www.oup.com

Oxford is a registered trademark of Oxford University Press.

Library of Congress Cataloging-in-Publication Data
DuPré, Athena.
   Communicating about health : current issues and perspectives /
Athena du Pré.—4th ed.
       p. ; cm.
   Includes bibliographical references and index.
ISBN 978-0-19-999027-6 (main text : alk. paper)—
ISBN 978-0-19-999028-3 (instructor's manual/test bank : alk. paper)—
ISBN 978-0-19-999029-0 (companion website)
   I. Title. [DNLM: 1. Communication.   2. Delivery
of Health Care.   3. Health Promotion.   4. Interprofessional
Relations.   5. Professional–Patient Relations. W 84.1]
613—dc23   2012048977

Printing number: 9 8 7 6 5 4 3 2 1

Printed in the United States of America
on acid-free paper

Brief Contents

Contents

PART III

Social and Cultural Issues 131

CHAPTER SIX Diversity in Health Care 132

BOXES

CHAPTER TWELVE **Public Health Crises
and Health Care Reform 310**

BOXES

CHAPTER THIRTEEN **Planning Health
Promotion Campaigns 342**

CHAPTER FOURTEEN **Designing and Implementing Health Campaigns 365**

Preface

My fascination with health communication began with people who were generous enough to share their stories with me. I've been lucky to occupy roles in which the marvels of health care have played out before my eyes.

- As a health news reporter, I stood, awed, in the hospital room of a woman who invited me to be there when the bandages were removed from her eyes and she saw her children for the first time in 20 years.
- As director of hospital public relations, I met other remarkable people, including a 34-year-old police officer, nestled into the left side of a hospital bed in his parents' front room, the right side reserved for his faithful canine companion, Shep, who, along with hospice, provided warmth and comfort during the final joyful and sad months of his life.
- Years later, as a health communication researcher, I met a young woman who said, "If you have a minute, I have a remarkable story to tell you." Indeed, she did. It forever changed my feelings about dying and convinced me that, maybe, the connections between people both living and dead are never lost.
- One of my greatest privileges has been befriending Samantha Rodzwicz, who, despite being paralyzed from the neck down, is the one of the most dynamic, energetic, and brilliant people I have ever met. She is the teacher and I the student. (Sam is pictured in Chapter 8.)

Stories such as these occur every day in health settings. They're the reasons we do what we do—whether that be designing health campaigns, caring for patients, serving in leadership roles, researching and teaching health communication, or studying the issues so that we and our loved ones will be better prepared when we are the patients.

In this edition of *Communicating About Health: Current Issues and Perspectives* my objective is twofold: (1) to update coverage of the latest issues and research (and there is a lot of exciting news to cover) and (2) to give voice to the stories of people who live and embody the issues we study. If I have been successful, you will find this to be an insightful, rich, and thorough overview of health communication. My wish is that readers come away with sophisticated knowledge about current issues and research, a real-life appreciation of the human side of health care and advocacy, and practical strategies for communicating more effectively and ethically about health.

My Approach

Because health care is so dynamic and complex, it is difficult to keep up with everything. We feel we're doing well to stay up to date in any one sector. That's understandable. But it's also the greatest weakness in the system, and it can be a fatal flaw. We miss opportunities for innovative teamwork. Our efforts are often duplicative and contradictory. And we often don't see the larger patterns at work. As the great systems theorist Peter Senge (2006) observes, "*Structures of which we are unaware hold us prisoner*" (p. 93).

In health care, this often equates to mistakes and duplications, expensive care that might have been avoided, well-intentioned campaigns that don't work, and administrative oversight that is cumbersome and distracting rather than smooth, supportive, and integrated. Effective communication isn't a nicety. It's good medicine, and it's good business.

If I have done my job well, the book is readable enough to serve as an introduction to the field. But as feedback from experienced health professionals bears out, this is not a skim-the-surface book. It offers deeps insights that are helpful even for experienced practitioners and researchers. By the book's end, readers should be able to speak knowledgeably, not just about one aspect of health care, but about how the many pieces fit together and influence each other.

Intended Audience

This book is designed primarily for people pursuing careers in the health industry and those with a research interest in health communication. This includes caregivers, health care administrators, marketing and public relations professionals, media planners and producers, public health promoters, educators, human resources personnel, researchers, educators, and others.

It may seem that such a diverse audience could not be served by the same text, and that is true to some extent. By all means, read other works as well. Explore specialized texts. But my advice is to read this book first or alongside the others. It provides something that specific-interest books cannot—a revealing overview of how various professions, cultures, and current concerns converge in health care. I believe that, where health is concerned, understanding the big picture is as important as mastering a particular skill set. Your success will be enhanced if you are able to speak knowledgeably about current issues in the health care field overall. (And truth be told, I'm counting on you to address some of the challenges in health care.)

My Background

I have a professional and a theoretical interest in health communication. In recent years, I have devoted myself to teaching health communication, studying health transactions, consulting with health care organizations, and writing books and articles on the subject. Earlier in my career, I covered health news for newspaper and television audiences and supervised advertising and public relations for a large medical center. In these capacities, I wrote news stories, directed public health campaigns, designed advertising, produced a monthly television program about health issues, assisted in strategic planning and marketing efforts, and worked alongside health caregivers and administrators.

As a former journalist, I understand the difficulties in keeping the public informed, and I am uncomfortably aware that unethical practices sometimes degrade the value of what the media has to say. My experience in a health care organization reminds me of how challenging it is to maintain morale, encourage open communication, and adjust to market pressures. As a scholar and researcher, I appreciate more than ever how important and difficult it is to manage the multiple goals and diverse influences on health communication.

Together, these experiences make me especially sensitive to the weaknesses and strengths of health communication. It is impossible to observe (and be part of) health communication efforts and believe that they are all good or all bad. You will notice throughout the book that issues are described in terms of their potential advantages and drawbacks. For instance, public health promotion is an immensely valuable way to inform and motivate people. However, promoters must be careful to avoid stigmatizing ill persons and making people unnecessarily anxious. I believe communicators are most effective when they have given careful thought and ethical consideration to the communication strategies available to them.

Another result of studying and working in the health industry is my immense respect for the diverse people who comprise it. I am frustrated by scholars who criticize the actions of health professionals and patients without also acknowledging what they are up against—time limits, stress, overwhelming emotional demands, and so on. I believe health communication can be improved in many respects, but it's naive to call for reform or expect it to happen without understanding and modifying the factors that influence it. This book provides insight about many of those factors.

Strengths of the Book

Communicating About Health has several advantages. For one, it offers up-to-date coverage of issues and research. It describes how managed care, telemedicine, health care reform, the Internet, and other factors are changing the nature of health communication. More than most health communication texts, this one goes beyond research data to explain the larger social issues and policies that influence health care and health advocacy.

Second, this book provides extensive coverage of diversity in health care. It describes culturally diverse ways of thinking about health and healing and reveals how such factors as gender, age, and race influence health communication. Readers are able to look at health care through the eyes of caregivers, patients, administrators, health promoters, and others who contribute to the process.

Third, *Communicating About Health* is a useful guide for people interested in improving their health-related communication skills. It includes suggestions for encouraging patient participation, providing social support, listening, developing cultural competence, working in teams, designing health promotion campaigns, and more.

Fourth, this text situates health communication within the contexts of history, culture, and philosophy. This gives a depth of understanding and allows readers to grasp better the significance of health communication phenomena. For instance, evidence that doctors tend to dominate medical transactions takes on added importance when readers understand the influence of science and technology on medicine. By the same token, managed care comes into focus in light of the way health care has evolved in the United States.

Fifth, this book is designed to promote critical thinking and discussion. It poses ethical considerations, discussion questions, and is supported by an instructor's manual that presents a wide range of class activities and discussion-starters. Additionally, case studies and interviews with health professionals bring health communication to life.

In summary, *Communicating About Health* is much more than a literature review. It explores the diverse perspectives of people involved in health communication and shows how they blend and negotiate their ideas to create communication episodes. The book integrates research, theories, current issues, and real-life examples. This blend of information enables students to understand the implications of various communication phenomena. At the same time, readers learn how they can contribute to health communication in a positive way as professionals, patients, and researchers.

Features in the New Edition

A great deal has happened in the last few years, including passage of the Affordable Care Act and the proliferation of eHealth. At the same time, research and theory continue to evolve, embracing a broader range of perspectives than in the early days of the discipline. This edition includes references to more than 400 works not cited in the third edition. To preserve the readable flow and overall length of the book, I have moved coverage of some material to the instructor's manual. (A detailed list of those changes appears in the manual.) Following is an outline of what appears in this edition.

Enhanced Features

I have preserved and enhanced features that were popular in previous editions, including the following:

- *Theoretical Foundations* segments in each chapter showcase important theories relevant to health communication.
- *Resource* lists suggest articles, books, organizations, and other means to continue exploring communication issues. In addition, new *Check It Out!* sidebars provide quick links to video footage and other resources.
- *Perspectives* boxes describe actual episodes of health communication as described by patients, professionals, family members, health care leaders, and others.
- *Communication Skill Builder* sections feature practical strategies for communicating with patients and caregivers, avoiding burnout, stimulating teamwork, designing public health campaigns, and more.
- *Career Opportunities* boxes throughout the book showcase professional options related to health communication, along with links to more information and job listings. This edition includes information about more than 125 careers.
- *Ethical Considerations* boxes present the pros and cons of issues such as paternalism, privacy, the politics of prevention, health care rationing, and more.
- *Can You Guess?* sidebars challenge readers to consider questions such as "Which state has the highest percentage of uninsured residents?" and "In which country do people have the longest life expectancy on earth?"
- An *Instructor's Manual*, available both in print and online at www.oup.com/us/dupre, features sample syllabi, test questions, class activities, audiovisual materials, and more.

New to the Fourth Edition

The following features are presented for the first time.

- A new chapter titled *eHealth, mHealth, and Telemedicine* describes the global impact of smart-phone and tablet technology, tailored health messages, and the Internet. You'll read about innovative efforts to use technology in ways never imagined just a few years ago.
- A new chapter titled *Health Care Administration, Human Resources, Marketing, and PR* provides in-depth coverage about the contributions and communication strategies involved in leadership, morale, service excellence, community engagement, and more—facets of health communication that affect everyone in health care. Coverage includes the latest theories and stories from professionals in the field. (The new chapters replace Chapters 9 and 10 of the third edition.)
- This edition includes a greater emphasis on both *theory* and *narrative*. I am indebted to reviewers who encouraged this combination. It turns out to be a powerful blend of depth and vivid detail.
- This edition expands coverage of communication involving *nonphysician caregivers*. As research has progressed, we know more about the communication issues affecting pharmacists, allied health personnel, dentists, therapists, and others.
- The new edition features a different format that allows for sidebar features (*In Your Experience, What Do You Think?, Check It Out!,* and so on) that stimulate critical thinking and discussion, not just at the end of the chapter, but as readers explore the text. The new look also includes more photos and graphics.

With this brief overview in mind, here is a more detailed look at components of the book.

Part I: Establishing a Context for Health Communication

The first two chapters provide an introduction to health communication. Chapter 1 establishes the nature and definition of health communication, current issues, and important reasons to study health communication. It also provides tips for making the most of features such as *Ethical Considerations, Theoretical Foundations,* and *Career Opportunities* boxes that appear throughout the book.

Chapter 2 provides an account of how health has been shaped by centuries of philosophy and scientific discovery. Understanding these issues allows for deeper appreciation of topics described in the rest of the book. The chapter culminates with a description of current issues in health care. The section on managed care is updated to describe the array of new options available.

Part II: The Roles of Patients and Caregivers

Part II focuses on interpersonal communication between patients and professional caregivers. Chapter 3 describes patient–caregiver communication in terms of who talks, who listens, and how medical decisions are made. It features a broader array of caregivers than in the past, thanks to emerging research about nurses, pharmacists, paramedics, physical therapists, technicians, and others. A new segment focuses on the philosophy and practices of narrative medicine. The chapter also includes an expanded discussion of power differences and communication as a collaborative interpretation, as well as updated coverage about the link between poor communication and malpractice lawsuits, the value of communication in reducing pain, and additional tips for engaging in motivational interviewing. The chapter also includes a list of journals relevant to health communication and career opportunities for people with expertise in health communication research. Integrative health theory, previously covered in Chapter 5, is now in this chapter, along with a new feature on the disclosure decision-making model. (Coverage of telemedicine now appears in Chapter 9.)

Chapter 4 examines health communication through patients' eyes, considering what motivates patients, what they like and do not like about health care, and how they express themselves in health encounters. This edition looks closely at how communication is influenced by the nature of an illness, patient disposition, and threats to personal identity. It includes information about communication skills training for patients and additional information about patient narratives, self-advocacy, and individuals' willingness to communicate about health. The chapter also includes new resources and career information for people who wish to serve as patient advocates. (I swapped the order of Chapters 4 and 5 in this edition so that readers may begin with patients' perspective, which is probably where most of us begin to understand health care.)

In Chapter 5, readers view health from the perspective of professional caregivers. As in Chapter 3, coverage includes a broader array of caregivers. The chapter describes the rewards of caregiving as well as the stress, competition, time limits, and self-doubt that often influence how caregivers communicate. A new segment examines the organizational factors that influence caregivers and spotlights a medical center that revolutionized patients' experience based on a Japanese-inspired model. The chapter features updated coverage of tips for communicating with difficult patients, communicating when time is limited, and disclosing medical mistakes. Interdisciplinary teamwork, previously covered in another chapter, was enhanced and moved here. Career information is expanded to cover more than 30 jobs in medicine, dentistry, nursing, and allied health.

Part III: Social and Cultural Issues

Chapter 6, Diversity in Health Care, was expanded from coverage about diverse patients to include diversity among health professionals as well. It presents information and tips on communicating effectively with patients who differ in terms of social status, gender, sexual orientation, race, language, ability, or age. The chapter also presents the latest figures on gender and racial representation among medical professionals, which lags behind diversity in the broader population. The section on health literacy is substantially updated and is followed by tips for serving marginalized populations. Case studies describe the experiences of a Spanish-speaking woman in an English-speaking hospital and a college student coping with a physical disability. The chapter features career information for diversity officers, interpreters, and Equal Employment Opportunity personnel.

Chapter 7 describes social and cultural conceptions of health and healing. It describes the increasing importance of focusing on global health and creating intercultural teams. Coverage of holistic medicine now appears in this chapter. The chapter also includes updated coverage about the health beliefs of Asians and Pacific Islanders, as well as Hispanic and Arab cultures, and a new sidebar contrasting Eastern and Western ideas about health. Coverage highlights the importance of cultural competence, examines culturally diverse ways of defining health, and describes the different roles patients and caregivers may be expected to play. The chapter includes a feature about the theory of health as expanded consciousness and suggestions for communicating more effectively across cultural lines. (The order of Chapters 7 and 8 is swapped in this edition.)

Part IV: Coping and Health Resources

Part IV focuses on the array of resources we may use to maintain and regain health, and when that isn't possible, to cope at the end of life.

Chapter 8 illustrates the importance of social support and provides tips for supportive communication. This edition features updated coverage about the role of communication in family caregiving and end-of-life experiences. A new section examines instances of social support "gone wrong"—episodes in which people's efforts to help actually hurt, and how we can avoid making the same mistakes. Another new section explores the notion of animals as supportive companions. The chapter includes an expanded discussion about theories that explain how and why social support is important to coping and good health. It also includes sections on transformative health care experiences and organ donation decisions. A *Career Opportunities* box showcases careers in social services and mental health.

Chapter 9, a new chapter, focuses on eHealth, mHealth, and telemedicine. It presents new evidence that, around the world, more people now have mobile technology than have electricity in their homes. We will explore how health communication specialists are trying to make the most of this new information resource to benefit big-city dwellers and people in the most remote regions of the world. The chapter addresses such questions as *Why and under what circumstances do people seek electronic health information? Is eHealth information mostly helpful or counterproductive?* and *How does eHealth communication compare with face-to-face transactions?* Theorists and researchers reflect on the implications of Web 2.0, the ability for people to actively create and share information with worldwide audiences. You will read about the profile of a typical ePatient and see how telemedicine is shrinking the distance between patients and providers in different locations. Information about medical information and technology careers is presented.

Part V: Communication in Health Care Organizations

Chapter 10 has been revamped to focus on the role of communication in health care administration, human resources, marketing, and public relations. You will follow a health care administrator in charge of marketing, public relations, and crisis management through the fascinating challenges that come up when one's job is to handle the unexpected, often while the cameras are running. The chapter is loaded with useful theories and expert tips for being a servant leader, promoting a shared vision, working in teams, and rewriting the rules by which health care organizations operate. It culminates with tips for service excellence from some of the best medical centers in the world.

Part VI: Media, Public Policy, and Health Promotion

Chapter 11 provides the latest information about health images in advertising, news, and entertainment. It features expanded discussions of direct-to-consumer drug advertising and media influences on obesity, alcohol and tobacco use, and body image. The chapter also includes a section on the international impact of entertainment-education and information about careers in health journalism. It includes tips for reporting health news, using interactive media to present health information, and developing media literacy.

Chapter 12 focuses on public health, crisis, and health care reform. The chapter opens with a series of mini-case studies about mad cow disease, AIDS, SARS, anthrax, and avian flu, presenting lessons about risk and crisis communication from each of these experiences. The chapter includes

a discussion of public health and an up-to-date exploration of health care reform, including the Patient Protection and Affordable Care Act of 2010 and a survey of health care models around the globe. Readers will learn more about universal coverage, multi- and single-payer systems, play-or-pay provisions, individual mandates, and more. A *Career Opportunities* box features information about careers in public health.

Chapters 13 and 14 guide readers through the creation and evaluation of public health campaigns. Both chapters include campaign exemplars and sample PSAs, as well as expanded coverage of campaign design resources and message framing. An updated section discusses the lessons of the critical-cultural approach as we contemplate the ethics of persuading people in diverse cultures to change health-related behaviors. These chapters showcase careers in health promotion and health campaign design.

Acknowledgments

A great number of people have contributed to the creation of this text. My first thanks go to Mark Haynes, Peter Labella, Erin Brown, Caitlin Kaufman, Grace Ross, Keith Faivre, and their colleagues at Oxford University Press for their remarkable guidance, enthusiasm, and good humor. I am also grateful to the following reviewers who suggested ideas for this edition:

Mariaelena Bartesaghi, *University of South Florida*
Maria Brann, *West Virginia University*
Ellen R. Cohn, *University of Pittsburgh*
Randa Garden, *Wayne State College*
Chris R. Morse, *Bryant University*
Loretta L. Pecchioni, *Louisiana State University*
Richard L. Street, Jr., *Texas A&M University*
Julie E. Volkman, *Emerson College*
Ken Watkins, *University of South Carolina*
Elaine Wittenberg-Lyles, *University of Kentucky*
Debra L. Worthington, *Auburn University*
Jill Yamasaki, *University of Houston*

I continue to be grateful, as well, to those who have edited and reviewed previous editions, including Peter Labella, Nanette Giles, Holly

Allen, Mariaelena Bartesaghi, Ellen Cohn, Michael Dennis, Stephen Haas, Amy Hedman, Haywood Joiner, JJ McIntyre, Jill O'Brien, Jim Query, Pam Secklin, Jiunn-Jye Sheu, Juliann C. Scholl, Sharlene Thompson, Kandi Walker, Catherine Woells, Kevin Wright, Mary L. Brown, Rebecca Cline, June Flora, Stephen Hines, Katherine Miller, Donna Pawlowski, Rajiv N. Rimal, Claire F. Sullivan, Teresa Thompson, Monique Mitchell Turner, and Gust A. Yep.

I would also like to thank colleagues and students who have contributed ideas, narratives, and feedback, most notably Jennifer Terry, Susanne Fillmore, Dawn Murray, Praewa Tanuthep, Beverly Davis Willi, Jennifer Seneca, Lori Juneau, Stefanie Howell, Melanie Barnes, Amy Jenkins, Bridget King, Micah Nickens, Samantha Olivier, Gwynné Williams, Brittany Jay, Dustin Saulmon, Vickie Payne, Chris Thomas, Nicole Yeakos, Drew Bryson, and Evelyn Briere.

I owe heartfelt thanks to Grant Brown, who inspired me throughout the process, and to Ken Brown, M.D., who served as my advisor on medical details, managed care, and many aspects of health care administration.

As always, I am indebted to mentors Sandy Ragan, Sonia Crandall, Jon Nussbaum, and the late Larry Wieder and Jung-Sook Lee. Heartfelt thanks also to Betty Adams and Cris Berard, who will always be the kind editors in my head. Finally, to Ron and my family (Jordan, Hannah, Ginger, Ed, Sarah, Andrew, Dale), who accommodated the many hours devoted to this project and provided endless support, I am deeply grateful.

Establishing a Context for Health Communication

There are decades when nothing happens; and there are weeks when decades happen.

—VLADIMIR ILYICH LENIN

In the last few years, decades of talking about health care reform burst forth to claim a space in daily conversation and news coverage. Passage of the Patient Protection and Affordable Care Act (Obamacare) in 2010 opened the way for the United States to become the last industrialized nation to offer health coverage to all citizens. As with any decision of this magnitude, it incited a mixture of controversy, optimism, concern, joy, and renunciation. No matter which of these describes your reactions, one thing is certain: It is an exciting time to study health communication. To contribute in meaningful ways, we must be up-to-date, well informed, and aware of the big picture. This section lays the groundwork for that. You can read the rest of the book in any order you like, but start here. In Chapters 1 and 2, you'll learn about the philosophical and historical journey that has led us to the current moment. Understanding that journey makes it easier to envision the future—and ways that we can make a difference in it.

CHAPTER ONE

Introduction

"COMPASSION IN A BAG"

This is a good day in the hospital. Tracy Porter marvels at the sight of her newborn grandson, Kingston James, in his car seat, ready to go home. "He looks so small in that!" she exclaims.

In some ways, this experience is a world away from a different hospital experience years ago, when Porter received "the call." It was from a friend of her son, Justin, then 16 years old, letting her know that Justin had been in an automobile accident and was on his way to the hospital. A 911 operator helped a frantic Porter identify the hospital and connect with a trauma surgeon there, who told her, "He's life-critical. You need to get here right away."

Anyone who has received such a call knows the feeling. Shock and adrenaline collide in a way that makes it hard to breathe. Only one thing seems certain, and it's a blinding, overwhelming imperative—you must get to your loved one's side as quickly as possible. You don't pack a bag, you don't grab your toothbrush, you don't think. You just go.

That seems far removed from this happy day. For one thing, Kingston's birth is a joyous, much-anticipated occasion. The newborn nursery seems a million miles from the trauma unit. And Justin—who lay comatose with a traumatic brain injury in 2004—is, today, a proud, first-time father.

But the distance isn't essentially so great. Determined that no one should feel as alone as she did back then, Porter carries a phone that connects her, via a hotline, with families who have themselves just received "the call" and need to talk with someone who has been through the same thing. And just across town—indeed all across the state—the nonprofit program that Porter began as a result of her family's experience is in full swing. The program is called Totes of Comfort & Hope. It ensures that the families of patients with brain injuries receive a free bag with the items people need but don't grab in a crisis—a soft pillow and blanket, toiletries, items such as playing cards to fill the time, and, perhaps most important, easy-to-understand information about traumatic brain injuries and related resources. The program operates in all 27 trauma units in Florida, thanks to Porter's efforts to raise money through donations.

Justin East and his mother, Tracy Porter, celebrate the birth of his son, Kingston James, 8 years after a traumatic brain injury nearly cost Justin's life. Today, the mother-son duo makes frequent public appearances to talk about the importance of safe driving and to raise awareness about traumatic brain injuries. (Photo by Brooke A. Page)

We'll return to Porter's story throughout the chapter to learn more about her family's experiences with health communication. But, first, let's consider: *How many instances of health-related communication can you identify in her real-life example?* There's the call from a friend, the conversation with the surgeon, Porter's contact with families in need, the printed material in the tote bags. And don't forget the bags themselves.

"Sometimes, giving someone a tangible thing takes the place of spoken words," says Porter. "Dr. Tepas calls it compassion in a bag." (Joseph Tepas III is a pediatric surgeon and a board member for the Totes of Comport & Hope Program.)

Episodes like this one remind us that we are all involved in health communication. Our ideas about health are influenced by health care professionals, friends, family members, coworkers, educators, advertisers, entertainers, public health promoters, and many others. Television medical dramas influence what people expect from actual health care encounters. At the same time, we influence the people around us with our own actions and thoughts about health.

In this chapter, we will consider what health and health communication are all about. We will

CHECK IT OUT! To read more about Totes of Comfort & Hope, watch a video about the program, and see how you might help or launch a similar program where you are, visit http://www.800tbihope.org/Home.html.

 WHAT DO YOU THINK?
Off the top of your head, define what *health* means to you. Then keep reading to see how your definition compares to that of the World Health Organization. In Chapter 7, we'll examine different ways of viewing health in cultures around the world.

examine philosophical perspectives of health and healing. Then we will focus on the importance of studying how and why people communicate as they do about health. The chapter concludes with a look at current issues that underline the importance of understanding health communication—whether one is a patient or a professional, a clinician or someone involved in leadership, technology, education, public health, advocacy, or one of the other roles integral to health care. (See Box 1.1 for a list of health-related careers featured throughout the book.)

The Philosophy Behind This Book

It's an exciting and challenging time to be involved with health. Perhaps more than ever before, health care leaders are open to innovative ideas. They are also facing critical challenges—to control costs, attract clients, earn employees' loyalty, and more. The changes are both destabilizing and exciting. In Richard T. Pascale's (1999) terms, it can sometimes feel like "surfing the edge of chaos" (p. 198). The good news is that disequilibrium opens the field to new ways of thinking and behaving. People involved with health care today have the potential to reshape and improve the system. In Chapter 10 we'll discuss innovative

BOX 1.1   CAREER OPPORTUNITIES

Profiles of More Than 125 Health-Related Jobs

Career boxes throughout the book showcase careers related to health and health care. Each box provides links where you can find more information and job listings. Here is a list of jobs profiled in each chapter.

CHAPTER 3
RESEARCH/EDUCATION
Consultant
Professor
Researcher

CHAPTER 4
PATIENT ADVOCACY
Case manager
Patient advocate
Patient care coordinator
Patient navigator
Social worker

CHAPTER 5
CAREGIVERS
Clinical laboratory assistant
Dental assistant
Dental hygienist
Dentist
Doctor of osteopathic medicine
Emergency medical technician
Hospitalist
Licensed practical nurse
Medical records technician
Medical doctor
Nurse practitioner
Occupational health/safety technician
Occupational therapist
Pharmacist
Pharmacy technician
Physical therapist
Physician assistant
Psychiatric technician or aide
Psychiatrist
Psychologist
Radiology technologist
Recreational therapist

Registered nurse
Respiratory therapist
Speech-language therapist
Surgeon
Surgical technologist

CHAPTER 6
DIVERSITY
Diversity officer
Health care interpreter
Equal Employment Opportunity (EEO) officer

CHAPTER 7
HOLISTIC MEDICINE
Acupuncturist
Chiropractor
Holistic nurse
Massage therapist
Midwife
Naturopathic physician
Nutritionist/dietician
Reiki practitioner
Yoga instructor

CHAPTER 8
MENTAL HEALTH
Mental health counselor
Social worker
Psychologist
Social service manager
Hospice/palliative care provider
Home health aide
Senior citizen services providers

CHAPTER 9
MEDICAL TECHNOLOGY
Computer and information systems manager
Health information administrator or technician
Software developer

CHAPTER 10
HEALTH CARE ADMINISTRATION
Chief financial officer
Chief operating officer
Departmental director
Director of human resources

Health information manager
Medical director
Medical office manager
Nursing director
President or CEO
Strategic planning director

HEALTH CARE HUMAN RESOURCES
Compensation and benefits manager
Customer service representative
Human resource manager
Recruiter
Training and development specialist

HEALTH CARE MARKETING AND PUBLIC RELATIONS
Advertising designer
Community services director
In-house communication director
Marketing professional
Pharmaceutical sales representative
Physician marketing coordinator
Public relations professional
Strategic planning manager

CHAPTER 11
HEALTH JOURNALISM
Health news editor/reporter
Health publication editor
Journal or magazine editor
Media relations specialist
Nonprofit organization publicity manager

CHAPTER 12
PUBLIC HEALTH
Business or billing manager
Communication specialist
Emergency management director
Environmentalist

Epidemiologist
Fundraiser
Health campaign designer
Health department administrator
Health educator
Health inspector
Health researcher
Media relations professional
Nonprofit organization director
Nutritionist/dietician
Nurse
Patient advocate or navigator
Physician
Public policy advisor
Risk/crisis communication specialist
Social worker

CHAPTER 13
HEALTH PROMOTION AND EDUCATION
Community health educator
Corporate wellness director
Fitness instructor
Health campaign designer/manager
Health information publication designer
Hospital-based health educator
Patient advocate or patient navigator
School-based health educator

CHAPTER 14
HEALTH CAMPAIGNS
Communication director
Director of nonprofit organization
Media relations specialist
Public relations specialist
Publication designer
Professor/educator

ways that people in health care organizations are pursuing these goals.

At the same time, we must always keep in mind that health communication is more than business and economics. It involves life and joy and, sometimes, heartbreak. Porter's experiences as a delighted, first-time grandmother and a distraught mother underscore the range of emotions that people experience relevant to health. At the same time, her passion in launching a nonprofit organization and volunteering her time remind us that caring for others is a noble calling.

A central theme of this book is that to be our best (and our best is required), we must seek to understand health communication from a wide range of perspectives. It isn't enough to know just one aspect and neglect the others. Health and the people involved in it make up an interconnected whole. Here are some examples:

Tips on Reading This Book

■ *Don't overlook the boxes and sidebars.* Sometimes a feature works better standing on its own. That doesn't mean it's less important than the rest. Key terms and theories appear in boxes as well as in the main text.

■ *Engage in critical thinking.* Questions in the margins prompt you to reflect on your viewpoints and experiences. Critical thinking—the ability to link abstract ideas to actual practices—is one of the highest forms of intellectual achievement. It distinguishes the wise and smart from the merely smart.

- It's not helpful if a patient is well treated, but his or her family feels distraught and uninformed.
- A well-meaning health campaign director unfamiliar with cultural ideas about health may create messages that are unappealing or offensive to the audience that he or she is trying to reach.
- A marketing/public relations director who doesn't understand the dynamics of patient–caregiver communication is unable to help shape and promote services that meet the needs of internal and external shareholders.
- A team member uninformed about health care administration or health care reform misses out on leadership opportunities and has relatively little chance to influence how organizations are run.
- Caregivers who do not communicate well among themselves can confuse patients and their loved ones with contradictory information.

The list goes on. That doesn't mean it's easy. Knowledge gaps are understandable, even among people who have been in health-related careers for some time. Ideas about health, health care, and prevention are changing rapidly. Whereas specialization was once encouraged, now effective health care scholars and practitioners are attuned to broader contexts and more diverse ideas. They consider situations from many perspectives. They must be aware of the historical, cultural, and market pressures that influence health. Success relies on their ability to encourage feedback, to listen, to analyze, to experiment with new communication techniques, and to sell their ideas to others.

This book is designed to give readers an up-to-date look at health communication from many perspectives. After establishing the context for health communication in Part I, we will begin, in Part II, with the interpersonal connections between patients and professional caregivers, then broaden the scope in Part III to consider the influence of diversity and culture. In Part IV, we explore health care resources, including social support and technology. Part V focuses on the ways that people use communication in health care organizations to lead, inspire, and support team members and, externally, to listen to and partner with members of the community. The book concludes, in Part VI, with coverage of health communication in the media, public health, health care reform, and health care campaigns. We move from micro-level, one-on-one communication, to macro-level issues such as public policy and mass media. Of course, in real life it's not so simple as that. We encounter all of these factors every day, in ways that blur the boundaries between them. Keep the interplay of these factors in mind as we focus on each of them.

Perhaps the most rewarding aspect of studying health communication is putting what we learn to good use. Throughout the book, *Communication Skill Builder* sections present practical tips for communicating effectively about health. Experts suggest strategies for communicating with diverse patients, presenting our concerns as patients, avoiding burnout, engaging in leadership and teamwork, listening, using social media to promote health, attaining service excellence, designing health campaigns, and more. (See Box 1.2 for ideas about how you can put your skills to work in a service-learning project or internship.)

What Is Health?

It sounds like an easy question, doesn't it? We know when we're healthy and when we're sick. At least that's how it feels most of the time. But sometimes we're not even sure ourselves. There's space in the middle. And depending on our personal and cultural perspectives, our very idea of being *healthy* can differ from other people's definitions of health.

The World Health Organization (WHO) defines **health** as "a state of complete physical, mental

BOX 1.2

Learn While You Make a Difference

Whether it's a service-learning project, an internship, or a volunteer effort, there are many ways that you can gain experience and learn about health care while you make a difference in people's lives. It helps to establish learning objectives and goals at the beginning and to reflect on what you have learned and accomplished when the project is complete. Here are a few ideas.

WORK WITH A NONPROFIT ORGANIZATION
- Help with strategic planning
- Create a media packet and marketing plan
- Publicize an event or program
- Provide assistance with training
- Recruit volunteers
- Help with an event already scheduled
- Conduct surveys
- Host a health fair booth
- Help develop a crisis management plan
- Stage a mock crisis for practice

PLAN, PUBLICIZE, AND HOST AN EVENT
- Fundraiser
- Awards banquet
- Celebration
- Clean-up or spruce-up activity
- Image-building outreach activity
- Health-enhancing event

ADVOCATE
- Focus on a particular need, risk, or group of people

- Research the issue
- Partner with people in need; honor their agenda
- Identify needed resources and/or policies
- Educate the public
- Meet with policy makers and community leaders
- Host strategy sessions
- Create coalitions and long-term plans

EDUCATE PEOPLE
- Host a public lecture
- Organize a symposium
- Hold a mini-conference
- Present communication workshops

RAISE MONEY
- Host a fundraising event
- Collect contributions
- Recruit sponsors and partners
- Sell items of value
- Host a chance drawing

HEALTH CAMPAIGNS
- Conduct market research
- Create a campaign or assist with one
  - Promote healthy behaviors
  - Raise awareness of risks
- Assess campaign exposure
- Evaluate outcomes
- Recommend what happens next

and social well-being and not merely the absence of disease or infirmity" (WHO, 1948). This definition, unchanged for more than 60 years, reminds us that *healthy* is not the opposite of *sick*. Being healthy means more than that. It's a state of harmony and equilibrium between many aspects of life. Health involves inner feelings, physical abilities, and relationships with others. Throughout the book, we'll discuss diverse theories about the nature of health and its relation to communication.

What Is Health Communication?

Health communication is shaped by many influences, including personal goals, skills, cultural orientation, situational factors, and consideration of other people's feelings. The definitions presented in this section emphasize the interdependence of these factors. As communicators, we influence—and are simultaneously influenced by—the people and circumstances around us. We rely on others to

WHAT DO YOU THINK?

Do you believe health is affected by moods and communication with others? Why or why not?

True Stories About Health Communication Experiences

In *Perspectives* boxes you'll read about the real-life experiences of people involved with health communication. These accounts represent the viewpoints of patients, loved ones, caregivers, executives, social activists, health campaign managers, and others. They provide insight about how people of different races, cultures, ages, languages, abilities, sexual orientations, and educational levels experience health communication. See Boxes 1.6 and 1.8 for the first in a series of *Perspectives* boxes that appear throughout the book.

help us meet goals and make sense of life events. Sometimes the most important thing we do is simply be present for others.

While Tracy Porter and her family camped for days in the hospital waiting room, hoping that Justin would regain consciousness, she says they felt profoundly alone. Other people were around, but no one seemed to be experiencing what they were. Gradually, that impression changed. As she researched the issue, Porter says she realized they were part of a much larger pattern. More than 1.7 million people sustain traumatic brain injuries in the United States every year (CDC, 2010).

"When I learned that, I didn't feel so alone any more," she says. "But if all these people had been there with this injury before I was, why wasn't anybody there to give me a hug and say, 'It's okay. I know how you feel'?" She determined that she would be that person for others. To date, the program she started has distributed more than 7,000 free tote bags, and she spends hours each week talking with families who need a hug, someone to listen, and a comforting presence during a difficult time.

Funding for each bag (the contents of which cost about $20) has come in large part from recipient families eager to help others by giving something back. But Porter says she's worried that she won't be able to keep up with the need, and she'd love to see the program spread across the country.

Defining Communication

To attempt a conversation with someone who doesn't understand you is usually neither satisfying nor productive. There's more to effective communication than putting thoughts into words. Understanding other people's perceptions and clearly expressing your own are important aspects of communication. The definition of **communication** offered by Judy Pearson and Paul Nelson (1991) underscores these concerns. As they put it: "Communication is the process of understanding and sharing meaning" (p. 6). The significance

of this definition becomes clear when we examine communication in terms of process, personal goals, interdependence, sensitivity, and shared meaning.

PROCESS

Defining communication as a process recognizes that people are involved in an ongoing effort to understand each other and the world around them. Meaning is interpreted in light of past, present, and future expectations.

Some factors that influence communication are set in motion before a word is ever spoken. For example, Porter's father was killed in an automobile accident 5 years before Justin's accident. "I had never lost someone close to me before," she recalls. "I didn't handle it well." But going through that process taught her something about grief and coping that she remembered when Justin was hurt. "I thought to myself, 'I'm never going to make it through this unless I focus on the positive,'" she remembers. She also realized that being well-informed helped her to feel more in control. "I'm the sort of person who needs information," she says. "The more I knew, the better I felt I could help Justin."

In Porter's case and others, the groundwork for communication begins long before the participants even meet. If we are to communicate effectively, it is important that we appreciate that everyone brings his or her own life context to an encounter, along with a unique collection of needs and expectations. In Chapter 3, we'll discuss narrative medicine, a movement that honors patients' stories as sources of information and as a therapeutic means of bridging the distance between people.

Just as communication has no set beginning, it has no definite ending either. People may reevaluate the meaning of a conversation long after it has ended. For instance, you might say to a friend: "When I began physical therapy, I thought my therapist was mean. But now I realize he was doing me a favor by making me work so hard." Porter says they nicknamed Justin's rehabilitation therapists "ninja nurses." "I learned a lot from them," she says. "They would flip him around and move him every which way. They taught me what you have to do with someone recovering from a traumatic brain injury." Fortunately, Justin recovered sufficiently within 6 months to return to his senior year of high school and to graduate, just a bit delayed. However, full recovery from such a serious injury can take years. It often becomes an ongoing part of life.

Porter says her family's needs and expectations have changed over time. Good communicators realize that it is helpful to know what people expect going into communication episodes and how they feel about them later. In health care situations this may mean asking about events leading up to an illness or health care visit, being attentive during it, and making follow-up phone calls or visits later. In Chapters 3 through 5 we'll explore the nature of patient–caregiver communication.

PERSONAL GOALS

One measure of effective communication is how well all participants feel their goals have been met. Knowing what people expect from a health encounter is a useful way to increase everyone's satisfaction. The main goal of caregivers is presumably to maintain or restore patients' health, but they may have other goals as well, such as saving time, preventing burnout, displaying their knowledge, and so on. Likewise, patients may have many goals, including the need to vent emotions, be forgiven, be reassured, or simply to be healed.

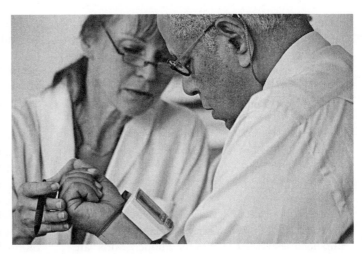

People may have many goals as patients, including the need to vent emotions, be forgiven, be reassured, or simply to be healed.

INTERDEPENDENCE

Although it's important to consider personal goals, communication ultimately relies on how well people work together. Defining communication as "understanding and sharing" emphasizes that no one communicates alone. Communicators are **interdependent**. That is, they rely on each other and exert mutual influence on communication episodes.

Communication is a process of acting, reacting, and negotiating. For example, if a waiting room receptionist seems curt and unfriendly, patients are likely to feel defensive. This may affect their willingness to be open about embarrassing or frightening concerns in the exam room later. We tend to react. But, if we are mindful about communication, we can also be proactive and can even transform our relationships and environments.

Health communication is, in large part, about relationships. Porter says the tote bags have had an unexpected benefit in that they enhance the bonds between families and professionals. Usually a social worker or nurse presents a bag to family members soon after their loved one is admitted. "It make their jobs a whole lot easier—giving something that will comfort and inform patients," says Porter, "and they get to feel good about it, too." Alisa Gormley, a nurse who distributes the totes, concurs: "You see them with that blanket around them. Or you see them brushing their hair with that brush, or whatever. You know that it did help somebody" (quoted by Banks, 2011).

Interdependence also serves to emphasize that everyone involved in a communication episode has some influence on it. Patients, family members, receptionists, and others often affect health communication as much as doctors do. Porter probably never realized 8 years ago that she would play a pivotal role in assisting thousands of other patients and their families.

SENSITIVITY

The best communicators are sensitive to other people's feelings and expectations. Public health campaigns are most effective when they are designed with the audience's concerns and resources in mind (Ledlow, Johnson, & Hakoyama, 2008). By the same token, people are most satisfied with physicians who listen attentively and seem to understand what they are feeling (Cousin, Mast, Roter, & Hall, 2012; Jangland, Gunningberg, & Carlsson, 2009).

Porter says that families in which someone has experienced a traumatic injury are often able to comfort each other because they have felt similar emotions. "We're part of a club we didn't volunteer to join," she says. "The second I hear an ambulance drive by, my gut says, 'Someone's going to get that phone call. Who's going to be there for them if not me?'"

Sensitivity is more difficult when communicators don't share the same experiences or expectations. For example, across cultural lines, a well-intended joke might seem offensive rather than kind. Interpreting subtle cues and responding to them appropriately requires an awareness of **cultural display rules** (ways of showing emotions in different cultures) and an understanding of personal preferences and expectations. To be effective, health communicators must be concerned enough to pay close attention to people's behavior and knowledgeable enough to recognize cultural and personal preferences that make people different.

In some ways, the health profession is a culture of its own, with a distinct language and artifacts. Porter sees this while coaching families, and she experienced it to some extent herself. Although health professionals often mean well, Porter says, they sometimes have a hard time connecting with

families. "It's hard for them to get too attached and become too personal or they couldn't do their jobs," she acknowledges, "but I'm approached by this person in a white lab coat and a name badge. They're trying to comfort me, but I don't always feel I have a shared experience with them."

In Chapter 7 we travel around the world, exploring the diverse ways that culture influences health and healing. For example, we'll contrast the Western concept of *fighting for one's life* with the Eastern belief that health isn't a battle, but *harmony*. In this way and many others, culture provides a rich context for understanding others and expanding our own ideas. The more we know about diversity, the more likely we are to be culturally competent communicators. On the other hand, people who don't understand and respect cultural differences often do harm even when they are trying to help (Dutta & de Souza, 2008). We will explore the idea of health disparities, social capital, and the health/power relationship in Chapters 6, 13, and 14.

SHARED MEANING

What an action means depends largely on the people and the circumstances involved. For instance, trading teasing put-downs with a friend means that you like each other, but the same put-downs from someone you barely know might make you angry. Meaning exists in the participants' mutual interpretation of it.

So how do people know if they're sharing the same meaning? Usually, they can tell by the way other people respond. A nod of the head, a smile, an angry look, or a question may signal how a conversational partner is interpreting the conversation. People send and receive messages constantly, although they may not be aware of it.

Feedback is tricky enough to decipher in person. It's even more difficult when communication occurs via computer or mass media. In Chapters 12 through 14 we will discuss best practices in public health and health campaigns, including the importance of partnering with audience members and involving them in interpersonal, dialogic communication.

Because communication is a cooperative process, it is inappropriate to blame one partner or the other when communication between them is unsatisfactory. In the past, scholars often blamed doctors for being insensitive to patients' wishes. However,

BOX 1.4 PERSPECTIVES

Making Connections

"When I first began working at a continuing care retirement community I would speak loudly, lean close to people, and draw out my words. Finally, a resident gave me a little advice: 'Just relax, we can hear you fine. You're the one that may need to listen better.' I began to listen to their stories, exchange jokes, and ask them for advice. I quickly realized I was surrounded by people with wisdom and history that far exceed mine."

—CHRIS

 IN YOUR EXPERIENCE

■ Have you ever felt like the underdog in a health care encounter?

■ If so, what contributed to this feeling?

■ Is there anything you or other people might have done differently?

theorists such as Teresa Thompson (1984) and Gary Kreps (1990) caution that patients should not be considered the underdogs in health situations. Patients are active agents who can influence the way in which health communication is conducted. For example, doctors are sometimes criticized for doing most of the talking in medical encounters. At the same time, however, patients are known to be particularly submissive around doctors. Whether patients realize it or not, they may contribute to the very dynamic they dislike.

Defining Health Communication

Kreps and Barbara Thornton (1992) define **health communication** as "the way we seek, process, and share health information" (p. 2). People seek and share messages and mingle what they hear and see with their own ideas and experiences. We are actively involved in health communication, not just passive recipients of information. A great deal of health communication involves professional caregivers, such as doctors, nurses, aides, therapists, counselors, and technicians. But we serve as caregivers for friends and loved ones as well. Chapter 8 demonstrates the value of social support when we are ill, healthy, and even (perhaps especially) when we cope with death and dying.

The History of Health Communication

Health communication emerged as a defined area of study in the late 1960s. Interest was spurred most

notably by researchers and practitioners in psychology, medicine, sociology, and persuasion who were attentive to the idea that communication is central to the process of health and healing (Kreps, Query, & Bonaguro, 2008, p. 5). It has also flourished as a component of communication, business, nursing, public health, and allied health programs, to name just a few.

One lesson that has emerged is that communication is not separate from health care, but is therapeutic in itself. It is also the vehicle through which people (both professionals and patients) learn about health and reach agreement about what's wrong and what should be done. Another contribution of health communication scholars has been to broaden our awareness of social factors that influence health. It's tempting to think of health in terms of personal choices—a good diet, an active lifestyle, regular checkups, and good information. But the evidence is clear (see Chapters 6 and 14) that these options are not available to everyone in the same measure. Health and life expectancy differ substantially between people of different races and between the residents of one neighborhood and another. This is because social issues are sometimes more important than individual choices in determining people's health status. It is important that we consider the role of communication not just in the exam or hospital room, but as a means of uniting people and addressing issues of social equity, justice, community resources, and the environment.

Health communication research also summons our attention to the power of persuasion. Communication—be it through news stories, PSAs, entertainment programming, or conversations with health professionals, neighbors, friends, or family members—has an impact on whether we smoke, exercise, drink and drive, get enough sleep, take part in health screenings, and so on. Persuasive

---

BOX 1.5 THEORETICAL INSIGHTS

The Basis for Health Communication

He who loves practice without theory is like the sailor who boards the ship without a rudder and compass and never knows where he may cast.

—LEONARDO DA VINCI

As we explore the field of health communication, theories connect the dots, just as constellations reveal patterns in the stars. Good theories make sense of diverse information and help us to get our bearings. They help us know, in advance, where we are headed and what paths are available to us. *Theoretical Insights* segments (sometimes in the text, sometimes in boxes of their own) showcase theories relevant to health communication. These theories address such issues as:

- What is health?
- How do we make sense of health crises?
- What behaviors enhance and compromise coping efforts?
- How do interpersonal relationships influence health?
- How does multiculturalism influence health and health care?
- How can health care organizations stimulate teamwork and innovation?
- In what ways do media messages influence our health?
- How do people respond to public health campaigns?
- What factors influence people to become more knowledgeable and proactive about their own health?

---

communication is a powerful tool. How, and under what circumstances, should we use it to influence people's behavior? What persuasive appeals are most effective? Which are unethical? We will examine answers to these questions and others in Part VI.

Today, health communication research is a thriving field. Notable publications include the journal *Health Communication,* first published in 1989 and still led by founding editor Teresa Thompson at the University of Dayton, as well as *Qualitative Health Research,* the *Journal of Health Communication, Communication & Medicine, The Routledge Handbook of Health Communication* (Thompson, Parrott, & Nussbaum, 2011), and many others. (See Box 1.5 for a list of relevant organizations, and see Chapter 3 for a more comprehensive list of journals.)

As you're probably beginning to appreciate, health communication is quite diverse. It unites interdisciplinary practitioners and scholars and covers a gamut of issues ranging from patient–caregiver interaction to cultural ideas about health, media images, public health efforts, health campaigns, health care administration, and much more. It also involves the work of scholars around the world—from Europe to Australia and New

Zealand, Asia, Canada, the United Kingdom, and the Americas (Thompson et al., 2011).

The following section introduces two approaches to health care that are fundamental to considering how and why people communicate as they do about health.

Medical Models

What causes ill health? If your answer is germs, you've probably been influenced by the biomedical model, which isn't surprising, considering that it has been the basis of Western medicine for the last 100 years. But if you believe that illness is caused by a variety of factors, including a person's frame of mind, your views more closely reflect the biopsychosocial model, which is gaining favor in today's health care system. Following is a description of each model and its impact on health communication.

The Biomedical Model

The **biomedical model** is based on the premise that ill health is a physical phenomenon that can be explained, identified, and treated through physical

BOX 1.6 RESOURCES

Health Communication Organizations and Resources

This book is designed to give you a rich and current overview of health communication. We'll visit a number of locations (social settings, doctors' offices, board rooms, movie theatres, and more) and look at health through different people's eyes. My hope is that, as you explore each perspective, your appreciation of the nuances that influence health and health communication will increase. Along the way you'll probably want to know more than I could fit into the book, so *Resources* boxes provide information about relevant websites, organizations, publications, and more.

To get you started, here is a list of organizations and websites you might wish to investigate for more information about health communication:

- American College of Health Care Administrators: http://www.achca.org
- American College of Health Care Executives: http://www.healthmanagementcareers.org
- American Communication Association: www.americancomm.org
- American Public Health Association: www.apha.org
- American Society for Healthcare Human Resource Administration: http://www.ashhra.org
- Association for Education in Journalism & Mass Communication: www.aejmc.org
- Centers for Disease Control and Prevention: http://www.cdc.gov
- Central States Communication Association: www.csca-net.org
- Coalition for Health Communication: http://www.healthcommunication.net/
- Eastern Communication Association: www.ecasite.org
- European Association for Communication in Health Care: www.each.nl
- European Public Health Association: www.eupha.org
- Health Care Public Relations Association: https://www.hcpra.org
- Health Communication Partnership: www.hcpartnership.org
- International Communication Association (see Health Communication Division): www.icahdq.org
- International Union for Health Promotion and Education: www.iuhpe.org
- National Cancer Institute: http://www.cancer.gov
- National Center for Health Marketing: www.cdc.gov/healthmarketing
- National Communication Association (Health Communication Division): www.natcom.org
- National Institute of Health: www.nih.gov
- National Prevention Information Network: www.cdcnpin.org/scripts/campaign/strategy.asp
- Pan American Health Organization: devserver.paho.org
- Public Relations Society of America, Health Academy: healthacademy.prsa.org/index.html
- South Asia Public Health Forum: www.saphf.org
- Southern States Communication Association: www.ssca.net
- U.S. Department of Human Services Health Communication Activities: www.health.gov/communication
- Western States Communication Association: www.westcomm.org
- World Federation of Public Health Associations: www.wfpha.org
- World Health Organization: www.who.int/en

means. Biomedicine is well suited to a culture familiar with engines and computers. "Repairing a body, in this view, is analogous to fixing a machine," writes Charles Longino (1997, p. 14). Physicians are like scientists or mechanics. They collect information about a problem, try to identify the source of it, and fix it. The focus is often reductionistic. That is, in accordance with the scientific method, health professionals try to isolate key variables by bracketing out extraneous information. A medical interview may sound a lot like this: "When did the symptoms start?" . . . "Does it hurt when I do this?" . . . "On a scale of 1 to 10, how bad is the pain?" . . . "Have you had a fever?"

Health communication influenced by the biomedical model is typically focused and specific. Doctors' questions require only brief answers (e.g., "Last weekend." "Yes." "Five." "No."). Patients may have little input, and talk is largely restricted to physical signs of illness (Roter, Stewart, et al., 1997).

Biomedical talk tends to have its own vocabulary, which can be puzzling and intimidating to patients. "When I walked into the trauma center," Porter says, "they told me Justin had suffered severe trauma to his brain, a subarachnoid hemorrhage in the sylvan fissure and right posterior fossa, frontal lobe contusions, diffuse axonal shearing injuries and a non-displaced vertical fracture of the c6 vertebrae. What I heard was 'brain damage, retarded, broken neck.'"

At its best, the biomedical approach is efficient and definitive. Medical tests and observations may yield evidence that can be logically analyzed and treated with well-established methods. One criticism of the biomedical model, however, is that it marginalizes patients' feelings and social experiences, sometimes to the extent of treating people as impersonal collections of parts or symptoms. People are often dissatisfied when caregivers don't listen to their concerns surrounding an illness, and they may not trust diagnoses if they feel their caregivers do not fully understand their problems.

The Biopsychosocial Model

The **biopsychosocial model** takes into account people's physical conditions (biology), their thoughts and beliefs (psychology), and their social expectations. From this perspective, illness is not solely a physical phenomenon but is also influenced by people's feelings, their ideas about health, and the events of their lives.

Caregivers influenced by the biopsychosocial model are likely to be concerned with patients' thoughts and emotions as well as the physical conditions of their illnesses. For example, consider the following dialogue, which occurred when I took my daughter Hannah to the doctor, hoping he could treat her poison ivy.

Doctor: *That must really itch. Is it driving you crazy?*

Hannah: *(giggling) Not really.*

Me: *I thought the ointment would help, but the rash seems to be getting worse.*

Doctor: *That was a reasonable treatment. I'm not sure why it didn't help. At any rate, I can put your mind at ease. . . .*

The doctor addressed Hannah's condition—and by acknowledging that the ointment was "a reasonable treatment," he greatly eased my anxiety as a parent. Hannah and I left feeling better both physically and emotionally. Plus, we had a prescription for medicine that cured the rash overnight.

This approach is supported by evidence that people's thoughts and emotions have an influence on their overall health. Researchers have long known that emotional stress tends to elevate people's heart rates and blood pressure. They are now finding that excessive stress reduces the body's resistance to disease (e.g., Lovell, Moss, & Wetherell, 2011). On the bright side, health is enhanced by good humor, a positive attitude, and social support (e.g., Gallagher, Phillips, Ferraro, Drayson, & Carroll, 2008).

The biopsychosocial model is appealing for its thoroughness and personal concern. The case studies in Box 1.6 and Box 1.8 illustrate out how grateful people can be to caregivers who go beyond strictly physical concerns. However, implementing a biopsychosocial approach is no easy task. At a time when health professionals are conscientiously conserving resources, broadening the scope of medicine may seem unrealistic. Some health professionals feel that it is too time-consuming to evaluate all aspects of a patient's well-being. And sometimes, as patients, all we really want is a diagnosis and a cure. You will read more about patients' perspectives in Chapter 4 and caregivers' perspectives in Chapter 5.

Although it is useful shorthand to speak of medical models, it is important to remember that models are only prototypes. As such, they are open to interpretation and blending. Few patients or caregivers operate solely within one model, nor would most people wish the entire health care system to adopt a single model. Ultimately, the best option may be the awareness that health can be approached in different ways and the versatility to use aspects of these models appropriately.

The Importance of Health Communication

Health communication is important to individuals, organizations, and society overall. It is crucial to meeting medical goals, enhancing personal well-being, saving time and money, and making the most of health information. Following are six reasons to study health communication. Each of these is addressed more fully in the chapters that follow.

Six Important Issues

First, *communication is crucial to the success of health care encounters*. Without it, caregivers cannot hear patients' concerns, make diagnoses, share

 **IN YOUR EXPERIENCE**

■ Have your health care experiences been characterized more by the biomedical approach or the biopsychosocial approach? How?

■ Which do you prefer and why?

their recommendations, or follow up on treatment outcomes. "Health communication is the singularly most important tool health professionals have to provide health care to their clients," write Kreps and Thornton (1992, p. 2). Patients who take an active role in medical encounters are more likely than others to be satisfied with their doctors, trust diagnoses, and carry out treatment regimens (e.g., Dillon, 2012; Jadad & Rizo, 2003; Tarrant, Windridge, Boulton, Baker, & Freeman, 2003).

BOX 1.7   PERSPECTIVES

A Memorable Hospital Experience

In my short 27 years I have visited hospitals in four states, and only one stands out in my memory: St. Jude Children's Research Hospital in Memphis, Tennessee. My family spent nearly 2 years of our lives walking in and out of the doors of St. Jude while my sister was being treated for leukemia.

Walking into the administrative office the first day we arrived was like being in grandma's house seated by a warm, open fireplace. During those first hours of our shock and fear over my sister's diagnosis, the hospital staff worked quickly on her paperwork without making us feel the least bit rushed. The warmth and tone of their voices was like that of a family member. We were assured we could always reach them—if not at work, at home! They were our new family.

The doctors at St. Jude stopped and spoke with families and patients and answered any questions they were asked. The doctors were not the only gems in the hospital, though. I remember two very special nurses, Jackie and Mary. One night my parents and I went to eat and were late getting back (it was shrimp night!). We found Mary, who had gotten off work 1½ hours earlier, reading to my sister. Jackie assisted my sister with manicuring her nails, even though it was

not part of her technical duties. The nurses at St. Jude stepped out of their textbook roles to accommodate the needs of their patients.

Members of the housekeeping and dietary staff were always helpful, too. When my sister thought she had an appetite for a hamburger or macaroni and cheese, they always did their best to get some up to her before she realized she did not want anything at all.

The last person I recall from the support staff was Mrs. Fran, our social worker. She was a dream, not just a friend you could talk to but one you could count on to take care of the little things you naturally forget in situations such as ours. When my sister died, Mrs. Fran was there for my family and made all the arrangements to get us back home to Louisiana.

There were many difficulties in dealing with the death of a loved one, and my sister was only 15. However, my parents and I feel an incredible debt to St. Jude. We have founded a fundraising chapter for St. Jude in Baton Rouge and I hope to pursue a career to help caregivers, families, and the public understand the importance of interpersonal communication skills in hospitals and other health care centers.

—GWYNNÉ WILLIAMS

? CAN YOU GUESS?

1. Does the United States spend more on national defense or on health care?

2. Order the following countries, from the one that spends the least on health care, per capita (dollars divided by the number of citizens), to the one that spends the most: Australia _____, Iceland _____, the United Kingdom _____, China _____, USA _____, France

3. Which, if any, of the following countries outranks the United States on the World Health Organization's ranking of national health systems? France, Japan, Cyprus, Saudi Arabia, Morocco, Chile, Costa Rica, Cuba, Colombia, Malta

Answers appear at the end of the chapter.

Interpersonal communication is crucial, considering that about 90 million people in the United States (roughly 1 in 2 adults) are unable to read more than a simple children's storybook. Added to that figure are people who, although they can read, have language differences and physical challenges that make it difficult to understand and use health information. All of these fall within the category of health literacy. People with health literacy challenges are usually less knowledgeable about health issues than others, and they may miss appointments, avoid medical care because they are embarrassed or frustrated, prepare incorrectly for surgery and other procedures, misinterpret the instructions for medications, and more. Experts estimate that health literacy challenges result in avoidable medical costs totaling more than $106 billion a year in the United States (Vernon, Trujillo, Rosenbaum, & DeBuono, 2007), and the loss in productivity and quality of life is immeasurable. Effective communication can offset the tragic and costly consequences of low literacy. We will focus on that more in Chapter 6.

Second, *the wise use of mass media can help people learn about health and can minimize the influence of unhealthy and unrealistic media portrayals.* Health promoters use communication skills to assess public needs, inform people about health issues, and encourage them to behave in healthy ways. Media consumers—especially those who rely on newspapers, magazines, and computers—are likely to be well informed about health issues and to take an active role in maintaining their own health (Koch-Weser, Bradshaw, Gualtieri, & Gallagher, 2010; Rains, 2008b). However, the media is also filled with glamorous images of people engaging in unhealthy behaviors, making media literacy especially important. In Chapters 11, 13, and 14 we will explore health images in the media, media literacy, and how to create effective health campaigns.

Third, *communication is an important source of personal confidence and coping ability.* Health professionals are less likely to experience burnout and less likely to leave the profession if they are confident and satisfied (Landon, Reschovsky, Pham, & Blumenthal, 2006). Likewise, patients cope best when they feel comfortable talking about delicate subjects like pain and death. And people involved in support groups often cope better and even live longer than similar persons who are not members. In short, good communication is conducive to good health.

Fourth, *effective communication saves time and money.* Caregivers who listen attentively and communicate a sense of caring and warmth are less likely than others to be sued for malpractice (Dym, 2008). Likewise, patients who communicate clearly with their caregivers have the best chance of having their concerns immediately addressed, which is likely to improve their health and save time and money.

Fifth, *communication helps health care organizations operate effectively.* Communication skills are useful in recruiting employees, establishing innovative teams, creating efficient systems, and sustaining service excellence. Studies show that supervisors' communication skills are one of the most important determinants of employees' satisfaction and their intention to stay on the job. Organizational leaders can also use communication to assess market needs and respond to patient preferences.

Sixth, *health communication may be important to you because the health industry is rich with career opportunities.* A background in health communication is an asset in a range of careers, including clinical care, public relations, marketing, health care administration, human resources, education, community outreach, crisis management, patient advocacy, and more.

Health care is a rare source of optimism in today's economic climate. Jobs are multiplying in health care more quickly than in any other industry. (See Figure 1.1.) The U.S. Bureau of Labor Statistics

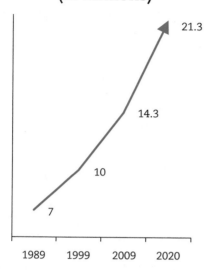

Job Growth in Health Care (in millions)

21.3

14.3

10

7

1989   1999   2009   2020

FIGURE 1.1 The job outlook in health care is better than in any other segment of the economy.

Source: Hatch & Clinton, 2000; U.S. BLS, 2012a

projects an increase of nearly 6 million jobs in health care and social assistance sectors between 2010 and 2020 (U.S. BLS, 2012a). As analyst Charles Lauer (2008a) puts it, health care is "an economic lifeboat in many communities" (p. 25).

To get an idea how large and dynamic the health industry is, consider these statistics. In the United States, health care accounts for $2,600,000,000,000 in domestic spending per year. That's $2.6 trillion ("National Health Care Expenditures," 2012). More than 14.3 million people are employed in the U.S. health care system, and 6 of the 20 industries expected to have the largest wage and salary increases are in health care (U.S. Bureau of Labor Statistics, 2012a, 2012b). In addition, several of the other career fields on that list are often associated with health care—computer systems design; employment services; and management, scientific, and technical consulting.

Reasons for the steep job growth in health care are threefold: (1) baby boomers are retiring, which is diminishing the current pool of professionals in health care, (2) health needs are simultaneously escalating as the average age of the population increases, and (3) health care reform has the potential to add 20 to 30 million Americans to health insurance rosters, qualifying them to receive medical care. Experts predict a particularly high demand for nurses, allied health professionals, people qualified to educate the public about health issues, and health care administrators. Communication skills are a valuable asset in these and every other aspect of the health industry.

Current Issues in Health Communication

If you watch the news you know that health care is in a state of rapid transformation. In 2012, in what has been called the most influential Supreme Court ruling in decades, the court gave the go-ahead to require all U.S. citizens to maintain health insurance (Liptak, 2012). That decision, paired with provisions of the Affordable Care Act passed in 2010, is expected to change the landscape of health care in the United States. Among other things, it will reverse a rising spiral in the number of uninsured Americans. (See Figure 1.2.) Researchers at the Robert Wood Johnson Foundation predicted that, without reform measures, the number of uninsured Americans would have risen to an unprecedented 66 million by 2019, but with reform, the number should drop to 26 million (Blavin, Buettgens, & Roth, 2012, Robert Wood Johnson Foundation, 2010). That's good news to many. It's worrisome to others. As you can imagine, more patients will mean a higher demand for resources, clinicians, administrators, pharmacists, health educators, PR and marketing professionals, medical technology specialists—you name it. It will also require a great initial expenditure before the country begins to recoup the investment in a healthier citizenry. We will explore the implications of the Affordable Care Act—pro and con—in Chapter 12.

Keep health care reform on your radar. But we won't jump into that topic immediately. First, we'll get a feel for where we've been and how we got here. In Chapter 2 you will learn more about current issues in health care by going back in time. Following the evolution of medicine from ancient Egypt to twenty-first-century managed care reveals a lot about where we are today. When we

BOX 1.8   ETHICAL CONSIDERATIONS

An Essential Component of Health Communication

Our customers routinely bare their bodies, as well as their souls, within our organizations. I can think of no other enterprise in our society where so much is placed in the hands of others.

—LARRY SANDERS, CHAIR OF THE AMERICAN COLLEGE OF HEALTH CARE EXECUTIVES

Sanders (2003) advises those who provide and study health care: "One of the most significant ways we can demonstrate how much we care about those we serve is to visibly display our personal commitment to operating with extraordinary integrity, ethics and morality each and every day" (p. 46).

It is imperative that people involved with health care understand the ethical implications of their actions and conduct themselves with honor and integrity. They must also be aware of the perceptions of others. If people perceive—rightly or wrongly—that health-related professionals are unethical, they may experience stress, avoid medical care, lie to health care providers, or withhold information to protect themselves.

I once studied a hospital unit in which several patients with AIDS were afraid to tell their caregivers about their diagnosis. The caregivers were justifiably angry that they might become infected because they were not aware which patients were contagious. However, the patients had a good point as well. They felt that their diagnosis would not be kept confidential, and they were probably right. Patient records were often left open on the counter of the nurses' unit, posted outside patients' rooms, and handled by more than a dozen employees, including clerks, secretaries, pages, and more. There was no reasonable assurance of confidentiality. Consequently the caregivers distrusted the patients, and the patients distrusted everyone in the organization. (HIPAA privacy legislation passed in 2003 has changed much of that. We will discuss that in Chapter 5.)

Many of the ethical dilemmas that people in health care face are essentially matters of communication. Issues frequently arise concerning honesty, privacy, power, conflicts of interest, social stigmas, media images, advertising, and persuasive messages about health. In most cases, there is more than one option, but no simple solution. What seems right in one situation may be wrong in another. Personal preference and culture, among other factors, shape what people want and expect. Even so, there is value in thinking through the implications and exploring diverse reactions with others.

An *Ethical Considerations* box in each chapter presents an ethical dilemma and a list of discussion questions and additional resources. I encourage you to discuss and debate these issues, eliciting diverse views. Don't be afraid to change your mind or to argue both sides of an issue. It's usually easier to behave ethically if you have thought the issues through *before* you find yourself in a real-life dilemma. Following are some questions you might ask yourself as you consider your options concerning ethical challenges posed in this book and elsewhere.

- Is this option legal?
- Is it honest? Is deception or omission of the truth involved?
- Who will be hurt? Who will be helped?
- Will the decision benefit me personally but hurt others?
- Are the results worth the hardship involved?
- Is it culturally acceptable?
- Will my decision compromise people's privacy or trust?
- Will my decision be demeaning or degrading to anyone?
- Is it fair? Will my action unfairly discriminate against anyone?
- Is the action appropriate for the situation?
- Have I considered all the options?
- How would I wish to be treated in the same situation?
- How would I feel if my decision or action were published in tomorrow's newspaper?

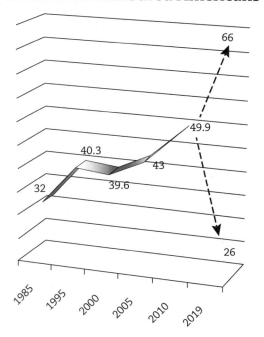

Millions of Uninsured Americans

FIGURE 1.2 Despite the introduction of managed care, the number of uninsured Americans continued to climb to an all-time high in 2010. Research sponsored by the Robert Wood Johnson Foundation predicted that the number of uninsured would rise to 66 million without health care reform but should drop to 26 million by 2019 with implementation of the Affordable Care Act.

Sources: Blavin, Buettgens, & Roth, 2012; S. Collins, Garber, & Davis, 2011; Hoffman & Schlobohm, 2000; Holohan & Chen, 2011; Robert Wood Johnson Foundation, 2010; "Uninsured in America," 2000

The United States spent more than 10 times as much on health care in 2010 as it did in 1980 ("National Health Care Expenditures," 2012). Even though the United States spends more on health, per capita, than any other nation, it nevertheless has lagged behind other industrialized nations in terms of equitable care for all citizens. The culprit, say many, is unwise use of resources. When researchers at the Commonwealth Fund issued a 2008 performance scorecard on the U.S. health system, they gave it an F (53%) on efficient use of health resources, citing uncoordinated patient care, avoidable hospitalizations, too-high administrative costs, and slow adoption of time-saving communication technology (Commonwealth Fund, 2008c). Improving these is mostly a matter of communicating more effectively.

Managed care, begun in the late 1980s, is one effort to monitor and reduce health expenses. However, some people worry that managed care has gone overboard, skimping on care in the zeal to cut costs. We will discuss these issues in Chapter 2.

As we look ahead, it's important to be well-informed about the options for health care reform. Terms such as *universal coverage, individual mandates, public option,* and *single-payer versus multipayer models* have entered the health care lexicon. In Chapter 12 we will explain these terms, survey health systems around the world, and explore the status of health care reform in the United States.

Prevention

Prevention has become a health priority for two main reasons: It increases people's quality of life, and it costs less than medical treatment. Although the first reason has always been true, the second has become an important concern in recent years. S. Renée Gillespie (2001) observes that the dual pressures of competition and cost-containment have created "a new conceptualization of the patient as both valued customer and dangerous consumer of health care resources" (p. 99). Within this framework, recruiting the "right" patients (those who don't require expensive care) may keep a health care organization in business. However, patients with expensive health needs can drain

understand the philosophy and events that have shaped the modern system, we are in a better position to decide what has worked well, where we went wrong, and where we should go next.

This chapter concludes with a brief overview of current issues in health care. We will discuss the influence of these issues on health communication throughout the book.

Emphasis on Efficiency

As demand for health services increases, there is more concern than ever that they be affordable.

BOX 1.9 PERSPECTIVES

Down, But Not Out

"Swing and a miss, strike three, and that's the ballgame! Bearcats win 7–1." It was an early April Saturday of my senior year as our baseball season was winding down. We were just 3 weeks from playoffs, and we had already clinched the area championship and an automatic berth to the state playoffs. However, in the last inning I felt a pain in my throwing shoulder. I assumed it would be better in a couple of days, but the pain increased as days went on. This wasn't a good sign, because as a senior, I was the ace of the pitching staff.

When my doctor, whom I have visited on several occasions throughout my athletic- injuries history, walked in he had a smile on his face and a cup of coffee. "Well, well, well, the superstar is in here again. You're a great kid and I like you, but I hate seeing you here in my office. That means something's wrong," he joked in an attempt to loosen me up. I always felt comfortable with him because he knew how to connect with me and assure me that whatever the problem was, he would get it fixed and get me back out on the field.

As it turned out, there was no tear in my shoulder. I didn't need surgery, but I did need physical therapy five days a week. The therapists were really great. They were very strict when it came to my rehab and throwing program. "Absolutely no throwing if you feel any pain whatsoever. You got it?" one therapist said to me. They treated me like royalty, even though I wasn't, and made sure I was doing the right things

to get healthy again. With the urgency to get back in the game quickly, they placed me on a fast-paced, demanding rehabilitation regimen. They made sure I received the appropriate amount of work every day, and they repeatedly asked me how my shoulder was coming along.

I can't say enough about how helpful and flexible they were with me. With my school schedule and baseball practice, it was tough for me to come in during office hours, so they sacrificed their own time to come in early and stay late for me. Not once did they complain. They always had smiles on their faces and always seemed positive and excited to be helping me. After 2 weeks of the well-conditioned rehab they put me through, I felt completely pain-free and ready to pitch again. "Now if you ever need to come in again for any therapy or some shoulder exercises, you just come on in. Don't hesitate. We'll be here," the head physical therapist told me. "Yes ma'am, I appreciate everything you all have done for me," I replied. I am thankful to have had those professionals who gave me their best effort and went to the absolute maximum to ensure that I was taken care of and treated properly. I can never repay them for what they did for me.

— DREW BRYSON

Drew went on to earn titles as Pitcher of the Year in Alabama, All-County Pitcher of the Year, and Most Valuable Pitcher of the Year, in addition to pitching for his college team. His future plans include a career in orthopedic surgery or physical therapy.

resources. It's in everyone's best interest to keep people healthy.

Prevention is cost-effective because it is usually less expensive to prevent diseases and injuries than to treat them. For example, it costs less to provide cardiovascular exercise programs than to perform open-heart surgeries. Prevention efforts are often led by diverse teams of physicians, nurse practitioners, physician assistants, dietitians, therapists, and others. The rewards are great, for both patients and caregivers. But so are the challenges. We will discuss both in Chapter 6.

Holistic medicine is gaining popularity as a means of maintaining good health. Nearly 4 in 10 Americans now use alternative therapies such as chiropractic, acupuncture, and relaxation therapy—and worldwide, 8 in 10 people use these therapies (National Center for Complementary, 2012). These methods are relatively inexpensive and are geared toward prevention and long-term health maintenance. As you will see in Chapter 7, holistic therapists often spend a good deal of time talking with patients about lifestyle choices and emotional well-being.

Prevention efforts are often led by diverse teams of physicians, nurse practitioners, physician assistants, dietitians, therapists, and others. The challenge is to develop the communication skills necessary for interdisciplinary teamwork and collaborative problem solving.

Patient Empowerment

It's easier than ever to be knowledgeable about health. It's the subject of cable television channels, magazines, best-selling books, news programs, advertisements, and extensive computer databases. News media in the United States release more than 3,500 health-related stories in a typical 18-month period (Kaiser Family Foundation, 2008). It's said that knowledge is power, and that may be the case in health care. The current Information Age coincides with a move toward **patient empowerment** (Hardey, 2008). Empowerment means that patients have considerable influence in medical matters. Their ideas count. They ask questions and state preferences, and they may visit doctors or other caregivers, not because they are ill, but because they would like information or feedback on a health issue.

Patient empowerment is also encouraged by increased competition in the health industry. People are now courted by health plans and medical centers vying for their business. Advertising appeals make it clear that health organizations are not simply a source of assistance but are part of an industry that relies on consumers.

Increased knowledge and the awareness that health agencies need patients' business may reduce the status difference between patients and their caregivers. As Tom Ferguson (1997) puts it:

> As we move farther into the Information Age, health professionals will do more than just treat their patients' ills—they will increasingly serve as their coaches, teachers, and colleagues, working side-by-side with empowered consumers in a high-quality system of computer-supported, low-cost, self-managed care. (para. 34)

It will be interesting to see if (and how) patients and caregivers adapt to the idea that they are well-informed partners working toward common goals. On the one hand, patient empowerment relieves some of the pressure on caregivers to "fix" people who do very little to maintain their own health (R. Kaplan, 1997). On the other hand, patient empowerment dispels the notion that people should simply follow doctors' orders. It's no longer enough (if ever it was) simply to tell patients what to do. Empowered patients want information and the right to make their own decisions. Changing expectations require new communication skills and different styles of interaction on the part of patients and caregivers.

Global Health Needs and Intercultural Competence

Travel, immigration, and the international exchange of food and products mean that diseases today are continually carried across national borders. The outbreak of severe acute respiratory syndrome (SARS) in 2003 provided a striking example of how quickly a communicable disease can spread around the globe. Within 100 days, the disease that began in southern China had killed more than 100 people in 20 countries. Remarkably, the world health community was able to contain the outbreak of SARS within a few months.

The AIDS epidemic has been far more difficult to keep in check. The number of new HIV/AIDS cases has leveled off since 2000, partly because of aggressive health promotion efforts (UNAIDS, 2008). Slower spread of the virus is an intermediate victory for health educators, but the situation remains critical. Some 33.3 million people (down from 42 million in 2003) are infected, and the spread is still rapid in some parts of the world, particularly sub-Saharan Africa and India.

In Chapter 12 we will focus on international teamwork and the intercultural competence necessary to deal effectively with SARS, AIDS, mad cow disease, avian flu, and more.

Changing Populations

Population shifts are also changing health care needs in the United States. One shift is toward an older society. In 2010, about 40.2 million people in the United States were 65 and older. By 2020, that age group will more than double, to 88.5 million. The upshot is that about 1 in 5 Americans soon will be 65 or older (U.S. Census Bureau, 2010b). Although many older adults are healthy, they are more likely than others to have chronic diseases, which will increase the need for medical care, assisted living facilities, social services, and home care.

The racial and cultural mix of American society is also changing. By 2042, people from current minority racial and ethnic groups will comprise the majority of the U.S. population (U.S. Census Bureau News, 2008). This presents an unprecedented richness of diversity. Unfortunately, it is anticipated that people from minority groups will still have disproportionately fewer educational and professional opportunities than others, meaning that the number of underprivileged individuals in the United Sates will probably rise. People with limited education and income are typically most in need of health care but are least likely to be informed about health issues and to utilize health services. The challenge is to provide affordable care to the people who need it and to use prevention efforts to keep people as healthy as possible.

Complicating the issue even further, diversity among health care workers is not expected to keep pace with the overall population. Currently, minorities comprise about 9% of physicians and 6% of registered nurses in the United States, which is far smaller than their representation (nearly 30%) in the population (Boukus, Cassil, & O'Malley, 2009;

The number of people 65 or older is expected to more than double between 2010 and 2020.

"Minority Nursing Statistics," 2009; U.S. Census Bureau, 2011b). As a result, the odds are that patients will be treated by caregivers who differ markedly from them in terms of knowledge, needs, and cultural beliefs. Communication is a valuable tool for meeting this challenge. It is important to understand and appreciate culturally diverse views of health and illness and to become skillful at intercultural communication (see Chapters 6 and 7).

Technology

Technology may address many of the issues just described. The ability to communicate with people across great distances may avail people of medical care, information, and social support that they would not otherwise receive. Through eHealth and telemedicine, information can be broadcast around the world or tailored (*narrowcast*) to meet the needs the needs of specific individuals. At another level, electronic medical records can save time, prevent mistakes, and help coordinate patient care. Some analysts predict that we will eventually have medical ATM-type cards or microchips inserted under our skin so that our medical profiles will be accessible anywhere we are, even if we are unable to answer questions.

In yet another application of medical technology, scientists have used computers to map nearly all the genes in the human body. This has the potential to unlock the mystery of many diseases, maybe even cancer. But for genetic testing and all the forms of technology just listed, questions about privacy, quality, cost, and access remain to be resolved.

An interesting dimension of emerging technology is the ability to facilitate "multimedia storytelling" by people who are not merely consumers of information but who are actively (and interactively) involved in creating messages themselves (Cozma, 2009). New media illustrate clearly that people have stories to tell and experiences to share. This process can be rich, therapeutic, and informative, says theorist Raluca Cozma, but she warns that it can divert attention away from scientific information, which is typically more complex and less emotionally immediate than personal stories. We will explore issues related to eHealth, mHealth, telemedicine, and Web 2.0 in Chapter 9 and in *Communication Technology* segments throughout the book.

In closing, although it may seem that the average person is not directly affected by changes in the health industry, that's far from the case. Changes influence the type of caregivers people are likely to see, what services are available, and what role individuals play in maintaining their own health. People who work in the health industry are likely to experience the stress and promise of change, the pressure to save money, the opportunity to use new technology, and the need to communicate effectively with a variety of people and to include them as partners in their own care and disease-prevention efforts. We are all influenced by health issues, not only in the United States, but around the world.

Summary

Effective health communication involves an extensive number of people. Physicians often seem to call the shots, but they are affected by a range of factors themselves, including budget limitations and public expectations. And doctors don't work alone. Nurses, therapists, technicians, counselors, public health experts, friends, and others also shape our health attitudes and behaviors. Health care administrators, media professionals, and public health promoters play important roles. Furthermore, everyday citizens affect the process more than they may realize.

In a context of rapid change, the most effective people are those who keep the larger picture in sight, are open to new ideas, and work with others to identify and implement options that serve multiple goals at the same time. The emphasis is on communicating as leaders and as team members. In this climate of change and consolidation, communication specialists can help assess community needs, market new services, keep people informed about changes, and facilitate team efforts to design high-quality, affordable care systems. Caregivers, administrators, and researchers who wish to influence the transformation of health care will need to draw on a range of communication skills.

Health communication is accomplished within a complex array of influences. It is partly the result of individual action and partly the result of social contexts and expectations. Participants in health care must strive not only to attain their personal objectives but also to maintain the good faith of those around them, without whom they cannot achieve long-term success. Social equity and opportunities are profoundly important in determining who is healthy and who is not.

With this philosophy it seems important to emphasize that, if health communication is good (or bad), we have a host of people to thank (or blame). Almost always we are among those people. We influence the process throughout our lives. We all have something to gain by understanding the process and, hopefully, something to contribute as well.

Two of the most popular ways of looking at health are the biomedical model, which assumes that disease is best understood and treated in physical terms, and the biopsychosocial model, which treats health as a broad concept that includes social, personal, and physical factors.

Health communication is important for several reasons. It allows patients and caregivers to share concerns and establish trust. It helps people to cope and to build self-confidence. Communicating well saves time and money and helps organizations to solicit, organize, and implement new ideas. Finally, media messages have the potential to improve or discourage healthy habits.

Health communication is especially important now as the industry and the public work toward a more affordable health system, disease prevention, patient empowerment, and treatment for a diverse population. The current health care system is quickly evolving, making the nature of medicine and the importance of health communication a dynamic and important consideration in the twenty-first century.

Key Terms and Theories

health
communication
interdependent
cultural display rules
health communication
biomedical model
biopsychosocial model
patient empowerment

Discussion Questions

1. Why is it important for people in any one aspect of health (e.g., campaign management, public relations, clinical care) to be knowledgeable about broader issues relevant to health?
2. How do personal goals, interdependence, and sensitivity affect the communication process?
3. How do communication partners establish shared meaning?
4. What are the implications of describing health communication in terms of seeking, processing, and sharing information?

5. Why is it important to study theories in conjunction with research about health communication?
6. What do you think of the case studies about St. Jude Hospital (Box 1.6) and the baseball player's physical rehabilitation (Box 1.8)? Have your experiences been mostly similar to these or different? How?
7. Why is it especially important that people involved in health care maintain high ethical standards?
8. What role can communication specialists play in efforts by health agencies to cut costs?
9. How does patient empowerment affect health communication?
10. Why should we be concerned about health crises around the world? What role does communication play in striving for global health?

Answers to *Can You Guess?*

1. The United States spends 4.3 times more on health care than on national defense (National Coalition on Health Care, 2008).
2. From least to most dollars spent, per capita: China ($81), UK ($3,064), Australia ($3,181), France ($3,819), Iceland ($5,154), United States ($6,350) (WHO, 2008b).
3. The only country on the list that does not outrank the United States is Cuba (World Health Report, 2000). We will examine the reasons in Chapter 12.

CHAPTER TWO

History and Current Issues

On one of my trips, I received an urgent call that my mother had been in a terrible accident, in which she had fallen asleep at the wheel and hit a tree. In the accident my father was killed and my mother had broken her neck, her sternum, one leg in three places, and the other leg just above the knee.... I took the first plane I could get to be by her side. I wondered if the nurses in ICU would be strict about how long I could spend with my mother. I pictured them telling me that I could spend only 10 minutes out of the hour with her. The more I thought about being chased out of ICU, the more I decided I was going to be belligerent about my rights to be with my mother as long as she wanted me there.... I finally arrived at the ICU waiting room.... As I walked into the unit, I was a time-bomb ready to go off if anybody tried to limit my time with my mother. When I entered her room, it was a shock to see her on the ventilator. Her head was in a steel halo with rods running from the rim into her skull. Her face was swollen beyond recognition. Her bandages made her seem twice as big.... Off to one side of her bed was a nurse facing a bank of electronic equipment with blinking lights. She was writing my on mother's chart. I hoped she didn't notice me enter the room as I went over to the other side of the bed and took my mother's hand. Not knowing if she was awake or not, I said softly, "Mother, this is Fred and I am here now to be with you." I felt a gentle squeeze and knew she heard and understood me.... As if on cue, the nurse turned around and looked at me. I thought, Here it comes. Give it your best shot, lady. *But instead, the nurse smiled and said, "My, my, my, you should see what your touch just did to your mother's vital signs. It's amazing. We need you here all of the time!"* (F. Lee, 2004, pp. 61–62)

This story, told by Fred Lee in his book *If Disney Ran Your Hospital*, illustrates many of the facets of modern-day medicine. Health care today is a mix of life-saving technology, institutional rules and guidelines, and, at its best, a deep appreciation for the role that compassion, love, and touch play as well. The example also points to the powerful role of communication. Lee reflects: "Could she have come up with a more perfectly timed thing to say? It was as if she had read my mind and in one gracious comment had made me feel needed and welcome, an essential part of the healing team" (p. 62).

Unfortunately, the opposite is also true. Lee's trepidation about being turned out from his mother's room reflects the reality that health care professionals and patients are sometimes at odds about what constitutes good care. To understand how and why health communication has evolved as it has, we take a journey through history in this chapter. You will see how ideas (some ancient, some modern) influence the way people think and talk about health today. You may be surprised to find that your assumptions about health care have roots in the philosophies of ancient Egypt, medieval Europe, or colonial America. By chapter's end, we will explore current issues, including the evolution of managed care.

Medicine in Ancient Times

Many Westerners date medicine to ancient Greece and think of Hippocrates as the first physician. This would make medicine about 2,000 years old, a period during which tremendous change has taken place. However, the first doctor in recorded history was actually Imhotep of ancient Egypt, who lived about 2,000 years before Hippocrates was born.

Imhotep

As the first known physician, **Imhotep** was part of an ancient medical community that is still admired for its vast knowledge. Translations of early texts suggest that Egyptians were aware of blood circulation and the functions of bodily organs thousands of years before the Western world attained that knowledge. A learned observer of archaeology once remarked that the accomplishments of ancient Egypt would make citizens of the modern world "blush for shame" (Thorwald, 1962, p. 15).

Imhotep was not only a healer but a priest, a sculptor, and an architect as well. He designed the first stone pyramid, which was built for King Zoser about 2600 B.C. In the centuries after his death, Imhotep attained godlike status. Some legends portrayed him as the son of Ptah, the Egyptian god of architecture. Others revered Imhotep as a medicine god and evoked his name in healing ceremonies.

Imhotep designed the Pyramid of Zoser and served as one of the first physicians in recorded history. Medicine at the time involved a mixture of physiology and spiritualism.

The ancient Egyptians took a **religio-empirical approach** to medicine, combining spiritualism and physical study. Healers were holy men such as Imhotep, but the ancients also recognized a physical component of illness (Thorwald, 1962). They developed an impressive variety of instruments, including surgical appliances, sutures, drugs, and immobilizing casts. Mummies show that the ancient Egyptians were prone to many disorders that plague people today, including dental ailments, cancer, and hardening of the arteries.

It is believed that Imhotep was the basis for the Greek god Aesculapius, whose name is mentioned in the famous Hippocratic oath (Garrison, 1929). In fact, historians believe that Hippocrates was strongly influenced by the writings of ancient Egypt.

Hippocrates

Hippocrates (460–370 B.C.) is often considered the founder of scientific medicine and Western medical ethics. Perhaps his most enduring legacy is the oath that bears his name.

The **Hippocratic oath** (Box 2.1) established a code of conduct for physicians that has influenced the Western world until the current day. In a collection of succinct sentences, the oath says a great deal about medical ethics then and now. For centuries, medical students took the Hippocratic oath when they received their degrees. The tradition has largely been abandoned, but most doctors are familiar with the oath and continue to be influenced by the ethical framework it presents.

Parts of the Hippocratic oath—particularly the appeal to medicine gods Apollo and Aesculapius—seem archaic today. More remarkable, however, are the issues that remain current. The oath's edict to "give no deadly medicine" is relevant to modern debates over physician-assisted suicide. Likewise, the mention of abortion and sexual misconduct could be straight from modern headlines, as could issues of patient confidentiality.

The oath's pledge not to "cut persons laboring under the stone," but to leave such work to specific practitioners, reflects the distinction in Hippocrates' day between medicine and surgery. It is believed that this passage refers to bladder and kidney stones, which were then extracted by surgeons but not by physicians (Edelstein, 1967).

Hippocrates' views on the nature of disease are as important as the oath that bears his name. During Hippocrates' era, many people believed that disease was God's punishment, and they were shamed by it (Amundsen & Ferngren, 1983). Hippocrates' ideas helped to dispel this notion. In place of spiritual explanations, he presented a rational/empirical model of medicine. From a **rational/empirical approach**, disease is best understood by careful observation and logical analysis.

Hippocrates promoted the idea of health as a harmonious balance between many factors, such as

---

BOX 2.1

The Hippocratic Oath

I swear by Apollo the physician, and Aesculapius and Hygeia, and Panacea, and all the gods and goddesses, that according to my ability and judgment, I will keep this oath and its stipulations—to reckon him who taught me this art equally dear to me as my parents, to share my substances with him, and to relieve his necessities if required; to look upon his offspring in the same footing as my own brothers; and to teach them this art if they shall wish to learn it, without fee or stipulation, and that by precept, lecture, and other mode of instruction, I will impart a knowledge of the art to my own sons, and those of my teachers, and to disciples bound by a stipulation and oath according to the law of medicine, but to none other.

I will follow that system of regimen which, according to my ability and judgment, I consider for the benefit of my patients, and abstain from whatever is deleterious and mischievous. I will give no deadly medicine to anyone if asked, nor suggest any such counsel; and in like manner I will not give to a woman a pessary to produce abortion. With purity and holiness I will pass my life and practice my art. I will not cut persons laboring under the stone, but will leave this to be done by men who are practitioners of this work. Into whatever houses I enter, I will go into them for the benefit of the sick, and will abstain from every voluntary act of mischief and corruption; and, further, from the seduction of females or males, of freemen and slaves. Whatever, in connection with my professional practice, or not in connection with it, I see or hear, in the life of men, which ought not to be spoken of abroad, I will not divulge, as reckoning that such ought to be kept secret.

While I continue to keep this oath unviolated, may it be granted to me to enjoy life and the practice of this art, respected by all men, in all time. But should I trespass and violate this Oath, may the reverse be my lot.

This version of the Hippocratic oath was published in 1910 by P. F. Collier and Son in *Harvard Classics* (Vol. 38). It was placed in the public domain in June 1993.

Hippocrates of ancient Greece made popular a rational/empirical approach to health care, moving away from spiritual interpretations of illness.

diet, contact with nature, relationships, and physical strength. He also advocated a balance between different body fluids, which he called body *humors*—blood, phlegm, yellow bile, and black bile (Moore, Van Arsdale, Glittenberg, & Aldrich, 1987). Thus, although Hippocrates strengthened the notion that physical factors are a significant part of disease, he acknowledged social and personal influences as well. In this way Hippocrates' philosophy was an early forerunner to the biopsychosocial approach.

The treatment of body humors had a substantial impact on the practice of medicine, forming the basis for bloodletting and other purging practices. Bloodletting involves lancing a vein or applying leeches to allow a portion of the patient's blood to drain from the body. It was believed that this would purge impure blood or balance blood levels with other humors. Other purging practices include vomiting, sweating, and the use of laxatives.

Bloodletting may seem archaic today (actually, it's still used in some rare cases), but Hippocrates' influence on health communication has endured through the centuries. By establishing medicine as rational and empirical, Hippocrates helped to shape the role of physicians as scientists and intellectuals rather than spiritualists. As a result, medical talk began to focus on physical, social, and personal

factors. If the rational/empirical perspective had never taken root, you might now visit a minister rather than a doctor when you become ill. By the same token, treatment and diagnosis might involve spiritual exploration more than physical remedies.

Hippocrates' ideas were not always well received, however. His views on medicine were overshadowed for a time when early Christianity brought about a resurgence of spiritualism in western Europe.

Medieval Religion and Health Care

Christianity dominated the course of Western medicine for hundreds of years during the Middle Ages, also known as the medieval period (A.D. 500–1450). Medical spiritualism, which waned but never fully died under Hippocrates' influence, was renewed with vigor.

Medical Spiritualism

As Donald Bille (1981) defines it, **medical spiritualism** is the belief that illness is governed by supernatural forces such as gods, spirits, or ghosts. Medical spiritualism was supported by the belief that Jesus performed healing miracles. Healing was so closely tied to Christianity that monks were the principal physicians during much of the Middle Ages (White, 1896/1925).

As the leader of the only recognized religion in medieval Europe, the Catholic Church was involved in making laws, allocating land and resources, and caring for the sick and homeless. As such, it had immense influence over people's well-being and way of life. The church's ideology affected the nature of health communication. From a spiritualist perspective, disease was treated through prayer and faith and, sometimes, through application of natural (God-given) substances such as plants. People generally believed that illness was manifested differently in each person (Thompson, 1990). As a result, patients' thoughts and feelings, faith, and behaviors were directly relevant to the subject of healing.

During a portion of the Middle Ages, the church banned the practice of secular medicine, particularly surgery. Surgeons were often regarded as sorcerers, butchers, and atheists (White, 1896/1925). Because the soul was believed to inhabit a persons'

Historians believe that the modern barber pole was derived from the image of white and bloodstained bandages swirling in the wind as they dried outside barbershops.

entire body, to cut into the body (before or after death) was to interfere with God's work.

Barber Surgeons

During the Middle Ages, health care was provided mostly by monks and by a limited number of secular practitioners, most of whom did not perform surgery. Barbers began offering surgical procedures in addition to hairstyling because they had the sharp instruments and public facilities necessary. **Barber surgeons** were called on to perform simple surgeries, bloodletting, and tooth extractions (Douglas, 1994). It is believed that the modern barber pole was derived from the image of white and bloodstained bandages swirling in the wind as they dried outside barbershops. If these images sound harrowing by today's standards, consider that during the time of barber surgeons,

people were still unaware of germs and had no effective anesthesia!

Although it's easy to regard the church as anti-progressive for discouraging secular medicine, it's perhaps understandable considering how dreadful surgery seemed at that time. As medical historian John Duffy (1979) describes it, prior to the 1860s surgery was "a grim and bloody business" requiring the surgeon "to be a strong, fast, forceful operator, ruthlessly immune to the screams and struggles of the patient" (p. 130).

Science and Magic

Monastic medicine varied from the scholarly to the superstitious. It was, in turn, praised and condemned. In cathedral schools such as Salerno in southern Italy, the clergy studied medical theory. These institutions became models for European medical schools to follow. The church founded the first hospitals as we know them and staffed them with its own learned practitioners, forming what Darrel Amundsen and Gary Ferngren (1983) laud as a "vast charitable institution" (p. 15).

In contrast to this academic atmosphere, however, was the exercise of **Christian magic,** the use of bizarre ceremonies and exorcisms condoned by the church (Amundsen & Ferngren, 1983). In an effort to disgust evil spirits into leaving a patient's body, for instance, the patient might be instructed to eat toad livers or drink rat's blood (White, 1896/1925). (In fairy tales to come, of course, these ingredients made up the imaginary contents of witches' brew.)

The church also became involved in selling fetishes and hosting miracles, some of which were later exposed as hoaxes. **Fetishes** were holy relics said to protect those who purchased them from calamities such as shipwreck, fire, lightning, and difficult childbirth (White, 1896/1925). Those who could afford to buy fetishes or visit holy sites made lavish offerings to the church in exchange for divine intervention.

The End of an Era

Ironically, as medicine advanced with the monks' practice of it, their work began to seem disturbingly secular and altogether overwhelming. The very technology and pharmacology they developed were at odds with the church's position on healing by faith and were diverting the monks from other spiritual pursuits (Ackerknecht, 1968). In 1311 the church forbade monks to practice medicine any longer.

As with any enterprise of such vast duration and involvement, the church's role during the Middle Ages had both positive and negative aspects. The church has been criticized for profiting from its caregiving role and for suppressing the development of secular medicine. At the same time, it has been lauded for helping to establish a compassionate perspective toward the ill and for founding institutions of care and learning that served as a model of Western medicine. Today, even in the context of high-tech biomedical care, this influence is reflected in the existence of church-funded and other nonprofit medical centers devoted to public service and in the presence of clergy and chapels in many hospitals.

Renaissance Philosophy and Health Care

From one extreme to another, the religious orientation of the Middle Ages was followed by the intellectual skepticism of the European Renaissance. The Renaissance began in the 1300s (overlapping with the Middle Ages) and continued into the 1600s.

Confronted with the age-old question "What is real?" artists and philosophers of the Renaissance looked to mathematics and matter for answers. Their theories changed the Western worldview, including the nature of medicine.

Partly in reaction to the religious dominance of the Middle Ages, Renaissance thinkers tended to be skeptical about anything they could not prove. **René Descartes** (1596–1650), an influential philosopher and mathematician of the time, introduced his method of doubt, prescribing that the thinker systematically doubt the existence of all things until that existence could be verified. (Such a method eventually led him to doubt his *own* existence until, realizing that he had to *exist* to be *doing* the doubting, he reached the famous conclusion "I think, therefore I am.")

The Principle of Verification

The **principle of verification**—do not believe it if you cannot prove it—changed the nature of health care. No longer were people considered ill based solely on their feelings. Instead, physicians and others began to look for verifiable signs of illness (a perspective consistent with today's biomedical approach).

Surgery and autopsies became acceptable. In fact, not only physicians but artists became interested in human dissection (Dowling, 1997). Renaissance artists, including Michelangelo and Leonardo da Vinci, studied the human body inside and out to make their representations of it more precise. Mathematical precision and a knowledge of anatomy became mainstream in both science and art.

The principle of verification affected health communication. If illness is physically verifiable, it follows that people may believe they are ill even though they really are not. This idea is still pervasive in Western medicine. You know this if you have ever gone to the doctor feeling ill and have been told that tests confirm you are "just fine." In fact, some people avoid going to the doctor because it seems a sign of weakness to complain about something that (medically speaking) is trivial or does not exist. (See Box 2.2.) My experience producing health campaigns bears this out. I once directed a campaign to encourage people to go to an emergency room if they experienced chest pains. The campaign was spurred by evidence that people were dying of heart attacks because they were afraid to go to the emergency room and find out, to their embarrassment, that they had nothing more than indigestion.

Cartesian Dualism

Renaissance thinkers were challenged to explain the relationship between body and soul. As mentioned, during much of the Middle Ages the soul was believed to inhabit the entire body. Descartes proposed an alternative in the form of a mind–body dualism.

Cartesian dualism (named for Descartes) contends that every person has a soul and a body but that the two are not the same. Descartes believed that the soul dwells only temporarily in the human body, a belief based on the conviction that the soul lives after the body dies (Cottingham, 1992). Furthermore, Descartes theorized that the soul was seated in the human brain (other animals being presumably soulless). Thus, in Descartes' view, the soul is most closely associated with the mind, not spread throughout the body.

The medical implications of Cartesian dualism are profound, including the separation of medicine

---

BOX 2.2 PERSPECTIVES

Sick in the Head?

After two months with a 101-degree temperature but no real discomfort, a 21-year-old woman presented her concerns to a doctor. "From the beginning, I got the feeling he really didn't want to see me," she remembers. "I waited 4 hours in the waiting room."

During a brief consultation, the doctor scolded the woman for smoking and prescribed two medications. "Those were to relieve the congestion in my chest (which I didn't have) and strep throat (which I also didn't have). We paid and left. I knew I didn't have strep throat, and I wasn't sick from smoking, but I took the medicine because it might help, and he was a doctor," says the woman.

The medicine made her feel worse, and the woman eventually went to a physician assistant who diagnosed a urinary tract infection and prescribed medication that provided immediate relief. Looking back, the woman muses: "I wondered why the first doctor was so incompetent. He came highly recommended. I guess he figured I was a young hypochondriac. I didn't really spend that much more time with the physician assistant, but she believed I was sick, where the other doctor obviously didn't."

This true story brings up an interesting question. What makes an illness real? Is it symptoms, lab tests, a certain look or demeanor? A by-product of organic medicine is the belief that an illness is not real unless it's physically verifiable, and society frowns on those who complain of "imaginary" conditions.

The phrase "sick in the head" is typically a put-down, an insult that suggests one is crazy or out of touch with reality. Yet, in reality, there's strong evidence that what people think does affect how they feel, germs or no germs.

WHAT DO YOU THINK?

1. How do you feel if a doctor tells you there is nothing wrong, but you feel sick?
2. If you feel sick but the doctor can find nothing wrong with you, are you sick?
3. How would you feel if you were told your illness was "all in your head"?
4. What would you do if you thought the doctor's diagnosis was incorrect?

---

into two branches, one for the mind and one for the body. From this perspective, disease (a physical condition) is distinguishable from illness (the condition as it is experienced). Of course, this distinction goes only so far. Few people would argue that the mind and the body have no influence on each other. Nevertheless, dualism was (and still is) accepted as a general principle. For the most part, medical doctors (e.g., internists, cardiologists, neurologists) consider it their primary function to treat physical ailments. Mental health is more the domain of psychiatrists, psychologists, social workers, and the like.

Health Care in the New World

Near the end of the Renaissance, European settlers began inhabiting North America. Despite our romantic notions of it, the New World was not a healthy place, physically or emotionally.

Health Conditions

The relatively good health enjoyed by Native Americans before 1600 was replaced by widespread epidemics after European settlers began arriving, and the early settlers fared little better. James Cassedy (1991) reports that 80% of the settlers in Virginia died between 1607 and 1625, and contact with settlers resulted in the death of 90% of the Native American population. The settlers suffered from exhaustion, malnutrition, and, very often, severe depression. In addition, both settlers and Native Americans were threatened by exposure to diseases uncommon in their homelands. Without the immunity that might have resulted from previous exposure, many died of conditions such as measles, dysentery, malaria, and the flu.

Health care consisted mainly of family efforts and home remedies. Caregivers were diverse, including physicians as well as folk therapists specializing in herbs, hypnosis, acupuncture, phrenology (based on the size and shape of the skull), and other forms of treatment. Many of these folk remedies remained quite popular until the late 1800s (Cassedy, 1991).

Hippocrates' Influence

People nostalgic for the age of humble country doctors may not wish to turn time back quite so far as the 1700s. Physicians in colonial America adhered largely to Hippocrates' idea of body humors, bloodletting, and purging. Early accounts describe patients who died after being induced to vomit 100 times or enduring days of sweating and bleeding (Cassedy, 1991). Cotton Mather, a Boston minister and healer, spoke out against such aggressive treatments. He once wrote:

> Before we go any farther, let this Advice to the Sick be principally attended to: *Don't kill 'em!* ... If we stopt here, and said no more, this were enough to save more *Lives* than our *Wars* have destroyed. (quoted by J. Duffy, 1979, p. 35)

It's no wonder that people preferred more gentle folk remedies and often summoned doctors only as a last resort.

Women's Role

In early America women played an important but unofficial role in health care. Most care was provided in the home, where women were expected to nurse ill family members. Schools of nursing had yet to be established. During the Civil War, female nurses and a small number of unlicensed female physicians were accepted as military medics, but the prevailing assumption was that most women were too delicate and uneducated to be doctors (Bonner, 1992). We will explore the role of women and ethnically diverse people more in Chapter 6.

THE RISE OF ORTHODOX MEDICINE

The Industrial Revolution was made possible by mass production and diverse power sources available in the United States by the late 1800s. Industrialization brought people to urban centers to work in factories and made health care a

Women such as nurse Clara Barton cared for wounded soldiers during the American Civil War, but women of the time were not accepted as physicians.

booming business. This dramatically widened the schism between what Cassedy (1991) calls **orthodox practitioners,** who were educated in medical schools, and **sectarians,** who practiced folk medicine taught to them by friends and family members.

Folk medicine had long been popular as a safer and less painful alternative to orthodox medicine (also referred to as *conventional medicine*). However, these advantages were diminished by the introduction of anesthesia and sterilization in conventional medical centers, medical research and technology, medical school reform, and a campaign to wipe out disease through orthodox medicine. Together these factors contributed to the decline of sectarian medicine.

Population Shifts

Industrialization increased the demand for medical care. The number of crippling injuries rose with the introduction of heavy machinery in factories and on farms (Cassedy, 1991). Contagion was also a threat in dense population centers, a factor aggravated by inadequate drainage and waste disposal.

Medicine became more lucrative, but also more demanding. Larger patient-to-physician ratios made house calls impractical and required physicians to develop more intricate methods of keeping records. Hospitals and clinics were opened to bring patients and doctors together. The image of the solitary traveling country doctor gave way to that of the physician situated at the hub of an overwhelming number of patients, professionals, and technical facilities.

Germ Theory

At about the same time, a scientific breakthrough helped hospitals and medical centers become safer and more appealing than in the past. That breakthrough was germ theory, which became widely accepted in the late 1800s through the work of Louis Pasteur.

Simply put, **germ theory** states that disease is caused by microscopic organisms (Twaddle & Hessler, 1987). The ramifications of such a simple notion are astounding. An awareness of microscopic agents has allowed communities to remove the threat of many contagious diseases, reduce the incidence of infection, and develop inoculations against smallpox, measles, polio, and other diseases. Based on germ theory, Joseph Lister revolutionized surgery by sterilizing medical instruments and environments (Raffel & Raffel, 1989). Hospital personnel began cleansing their instruments and separating people with contagious diseases from other patients.

Research and Technology

Medical centers made it possible to collect large amounts of patient data systematically and to acquire expensive technology. As research and technology advanced, so did the demands on health professionals to expand their knowledge, increase their patient loads, and track the health of a diverse population (Raffel & Raffel, 1989). With so many demands, it was necessary for physicians to limit the time they spent with each patient, promoting the idea that medical communication should be brief and to the point.

Medical developments also made it important for doctors to be well trained. Physicians increasingly gained legitimacy through attendance at medical schools, membership in medical societies, contributions to professional journals and research, and eventually, through laws requiring doctors to be state licensed. The American Medical Association (AMA) was organized in 1846 to unite doctors across the country and to speak on their behalf.

Campaign of Orthodox Medicine

In his book *The Silent World of Doctor and Patient,* Jay Katz (1984) makes a case that conventional practitioners in the early 1900s sought to distinguish themselves as the legitimate guardians of people's health. In Katz's view, this campaign was not entirely self-serving. Many people believed that scientific knowledge and technology could be used to eradicate disease. Whether conventional medicine was more concerned with this goal or with attaining professional dominance, the effect was the same. Folk medicine was largely discredited as quackery, and "orthodox" medicine gained a virtual monopoly over health care. As Katz describes it, this monopoly seemed to eliminate the need for physicians to explain or justify their actions:

> Since they no longer had to defend themselves against the criticism of rival groups, doctors asserted more adamantly, and now without fear of contradiction, that laymen could not judge medical practices and had to comply with medical orders. (p. 39)

Physicians' authority was considered unquestionable. Doctors were not expected to express doubts or uncertainties, and they were not to be influenced by the opinions of people (including patients) less educated than themselves.

The image of physicians as all-knowing authorities inspired public trust. But defining medical professionalism in terms of certainty and scientific expertise discouraged doctors from showing emotions or admitting doubts or mistakes (Katz, 1984). At the same time, patients and their loved ones were often silenced into submission. Soon, many patients were too trusting or intimidated to speak freely to their doctors (Katz, 1984).

The Flexner Report

One part of the campaign to promote scientific medicine took the form of medical school reform.

WHAT DO YOU THINK?

The Flexner Report led medical schools to focus intensely on science. In your opinion, what is lost and what is gained by this focus?

Prior to 1900, most medical schools in the United States were run as private businesses, oriented more toward profit than toward rigorous education (Cassedy, 1991). Such schools produced thousands of physicians with little knowledge of biology or physiology.

Disturbed by the low scientific standards in these schools, the AMA commissioned Abraham Flexner of the Carnegie Foundation to evaluate U.S. medical schools and make recommendations. The **Flexner Report**, published in 1910, was a stinging indictment. It charged that all but a few medical schools in the country—the notable exceptions were Harvard, Johns Hopkins, and Western Reserve—were lax in their coverage of biology and other sciences. The report also criticized medical schools for not offering more supervised, hands-on experience with patients.

Of the 155 medical schools he evaluated, Flexner recommended that all but 31 cease operation (Raffel & Raffel, 1989). In fact, nearly two-thirds of U.S. medical schools did close, unable to meet the reform standards (Twaddle & Hessler, 1987). Most of the schools that remained open were incorporated within universities.

The chief model for reform was Johns Hopkins Medical School, with its alliance to Johns Hopkins Hospital (both located in Baltimore, Maryland). Staff members at Johns Hopkins incorporated the most up-to-date knowledge of healthy ventilation, efficiency, and infection control. They emphasized science, laboratory and research experience, and clinical experience with actual patients (Raffel & Raffel, 1989). Following this example, medical school standards across the country became more demanding, and curricula began to focus intensely on organic aspects of disease as well as on clinical and laboratory experience.

The Decline of Sectarian Medicine

For the most part, sectarian healers were not prepared to fight the emerging dominance of

Folks medicine based on herbs, hypnosis, acupuncture, and other methods was largely discredited in the early 1900s, but the popularity of those methods has increased again in the past few decades.

conventional medicine. Americans were enamored with science and technology—both of which were firmly rooted in the camp of conventional medicine by the early 1900s. Moreover, there was little to unite diverse healers, and because their treatments promised gradual and long-term effects, outcomes were hard to isolate and measure (Cassedy, 1991).

Osteopathy and chiropractic were among the only sects to maintain popularity. Other forms of therapy, such as acupuncture and herbal remedies, faded from significance for several decades, at least in the United States. Interestingly, the very reasons that led to their decline—long-term results, low-tech methods—are now contributing to a resurgence of popularity as people seek to reduce costs and to prevent ill health. We will focus more on that in Chapter 7.

Twentieth-Century Health Care

Medicine began to depend ever more on technology, and by 1900 physicians were using x-rays to see inside the body. High-powered microscopes identified a long list of diseases, including malaria, influenza, pneumonia, tuberculosis, and more (Reiser, 1978). With the new technology, a small vial of blood could be the basis for dozens of diagnostic procedures. The phrase "a battery of tests" became common. The efficiency of technology, combined with people's confidence in it, made it an appealing option in medical care.

People's confidence in medicine grew, but as health care became high tech it lost some of the intimacy to which people were accustomed. Emotional concerns can seem out of place in the sterile, scientific atmosphere of clinics and hospitals, and caregivers trained in the sciences were not necessarily prepared to deal with psychosocial aspects of illness. In addition, doctors were so greatly outnumbered by their patients that it became difficult to establish close relationships with them all.

Social conditions affected medicine as well. Racial segregation continued well into the twentieth century. African American patients and caregivers were not allowed into most hospitals in the United States until the 1960s (a topic to be covered more thoroughly in Chapter 6). Even as the United States was building one of the most respected medical systems in the world, its benefits were not available to all citizens.

Specialization

The immense growth in medical knowledge and technology spawned an era of **specialization** in which doctors focused on particular aspects of health. Neurologists, allergists, radiologists, cardiovascular surgeons, and oncologists (to name a few) began limiting their practices to specific concerns. A patient with an ailment in any of these categories could see a specialist rather than a generalist, a prospect that was appealing but expensive. Before long, it became more prestigious and profitable to be a specialist than to be a general practitioner. This trend eventually led to a critical shortage of general practitioners—a shortage that continues today. It also changed the nature of health communication. Talk about broader concerns often seems out of place when seeing an expert who focuses on a specific body part or system.

Medicine and Free Enterprise

As health care evolved over the course of U.S. history, it came to be treated largely as a free-market

? CAN YOU GUESS?

1. What percentage of U.S. residents age 65 and older are uninsured?

2. Prior to the Patient Protection and Affordable Care Act passed in 2010, the number of uninsured residents in the United States was equal to the population of which state?

   a. Maine

   b. Alabama

   c. Oklahoma

Answers appear at the end of the chapter.

commodity. That is, consumers, commanding what buying power they could, were soon able to choose between a range of caregivers who charged fees for the care they provided.

Insurance became particularly important in the United States as health care costs rose to cover the expenses of medical technology, education, specialization, staffing, and facilities. The premise of insurance is to pool resources so that expenses are spread over a great number of people, saving any one subscriber from crushing debt. This assumes that most people will not require more than they contribute and that enough people will subscribe to establish an adequate treasury. These premises were about to topple.

Putting the Brakes on Health Care Costs

The strength of the United States after World War II made it a model for rebuilding countries, many of which received medical aid from the United States. However, a crisis was brewing. In this section, we discuss the financial dilemma surrounding health care that has given rise to managed care.

Health and Wealth

By the mid-1900s, Americans who could afford health insurance had access to specialists and facilities as superb as any in the world. It seemed for a while that no expense was too great, especially when the government or insurance companies were footing the bill.

The emphasis on individuality and the value of human life in the United States fostered the expectation of equal treatment for all and immense expenditures for the sake of single individuals (Balint & Shelton, 1996). In practice, of course, the system fell far short of that ideal. Discrimination has never been fully abolished, and the poor have always been underserved. Nevertheless, the ideology of individualism justified using every resource available for any patient deemed to be in need of it.

Problems

Eventually, the rising cost of health care became more than Americans could afford. The population increased as life expectancy lengthened. Today, U.S. residents live an average of 78.3 years—32 years longer than most settlers in colonial America (Taylor, 1999; U.S. Census Bureau, 2012). That is partly because of better living conditions and better medical care. Diseases once fatal have become treatable, allowing us to extend our lives, albeit sometimes with expensive long-term treatment.

It became clear by the 1960s that health care was too expensive. Health insurance rates became too expensive for many Americans. In 1965 the government stepped in with the creation of Medicare and Medicaid, publicly funded health insurance programs for impoverished children and pregnant women, people with disabilities, and people 65 and older. Even so, tens of millions of U.S. residents were still uninsured (McDermott, 1995).

A tragic spiral developed. As Americans were forced to drop their insurance coverage, insurance treasuries decreased, leading to rate hikes for those who continued to subscribe, forcing more people to drop their coverage, and so on. Government-sponsored health programs forecast bankruptcies, unable to keep up with rising medical costs and the growing number of uninsured people in need.

The United States also began to experience a shortage of primary care doctors, especially in rural and low-income areas. This was particularly lamentable because primary care physicians are valuable in tracking and monitoring people's overall care. Without primary care, the uncoordinated efforts of various specialists may lead to treatment duplications and unforeseen drug interactions. Moreover, systemic illnesses are more apt to go undetected by doctors with a very specific focus. Finally, many patients became discontent because specialists were not focused on them as whole persons.

Reform Efforts

Beginning in the late 1970s, several measures were initiated to curb costs and improve medical care. One was increased surveillance. Utilization review boards began to review patient records to identify treatment duplications and to see if costs were justified. Second, funding agencies (government and private insurers) began to require that patients see specialists only with referrals from primary care physicians.

Finally, funding agencies established specific reimbursement rates for health services. For example, **diagnosis-related groups** (**DRGs**) establish in advance what the funding agency will pay hospitals for specified procedures. One effect of set reimbursement rates is that funding agencies largely control the market value of health services.

A major player in this process is the government. In theory, the U.S. health system is private rather than government-funded, but the numbers tell a different story. The U.S. government will soon pay more than 50% of the nation's health care bill through Medicaid and Medicare ("National Health Expenditures," 2011). The government's proportion is already higher than that if you figure in health benefits for government employees and contractors, elected officials, state children's health insurance programs, and military-related health benefits as well. "It's not even a question of whether or not the U.S. government is going to get into the insurance business. We're there," says analyst Sara Robinson (2009, para. 8).

As a result, the reimbursement rates set for government-funded health plans have become a baseline of sorts. This is important because reimbursement rates limit the care that health agencies are willing or able to provide. If reimbursement rates are too low, health organizations may discontinue services or stop treating certain patients. Especially worrisome is funding for diagnostic tests, AIDS treatment, care for dying individuals, and long-term care. For example, in 2008 the U.S. legislature considered cutting nursing home reimbursements by two-tenths of a percent. That sounds small, but the measure would take $5 billion out of nursing home budgets in just 5 years ("Nursing Homes," 2008).

Reimbursement restrictions have had several effects besides influencing what services are marketable. First, health care organizations are under pressure to keep costs down. If their expenses fall below reimbursement rates, they get to keep the difference. However, if they exceed them, they take a loss. Furthermore, paperwork to justify procedures has increased, and health professionals accustomed to professional autonomy sometimes chafe under the scrutiny of third parties who second-guess their judgments.

Managed Care

Another response to cost containment was the creation of managed care. About 99% of U.S. residents with employer-sponsored health plans and about 87.6% of U.S. physicians now participate in managed care plans (Boukus, Cassil, & O'Malley, 2009; Henry J. Kaiser, 2011). **Managed care organizations** essentially coordinate the costs and delivery of health services. Whereas health decisions used to be made almost entirely by caregivers and patients, managed care organizations now recruit patients, match them up with caregivers and facilities, and monitor expenses. As such, managed care represents the influence of people (or entities) other than patients and caregivers. By managing resources such as money, labor, technology, and facilities, people in managed care organizations seek to make health care more efficient and affordable.

The easiest way to understand managed care (and how it compares to traditional health insurance) is to look at it from the consumer's perspective. Imagine that Sam is trying to decide between traditional health insurance and managed care options offered through his employer.

CONVENTIONAL INSURANCE

At one point, nearly everyone who had health insurance in the United States had conventional (also known as *indemnity*) insurance. Now that managed care has become the standard, this type of insurance is rare. Only 1% of employee-sponsored plans meet this description (Henry J. Kaiser, 2011). (See Figure 2.1.) But let's imagine that Sam's employer is one of the few that offers this option.

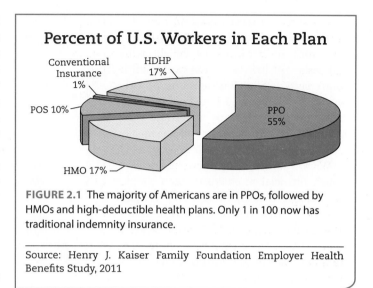

FIGURE 2.1 The majority of Americans are in PPOs, followed by HMOs and high-deductible health plans. Only 1 in 100 now has traditional indemnity insurance.

Source: Henry J. Kaiser Family Foundation Employer Health Benefits Study, 2011

Based on national averages, with indemnity insurance, Sam will pay a set monthly amount (his **insurance premium**) and the first $500 (his **insurance deductible**) of medical expenses he incurs every year. If Sam's expenses exceed his deductible, his insurance will pay 80% of the remaining medical bill and Sam will pay 20%. To prevent Sam from going into overwhelming debt, there is an upper limit, called a **catastrophic cap**, on the amount of out-of-pocket money he will be required to pay each year. Beyond that limit, insurance pays 100%. Amounts vary, but let's say that Sam's cap is $1,500 a year for covered services.

Conventional insurance is classified as **fee-for-service** because providers are paid (reimbursed) for specific care they provide. In other words, doctors, hospitals, physical therapists, and so on, make money only if patients use their services. Traditional insurance is also known as a **third-party payer** system because, as you can see, there are three parties involved—the provider, the patient, and the payer (insurance company). Practically speaking, this means that if Sam has knee surgery this year, he will pay the first $500 and 20% of the remaining medical bills in addition to his monthly premiums. The insurance company will pay the rest.

As mentioned, this is how almost all insurance used to work, meaning that it's quite possible that care providers overprescribed tests and treatment at times. For one thing, more treatment means more pay in a fee-for-services system. But also keep in mind that diagnostics is detective work. It's hard to know which medical tests will help solve the puzzle until the results are in. Furthermore, providers wary of being sued were (and still are) reluctant to overlook or undertreat concerns out of fear that they will be considered negligent if things don't go well.

With traditional insurance, there isn't much financial incentive to keep people well. Most policies don't cover routine checkups. That means that Sam would pay for those visits entirely from his own pocket. This is a significant difference between conventional insurance and managed care.

Here are two final considerations for Sam. Conventional insurance premiums are usually more expensive than other forms of health insurance. However, the advantage is freedom of choice. Under this type of plan, Sam may choose his own caregivers.

Next Sam considers managed care. The most obvious benefit is that his employer probably *does* offer some type of managed care plan, perhaps several types. This means the employer will help pay for Sam's monthly premium. Employers in the United States currently pay about 82% of the monthly premium for one-person coverage and 78% for family coverage (Henry J. Kaiser, 2011). The confusing part may be deciding which managed care plan to choose. So let's walk through the typical options. The averages presented here are based on the Henry J. Kaiser Family Foundation's 2011 study of employee-sponsored health plans.

HEALTH MAINTENANCE ORGANIZATION

A **health maintenance organization (HMO)** is designed to be more or less a one-stop shop for members' health needs. An HMO hires physicians and other care providers, who work directly for the HMO. Their salaries are covered by the premiums that members (like Sam) pay each month.

If Sam chooses an HMO through his employer, his portion of the monthly premium will probably be about $78 a month (for one-person coverage) and he will be charged a **copay** (usually $15, $20,

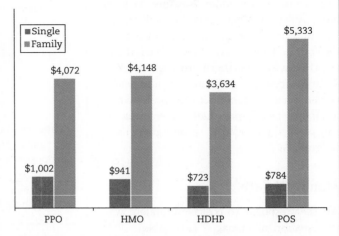

Average Yearly Premiums Paid by U.S. Employees

- ■ Single
- ■ Family

PPO: $1,002 / $4,072
HMO: $941 / $4,148
HDHP: $723 / $3,634
POS: $784 / $5,333

FIGURE 2.2 High-deductible plans have the lowest premiums, but they require a great deal out of pocket. Point-of-service plans offer the advantages of both HMOs and PPOs but have the highest premiums.

Source: Henry J. Kaiser Family Foundation Employer Health Benefits Study, 2011

or $25) every time he visits a doctor.[1] This includes checkups and preventive care visits. (See Figure 2.2 for a comparison of premium costs.)

Let's pause for a moment to look back in time. In the beginning, premiums and copays were usually the only costs associated with HMO membership. All other medical costs were absorbed by the HMO. Knowing that he would never pay more than $25 a visit, Sam would probably be more willing to have annual checkups and to see a doctor about minor health concerns than he would have been with conventional insurance. This incentive to seek wellcare is meant to save money in the long run, both for members and for HMOs, because, where health care is concerned, a pound of prevention is often less expensive than an ounce of cure.

These days about 29% of HMOs charge a deductible (usually $900 or so a year). Thus, the

---

[1]For now, let's leave prescription drugs, outpatient surgery, and hospital care out of the mix. With managed care, separate copays and deductibles usually apply to those services.

incentive to seek preventive and minor care is not quite as great as before. But if Sam needs a lot of medical care, HMO membership might still save him money. He can feel confident that he won't have exorbitant medical bills, no matter what. (With traditional insurance, even 20% of a major surgery bill is pretty high.) The trade-off is that Sam cannot choose any doctor he wants. He is limited to providers who work for the HMO, and he cannot see specialists (even if they are part of the HMO) unless such care is recommended by his primary care physician in the HMO. This is designed to avoid unnecessary visits and costs, but the approval process and limitations can be frustrating.

You guessed it: HMOs are not third-party payer systems. In their case, it's as if the insurance company and the medical center merged into one. And they are not based on fee-for-service. Instead, HMOs are **capitated systems**. They receive a set (capitated) amount, in the form of premiums (plus minor copays), no matter what care they provide. It is the job of HMOs to manage both the budget and the care.

Some people (including many physicians) worry that combining the insurance company with the medical center presents a conflict of interest. We will talk more about that shortly. First, let's continue the tour of managed care options.

PREFERRED PROVIDER ORGANIZATION

A **preferred provider organization (PPO)**, also in the managed care family, works a little differently. If Sam joins a PPO, he will pay a monthly premium ($83 on average) that is just a bit higher than HMO membership. He might also have a deductible. (About 81% of PPOs have deductibles, usually about $675 a year. See Figure 2.3 for more details.) The difference is that, as a PPO member, Sam's copay is not a prescribed amount. Instead, he pays a percentage of the medical bill.

Here's how it works. Rather than hiring care providers outright, as HMOs do, PPOs contract with independent care providers. The PPO agrees to put the provider on a "preferred" list if the provider

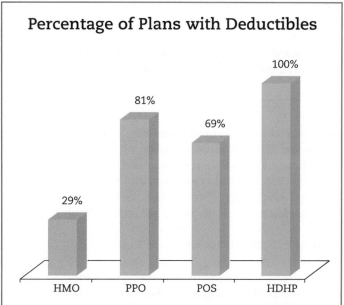

Percentage of Plans with Deductibles

FIGURE 2.3 Relatively few HMOs have deductibles, but most other plans do.

Source: Henry J. Kaiser Family Foundation Employer Health Benefits Study, 2011

offers services at agreed-on discount rates to the PPO's members.

Sam's copay is a percentage of this discounted fee. This means that he will pay different amounts for different services. It also means that he can choose any health care providers he wishes, with one caveat. As the name implies, providers on the "preferred" list cost less than those who are not. There are often higher copays and/or separate deductibles for providers not on the list. But unlike HMO members, Sam will receive *some* financial coverage no matter which caregivers he chooses. (As with conventional insurance, there's usually an annual catastrophic cap for PPO members.)

If Sam requires a lot of care or sees nonpreferred providers, he's likely to pay more as a PPO member than as an HMO member. But he has more freedom of choice. He may also encounter less conflict of interest because (1) PPO providers do not work directly for the managed care organization, so they may be spared some of the pressure to cut costs and speed up patient visits, and (2) they operate on a fee-for-service basis that gives them more incentive to prescribe (rather than avoid) tests and treatment.

These advantages may be why the majority of people with employee health plans choose PPOs (55% compared to 17% in HMOs).

HMOs and PPOs used to be the only two options in managed care. But a few others have emerged.

POINT OF SERVICE

Point of service (**POS**) plans combine features of HMOs and PPOs. If Sam chooses to see only preferred providers, the POS plans feels like an HMO. He pays a set, minimal copay every time he seeks care, and his primary care provider oversees his care and determines if he should see specialists or not.

However, Sam also has the option to see providers outside the network. At that point, the POS plan functions like a PPO. That is, Sam pays a portion of the medical bills, and he may have to meet a deductible. In sum, although Sam has greater choice than with HMO membership, there are still financial incentives to see preferred providers.

POS plans are relatively scarce. So far, about 10% of people with employee health plans subscribe to them. On average, monthly premiums are more expensive than HMOs and PPOs. About 69% of POS plans have deductibles, which are usually about $928 per year.

HIGH-DEDUCTIBLE HEALTH PLAN

Imagine that Sam is in excellent health and almost never seeks medical care. He may wonder, "Why should I pay such high premiums when I never meet the deductible anyway? My money goes in, but it doesn't come out—at least it doesn't come to me." And if he's really thinking long-term, he might also wonder, "Rather than paying high premiums, why can't I save that money for the future, when my medical bills are likely to be higher?"

These are the basic concepts behind **high-deductible health plans** (**HDHPs**). Members pay relatively low monthly premiums (about $60 per month in employer-sponsored plans). In exchange, their deductibles are two to three times more than for other plans (about $1,908 per year), and the catastrophic cap is several thousand dollars higher. HDHPs are typically coupled with other managed care plans. Thus, members enroll in either an HMO, a PPO, or a POS. The difference is in the out-of-pocket expenses they absorb.

Furthermore, membership in an HDHP qualifies one to invest in a tax-deferred **health savings account** (**HSA**). That's why you often see the abbreviations HDHP/SO (HDHP with a savings option) or HDHP/HSA. Sam and his employer can contribute to his HSA over time, creating a fund that he can use to pay for future medical expenses. As long as they invest the money while Sam is an HDHP member and he uses the money only for medical bills, Sam doesn't pay taxes on it.

The U.S. government approved tax breaks for HSAs in 2003 to give people an incentive to control their own health costs. After all, if you have a high deductible or are paying the medical bills from your own savings account, you might think twice before seeing a doctor.

Unfortunately, this is also the downside of HDHPs. Some people buy into them because they can afford the lower premiums but then find out that they can't afford the out-of-pocket costs that lie ahead. Reports abound of people who are insured but still cannot afford to buy prescription drugs or see a doctor. Even if Sam hasn't needed much medical care in years past, one accident or appendicitis attack can wreck his finances if he is not adequately insured.

Critics of HDHPs point out that premiums, once quite low, continue to rise and that the true audience for HDHP/HSAs have been the wealthy, who use them as tax shelters. The numbers bear this out. The average taxpayer in the United States makes $51,000 per year. The average income among people claiming HSA tax benefits is $133,000 (Woodbury, 2007). The most comprehensive study of HDHPs subscribers to date shows that subscribers save

WHAT DO YOU THINK?

■ Which type of health insurance do you prefer as a consumer? Why? What type would you prefer as a health professional?

■ Less than half of Americans fully understand their health insurance plans. Do you feel confident that you understand yours?

■ Do you worry that your doctor might not prescribe tests or treatments because he or she is being pressured to cut costs? Why or why not?

money, at least in the short run, but mostly because they tend to skimp on routine and preventive care (Buntin, Haviland, McDevitt, & Sood, 2011).

Another criticism is that enticing people to pay lower premiums further depletes the money available to pay for health costs across the nation. In Sam's case, maybe he hasn't needed insurance payouts so far, but the day may come when his benefits outpace his contributions. This only works if people at every need level are invested in the system.

As you can see, managed care has given rise to its own vocabulary, and the system and terms continue to evolve. For a handy synopsis of relevant terms, see Box 2.3.

ORGANIZATIONS' PERSPECTIVE

Managed care also affects hospitals, medical centers, treatment and diagnostic centers, and other organizations in the health care industry. These organizations

---

BOX 2.3

Managed Care at a Glance

managed care: A health care system in which income, resources, and health services are supervised by a managing body such as a health maintenance organization or preferred provider organization. Patients pay the organization a set fee each month to receive health services.

health maintenance organization (HMO): A managed care organization that offers enrollees a variety of health services for a set monthly fee and copays. Caregivers are usually employed directly by the HMO and provide services only to HMO members.

preferred provider organization (PPO): A managed care organization that pays independent caregivers a discounted fee for each service they provide to PPO members. Patients may visit providers not on the preferred list, but they pay higher fees to do so.

point of service (POS): A hybrid between an HMO and a PPO. Members may pay an established copay to see providers affiliated with the plan. But they are also covered (at a higher cost) if they see providers not on the list.

high-deductible health plan (HDHP): A managed care plan with lower-than-normal premiums but higher deductibles and out-of-pocket spending caps. Most HDHPs qualify members to establish tax-exempt health savings accounts.

health savings account (HSA): A tax-exempt savings plan (a lot like an IRA) in which people can set aside money to pay future medical bills. U.S. taxpayers qualify for HSAs if they are part of high-deductible health plans. Money saved can be used over many years' time.

health reimbursement account (HRA): Not to be confused with an HSA, a health reimbursement account (HRA) is a temporary fund in which an employee can set aside tax-exempt money for health care costs incurred within the plan year. For example, you might have $100 set aside from each paycheck before taxes. Your employer will use this money to reimburse you for medical expenses during the year. Typically, if you do not use the money in an HRA by year's end, you forfeit the balance.

premium: A membership fee paid by subscribers in a conventional insurance or managed care plan. Usually deducted from one's paycheck.

capitation: A set fee paid to cover a person's health needs, regardless of the care actually required.

catastrophic cap: An upper limit on the amount of out-of-pocket expense a subscriber is required to pay each year.

copay: The portion of a health care bill the patient is required to pay when services are rendered.

deductible: The amount of out-of-pocket medical expense an insured individual is required to pay before receiving financial assistance from the insurer. For example, you might pay the first $500 of your emergency room bill, and insurance will pay 80% of the remaining cost.

fee-for-service: The practice of being paid for specific care provided.

may contract with managed care agencies to provide care for their members, or they may offer their own managed care plans. Either way, their income is largely governed by the terms of managed care, with its reliance on discounts and capitated fees.

I was public relations director at a large medical center in the early 1990s, when managed care tipped the scales in our market. Prior to that point, we received daily census reports detailing how many patients were in the hospital. The higher the census, the greater was our revenue. But I remember a pivotal meeting at which the CEO said to us:

> We now rely on DRGs and capitation to such an extent that "beds filled" doesn't mean much. We could just as easily lose money on a patient as make money. And sometimes we make more money when the beds are empty!

What he meant, of course, was that capitation agreements provided us money even when patients didn't need care. But, on the flip side, reimbursements rates below previous market value meant that we had to cut costs or we would quickly find ourselves in a hole.

Capitation, discounted fees, DRGs, and other cost-curtailment efforts may be especially hard on not-for-profit medical organizations. These organizations are granted tax exemptions because they provide care for needy persons and they reinvest the money they earn in the organization rather than paying owners or stockholders (Bruck, 1996). However, even with tax breaks, making less money on insured patients means that these organizations have less surplus to cover the care of people who cannot afford to pay. And non-profit organizations are typically not at liberty to discontinue services that yield low reimbursements.

Overall, there are upsides and downsides to managed care. Following are a few considerations both ways. One note before we begin: In the parlance of health care, *insurers* include both conventional insurance companies and managed care organizations. However, as you have seen, as much as 99% of insurance policies are now managed care memberships. So when people talk about "insurers" these days, they mostly mean managed care organizations.

ADVANTAGES OF MANAGED CARE

Imagine yourself around the table at a health care center in the early days of managed care. You are present at a historical turning point. Rather than earning income after the fact for specific services you perform, the health center will now have an annual budget paid by member fees. It's not a huge budget. It's actually less than you made before. But it's predictable, so you can plan ahead. The beauty of capitation is the freedom to be proactive, to accomplish some things you could never do before. You have the opportunity—in fact, the obligation—to redesign how medical care is provided.

Physicians Joseph Dorsey and Donald Berwick were around that table. They were on staff at Harvard Pilgrim Health Care when managed care began. "Capitation gave us the flexibility to use our budget with creativity limited only by our imaginations and habits," they recall (Dorsey & Berwick, 2008, p. A9). The Harvard Pilgrim team invested in innovative and patient-friendly services such as reminder calls, after-hour phone access, extended clinic hours, time-saving technology, and more. They devoted themselves to providing better, more patient-centered care for less money than before. As a result, their patient/members made half as many visits to emergency rooms as the state average. "The innovations that managed care and capitation made possible were good for almost everyone" (Dorsey & Berwick, 2008, p. A9).

That's one advantage of managed care in its purest form—it gives health care professionals a means and an incentive to work together to provide innovative care in a cost-effective way. With managed care, there's a strong incentive to streamline processes and eliminate wasteful practices.

A related benefit is that managed care is designed to make health care more affordable. In a global sense, it is oriented to making the most of every health care dollar. At an individual level, membership in a managed care organization, particularly an HMO, curbs financial risk because subscribers pay set (or reduced) fees even if they need a lot of care. This can be especially valuable to people with chronic illnesses who benefit from regular treatment (Nussbaum, Ragan, & Whaley, 2003).

Third, managed care presents an incentive to keep patients well. In the long run, organizations make more money if people don't require costly treatments. And everyone stands to benefit if managed care invests in disease prevention and public education. (As you'll soon see, this potential has not been realized so far.)

So far we have talked mostly about the advantages for patients. But providers may also benefit from managed care. Working for an HMO has the potential to ease the administrative demands of running a private medical practice. The HMO handles facilities, maintenance, administrative and support staff (receptionists, nurses, and so on), billing procedures, marketing, and more. This can mean more stability, fewer headaches, and better working hours because providers can share the patient load with others in the organization. A physician I know says that managed care gave him his life back. He doesn't make as much money as before, but he's only on call one day a week, and he can schedule days off—luxuries he didn't have as a physician entrepreneur.

For health professionals who are just getting started and those worried about attracting new patients, managed care organizations can also offer the advantages of a ready-made caseload. Signing on as an HMO employee or a preferred provider means built-in advertising among hundreds or thousands of available patients.

DISADVANTAGES OF MANAGED CARE

Unfortunately, as the system has evolved, the disadvantages of managed care have become numerous. Public opinion about managed care has not been favorable since 1995. In 2006, *Modern Healthcare* magazine proclaimed: "Over the past 20 years, managed care has gone from industry hero to industry villain and then to health care has-been" ("Managed Care," 2006, p. 20). Nearly everyone agrees that the system is badly flawed. It may help as you read the following list of drawbacks to keep in mind that *something* had to be done. It is conceivable that we would be in even worse shape without the managed care revolution. But clearly, we still have a long way to go.

One disappointment is that the goal of cutting overall costs, thus insuring a greater proportion of the population, has not been met. Managed care may have slowed spiraling costs to some extent, but premiums have climbed steadily, as has the percentage of uninsured Americans.

To illustrate, managed care organizations originated in the mid-1980s and doubled in number during the 1990s. But, during the 1990s, health insurance premiums rose by 53%, far outpacing inflation and wage increases. And health care costs rose even more—by 57% in the same time frame (Economic Research Initiative, 2005). By the

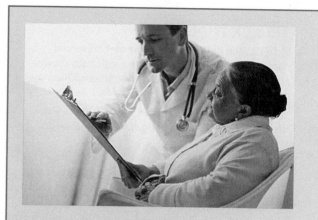

Potential Advantages of Managed Care
■ The potential for proactive budgeting and teamwork
■ Goal of making health care more affordable
■ Incentive to keep patients well
■ Less administrative load for practitioners
■ Ready-made caseload for practitioners

decade's end, the number of uninsured Americans didn't shrink. It grew by 23%, from 34.7 million to 42.6 million (Economic Research Initiative, 2005).

In 2005, the number of uninsured in the United States jumped from 44.8 million to 47 million in one year—the largest leap since 1992 (U.S. Census Bureau, 2007). In 2010, portions of the Patient Protection and Affordable Care Act (covered in Chapter 12) went into effect, allowing daughters and sons to stay on their parents' health plans until they are 26. That boosted insurance rates among young adults, but it wasn't enough to reverse the overall downward spiral. By 2012, 49.9 million Americans were uninsured, the largest number ever (U.S. Census Bureau, 2010a). To put that into perspective, consider that 49 million is more than the combined populations of Alabama, Alaska, Arizona, Colorado, Connecticut, Delaware, Hawaii, Idaho, Iowa, Kansas, Maine, Montana, New Mexico, North Dakota, Oklahoma, Oregon, South Carolina, Vermont, West Virginia, and Wyoming! (For more about the impact of being uninsured, see the *Check It Out!* sidebar on the next page.)

Some people assume that the uninsured are covered by programs such as Medicaid and Medicare. Actually, people in those programs count as *insured*. The 49.9 million had no insurance of any

CHECK IT OUT!

■ To view an online video about the causes and consequences of being uninsured, visit: http://www.kaiseredu.org/Tutorials-and-Presentations/Overview-of-the-Uninsured.aspx.

■ To take an online quiz about the uninsured, visit http://quiz.kff.org/uninsured/uninsured-quiz.aspx.

type—not even government-sponsored assistance. (We will talk more about these issues and health reform efforts in Chapter 12.)

Spokespersons for managed care say premium hikes are necessary because health expenses are rising and the population is getting older. However, critics charge that managed care organizations are making profits while patients and providers lose money. The average salary of managed care executives is nearly $200,000 a year (Economic Research Institute, 2012), a figure that has been rising even as industry spokespeople say premium hikes are necessary.

It is sometimes said that the United States doesn't have a health care system, it has an illness care system. Managed care was supposed to change that by shifting the focus to cost-saving prevention. That has not happened on the scale many people had hoped. This is mostly because prevention efforts cost in the short run but save in the long run. "I think that [the rising cost of premiums] is primarily due to the short-sighted nature of many of the for-profit companies," said a managed care executive on an anonymous survey. "The managed care plans don't think it's worthwhile to invest in prevention programs when people change their plans frequently, trying to get lower costs" ("Health Economics," 2003, p. 56). In other words, predictably enough, managed care organizations are often reluctant to invest in the long-term health of short-term members.

Critics are also troubled that managed care organizations sometimes pressure providers to limit care and speed up patient visits. Journalists have coined the phrase "death by HMO" to refer to instances in which people's health was hurt or destroyed when decision makers in managed care organizations refused to authorize expensive treatments or delayed approval until it was too late.

Some people worry that these incentives will interfere with caregivers' professional judgment. It is common for HMOs to withhold a portion of physicians' pay, to be awarded only if the treatment they prescribe comes in under budget and only if they see a specified (usually large) number of patients per day. Equally as worrisome are so-called **gag rules** that prohibit physicians from telling patients about costly treatment options. For example, if the doctor believes that a cancer patient might benefit from a certain treatment but the treatment is expensive or not covered by the health plan, the doctor would be disciplined for even mentioning it to the patient. Although the AMA and the federal government have banned the use of gag rules, many say they are at least implicitly enforced. About 31% of managed care physicians surveyed said they had avoided mentioning useful medical procedures to patients because those procedures were not covered by the health plan (Wynia, VanGeest, Cummins, & Wilson, 2003). Physicians worry that patients' mistrust is damaging their professional reputations and diminishing how much patients trust their doctors (Gorawara-Bhat, Gallagher, & Levinson, 2003). (To debate the managed care issue yourself, see Box 2.4.)

Fourth, patients in managed care lose some of the ability to choose or switch caregivers. Even with PPOs and POS plans, there is a strong financial incentive to see providers on the short list. To receive full benefits, members are limited to providers who participate in their care plans, and they may be forced to switch providers if they change employers or if their employers change managed care affiliations. Such disruptions may compromise the quality of patient–caregiver relationships. Some people are more worried than others. Less than half (44%) of older adults surveyed said they would switch doctors to save money (Tu, 2005). However, people ages 18 to 34 felt differently. A large majority (70%) of them would choose a lower-priced plan, even if it required them to change doctors (Tu).

Fifth, medical information becomes less confidential when patient records and caregiving decisions are scrutinized by members of a managed care organization. Of the 51 hospital patients interviewed by Maria Brann and Marifran Mattson (2004), 81% were concerned that their confidential medical information would be inappropriately shared by people within the health care organization. In an earlier study (Eastman, Eastman, &

BOX 2.4   ETHICAL CONSIDERATIONS

Classroom Debate on Managed Care

Managed care is currently the most controversial issue in health care. You have already been exposed to several viewpoints about it. Some people fear that managed care will lessen the quality of medical decisions by limiting what doctors can say and do. Others favor the managed care emphasis on wellness and applaud the effort to cut health care costs. There are other issues, both pro and con. Read up on the managed care debate (a few sources are listed at the end of this box) and develop your own viewpoints.

Hold a classroom debate. Divide the class into four groups: (a) those in favor of HMOs, (b) those who support PPOs, (c) those who propose specific alternatives, and (d) those who support HDHPs. Appoint team captains or have the instructor moderate. One group at a time should present its arguments, with time after each argument for questions and challenges.

(Make sure talking time is divided fairly among the participants.)

As the debate progresses, people may change their minds. If so, they should get up and move to the group that best represents their viewpoints.

SUGGESTED SOURCES

Anderlink, M. R. (2001). *The ethics of managed care: A pragmatic approach.* Bloomington, IN: Indiana University Press.

Bondeson, W. B., & Jones, J. W. (Eds.) (2010). *The ethics of managed care: Professional integrity and patient rights.* Dordrecht, The Netherlands: Springer.

Shapiro, R. S., Tym, K. A., Eastwood, D., Derse, A. R., & Klein, J. P. (2003). Managed care, doctors, and patients: Focusing on relationships, not rights. *Cambridge Quarterly of Healthcare Ethics, 12*(3), 300–307.

Ulrich, C. M., Soeken, K. L., & Miller, N. (2003). Ethical conflict associated with managed care: Views of nurse practitioners. *Nursing Research, 52*(3), 168–175.

Tolson, 1997), 80% of physicians surveyed said they might divulge sensitive information (such as drug abuse) to other members of a health maintenance organization, even if patients asked them not to tell.

Sixth, a great deal of energy in managed care is diverted to paperwork, authorizations, and procedures. Many caregivers say that it is nearly impossible to do their jobs well and meet the increased demand for paperwork. When Locum Tenens, a physician staffing agency, surveyed 2,400 physicians across the United States, only 3% were satisfied with the current health system. The most common complaint was frustration about the hassles and delays of managed care ("Physicians Report," 2008).

Of a similar mind, Bhupinder Singh, a New York general practitioner, told the *New York Times:*

> Thirty percent of my hospital admissions are being denied. There's a 45-day limit on the appeal. You don't bill in time, you lose everything. You're discussing this with a managed care rep on the phone and you think: "You're

Disadvantages of Managed Care

- Health care costs and the number of uninsured continue to rise
- Incentives to focus on prevention have not functioned as expected
- Health professionals are pressured to control costs and speed up visits
- Patients' choice of caregivers is often limited
- Patient privacy is at risk
- Paperwork and oversight are time-consuming and frustrating

sitting there, I'm sitting here. How do you know anything about this patient?" (quoted by Jauhar, 2008a, p. 5)

Likewise, Texas physicians surveyed about managed care gave the system a resounding thumbs-down (Greene, 2008). Here's a brief summary of what they said:

- Some 83% of the physicians have had to hire extra staff to help with the paperwork required by managed care;
- 65% feel that insurers make it needlessly cumbersome and time-consuming to get treatment options approved;
- 64% say that managed care payments to doctors are often late and less than promised; and
- 58% charge that insurers do not educate patients well about their coverage, copayments, and deductibles.

The discontent begins even before many physicians enter practice. Of more than 2,000 medical students surveyed, 35% strongly agreed (and only 5% disagreed) with the statement that "physicians have a responsibility to take care of patients regardless of their ability to pay" (E. Frank, Modi, Elon, & Coughlin, 2008, p. 140). But only 1 in 10 agreed that managed care, as it is currently implemented, does a good job at providing that care.

The extra paperwork translates to less time with patients. An extensive study of hospital nurses revealed that the nurses spent less than one-fifth of their time (just shy of 2 hours per 10-hour shift) providing direct patient care (Hendrich, Chow, Skierczynski, & Lu, 2008). The nurses spent the most time (nearly 4 hours per shift) doing required paperwork. (The rest was spent communicating with other care team members, getting supplies, moving between rooms, and so on.) Patients are frustrated by the red tape as well. Says one managed care Medicaid patient:

> It's hard to get a doctor who takes Medicaid. They send out a list of doctors who'll see us, but they don't tell you that only a few'll take new patients. Nobody wants Medicaid patients. The doctors hate dealing with us, the insurance is such a pain in the butt. (Gillespie, 2001, p. 109)

All in all, the managed care landscape is pretty unsatisfying and even downright frightening. It has changed significantly from the early days when, as physicians Dorsey and Berwick (2008) recall, "neither of us can recall a single instance of being told by management to withhold from a patient any care that we thought, based on evidence, could help" (p. A9). Dorsey and Berwick's initial optimism has turned to disillusionment. Now, they

charge, managed care has been "hijacked by insurance companies" such that physicians are "handcuffed" to procedures and limitations meant to save money today rather than provide high-quality care that will pay off in the long run (p. A9).

For some questions to ask as you consider various managed care plans, see Box 2.5.

MANAGED CARE AROUND THE WORLD

The United States is not the only country grappling with issues of health care costs and access. People in India, China, and Russia rank affordable health plans as the most important benefit an employee can offer (Korkki, 2008). The Japanese health care system, one of the best in the world, has traditionally offered care to every citizen without out-of-pocket expense. But the demands of a disproportionately older population threaten the solvency of the national system (Kakizoe, 2008). Similarly, leaders of the Singapore health system, which is ranked sixth in the world by the World Health Organization, are debating tough choices such as the need to improve patient–caregiver ratios versus investing in expensive cutting-edge medicines. Singaporean Minister of Health Khaw Boon Wan echoed the concerns of people throughout the world: "Our doctors and health care professionals are overworked, and at some point they need a life too. . . . But the patients keep coming" ("World-Class," 2008, np).

Summary

A historical perspective offers suggestions as to why patients and caregivers communicate as they do and why they devote themselves to certain topics but not to others. The ancient Egyptians established a basis for considering health in both spiritual and physical terms. About 2,000 years later, influenced partly by Egyptian ideals, Hippocrates of ancient Greece proposed a rational/empirical model for medicine. Within that model, illness was believed to reflect people's physical well-being as well as their harmony with nature and other people. Parts of the Hippocratic oath continue to influence Western medical ethics.

During the Middle Ages, illness was assumed to be a spiritual matter, to be treated with prayer and holy redemption. Patients' spirituality and behaviors were central to talk between patients and

---

BOX 2.5 RESOURCES

Before You Select a Managed Care Plan

Here are some questions to ask when reviewing health insurance plans.

1. What are my monthly premiums, and, if applicable, what portion of the premium will my employer pay?
2. Will I have copays? If so, how much are they?
3. Is there an annual deductible? If so, how much is it? (*If you are considering a family plan, ask if this amount applies to each person's care or to the family overall.*)
4. Does the deductible apply to preventive care visits?
5. Do separate deductibles or copays apply to preventive care, prescription drugs, outpatient surgery, hospital stays, or visits to nonpreferred providers?
6. Is there an annual catastrophic cap (a limit on my out-of-pocket) on expenses? If so, what is it? What expenses count toward this amount?
7. How many (and which) physicians and specialists are on the plan or the preferred provider list? (*It's a good idea to call a few of these before you sign on, to see if they are accepting new patients and to gauge how long patients typically wait to get an appointment. Just because a provider appears on the list doesn't mean he or she has time for more patients.*)
8. Are there conditions or treatments not covered by this plan? (*Managed care has not been particularly good about funding care for mental health and some other concerns. Ask in advance what's covered and what isn't.*)
9. Is it required that I establish a primary care physician? If so, who are my options? If an HMO, will I be able to see the same physician every time, or will I be required to see whomever is available?
10. To what extent will the plan restrict the prescription drugs I am able to buy with benefits? (*Every plan has formularies, which are lists of approved drugs that the plan covers. Some plans have long lists, and some have short ones. Particularly if you know which drugs you prefer or need to take, it's wise to ask in advance if they are covered.*)
11. Which hospitals are covered by this plan? If more than one, can I choose from among them?

---

caregivers. In the centuries that followed, fervor for accuracy and physical proof characterized the European Renaissance. Talk of faith or emotions was treated as inappropriate, even misleading, to scientific analysis. Cartesian dualism strengthened the separation of mental and physical factors. The basic assumption (which continues to influence medicine) is that patients' thoughts and feelings are largely separate from their physical conditions.

Today, the United States is renowned for its scientific, high-tech medical system. However, spiraling costs and overutilization have made it necessary to allocate health resources with care. Managed care, which developed from the need to rein in medical costs, has spawned new concerns about the quality of care Americans will receive from organizations that have a vested interest in saving money. Few are satisfied that managed care has lived up to its potential to cut costs, promote wellness, stimulate teamwork, and trim waste. Instead, managed care is often criticized for creating hassles and roadblocks, increasing paperwork, second-guessing doctors' judgments, and restricting patients' options.

The need to provide citizens of the world with excellent, affordable health care is a challenge worthy of our best efforts. Throughout the rest of the book, we will examine health care from multiple perspectives—both personal and global—to better understand the needs and opportunities that lie before us.

Key Terms and Theories

Imhotep
religio-empirical approach

Hippocrates
Hippocratic oath
rational/empirical approach
medical spiritualism
barber surgeons
Christian magic
fetishes
René Descartes
principle of verification
Cartesian dualism
orthodox practitioners
sectarians
germ theory
Flexner Report
specialization
diagnosis-related groups (DRGs)
managed care organizations
insurance premium
insurance deductible
catastrophic cap
fee-for-service
third-party payer
health maintenance organization (HMO)
copay
capitated system
preferred provider organization (PPO)
point of service (POS)
high-deductible health plan (HDHP)
health savings account (HAS)
health reimbursement account (HRA)
gag rules

Discussion Questions

1. Why was medicine in Imhotep's time referred to as religio-empirical?
2. How did Hippocrates' ideas about medicine affect the role of physicians and the nature of health communication? How did Hippocrates' ideas influence health care in colonial America?
3. How did the medical spiritualism of the Middle Ages affect health communication?

4. For what reasons (spiritual and practical) did the church ban surgery during the Middle Ages?
5. Based on the principle of verification, how do you know if you are ill? Who is better able to know the state of your health, you or a doctor?
6. What factors led to the rise of conventional ("orthodox") medicine in the United States?
7. How have reimbursement restrictions affected the health care industry?
8. How do fee-for-service and capitated systems differ from a consumer's perspective? From a care provider's perspective?
9. What are the potential advantages and disadvantages of managed care?
10. If you were able to change managed care for the better, what might you do?

Answers to *Can You Guess?*

1. Statistics indicate that only about 1% of uninsured Americans over age 65 are uninsured. This is largely because 90% of older adults in the United States qualify for Medicare benefits. Keep in mind, however, that unregistered immigrants, homeless individuals, and some other populations do not show up much on the statistical radar. And being insured does not mean that older adults have it easy. Many still pay large amounts for prescription drugs and long-term care.

2. It was a trick question. The number of uninsured Americans in 2012 was equal to the population of these states, plus much more. As you read, the number of uninsured people in the United States is equal to the total combined populations of Alabama, Alaska, Arizona, Colorado, Connecticut, Delaware, Hawaii, Idaho, Iowa, Kansas, Maine, Montana, New Mexico, North Dakota, Oklahoma, Oregon, South Carolina, Vermont, West Virginia, and Wyoming.

The Roles of Patients and Professional Caregivers

Each patient ought to feel somewhat the better after the physician's visit, irrespective of the nature of the illness.

—WARFIELD THEOBALD LONGCOPE

It's fitting that we begin our in-depth exploration of health communication at the most personal level—those moments when we look another person in the eye and seek to offer comfort and care, or, as patients, open ourselves to receive what another can do for us. There's something remarkable about the patient–caregiver relationship that makes it far more than a business transaction. In this section we will explore common patterns of patient–caregiver communication—from brusque, rushed, encounters that may leave us feeling exposed and disappointed, to moments of true connection and compassion that, whether or not they heal our bodies, comfort our souls. In Chapter 3, we explore the communication patterns that character-ize patient–caregiver communication—who talks, who listens, what stories are shared, and so on. Then, in Chapters 4 and 5, we'll immerse ourselves, first, in what it means to be a patient, and next, in what it feels like to be a professional caregiver, including the hopes, fears, joys, and frustrations of both roles. Hopefully, you will finish the section with an enhanced respect and appreciation for everyone involved.

CHAPTER THREE

Patient–Caregiver Communication

Ben noticed a lump in his breast just after his 58th birthday. Embarrassed about the problem, he avoided mentioning it to his wife for several months, thinking it would probably go away on its own. When she learned about it, his wife encouraged, then begged, Ben to see a doctor. In the next few months other family members joined her entreaties. Finally, Ben made a doctor's appointment. On the day of the appointment the family was anxious to hear what the doctor said. Imagine their surprise when Ben returned and said the visit went "just fine," but he didn't tell the doctor about the lump. When the shocked family asked why, Ben shrugged and said, "He didn't ask."

This true story illustrates some of the complex factors that affect patient–caregiver communication. Although it may sound foolish not to tell a physician about our health concerns, research suggests that episodes like Ben's occur quite frequently. In a classic study of 800 visits to a pediatric emergency clinic, 26% of the parents said they did *not* tell the doctor what concerned them most (Korsch & Negrete, 1972). In this case, Ben felt that the doctor did not encourage him or even give him a chance to share the information. Health professionals may see the matter differently, wondering why patients seem to play guessing games with them rather than coming to the point.

This chapter examines what happens during medical transactions—who talks, who listens, and how people behave. As you will see, communicating well is important for a number of reasons. Patient–caregiver communication has an impact on how well patients recover, how they tolerate pain, how much stress they experience, and whether people follow medical advice.

Moreover, health professionals are less likely to be sued for malpractice if they communicate effectively with patients. Physicians and dentists who have never been sued are observed to spend more time with patients, use more humor, and solicit patients' participation more often than doctors who have been sued (Dym, 2008).

Because patient–caregiver communication is so important, researchers and others tend to judge it by high standards. As you read about (and experience) patient–caregiver communication, you may be tempted to blame one party or another if the communication seems insensitive or ineffective. One of my students, when asked to sum up health communication literature, declared, "What I get is that doctors are mean and patients are dumb." Though most people might not be so blunt, experts and students alike are often guilty of similar assumptions.

Resist the urge to draw simplistic conclusions. Keep in mind that patients and caregivers work together to shape their communication patterns. Communication is a transactional process. No one communicates alone, and participants are not completely at liberty to behave as they might wish (Rawlins, 1989, 1992; Watzlawick, Beavin, & Jackson, 1967). Relational communication, or **transactional communication,** means that communicators exert mutual influence on each other such that the approach one participant takes suggests how the other might respond. For instance, if a physician acts like a parent, the patient is encouraged to behave in the complementary role of a child (and the other way around). Patients sometimes become frustrated with their caregivers' parent-like behavior, unmindful that they may have encouraged it by adopting meek and submissive roles themselves (Pendleton, Schofield, Tate, & Havelock, 1984). Stephen Bochner (1983) urges people not to consider patients and caregivers as adversaries but as "reasonable people of good will, trying to exchange views with other reasonable people of equally good will" (p. 128) in circumstances that are sometimes very challenging.

The chapter is divided into four sections. The first two describe and juxtapose physician-centered and collaborative communication. The third presents communication skill builders involving motivational interviewing, dialogue, narrative medicine, and tips for patients. The final section looks at efforts to create communication-friendly, healing environments.

Before we begin, here are a few notes about what appears in this chapter and what doesn't. First, content is guided in large part by published research, the majority of which focuses on physician communication. However, the field is gradually broadening to include more research about nurses, pharmacists, paramedics, physical therapists, technicians, and others. So I'm pleased to say that you will see references to communication with

a broader range of caregivers than ever before. (We'll also go into more depth about diverse caregivers in Chapters 5 and 7.) You will also notice that this chapter focuses on interactions with professional caregivers. This focus excludes the more than 60 million nonprofessional caregivers

---

BOX 3.1   RESOURCES

Journals That Feature Health Communication Research

Health Communication
Journal of Health Communication
Communication & Medicine
Social Science & Medicine
Journal of Applied Communication Research
Journal of Communication in Healthcare
Journal of Qualitative Health Research
Journal of the American Medical Association
Australian Journal of Communication
New England Journal of Health
American Journal of Public Health
Journal of Health and Social Behavior
Communication Monographs
Communication Quarterly
Communication Research
Communication Studies
Communication Yearbook
Critical Studies in Mass Communication
Critical Studies in Media
Developmental Psychology
Discourse and Society
Discourse Analysis
Human Communication Research
Journal of Communication
Journal of Personality and Social Psychology
Journal of Sociology
Language and Social Interaction
Medical Education
Medical Economics
Patient Care
Patient Education and Counseling
Annals of Internal Medicine
Annals of Family Medicine
Academic Medicine
Health Psychology

who care for ill or injured loved ones at home. Since the challenges and rewards of family caregivers deserve special attention, we will focus on them separately, in Chapter 8. Finally, this chapter focuses mostly on face-to-face communication, which, as you know, is now only part of the picture. We will look more closely at the impact of eHealth, mHealth, and telemedicine in Chapter 9. The impact of such technology has become so powerful that it merits a chapter of its own. All the same, keep in mind that communication is an integrated whole.

Medical Talk and Power Differentials

I sometimes ask students to imagine that two people arrive home. One says, "I'm hungry," and turns on the television, while the other person goes to the kitchen to prepare sandwiches. Who has more power in this situation? It's tempting to assume that the TV-watcher is in control. Ostensibly, he or she need only voice a need to have it fulfilled by the other person. If we go beyond initial impressions, however, it's not so clear. Perhaps the hungry person is a toddler or an adult with physical or cognitive challenges that make meal preparation infeasible. From that perspective, who has more power?

Let's apply that idea to health care. Since the Industrial Revolution, we have largely assumed that health professionals have the power. After all, they have the benefit of advanced education, access to technology, and social status. Moreover, the very definition of patienthood suggests someone who is in need and requires assistance from another. Also, since the Industrial Revolution, medical encounters have occurred mostly on professionals' turf rather patients'.

As a consequence, we sometimes speak in terms of *doctor's orders*, *patient compliance*, and the like. Medical communication is considered **physician-centered** if caregivers do most of the talking,

choose conversational topics, and begin and end communication episodes. We will examine some examples of the communication dynamics within that paradigm. As we do, keep in mind that, for the most part, power is not something one person can demand from another. Instead, power is granted. As you read the following examples, consider how the parties involved collaborate in the creation of a power differential, whether they realize it or not.

Knowledge and Power

One aspect of caregiver-centered communication involves unequal access to information. In the "I'm hungry" example, if we assume the TV-watcher doesn't know *how* to make sandwiches or isn't capable of making them, we may suppose that he or she is more dependent (thus, less powerful) than the other person. In much the same way, physicians' authority has traditionally been considered unassailable because they have knowledge and abilities that others don't have. J. Katz (1984) reflects on the long-standing belief that physicians should act on their own authority "without consulting their patients about the decisions that need to be made" (p. 2). For many decades, doctors even felt it would be unkind to "confuse" patients with medical details or "burden" them with making medical decisions (Katz, 1984). (See Box 3.2 for more on this issue.)

Added to the conviction that clinicians know best is the common belief that, if allowed, patients will waste time describing irrelevant details, so health professionals should keep a tight rein on medical interviews. It has been traditional to teach doctors, especially, to keep interviews brief and to the point, to assert themselves verbally and nonverbally, and to ask focused questions. In extreme cases, this results in a pattern in which patients are treated as if (and may act as if) they are ignorant or childlike. These asymmetrical exchanges are characterized by several communication patterns, which we will explore next.

Assertive and Nonassertive Behavior

Power is shared when people treat each other as partners. However, in a study of patient interactions by Richard Street Jr. and Bradford Millay (2001), physicians devoted only about 2% of their talking time to partnership-building and supportive

WHAT DO YOU THINK?

- In what ways do health professionals have power?
- In what way do patients have power?

BOX 3.2 ETHICAL CONSIDERATIONS

Therapeutic Privilege

Although Anna (age 68) is seriously ill, she feels relatively well and her spirits seem high. She often remarks to those around her that she's feeling much better and she's eager to talk of future plans. However, it is obvious to her caregivers and to her family that she will not live more than a few months. The family has asked Anna's physician not to tell her she is dying. They argue that she probably knows she's dying but that her behavior implies a request that people not bring up the issue. They feel that Anna's current happiness is what really matters at this point, and they are reluctant to impose bad news on her, particularly when there is nothing that can be done about it.

Therapeutic privilege is the prerogative sometimes granted to physicians to withhold information from patients if they feel that disclosing the information would do more harm than good. For many years, doctors withheld information from patients if they thought patients would be unable to understand it or would be distressed by it (Katz, 1984).

Robert Veatch (1991) argues that therapeutic privilege is indefensible because it's counter to the goal of making patients informed partners in their own care. Charles Lund (1995) takes a more moderate view. He asserts that physicians should almost always tell patients the truth, but he warns that blunt honesty is not always the kindest method of disclosure.

In some cultures, people prefer to shield family members from distressing news about their health. In Japan, for example, although people typically want to know the truth about their own health, they often insist that physicians shield family members from distressing diagnoses (Kakai, 2002). Based on cultural ideas about illness and death, they are afraid of destroying their loved one's hope and are fearful that talking about adverse outcomes might lead to their occurrence (Kakai, 2002).

WHAT DO YOU THINK?

1. If you were Anna's physician, would you tell her she does not have long to live? Why or why not?
2. If physicians withhold information, should they go so far as to lie if patients ask outright about their prognosis?
3. How do you respond to the argument that physicians can never be sure about patients' odds of recovery, so it's sometimes better to withhold information that might diminish patients' hopes?
4. What if you were the physician and a patient told you, "If this condition is terminal, don't tell me"? Would you withhold information even if it meant making treatment decisions on the patient's behalf?
5. What if patients do not say "Don't tell me" outright, but their actions seem to suggest that they don't want to know if the news is bad? Would you tell them?
6. Is it ever permissible to give a patient's family information without telling the patient? If so, under what circumstances?
7. If you were the patient, are there any circumstances in which you would wish information to be withheld from you?

communication. Patients supported the asymmetrical dynamic by devoting only 7% of their talking time to asking questions and assertively conveying their concerns. Indeed, patients rarely asserted themselves as active participants unless their doctors actively encouraged them to do so.

Similarly, in a study of online birthing stories, Carma Bylund (2005) found that only 57% of the narratives indicated that the women had participated in medical decision making (usually about pain medication), even though women who were active participants described their experiences using more positive emotional terms than other women.

Interruptions and abandoned utterances (when people stop talking and allow an interruption) also display a power differential. Physicians typically ask some version of "What seems to be the problem?" at the beginning of medical exams. That may seem like an easy question, but try answering it in a third of a minute! In a famous study, Howard Beckman and Richard Frankel (1984) studied 74 doctor's office visits and found that most patients talked for no longer than 18 seconds before the physician interrupted them and began asking specific questions. None of the patients who were allowed to keep talking took more than 2½ minutes. And notably, only 1 patient of the 52 who were interrupted returned to the original subject.

More recent research has revealed similar results. In a study published in 2005, researchers found that internal medicine residents interrupted patients 59% of the time after asking about their concerns. The interruptions occurred after patients had talked for an average of 16.5 seconds (Dyche & Swiderski, 2005). In the same study, residents began 37% of medical exams *without* asking patients about their concerns. Presumably, in those instances the residents felt they already knew what was on the patients' minds. But when researchers talked to patients afterward, they found that doctors who neglected to ask for input were 24% less likely than others to identify correctly and address the patients' main concerns.

We should note that interruptions are not always assertive or intrusive. They can be used to encourage further talk, as in "I understand," "Tell me more," or "Say that again." And doctors are not the only ones who interrupt. Patients do so as well. But when physicians interrupt patients, they tend to claim the floor or change topics (Li, Krysko, Desroches, & Deagle, 2004). In contrast, patients (especially female patients) typically interrupt their doctors to show cooperation. Female patients studied by Li and colleagues were 11 times more likely to offer cooperative interruptions than were male patients. But male and female patients were similar in that they yielded the floor 94% of the time when physicians began talking. In contrast, physicians yielded to patients' attempted interruptions only 68% of the time (Li et al., 2004). The researchers concluded that, much of the time, "physicians are firmly in charge of the process and/or content of the conversation" (p. 152).

When patients don't speak up, health professionals may have inadequate information with which to make diagnoses and suggest acceptable treatment options, and patients may feel frustrated and belittled, lamenting that they have wasted time and money addressing concerns that are not chief on their minds. One implication is that it is important to enlist patients' involvement in setting the medical agenda. That means not just asking, but asking in ways that encourage honest input.

John Heritage and Jeffrey Robinson (2006) found that patients' responses to doctors' question are shaped partly by the doctors' word choices. In their analysis of 302 patient visits, the researchers found that the open-ended question *"What can I do for you today?"* yielded the most detailed patient responses. But opening lines such as *"So you're sick, huh?,"* or *"You're having body aches"* (pp. 92–95) resulted in briefer, less detailed responses, probably because they imply that the doctor already understands what's going on. Patients may assume (rightly or wrongly) that the doctor has already reviewed their concerns and has identified the most important or salient of them (e.g., body aches). As Heritage and Robinson point out, the rules of polite conversation discourage people from repeating information that is (ostensibly) already known, so respondents may be dissuaded from saying very much. For their part, health professionals may not realize that the precise *way* they ask questions can have a powerful influence on what is said and what agenda emerges. (See Box 3.3 for more on this idea.)

As suggested by the tenets of transactional communication, physician-centered communication is a collaborative enterprise. Physicians are often assertive, but for their part, patients are typically quick to acquiesce. In a study of 72 patient visits with a family physician, Kandi Walker and colleagues (2002) noted that the patients displayed a general willingness to let the physician guide the encounters, and in various ways the physician conveyed that her understanding of health conditions was superior to the patients' (Walker, Arnold, Miller-Day, & Webb, 2002). For example, when a patient who had had kidney infections before said she recognized the symptoms of a current infection, the physician responded, "Let me take a look. Since I am the doctor here . . . " (Walker et al., 2002, p. 52). The patient briefly objected that she was sure of the diagnosis, but then she relinquished the argument and was relatively submissive during the remainder of the medical visit.

Doorknob Disclosures

The instant intimacy demanded in medical situations is tricky to manage. The caregiver may wish to get right to the point, but the patient may consider it extremely risky (or even rude) to disclose information in the first few seconds of the conversation. However, delaying disclosures or beating around the bush can waste valuable time, often at the expense of other people.

While studying interactions in a family practice office, I noticed that patients often began with small concerns, not their main worries. One woman said initially that she was suffering from a sore throat. Only halfway through the medical visit did she admit that depression was her biggest problem. In fact, she eventually told the doctor she had tried to commit suicide several days earlier. Many other patients blurted out their main concerns just as the physician was leaving the room. These so-called **doorknob disclosures** occur at what seems to be the last instant of the medical visit. The physician in such a situation can postpone the main concern until another time or, as more often happens, launch what is in effect **another** medical interview with the patient. All in all, it's worthwhile to earn patients' trust and for patients to be forthcoming early on in medical encounters.

Questions and Directives

Health professionals traditionally have used talking time mostly to ask questions and to issue **directives** (instructions or commands). For example, during physical therapy visits, therapists talk about twice as much as their patients, mostly asking about health history and giving instructions (Roberts & Bucksey, 2007). A Canadian study showed that medical residents, although assertive, are less so than physicians. In the episodes studied, residents asked 80% of the questions during medical exams (compared to physicians' 89%) and spent twice as long (about 19.7 minutes) with patients as did most physicians (Pahal, 2006). Pahal speculates that the residents are more comfortable extending exams

and entertaining patients' questions because they are not under the same time constraints as doctors and because, unlike doctors, the residents are not paid based on the number of patients they see.

As mentioned, doctors may keep medical conversations focused to save time and prevent patients from rambling. Patients tend to stammer and stutter, especially when they're afraid their doctors will disapprove of their behavior (du Pré & Beck, 1997). Ironically, these stutters and stammers, which may sound like wasted time, are often signals that the patient is working up to an especially important disclosure. The caregiver who too quickly diverts the conversation may lose important opportunities to learn what is on patients' minds.

Blocking

Research on patient–caregiver communication refers to **blocking**, a process by which caregivers steer talk away from certain subjects. For example, caregivers are sometimes observed to use topic shifts and questions to block complaints and to avoid patients' emotional disclosures (Jarrett & Payne, 1995). In one conversation, when a patient asked, "You know how you get sorta scared?," the physician responded, "How long were you on the estrogen?" (Suchman, Markakis, Beckman, & Frankel, 1997). In a different episode, when an 80-year-old patient told a doctor that she was "very nervous, very nervous" and said that she had recently suffered the sudden death of two friends and watched her husband committed to an intensive care unit, the physician simply asked, "Do you smoke?" (M. G. Greene, Adelman, & Majerovitz, 1996, p. 270).

More recently, Diane Morse and colleagues (2008) analyzed the doctor visits of people coping with lung cancer. Although the researchers identified 384 opportunities to display empathy with the patients' feelings, physicians actually expressed empathy only about 10% of the time, usually at the conclusion of the interviews. Morse and coauthors conclude that physicians' task-orientation blinded them to opportunities for compassionate, biopsychosocial care (Morse, Edwardsen, & Gordon, 2008).

The caregivers' responses may seem callous, but sometimes it's more that they don't know how to respond. Medical students, for example, often avoid emotional topics because they don't feel qualified or comfortable talking about them (Lumma-Sellenthin, 2009).

On the other hand, some caregivers are quite responsive and patient-centered. Michelle G. Greene and coauthors (1996) describe an encounter during which an 84-year-old patient told the doctor she was being pressured to provide care for a mentally ill family member. "They've been putting a lot of pressure on me and it's made me very nervous," the patient said. The physician responded, "Maybe there's a way I can help. Well, I can see [by] what you said that you have a lot of things on your mind. An awful lot of pressure and tension" (p. 273). The doctor wrote a letter that resolved the dilemma, and the patient thanked him profusely. The researchers point out that the caregiver in this episode acknowledged the woman's feelings, offered specific assistance, and reassured her that he was concerned.

Patronizing Behavior

Because of physicians' high social status and their extraordinary ability to influence people's lives, when patients aren't happy with the care they receive they may be reluctant to criticize or protest. It follows that patients of relatively low social status will feel this effect most strongly. The powerlessness of women and minorities in medical situations is sometimes quite shocking.

Critical theorists such as Alexandra Todd point out ways in which some doctors **patronize** patients (treat them as if they are inferior) by withholding information, speaking down to them, and shrugging off their feelings as childish or inconsequential. Many of these episodes involve **transgressions**, which are instances in which someone acts inappropriately toward another (Farber, Novack, & O'Brien, 1997). For example, Todd (1984) described an examination she witnessed during which the gynecologist exclaimed, "This is all girl" while examining a woman's breast for lumps. When the patient did not respond, the doctor repeated, "I *said*, this is all girl." After the exam, the physician told the woman to "get dressed like a good girl" and he would give her some "happy pills" (birth control pills) (p. 182).

Of course, patients sometimes behave badly as well. See Box 3.4 for tips on handling transgressions by both patients and professionals.

Even experts find health situations challenging. Health communication scholar Christina Beck describes her panic and frustration when a doctor refused to take her seriously (Beck, Ragan, & du Pré, 1997). Previously diagnosed with a hormone deficiency that had already caused one miscarriage, Beck pleaded with her new doctor to begin hormone replacement therapy at the beginning of her next pregnancy. Calling her "honey" and telling her "don't worry," the doctor declined to do so. Within weeks Beck suffered another miscarriage. Writing of the experience, Beck expresses regret that she, "a normally assertive, intelligent, and well-educated woman," didn't take a firmer stand or switch doctors.

Episodes such as these point to the pitfalls of a power inequity between patients and caregivers. Although most professionals do not abuse the power difference, when they do, patients may perceive that they have little recourse. This situation is particularly unfortunate for patients of low socioeconomic status, who may feel the effects of discrimination more than others but may not be at liberty to choose or switch doctors.

Why Do We Do It?

You may feel yourself becoming frustrated reading these examples. The reality is that patients don't usually like a lopsided power dynamic, but neither do health professionals. So, if neither side typically likes it, why do we engage in it?

Our reason is that we don't perceive that we have a choice. We may underestimate our options, concluding that "I *have* to take control because many patients either don't speak up or they talk too much," or "My doctor doesn't give me a chance to say much." Another lies with the power of social expectations. Accepted rules of politeness and professionalism may guide our actions, even if we don't particularly like them. In the current political climate in which doctors are criticized for being domineering, it's easy to forget that for many generations, society expected them to be dominant and patients to be submissive. By this point, professionals who want patients to be forthcoming may find some who are still uncomfortable doing so.

Health professionals do not have license to treat patients without their consent, nor can they require them to follow medical advice. They cannot even require people to show up for exams. However, patients may not perceive that they have

BOX 3.4

Stepping Over the Line

It's sometimes difficult to establish what behaviors are appropriate between a patient and a caregiver. Touch, personal disclosures, and body exposure usually reserved for intimate relationships are often required in medical settings.

Usually both parties recognize the boundary between intimacy (a unique sense of closeness, interdependence, and trust) and detached concern (the effort to understand another person, but with restricted emotional involvement). However, patients and caregivers sometimes cross the line. Farber et al. (1997) call actions that cross the line between intimacy and professionalism **transgressions** (from the Latin phrase meaning "to step across").

Transgressions frequently have painful and confusing results. Feelings of heartache, disappointment, guilt, and loss of reputation may result. Patients, typically in positions of lesser power, may feel violated or forced into behaving against their wishes. Professionals may feel harassed or embarrassed and may face legal action and loss of professional privileges.

Sexual contact is an obvious transgression, but other behavior can be inappropriate as well. Doctors say that patients sometimes transgress by demanding more time than the caregiver can afford, asking for money or favors, being overly flirtatious or seductive, giving frequent or expensive gifts, and even being verbally abusive, bringing or threatening to bring weapons, and shouting. Nurses are sometimes harassed by patients who grab them and make suggestive comments (Zook, 1997). Caregivers may transgress by making sexual advances, asking unnecessary personal questions, insulting patients, or sharing confidential information with others.

Researchers propose that transgressions may result from patients' vulnerability, their need for assurance, and the trust they place in their caregivers. Caregivers, too, may experience strong feelings (either positive or negative) in relation to patients, feelings that may be heightened by a sense of isolation from family and friends.

Following are some steps for addressing transgressions based on work by Pateet, Fremonta, and Miovic (2011), Farber, Novack, and O'Brien (1997), and R. Zook (1997).

- Take stock of personal needs and social expectations that may motivate a transgression (loneliness, need for approval, etc.).
- Establish clear boundaries for touch and talk, preferably in a list of prohibited behaviors that can be shared and distributed.
- Be careful not to send ambiguous or mixed messages.
- Seek the counsel of support groups, friends, and colleagues.
- Enlist the help of mental health professionals if it seems warranted.
- If possible, have others present during problematic transactions.
- Acknowledge transgression attempts and discuss them in a calm way with the other person.
- If inappropriate behavior does not stop, let the other person know you intend to take formal action. If it still does not stop, contact the health care management or the local medical society.

much choice in these matters. A powerful example is emergency room (ER) care. Across the country, emergency departments are often overcrowded and understaffed. This is partly because people who don't have insurance—and thus may be turned away from doctors' offices—often rely on ER care instead. For most hospitals, ER isn't a money-maker; it's a financial drain, hence the understaffing. The hectic, high-anxiety atmosphere affects both patients

 WHAT DO YOU THINK?

■ In your opinion, should doctors and patients work toward greater equity in medical conversations?

■ If so, what could patients do to help accomplish this?

■ What could caregivers do?

and professionals. While studying an urban emergency department for 6 months, Eisenberg, Baglia, and Pynes (2006) noted the enforced passivity of patients and their families, who were often required to wait for hours and watch people with more serious concerns (or more political clout) "jump the line" to be seen ahead of them. The researchers observe: "Patients are expected to play a 'sick role' in which they passively and cooperatively submit to the expert opinion of the professionals" (p. 205). In one case they witnessed, a father had brought his daughter in for evaluation after she fell and bloodied her nose.

> After waiting for 20 minutes, the man approached the window and asked when his daughter would be seen. "We have more serious cases, sir," replied the triage nurse. "This is serious," said the father. "But I saw her walk in," returned the nurse. "Yeah, but now she's complaining about a headache." "Well, if she fell on her nose, she's going to have a headache." (Eisenberg et al., 2006, p. 201)

The incident illustrates the powerlessness of the father to get immediate care for his daughter and the subtext—an environment in which caregivers are often too harried to feel compassion and patience. For a variety of reasons, health professionals are sometimes "ruled by the tyranny of the urgent" (Walsh, Jordan, & Apolloni, 2009, p. 176). "Not only are we short on time to speak, we are short on time to listen," say nursing professor Kenneth Walsh and colleagues (Walsh et al., 2009, p. 168). In these situations, cultural expectations, combined with the desire to stay in caregivers' good graces, may be enough to silence patients into submission, whether they follow doctors' advice when they leave or not.

Shifting Paradigm

The asymmetrical power dynamic is changing, albeit more slowly than some might wish. For one thing, as the public becomes more educated about health matters, many people are no longer content answering closed-ended questions and following doctors' orders. They wish to discuss options and participate in medical decision making. This can be frustrating for some health professionals, who may take patients' assertiveness as a sign of disrespect and long for the days when they didn't have to "de-educate" patients about what they consider erroneous information. A patient in Alex Broom's (2008) study overheard his doctor call him "difficult and overinformed" after he asked the doctor about information he had learned online (p. 101). However, many health professionals realize that well-educated and active patients are conducive to good health. Says Gail Weiss (2008), "It's the rare physician who doesn't acknowledge that now, more than ever, physicians learn from their patients" (para. 3).

Indeed, if patients don't speak up, it's difficult to know what they want and need. Physicians trying to guess may have a difficult time, considering that patient expectations typically differ according to anxiety level, age, education, and familiarity with the caregiver.

Kathryn Greene's (2009) **disclosure decision-making model** (**DD-MM**), designed specifically for health contexts, proposes that people decide whether to share information about health concerns based on three considerations:

- The *predicted outcome* of sharing the information (e.g., Will sharing this result in my being stigmatized? Will it assist with a good diagnosis and better care? Is the information relevant? Am I ready to hear what might result?);
- The *anticipated reaction* of the other person based on the quality of the relationship (e.g., Do I trust this person enough to share private information with him or her? How is s/he likely to respond? How confident am I in predicting his or her response?); and
- *Confidence and skills* (efficacy), as in, Can I present my concerns effectively? Can I find the right words? and Will I sound stupid?

In another study, Greene and colleagues (2012) studied people whose health concerns are not visually evident. They found that, if people felt that disclosing the concern might lead to severe consequences, they were likely to consider it highly relevant, but they were also likely to doubt their ability to present the information effectively. As expected, relational quality was associated with greater willingness to disclose. Together, these findings suggest that relationships are important, particularly when we have a serious concern that people are unlikely to know about unless we tell them.

Many people are also realizing that, although physician-dominated communication seems efficient in the short run, it is often counterproductive. Patients who perceive their physicians to be domineering talk less than others and are less likely to share information with them (Schmid Mast, Hall, & Roter, 2008). In contrast, patients who perceive their doctors to be caring are more at ease than other patients and share their feelings more easily (Schmid Mast et al., 2008). This is an advantage for medical decision making, and it's usually a more rewarding interpersonal dynamic. Gail Geller and colleagues (2008) found that physicians, nurses, and genetic counselors (particularly female caregivers) who feel that they are highly engaged with patients consider their work more meaningful and are less likely to experience burnout than other caregivers.

Finally, to return to the "I'm hungry" example, it's rarely productive to maintain a power differential if there's a good alternative. Perhaps the person watching TV *could* make sandwiches if he or she were more motivated or learned how. If this is the case, it would probably be better—for both people and for their relationship—to share the responsibility more equitably. For a long time, we considered patients to be passive participants who showed up at a doctor's office to say "I'm sick" and then expect to be cured ("I'll watch TV while you make the sandwiches.") It's become clear that health doesn't work that way. It involves relationship building and an ongoing, active commitment to healthy choices. Patrick Dillon (2012) found that patients remember more about treatment recommendations when they have played an active role in the medical encounter. Considering that what happens as a result of a medical encounter is typically more important than what happens *during* it, that's an important consideration. All in all, people have the best chance at long, healthy lives if they proactively strive for good health and, when they are ill, work with caregivers to design treatment plans that they can and will carry out.

All the same, it remains to be seen if leaders in managed care organizations and other agencies will recognize the expediency of collaborative communication or if they will continue to impose strict time limits as well as other limitations.

> 💬 **IN YOUR EXPERIENCE**
> ■ Have you ever had to make a difficult decision about whether to share a health concern with someone else?
> ■ If so, what factors did you consider?
> ■ Did you reveal your concern or not?
> ■ What happened as a result?

In summary, caregiver-centered communication isn't a thing of the past. However, the tide seems to be shifting toward something different. Some health professionals have always been careful to empower and listen to patients. And many others are beginning to orient themselves toward more collaborative communication, a topic we turn to next.

Collaborative Communication Model

As you know, one tenet of social interaction is that communication episodes are inherently collaborative. Therefore, it may seem a bit redundant to speak of a new trend toward **collaborative medical communication**. But, as the phrase is used, it signifies something more purposeful, namely participants' proactive desire to treat each other as peers who openly discuss health options and make mutually satisfying decisions (Balint & Shelton, 1996; Laine & Davidoff, 1996). The difference is between an implicit collaboration that may unwittingly support a power differential and an explicit desire to collaborate as equal partners. It is important to note that collaborative communication is neither entirely patient-centered nor caregiver-centered. Instead, participants work together as partners.

This section describes developments in the health industry that make collaborative communication appealing. It also describes communication techniques that support partnering behaviors.

Theoretical Foundations

Michelle, a 15-year-old caring for her 5-month-old daughter, seeks emergency care for excessive menstrual bleeding. Although Michelle was hospitalized 2 weeks earlier for asthma and suspects that the asthma and her current problem are the result of stress, she does not mention either the hospitalization or the stress to her doctors.

This true story, described by Amanda Young and Linda Flower (2002), illustrates what they call a *rhetoric of passivity* supported by participants' assumption that patients should go along with what caregivers say and do. The medical student caring for Michelle asks leading and closed-ended questions that do not encourage her to share her concerns. For her part, Michelle makes only brief replies and is not assertive about sharing her feelings. Consequently, Young and Flower report:

> Michelle leaves the hospital with a referral to see a gynecologist with no discussion of what she thinks is causing her problem—a list of stressors that would boggle the mind of a middle-class adult, let alone a 15-year-old single mother in the inner city. (p. 82)

Young and Flower (2002) propose an alternative model of communication based on a *rhetoric of agency* that recognizes patients as co-agents in health encounters. Their **model of collaborative interpretation** (**CI**) proposes that health communication is most effective when patients actualize the roles of decision makers and problem solvers and when caregivers function as counselors or friends who work alongside patients to help them achieve shared goals. This rhetorical shift relies on the mutual efforts of everyone involved. It cannot work if patients are unwilling to share their stories and take an active role in health care transactions. Nor will it work if caregivers adhere to a paternalist notion that they know what's best for patients. With the CI model, patients and caregivers, together, establish shared goals and work collaboratively to pursue them.

Importantly, the CI model does not privilege either patients or caregivers. Instead, as Young and Flower (2002) describe it, the goal is "an experience that validates the expertise of both patient and provider and that dignifies the patient's needs" (p. 89). Such a model can be difficult to create, especially since it is a new idea for many people. As a helpful guide, Young and Flower present a list of communication criteria that define collaborative interpretations. They include the following:

- Draw on each other's expertise by asking for details about past experiences with the health concern;
- Consider how the patient feels the health concern influences his or her lifestyle and physical, mental, and emotional health;
- Explicitly discuss both parties' interpretations of the health concern;
- Encourage both parties to share their goals and expectations;
- Develop a mutual sense of control by identifying strategies that you both feel are beneficial, practical, and acceptable.

Now let's take a closer look at research about the collaborative model.

The Emerging Model

In an issue of *Health Communication* devoted to "The Patient as a Central Construct," Robert Kaplan (1997, p. 75) forecast a move away from the "find it—fix it" biomedical model to an "outcomes model" that emphasizes long-term quality of life. The goal of the outcomes model is to minimize people's reliance on medicine and to maximize the importance of their everyday health and fulfillment. Oncologist Jamie Van Roen believes in this. She says:

> The first thing I do to try to make the relationship real is teach them [patients] to complain. I tell them I don't know what it's like to be the patient, to have cancer. It's a matter of control. Patients often feel like they have lost control of everything. I try to give it back. (quoted by Magee & D'Antonio, 2003, p. 202)

Significantly, this model requires a wide-angle focus that extends far beyond organic indications of illness. Diet, exercise, emotional health, attitude, and similar factors become issues of immediate concern. Caregivers such as nutritionists, exercise physiologists, counselors, and others are in a good position to help.

As caregivers' roles change, so may patients.' Indeed, the very term *patient* becomes problematic when the emphasis shifts to everyday well-being.

Patient connotes a person in ill health who seeks the services of a care provider. Some theorists suggest that the terms *health citizen* and *health decision maker* are preferable because they acknowledge that people are involved in health care all the time—not just when they seek professional assistance (Rimal, Ratzan, Arnston, & Freimuth, 1997).

As health becomes a way of life, not just an occasional excursion to the doctor's office, many people feel it is insensible to treat patients as passive or incidental components of the process. Patricia Geist and Jennifer Dreyer (1993) apply Eisenberg and Goodall's concept of dialogue to medical encounters. A **dialogue** is a conversation in which both people participate fully and equitably, each influencing the encounter in ways that make it a unique creation. When conversational partners engage in dialogue, they don't simply adopt ready-made roles; they create them to suit their own situations and preferences.

In the book *On Call: A Doctor's Days and Nights in Residency*, Emily Transue (2004) describes her first conversation with a patient she knew to have terminal cancer. Aware that he had been experiencing depression, Transue asked the man, "How are your spirits?" and he replied, "As good as you could expect them to be, I guess. . . . Not that I don't have my moments." Rather than brushing his words aside, Transue said, "Tell me about the moments" (p. 13). The patient shared with her that he sometimes considered taking his own life, but he stuck around to have more time with his beloved dog. Transue says that such details helped her understand the man better and provide the care he needed. Together, she says, they learned about dying and all the steps along the way.

Researchers suggest that patients and caregivers are typically more satisfied with dialogues than with one-sided conversations, but they may be afraid that dialogues will take too long or that others will not wish to take part in them (Geist & Dreyer, 1993). Those who take the risk may enjoy profound rewards. For example, even people who are highly frightened about dental care respond well when dentists and dental assistants show a genuine interest in them, engage them in conversation, and work hard to earn their trust (Kulich, Berggren, & Hallberg, 2003).

Likewise, John Suchwalko remembers a doctor's visit that changed his life and that illustrates a patient's perspective on collaborative

WHAT DO YOU THINK?

■ Do you feel the term *patient* is accurate when describing well people seeking to maintain their own health?

■ Brainstorm some other terms we might use. What's your favorite?

CAN YOU GUESS?

■ In which U.S. state do health professionals rank highest in terms of patient-centeredness?

■ In which state do they rank lowest?

Answers appear at the end of the chapter.

communication. "My blood pressure was off the charts, but I didn't feel anything," he says (quoted by Magee & D'Antonio, 2003, p. 49). He was also overweight, seldom exercised, was a smoker, and had high cholesterol. It's easy to imagine that a physician might convey disapproval. But Suchwalko's doctor, George Hanna, didn't. As Suchwalko describes it:

> The thing that impressed me about Dr. Hanna was that he didn't come down on me real hard. I didn't feel like I had been sent to the vice principal's office and he was wagging a finger in my face saying, "You better do this" or "You better do that." Instead he came across like he was a very knowledgeable friend. . . . From then on, I was on a diet, I started walking every day, and I came into his office every two weeks. He would talk to me, encourage me, keep me going. That helped a lot. (p. 49)

The collaborative model involves more than just doctors. For example, medical technicians and therapists also spend a great deal of time with patients and often form individualized ways of interacting with them. In the context of well-developed relationships, being collaborative means responding to the unique preferences of each person. Laura Ellingson (2011) describes dialysis technicians' commitment to "figuring out" patients and treating them in ways that they appreciate, even though

Collaborative communication involves give-and-take by patients and caregivers.

it means adopting a different interaction style with each patient.

Patient-centered care has been shown to enhance satisfaction, help overcome racial and ethnic discrimination, lower costs, and improve medical outcomes (Epstein, Fiscella, Lesser, & Stange, 2010). As a result, some funding agencies and health care advocates have begun to measure caregivers' proficiency at it. The Clinical Skills Assessment (CSA) exam, which is required of foreign-educated doctors seeking to practice in the United States, involves interacting with trained (standardized) patients. Physicians earn highest marks if they engage in rapport-building behaviors, are nonverbally attentive, encourage patients to tell their stories, ask follow-up questions, are tactful and respectful, present information clearly, and show empathy and support (van Zanten, Boulet, & McKinley, 2007).

Despite all of this interest and advocacy, partnership behaviors are not as prevalent as many wish they were. Ray Marks and colleagues (2010) compared responses to the Health Information National Trends Survey (HINTS) in 2003 and 2007. In the HINTS study, 3,000 to 5,000 people in the United States (representing a cross-section of the population) answered questions such as "How often did the providers you saw in the past 12 months involve you in decisions about your health care as much as you wanted?" (Marks, Ok, Joung, & Allegrante, 2010, p. 137). Overall, the results show that slightly more than half of those surveyed felt they were "always" included in decision making. Between 2003 and 2007, responses to that question became more favorable only for people earning more than $75,000 a year (61.7% in 2003, compared to 63.6% in 2007); *decreases* in patient participation were notable among Hispanic residents, people with limited education, and those without health insurance. (See Figure 3.1.) The authors conclude that communication skills training is needed to improve communication overall and to address disparities.

There are several reasons that caregivers may be reluctant to engage fully in collaborative communication. They may feel that the treatment is so straightforward as not to require collaboration. (Patients may or may not share this sense of routine.) The caregiver may worry that negotiating the decision will take too long, or that the process of shared decision making may feel uncomfortable, either because it's likely to be emotional or because there don't seem to be a lot of good options.

Paramedics in one study say that communicating about facts and procedures is fairly easy compared to communicating about uncertainty and outcomes, particularly when there's no easy solution to a patient's problem or when the prognosis is not good (Nordby & Nøhr, 2011). For that reason, they say, they sometimes keep a bit of distance so they don't "put a foot in it" or invite requests they will be unable to fulfill. At the same time, the paramedics describe episodes in which patients are deeply grateful for personal attention. For example, one paramedic was able to arrange for a patient in the final stages of cancer to go straight into a hospital room rather than wait in the hospital reception area first. The paramedic said of the experience:

> We tried to make everything as comfortable as we could, and when we were finished, I said, "I cannot say have a good recovery, but I hope we have contributed to making this journey as pain free as possible for you." The patient had tears in his eyes, and said that if there were angels on earth, then they had to be us. (Nordby & Nøhr, 2011, p. 220)

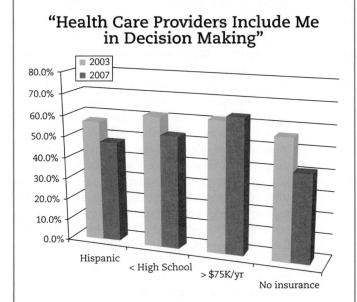

"Health Care Providers Include Me in Decision Making"

FIGURE 3.1 The percentage of U.S. residents who say that health care providers always involve them in decision making declined between 2003 and 2007 overall, most notably among Hispanic residents, people with limited education, and the uninsured. Overall, the only respondents who indicated an improvement were those who make more than $75,000 a year.

Source: Marks, Ok, Joung, & Allegrante, 2010

Health professionals are regularly involved in the types of highly charged conversations most other people experience only occasionally. In an essay about the "problematic art of conversation," three New Zealand nursing scholars propose that it may help to consider that conversations need not be about finding definitive answers, but instead about exploring ideas and reactions to them (Walsh et al., 2009). Conversation, they say, can be a form of "talking aloud" that improves the quality of relationships and, ultimately, the decisions that participants reach. Approached this way, conversations are nonadversarial. Parties do not square off for debates. Instead, they engage in an exploration as partners with different, perhaps, but equally valid perspectives. Walsh and coauthors suggest that "puzzle" is a better conceptualization than "problem" when it comes to exploring new ideas and that focusing on "purpose" (*What are we trying to achieve and why?*) is often more fruitful than focusing immediately on solutions (*Here's what I think we should do*).

All in all, collaborative communication can be rewarding for everyone involved. But it's not always easy. To help, here is a collection of communication approaches—motivational interviewing, dialogue, narrative medicine, and tips for patients—that may be useful in initiating and taking part in medical dialogues. The chapter concludes with a discussion of healing, communication-friendly environments.

Communication Skill Builders

Motivational Interviewing

We may as well admit it: Most of us *know* about healthy behaviors, but we don't always do them. We know we should work out more, eat less fast food, drink more water, get more sleep, and so forth. But sometimes other options seem more appealing or important. Even when we have the healthiest of intentions, once the day starts, a hamburger is a quick meal on the way to school, it's too hot or too cold to jog, and so on. A whole range of factors seems to keep us from doing what we intended. Theorist Brenda Dervin calls these *gaps*.

Dervin and colleagues propose that life is an enterprise in sense making (Dervin, 1999; Dervin & Frenette, 2001). They use the terms *nouning* and *verbing* to illustrate the point. **Nouning** implies that things are static and predictable. From this perspective, we decide to drink more water, and we do, as simple as that. But more often, life feels more like **verbing**, a process in which we continually make sense of changing circumstances because new information becomes available to us, our perspective changes, circumstances transform, or the like. As this occurs, gaps emerge in what we believe and in the actions available to us.

To employ a simple example, perhaps I'm determined to drink more water today, but the vending machine is out, a friend surprises me with a latte, or I run out of change. Now there is an unforeseen gap. To visualize what Dervin and colleagues call *gappiness,* imagine walking down a sidewalk, fairly certain about where you're going, and then finding that a significant section of the pavement ahead of you is missing. It may be an easy matter to bridge the gap, or it may not. But if you're to keep going in the original direction, you must bridge it in some way. In my example, bridging might mean finding a different vending machine, refusing the latte, or getting change. If I foresaw the gap, perhaps I planned ahead and brought a water bottle with me. Conversely, I might abandon the gappy path for now and resolve to try again tomorrow. This is a simple example. As you might imagine, it's often a lot more complicated. The main point is that life is inherently gappy. We continually adjust our goals and behaviors in light of changing circumstances. It's no wonder health professionals want to throw up their hands sometimes. Health (a noun) *is* really important. Yet for a wide range of reasons, people's actions (the verbs) don't always support that ideal.

This leads us to another concept that recognizes the verbing side of life—**motivational interviewing (MI)**. Stephen Rollnick and William Miller (1995) conceptualized MI as "a directive, client-centered counseling style for eliciting behavior change by helping clients to explore and resolve ambivalence" (para. 3). Let's break that definition down. As the wording suggests, MI was originally designed for use in psychotherapy, but it has since found utility in a variety of settings. It's most frequently applied to health-related behavior choices, but the basic premises of MI work in nearly every setting, including a casual conversation with a friend or an internal dialogue.

MI is appealing to many because it's patient-centered and nonconfrontational. The counselor/interviewer does not play a coercive or prescriptive role. That is, he or she doesn't tell the client what to do. In fact, although the interviewer may be knowledgeable about options, he or she doesn't presume to know what's best for the other person. Instead, the interviewer respects that people weigh a variety of factors when making decisions, so they almost always have mixed feelings (ambivalence) about change. The interviewer's job is respectfully and nonjudgmentally to ask questions about (elicit) a person's feelings, to help clarify those feelings, and to assist the person in making choices (resolving the ambivalence).

In one study, nurses used MI to help people experiencing cancer-related pain to examine their feelings about various treatment options (Fahey et al.,

2008). From a distance it may seem that a person in pain would naturally seek pain relievers, but as you probably know from personal experience (even considering a headache or sore muscle), the decision is more complicated than that. For one thing, there is no one right way to respond to pain. We might consider it weak to seek relief, or we may be afraid that we'll mute our body's natural warning signs. We might fear that we'll become addicted to pain killers, we may believe that they will make us groggy, and so on. (See Box 3.5 for more on the link between communication and pain.) MI practitioners respect this natural ambivalence and try to help people sort through it. MI is a true partnership. As Rollnick and Miller (1995) write: "The therapist respects the client's autonomy and freedom of choice (and consequences) regarding his or her own behaviour" (para. 4).

Following are some common techniques and assumptions of MI, illustrated with questions adapted from Miller & Rollnick (2002) and Fahey and colleagues' (2008) work with people experiencing pain and Gerry Welch and colleagues' (2006) work with diabetes patients.[1]

- *Set a respectful tone.* Explain the basic ideas of MI, and express a sincere commitment to listen to and learn from the other person.
- *Let the decision maker set the agenda.* Ask initial questions to help identify what's important to him or her. "Are you happy with the way things are?" "What's going well?" "Is there anything that could be better?" "Do you have concerns about pain?" "Why do you think you have pain?"
- *Gauge the decision maker's interest.* Keep in mind that change is self-motivated. If the issue isn't important to the decision maker, it's probably not fruitful to focus on it. "On a scale of 1 to 10, how important is it to you to reduce your pain?"
- *Explore ambivalence.* Remember that people almost always have mixed feelings about change, based on values, experiences, confidence level, perceived alternatives, and so on. "It sounds like

---

[1]As previously mentioned, our vocabulary is as yet inadequate to describe the partnering roles that people play in health scenarios. For clarity's sake, I refer to the people involved as *interviewer* and *decision maker*. You could insert a variety of terms in place of *decision maker—client, patient, friend, self.*

Ouch!

Sitting in a quiet reception room you read an article while waiting for your appointment. With little or no warning, a woman walks up to you, extends her hand, and abruptly hits you on the arm. Instantly your blood pressure rises as you become angry and confused. . . . Here's a second scenario. Same setting, but this time, as the woman approaches, she says, "There is a mosquito on your arm, hold still!" Then using the same motion, she gently hits your arm. Is your reaction the same? Most likely not.

This scenario, presented by Niki Henson (2007, p. 32), reminds dental assistants to tell patients exactly what to expect, even if it will hurt. Her words are right on target. Research is consistent that effective communication can modify people's experience of pain. For one thing, people with realistic expectations about pain are usually better able to cope, and they typically consider the pain less severe than others (Adams & Field, 2001).

Another factor is people's reluctance to ask for pain relief. Although 98% of abdominal pain sufferers in an emergency department were in pain, only one-third of them asked for pain medication (Yee, Puntillo, Miaskowski, & Neighbor, 2006). Patients may be afraid of inconveniencing the staff or of appearing weak. However, unresolved pain often slows recovery and is stressful for patients, their loved ones, and caregivers. Caregivers can help by educating people about what to expect and encouraging them to ask for relief when they are in pain.

It's hard to imagine a more challenging scenario than managing the pain of people who cannot express themselves clearly. In an attempt to help, nurses who care for people with dementia implemented a pain-assessment checklist to help gauge patients' comfort levels even when the patients could not articulate their feelings. Over 3 months' time the patients showed reduced signs of unresolved pain, and the nurses rated themselves less stressed and less likely to experience burnout than before (Fuchs-Lacelle, Hadjistavropoulos, & Lix, 2008).

---

eating sweets makes you feel unwell, yet you crave them. Is that how it feels?" or "What would change in your life if you had less pain?" or "What factors might prevent you from eating a healthy diet?"

- *Listen.* Let the decision maker do most of the talking.
- *Elicit–provide–elicit.* Ask a question, reflect your understanding of the answer, and ask questions to get a deeper understanding of the issue. "I hear you saying that you would enjoy being around loved ones more if you were in less pain, but you're worried that you might become addicted to the medication. Why does that worry you?"
- *Identify multiple options (including doing nothing) and weigh their merits.* "What options are you aware of?" "What are the advantages of your current diet? What are the disadvantages?" "What are the advantages of changing your diet? What are the disadvantages?"

 IN YOUR EXPERIENCE

Imagine that a friend is concerned because work commitments keep him from working out as much as he would like. Following are some 1-to-10 questions you might ask.

■ On a scale of 1 to 10, how concerned are you about this?

■ If 10 is working out as much as you want and 1 is not working out at all, where are you?

■ What would take to move 1 or 2 points closer to your ideal?

- *Partner; don't persuade.* If you'd like to suggest options or information, make sure they don't sound like prescriptions. "If you'd like, I'll tell you a bit more about . . . " "Here are a few things that work for some people . . . "

• *Roll with resistance.* Avoid arguing or convincing. Instead, try to understand thoroughly the decision maker's reluctance to change. "It sounds like you're interested in biofeedback, but you're not confident that it will work."

• *Gauge the decision maker's sense of confidence and self-efficacy.* "On a 1-to-10 scale, how confident are you that you can manage the pain by . . . ?" Keep in mind that confidence, in this case, is not simply a matter of positive attitude. Someone may be unconfident that she can engage in speech therapy twice a week because she doesn't have regular transportation.

• *Focus on small, incremental changes.* Often, we're not confident that we can make drastic changes, but small ones seem doable. "You indicated that your pain level is usually an 8 out of 10. What do you think it would take to get it down to a 6?"

• *Collaborate and empower.* Emphasize that you are partners in the process and that you'll work together and adjust the strategy as you go. "I hear you saying that you would like to try sugar-free snacks. Would you like to try that for 2 weeks, then come back and we'll see how it's going?" "What can I or other people do to help you reach your goal?"

This is but a brief overview of MI. Extensive literature charts its efficacy at helping people quit smoking (Bock et al., 2008), exercise more (Olson, Gaffney, Lee, & Starr, 2008), seek help when considering suicide (Britton, Williams, & Conner, 2008), and more. See Box 3.6 for more about MI.

Cultivating Dialogue

Following are some other techniques for encouraging collaborative communication. Although patients as well as caregivers may use these, the majority of the literature is addressed to caregivers, recognizing perhaps that patients are traditionally more likely to follow their caregivers' cues than the other way around.

NONVERBAL ENCOURAGEMENT

Researchers have noted several ways that caregivers can nonverbally encourage patients to take a more active role in medical encounters.

BOX 3.6   RESOURCES

More About Motivational Interviewing

Fahey, K. F., Rao, S. M., Douglas, M. K., Thomas, M. L., Elliott, J. E., & Miaskowski, C. (2008). Nurse coaching to explore and modify patient attitudinal barriers interfering with effective cancer pain management. *Oncology Nursing Forum, 35*(2), 234–240.

Miller, W. R., & Rollnick, S. (2002). *Motivational interviewing: Preparing people for change.* New York: Guilford Press.

Rollnick, S., & Miller, W. (1995). What is motivational interviewing? *Behavioural and Cognitive Psychotherapy, 23,* 325–334. Reprinted from http://www.motivationalinterview.org/clinical/whatismi.html

Welch, G., Rose, G., & Ernst, D. (2006). Motivational interviewing and diabetes: What is used, and does it work? *Diabetes Spectrum, 19*(1), 5–11.

• *Look interested.* Patients respond well when caregivers show interest in what they are saying, and they gauge caregivers' interest primarily based on their nonverbal cues (Nicolai, Demmel, & Farsch, 2010). The parents of pediatric patients are more satisfied with nurses, doctors, and other health professionals when they show attentive listening behaviors (e.g., eye contact, body orientation, encouraging nods) and seem friendly, open, and approachable (Wanzer, Booth-Butterfield, & Gruber, 2004).

• *Touch (cautiously).* People may interpret touch in a number of ways. Subjected to physical contact and proximity usually reserved for intimate relationships, some patients may feel defensive or violated. Others may regard touch as a sign of comfort or esteem. Nursing home residents perceived nurses who touched a resident's arm to be more affectionate and immediate than other nurses (Moore & Gilbert, 1995).

• *Allow silence.* Physician Frederic Platt, the author of numerous books and articles on patient–caregiver communication, says that asking the right questions is only half the challenge. The rest is waiting for the answer. "Pausing long enough to allow the patient to find that answer is hard," Platt acknowledges. "Nature and doctors abhor a vacuum; we rush to fill the silences. It works better if we can trust the silence to do its work" (Platt, 1995, p. 13).

- *Pay attention to nonverbal displays.* Partly because patients are so nonassertive verbally, physicians may use nonverbal cues to gauge patients' feelings as well as the severity of their symptoms (Mast, 2007). Patients tend to be more satisfied with physicians who are skillful at understanding body language and are able to display their own emotions nonverbally (Mast, 2007).

VERBAL ENCOURAGEMENT

The challenge has sometimes been to get patients to open up and share concerns. Suchman and colleagues (1997) lament lost opportunities for sharing emotions, asserting that "the feeling of being understood by another person is intrinsically therapeutic" (p. 678). However, many patients feel inhibited, fearing that they will seem inappropriate if they share their feelings. Some caregivers have overcome patients' inhibitions by using open-ended questions, treating people as equals, encouraging self-disclosure, coaching patients, and using humor. Here are a few tips.

- *Start on a friendly note.* When researcher Gretchen Norling (2005) asked people to describe an experience in which they felt a high degree of rapport with a physician, many said that the first few moments of a medical visit set the tone. They were most likely to feel rapport with the doctor if he or she shook hands, smiled, and engaged in a polite greeting and introduction.
- *Remember that small talk is no small matter.* Courteous comments such as "How are you doing?" and "What do you do for work?" have a significant impact on patient satisfaction and may enhance trust and rapport in ways that ultimately save time and improve medical care (Koermer & Kilbane, 2008, p. 75).
- *Use open questions.* Branch and Malik (1993) propose that skillful communicators can address

patients' concerns in intense but brief discussions. They observed five physicians who invited patients to expand the scope of medical talk with open questions such as "What else?" By listening attentively, the physicians were able to hear the patients' concerns in 3 to 7 minutes. The patients were satisfied, and the doctors won accolades as some of Massachusetts' most outstanding general physicians.

- *Don't rush.* Give patients a reasonable amount of time to express their concerns.
- *Avoid abrupt topic shifts.* If you suddenly change the subject, patients may wonder if they have offended you or if you have really been listening. To reduce misunderstandings, strive for smooth transitions, such as: "I appreciate your sharing these things; we're going to have to shift gears now and I'll ask you some different types of questions about your symptoms" (suggested by Smith & Hoppe, 1991, p. 464).
- *Determine the real issue* before *conducting the exam.* Keep in mind that patients often work up to their main concerns. Don't launch into a physical exam until you're sure of the main point of the visit. ("Is anything else on your mind today?") Ask "What else?" at least three times, or until the patient says, "That's all."
- *Listen for distress markers.* Remember that patients often stutter and stammer when they're working up to important disclosures. Don't change the subject before you know what's on their minds. Your reassurance will help them speak openly.
- *Ask for the patient's feedback.* Most people won't interrupt you to let you know they cannot follow your advice. You must ask, as in, "How do you feel about this option?" and "Is there anything that would make this hard for you to do?"
- *Reassure patients.* Keep in mind that people seek medical attention for many reasons—to be reassured, forgiven, comforted, cured. Words mean a lot ("You needn't feel embarrassed about this." "It's not your fault." "I understand.") Patients typically consider that physicians who are open and reassuring understand them better than doctors who seem controlling (Silvester, Patterson, Koczwara, & Ferguson, 2007). Annette Harres (2008) found that physicians can show empathy and invite response by using friendly tag questions such as "You're in pain, aren't you?" (p. 49).

- *Treat people as equals.* Status differences often inhibit open communication. For example, some physicians earn patients' trust (and gratitude) by disclosing some of their own feelings and reassuring patients who seem nervous or unsure (du Pré, 2002; Smith-du Pré & Beck, 1996).
- *Coach patients.* After researchers trained physicians and the parents of pediatric patients using the PACE model (present information, ask questions, check your understanding, express any concerns), the parents shared more information with the doctor, expressed their concerns more freely, and were more likely than other patients to verify the information the doctor gave them by asking additional questions and restating what they understood (Harrington, Norling, Witte, Taylor, & Andrews, 2007). Physicians trained in the model were more likely than before to encourage parents' questions and to engage them in collaborative decision making. And they accomplished all of this without significantly adding to the length of exams.
- *Consider using humor.* The use of mild, respectful humor seems to be a particularly effective means of minimizing status differences between patients and caregivers (Beck & Ragan, 1992; du Pré, 1998; Ragan, 1990) and helping family caregivers relieve stress (Bethea, Travis, & Pecchioni, 2000). Juliann Scholl (2007) studied communication at MIRTH (Medical Institute for Recovery Through Humor), a skilled nursing unit within a large hospital. Patients in the unit took part in at least two good-humor activities a day, including storytelling, entertainment, cooking, and more. Scholl found that conversational humor helped participants speak candidly without seeming like "bad patients" and fostered a sense of immediacy and friendliness.
- *Minimize distractions.* James Price Dillard and associates studied medical visits during which parents of newborns who were suspected of having cystic fibrosis found out for sure if their babies were ill (Dillard, Carson, Bernard, Laxova, & Farrell, 2004; Dillard, Shen, Laxova, & Farrell, 2008). Even during such important meetings, distractions often made it difficult for the parents to concentrate. The most common distractions were the infants themselves, followed by siblings who were also present. Other distractions included noises from children in nearby rooms, staff and equipment, phone calls, and announcements over the public address system (Dillard et al., 2008). The researchers suggest meeting in a quiet office, outside the hospital or clinic if necessary, and providing follow-up information that parents can take with them.

For an example of especially pleasing patient–caregiver communication, read the mother's story in Box 3.7.

Narrative Medicine

Anne had seen a lot of doctors over the years, but Dr. Falchuk was different. She could barely believe her ears as he sat before her:

> Falchuk offered a gentle smile. "I want to hear your story in your own words." Anne glanced at the clock on the wall, the steady sweep of the second hand ticking off precious time. Her internist had told her that Dr. Falchuk was a prominent specialist, that there was a long line waiting to see him. Her problem was hardly urgent, and she got an appointment in less than two months only because of a cancellation in his Christmas-week schedule. But she detected no hint of rush or impatience in the doctor. His calm made it seem as if he had all the time in the world. (Groopman, 2007, p. 12)

Actually, Anne's condition *was* urgent. Although she was eating 3,000 calories a day, she was unable to keep food down and she had become critically underweight (Groopman, 2007). The problem had persisted for 15 years, and although Anne was only in her thirties, her body's systems were crashing. Of the 30 or so doctors she had consulted before Dr. Falchuk, none had asked to hear her whole story, as he did. Instead, most doctors had asked only brief, closed-ended questions. Their subsequent diagnoses ranged from depression to bulimia, to irritable bowel syndrome, and more. Some felt that the illness was "all in her head." Most urged her to eat a high-carbohydrate diet of cereals and breads to gain weight. But her health kept deteriorating.

After listening carefully to Anne's story from beginning to end, Falchuk was the first to identify her

BOX 3.7 PERSPECTIVES

A Mother's Experience at the Dentist

When I first took Kathryn to the dentist, she was very apprehensive. She had never been before due to lack of dental insurance and money, and she only went to the doctor when she was really sick, which was once every 2 years or so. Most illnesses we handled at home, and the idea of preventive care was foreign to her. I knew she needed to go. I knew she wasn't brushing as good as she should, and I also knew that sometimes she lied to me about brushing at all. I couldn't watch her every minute.

When I remarried last year, we were finally fortunate enough to have dental insurance, only we found out there was a 1-year waiting period for anything other than cleanings. So I waited.

Finally, the year was up, and in July I took Kathryn to the dentist for the first time in her life. I tried in advance to make her understand that it was all right to be scared, but that did not mean that it was all right to whine, cry, and generally throw a fit. I told her again and again that I would never take her to anyone I didn't trust or anyone I thought would harm or hurt her unnecessarily.

On a Saturday morning we drove 40 miles to the dental center. Right away, the staff tried to make Kathryn feel at home. The receptionist greeted me and Kathryn by name and asked Kathryn if she was tired from getting up so early on a Saturday. But as I filled out the forms, Kathryn hid behind me, and she spent a lot of time trying to hug me and kiss my cheek. She always does this when she is nervous.

I found I was nervous as well. Not only could I not ease Kathryn's fears, but I found myself feeling like I was a bad parent for not bringing her to the dentist until she was 8. I wasn't sure, as nice as the receptionist was, if she would understand things like no money and no insurance. So we didn't talk about the fact that Kathryn should have been to the dentist years ago; we just talked about easy things, like the nice weather and my wedding pictures.

Soon it was time for Kathryn to go back. After taking x-rays the hygienist led us back to an examination room and found me a small stool to sit on so that I could stay in the same room. She was very friendly and made me feel comfortable. She was also nice to Kathryn and didn't put us down for not coming in sooner.

The cleaning was a little nerve-wracking, since it was a bit uncomfortable, and Kathryn has a wonderful gag reflex. But the hygienist never seemed to get upset, and she even talked to Kathryn as though she understood, asking her questions like "It's a little scary at first, isn't it?" and "Are you okay? We can wait a minute if you want to, but if we go ahead, we'll be done sooner." It was great that she was so understanding.

By this time, Kathryn was less apprehensive about me leaving the room for a few minutes. The dentist and I walked to the other end of the hall, where he explained that Kathryn had a lot of cavities. He recommended a series of four brief appointments to help Kathryn become more at ease as they repaired her teeth. He made me feel at ease, telling me what a pretty girl Kathryn was. Then he got serious and let me know he understood my concerns about not bringing her in sooner, but not to worry. The cavities were not severe, they were all in baby teeth, and although there were several, they would be easy to fix.

I collected Kathryn and stopped by the front desk, where the receptionist pulled out a surprise box and let Kathryn pick out what she wanted. The next visits were not as bad as Kathryn thought they would be. Every time she was a little happier and not so apprehensive about what would happen. Once she had been through the routine, she knew what to expect, and that helped. She said she liked everyone at the dentist's office. Once I brought a newspaper article I had written about Kathryn's school with her picture in it. The staff insisted on reading the whole thing and remarked what a good writer I was and how pretty Kathryn was. They also insisted on seeing my wedding pictures. It wasn't just something to be nice; they really wanted to see them.

I feel good taking Kathryn there because I know, no matter what, we will get the best treatment. Not only that, but we have established friendships with these people that will last. They truly believe they are there to serve, and they show that in everything they do. Just ask Kathryn. She'll tell you.

—DONNA

disease correctly. He suspected—and confirmed—that she had celiac disease, a severe allergy to the gluten found in many grain products (notably the same products that other doctors were urging Anne to eat). Falchuk's diagnosis and the subsequent diet change saved Anne's life. When Groopman (2007) interviewed Falchuk about the episode, he denied doing anything extraordinary. Listening to patients' stories *should* be a doctor's first priority, Falchuk said, avowing that "once you remove yourself from the patient's story, you are no longer truly a doctor" (Groopman, p. 2007).

Narrative medicine is an approach championed most notably by physician and medical school professor Rita Charon. It involves respect for people's stories and the awareness that storytelling unites both the teller and the listener in a unique and shared experience with profound implications for life and for healing (Charon, 2006). Charon proposes that narrative medicine is both an ideal and a method. It involves a commitment to deep and sincere listening, a belief in the power of stories to heal and to reveal what needs healing, and the courage to, as Charon puts it, "inhabit" another person's point of view for a while.

Charon (2009b) proposes that narrative medicine is a means of bridging the "chasms and divisions and discontinuities" of health care and the experience of being ill (p. 197). The disconnect may have blinded Anne's previous caregivers to the true problem. Falchuk was different from them in that he attentively listened to her. In doing so, he was able to identify what all the others had missed. Charon shares his belief that medicine, at its best, bridges the gaps between people. Genuine engagement, she says, requires the courage to face raw and uncomfortable emotions. But it also offers revelations and connections beyond imagining. As Falchuk, Charon, and many others agree, it's good medicine. Here are a few of the key principles involved.

Narrative medicine embraces the idea that storytelling is a natural way of making sense of the world. Any time people gather, even for a few moments, they tell stories. One person tells another what it was like to undergo surgery, have a baby, go on a blind date, or so on. Communication scholar William Rawlins (2009) proclaims, from personal experience and many years researching the topic, that "making stories with friends is good for the heart and the soul" (p. 168). This is especially true when we're trying to make sense of a serious occurrence such as a health event that interrupts the storyline we imagined for ourselves. "Sickness summons stories," writes narrative theorist Lynn Harter (2009, p. 141).

Moreover, people tell stories for some very compelling reasons. At a surface level, narratives are informative. They tell people of specific goings-on and perhaps prepare them to take part in similar circumstances. But at an even deeper level, narratives shape interpretations and viewpoints—some would say that they shape reality. In Charon's words, through the events of life and our stories about them "we become who are, discover who we are, accept who we are, rage or pleasure toward who we are" (2009a, p. 120).

Narrative medicine involves compassionate engagement and a respect for the uniqueness and wholeness of each individual. Here's a powerful example told by Charon:

> My first gesture after hearing out a woman with muscular dystrophy and impending respiratory failure was to sit as close to the patient as I could, thigh to thigh, my hands in my lap, trying to inhabit her climate of panicky despair so as not to leave her alone in it. And so we were on a search together right from the beginning. (2009a, p. 123)

Charon begins conversations with new patients by saying, "I will be your doctor, so I must learn a great deal about your body and your health and life. Please tell me what you think I should know about your situation" (2009a, p. 122). Then she listens, without writing or typing or any other activity that might distract.

Far from being a waste of time, listening without interrupting has enabled Charon to learn things that might have taken years to discover otherwise. "Having hastened the development of genuine listening and learning about the patient, I found

WHAT DO YOU THINK?

■ What's your opinion of Dr. Falchuk's approach?

■ Why do you think more doctors don't take this approach?

myself able to do things that mattered right from the beginning" (2009a, p. 122). But the process is not only for her benefit. Telling one's story has a value even more inherent. "The patient's body talks with the patient's self, in an odd and powerful way, while I, the witness, listen," Charon says, observing that we often come to understand and integrate facets of ourselves through storytelling (p. 122).

Narrative medicine embraces the idea that health professionals are not, and cannot be, all-knowing and all-powerful. Indeed, many would argue that the expectation that they should be omnipotent and infallible fosters a sense of distance and authority that is at odds with true engagement. From the perspective of narrative medicine, even when there is nothing a professional can do to cure a patient, the act of being present with that person is therapeutic and affirming. As Charon puts it, "one knows, one feels, one responds, and one *joins with* the one who suffers" (2006, p. 12).

Harter (2009) tells of a physician who includes in patient charts notes about what and whom they love and what they dream of doing. In the chart of Anna, a young woman with bone cancer, he included her prom and graduation photos, two life events he knew were important to her. Later, in a poignant meeting in which he had to tell Anna that her cancer had spread to her lungs, he asked, "What other chapters in your life do you want to write, Anna? How can I help you write those?" (quoted by Harter, 2009, p. 141). Rather than talking, he listened.

Narratives are important to health communication in several ways. As mentioned, patients naturally speak in narrative form, describing their concerns within a sequence of events that they consider relevant. Narratives often address a sophisticated array of factors simultaneously, and they may be a means of conveying what we wouldn't otherwise blurt out. Timothy Halkowski (2006) observed that patients often present a "sequence of noticings" that involve emerging indications of a potential health problem and what the patient did about them at each step. These narrative details may seem superfluous to caregivers, who may wonder, as one doctor I know puts it, why patients don't just come to the point and "bottom-line it." But for a patient, Halkowski says, these narratives allow patients to manage the dilemma of simultaneously impressing the doctor that one's concerns are legitimate

while avoiding being typified as melodramatic or overly self-concerned. The patient is able to present a number of indicators that are demonstrated as being relevant to the current concern, underscoring its status as real rather than imagined. Patients can also display that they were not actively looking for things to go medically wrong and can share useful information about what has or has not worked so far. This sequential narrative, Halkowski says, gives patients a mechanism for presenting their concerns in an informative and identity-supporting way.

This leads to another reason that narratives are important: They're loaded with information. A sensitive listener can detect cues to a person's hopes, fears, doubts, future intentions, and more. Particularly since patients are often nonassertive about expressing these feelings, caregivers may find that narratives offer valuable insights. Subtle cues may be the only indications that a patient is dissatisfied, in despair, reluctant to cooperate, overly anxious to please, or so on. All of these feelings can be directly relevant to the success of medical care.

Janice Brown and Julia Addington-Hall (2007) identified four types of narratives in the stories told by people with motor neurone disease (MND), a neurological disorder that gradually diminishes people's ability to move and speak. Most people with MND die in 3 to 5 years.

- *Sustaining narratives* emphasize hope and positive thinking. For example, one mother of two young children said she was grateful for what she could still do, even though her ability to walk and talk were ebbing. "I mean, I still feel I could be a lot worse off. I mean I know everything's hard work, but there's no pain it" (p. 204).
- *Enduring narratives* describe a process of stoically living through one's suffering, ambivalent about whether it would be better to live or to die. One man in the study, who could no longer move his hands or arms, said, "They say there's not much they can do about it, you have just got to take it" (p. 205). He said he had instructed caregivers not to resuscitate him if he had a heart attack because dying would be better than "sitting here like this" (p. 205).
- In *preserving narratives,* people describe illness as something to be conquered, with varying levels of confidence in their ability to do so. One participant in the study had turned to

holistic therapies in addition to pharmaceutical prescriptions, changed his diet, and eliminated chemicals from his home. "I am just willing to try anything," he said (p. 205).

- *Fracturing narratives* describe fear, loss, denial, and threats to self-concept. Said one woman with MND: "I try and remain optimistic and fear that if the day comes when I have to fully embrace this illness, possibly because of increasing symptoms, then I will totally fall apart. I am trying to postpone that moment" (p. 206).

The researchers reflect that caregivers can better understand people by listening to their narratives and appreciating that the narratives are likely to evolve over time.

Finally, there's something more to narratives—something less easily measured, but unquestionably powerful in the act of bearing witness to another person's story. As Richard Zaner (2009) expresses it, there is, in narrative, something between people "that does not belong exclusively to either person" (p. 170) but lives in the "terrain where wonder holds sway" (p. 170). Within that terrain, says Charon (2006), caregivers connect with others through a sense of genuine curiosity and concern, and they learn a great deal about themselves in the process.

If the move toward patient empowerment continues, narratives are likely to become more influential components of patient–caregiver communication. Geist and Gates (1996) describe the process as "movement from biology to biography" (p. 221). When caregivers listen and ask open-ended questions, they can learn a great deal, not only about patients' physical conditions, but also about their expectations and values (Eggly, 2002). How relevant are such factors to personal health? Very relevant, according to the integrative health theory (Box 3.8), which proposes that health is not an isolated condition, but an alignment between multiple factors.

Narrative medicine represents a move away from the historical divide between mind and body that we discussed in Chapter 2. Charon reminds us that narratives help to bridge the gap between people and between what she calls "the unstable gap between the body and the self" (2009a, p. 122), facilitating reconciliation between a person's body and his or her "totality of being" (p. 124).

We have focused a great deal on what caregivers can do to encourage effective communication. Let's turn to communication tips designed specifically for patients.

Tips for Patients

Here are a few suggestions from the experts.

- *Take stock.* Consider Rita Charon's question: "Please tell me what you think I should know about your situation." You needn't memorize or rehearse, but do give some thought to what you want caregivers to know, as well as your goals for the visit and your concerns at a physical, emotional, and social level.
- *Create a one-page health history.* In an easy-to-read format, present information about your health (medications, illnesses, hospitalizations, allergies, surgeries) and any diseases diagnosed in your immediate family. Bring a copy to all doctor visits and hospital stays.
- *Write down and rank-order your concerns.* Doctors like a list—*if* it helps them get a succinct overview of all your concerns and *if* the list identifies what you consider most important. (Keep in mind that you may not have time to go through all the items on the list in one visit. Bring an extra copy to share and to include in your chart.)
- *Prepare for the standard questions.* Be ready with answers to such questions as: What does it feel like? When? Where? For how long?
- *Choose health care providers carefully.* Find professionals who are well respected by their peers and who listen well and make you feel comfortable. Your feelings are as legitimate as your medications and health history. Find someone who pays attention to both.
- *Don't overlook valuable resources.* There are probably more people available to help you than you realize. For example, pharmacists are among the most knowledgeable but underutilized health experts. They can offer advice about prescription and nonprescription medications, address concerns, and serve as ongoing advisors and guides (Gade, 2007). Likewise, dieticians, athletic trainers, and others can help with health-related behaviors.
- *Know what treatment you're supposed to get, and make sure your caregivers know it, too.* As we will discuss in Chapter 5, medical mistakes do happen. Tell caregivers why you're at the clinic or hospital,

BOX 3.8   THEORETICAL INSIGHTS

Integrative Health Model

Health cannot accurately be reduced to a failure of body, identity, or behavior, say the creators of integrative health theory (Lambert, Street, Cegala, Smith, Kurtz, & Schofield, 1997). Instead, *integrative health theory* proposes that health is the alignment between interpretive accounts (assumptions and explanations), performance (activities and behaviors), and self-image (understanding of one's own identity).

Ideally, alignment is stable and enduring (the person is healthy), but a change in any one force can upset the alignment. Lambert and colleagues (1997) present the example of a man who feels healthy despite undiagnosed high blood pressure. However, once his condition is diagnosed and he begins taking medication for it, the man experiences a side effect (impotence). His interpretive account—that, as a healthy male and husband (his self-image), he should have a sexual relationship with his wife—is threatened by his inability to engage in sexual activity (performance). In short, "the impotence is a resistance that destabilizes his healthy alignment," write Lambert and associates. "When he realizes he is impotent, he no longer feels healthy" (p. 34).

Lambert and colleagues (1997) use the term *resistance* to describe factors that threaten alignment. The effects of resistance are not predictable or universal. The man in the previous example might respond by altering his self-image, redefining his ideas about being a good husband, or resuming sexual activity by ceasing the medication (Lambert et al.).

People may have a difficult time adjusting to resistance factors that seem small to others. By the same token, over time, people sometimes achieve alignment that others would not think possible. Marianne Brady and David Cella (1995) described the resiliency with which some cancer patients ultimately adapt to their illness: "Many even say they are strengthened by the experience and note an improved outlook on life, enhanced interpersonal relationships and a deepened sense of personal strength" (para. 13). Although their physical abilities may be compromised by the disease, these people apparently adjust other factors to achieve a new (even an improved) sense of alignment.

The integrative health model presents several implications for health communication. For one, it sets aside the centuries-old question of whether health is fundamentally a matter of mind or body. By rejecting reductionistic notions, it provides an inclusive definition of health that relies more on alignment between factors than isolation of any one element. From this perspective, a health examination would not be focused on identifying the "cause" of a health concern but in considering how it is situated within broader contexts.

Another implication is that restoring alignment may be simple or complex. Sometimes there is primarily one form of resistance. Lambert and coauthors (1997) give the example of an appendectomy that restores a young woman to full health. In her case, alignment is disrupted but quickly restored. In other situations, however, focusing on one resistance point may not help (or may even worsen) overall alignment. For example, amputating a limb may remove physical danger but plunge the patient into personal crisis. Considering this, the biomedical model may be appropriate for some medical encounters but woefully insufficient for others.

A third implication is that outcomes are neither static nor definitive. Lambert and colleagues (1997) write: "It is never known in advance which accommodations will be successful, nor is it known whether accommodations will themselves lead to the emergence of new resistances" (p. 35). Even when alignment is present, there is no guarantee it will stay that way. In fact, it almost certainly will be challenged. Because of this, health is viewed more productively as a process, as a temporal emergence, than as an outcome.

Finally, in the midst of this complexity, Lambert and colleagues (1997) argue that there is one constant: *The patient is always central in the process.* As an individual involved in the ongoing work of balancing identity and performance, a "patient is at the center of the aligned elements" and is "also the one doing the work of interactive stabilization" (p. 31).

WHAT DO YOU THINK?

1. In what ways do your daily activities support your self-image? How would you feel if you lost the ability to perform these activities?

2. Think of the last time you felt unhealthy. What resistance factors were involved? Was alignment restored? If so, how?

SUGGESTED SOURCES

Integrative health is based on the collective ideas of a number of theorists. For the rich background behind this theory, see the following:

Charmaz, K. (1987). Struggling for a self: Identity levels of the chronically ill. In J. Roth & P. Conrad (Eds.), *Research in the sociology of health care* (pp. 283–321). Greenwich, CT: JAI Press.

Corbin, J., & Strauss, A. L. (1988). Experiencing body failure and a disrupted self image. In J. Corbin & A. L. Strauss (Eds.), *Unending work and care: Managing chronic illness at home* (pp. 49–67). San Francisco: Jossey-Bass.

Goffman, E. (1974). *Frame analysis: An essay on the organization of experience.* New York: Harper Colophon.

Pickering, A. (1995). *The mangle of practice: Time, agency, and science.* Chicago: University of Chicago Press.

and make sure everyone agrees. This might prevent a wrong-side surgery or medication error.

- *Help set the agenda.* Be as clear as possible when making an appointment so that the caregiver knows your concerns and expectations. ("I'm experiencing sharp abdominal pains" and "I'd like an overall physical and a chance to ask some questions.")
- *Talk to the nurse.* Odds are you'll speak with a nurse before you speak with a doctor. Let the nurse know your concerns. He or she can help facilitate your visit.
- *Don't abuse the clock.* The reality is that caregivers must budget their time. Most are willing to listen when they appreciate that what you're saying is relevant to your concern. For your part, speak freely, but emphasize the relevance of what you want to share and avoid going off on tangents.
- *Take an active role.* Doctors usually understand patients' goals more clearly and share more information when patients ask questions and state their concerns, preferences, and opinions (Cegala, Street, & Clinch, 2007).
- *Acknowledge reservations.* If something prevents you from speaking frankly with a caregiver, let that person know ("I'm embarrassed," "I'm afraid," etc.).
- *Be assertive.* If your questions have not been answered or you don't agree with the advice given, state your feelings in a clear and respectful way. Walking away dissatisfied helps no one.

Next we look at efforts to create physical environments that are conducive to healing and open communication.

Healing Environments

I wanted to design a building where the healing process begins the moment a patient enters in the front door.

—César Pelli

Pelli, a design consultant to the Mayo Clinic, describes the careful attention he and others devote to the clinic's physical environment (Berry & Seltman, 2008, p. 41). Traditionally, medical settings come across as intimidating and sterile. The rooms are usually cramped and the furnishings austere. Some medical centers, such as Mayo, have committed to creating a different atmosphere, however. The idea is that environments that soothe and uplift can lower stress, reduce pain, keep people's spirits up, and facilitate better communication.

Mayo designers go so far as personally to examine each sheet of marble to be incorporated in floors and staircases to make sure that no unpleasant designs are suggested in the natural color variations. Their goal is to inspire confidence and health from the ground up. The clinic is famous for its art (much of it donated by grateful patients), soaring architecture, large windows, and live music. A grand piano is available in the main lobby of each Mayo campus. James Hodge, who chairs the clinic's art committee, says:

It is rare that someone is not playing the piano in the Gonda lobby. I've seen patients and visitors join in a sing-along—once patients and visitors were dancing. Another time a diva of opera paused and spontaneously sang. On another occasion, a well-known pop musician sang while a volunteer accompanied him on the piano. (quoted by Berry & Seltman, p. 42)

To see a couple of captivating performances in the Mayo lobby, visit the links provided in *Check It Out!*

Even supposed luxuries are considered part of the healing experience. When Serena Fleischaker donated chandeliers for a Mayo grand lobby, she explained that she wanted to provide a beautiful, soothing presence for people coping with hardship. "I want the Chihuly glass chandeliers to pleasantly distract people, to cause them to raise their eyes toward the heavens, to pause in the anxious interludes between appointments, to have a tiny respite from their suffering," she said (quoted by Berry & Seltman, p. 41). The clinic also features large windows, grand staircases, gardens, fountains, and quiet sitting areas.

Research supports that physical environments have a significant influence on health-related communication. Kreps and Thornton (1992) describe the subduing effect of confined spaces (small rooms, low ceilings) versus the stimulation of open spaces and windows. du Pré (1998) observed that communication in a doctor's office tends to be quieter and more private than in the open-air arrangement of most physical therapy units, where conversations are often loud and invite participation from anyone in earshot. With the goal of improving communication and emotional well-being, health practitioners and researchers are beginning to examine—and in many cases reshape—the environments in which patients and caregivers communicate.

Soothing Surroundings

One effort to restructure medical environments is led by **Planetree**, a nonprofit organization that helps medical centers establish pleasing and empowering surroundings. Planetree was founded in California in 1978 by Angelica Thieriot, who was dismayed by how "cold, impersonal, and lonely" she found U.S. hospitals compared to those of her native Argentina (Schwade, 1994, para. 23). (Planetree is named after the type of tree under which Hippocrates is said to have mentored medical students.)

Hospitals influenced by the Planetree model usually offer hotel-style rooms with accommodations for overnight visitors. Patients are encouraged to

CHECK IT OUT!

■ For an irresistible 74-second clip of a lively couple playing a duet in the Mayo Clinic atrium, visit http://www.youtube.com/watch?v=RI-10tK80k0.

■ For a performance by 15-year-old virtuoso Alex Walton-Creutz, whose mother is a regular patient at the Mayo Clinic, see http://www.youtube.com/watch?v=gYGEjER_h4g.

wear their own clothing, and soothing colors and adjustable lighting help to reduce the cold sterility common to clinical settings ("Patient Satisfaction," 2007). Rooms are equipped with thermostats so that patients can control the temperature. Treatment

BOX 3.9   PERSPECTIVES

Normal hospitals aren't this relaxing, I thought, when I entered the birthing center where my nephew Jacob was born. There were lush, green plants in every corner and ocean paintings on the walls. The staff was friendly and seemed excited to share the experience with us. Each time a baby was born, the sound of "Lullaby and Goodnight" softly flowed from overhead speakers. Finally my brother came out and announced with a grin, '8 pounds, 9 ounces, and 21 inches long.' My family jumped from their seats to hug him. It was Italian-family-overload at its best.

—NICOLE YEAKOS (SHOWN WITH NEWBORN JACOB)

areas allow patients to gaze at colored glass, gardens, or soothing displays as they undergo procedures.

Large windows are a key Planetree feature, allowing access to sunlight and a view of plants, flowers, and fountains. At some hospitals, "healing gardens" provide living displays of plants honored through the centuries for their curative properties, complete with labels describing the significance of each.

The Bergan Mercy Medical Center in Omaha, Nebraska, adopted the Planetree model to "humanize and demystify" its emergency services department (Lumsdon, 1996). An administrator remembers that the staff was initially indignant when it was proposed that they institute patient-centered care. They felt that they were already patient-centered. But soon, says the administrator, they became excited about ideas they had never considered before. Now the hospital staff keeps clinical equipment in handy closets (not out in the open) whenever possible, plays Disney movies to soothe frightened children, and uses dimmer switches to adjust room lighting. The hospital received only 2 patient complaints the year after changes were implemented, compared to 37 the year before (Lumsdon, 1996).

Easy Communication with Loved Ones

Sometimes a healing environment is more virtual than physical. Free online programs such as CarePages provide ways for people coping with health issues to post photos, news, and updates.

Loved ones can visit online and post comments of their own. I once received a CarePage invitation from a former student whose newborn baby was in intensive care. The website allowed the anxious parents to keep loved ones informed without calling everyone individually. They posted pictures of the baby and frequent updates about her condition. When I logged on, there were already dozens of messages from loved ones, ranging from "She is beautiful like her mother!" to "We know how worried you are. Our thoughts are with you at this difficult time." CarePages users can also take part in online forums and blogs with people in similar situations. (See *Check it Out!* for more information about healing environments.)

Summary

The traditional power difference between patients and caregivers is manifested in conversations in

WHAT DO YOU THINK?

■ In your experience, does the physical environment affect healing and communication? Why or why not?

■ If so, what elements would you find most appealing?

CHECK IT OUT!

■ *Putting Patients First: Designing and Practicing Patient-Centered Care* (Frampton, Gilpin, & Charmel, 2003)

■ Planetree website: www.planetree.org

■ CarePages website: www.carepages.com/support

BOX 3.10 CAREER OPPORTUNITIES

Health Communication Research

Professor
Researcher
Consultant

CAREER RESOURCES AND JOB LISTINGS

- Association of American Medical Colleges: www.aamc.org
- *Chronicle of Higher Education*: chronicle.com
- Coalition for Health Communication: www.healthcommunication.net
- European Association for Communication in Health Care: www.each.nl
- Health Communication Partnership: www.hcpartnership.org
- International Communication Association: www.icahdq.org
- National Communication Association: www.natcom.org
- Society of Behavioral Medicine: www.sbm.org
- Society of Teachers of Family Medicine: www.stfm.org/index_ex.html
- U.S. Bureau of Labor Statistics: www.bls.gov

which patients tend to acquiesce and physicians to dominate. With physician-centered communication, doctors do the majority of the talking and ask most of the questions (questions that usually stipulate brief responses). Unwittingly or not, patients often collaborate in the lopsided nature of these medical conversations by speaking hesitantly and abandoning topics when interrupted.

Although it may seem expedient for caregivers to keep a tight rein on medical interviews, ineffective patient–caregiver communication is hurtful for everyone involved. People who don't feel rapport with their caregivers are more likely than others to sue for malpractice, to experience heightened pain, to withhold information that may be important to an accurate diagnosis, to switch caregivers or avoid medical care altogether, and to distrust medical advice. Evidence suggests that good communication isn't merely a nicety; it's good medicine. Good communication (open, trusting, clear, and thorough) can help participants in medical encounters arrive at accurate diagnoses, mutually acceptable treatment plans, clear expectations, a shared sense of support and solidarity, and proactive strategies for health maintenance. What's more, effective communication can help ease patients' anxiety and pain and assist them in navigating the complexities of the health care system.

Many caregivers, far from being anxious to abuse the power granted them, are frustrated by the barriers it creates. They attempt to empower patients through the use of encouraging words and nonverbal gestures, touch, and humor. Collaborative communication is neither caregiver-centered nor patient-centered, but instead is dedicated to active partnerships.

Motivational interviewing is one technique for involving people as active participants in health-related decisions. The interviewer issues no orders or commands and makes no judgments. Instead, he or she asks questions to help decision makers explore the perceived advantages and disadvantages of various options.

Likewise, narratives are a key component of patient talk and may reveal much more than factual details. Storytelling usually reflects how people view the world, how they see themselves in relation to others, and what events are most significant to them. Information of this sort can give caregivers valuable insight and can provide a therapeutic way for them to authentically engage with patients.

Patients may respond to illness in many ways—from relief to terror—and may experience changes in their personal identity as a result of illness. Integrative health theory describes the importance of alignment and resistance in maintaining good health.

No matter what the medium or setting, communication between patients and caregivers is most effective when both sides are sensitive to each other's goals. For their part, patients can strive to communicate more clearly and assertively. Caregivers can show that they are sensitive to the challenges people face in communicating about issues that are often personal, fearsome, and uncertain.

Recognizing that the physical environment affects how people feel and how they communicate, some medical centers are redesigning facilities to include beautiful views, peaceful settings, amenities for family members, soothing music, and artwork.

Key Terms and Theories

transactional communication
physician-centered communication
therapeutic privilege
doorknob disclosures
directives
blocking
patronize
transgressions
disclosure decision-making model (DD-MM)
collaborative medical communication
model of collaborative interpretation (CI)
dialogue
nouning
verbing
motivational interviewing (MI)
narrative medicine
sustaining narratives
enduring narratives
preserving narratives
fracturing narratives
integrative health theory
resistance
Planetree

DISCUSSION QUESTIONS

1. What is the significance of regarding patient–caregiver communication as transactional?

2. Traditionally, physicians have had more control over medical conversations than patients have had. What factors contribute to the prevalence of physician-centered communication? Describe some of the communication patterns involved. How do patients' behaviors contribute to these dynamics? How do caregivers' behaviors contribute?

3. What is therapeutic privilege? What guidelines would you suggest for using this privilege?

4. Why might patients and caregivers commit transgressions? What are some methods for handling transgression attempts? Provide a few examples.

5. How could patients and caregivers lessen the likelihood of doorknob disclosures?

6. According to the disclosure decision-making model, what three considerations affect whether people disclose nonvisible health concerns to someone else?

7. Compare a "rhetoric of passivity" with a "rhetoric of agency." What are some communication strategies caregivers and patients can use to accomplish collaborative interpretation? Apply these to an example of your own.

8. Compare the assumptions of physician-centered and collaborative communication. How is the caregiver's role different in each model? How is the patient's role different? What are some of the reasons that many people are shifting from physician-centered to collaborative communication?

9. What are the assumptions and techniques of motivational interviewing? Would you enjoy being part of such an interview? Why or why not?

10. In what ways can caregivers use nonverbal communication to encourage patients' communication?

11. How can caregivers use verbal communication to encourage patients' communication?

12. Why are narratives important to health communication? What the main principles of narrative medicine?

13. Describe the four types of narratives identified by J. Brown and Addington-Hall (2007).

14. Describe integrative health theory. What is meant by *alignment?* By *resistance?*

15. How and why are some health centers restructuring their environments?

Answers to *Can You Guess?*

1. Based on surveys, caregivers in Vermont rank highest in terms of patient-centeredness and those in Arizona lowest ("State Scorecard," 2007). To find out how other states stack up, visit www.commonwealthfund.com and search for state scorecard.

CHAPTER FOUR

Patient Perspectives

I remember, as a child, the distinct smell of the doctor's office. It's different than any other odor, and it leaves a lasting impression. The smell of rubbing alcohol, the smell of medicines, and the smell of antibacterial soap on the doctor's hands. As a child, you don't know what to make of it.

These musings by a college student evoke vivid images of patienthood. Whatever else we remember of childhood, most of us will never forget the sensory alert of waiting anxiously to be seen by a doctor.

Being a patient can be a frightening experience, even as an adult. Uncertainty is guaranteed, and pain is a strong possibility. At the same time, though, there is the promise of relief, a cure, or a reassuring health assessment. (See Box 4.1 for a true story about one patient's experience managing uncertainty.)

In this chapter we look at health care situations through patients' eyes. We will investigate the informal socialization process that helps us learn how to behave appropriately, what we generally like and dislike, and what motivates us to follow (and, just as often, to ignore) medical advice. The chapter concludes with a discussion of illness and personal identity.

Patient Socialization

Being a patient often means suspending the rules of everyday interaction. In medicine, the touch and physical exposure usually reserved for intimate relationships occurs under bright lights in the company of strangers. The contrast can be challenging for both patients and caregivers. Recalling her early experiences as a doctor, Transue (2004) remembers a moment when it dawned on her that touching a patient had become something very different. As she administered CPR compressions to a hospital patient in distress, she struggled to compare it to other forms of touch:

> I think, irrationally, of lovers whose skin I have delighted in, clasped beneath my fingers, massaged, caressed. What framework can I find to encompass both these concepts, the thrilling touch of beloved flesh, and this strange doughy substance

BOX 4.1 PERSPECTIVES

The Agony of Uncertainty

It all began one day when I was in eighth-grade physical education class. As the class began to warm up and stretch, I noticed a knot on my knee. A month passed and the knot did not go away. In fact it grew from the size of a pencil eraser to the size of a quarter. My mother made an appointment with our family doctor, and I began to panic. I personally gave myself one year to live.

During my appointment the doctor asked questions like "Have you fallen down recently?" I was so distraught I felt like screaming, "I did not come in here for a bump and scrape!" But I just said no.

After ordering x-rays, the doctor said he could not tell if the knot was a cyst or a tumor and referred us to a bone and joint specialist. I was beyond scared. I was only 13 and had never had anything worse than the flu. I had so many questions, but there wasn't much chance to ask them. Every question I asked got a brief response, when what I really wanted was a full explanation and, above all, reassurance. The conversation went something like this:

Doctor: It looks like you have a cyst or a tumor. I'm going to refer you to a specialist.

Me: What does that mean?

Doctor: It means he will look at your knee and figure out what is going on.

Me: Is it serious?

Doctor: That's what he'll be able to determine.

Me: Well, OK.

I wasn't sure about the difference between a cyst and a tumor, and both sounded horrible. I was afraid the doctor would laugh if I said I was afraid of having cancer. Or had he just told me I *did* have cancer? I left not knowing, and I had to wait a month to see the specialist.

On the day of the appointment with the specialist, Dr. Benze, we waited 2½ hours to see him. However, his personality and gentle manner made up for the wait. Dr. Benze compassionately and carefully told me the lump (now the size of a small orange) was a tumor. When I began to cry, he explained that not all tumors are cancerous. He arranged to surgically remove the tumor in two days, and he promised to tell me everything about the surgery in advance and to share the lab results with me as soon as he received them.

On the day before surgery my mother and I visited the hospital to make arrangements. The admitting attendant was detached and unfriendly, but the nurses and doctors were wonderful. They tried to make me feel comfortable and relaxed. An outpatient nurse sat down with us and described in detail what would happen before, during, and after the surgery. I felt comfortable asking every question I did not feel safe asking the first doctor.

Suffice it to say that the surgery went well. The tumor was not cancerous, and I have had no more tumors. Overall, the experience was a positive one. The worst part was leaving the first doctor's office with so many fears and questions I never got to voice. Although the surgery was frightening, I felt better once people started telling me what was going on.

—SARAH

WHAT DO YOU THINK?

1. Do you think the first doctor could have communicated more effectively with Sarah? If so, how?

2. Do you think Sarah could have communicated more effectively? If so, how?

3. Sometimes doctors feel they will alarm or confuse patients (especially young patients) by giving them medical details. Do you agree?

4. How can patients help ensure that they get the information they want?

beneath my hands? What is skin, what are bodies?—these fragile, mortal shells that house us, all so much the same. (p. 45)

In one sense, it may be comforting for patients to realize that caregivers learn early on to separate intimate and professional touch. But, as patients, we are unlikely to find the distinction easy to make, particularly since our bodies are the ones being viewed and touched.

In emergencies or especially intense circumstances such as childbirth, modesty may not be on anyone's mind. But during routine exams, there's a fine line to walk, and evidence suggests that patients and caregivers walk it together, demonstrating in subtle ways that the body-as-examined is more an object than an intimate landscape. In a microanalysis of exam-room behaviors, Christian Heath (2006) described the process with which patients present themselves as clinical objects during potentially embarrassing or painful examinations. They typically lower their eyelids, turn their heads aside, and gaze into the middle distance. At the same time, health professionals typically avoid direct eye contact during sensitive exams, focusing instead on particular parts of the patient's body. This "body work," as Heath calls it, is a sophisticated, collaborative performance in which participants display that what might otherwise seem to be an intimate or callous infringement is—by mutual consensus—an acceptable, clinically approved interaction with its own rules of appropriateness.

As patients, we are invested in avoiding embarrassment and pain as much as possible. We are also involved in securing the good opinions of our caregivers. With our very well-being hanging in the balance, we are loath to have caregivers view us as whiny, crazy, annoying, or stupid.

How is it, then, that we come to understand which behaviors distinguish us as "good" patients? Unlike caregivers, patients are usually in medical situations only briefly and occasionally. Moreover, whereas caregivers-in-training are required to watch other caregivers, people seldom get to observe other patients. Thus, socialization into the role of patient is an imprecise process. We may feel we have been thrust center stage but don't know the script.

We apply our everyday knowledge to the patient role and generally display all the hesitancy you might expect. This section describes the Voice of Lifeworld, the typical power difference between patients and caregivers, and the dilemmas people face when they disagree with caregivers.

Voice of Lifeworld

Quite naturally, as patients, we interpret our health within the arena most familiar to us—everyday life. In contrast to the scientific Voice of Medicine that many caregivers use, patients speak what Mishler (1984) calls the Voice of Lifeworld. The **Voice of Lifeworld** is concerned with health and illness as they relate to everyday experiences. For example, a physician may understand back pain in terms of specific discs and muscles, but from a lifeworld perspective, the main issue is that the pain interferes with a person's ability to pick up a child or perform tasks at work. As patients, we're usually most concerned with how we feel and how our health affects our regular activities. When asked what's wrong, we typically describe sensations and events, as in, "I get a horrible pain behind my eyes when I try to read the newspaper. It really scares me."

In contrast to the Voice of Medicine—which is primarily oriented to evidence, measurement, and precision—the Voice of Lifeworld is more oriented to feelings and contexts.

FEELINGS VERSUS EVIDENCE

Patients and health professionals tend to make sense of health in different ways. As patients, we "know" we're sick (or healthy) based on how we feel. Through experience, comparisons with others, and gut instinct, we distinguish between feeling well and feeling ill (Mishler, 1981, 1984).

Health professionals, however, are typically taught to be empirical. Science holds that feelings can be distorted and unreliable. Caregivers "know"

 WHAT DO YOU THINK?

■ Have you ever found yourself unable to tell a health professional what you wanted to say?

■ If so, what held you back?

■ What factors would make it easier for you to communicate openly?

someone is sick based on observation and tests. You may recall from Chapter 2 that this emphasis on physical indicators has roots in the Renaissance principle of verification, the nineteenth-century discovery of germs, and scientific means of detecting illness using microscopes and other technology.

As a general principle, patients trust feelings, but caregivers trust evidence. Depending on which perspective the participants take, health care encounters may sound very different. Typically, lifeworld talk is more emotional, social, and contextual than medical talk.

As we saw in the description of collaborative interpretation (CI) and narrative medicine in the last chapter, some patients and caregivers frequently integrate medical and lifeworld voices. But evidence suggests that, for many people, the integration feels unfamiliar and difficult. Indeed, lifeworld concerns can seem problematic from a medical perspective (Waitzkin, 1991). They may seem irrelevant to the medical condition, they may seem relevant but fall outside caregivers' power to control, or they may be uncomfortable to discuss. "Under these circumstances doctors typically interject questions, interrupt, or otherwise change the topic, to return to the voice of medicine," Waitzkin says (p. 25).

SPECIFIC VERSUS DIFFUSE

One result of their disparate philosophies is that caregivers are often precise, whereas patients are diffuse. To illustrate, a doctor hears "pain behind the eyes" and wants to know exactly where, how strong, how long. Patients, however, may be concerned with surrounding issues, such as the scariness of the pain (*Will I die? Can I still be a good parent? Am I going blind? Do I have a tumor? What have I done to deserve this?*). Although both mean well, caregivers may be frustrated when patients

"go on and on," and patients may feel rebuffed when caregivers seem uninterested in their feelings.

As patients, we tend to be diffuse in our perception of what causes illness. Unlike doctors, who typically strive to find the cause of an illness, patients often perceive that it has multiple causes, common among them stress and relationship issues. Consequently, physicians' scientific specificity may seem sorely deficient in explaining illnesses as patients perceive them. People may leave exams wondering if their caregivers really understood their problems at all.

Patients may also have numerous goals that take precedence over purely physical healing. We may wish to vent emotions, confess, or be reassured, forgiven, or comforted during a medical visit. These goals may be in direct opposition to some caregivers' efforts to set aside what they consider extraneous factors and focus on measurable ones.

All in all, as patients, we tend to interpret illnesses in the broad context of everyday life, whereas many caregivers are taught to reduce diseases to their simplest, most measurable parts. Of course, the differences described do not hold true for all patients or all medical professionals. Some caregivers are very sensitive to their patients' emotions and life experiences, and some patients are precise and oriented to biomedical concerns. Even so, understanding that patients and caregivers have traditionally been

WHAT DO YOU THINK?
What is the best term to describe professionals who assist others in maintaining and restoring health? A few options are *clinicians, health providers, health care providers, health professionals,* and *caregivers.* You may have other ideas. Which do you prefer?

BOX 4.2 PERSPECTIVES

Feeling Insignificant

I have been to two different clinics for the same concern. At one, I saw a doctor within 15 minutes. The staff was extremely friendly and helpful. At the other clinic, I was not met by a staff member, but rather by a sign-in sheet and a number. I immediately felt insignificant. After a long wait I finally was called back to my own room, where I sat for another hour and a half. The doctor was unfriendly and said, "There is not much I can do," even when I told her what treatment had worked last time. That visit made me feel as if no one cared.

—DUSTIN

socialized to regard illness differently may help both sides understand each other better.

The Voice of Medicine and the Voice of Lifeworld overlap to a large extent when the goal is *preventing* disease and injury rather than just *treating* them. Prevention is, by nature, a diffuse topic involving an array of risk factors and lifestyle decisions. Furthermore, talking about prevention is usually not as emotionally intense as talking about existing illness. Some speculate that a third voice will emerge that will combine medical and lifeworld voices in the context of prevention.

Next we turn to some factors that define particular patient experiences, including the nature of the health concern, the personalities involved, and participants' communication skills.

Patient Characteristics

Although, as patients, we would like to maintain our caregivers' positive regard, we may have goals that are at odds with their preferences. For instance, we may doubt the validity of a diagnosis or may wish to reiterate information that the caregiver has dismissed as unimportant. Sometimes, we would like to be assertive and inquisitive, but we don't feel well enough informed to do so. In this section we will look at challenging situations from patients' perspective.

Nature of the Illness

If we have a condition that is chronic or hard to define, we may feel like a nuisance to caregivers. Situations such as this present a dilemma. We must either risk the caregiver's disapproval or leave feeling that nothing much was accomplished. Either choice has negative consequences.

What do most of us do? Evidence suggests that we usually abandon or delay pursuit of our goals rather than challenge our caregivers (Dyche & Swiderski, 2005). This may be because a damaged identity is hard to mend, whereas specific goals can usually be pursued at a later date. We may hint at our feelings, but seldom do we assert them. Instead, dissatisfied patients tend to switch caregivers or go back to them again and again, perhaps hoping for the right conditions in which to accomplish their goals. All the while, caregivers may be unaware of their dissatisfaction.

The problem is especially difficult for people with multiple concerns. For example, a patient with depression may feel that other concerns are brushed aside as psychosomatic even when they're legitimate. Gillespie (2001) describes the frustration of low-income patients experiencing depression and chronic health problems:

> They resented feeling as though they had to prove or stress how sick they "really" were, especially since they felt this account might also label them as neurotic. They had to hide their upset because showing it only leant further evidence to potential neuroses. (p. 109)

Patient Disposition

Our backgrounds and personalities also influence how we communicate as patients. After reviewing patient–caregiver literature, Jeffery Robinson (2003) concluded that a number of factors persuade patients to temper their participation in medical dialogues:

- We may think it is appropriate to be passive.
- We may be too fearful or anxious to be assertive.
- We may not know or understand enough to participate in medical discussions.
- We may be discouraged by caregivers' communication styles.
- Socioeconomic factors such as education level may influence how actively we participate.
- The nature of the medical visit (routine or symptom-specific) may influence our behavior.
- The length of the visit and the people present may influence our involvement.

A number of studies support these ideas. As patients, we are more likely to be **self-advocates**—actively seeking health information, comfortable talking about health concerns, and assertive about seeking care—if we are well educated (Street, Gordon, Ward, Krupat, & Kravitz, 2005) and if we are confident we can make a difference in own health (Curtin et al., 2008). Cultural factors play a role as well. African American patients are typically less likely than European Americans to self-advocate about health concerns (Street et al., 2005; Wiltshire, Cronin, Sarto, & Brown, 2006).

BOX 4.3   CAREER OPPORTUNITIES

Patient Advocacy

Health educators work in health care organizations, government agencies, universities, and other organizations. The job requires a bachelor's degree or higher and typically pays about $45,800 a year. Demand is expected to increase much faster than average, with a 37% increase in positions between 2010 and 2020 (U.S. Bureau of Labor Statistics, 2012a; McNamara, 2009).

Patient navigators help individual patients and their families locate providers, make appointments, and handle insurance, language and communication, transportation challenges. The nonprofit Harold P. Freeman Patient Navigation Institute in New York City offers training, as do the Center to Reduce Cancer Health Disparities, the National Cancer Institute, and others. National salary and job outlook data are not yet available (U.S. Bureau of Labor Statistics, 2012a; McNamara, 2009

PATIENT ADVOCACY POSITIONS
    Patient advocate
    Patient navigator

Social worker
Case manager
Patient care coordinator or consultant

CAREER RESOURCES AND JOB LISTINGS
- Patient Advocate Foundation: www.patient advocate.org
- National Patient Advocate Foundation: www.npaf.org
- Patient Navigator Outreach and Chronic Disease Prevention Demonstration Program: http://bhpr.hrsa.gov/nursing/grants/patientnavigator.html
- National Association of Social Workers: www.socialworkers.org
- Council on Social Work Education: www.cswe.org
- Case Management Society of America: www.cmsa.org
- National Organization for Human Services: www.nationalhumanservices.org
- U.S. Bureau of Labor Statistics Occupational Outlook Handbook: www.bls.gov

Communication Skills

Patients who are at ease and confident about their ability to communicate effectively with caregivers are more satisfied than other patients with the care they receive (Chou et al., 2010). It follows that we may benefit from communication skills training programs that prepare us to communicate effectively with medical providers. Although the results are mixed and patient education programs are scarce, there has been modest success in this area. During training sessions, patients are usually instructed and encouraged to ask questions, provide information, and verify their understanding of information (Bylund, D'Agostino, Ho, & Chewning, 2010; Cegala & Broz, 2003). One reason skills training has not been more effective is that, even if we are trained *how* to pose questions, we may not know *what* to ask. Donald Cegala and Stefne Broz reflect:

Most patients do not formulate questions until they have had time to process what the physician has said or do not realize their lack of understanding until they try to follow the recommended treatment or explain their illness to someone. (2003, p. 10)

Even well-educated patients with good communication skills may find themselves out of their depth conversing about medical topics on the spot. Nevertheless, Cegala and Broz (2003) conclude that even modest improvements can enhance medical care and reduce the length of medical visits.

In his book *How Doctors Think*, Jerome Groopman (2007) offers behind-the-scenes insights for patients so they can more actively assist their doctors. A physician himself, Groopman attests: "Doctors desperately need patients and their families and friends to help them think. Without their help, physicians are denied key clues to what is really wrong" (pp. 7–8). Following are some of his suggestions.

Keep in mind that doctors' emotions may sometimes influence their judgment. As Groopman (2007) puts it, "Patients and their loved ones swim together with physicians in a sea of feelings" (p. 58). Sometimes, he says, patients can help doctors put things in perspective. He shares an example during which a patient told his doctor, "Don't save me from an unpleasant [medical] test just because we're friends" (p. 58). His gentle remark helped the doctor realize that she had been tempted to do just that. In another case, a middle-aged woman whose previous doctors had written off her symptoms to menopause helped her new doctor see beyond that stereotype by saying:

> I know I'm in menopause, and all five doctors have told me that's the cause of my problems. And two told me that I'm crazy. And, frankly, I *am* a little crazy. . . . But I think this is something else, that what I'm feeling is more than just menopause. (Groopman, 2007, p. 56)

Her doctor listened, and the patient was right. She had a rare tumor that, if left untreated, might have threatened her life. Groopman concludes that patients can help doctors by acknowledging emotions out loud rather than leaving them unspoken.

Recognize the limits of emergency medicine. An assessment in the ER is typically only a snapshot attempt to find a problem. ER doctors do not usually have the benefit of long-standing relationships with patients or full access to their medical records. Thus, their evaluation is incomplete at best. Groopman declares, "The last thing I want is a patient to leave the ER and say, 'The doctor said there is nothing wrong with me'" (p. 74). If the concern is serious, follow-up care and further assessment are essential.

Beware of your own stereotypes. Caregivers are sensitive to discrimination, just as patients are. Groopman tells of doctors whose patients take one look at them and, based solely on the doctor's skin color, demand to be seen by someone else. JudyAnn Bigby, an African American physician who oversees residents, recommends that residents who are female or from minority cultures always wear their lab coats and name badges and keep their stethoscopes visible. Even so, she says, "they

will sometimes be asked if they have come to take the meal tray" (p. 96). Patients are responsible for showing health professionals the same respect they wish to be shown themselves.

Accept medical uncertainty. As patients, we often find comfort in believing that our caregivers know exactly what's wrong with us, but that isn't always the case. Sometimes the underlying causes of an illness are revealed only gradually with persistent investigation over time. A false sense of certainty can blind both professionals and patients to the real or multiple causes of an illness. Groopman encourages patients not to criticize doctors for uncertainty or pressure them into acting more certain than they feel.

Ask questions. Caregivers are subject to cognitive errors and limitations, just like everyone else. Groopman admits, "Sometimes I come to the end of my thinking and am not sure what to do next" (p. 264). He encourages patients to stimulate physicians' thinking and communication by asking such questions as: What else could this be? What's the worst-case scenario? What should I expect next? Is it possible I have more than one problem? Is there any evidence that doesn't fit?

In the next two sections we look at factors that contribute to patient satisfaction and patient–caregiver cooperation.

Satisfaction

As patients, we seem to have many grievances about medical care, but we're moderately satisfied overall. About 70% of adults in the United States say their overall care is excellent or very good (Chou et al., 2010). Yet patients have a number of serious complaints. Slightly more than half say they are unhappy with doctors' level of caring, rude staff members, and cumbersome check-in and check-out procedures (Feldman, 2008). Feldman's study reveals that patients' greatest complaints concern time. Here are the percentages of people who agree with the following statements:

> 81%—I wait too long in the doctor's lobby.
> 50%—I wait too long in the exam room.
> 58%—My doctor doesn't spend enough time with me.
> 62%—My doctor doesn't answer all my questions and seems rushed.

? CAN YOU GUESS?

Which is the healthiest place to live—the United States, Germany, New Zealand, Australia, Canada, or the United Kingdom?

The answer appears at the end of the chapter.

From patients' perspective, time is an important consideration, and their experiences could be significantly improved by minimizing waits and establishing mutually appealing time frames for medical interactions. (In Chapter 5 you will read about a cancer center that did just that, reducing wait times by 50% and making better use of caregivers' time in the process.)

Satisfaction with hospital care in the United States is good, but there is room for improvement. Some 63% of U.S. hospital patients rate their care 9 or 10 on a 10-point scale (Jha, Orav, Zheng, & Epstein, 2008). However, only about 67% say they would recommend the hospital to a friend (Jha et al., 2008). The most frequent complaints are ineffective pain management and unclear communication at discharge. Conversely, satisfaction is highest when there are low nurse–patient ratios and positive health outcomes. Overall satisfaction is significantly higher at not-for-profit hospitals than at their commercial counterparts (Jha et al., 2008).

Researcher Ashish Jha encourages hospital staff members to do better. But he also encourages us to be more assertive about asking questions and voicing our discontent as patients. "The more engaged patients are, the better the care they will receive and the better the care all of us will receive, because they will drive the change for better systems of health care" (Jha quoted by Reinberg, 2008, para. 6).

As patients, we have strong opinions about doctors and nurses. We know what we like—plenty of information, a chance to participate in decision making, and a sense of being heard and respected (Jangland, Gunningberg, & Carlsson, 2009). We want to know we can speak freely, and we want to feel confident that our doctors won't turn against us if we seek second opinions (Jadad & Rizo, 2003). Another strong predictor of patient satisfaction is the sense that caregivers are concerned about us and have empathy for what we're feeling (Cousin, Mast, Roter, & Hall, 2012). In operational terms, we like health professionals who listen, ask questions, keep us well-informed, and encourage us (Jadad & Rizo, 2003). In the next section we take a closer look at what patients like and dislike about health care experiences.

Attentiveness and Respect

Patient satisfaction is more closely linked to caregivers' communication than to their technical skills (Tarrant, Windridge, Boulton, Baker, & Freeman, 2003). This may be because it is difficult to judge technical skills and because we tend to assume that caregivers are technically competent. It may also reflect how important communication skills are to diagnosis and treatment. In the article "I Am a Good Patient Believe it or Not," Alejandro Jadad and Carlos Rizo (2003) conclude, after interviewing patients: "In most cases it would not take fancy technology, extra time, or increased costs to satisfy what patients 'want.' It would take only an assertive patient and a confident healthcare provider who is willing to listen" (para. 6).

There is some evidence that pediatricians lead the pack in terms of patient/parent satisfaction. When researchers ("Patient Perceptions," 2006) asked people if their doctors (or their children's doctors) "listened carefully, explained things clearly, showed respect, and spent enough time" with them, about 73% of patients' parents said yes, compared to 61% of people 65 and older and about half of middle-aged adults and young adults. Parents of pediatric patients were the most satisfied of all, and they were most appreciative when doctors self-disclosed about their own experiences and feelings (Holmes, Harrington, & Parrish, 2010).

It's no surprise that, whatever our age, we like caregivers who seem to take us seriously and like us back (Grant, Cissna, & Rosenfeld, 2000). This impression is enhanced when caregivers are courteous and nonverbally expressive, maintain eye contact, ask about our coping strategies, and encourage us and our families to participate in medical decision making (Hart, Kelleher, Drotar, & Scholle, 2007; Koermer & Kilbane, 2008). (See Box 4.3 for a discussion about patient satisfaction and whether we put too much stock in it.)

Caregivers also get high marks for listening attentively and acknowledging our emotions without trying to control us (Grant et al., 2000). In

Is Satisfaction Overrated?

In a *New York Times* editorial, oncology nurse Theresa Brown (2012) proposes that a focus on patient satisfaction might diminish the quality of medical care. She worries that health professionals might cut back on painful, but important, procedures and overinvest in pleasing amenities that do not improve health outcomes. "Evaluating hospital care in terms of its ability to offer positive experiences could easy put pressure on the system to do things I can't, at the expense of what it should," says Brown (para. 11).

WHAT DO YOU THINK?

1. Are patients likely to rate medical care more favorably if it's pleasant? If so, are there ways to help them better understand?
2. Do you think it is more effective to rate health care centers on the basis of health outcomes than on patient satisfaction?
3. What do you say to those who feel that ratings based on health outcomes will penalize health care centers and professionals who take on high-risk and end-of-life cases?
4. In your opinion, what is the best way to rate the effectiveness of health care?

must discuss patients and their conditions, but they should do so in private. Making statements where others might overhear them threatens patients' privacy and reduces them to symptoms rather than complete persons.

- *Curt, discourteous, or disrespectful communication.* Patients say they resent it when caregivers neglect to introduce themselves or when they ignore them, don't listen attentively, or talk down to them. Some patients also prefer not to be addressed by first name.
- *Compromised appearance.* Patients typically report feeling most dignified when they are allowed to wear their own clothing and jewelry.

Satisfaction may vary by health concern. Overall, the least satisfied patients are those with chronic, hard-to-cure conditions, such as headaches and back pain (Tan, Jensen, Thornby, & Anderson, 2006). In contrast, obstetric, cancer, and heart patients are more satisfied than average, perhaps because these conditions are typically treated as more serious and legitimate.

Convenience

We also like it when things run smoothly. Satisfaction is enhanced when the wait is not long and when our health plans are covering the costs (Bleustein, Valaitis, & Jones, 2010; Fenton Jerant, Bertakis, & Franks, 2012). Hospitals in recent years have begun efforts to streamline paperwork and admitting procedures, realizing that patient satisfaction relies on more than skillfully performed medical procedures. The staffs of some hospitals are experimenting with check-in centers at which patients arriving for surgery or emergency care can key in their information (health history, payment information, health concern) at one of several private computer kiosks, rather than waiting for staff members to interview them (Huvane, 2008). In many cases this has reduced overall wait times. (Patients who prefer can still register with staff members.)

Convenience is also a factor in the creation of retail clinics in drugstores and department stores across the country, as well as extended-hour clinics and open-access clinics available to people who haven't made appointments in advance (Lowes, 2008b).

contrast, we're displeased when we feel our dignity has been compromised (Milika & Trorey, 2008). Some of the most commonly perceived threats to dignity include the following (from Milika & Trorey):

- *Invasions of privacy.* Patients surveyed say they feel dishonored when staff members allow them to be physically exposed to others or carelessly allow others to read or overhear their confidential information. Before he retired, physician John Egerton (2007) had a rule for his front-office staff: "Avoid mentioning the patient's name and diagnosis in the same sentence" (Milika & Trorey, 2008, para. 6.) For instance, never say, "John Smith has prostatitis again" or "Helen Will has head lice" (para. 6). Naturally, caregivers

What Patients Like

- Attentiveness
- Respect
- Convenience
- Privacy
- Empathy
- Sense of control
- Genuine caring

A Sense of Control

As patients, we appreciate being well informed and actively involved in our care. Although we appreciate doctors' advice, only about 20% of us want our caregivers to make decisions without us ("Reality Check," 2008). This applies to everyday decisions as well as major treatment options. One hospital patient interviewed said he appreciates it when nurses who bathe him wash body areas he can't reach and then ask, "Would you like to do the rest for yourself?" (quoted in Milika & Trorey, 2008, p. 2713). He says he feels respected when he is given choices, and this one allows him to maintain dignity and take care of private needs himself as much as possible.

Other patients echo the same sentiment. A man with diabetes in Ciechanowski and Katon's (2006) study describes his favorite doctor this way:

> He doesn't just come in, do your treatment and leave. He kind of talks, you know, "How are things going? Tell me about yourself," and he has a fabulous memory. He remembers about those things that you tell him. . . . I don't know if it's just a really good memory, or he puts notes in the chart, or whatever, but it's just . . . he makes you feel comfortable coming in. (p. 3074)

This leads us to the next discussion of how, as patients, we tend to define interpersonal warmth.

Genuine Warmth and Honesty

When Susan Harris and Edith Templeton (2001) conducted focus groups involving women with breast cancer, they asked participants to rank order the most positive elements of communication with their doctors. Beginning with the most important quality, the women listed: (1) physicians' active listening, (2) physicians' awareness about the depth of the patient's knowledge, (3) honesty, (4) partnership, (5) interest in the patient as a person, and (6) touch. Focus group participants said they appreciate it when doctors encourage them to audiotape medical sessions and when they offer them photocopies of lab results. Said one woman in the study: "It was helpful for me to get the information, important to have the hard copy in my hand. It gave me a sense of 'power.' I could question and read it through" (p. 446). Many women said they appreciate it when their doctors don't "mince words" but instead are honest and up-front about their conditions. They said they are deeply grateful when doctors don't seem rushed and when they extend human kindness and encouragement. Said one woman: "I'm very grateful my GP didn't feel he had to maintain some kind of professional distance. I was freaking out. I needed a hug" (p. 446).

Cooperation and Consent

Let's go back to a summer day in 2008 when Tiger Woods limped up the sloping hill of Torrey Pines golf course to where his ball lay on the green. He made the final shot to finish one stroke ahead of his nearest competitor after a grueling playoff in a golf tournament that included 91 holes. Woods won the 2008 U.S. Open, thrilling fans but confounding his doctors, who had urged him not to play because of a knee injury.

In this respect Woods isn't so different from the majority of us. Although we're unlikely to challenge our doctors' advice in person, only 50% to 60% of us follow medical advice completely or most of the time (Martin, Williams, Haskard, & Dimatteo, 2005). Some of the advice we're prone to ignore includes the following: avoid dangerous and unhealthy behaviors, undergo recommended health screenings, see a specialist, make regular doctors' appointments, take prescribed drugs as directed, exercise often, eat healthy foods, and so on.

As Michael Burgoon and Judee Burgoon (1990) observe, it's curious that we don't follow medical advice more closely, considering that we pay for the advice, presumably stand to benefit from it, and typically revere the expertise of medical professionals. In the next section we explore some of the reasons that we may not follow through. Then we will examine caregivers' stake in getting patients to perform medical regimens and look at policies concerning informed consent for medical treatment.

Reasons for Noncooperation

If, as patients, we don't follow medical advice, it doesn't necessarily mean we are lazy or indifferent about our health. A number of more legitimate concerns may affect our decisions.

For one, medical recommendations may be impossible or impractical to carry out. We may be unable to afford prescribed medications or may be physically incapable of performing suggested routines (Frankel & Beckman, 1989). For example, patients who miss dialysis treatments often report that no one is available to drive them to and from appointments (Gordon, Leon, & Sehgal, 2003). Likewise, low-income patients may have little choice concerning their exposure to "avoidable" health threats. As Gillespie (2001) describes it:

> Low-income families live in older homes filled with lifetimes of dust and molding timber. They breathe the air polluted by factories that never cease production and by the cars of daily downtown professionals who sleep in clean, suburban air each night. Often depressed, they are more likely to smoke and less likely to eat well. Many sleep on the floor, knowing that the asthma this triggers could kill them, but afraid that a stray bullet shot through the window will do so sooner. (p. 114)

In other situations, recommended regimens may be so foreign to us that we can't easily integrate them into our lifestyles. For instance, we may consider it inconceivable to remove red meat completely from our diet. Or, like Tiger Woods, we may feel that some goals and obligations are too important to miss, even if it means risking a personal illness or injury.

Second, we may not agree with the doctor's assessment or treatment recommendations. Research suggests that we're likely to distrust diagnoses and ignore medical advice if we're unable to describe our concerns during medical visits (Frankel & Beckman, 1989). We may also deny diagnoses that threaten our self-image. It may be

IN YOUR EXPERIENCE

Patients may not follow medical advice for any of the following reasons:

- ■ Impossible or impractical
- ■ Unaffordable
- ■ Unclear understanding
- ■ Culturally or personally unacceptable
- ■ Diagnosis seems incorrect
- ■ Treatment seems unneeded or unhelpful
- ■ Unpleasant side effects

Have you ever ignored or did not follow the medical advice you were given? Did any of the reasons for non-cooperation in this list apply? If not, what was the reason?

difficult to admit obesity, hearing loss, depression, sexually transmitted diseases, and the like.

Third, we may stop medical routines prematurely if we perceive that they have no effect or if our symptoms cease (Forrest, Shadmi, Nutting, & Starfield, 2007). For example, it is difficult to get people to remain on treatment for conditions such as high blood pressure because they cannot directly perceive that the medicine has a positive effect.

Finally, we may stop taking medication if we experience unpleasant side effects (Löffler, Kilian, Toumi, & Angermeyer, 2003). Rather than contact the physician for alternate instructions, we may try other methods or conclude that the cure is worse than the disease.

These factors are exacerbated when caregivers don't encourage us to express our concerns and reservations at the time they give medical advice. Evidence suggests that many people leave their doctors' offices knowing they cannot or will not follow through with the advice given, but they don't feel free to say so. Doctors who assume that patients should follow orders regardless of their circumstances may be discouraged when treatment outcomes are less than optimal. What's more, if we don't feel comfortable talking with the caregiver, we may be reluctant to be honest about not following his or her advice.

Caregivers' Investment

It may be tempting to assume that, if patients don't follow medical advice, they have only themselves to blame. But caregivers may (justly or unjustly) be blamed as well. Lack of patient–caregiver cooperation often results in harmful health outcomes. Nonadherence is linked to diabetes treatment failures (Joy, 2008), increased hospitalization for heart failure (Fonarow et al., 2008), and asthma-related complications and deaths (Gillisen, 2007), to name just a few. These are not just patients' problems.

Caregivers' careers may be damaged by excessive treatment failures. With capitation and restricted reimbursements, health care organizations lose money on patients who do not improve as expected. Consequently, hospitals may refuse to grant doctors privileges if their treatment outcomes are below par, and medical groups may deny them employment for the same reason. Doctors' reputations among patients may suffer as well. Physician Wesley Sugai of Kailua-Kona, Hawaii, says he does not treat patients who chronically ignore medical advice without explanation.

> As a rural solo pediatrician, I have neither the time nor the desire to try to convince parents about the importance of childhood immunizations, follow-up with specialists, or medications. . . . I tell parents that I have to be able to trust them to carry out the treatment plan, just as they must trust me to prescribe the proper therapy. If neither of us trusts the other, then the patient–doctor relationship is nonexistent and we must go our separate ways. (Sugai, 2008, p. 14)

Sugai says that he does work with patients who are up-front about reservations or limitations that affect their health behaviors. All in all, it's important for patients who can't follow treatment advice or who don't agree with it to be up-front in negotiating more suitable options with their doctors.

Public health is at stake as well. Good communication and healthy behaviors can avert pandemics and reduce spending on preventable illnesses and injuries. In the United States, the cost of preventable hospitalizations is about $26.4 billion per year, equal to about 10% of total health costs ("National Healthcare Quality," 2011). Analyst Bill

Clements (1996) advises: "Make no mistake about it: Bad communication costs you money" (para. 3).

Considering these factors, how far should caregivers go to gain patients' cooperation? Some doctors are trying cash rewards (see Box 4.5). Others are trying to involve patients more in medical decision making. As the next section illustrates, over time, public policy has changed concerning patients' role in medical decisions.

Informed Consent

For centuries, physicians considered it wise to tell patients only as much as they could understand

---

BOX 4.5

Cash for Cooperation?

Communication is important, but can it stack up to cold, hard cash? Maybe not. Some medical centers have had success with innovative cash-for-compliance programs that reward patients for healthy behavior. Incentives include cash or cash coupons (usually $4 or $5 or a chance to win from $25 to $100) for keeping appointments, maintaining healthy blood pressure (for hypertensive patients), reaching weight-loss goals, immunizing children, or abstaining from drug abuse.

Program sponsors say it is less expensive to offer cash prizes than to pay staff to work overtime or call patients, and everyone stands to gain if incentives reduce unnecessary care and keep serious health concerns from escalating. It's not clear, however, if patients will develop the motivation to continue the behaviors without the rewards.

WHAT DO YOU THINK?

1. Would you be more likely to engage in healthy behaviors if you might receive a cash award or prize for doing so?
2. If you said yes, would you be likely to cease those behaviors if the reward were no longer available?
3. Do you think reward systems are a good idea? Why or why not?

(in the doctors' opinion) and nothing that might dissuade them from following medical advice. For example, if a doctor judged that the potential advantages of a drug outweighed its possible side effects, the doctor might not tell the patient about side effects, for fear the patient would not take the drug (Katz, 1995). Likewise, although doctors have always been required to get patients' permission before they operated on them, they have not been required to tell patients about the risks involved.

In most cases physicians were presumably following their best judgment. In some cases, however, patients were subjected to risks, even to deadly medical experiments, without their knowledge. One example is the **Tuskegee Syphilis Study** conducted in Alabama (Box 4.6).

BOX 4.6   ETHICAL CONSIDERATIONS

Patients' Right to Informed Consent

During the infamous Tuskegee Syphilis Study, which began in 1932, some 600 African American men were enrolled without their knowledge in a medical experiment. They were patients of the Public Health Service in Macon County, Alabama, and the experiment was conducted by the U.S. government through the Tuskegee Institute in Alabama.

Although medical researchers knew that 399 of the men had syphilis, the men were not told. Doctors simply told all the men they had "bad blood" and provided them with medicine, meals, and burial expenses. However, the medicine was not really medicine at all. It was a harmless but ineffectual placebo.

The study was designed to help medical researchers learn more about the effects of syphilis among African Americans. Syphilis is a sexually transmitted disease that affects the bones, liver, heart, and central nervous system. In advanced stages, it can cause open sores, heart damage, tumors, blindness, insanity, and death. When the study was begun, there was no effective treatment for syphilis. However, by 1940, penicillin was known to be effective at treating and even curing it.

The syphilis patients in the Tuskegee experiment were not given penicillin. Instead, researchers continued to watch the disease progress until the experiment was called off in 1972, some 40 years after it began.

When details of the Tuskegee study were made public, there was an angry outcry. Some likened it to the Nazis' medical experiments on Jewish prisoners during World War II. The courts eventually ordered the federal government to pay the men and their families a total of $10 million for the injury and indignity they had suffered. Twenty-five years after the end of the experiment, President Bill Clinton publicly apologized for the government's behavior in May 1997.

Now, before patients are given medical treatment (experimental or otherwise), they must be fully informed, give consent, and be aware that they can cease treatment at any time. It is hoped that informed consent will prevent atrocities such as the Tuskegee Syphilis Study. But informed consent is sometimes hard to apply. Jauhar (2008b) describes the ethical challenges of informed consent in some instances:

> [An] issue I continue to struggle with today is how to balance patient autonomy with the physician's obligation to do the best for his patient. As a doctor, when do you let your patient make a bad decision: When, if ever, do you draw the line? What if a decision could cost your patient's life? How hard do you push him to change his mind? At the same time, it's his life. Who are you to tell him how to live? (p. 233)

Jauhar (2008b) describes a particularly difficult case when a hospital patient, Mr. Smith, began to cough up blood and have trouble breathing. His condition quickly deteriorated, and doctors knew they would have to act quickly to save his life. Their only hope was to insert a temporary breathing tube. But the patient adamantly refused. In his mind, being intubated seemed a worse fate than death. Mr. Smith's fear seemed irrational, yet he was coherent and capable of communicating—thus he was capable of giving (or refusing) informed consent. As the doctor responsible for Mr. Smith's care, Jauhar faced a dilemma. He could honor the patient's wishes and allow him to die, or he could overrule the patient and insert the breathing tube by force. What would you have done?

Jauhar chose to insert the breathing tube, although the staff had to restrain Mr. Smith physically to do it. During the procedure Jauhar worried that the patient would hate him for disobeying his wishes. " 'If you live through this,' I whispered to Mr. Smith, 'I hope you can forgive me' " (Jauhar, 2008b, pp. 236–237). Two weeks later, as Mr. Smith neared recovery, Jauhar stopped by his room and told the patient he was responsible for the decision. The patient considered his response for a moment. "I've been through a lot," he finally said, his voice still hoarse from two weeks of intubation. . . . But thank you" (p. 237). This is an extreme case, but it illustrates some of the ethical dilemmas involved in informed consent.

WHAT DO YOU THINK?

1. Do you agree with Jauhar's decision? Why or why not? What would you have done in his place?
2. Sometimes medical information is difficult to understand fully. How should we establish if the consenting person is informed enough to give consent?
3. Some people, such as those with terminal illnesses, are willing (even anxious) to try untested therapies. Researchers may not know what results to expect, and they may even anticipate negative outcomes. Who should decide whether the patient undergoes untested therapies? Should public money be used in these cases?
4. In medical research, is it ever justified to deceive people (as in giving placebos) to make sure they are not just responding to the power of suggestion? If so, under what conditions?
5. Sometimes it is in the best interest of society or health care workers to know if a person has a contagious disease (such as AIDS). If the person doesn't consent to a test for that disease, do you think it should be permissible to perform the test without the person's knowledge? (A vial of blood may be used for a variety of tests without the patient's knowledge.)
6. On what grounds, if any, should health professionals judge whether a patient is emotionally capable of making a life-or-death judgment about emergency treatment?

Public outrage over the Tuskegee Syphilis Study and others like it led the U.S. government to pass informed-consent laws. **Informed consent** means that patients must (a) be made fully aware of known treatment risks, benefits, and options; (b) be deemed capable of understanding such information and making a responsible judgment; and (c) be aware that they may refuse to participate or may cease treatment at any time (Ashley & O'Rourke, 1997). When patients are children or are otherwise unable to make decisions, close family members may be allowed to consent on their behalf.

Informed-consent requirements are designed to allow us enough information so that we can make knowledgeable judgments about our own care. Some theorists believe that health care should go even further toward including patients in treatment decisions. As early as 1973, medical analyst Harold Walker predicted that doctors would become less authoritarian and more persuasive. The difference is subtle but important. From an authoritarian perspective, we are expected to *comply* with doctors' orders. From a persuasive perspective, however, we take an active role in decision making as patients. We *cooperate* in the process as informed and influential participants.

If we are included in decision making as patients, it may be possible to overcome or accommodate many of the factors that keep us from following medical advice. The caregiver who is aware of our financial and physical limitations, cultural reservations, denial, or discouragement is better able to negotiate more acceptable options with us or provide information that may assuage our reservations. At the very least, patients and caregivers can establish outright what each is willing to do. This may ultimately be less frustrating than allowing our differences to go unspoken.

Informed consent is a victory for patient empowerment. However, the terms are sometimes hard to apply, even when people try hard to do so. For example, a long list of complications (many of them extremely unlikely) might result from a simple procedure. It may be impractical or impossible to list every possible outcome. However, physicians may be accused of negligence if an unlikely outcome results and the patient was not warned about it in advance. Language differences also present challenges. It is sometimes difficult to understand medical terminology. In focus groups, Spanish speakers in the United States with literacy challenges said that consent and privacy forms that had been translated into Spanish were too long and wordy, the fine print aroused their suspicious, and they felt rushed to comply without fully understanding the forms or discussing them with family members (Cortés, Drainoni, Henault, & Paasche-Orlow, 2010). (We'll talk more about health literacy challenges in Chapter 6.)

On the bright side, when they are available, multimedia presentations about medical procedures often increase understanding prior to informed consent. Melissa Wanzer (2010) and colleagues had the parents and guardians of children who were recommended for endoscopies view a 4-minute video about hospital procedures and endoscopies and an interactive presentation about informed consent, including optional voice-over and a true-false quiz they could take as many times as they liked at their own pace. Compared to parents and guardians who simply reviewed informed consent forms with a physician, those who took part in the multimedia presentation understood more about the procedure and were subsequently less anxious about it and more satisfied with the care their children received (Wanzer, Wojtaszczyk, Schimert, Missert, Baker, Baker, & Dunkle, 2010).

Partly because complete disclosure is so difficult to define, the courts have been somewhat reluctant to hold physicians responsible for informed-consent violations except in clear-cut cases. Review Box 4.6 for ethical implications concerning informed consent.

Acknowledging that, as patients, we make decisions based on a number of factors outside formal medical settings, in the next section we examine how illnesses can affect our sense of identity.

Illness and Personal Identity

To understand the effects of illness on personal identity, consider for a moment who you are. A

> **CHECK IT OUT!**   To view a video about gastrointestinal endoscopies by the American Gastroenterological Association, see http://www .youtube.com/watch?v=vItktDQo-mE. Videos about many other procedures are available online as well. Just be sure to select videos by experts in the field.

few words might come to mind: student, son, daughter, parent, athlete, kind, smart, energetic, and the like. To the extent that you and the people around you agree on these roles and descriptions, they make up your identity. They define who you are, and you are not likely to change in unforeseen, significant ways. **Personal identity** is a relatively enduring set of characteristics that define a person.

At first consideration, having an identity may seem easy. You simply are who you are. However, the deeper reality is that you work hard to "be" who you are. People generally want to be viewed favorably and to feel good about themselves. Therefore, they act in ways that are consistent with the positive image they wish to portray (Goffman, 1967). Like other people, you're probably invested in maintaining the qualities and talents that make you unique. Very often, this requires a great deal of work (studying, listening, practicing, rehearsing, exercising, etc.). These behaviors are not "you," but they do support the identity that helps you and others understand you.

What if you were suddenly unable to maintain the behaviors that seem to make you who you are? What if you lost your memory and could no longer pass a test? What if your looks or your ability to talk or walk changed substantially? These are extreme examples, but even minor illnesses and injuries can interfere with our ability to "be" who we are. If the effects are short-lived, we probably don't experience a serious crisis of identity. However, long-term effects can change how we see ourselves and how others treat us.

Michael Arrington (2003) interviewed men with prostate cancer, the treatment of which may render men impotent and incontinent. One man in the study, Walsh, describes his struggle to reconcile his sense of self and manhood with his inability to have an erection:

And the final thing was to know myself. Do I know what's happening to me? Do I understand, in my own anxieties, how important, as I look back on it, the whole sexual experience of my own sexuality has been to me? Have I overloaded myself with that or not? Have I given it too much value in life? Are there things in life that are maybe more important to me personally than that? I think that evaluation and that process is one that I have given a lot of time and attention to, being the kind of a person I am. (p. 35)

Some men in the study chose various methods (pumps, injections, pills) for simulating erections, but others felt that such solutions were phony and inauthentic. Said one man:

Come on. That's not sex. That's, forget that stuff; that's not gonna cut it with me. I'm just done with it, that's all. . . . It's not a natural thing when you do that. I just don't, uh, want to be an artificial man. (p. 38)

Thus, the men either found new ways to achieve or define sexual performance or they redefined its importance in their lives. For example, one participant in the study said that men who cannot find other ways to please their partners sexually are "piss-poor lovers" anyway (Arrington, 2003, p. 39).

In addition to personal identities, we have **social identities,** characterized by perceived membership in societal groups such as "teenagers," "Hispanic Americans," and "retired persons" (Harwood & Sparks, 2003). Based on the groups with which we identify, we may expect ourselves (and others like us) to think and behave in particular ways. For example, we may be surprised when a youthful friend reveals that she has a serious heart condition and we may thereafter view her as "older" than her peers (Kundrat & Nussbaum, 2003).

When we are diagnosed with an identity-threatening illness, it may become part of our identity as well. Jake Harwood and Lisa Sparks (2003) call this a **tertiary identity**—a label that defines simultaneously the illness and our alignment toward it. For example, during a leadership retreat, a colleague of mine introduced herself to the group as, among other things, a "breast cancer survivor." The group responded with applause and hugs. Surviving cancer was treated as courageous and admirable, and

I believe group members felt a sense of intimacy that she had shared this news with them. Harwood and Sparks propose that a number of tertiary identities are available to people with the same health conditions. For example, my colleague might have said, "I'm a cancer victim" rather than a "survivor." I believe the crowd would have been sympathetic, but their reaction (and their image of her) would have been somewhat different. Perhaps even more important, different wording would reflect something important about the way she viewed her *own* circumstances.

This section examines how we manage our identities in the life-altering circumstances of ill health.

Reactions to Illness

As patients, our reactions to illness may be surprising and unexpected, even to us, personally. Kathy Charmaz has studied the way that people with long-term illnesses seek to reconcile their previous identities with the changed circumstances in which they find themselves. She has identified four stages common to the process. First, people typically take on a **supernormal identity**, determined not to let the illness stop them from being better than ever. This stage is usually followed by a sense of **restored self**, in which people are not quite as optimistic but typically deny that the illness has changed them. The third stage is **contingent personal identity**, in which people admit that they may not be able to do everything they could previously do and they begin to confront the consequences of a changed identity. The final stage, **salvaged self**, represents the development of a transformed identity that integrates former aspects of self with current limitations (Charmaz, 1987). Of course, not everyone goes through every stage or spends the same amount of time in each stage. However, Charmaz's model illustrates that illness and identity are sometimes intertwined and that we actively try to manage our identity when illness threatens our ability to behave as we normally would.

In the case study "I Want You to Put Me in the Grave with All My Limbs" (Sharf, Haidet, & Kroll, 2005), a woman with a family history of diabetes says she would rather die at age 60 than experience amputation. Many of us shudder at such a choice, but for her, the devastation of losing a limb is familiar and distinctly identity threatening. She explains:

> My grandfather had no legs; my dad has no legs, and part of his chest is missing, and part of one hand is missing, and he can only see out of one eye, but not very good. Also, my dad's brother has one hand missing, and one leg missing and so forth. And so it goes in the family. (Sharf et al., p. 43)

Sometimes our abilities are not substantially altered by our health conditions, but we may be surprised or dismayed to have a condition that seems to clash with our established beliefs. For instance, an unmarried high school teacher may be horrified to learn that she is pregnant and may wonder if her pregnancy will affect students' image of her or cost her job.

It can be useful to ascertain whether people consider their health conditions to be identity threatening and how they react to that possibility. Patients may feel determined, ashamed, victimized, or even relieved by diagnoses. Some respond to illness with a zealous determination to "beat" it, as if it were an enemy. Others interpret illness as punishment. For others, it is comforting to have a name for the illness and perhaps a plan for dealing with it.

Leigh Ford and Brigitte Christmon (2005) illustrate this diversity well with narratives from women who have had breast cancer or feared that they might. One woman, Helen, described the nausea and fatigue of undergoing chemotherapy while doing her best as a wife and mother. She says, "It was a terrible time for us, but when I look back at it now, I feel nothing but pride in our resilience as a family and in the love that allowed us to make this work" (p. 160). Another woman said she put her faith in God when she didn't know what lay ahead. A third challenged the "corporatization of breast cancer," saying:

> Breast cancer is now part of the market economy. We have pink ribbons and scarves and bears and T-shirts and coffee mugs and wind chimes and breast cancer candles and tchotchkes galore. There is something offensive about this. Most of these items advertise that "part of the proceeds go to breast cancer research." I wonder how much—and to what end? I prefer a straight

business transaction—at least the motives and agenda are clear. (p. 165)

She also questioned the pink-ribbon movement's emphasis on feminine beauty, optimism, and survival—to the extent of ignoring the deadly and devastating aspects of breast cancer. "If you refuse to enact the role of the noble survivor," she said, "you are invisible and marginalized, not just by mainstream society but also by most other women who have experienced this disease" (p. 163). Samantha King (2010) agrees, calling the pink campaign largely a "tyranny of cheerfulness" depicting breast cancer survivors as "youthful, ultrafeminine, slim, light-skinned if not white, radiant with health, joyful and proud" (p. 287).

These diverse reactions can be informative. We may assume that people who are upbeat are "taking it well" or are "strong." But in some instances they are hiding deeper feelings or harboring unrealistic expectations. Others may feel their illness is degrading or is unfair. People who seem relieved may have expected something worse (it might be helpful to know what), or they may simply be glad to escape part of the dread and uncertainty of not knowing. In the case of extended illnesses, reactions are likely to vary considerably even within one person.

Summary

In contrast to the well-established ways in which caregivers are socialized, we learn how to be patients mostly through life experience and watching others (including our caregivers). As patients, we often communicate in hesitant and nonassertive ways because we're uncertain what is expected of us, and we're afraid to seem rude or ignorant.

Although a caregiver may conceive of health as a biological phenomenon to be identified by its physical manifestations, as patients, we usually interpret illnesses in light of their effects on everyday activities. The Voice of Lifeworld is concerned with feelings and events. Patients' communication and their willingness to self-advocate are influenced by a variety of factors, including the nature of their illness, their personality, and their communication skills. Throughout this chapter, we have examined suggestions by experts on how patients can be more active participants in medical encounters.

Patient satisfaction is often based more on how caregivers listen and empathize than on perceived technical competency. We typically prefer doctors who seem interested, genuinely caring, and sympathetic. We also appreciate having a sense of control and being treated with dignity. As a whole, we tend to have serious complaints but still consider ourselves satisfied overall with our doctors' care.

Overall, our adherence to medical advice is notoriously low for a range of reasons, including limited money and resources, mistrust of the diagnosis or treatment plan, a sense that the illness is cured, and a perception that the treatment (including drug side effects) is worse than the disease. Although we may have good reasons for not following medical advice, the results can be disastrous for us, for doctors, and for the public. Many health advocates urge patients and caregivers to be more explicit about negotiating treatment options that are practical and acceptable.

Ethical principles and U.S. laws stipulate that patients be well informed about health choices and allowed to decide for themselves what care they will and will not receive. Informed-consent laws protect people from atrocities such as the Tuskegee Syphilis Study, but some cases fall within a gray zone in which it is difficult to determine when patients are too distraught or fearful to make informed choices.

Illness can affect people's very identity. Evidence suggests that we work to maintain our identities, even when illness changes our patterns of behavior.

Now that we have considered patients' perspectives, we will explore how health communication looks through caregivers' eyes.

Key Terms and Theories

Voice of Lifeworld
self-advocates
Tuskegee Syphilis Study
informed consent
personal identity
social identities
tertiary identity
supernormal identity
restored self
contingent personal identity
salvaged self

Discussion Questions

1. What is the Voice of Lifeworld?
2. How is a patient's philosophy of health and illness traditionally different from a doctor's?
3. As patients, how do we tend to behave when our goals are different from those of our caregivers?
4. What advice does Jerome Groopman (2007) offer to patients for helping their doctors?
5. What factors are linked with patient satisfaction? What communication behaviors are associated with these factors?
6. What are some factors that patients tend to associate with a loss of dignity?
7. What reasons might patients have for not following medical advice?
8. How does patient–caregiver cooperation affect patients and caregivers?
9. What are the stipulations of informed consent? What are some ethical considerations associated with informed consent?
10. What are the four stages in Charmaz's (1987) model of identity management during chronic illness?

Answer To *Can You Guess?*

1. Of the countries listed, Australia ranks highest in terms of health and longevity (Davis, Schoen, & Stremikis, 2010).

CHAPTER FIVE

Caregiver Perspectives

I was asked to see Mrs. B, who had just been diagnosed with pancreatic cancer. . . . Her husband asked numerous questions about the toxicity of the treatment regimen and about difficult quality-of-life issues. I answered his questions, then turned to Mrs. B and asked for her thoughts and feelings. To my surprise, she was engrossed in filing her fingernails and watching television. When she saw me looking at her, she said, "I'm sorry. I wasn't listening to your conversation. What did you say?" (Urba, 1998, para. 13)

After feeling surprised by the woman's conduct, physician Susan Urba (1998) realized what was happening. The patient was overwhelmed by the information, unable to listen anymore. "She was too polite to ask us to leave, so she protected herself the only way she could. With her fingernail file and remote control" (Urba, 1998, para. 14). From this encounter and others like it, Urba says she has learned a valuable lesson, reflected in the title of the article, "Sometimes the Best Thing I Do Is Listen." She reflects that "the most important healing is done by the patient, and the physician can only have a small role in that process" (last para.).

Urba's experiences bring to mind the privileges and pressures of working every day with human life. Whether you are a technician, a physical therapist, a dentist, a pharmacist, a physician, or another of the many professionals we will discuss in this chapter, the odds are you will experience many of the same challenges and rewards of communicating with people who need your help. Like Urba, you may be puzzled and frustrated when people seem to ignore medical advice or, at the other extreme, try to call the shots themselves. But perhaps, like her, you will see something deeper—the vulnerability and beauty of human nature and the role that communication plays in connecting people.

In this chapter we look at health care from the diverse perspectives of professional caregivers. We begin at beginning, with the factors that lead us to careers as caregivers and how candidates are selected, educated, and socialized. Then we follow the path of caregivers-in-training through initial clinical experiences and into the professional domain. Along the way we will focus on issues related to time, autonomy, maturity, confidence, and satisfaction. Then we will zero in on three issues: medical mistakes, stress and burnout, and interdisciplinary teamwork.

Teamwork is a promising, but not always easy, opportunity to maximize effectiveness and reduce the stress of caregiving.

As you read, maintain a broad focus on what it means to be a caregiver. Many people think of medicine mainly in terms of doctors; indeed, most of the research still focuses on physicians. But of course they cannot do it all, and it's unrealistic to expect physicians to cover all the bases. In recognition of the interdisciplinary nature of health care, I have incorporated research (when available) and career information about a wide range of caregivers.

One more thing—I speak in terms of "you" and "us" throughout the book because I hope you'll try on various roles and seek to understand how they feel—as if you were actually in those roles yourself. Whether or not you plan to become a professional caregiver, it's the best method I know for developing true empathy.

Gaining Entrance

Let's start with the reality that not everyone is allowed to become a professional caregiver. Only about 39% of the people who apply to U.S. nursing schools and 45% of those who apply to medical schools each year are accepted (American Association of Colleges of Nursing, 2012; Association of American Medical Colleges, 2011). The numbers are limited based on schools' resources and applicants' qualifications. Across the board, admission requirements may be as simple as a high school diploma for medical aides and non-technical assistants. A college degree or higher may be required for admission into other fields.

Likewise, qualifications to enter professional fields differ. Technicians must typically complete specialized training and apprenticeships before being licensed. The qualifications to become a physician, psychologist, pharmacist, dentist, or rehabilitation therapist (e.g., respiratory, speech, recreation, physical, occupational) require graduate-level coursework, internships, and sometimes postgraduate residencies and fellowships.

High rank is usually associated with a focus on science and technology such that applicants may be evaluated in large part based on their aptitude for the sciences. This is good and bad. Few people question the value of biology and physiology, but

---

BOX 5.1 CAREER OPPORTUNITIES

Physicians and Surgeons

- Physicians and surgeons work in medical practices, hospitals, universities, and other organizations caring for patients, serving in leadership roles, and sometimes teaching and conducting research.
- Shortages are expected in general and family practice, internal medicine, and obstetrics/gynecology, particularly in rural areas of the country ("Physicians and Surgeons," 2008).
- Annual salaries range from $407,300 a year for anesthesiologists to $205,400 for internal medicine specialists and $189,000 for family practitioners.
- The job outlook is better than average, with a 24% increase in the number of positions expected between 2010 and 2020.

SOURCE: U.S. Bureau of Labor Statistics, 2012b

---

as you will see, some feel that caregiver education programs should be equally concerned about ethics and social skills.

Let's assume you applied and were accepted into a caregiver education program. Your first exposure is likely to involve science and anatomy, so let's examine that next.

Science-Based Curriculum

It's said that the average medical student learns 10,000 words that are not in general use outside medicine. The content is also voluminous in other fields. It's a steep learning curve, and what happens along the way can have profound implications for health communication.

Students are often overwhelmed with the amount of work and its critical nature. It's not unusual for medical students to spend 12 to 18 hours a day in the lab or studying. At least 50% of medical students say they are burned out, and 10% have had thoughts about suicide (Liselotte et al., 2008). A whopping 92% of nursing students surveyed report stress levels so high that they interfere with their everyday activities (Hensel & Stoelting-Gettelfinger, 2011). Ironically, studying health can be an unhealthy process. High stress sometimes endangers students' health and interferes with their learning. Nursing students who experience burnout engage less in learning experiences, do not adapt as well to professional life, and are more likely than others to leave the profession (Rudman & Gustavsson, 2012).

Sometimes the compassionate elements of caregiving are overshadowed by personal stress and by a curricular emphasis on the body as a mechanism. Analysts often point to the use of cadavers in this regard. Students preparing to become physicians, rehabilitation therapists, and dentists typically dissect cadavers to learn about the body. That's mostly a good thing. But Alan Bonsteel (1997) argues that an overreliance on cadavers encourages us to regard the body as an inanimate object. There's no need to communicate with a cadaver, treat it gently, or wonder about its feelings, he says. Bonsteel urges educators not to portray people as impersonal "biological systems," but as individuals with feelings and emotions. He maintains that "cold, clinical" professionals result from programs that concentrate on science but neglect interpersonal communication, social issues, and ethics.

Another issue is that, pressured to learn a great deal in a short amount of time, students may memorize information without understanding it, a process called **rote learning**. In this situation, you may do well on multiple-choice exams but may be incapable of applying the information to actual situations. Among students in traditional medical curricula, about half (49%) said they didn't understand the scientific information they learned for tests (Regan-Smith et al., 1994). One student said that studying science was like memorizing a chant "yet not comprehending a word of it" (para. 7).

Another promising alternative is **problem-based learning** (PBL), which challenges students to apply information to actual scenarios rather than simply memorizing it. For instance, you might be presented with a case study and asked to analyze the patient's condition and identify factors relevant to the patient's health. PBL is positively correlated with caregivers' competence later in their careers, particularly with their ability to communicate about complex health matters (Koh, Khoo, Wong, & Koh, 2008).

WHAT DO YOU THINK?

■ Which do you prefer as a student—rote learning or problem-based learning (PBL)? Why?

■ Would you rather have a caregiver who learned via rote or PBL?

Another useful technique is videotaped role-playing, in which students conduct interviews with trained mock patients (sometimes called *standardized patients*), practicing their responses to realistic symptoms and emotional concerns that the "patients" present. Usually, students review the videotapes with communication specialists and the mock patients involved.

Communication Training

Traditionally, communication skill training has been a minimal part of caregiver training. But it is emerging as a new priority, supported by evidence that communication can be instrumental in making good decisions, reducing costs, improving health outcomes, raising patient satisfaction, and minimizing mistakes and misunderstandings (Epstein, Fiscella, Lesser, & Stange, 2010).

Spokespersons for the Accreditation Council on Graduate Medical Education (ACGME) have proclaimed that "effective communication skills are at the heart of quality patient care" (p. 20) and are essential to leadership and teamwork. The council defines communication competence as the ability to:

- create and sustain a therapeutic and ethically sound relationship with patients;
- use effective listening skills and elicit and provide information using effective nonverbal, explanatory, questioning, and writing skills; and
- work effectively with others as a member or leader of a health care team or other professional group. (ACGME, 2006, p. 20)

We will focus on these skills in this chapter and throughout the book.

The ACGME standards are having a sweeping impact. Analyst Larrie Greenberg (2004) predicts that they "could have the greatest impact on medical education as a continuum since the Flexner Report" put the focus squarely on science (2004,

BOX 5.2 CAREER OPPORTUNITIES

Dentistry

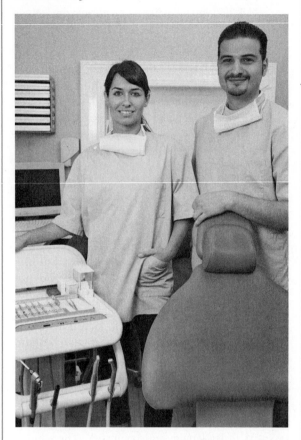

- **Dentists** with doctoral or professional degrees make an average of $143,000 a year. The need for dentists is expected to increase 21% between 2010 and 2020.
- Dental specializations include oral and maxillofacial surgery, orthodontics, and prosthodontics.
- **Dental hygienists** with associate's degrees earn an average of $68,250 a year, and the job outlook is much better than average, with need expected to increase 38% between 2010 and 2020.
- **Dental assistants** make an average of $33,500 per year. The number of positions is expected to increase 31%.

SOURCE: U.S. Bureau of Labor Statistics, 2012b

p. 1398). And momentum is growing. Organizations including the Institute of Medicine and the American Nursing Association have echoed the call for more communication training in caregiver training programs.

Research about the impact of communication skills training is promising. We have learned that the most effective programs employ a range of experiential activities (e.g., role-playing, observations, discussion) rather than relying on large, lecture-based formats (Lundine, Buckley, Hutchinson, & Lockyer, 2008). We have also seen patient satisfaction scores rise among the patients of physicians who take part in communication skills training, probably because those doctors tend to give more information, show more sensitivity, and address a greater variety of patients' lifestyle behaviors than others (Haskard et al., 2008). Likewise, nurses are typically more confident about their ability to interact effectively with patients after communication skills training (Wilkinson, Perry, Blanchard, & Linsell, 2008), and communication skills training results in improved performance and better health outcomes when it involves physiotherapists, speech and language therapists, physical and rehabilitation therapists, and occupational therapists as well (Parry, 2008).

With the evidence mounting, many advocates say we haven't gone far enough. They urge the creation of more communication courses, including classes on delivering bad news (Zakrzewski, Ho, & Braga-Mele, 2008), working with patients to set medical agendas (Rodriguez et al., 2008), and more.

Socialization

We have discussed the coursework, but becoming a caregiver is not strictly a matter of studying hard. It's also a process of **socialization**—learning to behave appropriately within a specific community. School is often the first place we begin to learn what it means to act and talk like a professional caregiver. The process can be transformational. Medical school, for example, has been called the "longest rite of passage in the Western world" (Bonsteel, 1997, para. 3). Few other experiences are so extensive and life altering. The intensity, uniqueness, and isolation make high-intensity caregiver education programs especially hospitable arenas for socialization.

One impact of socialization into a specialized community (such as health care) is that members, once socialized, may have expectations and practices that differ substantially from others. In Chapter 3 we talked about the Voice of Lifeworld typically spoken by patients. In contrast, caregivers in the United States are expected to be proficient in what Harvard University medical professor Elliot Mishler (1984) calls the **Voice of Medicine**. As the vocabulary of traditional biomedicine, this voice is characterized by carefully controlled compassion and a concern for accuracy and expediency.

The Voice of Medicine is designed to help people. One limitation, however, is that it doesn't provide caregivers with much of a vehicle for sharing emotions or soliciting emotional responses. Instead, it is characterized by medical terminology and attention to physical details. For the most part, patients' individuality is treated as less important than their physical conditions. However impersonal it may sound, the Voice of Medicine answers to the extraordinary demands of time and emotion exacted from caregivers and suits society's image of caregivers as stoically objective and in control. As you read this section, consider the pros and cons of the Voice of Medicine.

Now let's trace some of the factors that influence the socialization process. As we do, we will move out of the classroom and start to involve experiences in clinical environments. As you will see, this going-public phase is an important step in donning the identity of a health professional.

HIDDEN CURRICULUM

Socialization occurs partly as a result of the **hidden curriculum**, that is, the attitudes and practices that others model, even though they don't explicitly teach them. What we *do* often matters even more than what we teach. As medical professor Michael Wilkes says:

> We can teach extensively about the appropriateness of respecting different cultures, different beliefs and different health practices, but when the student hears a resident dissing a patient's mistaken notions of disease, or hears them making fun of a patient's body, the lesson is clear—to be a part of the "club," this is the expected behavior. (quoted by Lauer, 2008b, p. 50)

Wilkes and others warn that, very often, seeing is doing when it comes to shaping new professionals. True change comes through modeling the behaviors that we want others to adopt.

ISOLATION

Intense caregiver programs typically involve both physical and experiential isolation. Long hours mean less time hanging out with family and friends. At the same time, the uniqueness of your experiences can make you feel different from others.

Emily Transue (2004) recalls the initial shock of clinical work. "I had woken up that morning having never seen a death, and by lunchtime I had been part of one," she says. "Nothing in medical school or in life had prepared me for that moment. . . . I felt wrenchingly and terribly alone" (p. 1). As she felt herself being transformed by the experience, Transue wondered if the people she loved could still relate to her. "Would they understand what I had just seen and done? Would I be inevitably separated from them by this experience and those that would follow it?" (p. 1).

Being different from others can be a special feeling. It can also interfere with relationships and with communication, particularly when you're not sure where you fit into the scheme of things.

IDENTITY IN LIMBO

The process of framing a new identity typically involves a phase during which you feel you're in limbo—no longer a lay person but not yet accepted as a professional. And some rather harsh rituals sometimes signal that newcomers must earn their way into the community.

In many ways, caregiver education is like military boot camp. As a newcomer, you're apt to feel stripped of your previous identity and doubtful about your self-worth. As in the military, health care observes a strict hierarchy, and those at the lowest levels are reminded in many ways of their lowly status. Interns are sometimes referred to as "the dirt on which the ladder stands" (Hirschmann, 2008, p. 59) and as those who get "pimped first, blamed first, and thanked last" (Jauhar, 2008b, p. 201).

Dietetic students in a Canadian study describe a dynamic in which preceptors often assert that they have superior power by withholding information and demoralizing the students (MacLellan

& Lordly, 2008). Said one student in the study: "Sometimes it feels as though interns, we are put at the bottom of the priority list. . . . I sometimes feel as though my ideas and input are disregarded without any consideration" (p. E87).

Role theory explains such behavior by proposing that social roles are defined by unique sets of rights, responsibilities, and privileges (Mead, 1934). By asserting their power, preceptors may be sending the message that the initiates haven't yet earned the privileges and rights of full-fledged practitioners. It's a powerful message underscored in many ways. For example, the phrase *medical student abuse* appears frequently in published literature. Tales are told of medical students being cursed, slapped, kicked, punished, and worse. Among graduates of 16 medical schools in the United States, 84% said they had been belittled in medical school and 42% said they had been harassed by professors, residents, classmates, or patients (Frank, Carrera, Stratton, Bickel, & Nora, 2006). Only 13% of those surveyed considered the abuse severe, but those who did suffered significant losses in mental health and were more likely than others to regret choosing medicine as a career.

Students and interns are further reminded of their place with public pop quizzes in which personnel of higher status can publicly challenge them to answer questions and make diagnoses. And novices may be called on to do **scut work**, menial chores that no one else wants to do. It's commonly accepted that some of these chores are assigned mainly to punish or humiliate the novices.

The stress can be tremendous. Although you often have immense responsibility as a student, you often have less experience than the professionals around you. Medical and nursing students frequently report having insomnia, nightmares, and depression. Many are haunted by decisions or oversights that resulted in adverse patient outcomes. In *Intern: A Doctor's Initiation*, Sandeep Jauhar describes the computer-access password assigned to him by the hospital staff when he began his internship: "bogus doctor" (2008b, p. 45). Likewise, after experiencing a patient's death, a nursing student in New Zealand wrote to a professional journal to ask more experienced colleagues:

How do I protect myself and still engage on a deeper level with patients? How do I avoid burnout? . . . Am I just being a laughable year-one student, with hopes and dreams in need of a reality check? . . . I am left doubting what kind of a nurse I am going to be. (Kenyon, 2006/2007, p. 4)

Many students new to clinical experience relate to Jauhar's sentiment: "It seemed like the only people I wasn't scared of were my patients. They were as much at a loss in this place as I was" (2008b, p. 113).

In the midst of this, there's usually little time to get your bearings. The expectation that students will move expeditiously from observers to participants is reflected in the traditional clinical battle cry, "Watch one, do one, teach one" (Conrad, 1988, p. 326). Learning on the job can be a frightening experience when human lives (including your own) are at stake.

But, gradually, even as they are being cast as peons within the system, students often begin to see themselves as different, even superior, to those *outside* it.

PRIVILEGES

It's exhilarating to be part of the action and learning at a rapid pace. Medical interns sometimes say that, as much as they long for a day off, when it comes, they feel adrift and left out. When things got really tough, Transue (2004) reminded herself: "I will never learn as much in any year of my life as I will in this one. I may never have the same intensity of experience. I intend to make the most of it" (p. 34).

To be granted access to wonders seldom witnessed can also be a heady experience. Perri Klass, whose medical school memoirs were published as the book *A Not Entirely Benign Procedure* (1987), recalls a heady sense of wonder dissecting cadavers, reflecting that she was doing something "normal people never do" (p. 37). Klass compared the sensation to initiation into a priesthood.

In these ways and others, you get an early dose of the responsibilities, but also the privileges, that go with being a caregiver. Sometimes, as students begin to feel more like professionals, the emotional distance between them and their patients widens, as we will discuss next.

WITHDRAWAL AND RESENTMENT

The rigors of clinical experience can lead to darker aspects of socialization. Confronted by overwhelming demands, it's not surprising that students often begin to regard patients as enemies. Phillip Reilly, author of *To Do No Harm* (1987), remembers the extreme exhaustion during his residency that led him to resent the neediness of a comatose patient: "He was an enemy, part of the plot to deprive me of sleep. If he died, I could sleep for another hour. If he lived, I would be up all night" (p. 226). Another resident recalls hoping that a patient would die so that she wouldn't have to update his chart. She ruefully recounts: "But you know what? I had to write a note anyway, and fill out a death certificate, and deal with the morgue, and call the attending and the family. So it didn't really save me any time at all" (quoted by Jauhar, 2008b, pp. 119–120).

Medical professionals sometimes refer to patients in derogatory terms such as *drain circlers* and *gomers*. The first is a reference to patients who are expected to die (go down the drain) soon. The second, an acronym for "get out of my emergency room," generally refers to older patients who have little chance of recovering and are seen as wasting valuable time and space. Jauhar (2008b), jaded by sleep deprivation and the seemingly endless demands of residency, wrote in his diary:

> Nature did not wire into us the desire to take care of our aged. Maybe that's why the contempt, the frustration, with gomers. They are heavy, dead evolutionary weight. They sap our resources. We don't want to take care of them. Baby shit doesn't smell. But gomer shit smells the worst. (p. 90)

During medical school, students' empathy for patients typically decreases, especially among male students who are not specializing in primary care or psychiatry (Newton, Barber, Clardy, Cleveland, & O'Sullivan, 2008). Empathy typically plummets even more during their internships (Rosen, Gimotty, Shea, & Bellini, 2006). Many medical school graduates report that, by the end of their intern year, they are less overwhelmed than before, but also less compassionate and less emotionally available. As an intern, Jauhar (2008b) wrote:

> Do doctors care? I don't know. I don't see a lot of caring. Maybe I myself don't care, or care selectively, which is hypocrisy, which I despise. No, I don't see much attention to the psychosocial aspects of medicine. There is lip service, but by and large, no one seems to pay it much mind.

WHAT DO YOU THINK?

■ What is your reaction to residents' admission that they sometimes yearn for a dying patient to go ahead and die so that they can finally get some rest?

■ Can you imagine feeling a similar way under the same sort of pressure?

> Like this morning. Steve had no interest in holding Camille's mother's hand, in asking her why she was crying. . . . I myself didn't make an effort, not because I was uncomfortable but because there was so much to do. I thought it best to spend my time doing what needed to be done. (p. 90)

If you're persuaded by the curriculum or your mentors that disease is best understood in physical terms, depersonalizing patients begins to feel acceptable. Focusing on specific, organic concerns is more familiar and less emotionally exhausting than thinking in terms of unique individuals.

To counteract this tendency, some schools have made empathy a part of the curriculum. The Northeastern University School of Pharmacy in Boston implemented a program in which pharmacy students learn about nutrition and weight management and then, for a week, model the behaviors they would recommend to an obese or diabetic person (Trujillo & Hardy, 2009). The students are asked to calculate what portion of a limited family budget would be available for food purchases after subtracting medical costs, and then design a grocery list and shop for the recommended foods. Five months after the exercise, the students reported that the experience was still with them. They felt more confident counseling people about dietary matters and more sympathetic toward people with weight problems, especially those trying to buy healthy foods with limited financial means. Said one student, "This activity really made me realize how important it is to understand someone's culture and income level before recommending lifestyle changes" (p. 6).

Implications

It's natural to feel a mixture of awe and outrage over what some people go through on the way to becoming professional caregivers. Abuse and resentment can seem antithetical to a caregiver role. Indeed,

BOX 5.3 CAREER OPPORTUNITIES

Pharmacy

- *Pharmacists work* in retail establishments, clinics, and hospitals. They dispense medications and counsel people about side effects, diet and stress, treatment of minor health concerns, and other health issues.
- A doctoral or professional degree is required. Pharmacists make an average of $111,600 a year. The job outlook is good, with a 25% increase in positions expected between 2010 and 2020.
- *Pharmacy technicians* usually make about $28,400 a year. A training program after high school may be required. Demand is expected to increase 32%.

SOURCE: U.S. Bureau of Labor Statistics, 2012b

efforts are under way at some universities and medical centers to revamp the way things are done. (See Box 5.4.) However, the conditions described here are still common.

Whether justified or not, intense demands and demoralizing rituals endure partly because they serve several functions. The high-pressure environment may prepare students for the actual demands of practice, which require great patience, endurance, and emotional control. If you're put to the test early on, you may be better prepared to handle immense pressure later.

Second, a clearly established chain of command (power difference) may help health care teams make decisions and carry them out. Decisive, centralized decision making reduces the likelihood that caregivers' efforts will be disorganized and uncoordinated.

Third, the hardships may strengthen group membership. Students often say they feel a bond with people who went through the process alongside them. The result is often an enduring sense of camaraderie.

Fourth, the hardships serve collectively as a **rite of passage,** a challenge that qualifies students for advancement. Graduates may feel an extraordinary sense of accomplishment as they qualify for higher rank by surviving the harsh years as an initiate.

On the downside, caregivers may come to identify with each other more than they identify with their patients. They may also feel that, based on their experiences, others are in no position to question their judgment. For example, after they are licensed, doctors may chafe at questions and comments that seem to challenge their authority, reasoning that they have now earned the right to call the shots. Such assumptions may cause patients and coworkers to consider them arrogant and bossy. Another danger is that harsh conditions early on imply that you should be stoic and self-sacrificing as a professional. With excessive work and minimal opportunities to relax or vent emotions, you may end up in worse shape than your patients. We'll talk more about burnout later in the chapter.

To segue to the next section on a positive note, there's evidence that caregivers bounce back and regain at least a portion of their idealism and compassion once they are in the field. Following their

BOX 5.4

Medical School Reform

Juggling 8 courses with 35 hours of lecture per week, Audrey Young takes a deep breath and looks at her desk, which is stacked 2 feet high with papers. It's her second year of medical school, which she recalls as "the hardest stress" of an arduous process.

In this and other reflections in her book *What Patients Taught Me: A Medical Student's Journey*, Young (2004) describes a medical school experience that began with 2 years of intense studying and lectures. Regrettably, she says, she "didn't set foot in a real clinic or talk with a practicing doctor for months" during that time (p. 39).

Traditionally, medical students have been required to learn massive amounts of scientific material in their first 2 years, followed by 2 years focused on clinical experience. Within that model, students have only a delayed opportunity to apply what they are learning. And when they do face actual patients, they may find themselves at a loss to remember everything they crammed to learn. One intern describes what happened when a pulmonologist asked her, "What do you think of when you see a nodulorecticular pattern?"

> *You want an honest answer?* I think to myself. *When I see a nodulorecticular pattern on chest x-ray, I think: nothing.* I know we learned about this in med school, but my mind is drawing a complete blank. Worse, I'm panicking, thinking: *What am I doing here? How am I supposed to succeed as an intern if I can't even remember the differential diagnosis of a nodulorecticular chest x-ray?* (Transue, 2004, p. 16)

This isn't unusual. In fact, some people maintain that separating science and application interferes with learning. Moreover, linking the medical school curriculum with actual patient care may humanize the process by continually reminding medical students of the interpersonal dynamics involved. Here are a few examples of medical schools that have broken the mold.

Some schools, such as the University of California at San Francisco, are experimenting with integrated medical curricula in which information from various disciplines is woven together, along with clinical experiences. This method may help students to develop integrated knowledge and to apply it immediately in natural contexts. The new method is not without challenges, of course. Faculty who are accustomed to structuring their own classroom experiences are challenged to work, instead, as part of multidisciplinary teams. Students sometimes feel the information is less organized than in the traditional one-subject-per-course curricula, and they are apprehensive about being immersed in complex concepts before they have mastered the fundamentals (Muller, Jain, Loeser, & Irby, 2008). After studying the program, Muller and colleagues suggest that faculty can overcome these challenges by providing an overall "conceptual scaffolding" for students at every step.

A program at Harvard Medical School requires students to participate in a 3-year course on doctor–patient relationships. The program is designed to create "humanistic physicians" who appreciate social and psychological aspects of illness and embody ethics, warmth, and sensitivity. The course makes use of small-group discussions to help students explore their own feelings and philosophies and work together to develop communication skills.

Pediatric residents at the University of California (UC), Davis, don't just train in hospitals and clinics. They also work as advocates in the community, actively partnering with various groups to improve the overall health of children in the community. "Physicians have a greater responsibility to their patients beyond telling them what will keep them healthy," says Richard Pan, a UC physician who developed the program. "We need to be in our patients' communities and neighborhoods working with families" ("Getting Doctors Out," 2002, para. 3). The program has won numerous awards, and research shows that physicians tend to maintain their community-oriented focus after they transition into licensed medical practice (Paterniti, Pan, Smith, Horan, & West, 2006).

internships, for example, it's common for physicians to rediscover the reasons that they went into medicine. Jauhar—who was quite candid about the callousness he and others developed as interns—remembers a house call later on when he forgot his stethoscope, blood pressure cuff, prescription pad, and all the rest. "Without my tools, I couldn't follow my usual procedures, so I just sat at his bedside, stroking his hand. Afterward, in the kitchen, I sat with his wife and had a cup of tea," he remembers (2008b, p. 177). On his way home, Jauhar reflected on the sense of peace and satisfaction the encounter had given him. And his kindness was not forgotten. Two years later, the patient's wife wrote to thank him again and say she would never forget his thoughtfulness. (Jauhar now directs the Heart Failure Program at Long Island Jewish Medical Center.)

Next, let's move from the education phase to professional practice to examine other factors that influence the way caregivers communicate.

Systems-Level Influences on Caregivers

Once they join the ranks of medical professionals, caregivers are influenced by a range of factors including organizational protocols, time constraints, competition, and autonomy. These factors can sometimes be quite frustrating. On the good side, most caregivers say the frustrations are tempered by unforgettable moments in which they connect with patients and know they are making a difference.

Let's start our discussion of system theory with an example.

Theoretical Foundations

The cancer center administrators were stunned. First the CEO had insisted they consult Toyota management specialists. Then they learned they were to call their Japanese guides "sensei," meaning master or teacher. Now a sensei was handing them a skein of blue yarn, asking them to show, on a map of the medical center, the path patients take in the process of receiving care.

By the time they were done, representatives from the Virginia Mason Cancer Center in Seattle had created a maze-like web that went back and forth, up and down various floors, circled back over itself, and demonstrated clearly that patients—many of whom were quite sick and depleted—were put under ridiculous emotional and physical stress just to get treatment (Mars, 2011). Charles Kenny, who wrote a book about the experience, observes that the team members were horrified to realize that "they were taking these patients, for whom time is absolutely the most precious thing in their lives, and they were wasting huge amounts of it" (quoted by Weinberg, 2011, para. 6).

Months later, a different sensei met with Virginia Mason Medical Director Robert Mecklenburg and a team of employees. In that meeting the sensei pulled out a map of the medical center. Here's an excerpt from a *99% Invisible* podcast (Mars, 2011) in which Weinberg described what happened next:

> The sensei kept pointing to these areas and saying, "What is that?" and Dr. Mecklenburg would say, "Well, that's a waiting area." And this happened over and over again. And as this was happening, the sensei seems to him to be getting increasingly angry. And he says to Mecklenburg, "Why are there so many waiting areas throughout this facility? Who is waiting there? What are they doing? What are they waiting for?" And Dr. Mecklenburg says, "Those are our patients. They're waiting for us." And the sensei—long pause—looks quite furious, looks directly at Dr. Mecklenburg and in front of Mecklenburg's team, says to him, "Aren't you ashamed?" And Dr. Mecklenburg said that at that moment he *was* ashamed. He was absolutely ashamed.

This story illustrates the power of a system. No one at the cancer center particularly wanted patients to exhaust themselves traversing the large facility or to waste time waiting in one area after another, but they had probably never questioned the necessity of it.

Hospitalists: An Emerging Career

Hospitalists are physicians who work directly for hospitals, visiting and monitoring patients.

- Because hospitalists know the hospital even better than other doctors do, they may be better able to help patients understand and navigate the system (Volpintesta & Kanterman, 2008).
- Potential downsides are that hospitalists are less familiar with patients and their conditions than their regular doctors, they are sometimes stretched thin caring for a wide range of patient needs, and patients don't have the comfort of dealing with doctors they already know and trust (Fisher, 2008).

Systems theory awakens us to the presence of **organizational processes**, which are habitual or prescribed ways of doing things, and **organizational culture**, which comprises members' basic beliefs and assumptions about an organization, its members, and the organization's place in the larger environment (Schein, 1986). To the extent that these behaviors and assumptions become part of everyday thinking, they contribute to the culture of an organization and the socially constructed identities of people within it.

The problem is that familiar routines and structures often have a taken-for-granted quality that blinds us to alternatives. We become, as systems theorist Peter Senge (2006) puts it, "prisoners of systems" that we ourselves create. If team members at Virginia Mason were frustrated about the numerous delays and waiting areas, they probably felt they had no choice but to perpetuate the process. It is a tenet of systems theory that, while everyone may be trying to do his or her best, good intentions cannot overcome a poorly designed system. What is required is that we redesign the system itself.

The staff of Virginia Mason did just that. Once the Japanese guides opened their eyes to the injustices of the system, team members decided to rethink everything. Before long, they moved doctors out of their window-front offices and converted the perimeter of the building into a beautiful, sunny pathway with water-front views that patients can easily follow in a logical progression when it's necessary to move from one area to another. The staff now provides educational and entertaining options on the relatively rare occasions when people have to wait.

These changes have reduced the average time that patients spend in the medical center by 50%, and Virginia Mason skyrocketed to the top 1% in the nation in terms of safety and efficiency, earning a 37% reduction in the company's insurance premiums (Kenney, 2010; Weinberg, 2011). The system continues to evolve, but it is both kinder and more efficient than it used to be. The staff now cares for more patients in less time, which is good for patients and for the bottom line. Profits are up, but the greatest satisfaction, say team members, is doing what's right for their patients.

The relevance of this to caregivers is that we are all affected by the systems in which we operate. Because patients and their families interact more closely with caregivers than anyone else, they may assume that caregivers call all of the shots. The reality, however, is that many of the conditions that establish what happens in patient–caregiver communication are established at a system, not an individual, level. The Virginia Mason example demonstrates this and perhaps offers some encouragement that, if we are not happy with a system, we may be able to improve it. After all, as Senge (2006) points out, even small changes to a system can have potent implications.

Let's examine some of the systems-level factors that influence caregivers' communication and satisfaction.

Time Constraints

One consideration is the time budgeted for patient interactions. When time is in short supply, expediency may seem like the only alternative to turning away people in need. Even adding a few minutes to each patient visit soon adds up. Consider that, if you spend 15 minutes with each patient, you can see 32 patients in an 8-hour day. If we add just 5 minutes to each visit, however, the number of patients drops to 24 per day. In one month, you'll be 172 visits behind, and in one year, 2,064 visits behind. Consequently, some professionals feel that they must get right to the point with patients if they are to see everyone who needs care.

BOX 5.6 CAREER OPPORTUNITIES

Emergency Personnel

Emergency medical technicians (EMTs) and *paramedics* make about $30,400 a year. The job outlook is good, with the need expected to rise 33% between 2010 and 2020.

SOURCE: U.S. Bureau of Labor Statistics, 2012b

💬 IN YOUR EXPERIENCE

■ How do you respond to some caregivers' argument that they must limit patients' input so that they can keep visits within a particular time limit?

■ In your opinion, how can patients help manage time effectively?

Unfortunately, this game plan often backfires because it results in follow-up visits that might have been avoided, poorly developed relationships, misunderstandings, and other time-intensive outcomes. It has proven more effective to engage in communication that is open and inclusive but doesn't take longer than the average medical exam. We will return to this topic later in the chapter.

Time constraints may affect the amount and type of information that patients and caregivers share. Pressed for time, caregivers may seem rushed and impatient. Although it's tempting to blame caregivers for this less-than-hospitable demeanor, researchers have found that caregivers don't like time constraints any more than patients do. Caregivers rate themselves more satisfied when they have adequate time to spend with patients (Kisa, Kawabata, Itou, Nishimoto, & Maezawa, 2011; Tellis-Nayak, 2005).

Research indicates that caregivers who are worried about time constraints often limit talk to specific physical indicators. For example, doctors may reason that people have numerous sources of emotional support—friends, family members, clergy, counselors, and others—but they are the only ones qualified to diagnose physical conditions and prescribe treatments. Therefore they may devote the brief time available to the physical concerns they are uniquely qualified to assess and treat.

Interestingly, although they may consider the biomedical approach a means of saving time, caregivers are typically not satisfied with interviews that focus on strictly biological indicators. Physicians in private practice are most likely to enjoy their jobs if they have good relationships with their patients (Bell, Bringman, Bush, & Phillips, 2006).

One option is to make the most of caregivers at every level. For example, midlevel providers such as nurse practitioners (NPs) and physician assistants (PAs) now handle routine and minor concerns in some medical offices, which frees physicians to spend more time with seriously ill patients. Patients are typically satisfied with NPs and PAs because they are often less rushed than doctors and they tend to focus on social and personal concerns in addition to biomedical matters (Charlton, Dearing, Berry, & Johnson, 2008; Cipher, Hooker, & Sekscenski, 2006; Laurant et al., 2008).

There is also evidence that discussing emotional concerns may not be as time-consuming as it seems. A range of studies suggests that patients' emotional

BOX 5.7 CAREER OPPORTUNITIES

Midlevel Providers

Two types of midlevel providers are nurse practitioners (NPs) and physician assistants (PAs), both of whom are specially trained and state licensed.

- NPs and PAs are of equal status, about midway between that of doctors and nurses.
- For minor health concerns, they function much like doctors, performing routines exams and minor biopsies, suturing cuts, and so on.
- Annual salaries range from $80,000 to $89,500.
- The need for midlevel providers is expected to rise 30% between 2010 and 2020.

SOURCE: U.S. Bureau of Labor Statistics, 2012b

concerns can often be addressed in a brief amount of time (Branch & Malik, 1993; du Pré, 2002; Smith & Hoppe, 1991). An extensive study of medical visits revealed that biomedical visits took about 20.5 minutes each, whereas biopsychosocial visits took about 19.3 minutes (Roter, Larson, Sands, Ford, & Houston, 1997). Jeffrey Rudolph (2008) offers the following tips for bonding with patients when time is limited:

- *Start strong.* Shake hands, look the patient in the eye, inspire trust from the beginning.
- *Don't interrupt, and don't multitask.* Give the patient your full attention.
- *Empower patients.* Provide information, web links, follow-up phone calls, and other means of encouraging the patient's active involvement during and after the encounter.
- *Don't end the visit before you ask if the patient has other questions or concerns.* You're not actually saving time if the patient leaves without knowing what to do next. And even if you make a note to address some of the concerns on the next visit, it's ultimately more efficient to encourage full disclosure than to remain in the dark about what a patient wants and needs.

Now let's look at another factor that affects caregivers.

Autonomy

Caregiver autonomy is an issue in this age of managed care and fiscal reform. **Professional autonomy** means that caregivers work independently, making decisions without much supervision. Traditionally, physicians have had considerable autonomy and other caregivers have had variable, often limited, input about treatment decisions. With managed care, even doctors are likely to feel that multiple people—some of them far away—are weighing their decisions. Most physicians' are frustrated with managed care. As you may recall from Chapter 2, only 1 in 10 doctors in the United States feels that managed care is providing good care for patients in financial need (Frank et al., 2008).

Specialists are particularly sensitive to the effects of managed care since they must rely on referrals from primary care physicians, but nearly all doctors are affected. Physician Bhupinder Singh traded private practice for hospital work to get away from the red tape. He recalls:

I'd write a prescription, and then insurance companies would put restrictions on almost every medication. I'd get a call: "Drug not covered. Write a different prescription or get preauthorization." If I ordered an M.R.I., I'd have to explain to a clerk why I wanted to do the test. I felt handcuffed. It was a big, big headache. (quoted by Jauhar, 2008a, p. 5)

BOX 5.8 CAREER OPPORTUNITIES

Osteopathy

Doctors of osteopathic medicine (DOs) go to medical school, complete internship and residency requirements, and function as physicians. Their focus is on holistic health and enhancing the body's ability to heal itself through physical strength and skeletal alignment, accomplished, in part, through physical manipulation of the body (American Association of Colleges of Osteopathic Medicine [AACOM], 2012). They make up 7% of physicians in the United States (AACOM).

Unfortunately, hospital work has not been much better. "Thirty percent of my hospital admissions are being denied. There's a 45-day limit on the appeal. You don't bill in time, you lose everything," Singh says (Jauhar, 2008a, p. 5).

Caregivers may also feel constrained by economic pressures and government regulations. They must answer not only to their employers, but also to funding agencies and patients who have strong (but often conflicting) interests in medical decisions. (See Box 5.9 for information about the impact of federal privacy regulations.)

In summary, systems can help us succeed or can make the going very rough. The best-designed

---

BOX 5.9 ETHICAL CONSIDERATIONS

Privacy Regulations Incite Controversy

In recent years some people have been outraged to learn that health care providers have sold or carelessly leaked their "confidential" medical information to others. For example, a Florida state worker was able to download the names of people diagnosed with AIDS (Barnard, 2003). Companies, including Eli Lilly pharmaceuticals and CVS Pharmacy, have been charged with selling the names of patients on Prozac and other drugs (Ho, 2002; "Medical Records," 2001). The problem has grown since the advent of computer databases that make it easy to transmit medical data that was once stored only in doctors' filing cabinets (Conan, 2002).

New federal regulations went into effect in 2003 to prevent these types of privacy violations. The Health Insurance Portability and Accountability Act, better known as HIPAA, provides patients increased access to their own medical records and regulates who else may see them. The new regulations—which present a number of implications for health communication— have provoked a good deal of controversy.

One area of controversy involves the mandate to inform patients of privacy regulations. HIPAA requires health care providers to give every client a written copy of the organization's privacy policies. As a consumer, you have probably encountered this in the form of *HIPAA Alert* or *Patient Privacy* statements that doctors, pharmacists, health plans, dentists, and others ask you to sign. On the surface, this seems like a positive measure. Patients are informed up front about the measures being taken to protect their privacy and their right to file a grievance if the rules are not upheld. However, the process is less than perfect.

For one thing, the forms can be lengthy and difficult to understand, especially for people with limited reading skills. Compounding this is the implied or explicit demand that patients sign the forms whether they understand them or not. According to the U.S. Department of Health and Human Services, it's not necessary for patients to sign this form to receive care or services (Health Privacy Project, 2003). However, based on confusion about HIPAA standards (the act is about 400 pages long) and fear of incurring costly fines for noncompliance, a number of health care providers have refused to treat patients who don't sign the privacy notices.

The most serious complaint about the privacy notices is that they do not give patients a choice about how their medical information will be used. Early on, legislators envisioned the forms as consent letters. Patients could say yes or no to receiving information about the latest drugs or treatment options associated with their medical needs. For example, if you're on a drug commonly used to treat AIDS, you might appreciate receiving updates and promotional information about related drugs. However, you might feel that putting such information in the mail is a violation of your privacy. Says one physician, "When my postman knows what diseases my wife has, that's not appropriate" (Barnard, 2003, para. 19). Others worry that, if these mailing lists are in circulation, the information will be used to discriminate unfairly against them. One man, who mistakenly receives information meant for people with hepatitis C, wonders:

> What happens now with—my wife and I are going to be refinancing our house, and what if somehow the erroneous information that I have hepatitis C finds its way from an insurance

company or a pharmacy, a manufacturer, something like that, into someone's financial database and they say, "Well, jeez, we don't want to lend money to someone who has hepatitis C"? (Conan, 2002, transcript p. 7)

Under HIPAA regulations, health care providers cannot sell their mailing lists to others. However, they can accept money to send information to patients themselves as long as the information is health related. Either way, the information is in the mail. Janlori Goldman, director of the Health Privacy Project, says: "They don't have to tell the customer they're doing it, and they don't have to give the customer the chance to opt out" (quoted by Conan, 2002, transcript p. 6).

Despite HIPAA's shortcomings, it does emphasize providers' legal responsibility to maintain privacy. In 2008, Lawanda Jackson, an administrative specialist who had previously worked for the UCLA Medical Center, was indicted for selling celebrities' medical information to the media. Jackson pled guilty, but she died before the trial began. If she had been convicted, she faced a maximum 10-year jail sentence and $250,000 fine ("Former UCLA," 2008). Less obvious breaches of confidentiality are harder to identify and eliminate. Perhaps the most common breaches involve overheard conversations about patient care and leaving patient paperwork (such as registration forms) where others can see it (Brann, 2007). In one study, 81% of patients interviewed expressed concern that their medical information would be inappropriately shared with people in the organization not responsible for their care (Brann & Mattson, 2004).

There isn't room enough to outline all the provisions of HIPAA or to describe the pros and cons of each, but here a few of the mandates.

- Health care clients must be assured of confidential environments.
- Health care clients around the country have the right to see their medical records and suggest changes.
- People who believe their medical privacy has been violated can register a complaint with the

U.S. Department of Health and Human Services. Some people feel that this regulation should have included the provision for patients to sue for breaches of confidentiality. That right is not guaranteed under HIPAA.

- HIPAA requires that health care providers adopt a standardized set of codes, train staff about privacy regulations, and appoint a staff member to oversee implementation of HIPAA. The benefits are that medical information will be easier to share and compare and privacy will be a top-agenda item. The drawback is that the transition is costly and time intensive. Some medical professionals say the regulations allow even less time for patient care in already short-staffed medical units.

WHAT DO YOU THINK?

1. Have you been asked to sign a HIPAA Alert? Did you understand the information provided? Did you feel that you had to sign?
2. Under what circumstances, if any, would you like to receive health-related information through the mail? Do you feel it's important that people have an opportunity to opt out of such mailing lists?
3. Have you ever felt that you had to discuss confidential medical information within earshot of others (e.g., at a pharmacy counter or during a medical visit)? Do you feel this is a serious problem? If so, what would you do to fix it?
4. Some people believe the private-environment regulations are too strict. For example, an orthodontist who previously encouraged patients and families to move throughout the clinic and get to know staff members issued an HIPAA Alert saying, "We must now regretfully restrict all patients and friends to the reception seating areas only." What is your opinion of this?
5. How far do you think the federal government should go to enforce privacy regulations? Do you agree with adding staff members, more paperwork, and oversight committees? Would you suggest other or additional measures?

systems are typically built on shared values, team-work, and input by people at every level (Senge, 2006). Caregivers typically say they don't mind working hard to help patients. They just don't like struggling with rules and limitations that are antithetical to high-quality care. It remains to be seen how the health care system will evolve, but one thing is for sure—we'll be prisoners of the system unless we take an active role in shaping it for ourselves.

Now that we have looked at some the external factors that influence caregivers, let's shift our focus to the emotional health of caregivers.

Psychological Influences on Caregivers

Health care can be emotionally challenging, and research suggests that many caregivers are woefully ill prepared for it. As a result, they may act in ways that puzzle or wound others, even as they are themselves reeling under the pressure. In this section we will discuss how caregivers are affected by emotional maturity, confidence (or self-doubt), and satisfaction.

Maturity

As mentioned in the section on education, medical schools, in particular, have been criticized for allowing students little time to develop and mature as individuals. The intense workload can isolate students from normal activities and emotional development. As a result, according to Wayne Weston and Mack Lipkin, Jr. (1989), many students progress through medical school "in the throes of delayed adolescent turmoil" (p. 46).

Patients look to caregivers not only for technical advice but also for wisdom and understanding. However, caregivers sometimes have less everyday life experience than the patients who turn to them for guidance. As Weston and Lipkin put it, we "may know precise drug treatment but stand empty-handed and mute before the patient who desperately needs counsel and support" (1989, p. 45).

As a result, caregivers may avoid emotional matters or offer stiff platitudes such as "I'm sure it will all be fine." Patients are likely to sense the insincerity and may feel that their concerns have been brushed aside as unimportant. Seldom do patients realize that caregivers may not *know* how to respond, having never experienced or been prepared for the situation at hand.

At the same time, we all have emotional hot buttons. When one of these sore spots is touched, the emotional response can surprise the caregiver and the patient, although neither may understand it (Novack et al., 1997). For example, you may feel resentment, disgust, or sexual attraction for a patient, may become overly protective, or may wish to have nothing to do with him or her. Novack and coauthors point out that personal biases are unavoidable, but caregivers will have a hard time putting their feelings in perspective if they don't take time to acknowledge and understand them.

On the positive side, a sense of being "in this together" often fosters supportive relationships, which can mean a lot. A first-year physical therapist reflected on the support of more experienced therapists this way: "If work was a lake, I feel there is always someone next to me in a boat with an outstretched hand" (Black et al., 2010, p. 1765).

Confidence

It's natural to feel like an imposter when you adopt a new role. Caregivers say they sometimes doubt their capacity to cure and understand the people they treat, and they wonder what gives them the right to make decisions and know others' most intimate secrets. Your confidence may also be shaken by mistakes, a topic we will cover later in the chapter.

Socialized to be confident and in control, for example, caregivers may hide their self-doubt behind a protective gruffness or arrogance. The message is "Don't get too close," not because you dislike people but because you're intimidated by their appraisals. Patients are likely to misinterpret this behavior as cold and distant.

Caregivers' self-doubt may be more of an issue as patients become more knowledgeable and assertive. While it was once assumed that patients could not understand the details of their conditions, today patients may know more than their caregivers about particular experimental procedures or the latest research. Professionals cannot be expected to know offhand the latest details of every medical condition. Still, caregivers may feel defensive or inadequate when they don't.

Caregivers may also restrict communication because it is difficult to refuse patients' requests even when they aren't merited. Tanya Stivers (2002) studied what happened when parents of pediatric patients suggested "candidate diagnoses" rather than asking their doctors' opinions. In most cases (82% of them), the parents suggested conditions that could be treated with antibiotics, apparently eager to secure prescriptions for them. It often worked. Even when the physicians disagreed with the diagnoses and believed that the children's conditions wouldn't be improved with antibiotics, they prescribed them 62% of the time. Stivers concluded that health professionals, like other people, are sometimes susceptible to interpersonal pressure.

Satisfaction

Research to date has largely considered caregivers' satisfaction secondary to patients'. Most people seem to take it for granted that caregivers' satisfaction is either guaranteed or irrelevant. However, unsatisfying communication is linked to stress and burnout and to high employee turnover rates. Physicians who are dissatisfied are two to three times more likely than others to leave the profession (Landon, Reschovsky, Pham, & Blumenthal, 2006). For these reasons, scholars such as Ashley Duggan (2006) urge researchers to give more attention to caregivers' emotional well-being. To date, the small amount of satisfaction research is limited mostly to doctors and to nurses. We will review what has science has taught us so far.

For one, we have learned that doctors are usually quite satisfied with medical visits, sometimes more than their patients. Patients who are friendly

---

BOX 5.10   CAREER OPPORTUNITIES

Technicians and Technologists

- *Medical records* and *health information technicians* with an associate or bachelor's degree earn about $32,350 a year. The need is expected to increase 21% between 2010 and 2020.
- *Psychiatric technicians* and *aides* with on-the-job training make about $26,900 a year. Demand is expected to rise 15% between 2010 and 2020.
- *Surgical technologists* with an associate or bachelor's degree earn about $39,900 a year. Jobs are expected to increase 19% between 2010 and 2020.
- *Occupational health and safety technicians* with a high school diploma or associate's degree earn an average of $45,300 per year. The job outlook is about average, with a 13% increase expected.
- *Radiology technologists* with an associate's degree earn about $54,300 a year. The job outlook is better than average, with an increase of 28% expected between 2010 and 2020.
- *Clinical laboratory assistants* with a bachelor's degree usually earn $46,800 a year. The number of positions is expected to rise at an average level (13%).

SOURCE: U.S. Bureau of Labor Statistics, 2012b

---

and upfront about their needs help physicians avoid burnout (Halbesleben, 2006). This may be because 88% to 94% of medical students say they want to be a doctor so they can "make a difference" ("Minorities," 2005). Even when patient care is highly challenging, helping others is energizing and rewarding.

Dealing with the nonmedical aspects of medicine is another story, however. Of 2,400 physicians surveyed, only 3% said that they are *not* frustrated by the "business" aspects of being doctors ("Physicians Report," 2008). Their frustrations involve hassles over reimbursement, medical liability issues, being overworked, and feeling overwhelmed by regulations and policies.

Grace Terrell (2007) proposes that physicians may be especially disappointed when things do not go well because they have invested so much in becoming doctors. She writes:

> Doctors have sacrificed. They have suffered. They really have. For a profession built upon delayed gratification it is not fair that, at the end of all the hard work and sacrifice and all that training and achievement, we go up against managed care, Medicare, six-figure student loans and malpractice. (p. 14)

The rewarding aspects of the job mostly involve helping people, whereas the negative aspects center on obtrusive oversight, time limitations, and a sense of being unappreciated.

For their part, nurses are most satisfied when they have a reasonable workload and feel a sense of personal satisfaction. They are also sensitive to issues of autonomy and respect. Nurses are most likely to stay in the profession if they feel that people recognize and honor their efforts and involve them in decision making. Many report feeling dissatisfied because doctors or supervisors do not give their opinions enough credence (Tourangeau & Cranley, 2005). (We will talk more about interdisciplinary teamwork later in the chapter.)

It is a testament to caregivers' commitment that most stay in the profession even with the pressures levied on them. Although they are almost universally frustrated by the hassles, 72% of physicians surveyed in one study said they would choose medicine all over again, knowing what they know now ("Physicians Report," 2008). Pamela McKemie, who supervised the study, said that most doctors surveyed stay in the profession because of "the satisfaction of doing something that matters, the intellectual stimulation of solving clinical challenges, or the thrill of actually implementing medical procedures" ("Physicians Report," last paragraph).

We will focus now on two issues that can be distressing to caregivers—burnout and mistakes—and one that holds promise for improving the first two, interdisciplinary teamwork.

Stress and Burnout

Helping people can be extremely hazardous to your physical and mental health.

—PSYCHIATRIST JAMES GILL
(QUOTED BY WICKS, 2008, P. 21)

Health care is emotionally demanding, as evidenced by high substance abuse and suicide rates among professional caregivers. In the United States, 300 to 400 physicians a year commit suicide, which is two to three times the average number of students in a medical graduating class (American Foundation for Suicide Prevention [AFSA], 2008; "Struggling in Silence," nd). Suicide and substance abuse are more prevalent among health care professionals than in any other profession, mostly because of intense emotions and stress and a high incidence of depression ("Exposure to Stress," 2008). When medical professionals abuse drugs, it may be difficult for coworkers to know what to do. (See Box 5.12 for a true story about one staff member's response to a physician's substance abuse.) Allied health professionals are also prime candidates for burnout, as you will see in this section.

Stress refers to physical and psychological responses to overwhelming stimuli. Stress is

---

BOX 5.11   CAREER OPPORTUNITIES

Nurses

- *Registered nurses* (RNs) are the largest segment of health professionals, and 48% of them work in general medicine hospitals. Most of the others work in doctors' offices, specialized hospitals, nursing homes, and home health agencies (5% to 8% in each).
- RNs complete associate's or bachelor's degrees in nursing and are state licensed.
- The number of jobs for RNs is expected to grow 26% between 2010 and 2020.
- Annual salaries range from $58,000 to $66,600.
- *Licensed practical nurse* (LPN) and *licensed vocational nurse* (LVN) positions usually require a year or so of specialized training after high school. Annual salaries average $40,400, and demand is expected to increase by 22%.

SOURCE: U.S. Bureau of Labor Statistics, 2012b

BOX 5.12 PERSPECTIVES

Blowing the Whistle on an Impaired Physician

As manager of a small community clinic, having to identify an impaired physician was not on my agenda. Clinic operations were going smoothly and patients seemed to like the clinic and the physician, Dr. Havard (not his real name). I knew things about Dr. Havard, such as his turbulent relationship with his ex-wife and his constant financial difficulties. However, he seemed to be a caring and sensitive doctor. Several months into his employment at the clinic, I started noticing strange behavioral changes in Dr. Havard, such as being chronically late for work and his inability to account for missing narcotic samples.

I thought Dr. Havard's actions were suspicious, but I did not know they were signs of an impending problem until I received a phone call from a representative of an Internet pharmaceutical company. The woman on the other end of the phone explained to me that large quantities of a prescription narcotic had been ordered for the clinic. I explained to her that the physician does not dispense narcotics on the premises because of the potential of robbery. After several similar phone calls from various companies, I approached Dr. Havard with the information. He said, "It's all a mistake. I'll take care of it."

I knew that he was not going to resolve the situation, and the phone calls became more frequent, demanding payment in excess of $20,000. I notified the clinic administrator, whose office is in a neighboring city. When I originally reported the problem, the administrator told me to "watch and listen." A week later, while working in my office, I received a phone call from a local pharmacist, who explained

to me that a clinic patient presented a prescription for the same narcotic with authorization for three refills from Dr. Havard. She called because she knew it was rare for Dr. Havard to write prescriptions for such a large quantity of narcotics. When I asked for a description of the patient, she described Dr. Havard to a "T." After my initial shock, I called the administrator back and explained the situation. The next day, the administrator confronted Dr. Havard and asked if he had written the prescription. He denied it and said he didn't know who the patient was. I was given the "go-ahead" to treat the prescription as stolen and contact the Sheriff's Department.

Soon after the incident, Dr. Havard was drug tested and suspended from employment because he tested positive for narcotics and could not produce a legitimate prescription. When sheriff's deputies caught up with him, he confessed to writing the prescription for a "relative." He was offered assistance through the state's impaired-practitioners program. The program offers confidential counseling and assistance and the chance to resume practice.

I felt that I was ruining Dr. Havard's career by turning him in. However, I had an ethical and moral obligation to report him to his superiors to protect his patients.

—DENISE

WHAT DO YOU THINK?

- If you discovered that your doctor was abusing narcotics, would it change your opinion of him or her?
- Would you want the doctor to undergo counseling and have a second chance to practice medicine? Why or why not?

considered a major cause of burnout among caregivers, but other factors (such as boredom and feeling unappreciated) also contribute.

Burnout is actually a combination of factors. In her 1982 book *Burnout: The Cost of Caring,* Christina Maslach describes burnout as emotional exhaustion, depersonalization, and a reduced sense of personal accomplishment. In Maslach's

words, **emotional exhaustion** is the feeling of being "drained and used up" (p. 3). People experiencing emotional exhaustion feel that they can no longer summon motivation or compassion. **Depersonalization** is the tendency to treat people in an unfeeling, impersonal way. From this perspective, people may seem contemptible and weak, and the individual experiencing burnout may

Nervous Patients, Friendly Staff

The summer after my freshman year I volunteered at a small outpatient surgery center. I changed bed sheets, shredded old patient files, and even observed surgeries with patients' permission. Most of my time was in pre-op, where patients were prepped for surgery. I notice how nervous most patients were. They often cried and sought comfort from family and staff members. The staff was friendly and personable with every patient. They even joked or told funny stories to calm people's nerves. That made an impact on me.

—VICKIE

resent their requests. A **reduced sense of personal accomplishment** involves feeling like a failure. People who feel this way may become depressed, experience low self-esteem, and leave their jobs or avoid certain tasks.

Causes of Stress

There are several common causes of stress among health care employees. Stress is a major cause of burnout, but it's not the only cause.

CONFLICT

Stress can result from many factors, including competing and ambiguous demands. Nurses report feeling stressed when they have more tasks than they can complete, when they must work holidays or weekends, when their efforts are frequently interrupted by phone calls and conflicting demands (Gelsema et al., 2006), when physicians behave inappropriately and disruptively (Rosenstein & O'Daniel, 2008), and when they perceive that the organization does not reward or support them (McGowan, 2001). Nurses also report a high degree of stress when they are required to carry out treatment decisions they believe to be inappropriate or harmful to patients (Catlin et al., 2008). These situations place them in a **double bind**, meaning there are negative consequences no matter which option

they choose. In contrast, nurses report less stress when they perceive that coworkers and supervisors are supportive and when they feel that they have some control over their work environments and procedures (Gelsema et al., 2006).

Robert J. Wicks (2008) proposes that our energy and compassion aren't knocked out of us with one punch. More likely, they drain slowly, almost unnoticeably. "The causes of burnout are often so quiet and insidious that we fail to notice them until they have caused a great deal of harm," Wicks says (p. 18).

EMOTIONS

Intense emotions can cause stress and lead to emotional exhaustion. Although caregivers work in emotionally charged situations, they are expected to remain calm most of the time (Pincus, 1995). It can be difficult to be caring and compassionate yet keep personal emotions in check. (See Box 5.14 for tips on dealing with difficult patients.) To cope, caregivers often develop what Harold Lief and Renée Fox (1963) call **detached concern**, a sense of caring about other people without becoming emotionally involved in the process. Some degree of detachment is useful to keep from feeling overwhelmed. However, the expectation that health professionals will squelch or avoid their own emotions may lead them to become apathetic, cynical, and confused.

In "Blood, Vomit, and Communication," Krista Hirschmann (2008) describes what she learned while following medical interns through several 24-hour hospital shifts. At one point she asked the interns how long it took to become cynical. "A week," said one. "About a day," said another (p. 64). It may sound like an exaggeration, but Hirschmann had much the same experience herself.

Hirschmann (2008) was emotionally affected by the first death she witnessed, that of a 76-year-old man named Sumner. As staff members rushed into the man's room, Hirschmann looked at Sumner stretched out on the bed, "completely naked, except for his black nylon socks," restrained hand and foot as the room became a "jungle of IVs and wires" (p. 67).

By contrast, during her second observation, a month later, Hirschmann (2008) was exposed to a patient she dubbed Turkey Woman. The woman was rushed into the ER, near death. Although she

BOX 5.14 **COMMUNICATION SKILL BUILDER**

Dealing with Difficult Patients

Some patients bring out the best in their caregivers. Others—a small percentage but powerful nonetheless—evoke defensiveness and anger. Experts offer the following tips for communicating effectively with people who are stressed, tired, and worried, without becoming too frustrated yourself.

- *Treat complaints as opportunities.* Frustrated patients and family members may want or need something they are afraid to ask for outright. Their emotion can be a signpost calling your attention to it. Physician Calvin Martin recalls an aggressive patient who threw things at the staff and yelled at everyone around him. "He knew he was dying, but everyone else was denying it," he says. Once the doctor learned the problem and was honest with the patient, his entire demeanor changed. "He was wonderful after that," Martin recalls (quoted by Magee & D'Antonio, 2003, p. 163). He says, "In medical school they tell you that 75% of the people you are going to see have nothing really wrong with them. That's not true. I think they all have something real, but we are just not finding it" (p. 164).

- *Empower team members to handle problems before they grow.* Most nonclinical problems start as minor annoyances—a phone call not returned, an appointment mix-up. A quick and thoughtful response (even if the patient hasn't complained) can usually save a great deal of time and stress down the line.

- *Invest in patient relationships.* In *The Field Guide to the Difficult Patient Interview,* Platt and Gordon (2004) propose that "engaging our patients in a partnership with us" and "enlisting them in following our recommendations" are the hallmarks of effective caregiver communication (p. 3). They encourage caregivers to take the time to know patients and establish mutual trust and rapport. "Spending more time early in our patient encounters saves time in the long run," they maintain (p. 3).

- *Show empathy.* Demonstrate through words and nonverbal cues that you understand what the patient is experiencing. Listen attentively, paraphrase to check your understanding, and ask for clarification until the patient confirms that you understand what he or she is trying to express (Platt & Gordon, 2004).

- *Display curiosity.* If a patient hints at a grievance or a concern that she or he is reluctant to share, show a gentle and encouraging interest in hearing more. Platt and Gordon (2004) use the example of a patient who refuses to say how much she smokes. They propose saying, "That is really interesting! Of course you don't have to tell me. But I am enormously curious to understand why you don't want to tell me. Can you help me understand that?" (p. 118).

- *Try a little humor.* If the patient shows an inclination toward it, you can sometimes use gentle humor to clear the air. Transue (2004) recalls a hospital patient who did nothing but complain about the food, the service, and the interruptions. She recalls thinking to herself: "I'm pretty sure there's humor under his crabbiness, but I can never quite pin it down" (p. 100). One day the man declared that he wouldn't leave the hospital until the food there improved. Several days later, after checking his lab results and vital signs, Transue was prepared to discharge him, but she asked first, "Has the food gotten any better?" She recalls:

He stares at me for a long moment. Finally he bursts out laughing. "How do you think I'll answer that . . . Has the food gotten any better. You get out of here—" . . . I wave and walk away, listening to him laugh." (p. 101)

---

had requested DNR (do not resuscitate) status the previous day, that request was not yet in her paperwork, and the medical team was obligated to try to keep her alive. As Hirschmann watched, the team quickly stripped the woman of clothing so that they could more easily insert needles and a catheter, but thick rolls of body fat inhibited their efforts. Then the unconscious woman began to vomit up the Thanksgiving dinner she had eaten earlier, filling the air with a thick, unpleasant odor and making it difficult to insert tubes down her throat. Hirschmann, who was weary of dealing all day with nameless "unconscious bodies" and was too tired to imagine their lives outside the hospital, found herself thinking: *"Come on lady, just get it over with, and die"* (p. 69). Later she reflected on her "2-day transformation" from an idealist to a detached observer and her very different emotional responses to the two patients.

Hirschmann's honest account forces us all to consider how we would think and behave in similar circumstances. It's tempting to imagine that we would remain as compassionate on day 2 (and year 2 and decade 2) as we were on day 1. But none of us are entirely immune to emotional hot buttons and fatigue.

Ironically, the very qualities that draw people to careers in health care make them especially prone to burnout. The **empathic communication model of burnout** proposed by Katherine Miller and associates suggests that health care is appealing to people who are concerned about others and are able to imagine others' joy and pain (Miller, Birkholt, Scott,

& Stage, 1995; Miller, Stiff, & Ellis, 1988). These people are typically responsive communicators (able to communicate well with people in distress), but they may easily feel overwhelmed by constant exposure to emotional situations. Regrettably, caregivers typically receive little instruction on how to care for themselves or manage their own stress and burnout.

COMMUNICATION DEFICITS

Communication plays a significant role in stress and burnout. Caregivers are affected by the amount of information they receive, their confidence as communicators, and how involved they are in decision making. Too much information can make people feel overwhelmed. Too little information can make them worried and uncertain (Maslach, 1982).

Other evidence suggests that people are more susceptible to burnout if they don't feel they are skillful communicators. First-year physical therapists, among others, experience greater confidence as their communication skills improve (Black et al., 2010).

As a caregiver, you are more likely to feel stressed and that you have inadequate social support if you perceive that your communication skills are below par (Wright, Banas, Bessarabova, & Bernard, 2010). Interestingly, the critical factor seems to be *perceived* communication competence rather than observed behavior. When Ratanawongsa and colleagues (2008) studied actual patient–caregiver interactions, they found that doctors' actual communication competence didn't correlate with their self-reported stress and burnout levels, although their perceived communication competence did. They concluded that people who feel they have communication deficits are more likely to burn out than others, even if their actual communication behaviors look the same to observers.

As Kevin Wright and colleagues (2010) point out, the link between stress and communication makes sense in the context of the **Relational Health Communication Competence Model** (Kreps, 1988; Query & Kreps, 1996), which proposes that communication competence is positively associated with social support and emotional resilience. A sense that we communicate well may enhance our confidence and our relationships, two factors known to buffer stress.

BOX 5.15   CAREER OPPORTUNITIES

Mental Health Professionals

- *Psychologists* earn about $68,700 a year. Positions are expected to rise 22%. Requirements typically include a doctorate degree and state license.
- *Psychiatrists* have medical degrees. They typically make about $200,700 a year.
- *Social workers* earn bachelor's or master's degrees. They number of positions is growing at the faster-than-average rate of 25%. Social workers make an average of $42,500 per year.
- *Mental health counselors* and *marriage and family therapists* have master's degrees and state licenses. They make about $40,000 per year. The need is expected to increase 37% between 2010 and 2020.

SOURCE: U.S. Bureau of Labor Statistics, 2012b

WORKLOAD

An excessive workload or a highly monotonous one can cause stress. Because overnight hospital stays are now limited to people who are very sick or badly hurt, nurses and residents may be continually involved in difficult, intense situations. At the other end of the spectrum, some caregivers must cope with monotonous, repetitive tasks. Laura Ellingson (2007) studied staff members at a dialysis care center, where they are required to perform the same unpleasant routines over and over. Many of the caregivers said that they break the monotony by focusing on the unique qualities of each patient. As one put it: "Our job is repetitious, but the patients are not. Yeah, they all have the same illness, they have kidney failure, but each person is different, so that's what makes it different every day" (p. 109).

OTHER FACTORS

Stress does not affect everyone in the same way, nor does it always lead to burnout. People are able to tolerate different levels of stress before they experience burnout. Studies show that stress is more bearable if you feel that you are appreciated and are performing important services. A British study (Ramirez et al., 1996) found that surgeons had higher stress levels than most doctors. But because surgeons were highly satisfied and publicly respected, they were less likely to experience burnout than other professionals, such as radiologists. Radiologists were the least stressed but also the least satisfied of those surveyed. They experienced the highest burnout rate, apparently because they felt isolated and unappreciated.

Effects of Stress

Stress and burnout affect people physically and emotionally, causing sleeplessness, fatigue, weight changes, digestive disorders, headaches, and more. People experiencing burnout are also at elevated risk for heart disease and other stress-related conditions. Psychological symptoms include reduced self-esteem, depression, defensiveness, irritability, and a tendency toward accidents, anger, and emotional outbursts. Burnout also makes it more likely that you'll be apathetic, miss work, and leave the profession (Paris & Hoge, 2010). What's more, there is

exploratory evidence linking physician burnout with patient outcomes. In one study, patients of high-burnout physicians were less satisfied than other patients. They tended to recover more slowly and to leave the hospital later than the patients of physicians who were not burned out, apparently because the emotionally exhausted physicians were less attentive to details and because their relationships with patients were not as open and trusting as they could have been (Halbesleben & Rathert, 2008).

HEALTHY STRATEGIES

Caring for patients all day can be draining. But patients and friends can offer remarkable insights about life and happiness as well. Many analysts suggest that gratifying patient–caregiver relationships are the best antidote for burnout. Being a caregiver is difficult, attests George Hanna: "It can be exhausting. But don't let anyone tell you it's not rewarding. . . . It's worth it to put in the time and to let yourself care. It's better for the patients, but in the end, it's a lot better for you, too" (quoted by Magee & D'Antonio, 2003, pp. 53–54).

With a similar conviction, Wicks (2008) remembers visiting a dying friend in the hospital who asked him about the "good things" he had been doing:

> As I started to launch into an obsessive (naturally well-organized) list of my recent academic and professional accomplishments, he interrupted me by saying, "No, not that stuff. I mean what really good things have you done? When have you gone fishing last? What museums have you visited lately? What good movies have you seen in the past month?" (Wicks, p. 45)

Wicks reflects that, in dying, his friend understood life better than he—in the "arrogance of good health"—did. Here are a few of Wicks' suggestions for avoiding burnout, from his book *The Resilient Clinician*.

- *Hold daily debriefings with yourself.* Honestly assess your own emotions and hot buttons. Reflect on such questions as: What made me sad? Overwhelmed me? Sexually aroused me? Made me extremely happy or even confused me? (p. 31).

- *Resist the urge to put off the "good stuff."* Wicks recommends making time for quiet walks, meditation, laughter, listening to enjoyable music, having friends over for dinner, daydreaming, being in nature, making love, and journaling.
- *Be mindful about what makes you happy.* Frequently consider your answers to the following questions: What is my heart's desire? What is truly important to me? How do I most want to live?
- *Design your own time pie.* What size slice will you give to serving others, learning new things, spending time alone, being creative, relaxing with family, and so on?
- *Seek the company of people whose presence replenishes you.* A good friend who listens without judgment or who helps you find the humor in a tense situation can ward off burnout. Transue (2004) remembers a playful conversation with a fellow intern who asked her, "Do you really want to be a doctor for the rest of your life?" Laughing, Transue responded, "I don't even want to be a doctor for the rest of the week, especially" (p. 75).

Let's turn, now, to a topic of particular stress for caregivers—one that often boils down to an issue of communication.

Medical Mistakes

"DOCTOR AMPUTATES WRONG LEG"

The headlines told a shocking story. A Tampa surgeon, Rolando Sanchez, had mistakenly removed Willie King's left leg rather than his right one. It's easy to imagine the anguish of a patient with one good leg and one bad leg, awakening to realize the good leg is gone. "Now he'll be without any legs at all," mourned the patient's brother ("Florida Hospital," 1995, para. 4).

Why Mistakes Happen

The Willie King case is horrifying. But the public didn't hear the whole story. In his book *Medical Errors and Medical Narcissism*, clinical ethicist John Banja (2005) relates the behind-the-scenes facts of the case. First, King did not have one good leg and one bad leg. He suffered from diabetes and related vascular diseases to such an extent that open sores on both legs had developed gangrene, his skin was cold to the touch, and it was nearly impossible to detect a pulse in either leg. The left leg (which was mistakenly amputated) was actually worse than the right, and King was aware that he would lose both legs before long. He chose to have the right leg amputated first because it was the more painful of the two. So it wasn't an easy choice between good leg and bad leg. But a cascade of communication errors contributed to the mistake as well.

Someone dropped the ball. Who? There's no easy answer, says Banja (2005). The public might imagine a distracted, careless, or bumbling surgeon. However, Dr. Sanchez was anything but. He was "at the height of a sterling medical career" (Banja, 2005, p. 9), having served as chief resident among his colleagues at New York University School of Medicine and professor at Albert Einstein College of Medicine before returning to practice in his native Tampa. The mistake ended with him, but it began much earlier.

Because of a miscommunication between Dr. Sanchez's office staff and the surgery department at the hospital, the surgical staff incorrectly listed the procedure as a left-leg amputation. A hospital nurse detected the error and told another nurse about it. That nurse put a surgery-schedule correction notice on a clipboard, which she gave to another nurse. Each nurse began a sequence of remedial events. But the sequence was somehow interrupted. The correction never made it to the official surgical log or to the blackboard in the surgery unit.

Yet another correction opportunity arose just prior to surgery, when King told a nurse that his right leg was to be amputated. She noted this on his record but prepared his left leg. When the surgeon entered the room, King's body was draped, except for the left leg, which was braced and ready for the operation. Sanchez confirmed, by looking at the blackboard, that this was the intended leg, and he was nearly done with the surgery before the medical team realized the error.

It is easy to see, in retrospect, that the mistake might not have happened if people had communicated more clearly with each other or if the surgical team had consulted King's consent form (which correctly indicated his right leg) rather than relying on the blackboard or surgery schedule. But at the time, people were following standard procedure, and the error occurred because of system and communication breakdowns that were beyond any one person's control (Banja, 2005).

Banja (2005) points out the systemic nature of this mistake and others like it. "Well-trained, well-motivated people make errors all the time," he says (p. 11). Medical mistakes are often the result of ineffective communication—sloppy handwriting, forgotten or delayed instructions, busy shift changes in which there isn't time to talk about everything in a patient's chart, and so on. Small omissions and misunderstandings can quickly lead to critical breakdowns.

In 2007, another high-profile case hit the news when three newborns at Cedars Sinai Medical Center in Los Angeles (two of them were twins born to movie star Dennis Quaid and his wife Kimberly) were mistakenly given 10,000 units of the blood thinner Heparin rather than the 10 units they were supposed to have. The error occurred because a technician mistakenly put prepackaged vials containing adult dosages in the infant nursery cabinet. Because the packaging was similar to that of infant dosages, a nurse administering the drug to newborns didn't notice the discrepancy. The California Department of Health fined the hospital $25,000 for the mistake, and the Quaids sued the drug manufacturer for negligence in packaging. (Fortunately, the babies recovered.)

What Happens After a Mistake?

People who are hurt by medical mistakes often say they just want an apology, to feel that they are getting the full story, and reassurance that the organization is taking steps to avoid similar errors in the future. It can be agonizing not to know exactly what caused a loved one's death or suffering. Dale Ann Micalizzi (2008) recalls her own bewildered grief when her 11-year-old son died following a relatively minor surgery to treat an infected cut on his ankle.

Micalizzi says her family didn't want to sue. She works for an HMO herself and understands the intricacies of medical settings. But otherwise, no one would tell them what happened. "We were owed the truth," she says. "Money wasn't an issue for us" (2008, para. 12). Micalizzi describes sitting in a courtroom 3 years later, seeing the defense team consult a 6-inch-thick binder containing her son's medical records and reports from the hospital

WHAT DO YOU THINK?

Many people hurt by medical errors say they just want an apology, the full story, and assurance that future errors will be prevented.

■ If a family member of yours nearly died from a medical error, do you think these factors would influence your desire to sue for malpractice? Why or why not?

■ What other factors might influence how you felt?

investigation. "This was information that I had begged to see for such a long time and have still never seen," she says. "In the intervening time I had searched for the truth, only to hit my head against walls of silence" (para. 8).

Errors can happen in any organization, in or out of health care. But medical mistakes are particularly hard to handle because the stakes are so high and because caregivers are not expected to commit errors. When doctors' mistakes are brought to light, they may suffer more than most professionals from feelings of guilt and inadequacy, recriminations from others, and legal action. Even if others are involved in medical mistakes, it is typically physicians who are sued. And they may feel personally responsible, even when events were out of their control.

On the one hand, it's hard to deal with guilt and self-blame in isolation. Ethical guidelines and a sense of fair play encourage health professionals to make full disclosure to patients and their loved ones, to apologize, and to take corrective action. Likewise, hospitals' contracts with insurers typically stipulate that the hospital will promptly report medical errors when they occur. However, caregivers may be discouraged from admitting mistakes by their own sense of distress, by fears about their reputation, by ego needs that make them loath to admit fallibility, and by reluctance either to blame others or to accept blame for what is often a systemic chain of events involving numerous people (Banja, 2005).

Of 39 physicians who described medical mistakes in Joyce Allman's (1998) study, the doctors' most common emotional reactions were remorse and anger. Several said they considered giving up medicine in the wake of a mistake. Most of the doctors had disclosed the mistake to another physician, but two of them had told no one at all, afraid their peers would think less of them and/or they would be sued.

Mistakes do happen. In a survey of 53 family physicians, the doctors recalled an average of 10.7 significant mistakes each, and the average number of deaths from their mistakes was 1.2 per physician (Ely, Levinson, Elder, Mainous, & Vinson, 1995). Several doctors experienced grief over their mistakes, even when the results were not serious. One remembered making a serious mistake because he was ashamed to ask for help: "I think in medical school and often through your training programs is the time when you're most made to feel that asking and calling on people for help is an error" (Ely et al., 1995, para. 42).

Banja (2005) proposes that health professionals may rationalize not saying anything because they believe no permanent harm was done, the error probably didn't change the outcome (e.g., "the patient would have died anyway"), knowing about the mistake would only make the family feel worse, or the mistake wasn't anyone's fault, just something that happened.

Added to people's natural reluctance to admit mistakes are more tangible considerations, such as "Who will be held responsible?" and "Who will pay?" Malpractice insurance policies often include a clause that revokes coverage if the physician admits culpability (Banja, 2005, p. 22). Thus, although patients yearn for an apology and an explanation, and physicians may desire to give them, physicians may realize that, if they own up to mistakes, they are on their own if lawsuits ensue.

The issue is not only who will pay for a malpractice judgment. It's also who will pay for remedial care. For example, if a hospital stay is extended or a patient is transferred to an intensive care unit because of a medical error, who pays for the extra care? In recent years, many insurance companies have declared that they will not pay costs associated with what they call *never events*. **Never events** are loosely defined as clear, preventable errors with serious consequences. "Think wrong-side surgery," says Dennis Murray (2007, p. 18). The idea is that hospitals with a strong financial incentive to avoid never events will be more diligent about preventing them, identifying their root causes if they do occur, and avoiding future tragedies.

But the issue isn't black and white. A gray zone surrounds less obvious avoidable outcomes such as infections. If a patient contracts an infection in the hospital, was the staff negligent? In many cases it's hard to say what constitutes negligence versus a reasonable (but imperfect) standard of care. David Burda (2008) worries that insurers will become so stringent that medical professionals will live in fear of trying new procedures. Even if the standard options are not working, professionals may feel they cannot step out of bounds for fear of being either sued or refused payment. And Burda warns that caregivers who are terrified of making mistakes won't learn very much, and they will probably order so many precautionary tests that precious medical resources will be squandered.

Medical mistakes (and perceived mistakes) aren't only expensive. They can be demoralizing and humiliating. Although many new residents consider that doctors are likely to be sued at least once (Noland & Walter, 2006), it can be devastating when it happens. Family physician Steven Erickson (2008) remembers being sued over a difficult birth that resulted in the baby's having brain damage. In the courtroom, he weathered aggressive questioning by the plaintiff's attorney, all the while worrying that his colleagues, family, and friends would think less of him and doubt his judgment. Erickson won the case, but embarrassment and fear of future lawsuits shadowed him for a year, until he met a new patient, Roger. Roger had just moved to town, and he and his wife had chosen Erickson to be their doctor based on their son's recommendation. A year earlier, their son had served on the jury that heard the malpractice case against Erickson. Roger said that, as a farmer, his son had explained to fellow jurors that births do not always go perfectly even when the doctor is honest, competent, and doing his or her best. Writes Erickson:

> I thanked him for his candor and finished up the visit, all the while fighting to maintain my composure. But as I walked back to my office, my eyes welled up and I was crying. After all the embarrassment and self-doubt my malpractice case had engendered in me, there was a juror who not only believed my defense, but trusted me enough to refer his elderly father and mother to me. (p. 33)

Erickson's words remind us that—while we should guard citizens' right to reasonable legal recourse if they have been badly treated—lawsuits have many costs, emotional and financial. Very often, patients wish to avoid lawsuits just as much as doctors do, but a variety of human and systemic restraints may stand between them. When it comes down to it, the factors that lead to mistakes—and the factors that determine what will happen afterward if mistakes are made—involve mostly one thing: communication. If by communicating more effectively we can save lives and prevent some of the anguish that bereaved families and guilt-ridden professionals feel, surely it's worth the effort.

Communication Skill Builder: Managing Medical Mistakes

Following are some tips from the experts on how to avoid misunderstandings, disappointments, and lawsuits.

FROM THE BEGINNING

- *Establish trust.* Invest in open and trusting relationships with patients from the very beginning. Be sincere, polite, friendly, and engaging. Patients are less likely to sue doctors whom they like and trust (Boodman, 1997), and it is easier to share decisions and to admit mistakes with people one knows and trusts.
- *Invite feedback.* Patients who play an active role deciding on treatment options are more likely to consider them worthwhile, even if things don't work out perfectly.
- *Respond to complaints and requests as quickly as possible.* Patients who perceive that you don't care or aren't paying attention are more likely to assume you have neglected other aspects of their care. When you are unavoidably delayed, apologize, explain why, and express your sincere concern.
- *Show that you care.* Don't assume that patients know you care. Be explicit, as in "I don't know if we can eliminate 100% of your pain. But I think, if we work together, we can do a lot. It would make me happy to see you smiling and walking again."
- *Create realistic expectations.* Brushing aside patients' concerns, as in saying "There's nothing to worry about," may set them up to be disappointed and even to file lawsuits, down the line.

Attorney S. Allan Adelman (2008) suggests: "You can't always prevent undesirable outcomes, but you can help create realistic expectations" (p. 14).
- *Put it in writing.* "Document, ad nauseam," recommends Ralph Caldroney (2008), a family physician who has never been sued in 30 years of practice.
- *Don't be shy about giving referrals.* If another doctor can help, or the patient wants a second opinion, be supportive. Don't cast yourself as the roadblock that kept the patient from exploring all avenues (Caldroney, 2008).
- *Don't forget the family.* Keep in mind that family members often have opinions and fears of their own. Invite their input, and nurture those relationships as much as possible.
- *Own up to small mistakes.* Showing that you have nothing to hide can engender trust.

IF AN ERROR DOES OCCUR

Banja and Geri Amori (2005, p. 178) recommend the following five-step guide to telling a patient or his or her loved ones about a medical mistake:

1. Rehearse how you will disclose the information.
2. Deliver it as simply, truthfully, and clearly as possible.
3. Stop talking and listen.
4. Assess how the news is being received.
5. Respond empathically.

Banja and Amori recommend using the word *error* or *mistake* rather than blurring the issue with terms such as *unintended outcome* or *unexpected occurrence.* They also coach health professionals to tell the people affected: (1) when and where the error occurred, (2) what harm resulted, (3) what actions have been taken to offset the harm, (4) actions being taken to prevent future errors, (5) who will be caring for the patient and how, (6) a description of systemic factors that contributed to the error, (7) the costs of responding to the error and how they will be handled, and (8) information about counseling and support resources. They also recommend that the speaker "apologize profusely" and mean it (p. 185).

Finally, don't let doubt and remorse cripple your confidence. It's easy to obsess about what might have happened—if only you had stopped by one more time, ordered one more test, put a request in writing rather than called it in, and so on. These are not necessarily errors, just limitations in the amount a person can do.

The chapter concludes with a communication strategy that has the potential to ease some of the pressure on health care professionals.

Interdisciplinary Teamwork

It hardly seemed possible. Michael Hulshouser, a 48-year-old father of two, had become so ill that he was paralyzed from the neck down. Doctors diagnosed Guillain-Barré, a rare neurological disorder that can cause weakness, paralysis, and even death. "I had given up," Hulshouser says. But, inspired by his two children, he set an ambitious goal. "My son said all he wanted for Christmas was for me to be able to walk," he remembers. In October 2008, Hulshouser checked into Methodist Rehabilitation Hospital in Dallas. By February, he was on his feet again with the aid of a walker. Hulshouser credits a number of people for his remarkable recovery. "They brought me back," he says. By "they" he means his doctors, nurses, health aides, and even the hospital chef, who honored his special requests for delicious, inspiring food. "I've gained over 25 pounds since I've been here," Hulshouser says. ("Recovering Hope")

This is just one example of the teamwork that characterizes health care at its best. Multidisciplinary teams may include social workers, recreational therapy, psychologists, dieticians, pain specialists, and people in many other fields. In this section we will look at the rewards and challenges of interdisciplinary teamwork.

Simply defined, a **team** is "a set of individuals who work together to achieve common objectives" (Unsworth, 1996, p. 483). Teamwork is nothing new to health care, but the rules and reasons for teamwork are changing. To apply the terminology of management guru Peter Drucker, health care teams used to function like baseball teams, but now they must act like doubles tennis partners. Drucker (1993) writes that (managerially speaking)

BOX 5.16 CAREER OPPORTUNITIES

Physical Rehabilitation Teams

- *Physical, occupational,* and *speech-language therapy* positions typically require a graduate degree and state licensing. Salaries range from $67,000 to $76,000 a year, and the need is expected to rise between 23% and 39%.
- *Recreational therapists* (requiring a bachelor's degree) usually make about $39,400 a year, and the job outlook is average, with a 17% increase in positions expected.
- *Respiratory therapists* (requiring an associate's degree) usually make about $54,300 a year, and a 28% increase in positions is expected.
- *Assistants* in the fields mentioned above with specialized associate's degrees make about $49,000 a year and *aides* with high school diplomas about $23,700.

SOURCE: U.S. Bureau of Labor Statistics, 2012b

a doubles tennis game is different from a baseball game. In baseball, each player is assigned a position, with a specific set of tasks to perform. The pitcher pitches, the catcher catches, the batter bats, and so on. The game is specialized and precise. Doubles tennis is different—faster, less precise. Players have basic positions but must always be poised to help each other, and there is scarcely time to stand still.

To flourish, health care teams must function like tennis partners, argees Mary Fanning (1997). They must be ready for the unexpected and must be prepared to help each other. Caregivers used to play their positions with little overlap (like baseball players). A patient might see a physical therapist, a nurse, a doctor, and a laboratory technician—but one at a time, never all together. Technically, the caregivers were working toward the same goal, but they contributed in specialized ways, independently. The problem is that team members who don't communicate with each other are likely to drop the ball. Lack of communication can lead to duplicated efforts, costly (and sometimes life-threatening) delays, frustration, and wasted time. Teamwork can minimize the waste and frustration. However, as with leadership, teamwork isn't always easy to accomplish.

An organization famous for teamwork is Mayo Clinic. There's a saying at Mayo that "teamwork is not an option" (Berry & Seltman, 2008, p. 51). The medical center is unusual in that, although it is one of the largest in the world, it is a truly integrated system. To appreciate how, let's consider a patient-care scenario somewhere else. Typically, a patient with a serious health concern schedules an appointment with a primary care physician, who refers her to a separate facility for diagnostic tests, where the staff sends her back to the doctor for results, who refers her to a specialist in a different location, who might recommend surgery at still a different place, and so on. The patient probably has to make appointments with each provider separately, supply her health history and insurance information at each office, and perhaps wait weeks or months between appointments. The physicians involved with the patient's care probably do not work directly for the hospital, nor are they likely to have an easy or quick way to communicate with each other or to review an overall medical chart for the patient. (In many cases, there is no overall patient chart. Instead, each doctor maintains a separate chart detailing his or her work with the patient.)

In contrast, Mayo Clinic is a fully integrated system of doctors, specialists, therapists, hospitals, laboratories, and everyone and everything else needed to provide comprehensive medical care. Everyone involved—including the physicians—works for the clinic. They are linked with sophisticated communication technology and, very often, close enough proximity to allow face-to-face conversations about patients. The Mayo team practices what they call "destination medicine." When patients go there for serious health concerns, they should be prepared to stay in town for a few days. In that time, they will probably be seen by several specialists, have diagnostic tests done, and undergo treatment—all on the same campus. Even surgeries are typically scheduled on a next-day basis. The whole process—from the initial consultation, through visits with specialists, diagnostic tests, and even surgery and recovery—might take 3 to 5 days, compared to weeks or months elsewhere.

Mayo's streamlined efficiency is supported by an organizational culture that values and rewards teamwork as well as a carefully designed infrastructure. All appointments are made through one centralized system. This saves time and energy and allows the staff to properly coordinate the timing and sequence of tests and treatments. Pathologists and radiologists immediately evaluate diagnostic test data, usually before the patient leaves the office, in case more data is required. The results are immediately posted in the patient's electronic medical record. Every caregiver has instant, online access to the patient's comprehensive medical record, including all test results and other physicians' notes. This makes it feasible for everyone to get the full picture, to avoid delays or duplications, and to work effectively as a team. All the while, physicians are free to collaborate and to refer patients to each other without loss of income because they are all on salaries and are all part of the same team. "It's like you are working in an organism; you are not a single cell out there practicing," says Mayo physician Nina Schwenk. "I have access to the best minds on any topic, any disease or problem I come up with and they're one phone call away" (quoted by Berry & Seltman, 2008, p. 53).

Advantages

One advantage of teamwork is that members are able to apply multiple perspectives to a problem, enhancing innovation and creativity. This applies to overarching issues, such as new cost-cutting measures and service lines, and to everyday dilemmas.

Another advantage is that interdisciplinary teamwork blurs the line between departments and presents new opportunities for diverse employees to take part in decision making, which is linked to job satisfaction and retention. One result is that doctors and nurses are again playing a major role in health care management.

Third, teamwork reduces costly oversights that may occur when people are devoted to highly specialized tasks. Health care organizations can no longer afford (if ever they could) the oversights that result when team members don't communicate well with each other. Ask any hospital employee about patients who have gotten "lost in the system." Usually the story is that the patient is scheduled for a series of treatments or tests, but somewhere along the way everyone assumes that the patient is with someone else—until they realize the poor soul has spent hours lying on a gurney in the hallway.

Physical Fitness and Diet

- *Dieticians* and *nutritionists* have a bachelor's degree or higher in the field, and the average salary is $53,300. Higher-than-average job growth of 20% is expected.
- *Athletic trainers* are required to hold a bachelor's degree or master's degree in the field. The average salary is $41,600 a year, and demand is expected to increase 30%.
- *Massage therapists* complete training after high school and certification or licensure requirements. They earn about $35,000 a year, and job growth is higher than average.
- *Fitness trainers* and *instructors* with high school diplomas work mostly in fitness and recreation centers. They typically make about $31,000 a year. Demand is expected to increase 24%.

SOURCE: U.S. Bureau of Labor Statistics, 2012b

Bureaucracies are especially vulnerable to these kinds of oversights because many tasks don't fall squarely within the boundaries of any job description. Teamwork encourages people to look at the larger picture and pitch in, even with tasks that are not specifically assigned to them. For example, nurses who notice that lab results have not arrived on time may take the initiative to find out if tests were run and why results are delayed. This extra effort can save time and money in the long run.

Fourth, teamwork is well suited to biopsychosocial care. Members of some organizations have concluded that the best way to keep patients healthy is to pay attention to their broad range of concerns. As physician Alan R. Zwerner advises:

> The dog ate a 100-year-old patient's glasses, and she's not eligible for a covered pair for another year? Give her a pair. Free. It could prevent a fall that would break her hip. There is a reward for quality care, patient satisfaction, and doing the right thing at the right time. (quoted by Azevedo, 1996, para. 22)

Teams can help provide care that simultaneously addresses a variety of issues such as patients' personal resources, nutrition, exercise, psychological well-being, and more. The object is not to replace physicians with teams, but to help physicians provide broader care than they can provide alone. Interdisciplinary care teams can provide more complex biopsychosocial care than could any one caregiver.

Finally, team members may benefit from their involvement with coworkers. Teamwork allows professionals to share the immense responsibilities of health care, provide mutual support, and learn from each other.

Difficulties and Drawbacks

None of this means that teamwork is easy. Although it presents many advantages, there are potential disadvantages as well.

For one thing, teamwork takes time. If a quick decision is needed, an individual may be better qualified to make it. Some nurses in Julie Apker's (2001) study appreciated opportunities to be part of shared-governance teams. Others felt overwhelmed.

Said one nurse: "I don't feel it's fair to give someone a project if they don't have time" (quoted by Apker, 2001, p. 125).

Second, especially if they are rushed or intimidated, team members may resort to **groupthink**, that is, going along with ideas they would not normally support (Janis, 1972). Third, busy schedules make it hard to schedule meetings, especially if the organization is not supportive in allowing time for teamwork.

Finally, teamwork can also be particularly difficult because health professionals from different disciplines often have very different ideas about health, which creates the potential for competition and conflict. Status differences can cause rifts and intolerance. Health care is often characterized by what Kreps (1990) calls **professional prejudice**. Some professions are considered more prestigious than others, which means that people without impressive titles (including patients) may be excluded from discussions even though they have valuable information and ideas to share. Low-ranking and nonclinical personnel may be treated with less respect than doctors and nurses, and nurses may be treated as subservient to doctors.

Status differences can provoke animosity between coworkers and lead to turf battles in which members of one department or profession assert that they are more important than another, thus more deserving of new equipment, pay raises, additional staff, or the like. Unfortunately, efforts to cut expenses and limit resources have aggravated this long-standing competitiveness in many institutions.

A study of 320 doctors and nurses revealed that 73% of the physicians felt they collaborated well with nurses, but only 33% of the nurses agreed (Thomas, Sexton, & Helmreich, 2003). The discrepancy may lie in their different expectations. Whereas physicians were mostly satisfied with the communication, nurses reported feeling left out and intimated about expressing themselves freely with doctors.

Nurses and other caregivers who feel they are supported by peers and supervisors are likely to report wrongdoing, which may save lives and prevent lawsuits (Orbe & King, 2000). By contrast, caregivers who feel excluded are more likely to feel emotionally exhausted and to leave their jobs (Ellis & Miller, 1993).

Following are some tips for working through tricky communication dilemmas such as these.

Communication Skill Builder: Working in Teams

Honor the contributions of every individual. Few organizations honor this ideal more than Mayo Clinic. Denis Cortese remembers his early experiences as a physician at the clinic (related by Berry & Seltman, 2008, p. 44). "I was unaccustomed to have a desk attendant tell me, a physician, that I needed to adjust my schedule to see a patient right away," Cortese says. But then another physician pulled him aside. "He explained that at Mayo Clinic, the focus is always on the patient. And whichever member of the staff is interacting with the patient deserves our full support," Coretese recalls. "I've never forgotten that lesson." Cortese is now CEO of Mayo Clinic.

Take time to build trust and camaraderie. When quick or important decisions are needed, the investment will pay off.

Conduct team meetings with the goal of involving everyone. Minimize distractions and sit so that all members can easily see each other. Establish ground rules for attendance, discussions, and decision-making. Before trying to solve a problem, make sure group members agree on the nature, importance, and cause of the problem. Encourage all group members to contribute ideas, and strive to find creative options that meet numerous goals simultaneously. Summarize group discussions and decisions out loud to clarify the group's viewpoints and perspectives.

Develop a deep understanding of what each team member has to offer. People bring unique talents and perspectives as well as professional backgrounds. Get to know each other and correct the fact that one group of professionals is often unclear on what another group is trained to do.

Be aware that conflict is a natural part of group work. Group members who remain committed to the task often work through the conflict to achieve a mutual sense of accomplishment.

Monitor the health of the team. "Diagnose communication errors as you would any illness," recommend Eduardo Salas and colleagues (2008, p. 333), adding, "Examine the team and look for symptoms, then treat the symptoms through team learning and self-correction."

Summary

We have looked at health care through the eyes of caregivers, including the joys and challenges involved in such a role. Becoming a health professional typically involves a socialization process. Training programs and clinical experiences serve a powerful role in preparing people, helping them accept the immense privileges and responsibilities of practice, and also in suggesting what communication strategies are helpful and appropriate. As students become professionals, they typically adopt the communication styles, logic, and attitudes of their mentors, for better or worse. They also reflect the focus of their academic studies. Traditionally, caregiver-education programs have focused more on instilling technical competence than on preparing caregivers to deal with the diverse emotions and personalities they will encounter. Ultimately, this may be unsatisfying for both patients and caregivers. Emerging guidelines establish communication as a core competency for caregivers, recognizing that it can help save time and money, improve medical outcomes, and prevent much of the frustration that patients and caregivers feel. Reform efforts are underway that focus on knowledge, communication skills training, and clinical experience integrated with science education.

The way caregivers communicate also reflects professional pressures. Patients may be quick to assume that caregivers don't want to spend time with them, when caregivers may have little say in the matter themselves. Indeed, time constraints are often as frustrating to professionals as they are to patients. Autonomy is another factor in this age of oversight and cost-cutting. The added scrutiny of managed care may add to job stress. All in all, sometimes a gruff demeanor hides a caregiver's feelings of burnout, uncertainty, and self-doubt.

Caregivers are expected to be quick but thorough, strong but emotionally accessible, always available but never tired, and honest but infallible. Understanding these conflicting demands may help people understand why caregivers communicate as they do. Considering the pressures they face, it's no wonder that caregivers experience higher-than-average rates of suicide and substance abuse. It is vital that we identify healthy solutions.

Systems theory encourages us that we can change customary ways of doing things and avoid simplistic assumptions and shortsighted solutions. Well-designed systems can save time and improve the health care experience for everyone involved. They can also help to minimize the number and severity of medical mistakes, which typically result from miscommunication.

A great deal of evidence suggests that doctors are least likely to be sued if they build strong and trusting relationships with patients, take time to discuss treatment options and consequences carefully, and thoroughly describe their decision processes in writing. When mistakes do occur, disclosing them compassionately and fully can prevent lawsuits, provide comfort to those affected, and relieve some of the guilt that caregivers feel.

Health care teams may include physicians, nurses, hospitalists, mental health specialists, midlevel providers, allied health personnel, and others. Interdisciplinary teamwork isn't always easy, but it offers extraordinary rewards in terms of quality decision making, shared responsibility, and holistic perspectives of people's health.

As stressful as it is, health care can also be richly rewarding, and most caregivers consider it immensely gratifying to help patients. As any caregiver will attest, there's no such thing as a routine day. In the next unit, we will look at diversity among people and in cultural ideas about health and healing.

Key Terms and Theories

rote learning
problem-based learning (PBL)
socialization
Voice of Medicine
hidden curriculum
role theory
scut work
rite of passage
organizational processes
organizational culture
professional autonomy
stress
burnout
emotional exhaustion
depersonalization
reduced sense of personal accomplishment
double bind
detached concern

empathic communication model of burnout

Relational Health Communication Competence
  Model

never events

team

groupthink

professional prejudice

Discussion Questions

1. What are the implications, both good and bad, of focusing extensively on science during caregiver education?

2. How does role theory help to explain the initiation process in which caregivers-in-training are reminded of their status as novices?

3. What are the advantages and disadvantages of the way that professional caregivers are typically socialized?

4. How does sleep deprivation typically affect people? On the whole, do you think it's a good idea or a bad one to limit the work hours of medical residents? Why?

5. What do you think of the transformation at Virginia Mason Cancer Center? Do you think other medical centers could do a better job than they currently do at accommodating patients and limiting wait times? Are there other processes you'd like to see improved?

6. How might time constraints affect patient–caregiver communication? How do you respond to some physicians' argument that they must limit patient's input so they can keep exams within a particular time limit? How can patients help with this?

7. What are some tips for bonding with patients when time is limited? Which of these do you consider most important? Why?

8. Describe the provisions of the Health Insurance Portability and Accountability Act (HIPAA). What are the implications for health communication?

9. What are some of the "business" aspects of medicine that frustrate caregivers and contribute to burnout?

10. What factors are linked to caregiver satisfaction?

11. What do you think of the "Blowing the Whistle" case study? Why do you think substance abuse is higher than normal among health care providers?

12. What factors contribute to stress and burnout among caregivers? Does high stress always lead to burnout? Why or why not?

13. What do you think about Hirschmann's ethnography of medical interns? Were you surprised that some interns said they became cynical in a day or a week and that Hirschmann became frustrated with difficult patients within a couple of days? Why or why not? What factors do you think contribute to that pattern?

14. What are some communication techniques for dealing with difficult patients?

15. What are some strategies for avoiding burnout as a caregiver?

16. In the case of Willie King, who do you believe should be held responsible for amputating the wrong leg? Why? Who, if anyone, should be sued? Who should pay the extra medical bills?

17. Who do you think should be held responsible in the Cedars Sinai case? Why?

18. What do you say to doctors who are devastated by a mistake and want to apologize yet are afraid that doing so will invalidate their malpractice coverage and possibly destroy their careers?

19. What are some tips for avoiding and handling medical mistakes?

20. What are the advantages of interdisciplinary teamwork? The challenges? What communication strategies do experts suggest?

Social and Cultural Issues

If you watch how nature deals with adversity, continually renewing itself, you can't help but learn.

—BERNIE SEIGEL, MD

We can become so caught up in our own view of health and healing that we forget that these are largely cultural constructs. In some cultures, *healing* evokes images of science and technology, in others the power of Mother Nature and meditation. Bernie Siegel, who has taught us that love and laughter should be part of the mix, reminds us not to overlook the power of nature, either. Sadly, diversity sometimes becomes the basis for discrimination and exclusion, such that the color of our skin is a factor in how long we're likely to live, not because we're born with different genetic blueprints, but because social resources and discrimination affect our health. In this section, we will sample a rich variety of cultural perspectives about health and healing. We will also look at the link between health and race, socioeconomic status, literacy, and other factors. As you will see, effective communication is our most promising means of learning about, celebrating, and integrating diverse ideas.

CHAPTER SIX

Diversity in Health Care

She was in a motorized wheelchair that she controlled with her only usable finger. I could not understand her guttural speech or her facial contortions. She could not consistently hold her head up or control her drooling. After a few desperate moments, I asked her if she knew how to use a typewriter. She managed to make me understand a "yes" answer, and I ran out of the room to locate a typewriter on a movable stand. Pleased with my ingenuity, I stood next to her expecting some limited request. My smugness gave way to sheer awe as she painstakingly, letter by letter, tapped out with her left fourth finger the question: "What are the risks for me taking the birth control pill?" (Candib, 1994, p. 139)

In this account, Lucy Candib (1994) recalls a young woman who taught her to respect each patient as an individual. It may be tempting to group people within impersonal categories. However, there is extraordinary diversity among the people who seek health care.

Regrettably, diversity among health professionals still does not reflect the diversity in the population overall, so many people are likely to see caregivers with whom they have a limited amount in common. This can be a disadvantage. Communication scholars have long observed that people who are similar to each are likely to understand each other better.

This chapter explores diversity among both patients and caregivers in terms of status and literacy level, gender, sexual orientation, race and ethnicity, language, disabilities, and age. As you will see, each of these has an impact on health communication, especially when patients' and caregivers' assumptions are quite different. *Communication Skill Builder* sections throughout the chapter provide tips on overcoming these differences. But first, let's consider two questions: *Why should we worry about diversity in the first place?* and *How can we communicate most effectively?*

Theoretical Foundations

At a cultural level, **ethnocentrism** is the conviction that what is familiar is more right or moral than the alternatives. It's a natural tendency, but it steers us in the wrong direction, says physicist/philosopher David Bohm.

Bohm (1994, 1996) called it called **the problem of thought**—our tendency to leap to conclusions based on limited and fragmented information. One problem is our inclination to categorize. We all too frequently label people—old, young, rich, poor, male, female, virtuous, evil, and so on. We also perceive distinctions between cities, states, religions, races, genders, countries, and even between different departments within the same company. The problem, Bohm asserted, is that any distinctions we might make are trivial compared to the overriding law of nature and humanity— *that everything is connected in an interdependent whole.* The universe, from atoms to global social issues, is defined by nothing so much as holism. When we lose sight of that and begin to perceive things as categorically different from each other, Bohm charged, our thinking becomes distorted and fragmented.

To make matters worse, we assign values to different categories so that our thinking is not only fragmented, it is prejudicial. We value some groups more than others (Bohm, 1996). The results of such assumptions are often tragic. Fragmented thinking and prejudice lead to war, injustice, hatred, exploitation of the environment, lost opportunities for collaboration, and more.

It's even worse when we consider, as Bohm (1994) did, that the most problematic aspect of all is our perception of certainty—the conviction that we *know* what is right and true and real, when actually, we make assumptions based on very limited exposure and our own faulty means of processing that information.

It sounds pretty grim: As humans, we are more or less hardwired to be prejudiced and to be devout in our conviction to these prejudices. But Bohm (1996) proposed a saving grace, a means of overcoming, to a large extent, the problem of thought. The antidote, he felt, is a willingness to accept how much we don't know and a deep and sincere curiosity to learn about people and ideas beyond the scope of our own experience. Thus, a paradox emerges: The best way to overcome fragmented thinking and prejudice is not to *ignore* diversity, but to open our minds to it. In embracing new and diverse ways of thinking, Bohm proposed, we develop a more sophisticated appreciation of the world and we

> **CHECK IT OUT!** For more on "the problem of thought," read the following books by David Bohm:
> - *On Dialogue* (Routledge & Kegan Paul, 1996)
> - *Thought as a System* (Routledge, 1994)
> - *Wholeness and the Implicate Order* (Routledge & Kegan Paul, 1980)
>
> Also see the feature on the Theory of Health as Expanded Consciousness in Chapter 7 for more about Bohm's influence.

become more capable of seeing the holistic interdependence that unites all things. In a nutshell, we *are* diverse. But there is no "us" and "them." What affects one of us affects all of us.

So the best answer to the question "Why worry about diversity?" may be because, as humans, we're not very good at it. It takes effort. But the effort is worth it in terms of intellectual growth and awareness and in terms of improving the conditions within which we all live together. And open communication seems to be one of the main things we can do to overcome the gaps that differences can create.

With that in mind, let's start with a fundamental difference, socioeconomic status.

Status Differences

When high-status caregivers communicate with poor and illiterate patients, their life experiences are likely to be so different that they have a hard time understanding and warming up to each other. People of low **socioeconomic status** (a combined measure of such factors as income, education, and employment level) are consistently less satisfied with medical care than other people are (Becker & Newsom, 2003).

Research supports that misunderstandings occur for several reasons when caregivers interact with low-SES patients. First, low-SES patients typically ask fewer questions than others and reveal less about their health concerns (Fowler, 2006). This occurs despite evidence that they are typically more fearful about their health than most people and

---

💬 IN YOUR EXPERIENCE

■ Have you ever felt that you were regarded as having lower social status than a caregiver who was treating you?

■ If so, what cues gave you this impression?

■ What was the result?

■ What would have improved the situation?

---

are less able to judge the severity of their illnesses themselves (James et al., 2008).

Second, although low-SES patients are more likely than others to follow doctors' advice, they may not be receiving much information or guidance. In a study of nearly 6,000 patient interactions, physicians were more likely to discuss cancer screening with patients of high, rather than low, SES, particularly if the high-SES patients were well educated (Bao, Fox, & Escarce, 2007). For all tests except mammograms, doctors were twice as likely to discuss cancer screening with patients who were college graduates as with patients who had not finished high school. Race and ethnicity also played a factor. White and Black patients were significantly more likely than Hispanic or Asian patients to take part in detailed discussions with their doctors. Bao and colleagues speculate that the difference lies partly with patients and partly with doctors. Low-SES patients may initiate fewer discussions because they are not knowledgeable about the issues, they are intimidated by doctors, and/or cultural mores dissuade them from questioning their doctors. For their part, doctors may perceive (rightly or wrongly) that low-SES patients will not be interested in, or capable of understanding, details about their health.

Third, low-SES patients are less likely than others to benefit from written materials. About 1 in 2 adults in the United States is unable to read above an 8th-grade level (National Commission on Adult Literacy, 2008), and some adults who can read are not proficient in English. Some U.S. hospitals report a 300% increase in the number of Spanish-speaking patients since 1998 (Brice, Travers, Cowden, Young, Sanhueza, & Dunston, 2008). Worldwide, about 774 million adults (two-thirds of them women) cannot read (UNESCO, 2008). In the United States, literacy is a special challenge for non-English-speaking patients, many of whom cannot read medical consent forms or instructions on medications. Unlike other patients—who may be exposed to health information via pamphlets, cable television, newspapers, computers, and other means—low-income and literacy-challenged patients are likely to rely strictly on their doctors and on advice from people they know. (We'll talk more about language and health literacy in a bit.)

Fourth, it may be especially tricky to negotiate treatment decisions when patients have limited means. Physicians surveyed by Susannah Bernheim and associates (2008) said that, ideally, SES should not be a factor when making treatment decisions, but practically speaking it often *is*, because the patient's work schedule limits what he or she can do (for example, report for physical therapy three times a week), because some medications are too expensive for low-income patients to afford, and because it is difficult to find specialists or therapists who will care for patients of limited financial means. Said one doctor in the study:

> He [a patient] was a trucker . . . we really had to tailor the medication. He did not have any proper time to eat, and you know, he did not have time to come to his appointments. We have to tailor his appointments according to his travel schedule. It is not optimal, but we do the best we can. (p. 56)

In this and other ways, physicians surveyed say they do their best, but they are often constrained by factors outside their control (Bernheim, Ross, Krumholz, & Bradley, 2008).

Finally, preconceived notions can be a stumbling block to communication between caregivers and low-SES patients. Although we have been talking in generalities, there are immense differences among people who fall into the category of low SES. One group of low-income patients seems particularly dissatisfied with the quality of patient-caregiver communication—young people with low incomes but high literacy skills (Jensen, King, Guntzviller, & Davis, 2010). Evidence suggests that they expect to be actively engaged in medical talk and are disappointed when they feel rushed or belittled. They may be right in sensing prejudice. Many of the general practitioners whom Sara Willems and colleagues (2005) interviewed consider that people are impoverished mostly because they don't try hard enough to overcome their circumstances. Said one doctor: "They don't want to change their situation, . . . they are used to it. They no longer have the courage to change it" (p. 179). Physicians interviewed also tend to view low-SES patients as indifferent about staying healthy. As one doctor put it, "They are not interested in their health. They don't see the advantage of, for example, healthy food" (p. 180). Although these were common viewpoints, some doctors in the study *were* vigorous advocates of seeking care for impoverished patients and actively trying to help them improve their neighborhoods and living conditions (Willems, Swinnen, & De Maeseneer, 2005).

Health Literacy

About 90 million people in the United States suffer from health literacy challenges and the consequent health risks ("Health Literacy," 2003). Health literacy involves reading and understanding health information, but it's more than that. As defined by the World Health Organization (WHO), **health literacy** "represents the cognitive and social skills which determine the motivation and ability of individuals to gain access to, understand and use information in ways which promote and maintain good health" ("Health Promotion Glossary," 1998, p. 10). This definition emphasizes that it's not enough to read and write. To be literate about health, people must also:

- understand the language in which information is conveyed (be it English, Spanish, statistical jargon, legal talk, or some other language variant);
- have access to reliable and relevant information;
- be interested in health-related information;
- have the social skills to discuss health matters with others;
- have adequate hearing and/or vision to get the information;
- understand how to apply the information; and
- be willing and able to put health information to effective use.

Regarded in this way, it's clear that none of us is entirely health literate. Medical information is often baffling, even to well-educated individuals. A study by J. D. Power and Associates (2008) revealed that less than half (45%) of people across the United States fully understand their health plans. About 1 in

Literacy Challenges

FIGURE 6.1 In a study of nearly 6,000 people in the United States, more than half said they have trouble reading, they don't feel confident filling out medical forms, and they need someone to help them in the doctor's office or hospital (McBride & Cantor, 2010). As you might expect, these people are significantly less satisfied than other patients with the care they receive.

5 Americans is unable to read a prescription bottle, 1 in 2 cannot understand a medical brochure, and 3 in 5 cannot understand a consent form (AMA, 2003). Even people who read well may be hampered if they are not also able to do math, see and hear well, and speak and understand English proficiently. In a study of 24 older adults, more than 80% said they had had problems communicating with their doctors. The most frequent challenge (reported by 54% of the respondents) involved difficulty understanding spoken information. About 29% of the misunderstandings occurred because they had difficult seeing or hearing, and 21% because of difficulty remembering precise information (Hickman et al., 2009).

Emotions play a role as well. People who are otherwise highly literate may feel so overwhelmd by medical information that they cannot pay close attention to it. And sometimes information is so complex that people cannot be expected to understand it. When we consider that 8 in 10 people cannot understand a Medicaid application (AMA, 2003), it seems that the real problem is the form rather than the readers.

Low literacy is masked by embarrassment. People are often too ashamed to admit they can't read or understand medical information (Bernhardt & Cameron, 2003). Even friends and family members may not realize it. At a briefing to launch the AMA's new health literacy initiative, physician David W. Baker said:

We find that a lot of people have gone through their lives and listen to the radio, watch television and don't read their newspapers too often but can get by pretty well with minimal reading skills. . . . They come into the health care setting and they are all of a sudden faced with medications and instructions and all of this information written at too high a level for easy comprehension. (AMA, 2003, para. 7)

Embarrassment and frustration may discourage people with literacy challenges from pursuing medical care and may lead them to take medicine incorrectly, overlook health risk factors, and miss out on important information.

Unaddressed health literacy challenges contribute to worsening health and higher expenses. In the United States, costs incurred because of health literacy challenges are estimated at $106 billion to $238 billion a year (Vernon, Trujillo, Rosenbaum, & DeBuono, 2007). That's enough money to insure more than 40 million people.

About 90% of patients with literacy challenges say it would be helpful if their doctors understood their limitations (Wolf et al., 2007). Most people, even those with literacy challenges, are in favor of simple questionnaires that allow health care providers to identify people with reading and math challenges (B. Ferguson, Lowman, & DeWalt, 2011; Vangeest, Welch, & Weiner, 2010). An easy-to-use talking touch-screen program is being tested now for just such a purpose (Yost et al., 2010). Clearly, compassionate communication is required to help people with literacy challenges feel comfortable asking for help.

The American Medical Association (AMA) and cosponsors have launched *Ask Me 3,* an effort to minimize the literacy gap. *Ask Me 3* is a simple program that prepares patients to ask questions and seek clarification when they talk with medical professionals. People are encouraged to ask their doctors, nurses, and pharmacists these three questions:

• What is my main problem?
• What do I need to do?
• Why is it important for me to do this?

Simple and attractive *Ask Me 3* materials reassure people that "Everyone wants help with health information. You are not alone if you find things confusing at times." Handouts suggest options for patients who feel confused. For example, if they

"I practiced medicine in a rural coastal Alabama shrimping village. I saw first-hand . . . [that] health professionals cannot assume that everything we tell our patients is perfectly clear to them. Being health literate is just as important for clinicians as it is for patients."—Regina Benjamin, Surgeon General of the United States (AP Photo/ Jacquelyn Martin)

do not understand answers to the suggested questions, people are encouraged to say, "This is new to me. Will you please explain that one more time."

Other promising avenues include using interactive computer modules (some of them multilingual) and videos about treatment options so that people with literacy challenges can better understand the risks and benefits before they consent to undergo procedures (Bickmore et al., 2010; Jibaja-Weiss & Volk, 2007; Leeman-Castillo et al., 2007; Shue, O'Hara, Marini, McKenzie, & Schreiner, 2010). Because these formats present information both visually and verbally, they help overcome many communication barriers, particularly when designers take into account that some users will have limited reading and computer skills. The problem may be inducing people with literacy challenges to try them. Internet sites meant for people with literacy challenges tend to be used more by people who are already information rich than by people who find health communication challenging, perhaps because the latter have more limited access to computers and because they are less confident using them (Sarkar et al., 2010).

When we overcome access issues, the results can be extraordinary. An easy-to-understand training program for parents about treating children's minor health concerns resulted in 58% fewer emergency room visits, 42% fewer doctor visits, 29% fewer school-day absences, and 42% fewer work days missed by the primary caregiver (Herman & Jackson, 2010). The researchers estimate that each family in the study saved about $450 per year in health care expenses, and since more than 9,000 families were involved, the total savings were more than $5 million (Herman & Jackson, 2010).

Communication Skill Builder: Surmounting Status and Literacy Barriers

The unfortunate result of status-related communication barriers is that the neediest people often receive the least amount of information and attention. Experts offer the following ideas for improving communication between caregivers and people with health literacy challenges.

- *Caregivers: Be attentive and respectful.* Try to identify patients' needs and respect their contributions. Double-check patients' understanding of verbal information, listen attentively, and don't be put off by colloquialisms. In an article titled "All I Really Need to Know About Medicine I Learned from My Patients," physician Dwalia South (1997) says that most patients don't have large medical vocabularies. They describe unfamiliar lumps and bumps as "hickeys" and "doodads." Nonetheless, people know a lot about their own bodies, and smart caregivers take patients' knowledge seriously.
- *Caregivers: Let patients know what is expected.* Bochner (1983) suggests that low-SES patients

WHAT DO YOU THINK?

Experts point out that we all have literacy challenges to some extent. What factors might affect your ability to understand complex medical information?

may be tongue-tied by intimidation or may simply be unaware of what is expected of them. He encourages doctors to socialize patients into the medical context by explaining routines and encouraging them to participate in discussions.

- *Patients: Be explicit about feelings and questions.* Don't assume that caregivers understand your concerns. Instead, make an extra effort to express your feelings and questions. You can improve communication by overcoming your reluctance to speak up.

Now we'll look at a different type of diversity that affects us all.

Gender Differences

About 150 years ago, a father received a letter from his daughter, saying she wished to become a physician. He replied: "If you were a young man I could not find words in which to express my satisfaction and pride . . . but you are a woman, a weak woman; and all I can do for you now is to grieve and to weep. O my daughter! Return from this unhappy path. (Bonner, 1992, p. 11)

Well into the 1900s, many people believed that women lacked physical strength and intelligence and were too emotionally unstable to practice medicine (Bonner, 1992). Furthermore, they considered it scandalously immodest of women to touch and see portions of other people's bodies.

In this section we look at historical patterns that have restricted women's ability to serve as physicians until the last few decades. After that, we consider whether male and female caregivers communicate differently or not.

Women in Medicine

Women's involvement with medicine involves a fascinating history. In ancient cultures, women were

The first woman in the United States to receive a medical degree was Elizabeth Blackwell in 1849. She had to leave North America to find a hospital willing to host her clinical training, and when she returned to the states, she was forced to open her own clinic because no hospital would grant her privileges to practice. (Schlesinger Library, Radcliffe Institute, Harvard University)

considered skillful and intuitive healers, primarily because of their "cosmic link" to the earth and the birth of new life (Achterberg, 1991). During the Middle Ages, however, Christianity depicted women as the embodiment of original sin and decreed that church positions be restricted to men. Women who continued to practice healing arts were often regarded as heretics and witches. They were tortured and burned by the thousands when plagues ravaged Europe and women were accused of using witchcraft to spread the disease (Achterberg, 1991).

Women were further excluded from medicine during the sixteenth century with the advent of scientific medicine. Largely prohibited from academic pursuits, women were not seen as qualified caregivers because they lacked formal scientific knowledge

(Achterberg, 1991). By 1859, about 300 women had graduated from U.S. medical schools. However, they were denied privileges in established hospitals and were forced, instead, to open their own clinics and hospitals, specializing mostly in homeopathic and herbal medicine (Bonner, 1992). For centuries, virtually the only time female physicians were allowed to practice alongside men in the United States was when they were needed to treat soldiers on the battlefield.

As late as 1970, only 9% of medical students in the United States were female (Waalen, 1997). At that time the Women's Equity League filed a class action suit against all U.S. medical schools, accusing them of unfair discrimination. Continued efforts by women's groups and civil rights leaders led to affirmative actions laws, requiring schools and businesses to accept qualified minority applicants, including women.

Female representation increased substantially after that. By 2002, 44% of medical students in the United States were women ("Educational Programs," 2002). And for the first time, in 2005, there were as many female as male medical students in the United States. Their numbers have remained roughly equal in the years since then ("Diversity in Medical," 2008).

The story doesn't end there, however. Female physicians still make only 63% as much as their male counterparts ("Investigating," 2008), partly because women usually specialize in lower paying specialties such as pediatrics and family medicine and are vastly underrepresented in high-paying specialties such as neurosurgery, oncology, and cardiology. Female physicians are half as likely as males to be surgeons and twice as likely to be pediatricians (Magrane, Lang, Alexander, Leadley, & Bongiovanni, 2007, Table 2). Although female medical students perform as well as their male counterparts, women consistently underestimate their abilities because they receive less encouragement, have fewer role models, and endure more discrimination (Blanch, Hall, Roter, & Frankel, 2008). Gender inequities persist in medical school faculty positions as well. Women hold about 41% of entry-level professor positions in U.S. medical schools, but only 18% of the highest-ranking teaching positions (Leadley, 2009, p. 4). And male department chairs outnumber female chairs nearly 8 to 1 (Magrane et al., 2007, Table 9).

Sex Differences and Communication

Overall, research does not show dramatic differences between the way male and female caregivers communicate with patients. There are often slight differences, though, which are more as a matter of style than ability. For example, there is no significant difference in emotional intelligence between male and female medical students (Stratton, Saunders, & Elam, 2008), but female patients and female caregivers tend to be more nonverbally expressive in health care situations than men are, to engage in more partnership-building behaviors, and to reveal more personal information about themselves (Gabbard-Alley, 1995, 2000). Female caregivers also tend to display more interest in patients' life contexts and feelings, possibly because they are often trained to be primary caregivers (Christen, Alder, & Bitzer, 2008). Furthermore, women are more likely than men to attend medical school for the purpose of treating underserved people and to maintain that commitment until graduation and beyond (Crandall, Volk, & Loemker, 1993; Shannon, 2006).

Research in the United States indicates only slight differences between the preferences of male and female patients. Men typically have no strong preference concerning the sex of their doctors. Women indicate a slight preference for female caregivers and women's clinics (Bean-Mayberry et al., 2003; Piper, Shvarts, & Lurie, 2008), and women more often prefer caregivers (especially female caregivers) to communicate in a caring and compassionate manner (Schmid Mast, Hall, & Roter, 2007). These slightly different preferences may reflect gendered socialization and historic patterns of discrimination. Women are typically socialized to prefer affiliative communication in general, and, as patients, women are typically more wary than men of encountering sexist attitudes.

Unfortunately, even though things are improving, there is a long history of brushing aside women's health concerns. The phrase "hysterical" comes from the Latin word *hysterika*, meaning womb or uterus, and reflects a belief dating back to ancient Greece that women are overly emotional and histrionic, particularly where their health is concerned. Vestiges of that belief remain. A New Zealand study revealed that male doctors were more likely than female doctors to assume that female patients had

WHAT DO YOU THINK?

Does it matter to you whether the caregivers you see are male or female? Why or why not?

a hidden agenda and were exaggerating their symptoms. For their part, female patients were more timid when interacting with male doctors than with female ones. Again, familiarity seems to foster trust and openness (Gross et al., 2008).

Although women have historically been treated as less capable than men in health settings, female patients today are typically better informed about health issues than male patients are. This is probably because women are most often targeted as consumers, they utilize medical services more than men, and they typically feel more responsible for the health of family members ("Women Most Active," 2003).

Although we noted some differences between men and women here, it's important to note that gender may be less important than other factors in shaping how health professionals communicate. Medical socialization, professional constraints, and personal style mitigate some of the differences between male and female speech. Patients are sometimes surprised to find that there is actually less difference than they expect between the communication styles of male and female caregivers (Gorter, Bleeker, & Freeman, 2006).

In the next section we discuss **heterosexism**, the assumption that people's romantic relationships involve members of the opposite sex.

Sexual Orientation

In the article "Do Ask, Do Tell," physician Jennifer E. Potter (2002) asserts that gay and lesbian individuals often receive substandard care because doctors are not aware of, or misunderstand, their sexual orientation and behaviors. Potter recalls her own experience as a teenager, when, after telling her family physician that she was attracted to girls, he laughed it off as a "phase a lot of girls go through" (p. 341). Later, a psychiatrist tried to "cure" her of homosexual tendencies, and doctors urged her to use birth control, never considering that she might be sexually active with women rather than men. Although Potter regarded the prescription for the pill "absurd," previous experience told her to keep the truth to herself. Even as a student at Harvard Medical School, Potter says she was encouraged to keep her lesbianism secret.

Fear of social rejection can rob lesbian, gay, bisexual, transgender (LGBT) individuals of comfort and acceptance. Potter (2002) describes the temptation to "pass" as heterosexual: "On the face of it, maintaining silence makes almost everyone happy" (p. 342). But pretending to be heterosexual felt like lying by omission. She says that pretending to be someone she wasn't eroded her self-respect, unwittingly put her in cahoots with people who wished to ignore and invalidate homosexuality, and made her feel isolated. She could not introduce her long-term partner to friends or invite her to professional and social gatherings. Now, although Potter is open with her close friends and associates, some people still presume she is heterosexual. Although it may seem inappropriate or awkward to reveal her sexual orientation to new acquaintances, misunderstandings can make people feel embarrassed or deceived. Potter reflects: "Coming out is a process that never ends. Every time I meet someone new I must decide if, how, and when I will reveal my sexual orientation" (p. 342).

Discrimination is a particularly threatening possibility when one's health is at risk. For example, some gay women with cancer say they fear they will receive substandard care if they reveal their sexual orientation to their doctors (Matthews, 1998). However, keeping quiet presents risks as well. Although a vaccination against hepatitis A is recommended for men who have sex with men, a study in Birmingham, Alabama, revealed that only 34% of gay African American men there had been vaccinated (Rhodes, Yee, & Hergenrather, 2003). The researchers found that men who had open communication with their caregivers were more likely than others to be aware of the hepatitis risk and to seek the vaccination.

The tell-or-not dilemma may be especially difficult for older adults. A Canadian study revealed that homosexuality among older adults was largely ignored by society and by health care providers (Brotman, Ryan, & Cormier, 2003). Moreover, older adults who are homosexual may be especially

Reality Beats Prejudice

When Barney Frank announced in 2012 that he would not run for reelection after serving more than 30 years as a U.S. Representative, a reporter asked how he felt about being one of the first public officials to be openly gay. He replied:

> I think one of the great success stories in America is the extent to which we have overcome prejudice based on being lesbian or gay, bisexual, transgender. It's not completely gone but the end is in sight. And I am proud of my role in that. I think coming out was a big part of it because reality beats prejudice. (James, 2012, audio interview)

sensitive to societal stereotypes and lack of acceptance, although they may be in long-term relationships that are important to their happiness.

If partners are not married, they may be denied visiting privileges and information when one of them is sick or injured. Internist Suzanne Koven reflected on this in a recent column in the *Boston Globe*:

> Not long ago I fractured my shoulder and needed surgery. . . . My husband of 30 years did all the things a loving spouse would be expected to do: He fluffed my pillows and put toothpaste on my toothbrush (try doing that with one arm!) and overlooked my crankiness. . . . He spoke with the surgeon on my behalf; he signed

me out when I was discharged; health insurance through his employer covered my medical expenses. Right now, thousands of couples in the United States can't take these things for granted as we did. Lesbian and gay couples who are as deeply committed as my husband and I are, who've shared private jokes and dumb arguments, budget-making and childrearing just as we have, can't count on being able to fully support one another when one of them is ill or injured . . . The extent to which LGBT people are able to support their loved ones during illness is . . . crucial. (Koven, 2012, para. 1–3)

In the United States (although not in other countries), a disproportionate number of HIV/AIDS cases have occurred among homosexual males, adding to the stigma and stress they may already feel. In a study of homosexual couples in which one or both partners has HIV/AIDS, Haas (2002) found that primary relational partners provided the majority of support during the illness. Ignoring or minimizing the importance of these relationships can have serious consequences for people's coping abilities.

Caregivers who avoid talking about sexuality are not necessarily prejudiced against it. They may be embarrassed or uncomfortable with the subject or feel that it lies outside their expertise. Richard Gamlin (1999) proposes that nurses should strive to become more comfortable with their own sexuality and should use role-playing to gain experience talking about sexuality with patients. Caregivers who are comfortable discussing sexuality are more likely than others to help patients feel comfortable as well. In one study, adolescents said they think it's important for their caregivers to know their sexual history, and they are most comfortable revealing this information when caregivers ask about sexual issues directly (Rosenthal et al., 1999).

In summary, like everyone else, LGBT patients are adversely affected when they feel they cannot be open with their caregivers. As you will see in the next sections, a similar fear of discrimination influences people of different races.

Race

Racism can make you sick. That is the conclusion of studies linking race to everyday well-being,

IN YOUR EXPERIENCE

Have you ever felt unfairly discriminated against because of your sex, sexual orientation, appearance, race, gender, ability, or ethnicity in a health care setting or another situation? If so, how?

medical care, and life expectancy. As this section shows, people of nondominant races and ethnicities are at a disadvantage where health and longevity are concerned. We will look at those patterns, and then consider how racism has influenced health professionals.

Racism is discrimination based on a person's race. People belong to a certain race if they share a hereditary background or common descent, such as European or African (Merriam-Webster, 1999). Practically speaking, people often judge race by visible characteristics such as skin color. Because the Black/White distinction is so visible, it's the basis for a great deal of racism, with direct and indirect effects on health.

In the United States, race is associated with life expectancy. The average life span of an African American male is 71.8 years, which is nearly 7 years shorter than the overall male average in the United States (Murphy, Xu, & Kochanek, 2012). Likewise, African American women live an average of 78 years, which is more than 3 years shorter than the American average for women. The good news is that the disparity has shrunk in recent years. The bad news is that it still exists at all.

Research shows that the link between health and race is social rather than biological. In other words, people of minority status do not suffer ill health because of the genes they are born with but because of what occurs during their lifetimes (Bhopal, 1998).

Different Care and Outcomes

Race is linked to health and to health care. A 2003 report by the U.S. Institute of Medicine revealed that Hispanic Americans are twice as likely as others to die from diabetes, and African Americans are significantly more likely than others to die from cancer, heart disease, and AIDS (Smedley, Stith, & Nelson, 2003). Part of the reason is that

CHECK IT OUT! Healthy People 2020 is a nationwide program uniting the efforts of people across the United States. The goal is to reach key milestones by the year 2020, such as reducing health disparities, tobacco use, and obesity, and improving personal health and environmental conditions. The program is sponsored by the U.S. Department of Health and Human Services.

■ To watch a brief video about the program, visit http://www.youtube.com/watch?v=IJzSxm45b18.

■ The Healthy People 2020 website is available at http://www.healthypeople.gov/2020.

they receive different care. For example, African Americans are less likely than European Americans to receive advanced cardiac therapy while they recover from heart attacks (Peterson et al., 2008). Similarly, in an extensive study of more than 20,000 people with cancer in the head or neck, Molina and colleagues (2008) found that White patients lived an average of 40 months, compared to 21 months for African Americans. The difference was significant even when researchers controlled for age, income, and other health concerns.

Only slightly more promising is evidence that Black patients live about as long as White patients (approximately 6 years) following their first hospitalization for heart failure (Croft et al., 1999). However, Black patients are typically younger than White patients, so, although their response to initial treatment is roughly the same, they experience ill health sooner in their lives and often die at a younger age.

Explanations

There are several explanations of why people of different races seem to receive different medical care and may respond differently to it. Overall, differences seem rooted in distrust, high risk, lack of knowledge, limited access, and ineffective patient–caregiver communication.

DISTRUST

People of color are less likely to pursue medical attention than others because they distrust the medical establishment. This is based largely on historic

patterns of discrimination such as the Tuskegee Syphilis Study described in Chapter 4 (Meredith, Eisenman, Rhodes, Ryan, & Long, 2007). In the United States, members of racial and ethnic minorities are more likely than European Americans to feel that their doctors fail to listen, to show respect, and to explain things clearly ("Doctor–Patient Communication by Race/Ethnicity," 2008). About 14% of Asian Americans feel this way, 12% of Hispanic Americans, and 11% of African Americans—compared to 9% of non-Hispanic White Americans.

Distrust may cause people to underutilize health services and to doubt the validity of medical advice (Armstrong et al., 2008). This could contribute to the comparatively low number of medical interventions among African Americans and Hispanics. They may be approved for prescriptions they never fill and may decline to undergo medical procedures if they distrust their doctors' judgment. Or they may never see a doctor at all.

HIGH RISK, LOW KNOWLEDGE

A second explanation is that members of minority races are not well informed about health issues even though they are often at high risk for them. African American men are significantly less knowledgeable about prostate cancer warning signs than White men in the United States, although African American men are twice as likely to die of prostate cancer (Weinrich et al., 2007). Members of minority races may also be at high risk for disease because a disproportionate number of them are of low socioeconomic status. With limited resources, they may suffer from poor living conditions, unhealthy diets, and insufficient access to health information and health services (Baldwin, 2003). For example, people with limited resources are often forced to live in violent and polluted neighborhoods (Ahmed, Mohammed, & Williams, 2007).

Health risks are greater, partly because of the stress of dealing with negative social feedback. A survey of Black, White, Hispanic, and Asian individuals shows that ill health is higher among people who are subjected to everyday discrimination such as poor service, insults, and being treated as inferior or stupid (Gallo, Smith, & Cox, 2006).

Despite their high-risk status, members of minority races may be relatively unaware of health issues because, on average, they don't use or trust mainstream media as much as White audiences and because many health messages are not designed to appeal to minority audiences. Individuals who are not well informed about health services and disease warning signs are more likely than others to become seriously ill before they seek medical attention (Ferguson et al., 1998). If African Americans are sicker than others when they seek medical care, that factor might explain (in part) why they don't respond to treatment as well and why they don't undergo the same procedures as other patients.

ACCESS

A third explanation is that members of minority groups have comparatively low access to advanced medical facilities. In the United States, more than 3 out of 4 uninsured residents do not undergo recommended health screenings (Cantor, Schoen, Belloff, How, & McCarthy, 2007). Table 6.1 shows health statistics related to race and ethnicity. As you can see, infant mortality rates are dramatically higher among African Americans than among other groups, and Hispanic Americans are more than twice as likely as White Americans to be uninsured and to lack a regular source of medical care (Cantor et al., 2007).

Individuals with low incomes may not qualify for care in high-tech medical centers, and such centers are not likely to be located in impoverished neighborhoods. Consequently, residents of these neighborhoods are less likely than others to end up in hospitals that offer advanced-care treatments such as bypass surgery and chemotherapy. Even

emergency response time may differ by social class. Canadian researchers report that residents of affluent neighborhoods usually get quicker ambulance service than people in poor neighborhoods and that the best paramedic crews are typically dispatched to rich neighborhoods (Govindarajan & Schull, 2003).

Moreover, patients who cannot pay their initial medical bills may be discouraged from seeking further care. Sora Chung (2008) says she's seen patients who felt they couldn't see their doctors because they still owed $25 on their bills. And the access gap grows. Between 500 and 1,000 physicians in the United States have converted to **concierge medical practices**, which offer better-than-average patient–staff ratios and longer exam times, but only to patients who can afford to pay more than their insurance will cover. Concierge practices are one way around the frustrating limitations and reimbursement tables of managed care, and the special attention is nice for patients who can afford it, but many worry that out-of-pocket services will widen the gap between the health rich and the health poor (Lowes, 2008a). In short, low-income individuals may receive care that is less advanced and less personalized because the medical facilities available to them do not offer it.

PATIENT–CAREGIVER COMMUNICATION

Finally, medical care may differ because of poor communication across racial and ethnic lines. In a study of pediatricians and parents (Brown, Ueno,

Table 6.1 **U.S. Statistics Relevant to Health Care, Race, and Ethnicity**

	Percentage of Members in Each Category Who Fit the Description at Left		
	WHITE AMERICANS	**BLACK AMERICANS**	**HISPANIC AMERICANS**
Uninsured	13.2%	19.3%	34%
Have not visited a doctor in 2 years	17%	9.4%	18.7%
Needed to see a doctor in last year but were unable to afford it	11%	18.9%	17.9%
Over age 50 who did not undergo recommended health screening	58.1%	63.8%	64.3%
Without a usual source of medical care	17.2%	22.5%	35%
Infant mortality per 1,000 live births	5.9	13.7	6.3

Source: The Commonwealth Fund Commission on a High Performance Health System (Cantor, Schoen, Belloff, How, & McCarthy, 2007)

Smith, Austin, & Bickman, 2007), when parents and doctors were of the same race, they shared more laughter during the exam. When they were of the same gender, the parents asked more biomedical questions than other patients. And when doctors and parents were both highly educated, they shared more laughter, more expressions of concern, more self-disclosure, and more biomedical information. The authors speculate that similarities increased the participants' sense of comfort and affinity.

However, patients and caregivers may be uncomfortable with people who are different from them, may misinterpret communication cues, or may allow stereotypes to interfere with their judgment. Members of racial and ethnic minorities often feel that medical personnel are reluctant to implement costly procedures they might use to treat other patients. An African American participant in Meredith Grady and Tim Edgar's (2003) study remembers being diagnosed with diabetes and the diagnosing physician's reaction:

> He said, "I need to write this prescription for these pills, but you'll never take them and you'll come back and tell me you're still eating pig's feet and everything. . . . Then why do I still need to write this prescription?" And I'm like, "I don't eat pig's feet." (p. 393)

The patient was left to wonder how the doctor's prejudicial assumptions affected other decisions as well.

The idea that stereotypes affect physicians' judgment is supported by research. Some 55% of doctors surveyed say they believe White patients receive better care than minority patients, and nearly 2 out of 3 have personally witnessed such episodes ("Physicians Are Becoming," 2005). When Clara Manfredi and colleagues (2010) studied 248 African American and 244 European American cancer patients, they found that, all else being equal, the Black patients were less often referred to cancer specialists than the White patients were (Manfredi, Kaiser, Matthews, & Johnson, 2010). It's a familiar theme. A decade earlier, Schulman and colleagues (1999) videotaped actor/patients describing chest pains using the same words and gestures, wearing identical clothing (hospital gowns), in the same setting. The patients differed only in terms of age, sex, and race. Doctors who viewed the patients' videotaped presentations of symptoms were significantly more likely to recommend heart catheterization for White male patients than for female or Black patients. This suggests that—all other things being equal—racial and sexist stereotypes do influence physicians' judgments. These stereotypes are likely to affect how doctors perceive patients' conditions and the treatment they recommend. (See Box 6.2 for a discussion of ethical principles when allocating health resources.)

In summary, research shows that racism affects health and health care in varying degrees depending on the level of patients' trust, their knowledge and health risk, access to medical information and services, and stereotypes affecting patient–caregiver communication. Many of these issues can be addressed with more effective communication. Verbal and nonverbal signs of acceptance are appreciated. In one study, African American and Latino American patients said they felt more comfortable with caregivers who had culturally sensitive artwork, reading material, and music in their offices (Tucker et al., 2003).

A new type of discrimination—based on health conditions that haven't even surfaced yet—may loom ahead. See Box 6.3 for information about the pros and cons of genetic testing.

Racial Diversity Among Health Professionals

In the context of overcoming health disparities, it is germane to consider that the racial and ethnic diversity of America is underrepresented in the health professions. Although African Americans and Hispanic Americans together make up 30% of the U.S. population, only 9% of the country's physicians and 6% of registered nurses (RNs) are from these groups (Boukus, Cassil, & O'Malley, 2009; "Minority Nursing Statistics," 2009; U.S. Census Bureau, 2011b). It is a regrettable imbalance because, for one thing, caregivers from underrepresented groups are often more willing and more capable of serving people in those communities.

Let's take a closer look at racial integration in health care.

HISTORIC PATTERNS OF ACCEPTANCE

Well into the 1960s, African Americans were barred from most hospitals in the United States (Cassedy,

BOX 6.2 ETHICAL CONSIDERATIONS

Who Gets What Care?

Doctor, do everything you can!

Is it ever justified for a doctor to do less than everything possible? Conventional American wisdom says no. Americans have come to expect that physicians will provide the best possible care, cost notwithstanding. However, it has become too expensive to do everything possible for every person.

For example, after Oregon officials decided to remove organ transplants from the list of procedures covered by Medicaid, media stories abounded about people who were being allowed to die. One of the highest profile cases was 7-year-old Colby Howard, whose life depended on a $100,000 bone marrow transplant. His family went public asking for donations, and they raised $700,000, but Colby died before they could raise enough. Floyd McCay, a spokesperson for the Oregon governor's office at the time, said:

> We are rationing health care on the basis of price. The state shouldn't have to pay for these things to begin with. But as long as they are forced to make decisions, you will have children with names and faces that will die or have severe difficulties. (quoted by Egan, 1988, para. 10)

An Oregon physician explained that, for the price of one organ transplant, the state could fund prenatal care for about 25 pregnant women, an investment with broader implications and the potential to avoid expensive care for premature and unhealthy newborns.

Many people feel that if the U.S. health system is to survive, it is necessary to make judgments about who gets what care. Health care leaders are being called on to eliminate excessive and unnecessary procedures. The question is: *Where is the line between necessary and unnecessary?*

One option is to provide care to those people who can afford it. This option places underprivileged persons at a disadvantage and may create a deeper schism between people of high and low socioeconomic status. All in all, few people are willing to allow low-income citizens to suffer in ill health.

Another option is to give priority to procedures that are known to have high success rates. For instance, a procedure that gives patients a 30% chance of survival may be granted priority over one with a 20% survival rate. This seems logical, but it's difficult to allow patients to go untreated when there is even a 1 in 5 chance of saving their lives. As Norman Levinsky (1995) points out, statistics are merely generalizations, and every patient is unique. There is no guarantee that a risky procedure will fail or that a tried-and-true one will succeed. Moreover, statistics vary, and sticking with well-established procedures diminishes the chances of developing new, better ones.

Still another option is to provide care for people who are likely to enjoy the highest quality of life as a result. From that perspective, it might be more important to fund expensive treatment to help a young child walk than to help an 85-year-old use his legs again following a stroke. Levinsky (1995) warns that such judgment calls are likely to lead to unfair discrimination. He wonders how it is possible to judge people's quality of life, and warns that such judgments are likely to be biased against people who hold values different from those of the medical decision maker.

As you can see, deciding how health resources will be allocated is no simple matter. To get an idea of how difficult it is, try answering the following questions.

WHAT DO YOU THINK?

1. If one person can afford expensive treatment but another cannot, is it okay to refuse care to the less affluent person?
2. If there is a slight chance that an expensive experimental drug will prolong a dying person's life, should the insurance company or health organization pay for use of the drug?
3. If two patients suffer from the same condition, should they be treated differently? What if one is a child and one is very old? What if one is famous and the other is unknown? What if one is homeless and the other is a community leader?
4. If you could fund only two of the following procedures, which would you choose? On what criteria would you base your choices?

a. Surgery to help an infertile couple conceive a child

b. Plastic surgery to improve the appearance of a person born with a facial deformity

c. Chemotherapy for a very sick person

d. Drug therapy that might prevent a person from getting AIDS

5. Who should decide which care will be funded? Doctors? Funding agencies? Community members? Patients? Legislators?

6. If research is able to develop improved treatment options but the cost of the research significantly raises health care costs, should the system continue to fund research? What if higher costs mean some people will lose their insurance?

7. Doctors say one reason they over-treat patients is because they may be sued for malpractice if they don't do everything possible. How would you resolve this dilemma?

BOX 6.3

Genetic Profiling: A View into Your Health Future

The crystal ball says you will live a long and healthy life.

It's hard to put much stock in such a prediction. But scientists have come up with something better. They did it by unlocking the codes that make up our genetic blueprints. To understand how, let's review some basic biology.

The cells in our bodies are home to DNA (deoxyribonucleic acid) molecules. Sequences of DNA, called *genes*, serve as a living instruction book for cellular activity. Genes determine our eye color and other physical features we inherit from our parents, how our bodies react to the environment, how we metabolize food, what diseases we're likely to get during our lifetime, and more. There are 20,000 to 25,000 genes in the human body.

In 2003, scientists around the world completed the Human Genome Project, a 13-year odyssey during which they catalogued nearly all of the genes and chemical base pairs (about 3 billion of them) in the human body ("Human Genome," 2008). For example, the gene Zbtb7 (rather cleverly code named Pokémon) enables other cells to become cancerous, but when inactive, it seems to inhibit cancer (Maeda et al., 2005). Scientists are still investigating what makes genes such as this one seem to turn on and off.

Sophisticated knowledge of genetics better enables medical scientists to look into our future—or at least the future to which we are genetically predisposed. For example, you might have genetic testing done early in life to find out if you're predisposed to various forms of cancer, liver disease, Alzheimer's disease, or other conditions known to have a genetic link. Being predisposed to these diseases doesn't mean you'll necessarily get them. In fact, that's the main promise of genetic testing. You might find out in time to lower your odds. For example, you might engage in more preventive behaviors if you know you are at high risk. Your doctor might start screening you for the identified conditions earlier than usual and, in some cases, begin preventive therapies. Focusing on genes might also help medical scientists design new ways of treating and preventing diseases.

RELIGIOUS PERSPECTIVE

But there are potential downsides. For one, some people see genetic testing as overstepping the boundaries between science and religious faith. In a series of focus groups, participants expressed a great deal of ambivalence about the issue. Some participants who believe in God said they feel that God's role ends at creating the genes that make a person unique; therefore genetic testing is not contradictory to their values. But some focus group members were openly apprehensive that, in deciphering the genetic code, scientists are "trying to do God's work" or "making changes to something that you are not supposed to be bothering" (Harris, Parrott, & Dorgan, 2004, p. 112). Participants were especially inclined to feel this way if they believed that God plays a role in illness and healing to the extent of changing a person's genetic structure after birth and/or if they feared that genetic profiling would be used to identify some people as worthier or superior to others (Harris et al., 2004).

Another conflict between genetics and some people's religious faith lies in scientists' efforts to chart human history through genetic markers. In a *National Geographic* article titled "The Ultimate Family Tree" (2005), scientists with the Genographic Project describe genetic evidence that they believe links people around the world to African ancestors 60,000 years ago. Some people consider this evolutionary perspective contradictory to their religious beliefs.

For the most part, however, people seem not to consider genetic profiling to be a direct challenge to religion. After a survey of 858 people, a research team led by Roxanne Parrott (2004) concluded that respondents' religious faith did not predict most people's attitudes about genetic testing. Media exposure was a more powerful antecedent. Religious faith was not wholly irrelevant, however, because intrinsic religiosity (the degree to which an individual bases his or her worldview on religious beliefs) is often related to the type of media that person uses and trusts. The researchers suggest continued investigation to better understand the overlap between religion and health (Parrott, Silk, Krieger, Harris, & Condit, 2004).

FEARS OF DISCRIMINATION

Another reservation concerning genetic testing is people's fear that the results will be used against them or their family members. So great is this fear that scientists sometimes have a hard time finding participants for research projects on the subject (Hudson, Holohan, & Collins, 2008). The issue is likely to become even more prominent when genetic testing is made available to the public.

To help ease those fears, U.S. lawmakers approved the Genetic Information Nondiscrimination Act of 2008 (better known as GINA). GINA stipulates that health insurance companies cannot refuse health coverage on the basis of genetic test results, nor can they require people to undergo genetic testing. By extension, GINA rules out informal genetic profiling, such as basing a person's insurance rates on a family history of heart disease. In the past, health insurance companies could figure family history into the price of your coverage. GINA now forbids that practice.

GINA also stipulates that employers cannot judge job applicants or current employees on the basis of genetic profiles. That is, they cannot hire, fire, promote, or refuse to promote anyone because of genetic propensities. Nor can employers require, request, or purchase genetic test results on any employee. (This doesn't apply to tests designed to monitor the effects of workplace exposure to dangerous materials. Those are still allowed.)

"GINA is the first major new civil rights bill of the new century," said Senator Edward Kennedy, a cosponsor of the bill, along with Olympia Snow (quoted by Hudson, Holohan, & Collins, 2008, para. 6). Many applaud the forward-thinking nature of the legislation, which was passed before the issue became a widespread concern.

It is important to note what GINA does not cover, however. The stipulations don't apply to life insurance, long-term care insurance, or disability insurance. And GINA doesn't apply to the U.S. military, the Veterans Administration, or Indian Health Services, because they are governed by a different set of laws.

WHAT DO YOU THINK?

1. If it were affordable, would you undergo genetic testing? Why or why not?

2. Are you worried that genetic test results may be used to discriminate unfairly against individuals or groups of people? Why or why not?

3. Suppose your test results show a genetic propensity for a disease that, so far, we don't know how to prevent. Would you want to know? Why or why not?

4. Do you think genetic test results would strengthen your resolve to engage in healthy behaviors?

Jocelyn Elders, the first African American U.S. Surgeon General, served in 1993 and 1994. (AP Photo/Dennis Cook)

1991). They could neither be treated nor practice medicine alongside White citizens. Members of other minorities were also discouraged from becoming doctors and often had little in common with the physicians they were allowed to consult.

Of necessity, African Americans formed their own medical societies and hospitals.

By 1910 the United States was home to nearly 100 hospitals and 7 medical schools catering to African American citizens (Duffy, 1979). Denied membership in the AMA and other medical societies, African American doctors formed their own. In 1895 they founded the National Medical Association. (The organization remains active with a current membership of 30,000).

African American hospitals and universities suffered from meager funding and harsh criticism. Not until the 1960s did the United States implement affirmative action laws and ban segregation in federally funded hospitals. No longer would federal money be used to build "separate but equal" facilities (Duffy, 1979). (See Box 6.4 for more on affirmative action.)

There have been some signs of increased acceptance. In the 1990s, Jocelyn Elders became the first African American U.S. Surgeon General, and her successor, David A. Satcher, became the second. In the same decade, the AMA inaugurated its first female president, Nancy W. Dickey. But even then, following decades of racist policies, less than one-third of minority doctors in the United States were AMA members (Foubister, 1997).

In 2008, the AMA issued a formal apology for its history of racial discrimination. Ronald Davis (2008) wrote on behalf of the association, remarking that, "the AMA failed, across the span of a century, to live up to the high standards that define the noble profession of medicine" (p. 323). He concluded:

> The medical profession must have diversity in the physician workforce—equivalent to that in the general population—and equity in health care delivery for all persons. . . . To some, whether looking back or looking forward, attaining equality of opportunity in medicine may seem an audacious goal, but it is not optional for the medical profession. It is within reach, and the nation will celebrate the day when racial harmony is achieved in health care for the benefit of patients, communities, and the medical profession. (p. 325).

COMMUNICATION EFFECTS

Physicians from underserved groups are usually well qualified to care for minority patients and more willing than their peers to provide such care. About 48.7% of minority medical students say they will provide care for the underserved, compared to 18.8% of White students, and 16.2% of students from non-White minority groups who are already well represented in medicine (mostly Asian Americans and Americans with ancestry from India, Pakistan, and the Pacific Islands) (Saha, Guiton, Wimmers, & Wilkerson, 2008). And contact with diverse classmates seems to help others become more sensitive to cultural differences as well. Medical students whose classmates are highly

BOX 6.4 ETHICAL CONSIDERATIONS

Is Affirmative Action Justified or Not?

Everyone wants the best doctor possible. The question is whether race and ethnicity have a place in that equation. Based on civil rights legislation passed in the 1960s, state *affirmative action* laws require publicly funded universities to give preference to minority applicants who meet admission requirements. Contrary to what many believe, affirmative action does not require acceptance of unqualified persons, nor does it set quotas requiring a certain number or percentage of minority members. Institutions are under no obligation to accept individuals who do not meet qualifications. However, if minority applicants meet the established criteria for admittance, they may be chosen even if nonminority applicants also meet or exceed the criteria. Affirmative action is meant to offset historic patterns of discrimination that have limited opportunities for women and minorities and have resulted in them being significantly underrepresented in professional positions.

Controversy over affirmative action escalated when nonminority applicants who met (or exceeded) the minimum requirements for medical school admission were passed over in favor of minority candidates. In 2003, after three White students sued because they were not accepted into the University of Michigan, the U.S. Supreme Court ruled that the university can give minority applicants special consideration, but it cannot continue its policy of granting minority candidates a portion of the points needed for a favorable admission review (Newbart & Grossman, 2003).

Opponents of affirmative action argue that prospective doctors should be chosen only on the basis of their academic qualifications. In 1996 the California Board of Regents banned state schools from considering the race and ethnicity of university applicants. Courts in Texas did the same after White students sued because they were denied admission to the University of Texas law school. In 1999 Florida governor Jeb Bush removed race from consideration in state university admission programs, effectively ending affirmative action in that state's higher education system. Mississippi, Washington, and Louisiana have followed suit. The number of minority applicants to medical schools in those states has dropped 17%, compared to a 7% drop in other states (AMA Minority, 2008).

People who favor affirmative action argue that the public is poorly served by physicians who do not reflect the diversity of the overall population. Research shows that exposure to diverse classmates helps doctors become more open-minded and aware of cultural differences. For example, medical students at Harvard and the University of California agreed that sharing classes with diverse students helped them become better doctors (Whitla et al., 2003). And minority caregivers are especially willing and able to serve minority patients who are currently least served by medicine and most at risk for health problems (Mitka, 1996).

WHAT DO YOU THINK?

1. Do you feel medical schools should consider sex, race, and ethnicity when reviewing applicants? Why or why not?
2. How do you respond to the argument that affirmative action sometimes allows people to be accepted into medical school even though others' credentials are higher?
3. How do you respond to the argument that affirmative action is needed to help the medical profession more closely reflect the concerns and backgrounds of patients?

diverse are 33% more likely than others to feel confident in their ability to care for minority patients and 44.2% more likely to advocate equitable care for everyone (Saha et al., 2008).

As it stands, patients from minority races and ethnic groups in the United States are likely to be treated by doctors whose backgrounds are different from their own. Levy (1985) observes that physicians may be more critical of, and less comfortable with, patients of another race. Or they may be overly paternal or condescending. Caregivers may also under- or overestimate cultural differences

WHAT DO YOU THINK?

■ After reading about historical patterns of prejudice in health care, what do you think about the current system?

■ Have you ever felt discriminated against as a patient, student, or professional? If so, how?

■ Do you have a preference for the race, ethnicity, or sex of caregivers? If so, why?

(Daly, Jennings, Beckett, & Leashore, 1995). As a result, they may consider behavior abnormal because it doesn't conform to their expectations or may perceive unhealthy irregularities as mere cultural differences. Caregivers may not be aware that they are acting differently or offensively. However, members of minority groups may be especially sensitive to communication that seems disrespectful or dismissive, as they usually fear discrimination or humiliation more than most people (Levy, 1985).

Language Differences

Every day, I jotted [Spanish] vocabulary words on index cards and studied them before each shift. Commuting to work, I recited road signs and license plate numbers in Spanish. I even rolled my Rs.

—PHYSICIAN HAROLD JENKINS (2008, P. 42)

Spanish-speaking nurses have encouraged Jenkins. They're not put off that he can only speak in the present tense and that his pronunciation is sometimes a bit off. (One nurse was amused when Jenkins asked a patient to "vacuum deeply" instead of inhaling.) They give him a thumbs-up for trying. His patients appreciate the effort as well. Jenkins says he feels like a better doctor when he can understand and speak at least a bit of the patients' language.

He's right. It's hard to offer quality care across a language gap. A physician at Maimonides Medical Center in New York asserts:

It is great training for your young residents to understand that when you walk up to a person from another country who speaks another language, that is a risk—period. It's as much of a risk factor as diabetes or anything else . . . if you had an internal point system to admit the patient, you should add 25% of risk. (quoted by Salamon, 2008, para. 5)

Cognizant of the risk, Maimonides employs more than 30 patient representatives who help families and interpret when needed. And medical center president and CEO Pamela Brier has implemented a "Code of Mutual Respect," complete with staff training sessions on communication and diversity appreciation. The extra effort is worth it, says Brier:

Communication problems are what cause mishaps that can harm patients. I mean communications between doctor and nurse, nurse and clerk, housekeeper to nurse or doctor, everybody. The idea of the "Code of Mutual Respect" for me was to make the place safer and medical care better. (quoted by Salamon, para. 9)

It is her conviction that good communication is good medicine and good business.

Nearly 21 million people in the United States don't speak or understand English proficiently (Gany & Ngo-Metzger, 2008). Non-English speakers are predictably less satisfied than others with medical care (Weech-Maldonado et al., 2003). (Box 6.5 describes the experiences of a Spanish-speaking woman in a U.S. hospital.)

Language barriers can be frustrating for patients and caregivers. It's difficult to make an accurate diagnosis if the caregiver can't fully understand what the patient is experiencing. And even if the diagnosis is correct, it's hard to ensure that patients are fully informed concerning their medical options.

For the most part, the U.S. health system has not kept pace with the rising number of Spanish-speaking residents. At one urban children's hospital, 68% of residents speak little or no Spanish, yet most say they care for patients with limited English proficiency "often" or "every day" (O'Leary, Federico, & Hampers, 2003). Most of the residents feel that Spanish-speaking families understand the diagnosis only "sometimes" or "never," and 80% of the residents say they avoid caring for these patients whenever possible.

In many medical settings, family members and bilingual employees fill in as untrained interpreters.

BOX 6.5 PERSPECTIVES

Language Barriers in a Health Care Emergency

Picture yourself in Mexico at a hospital trying to get someone, anyone, to help make a terrible pain in your stomach go away. You hear: "Tu no hablas Español, y nadien te puede entender." In other words, "You don't speak Spanish, and no one can understand you." Finally, you find a first-year English student, a schoolboy, who attempts to translate. Next, you find yourself in a room, half-clothed, wearing a hospital robe, wondering: Did the boy understand me? Did the doctors understand him? What is wrong with me? What is happening?

Perhaps this will give you some idea what it's like for Spanish speakers in the United States health care system. This is a true story about my mother, Maria, and her mother, Consuelo, Cuban Americans trying to deal with the frustrations, anxieties, and fears of communicating with medical professionals who speak a different language.

THE STORY

Consuelo had been showing symptoms for some time before finally agreeing to see a doctor. Now that she had moved to a new city with little to no Hispanic culture, she wondered fearfully if she would be able to communicate with doctors. But this time the pain was intense, and at least she had her daughter, Maria, to help her communicate. Consuelo wanted very much to be understood, and maybe this time she would be. That thought finally gave her the courage to see a doctor.

At the doctor's office Consuelo could tell something was wrong. She was now in her early 60s and knew her diabetes was not getting any better. She understood enough of the conversations between the doctors and her daughter to gather that she needed a heart catheterization. Maria was not giving her all the details, but Consuelo could sense from her body language that the procedure was serious. She was right. A few moments later she found herself being wheeled off to the operating room for an emergency catheterization—without Maria. Now she felt more scared and afraid, knowing she had no means of communicating with the people around her and unsure what they were doing or why.

Before the procedure the surgeon needed Consuelo to understand the process and answer some questions. This was no easy task. Once again, as Consuelo had feared, she was unable to communicate. By this time, she began feeling extremely anxious and frustrated that neither the surgeon nor any of his assistants could understand what she was saying. Finally, after what seemed decades, the surgeon summoned Maria to the operating room after finding no one else who could translate.

For Maria, the experience involved mixed emotions. She had accompanied her mother many times before to the hospital but had never been allowed inside the operating room. Now that she was there, she felt more anxious than ever. First, she wanted to do a good job because she felt her mother's life depended on it. Second, she felt uneasy being in the room because she was unfamiliar with the environment. Consequently, Maria did not know how she should act, what she should say, or what was expected of her. She also had to fight her emotional reactions at seeing her mother on the operating table. However, Maria was relieved to be able to be with her mother and decided to concentrate on positive feelings to get them both through the experience.

When Consuelo was back in a hospital room after the procedure, the doctor broke the news that Consuelo needed open-heart surgery and would soon be transferred to a larger hospital. Once again, Consuelo could tell something negative was being conveyed, but knew she would have to wait until the conversation was over to get the full story from Maria. Waiting only added to her anxiety. A few times, Consuelo tried to interrupt, but was only chastised by Maria for interfering with her efforts to understand the implications of what the doctor was trying to tell her.

Unfortunately, although the larger hospital was located within a predominantly Hispanic community, few doctors and nurses there could speak Spanish. That meant that Maria and her husband, Jesus, would have to take turns staying at the hospital to translate for Consuelo. But the difference in Consuelo's outlook was remarkable. After only a few hours in the new hospital, she started to feel better about herself and less depressed. This was because the new physicians, regardless of whether they spoke Spanish or not, attempted to speak to her in Spanish and to understand what she was saying. Consuelo recalled one young physician who would walk into her room saying, "Buenos dias," bringing a smile to her face, and then leave saying, "Buenas noches," despite the time of day, making her laugh. These small gestures made all the difference to Consuelo.

Maria noticed that her mother began to light up whenever a doctor entered the room. She also noted that the doctors were no longer looking at her but talking directly to her mother instead. Maria was still translating, but she was no longer the focus of their conversation. In return, she noticed that her mother seemed more attentive and willing to follow the doctors' advice. A few times, Consuelo even answered the physicians in English with responses such as "Yes" when she understood what they were saying. This in turn would make them laugh and rub her hand as a sign of acceptance and reward. And if this were not enough, Consuelo was introduced to a Spanish-speaking nurse at the hospital who would occasionally visit, making her feel even more at home.

The surgery went well, but following it, Consuelo was paired with a therapist who could not speak Spanish and made no effort to communicate with her. She began to feel depressed and frustrated again. But she learned to get over this new obstacle quickly after talking about her feelings with her family. They found a way to make her realize that her good experiences at the new hospital far outweighed the bad ones, and soon Consuelo was able to ignore the therapist's behavior and move on with her treatment.

Consuelo was in the hospital for about a month. In that time she learned a lot about what she liked and did not like. As a result, she asked Maria to help her look for doctors who would be as attentive with her as the hospital doctors had been. Now Consuelo has at least one doctor she likes very much who speaks Spanish.

— MARIE

WHAT DO YOU THINK?

1. How might you have acted if you were Consuelo? If you were Maria?
2. Do you think hospitals should do more to accommodate non-English speakers? Why or why not?
3. How could Consuelo have eliminated some of her anxiety?
4. What could the first surgeon have done to help both Maria and Consuelo feel more at ease?
5. Researchers have found that people are more fearful about medical visits if they feel socially alienated and disconnected from their environments. What might we do to ease these feelings?
6. Have you ever been in a situation in which you have had to communicate with someone who did not speak the same language as you? How did you handle the situation?

It's not uncommon for members of the housekeeping staff to do most of the interpreting, although they may speak English poorly themselves and have little knowledge of medical terminology. Even interpreters who are fluent in both languages may have a hard time fully conveying the speakers' tone and intent. Sometimes a direct translation isn't easy or possible. For example, exclamations such as "okey dokey," "geez," and "oh boy" are used to convey more than their literal meaning. They may be meant to express sympathy, claim or relinquish a turn at talk, encourage the other person to go on, call attention to something, or so on, but their intended meaning can easily be lost in translation (Vickers & Goble, 2011).

In a South African study involving interpreters between English-speaking pharmacists and people with HIV who speak Setswana or Sesotho, the participants were happy with interactions in which interpreters not only translated what was said, but, when appropriate, clarified wording that might easily be misunderstood, acted as advocates for clients, or just stood by to make sure the participants understood each other when they communicated without translation (Watermeyer, 2011). At least one customer was frustrated, however, when she felt left out of the conversation, as if the pharmacist were talking to the interpreter rather than to her. She waived off the interpreter and chose to speak for herself as best she could. Watermeyer concluded that "one size" does not fit all where interpreters' services are concerned.

Medical center managers may be hesitant to incur the expense of professional interpreters because guidelines for reimbursement are unclear in many states. California has led the nation in this regard. Based on the Medical Interpreter Law passed in 2009, health insurers there are now responsible for making sure that patients have adequate language assistance.

Other efforts are underway as well. Wake Forest University School of Medicine has piloted a training program to help physician assistants work effectively with interpreters and Spanish-speaking patients. After a 4-hour training session, 94% to 97% of students were able to demonstrate proficiency in role-play scenarios that involved interpreters and non-English-speaking patients (Marion, Hildebrandt, Davis, Marin, & Crandall, 2008). Members of other organizations report success using trained interpreters who are either present in the exam room or linked via telephone or videoconference technology (Jones, Gill, Harrison, Meakin, & Wallace, 2003). Some medical centers are even experimenting with remote simultaneous interpreting similar to that used at the United Nations, which is particularly quick and accurate (Gany et al., 2007).

For useful resources on becoming a diversity officer or medical interpreter, see Box 6.5 and read Elaine Hsieh's (2006) excellent article "Understanding Medical Interpreters" in the journal *Health Communication*.

Disabilities

Joanne had time for a cup of coffee and a chance to read the newspaper. Friday was the day that the personal ads ran in the paper. Joanne reads these ads without fail, trying to picture what kind of man would write advertisements to find dates. Although she sometimes thought about answering one of these ads, she never did. What would she say? "Woman, 28 years old, math whiz, attractive, red hair, green eyes, likes movies, jazz,

---

BOX 6.6 CAREER OPPORTUNITIES

Diversity Awareness

Diversity officer
Health care interpreter
Equal Employment Opportunity (EEO) officer

CAREER RESOURCES AND JOB LISTINGS

- American Hospital Association's Institute for Diversity in Health Management: www.diversityconnection.org
- National Council on Interpreting in Health Care: www.ncihc.org
- Registry of Interpreters for the Deaf: www.rid.org
- U.S. Equal Employment Opportunity Commission: www.eeoc.gov
- U.S. Bureau of Labor Statistics Occupational Outlook Handbook: www.bls.gov/oco

---

loves to cook, uses a wheelchair to get around." No, she just couldn't picture it. (Braithwaite & Japp, 2005, p. 175)

Individuals with disabilities are often confronted with frustrating dichotomies. For one, people tend either to treat their disabilities as the most important thing about them or self-consciously to avoid the issue entirely. Health professionals have typically not received much training on how to communicate with people who have disabilities. Consequently, when treating these individuals, physicians often focus on the disability and ignore medical concerns that are not directly related to it (Braithwaite & Thompson, 2000). On the other hand, well-meaning acquaintances may consider it taboo to talk about the disability. A woman described by Dawn Braithwaite and Lynn Harter (2000) said she initially appreciated it when her future husband did not make a big deal about her disability when they met. But after several months of getting to know each other, she was exasperated that he never even mentioned the subject. Eventually she brought it up, to end the awkward silence.

Another dichotomy concerns the way persons with disabilities are regarded by society. Sally Nemeth, a health communication scholar who is blind, reflects that people with disabilities are often cast "either as heroic super crips or as tragic, usually embittered and angry, unfortunates worthy only of pity and charity" (Nemeth, 2000, p. 40). The reality is that people with disabilities are much like anyone else.

It's frustrating to be treated as helpless or unsophisticated. Health professionals (and others) tend to treat individuals with disabilities as if they are childlike—speaking slowly and loudly to them even when that's not necessary and giving instructions rather than asking for their opinions. People may avoid talking to children with disabilities about sensitive subjects such as sex. I remember attending the wedding of a friend, Melissa, who had been deaf since age 6. Although Melissa was well into her twenties when she married, her family realized on the eve of her wedding that she knew nothing about birth control. The school Melissa attended did not provide sex education to students with disabilities, and her parents had always considered her too sheltered to need such information.

People whose disabilities are invisible to others may encounter unique difficulties. They face the dilemma of either keeping their illnesses a secret or revealing them to others and risking a changed social identity. Some individuals, particularly men, may be loath to admit disabilities they think will make them seem dependent or pitiful (Moore & Miller, 2003). A study of people with heart disease revealed that they often consider themselves older than their same-age peers, largely because of physical limitations and attention to end-of-life issues typically associated with older people (Kundrat & Nussbaum, 2003). (For more about the frustration of invisible disabilities, see Box 6.7.)

These challenges have an effect on health communication. Individuals with disabilities are typically less satisfied with managed care providers than with doctors they choose themselves, mostly because doctors on a provider list may not be knowledgeable about or comfortable dealing with disabilities (Kroll, Beatty, & Bingham, 2003). And because of the need for trust and familiarity, it may be particularly stressful for persons with disabilities to change doctors (O'Connell, Bailey, & Pearce, 2003). Physicians admit that they *do* often feel uncomfortable caring for people with disabilities, particularly if they involve mental impairments (Aulagnier et al., 2005).

Avoid treating people with disabilities as if they are child-like. Most are quite capable and wish to be treated like everyone else.

On the bright side, even brief training sessions tend to help caregivers interact more confidently and sensitively (Tuffrey-Wijne, Hollins, & Curfs, 2005). In a training program piloted by Ashley Duggan and colleagues (2009), medical students interacted with trained standardized-patient educators with disabilities, then took part in interactive feedback sessions about the experience. The medical students acknowledged that the patients' disabilities and appliances sometimes made them feel awkward and uncomfortable, they were unsure whether to talk about the disability or ignore it, and their advice was sometimes off the mark, as when one medical student advised a wheelchair user to ease the symptoms of her tendonitis by not using her shoulder. The student later told the mock patient, with chagrin: "Your arms are your mobility and independence, and I'm telling you to stop you using them" (Duggan, Bradshaw, Carroll, Rattigan, & Altman, 2009, p. 804).

BOX 6.7   PERSPECTIVES

"My Disability Doesn't Show"

Dear Editor,

Since receiving my handicapped hangtag two years ago, I have been rudely approached by so many people that I've lost count.

I am a 44-year-old female, tall, thin, and do not walk with a cane, nor am I in need of a wheelchair. My handicap is internal, from two major back surgeries, and although I do have pain while walking, I walk with confidence. By simply looking at me, one would not know that I have a handicap.

Since using my handicapped hangtag, I have been rudely approached by, not only people off campus, but from just as many students on campus. I have heard it all, from "You sure look handicapped" or "You must really be handicapped from driving a car like that (a 1992 Firebird)," to "How can I get one of those (a handicapped hangtag)?" These comments not only hurt my feelings but are truly insulting, especially since I received my back injuries from serving my country while in the military, and the scar on my back extends from my neck to my buttocks.

I would like to educate everyone on campus, as well as people off campus, that not all handicaps are visible. Not everyone with a handicap is over 60, nor do they have to walk with a cane, nor do they have to be in a wheelchair.

In order to receive a handicapped hangtag, the Department of Motor Vehicles requires that one must have limitations of walking because of arthritic, neurological or orthopedic (which I have) conditions, and one must have a disability rating of 50% or greater. My disability rating is 80% and is permanent.

The last comment came January 28th by a student getting into his blue truck, which was parked next to me in front of the campus police station. The young man made the normal comment that I did not look handicapped. Normally I usually just tell people if they have a problem with me to take my license plate number and report me, but this time, I lost it and told this guy to mind his own business, and added a few explicit words to boot.

I would like to see people stop stereotyping others based on their looks and think before they inadvertently insult someone, because it really does make me feel bad, and I have every right to use my handicapped tag.

—BEVERLY DAVIS

Source: Copyright © 2003 by *The Voyager*, the student newspaper at the University of West Florida. Reprinted by permission from *The Voyager* and Ms. Davis.

Following are some tips from the experts.

Communication Skill Builder: Interacting with Persons Who Have Disabilities

- Talk to people with disabilities directly, not to their interpreters or companions.
- Remember to identify yourself to sight-impaired persons.
- Treat adults with disabilities as adults.
- When a person with a disability is difficult to understand, listen attentively, and then paraphrase to make sure you heard correctly.
- Whenever possible, sit down when speaking to people in wheelchairs so that you can communicate at eye level.
- Relax! For example, don't be embarrassed if you accidentally say "See you later" to a blind person.
- Don't insist on helping people with disabilities. If they don't ask for help or if they decline your offer of assistance, respect their wishes (Soule & Roloff, 2000). Keep in mind that it's discouraging regularly to "owe" people gratitude for their assistance, especially when the assistance is unnecessary. (It's okay to extend the same common courtesies you would offer an able-bodied friend, such as holding a door open.)
- Heed the wisdom of Thuy-Phuong Do and Patricia Geist (2000), who remind us: "Everyone is othered to some extent; we all possess disabilities, whether visible or invisible" (p. 60).

As you are probably gathering by now, the concept of being "othered," or treated as if you do not belong, is demoralizing in everyday life and particularly in medical transactions. As the following section shows, age can be a source of "othering" as well.

Age

Aging alone is rarely viewed in a positive light and thus has led many to depict aging as a time of great loss and decline.

—JON NUSSBAUM (2007, P. 1)

In his presidential address to members of the International Communication Association, Nussbaum (2007) challenged scholars to reconsider social assumptions about aging. "Aging alone has also been a favorite of the great poets, playwrights, and novelists, who love to make us feel the 'horribleness' of our lonely human existence," he said (p. 1). But that idea, he argued, is more cultural myth than objective reality: "My mission is to spread the news that we are not purely or even remotely organisms that exist only within our own skins" (p. 1). Nussbaum proposed that it is possible to age happily and that the nexus of sustained quality of life is effective communication, as evidenced by people's ability to manage interpersonal conflict, develop relationships, manage uncertainty, share thoughts and ideas, and more.

Researcher Douglas Friedrich, author of *Successful Aging*, agrees. "Successful aging is within the grasp of most of us, especially if we develop coping or preventive strategies early in the life span and maintain them" (Friedrich, 2001, p. 157). Based on his own research and an extensive review of the literature, Friedrich concludes that lifestyle choices with the greatest influence on aging involve diet, exercise, safety precautions, healthy relationships, and a positive attitude. Many or all of these rely on communication—being well informed and interpersonally skillful.

In this section we examine the communication practices that affect people throughout their lives. We focus first on children and then more extensively on older adults. As you will see, both groups use health care services a great deal, and their communication is profoundly affected by the assumptions of people around them.

Children

She gots bad monsters inside her tummy that try to eat her up.

—4-YEAR-OLD SOPHIA EXPLAINING HER MOTHER'S BREAST CANCER

This quote, from Jenifer Kopfman and Eileen Berlin Ray's (2005) case study "Talking to Children About Illness" (p. 113), helps illustrate the way children make sense of illness. Although their conceptualizations may seem naive, children are often remarkably attuned to the ramifications of illness experiences. When Sophia's young friend Ethan asked her what color the monsters were, she said, "I think they're orange 'cause orange's a gross color" (p. 113). She went on to explain what happened when her mother received chemotherapy:

> She always gives me lots of hugs and kisses before she gets her medicine from the doctor 'cause she says it makes her throw up and be tired after she takes it, and I hafta be quiet and let her sleep and not ask for too many hugs and kisses until she feels better again. (p. 113)

After that, Ethan showed Sophia his "scary monster face" and they dashed off to play.

Communicating with children can be challenging because their perceptions are often different from those of adults. For example, children may perceive that painful medical treatments are a means of punishment (Hart & Chesson, 1998). Moreover, children may be unsure of how to express their feelings or may be afraid to speak freely in front of people they don't know.

Bryan Whaley and Tim Edgar (2008) outline the phases of development in which children conceptualize illness with increasing degrees of sophistication. In the **prelogical conceptualization** phase (roughly ages 2 to 6), children define illness as something caused by a tangible, external agent, such as a monster or the sun. In the **concrete-logical conceptualization** phase (ages 7 to 10), children begin to differentiate between external causes, such as wind and cold, and internal manifestations, such as sneezing and talking funny. In the **formal-logical conceptualization** phase (ages 11 and older), children are remarkably adept at envisioning the complex influence of agents they cannot readily see. Whaley and Edgar share the following example of formal-logical conceptualizing from Bibace and Walsh's (1981) study, in which they asked children older than 11 to explain various illnesses:

> Have you ever been sick? "Yes." What was wrong? "My platelet count was down." What's that? "In the bloodstream they are like white blood cells. They help kill germs." Why did you get sick? "There were more germs than platelets. They killed the platelets off." (Bibace & Walsh, p. 37)

When researchers asked 200 children being seen in an emergency department if they would prefer a male or female doctor, 78% of the boys and 80% of the girls expressed a preference for a female (Waseem & Ryan, 2005). In contrast, 60% of the parents preferred a male doctor. None of the children and only 21% of the parents said they would like "the best" physician, regardless of gender. (AP Photo/ Gary Kazanjian)

This is clearly a far more sophisticated explanation than Sophia's concept of orange monsters, which is a good reminder that children's ideas typically evolve over time.

Parents can be both a help and a hindrance in caring for young patients. Many times, parents have valuable information about their children's conditions and are able to comfort them as no one else could. Parents may become especially frustrated if their concerns are not taken seriously or if they don't feel well informed about their children's health needs (Kai, 1996). And rightly so. Parents are the children's principal caregivers, and their responsibility does not end at the doctor's office or hospital. However, it can be difficult for caregivers to attend to young children *and* manage the complex emotions of their parents. Parents tend to be especially anxious, guilty, and uncertain where their children's health is concerned.

When children are hospitalized, parents and professional caregivers may have conflicting ideas about what care each of them should provide. It may be unclear who is to feed the child, change bandages, and perform other tasks. With nurses' input, R. J. Adams and R. Parrott (1994) drafted a list of tasks parents should perform for their hospitalized children. By sharing the list with parents (orally and in writing), the nurses were able to reduce parents' uncertainty and their own. As a result, the nurses were more satisfied with their jobs, and the parents were more confident in the care their children received.

COMMUNICATION SKILL BUILDER: TALKING WITH CHILDREN ABOUT ILLNESS

Bryan Whaley, who has conducted extensive research about children in health situations, and colleagues offer this advice for explaining illnesses to children:

- *Let children set the tone.* Determine what the child wants and needs to know before launching into explanations the child may find incomprehensible, distressing, or simply irrelevant to his or her concerns (Nussbaum, Ragan, & Whaley, 2003; Whaley, 1999; Whaley & Edgar, 2008).
- *Pay attention.* Notice how the child conceives of illness and medical care. Ask questions and invite children to describe (and perhaps draw) their images of medical care and illness (Whaley, 2000).
- *Go easy on medical terminology.* Usually, children are more interested in how an illness will influence their lives and activities than the precise germs, tests, and scientific names involved.

As Whaley (1999) puts it, "Disease and etiology appear inconsequential or of negligible concern to children" (p. 190).

- *Talk about illness as something normal.* Children are typically reassured to know that their illnesses are normal and manageable. Speaking of an illness as a crisis or mystery may interfere with the child's coping ability (Whaley, 1999).

Buchholz (1992) adds that children benefit from honesty. Like adults, children usually cope better if they have a realistic idea of what to expect from health care experiences. Adults should also keep in mind that prior experience with medical procedures may not diminish children's fear and anxiety (Buchholz, 1992). Experienced youngsters may be all too aware of how frightening and painful procedures can be.

Older Adults

Experts predict that 1 in 5 Americans will be 65 or older by the year 2050 (U.S. Census Bureau, 2009). Population shifts will likely change health care needs and transform our understanding of the aging process. The outdated notion that "growing old cannot possibly be a positive experience and surely will be a time of great sadness, depression, and failing physical capacities" is likely to be revealed as more stereotype than reality (Nussbaum, Ragan, & Whaley, 2003, pp. 187–188). As with all stereotypes, the belief that all members of a group are alike in some way (e.g., sad, fun, weak, jovial) never holds water. **Ageism** is discrimination based on a person's age. It occurs when people judge others by preconceived notions about their age group, as when managers refuse to hire people over 65 because they believe employees of that age aren't productive.

? CAN YOU GUESS?

1. Around the world, in which country do people have the longest average life expectancy?

2. In which country are peoples' lives the shortest?

3. How does the average life span for men and women in the United States compare?

Answers appear at the end of the chapter.

Ageism results largely from negative stereotypes of older adults. Health personnel sometimes reinforce these stereotypes by referring to older patients in such derogatory terms as "coffin dodgers" and "digging for worms" (Fowler & Nussbaum, 2008). Ageism is also reinforced by media portrayals of older adults as unhealthy, lonely, unhappy, and irritable (Robinson, Callister, Magoffin, & Moore, 2006).

People with ageist beliefs are unlikely to regard older adults as unique individuals who can change, learn, react, and grow physically stronger. Instead, they tend to patronize seniors by speaking very slowly to them, using baby talk, and restricting conversations to happy subjects (Hummert & Shaner, 1994). They may even avoid communicating with older adults (Giles, Ballard, & McCann, 2002). Young people in Japan, the Philippines, and the United States tend to feel that older adults are less accommodating than their peers and that communication with older adults is based on obligatory signs of respect (Ota, Giles, & Somera, 2007). Youth in all three countries said they are likely to avoid communicating with older adults who are not part of their families. Among those studied, American youth were the least likely to say that older adults deserve respect, but they were the most willing to talk with older adults—a sign, perhaps, that the generation gap feels smaller in the United States than in the other countries.

Social beliefs about growing older often have profound implications for people's identity. When Laura Hurd Clarke and Meredith Griffin (2008) interviewed women ages 50 to 70, many of them said they actively engage in beauty work to maintain a youthful appearance because they believe that, if they don't, they will become "invisible" in society's eyes. As one woman in the study put it: "Be young or you're not counted" (p. 660). Another expounded:

> We won't love women if they're not lovely. Our society says that from the beginning. And for women who are older, we're invisible anyway. If you're considered ugly and old, ageism is awful and it's so prevalent. As a woman, we always look to someone else to see if we're okay. And as you get older, you get less and less okay, and people look at you less and less. . . . It gets down to "Well, you're old. You can't look good anyway."

So, I think it's about trying to look young, youthful, perky, and put on this "See I'm lovely, you can love me" kind of thing. (pp. 660–661)

Women in the study said they feel immense pressure, both from the idea that women's worth is inherent in their appearance and from the notion that feminine beauty is inherently youthful.

Based on the idea that getting older is a process of decline, people often assume that natural signs of aging (hearing loss, vocal changes) indicate cognitive decline. Young adults tend to underestimate the cognitive abilities of older adults with known hearing loss, although they score them highly on wisdom and visual memory (Ryan, Anas, & Vuckovich, 2007).

Despite Western society's cynical views about aging, many older adults enjoy good health, rewarding relationships, and a positive outlook on life (Nussbaum, Ragan, & Whaley, 2003). When Laurie Schur and Lisa Thompson interviewed women 80 and older for the video documentaries *Greedy for Life* (2008) and *The Beauty of Aging* (2012) they found that some of the women were frustrated with the effects of aging, but most said they were having the time of their life. A 97-year-old woman in the video said: "A few years ago someone asked me what time of my life did I like best and I said 'now.'" Another one said, "I see women 50 and 60 decide to give up on life and go sit down somewhere, don't look forward to a future. Even at 82 years old I've still got things that I want to do."

And life's milestones aren't what they used to be. Physicians report that baby boomers have different health needs than their parents at the same age. For instance, because they're more athletic, middle-aged people today have more sports injuries than prior generations ("Getting Old," 2003).

Not all older adults accept ageist beliefs about their health. My grandmother, for one, once stomped angrily from a doctor's office after being told she "was just getting old." As she left, she declared, "I don't owe you a cent. I knew how old I was when I came in here." James McCague, a columnist for *Medical Economics*, uses his 85-year-old aunt as an example of changing attitudes among older adults. When his aunt insisted on having bypass surgery despite her age, her doctor told her she was "quite functional" for an 85-year-old and was not a candidate for the surgery. To this she retorted, "I am the sole caretaker of my 90-year-old sister. I can't be just 'functional.' I want to be as healthy as I can be" (McCague, 2001, p. 104). The physician performed the procedure, and McCague reports that the last time he checked, his aunt was out applying for a passport! A physician himself, McCague reflects on changes among elderly patients:

> The elderly patient does not report symptoms with resignation; the questions ask for a solution. The elderly patient does not want his [or her] questions taken within the context of his age and, more important, is angry when the physician does so. Elderly patients today see medicine like everyone else—as a commodity to which they have the right to equal access. . . . That hope, that wonderful "great expectation" of the human species, is the crux of the demand of the elderly and, while we physicians need to moderate or shape it, we must never ignore or ridicule it. (p. 104)

THEORETICAL FOUNDATIONS: EFFECTS OF AGEISM

Despite changing trends, reconciling Western society's negative view of aging with new ideas about

---

CHECK IT OUT! To see a excerpt from Schur and Thompson's video, type "The Beauty of Aging trailer" into the search window of You Tube. To learn more about the video and others like it, visit http://www.beautyofaging.com/the-filmmakers.html.

WHAT DO YOU THINK?

■ Do you think people typically become less attractive as they age? Why or why not?

■ What are the implications for older adults' social status and their appeal as relationship partners and community members?

getting older is still a challenging enterprise with numerous implications for health communication. When people believe (rightly or wrongly) that older adults have diminished capacities, they tend to change their behavior toward them. For instance, people may speak more loudly to accommodate a hearing loss or move closer to accommodate an elder's shortsightedness. To **accommodate** is to adapt to another person's style or needs.

In some cases, accommodation is useful and appreciated. According to **communication accommodation theory**, people tend to mirror each other's communication styles to display liking and respect (Coupland, Coupland, & Giles, 1991). It is called **convergence** when partners use similar gestures, tone of voice, vocabulary, and so on. On the other hand, **divergence** is acting differently from the other person, as in whispering when the other shouts. Divergence implies that the partners are socially distant. They may be asserting uniqueness, pursuing different goals, or displaying that they don't understand or don't like each other.

To illustrate, patients who are baffled by their doctors' rapid explanations may converge by speaking rapidly themselves or by being silent to accommodate the physicians' speech. However, patients may diverge by paraphrasing the explanations more slowly to make sure they understand them. Socially speaking, divergence is risky, in that it shows the participants to be somewhat out of sync. Extreme divergence may seem disrespectful or rude.

People often mirror the behaviors of their conversational partners without really thinking about it, especially if they like each other. Accommodation can spiral, however, so that feedback encourages people to escalate their behaviors toward each other. For instance, when a dear friend speaks loudly and slowly to an older adult, the older person may respond in a similar way, which may reinforce the friend's belief that he or she is a bit slow and hard of hearing. In turn, the friend may accommodate even more, and so on. Thus, what was intended to be accommodation has become **overaccommodation**, an exaggerated response to a perceived need.

Especially if the overaccommodation is pervasive (everybody seems to do it), older individuals may begin to believe that they are indeed of diminished capacity, and they may behave in line with that expectation (Ryan & Butler, 1996). In short, they start to "do" being old, as society has defined it.

Older adults usually have no control over the cues that suggest to others that they are aging. Indeed, they may have a hard time dealing with these cues themselves, although the cues may not be signs of significantly reduced ability at all (Nussbaum, Pecchioni, Grant, & Folwell, 2000; Ryan & Butler, 1996).

An older sounding voice is one example. In one study, people whose voices sounded old were perceived by others to be older than their contemporaries and even perceived *themselves* to be older (Mulac & Giles, 1996). An "old" voice is quivery and breathy, with prolonged vowel sounds and extended pauses between words. These characteristics are certainly not signs that the speaker is less intelligent or is physically impaired in any significant way, but they may be enough to spur accommodation and overaccommodation.

Ironically, a great number of accommodating behaviors are unnecessary. Contrary to the assumption that older people are worse communicators than others, they are sometimes better. Mark Bergstrom and Jon Nussbaum (1996) found that respondents over age 50 handled conflict more cooperatively and productively than young adults, who were apt to be confrontational and judgmental. There is also evidence that older adults compensate for deficiencies in some areas by becoming stronger in others. For example, many become especially good at reading nonverbal cues if their hearing diminishes (Fowler & Nussbaum, 2008).

Older adults are not as helpless as many people think. "What's important to remember about people over age 65 is that while many begin to experience some physical limitations, they learn to live with them and lead happy and productive lives," says a spokesperson for the American Psychological Association ("Older Adults' Health," nd, p. 1). According to the most recent U.S. census, today's older adults are better educated, healthier, and more affluent than any generation before them. They are also socially engaged. Indeed, they are more likely to vote than younger people are. And only 4.5% of people ages 75 to 84 live in nursing homes. The reality is that accommodating behaviors are usually unnecessary.

IMPLICATIONS OF AGEISM AND OVERACCOMMODATION

Ageism and overaccommodation present several implications for health communication. For one, older adults are usually treated by caregivers who are significantly younger than they are. Relatively unfamiliar with the diversity in the older generation, young people are likely to rely on stereotypes. They may lump elders into simplistic categories, such as frail, mild-mannered grandparents, or worse, cantankerous grumps.

Second, people may not try very hard to maintain or restore older people's health. Research indicates that people expect older adults to be ill and confused. As a result, they tend to shrug off elders' illnesses and emotional distress as unavoidable and untreatable. In short, if they don't believe older people can change, people don't try very hard to help them.

Third, studies support that treating people as if they are helpless encourages them to believe it. Margaret Baltes and Hans-Werner Wahl (1996) found that, at home and in nursing homes, caregivers encouraged elders to be dependent by being attentive and supportive when the elders needed help, but caregivers discouraged or ignored them when they seemed independent. The authors conclude that caregivers are sometimes overresponsive in ways that encourage learned helplessness among older adults.

Fourth, caregivers tend to underestimate older adults' desire for information. Caregivers may assume they are not interested in medical details, are incapable of understanding them, or will be unduly frightened by risk factors. However, research suggests that most older adults are interested and are capable of understanding and assessing risks. In fact, because of long-standing experience, older adults often have more extensive medical vocabularies than younger people. Reflecting this, seniors' satisfaction with medical care is most closely linked to how well caregivers listen, how concerned and attentive caregivers are, and how actively they, as patients, are included in decision making about their own care (Atherly, Kane, & Smith, 2004).

COMMUNICATION PATTERNS

Although older and younger adults are not as different as caregivers (and others) may imagine, it is worth noting several communication patterns that distinguish older adults' behavior in medical contexts. For example, because they may

IN YOUR EXPERIENCE

■ To test the effects of communication accommodation, try altering your speech and observing how your conversational partners react. Does he or she converge (e.g., whisper if you whisper) or diverge?

■ How would you react if everyone started speaking unusually slowly or loudly to you?

■ Start to notice if you tend to change your communication patterns around older adults. Do you or not? If so, in what ways?

WHAT DO YOU THINK?

■ Ask older people you know which term(s) they prefer from the following list and why: *elders, seniors, elderly, older adults, senior citizen*.

■ What did you learn about their preferences?

■ It's common for people in their eighties and nineties to say they don't feel old or consider themselves "seniors" or "elderly" at all. Did any of the people you talked to feel that way? What do you learn from that?

have been taught to respect authority figures by not interrupting, older adults may be reluctant to ask questions and assert themselves with doctors, despite their desire to participate and be well informed (Nussbaum, Ragan, & Whaley, 2003).

Conversely, some older adults become what Fowler and Nussbaum (2008) call *extreme talkers*, chatting incessantly about topics that may seem irrelevant to their health concerns. Given time constraints in medical organizations, "it is quite easy to imagine communication with patients who have a tendency to stray from the matter at hand being quite frustrating" to doctors and others, say Fowler and Nussbaum (p. 165).

Third, caregivers may be put off by the presence of loved ones who often accompany older adults to medical visits. According to Nussbaum, Ragan, and Whaley (2003), very often "the companion will ask more questions, will cause the medical encounter to last significantly longer, and will expect more information regarding the health of the older

You can expect to live about 30 years longer than your great-grandparents. Put another way, if you think of life in roughly 25-year increments, their lives had two acts. Yours will probably have three. Jane Fonda, vibrant in her late seventies, challenges people to consider what they will do with the unprecedented gift of "life's third act." (Sipa via AP Images)

patient than the older patient normally seeks" (p. 192).

Finally, the fast pace of medical contexts may be incompatible with older adults' health needs, which (although they are not necessarily debilitating) are likely to be more numerous and chronic than those of younger patients, making it infeasible to cover them during a quick visit (Nussbaum, Pecchioni, Grant, & Folwell, 2000).

PROMISING OPTIONS

Even brief training sessions have been effective in dispelling ageist assumptions among medical students and health professionals (Christmas, Park, Schmaltz, Gozu, & Durso, 2008). Although not yet widespread, such educational programs may help change the way older adults are treated in medical situations.

Technology provides another resource. The next section discusses communication technology as it affects seniors. The chapter concludes with a *Communication Skill Builder* for reaching marginalized populations.

COMMUNICATION TECHNOLOGY AND OLDER ADULTS

Advanced technology can be a benefit or a liability for older adults. From one perspective, access to online health information and interaction expands opportunities for adults with limited mobility. On the other hand, older adults who don't keep up with technology may have difficulty finding and keeping jobs and staying in the mainstream of a technology-savvy society (McConatha, 2002). There is some evidence that older adults are rising to the challenge. "It's clear that older adults, like their younger counterparts, don't want to be left behind on the information highway," writes Donald Lindberg (2002, p. 13). Around the world, individuals over age 55 make up the fastest-growing segment of Internet users (Hopkins, 2007).

Older adults who are proficient at using online resources may benefit from a greater sense of control over their environment and personal fate. They may also feel less isolated and more informed about choices and options. Based on these ideals, Douglas McConatha (2002) proposed what he called the **e-quality theory of aging**, which posits that older adults benefit as both teachers and learners when they "use, contribute to, influence, and express themselves" in electronic environments (p. 38).

Based on experience working with older adults in an assisted living facility, David Lansdale (2002) notes that residents experienced a new sense of freedom when they learned to use an online computer made available to them. Lansdale applies the metaphors of "driving" and "going back to school." He writes:

> *Driving* is the antidote to helplessness. One of the most exciting events in adolescence comes with access to the keys to the car, and the

freedom it promises. At the other end of life's continuum, an elder is often forced to relinquish the keys, often one of the more trying transitions of a lifetime. (p. 135)

Lansdale says that older adults who begin using the computer are free again to "go" where they please and choose their own paths and experiences. At the same time, they can relieve boredom and feel that they are participating in life beyond the facility's borders. Similarly, by "going back to school" via the Internet, many older adults find pleasure in expanding their knowledge and skills. This provides a striking contrast to the view of aging as a steady decline in intellect and abilities.

The Internet may even serve as a modern equivalent to a house call. In their study of Internet use among people ages 63 to 83, Wendy Macias and Sally McMillan (2008) report that many seniors are "bringing the physician and health information into their homes through the Internet" (p. 38). The Web allows them to take their time, learning as much or as little as they like about a health concern without being constrained by someone else's timetable. One woman in the study said:

> When my husband had his shoulder replacement, he could not get in to therapy right away, and that's when I went in to the websites and was able to print actual diagrams and information about what . . . to do, so then when we finally got in to the therapy and back to the doctor, he said this was very good. (p. 38)

Although participants in the study sometimes felt overwhelmed by the volume of online information and unsure what information to trust, they generally appreciated the opportunity to research their own concerns and issues affecting their friends and family members.

Communication Skill Builder: Reaching Marginalized Populations

As this chapter has shown, people may be marginalized on the basis of many factors, including status, literacy, gender, race, sexual orientation, language,

disability, and age. All have implications for health and health communication. Leigh Arden Ford and Gust A. Yep (2003) offer the following suggestions for understanding and improving health-related communication with members of marginalized populations.

- *Do not impose your worldview.* Instead, seek to understand and work within the worldview of the people involved. Allow for multiple meanings.
- *Establish open dialogues in which people can communicate openly and honestly.* Strive for understanding. Allow meanings to emerge.
- *Strive to communicate in culturally acceptable ways.* Develop new skills and awareness.
- *Listen to people rather than telling them what do or think or how to act.*
- *Empower people to use their own skills and resources.*

Summary

Patients are quite diverse. Unfortunately, caregivers in the United States still aren't. That is worrisome because it's tempting to stereotype what is unfamiliar to us, and such categorizations can affect treatment decisions and advice and lead to strained relationships and misunderstandings.

Patients of low socioeconomic status are typically more fearful and less informed than others, but they talk less during medical exams and are likely to be treated within a strictly biomedical model. In addition to the communication challenges, practical considerations such as financial constraints, inflexible working schedules, and lack of transportation may limit the care they are able to receive.

Low health literacy is an invisible epidemic affecting 1 in 2 adults in the United States and 774 million people worldwide. The consequences of health literacy challenges include hundreds of billions of dollars of avoidable expenses, unnecessary suffering, frequent misunderstandings, reduced productivity, shame, and premature death. Better communication is the answer. Patients and caregivers can most effectively bridge literacy gaps if they develop trust, acknowledge and reconsider stereotypes, make the most of face-to-face communication, and encourage questions and open dialogue.

Female patients and caregivers in the United States are typically more expressive and self-disclosive than their male counterparts. There is some evidence that female patients and female physicians are especially trusting and comfortable together. Overall, however, the communication styles of male and female caregivers are probably not as different as people assume.

Sexual orientation can be a difficult subject for both patients and caregivers. Caregivers may feel out of their depth discussing sexual issues, although ignoring them may compromise medical care because some health risks are related to sex and because close relationships are crucial to coping. For their part, patients may be reluctant to bring up the issue for fear of being negatively judged.

Although members of racial minorities are often at high risk for disease, their health may suffer because they don't trust doctors and because they have limited access to medical facilities and health information. Some evidence suggests that doctors treat African Americans and Hispanics differently from White patients. We have yet to fully transcend decades of racist and segregationist thinking in the United States, and the impact is fewer professional opportunities and shorter lives for members of racial and ethnic minorities.

Health care is influenced by the social climate surrounding it. Civil rights advancements since the 1960s have brought unprecedented diversity to medicine. Women doctors are now present in numbers nearly equal to their portion of the population, but the proportion of minority doctors is still only half that of the population overall, and women and minorities still experience the lingering effects of discrimination. Affirmative action laws are active in some states but not others.

A new source of health information (and potential discrimination) looms ahead in the form of genetic profiling. Emerging knowledge about human genes is expected to foster breakthroughs in medical science. Already, people who understand their genetic predisposition for various diseases may be able to offset their risks and take part in early screening procedures. The Genetic Information Nondiscrimination Act of 2008 is designed to minimize the risk that genetic risk factors will be used to penalize people in terms of employment and health insurance.

Some risk factors are not genetic, but social and linguistic. People in the United States who do not speak English well are at a disadvantage as patients. One physician estimates that their risk level is elevated by 25%. Patients baffled by language differences may agree to procedures they don't understand or may be so frustrated that they don't return for further care. Caregivers can be frustrated also and may be held liable if adverse outcomes result. The good news is that community interpreters and long-distance interpretation services have mostly pleasing results if they are used. Still, people who are not proficient in English may wish to bring a friend or relative along, since interpreters are sometimes not available.

Many people treat individuals with disabilities as if they are childlike or incapable of contributing to conversations and decisions. These assumptions may seriously limit communication between them and their caregivers. Moreover, the same attitudes can make it difficult to cope on a daily basis. Although people mean well, their actions may stigmatize and isolate individuals with disabilities. Suggestions are presented to make communication more equitable and respectful.

Children frequently undergo routine exams and emergency care, but they may have a difficult time dealing with the foreign atmosphere, strangers, and threat of pain that medical care poses. Parents can help, but their role is somewhat ambiguous. Caregivers may feel that parents are either too demanding or not helpful enough.

Finally, older adults may be typecast in ways that affect their personal identities and the health care they receive. Ageist assumptions that older people are less healthy and less intelligent than others may cause people to write off legitimate health concerns as unavoidable signs of old age. Communication accommodation behaviors are often unnecessary and can be stigmatizing, especially if carried to extremes.

Unfair discrimination is especially worrisome in the current climate, in which medical services are being rationed to save money. Decision makers are cautioned not to make assumptions based on social prejudices.

Key Terms and Theories

ethnocentrism
the problem of thought
socioeconomic status

health literacy
heterosexism
racism
concierge medical practices
affirmative action
prelogical conceptualization
concrete-logical conceptualization
formal-logical conceptualization ageism
accommodate
communication accommodation theory
convergence
divergence
overaccommodation
e-quality theory of aging

Discussion Questions

1. Describe aspects of what David Bohm calls the problem of thought. Apply these principles to an episode of health communication you have experienced or heard about. What does Bohm suggest as the best way to overcome the problematic nature of the typical thought process?

2. Describe five reasons misunderstandings might occur between patients and caregivers of different socioeconomic status.

3. What abilities are considered when assessing health literacy? How prevalent is low health literacy in the United States? What are the consequences?

4. Describe three tips for improving communication between patients and caregivers of different socioeconomic or literacy status.

5. What are some of the reasons that discussion of sexual orientation is important yet challenging in medical transactions?

6. What are some explanations of why people of different races seem to achieve different health outcomes?

7. What guidelines do you suggest when deciding who gets medical care (see Box 6.2)?

8. Are you concerned that, if you have a genetic profile, the information might be used against you? Why or why not? Are you interested in knowing your genetic profile? Why or why not?

9. Describe pivotal points in the history of racial and gender acceptance in health care in the United States.

10. Do you think affirmative action should be maintained or abolished as a factor when selecting students for caregiver education programs (Box 6.4). Why do you feel that way?

11. What did you learn from the case study "Language Barriers in a Health Care Emergency" (Box 6.5)?

12. What are some promising options for bridging the language gap?

13. What two frustrating dichotomies do people with disabilities often face?

14. What are some tips for communicating effectively with people who have disabilities?

15. Describe the three phases of conceptualization that children experience as they mature.

16. What are some tips for communicating with patients who are children?

17. How do ageist assumptions affect health communication? Describe communication accommodation theory.

Answers to *Can You Guess?*

1. The longest-living people in the world are women in Japan, who live an average of 86 years.

2. The shortest average life span occurs among men in Malawi (southeast Africa), who live an average of 44 years.

3. In the United States, men live an average of 76 years and women 81 years. *Source: World Health Organization, 2012.*

CHAPTER SEVEN

Cultural Conceptions of Health and Illness

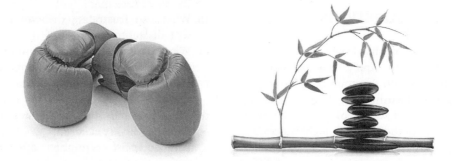

I f you found out you had a serious illness, which of these photos would best characterize your response? Would you resolve to fight the disease, or would you seek a sense of peace and balance? The difference is largely a cultural one.

From a Western perspective, illness is usually regarded as an attack, and people are encouraged to "fight" for their lives. From an Eastern perspective, ill health is more commonly regarded as the result of an imbalance. From that perspective, the healthiest option is to seek harmony and peace.

The metaphors could hardly seem more different—one based on doing battle, the other on seeking peace. But they do have some aspects in common, and together, they open our eyes to the reality that health and healing are, in many ways, cultural constructs. Understanding divergent concepts of health can improve our communication with people whose perspectives are different from ours. And there's another benefit as well—the opportunity to reflect on our own cultural assumptions and make choices about what's important to us personally. Although the implications of illness metaphors are powerful, they are so engrained in culture that we may not stop to think about them very much.

In this chapter we examine the impact of culture on health and healing. We will explore world cultures including Asian, Hispanic, and Arab, as well as smaller groups such as Native Americans, African Americans, African tribes, aboriginal communities in Canada, and others. We will examine different ways of thinking about health, some of the role sets that patients and caregivers embody, and experts' suggestions for communicating effectively with diverse others. The chapter concludes with a focus on two perspectives that, while larger than any one culture, display some of the concepts we discuss throughout the chapter. The first is holistic medicine, which is mostly reflective of an Eastern approach. The second is a cultural analysis of Viagra marketing, which reflects a Western idea of medicine pushed to an extreme. But first, let's look more closely at the Eastern/Western comparison we have already begun.

> **Culture** refers to a set of beliefs, rules, and practices that are shared by a group of people. Cultural assumptions suggest how members should behave, what roles they are expected to play, and how various events and actions should be interpreted.

Eastern and Western Perspectives

As you read more about Eastern and Western worldviews here, consider which are most familiar to you and which you find most appealing. Keep in mind that it's not necessary to choose one over the other. You might integrate elements from both into your way of thinking and behaving.

West

Western ideas about health have been shaped largely by a reverence for science. (Think germs, microscopes, x-rays, and so on.) The body, especially when ill, is regarded as a complex and unpredictable space vulnerable to invasion by forces (bacteria, viruses, allergens) beyond most people's understanding. These metaphors are evident in the words people use. For example, when Juanne Nancarrow Clarke and Jeannine Binns (2006) studied heart disease coverage in popular magazines in the West, they found that the words used most often depict the human body on the verge of war or disaster (*heart attacks, asthma attacks, risk factors, warning signs*). Within that menacing metaphor, the appropriate response is to be vigilant (*watch for warning signs*) and ready to engage in combat (*fight* disease). Members of Western cultures applaud people who are ill for being *strong* and *real fighters*. Regaining good health is portrayed as a battle against malicious foes that have occupied the body-fortress. One *fights for one's life* and, if victorious, *triumphs* over disease. Otherwise, people are said to *lose their battle* with heart disease, cancer, or any number of other diseases.

In the Western context, observe Clarke and Binns (2006), illness is a siege, and medicine is the cavalry ready to come the body's defense. Medicine is described in such optimistic and glowing terms as *life-saving, state of the art,* and *tried, tested, and true*. Some medications (like Viagra, which we'll talk about later) are even heralded as "miracle drugs" (Baglia, 2005, p. 28). All in all, the body is mysterious, but "the medical world is largely unquestioned and portrayed as if it is beyond criticism," conclude Clarke and Binns (2006, p. 45).

If you were raised in a Western culture, the idea of "being strong" and "fighting for your life" may make perfect sense. How else would you view disease? Actually, *quite* differently, if you subscribe to an Eastern worldview.

East

A classic intercultural exercise is to show people a picture of a snow-covered tree limb on the ground. People from Western cultures typically say the limb broke because it was too weak. People in traditional Eastern cultures say the opposite—that it broke because it was too strong, therefore too inflexible to bear the wind and weight. The Eastern idea of strength involves being supple and flowing. Tai chi, qigong, karate, and tae kwon do are methods of building spiritual and bodily awareness, flexibility, and fluid strength.

Whereas Westerners are typically urged to take action at the first sign of illness, the Eastern way is to strive for health and balance all of the time. Rather than regarding the body suspiciously, Easterners are more likely to consider the body a natural place of harmony and well-being. They typically believe that the best way to maintain good health is to honor the body and follow its rhythms.

WHAT DO YOU THINK?

■ Are there ways in which the Western viewpoint is appealing to you? If so, how?

■ Are there ways in which the Eastern perspective is appealing to you? If so, how?

■ On balance, which feels more familiar? More appealing?

Thus, rather than "fighting" an illness and using "strength" against it, people influenced by Eastern thought are more likely to focus on balance, harmony, and flexibility.

Traditional Eastern medicine is based on awareness of subtle energy patterns such as *Qi*, yin, and yang, which we will discuss later in the chapter. Interventions are typically mild and designed to enhance the body's natural functioning. Aggressive interventions such as surgery and strong drugs may be viewed suspiciously as interfering with the body's natural rhythms. We sometimes depict traditional Eastern medicine as *health from within* and Western medicine as a *cure from without*.

Of course, the dichotomy is not absolute. Eastern countries have high-tech medical centers and a full array of treatments, and Westerners often engage in harmony-enhancing activities and therapies such as massage, meditation, and yoga. Likewise, narrative medicine, discussed in Chapter 3, is a good example of an approach that spans the East/West difference in many ways. In the West, the lines between Eastern and Western therapies are not as rigid as they once were. Still, it's helpful to highlight their essential differences so that we can better understand the shades in between.

A Profile of Cultures

An Asian immigrant to the United States reports a perplexing set of symptoms, including a sense of heaviness and insomnia. Physical tests can detect nothing wrong. The patient attributes his illness to "too much wind" and "not enough blood," conditions resulting from his past immoral behavior. He is simultaneously being treated by a folk healer with meditation and herbal therapies. The American physicians eventually conclude

BOX 7.1 RESOURCES

More About Culture and Health

- Dutta, M. J. (2008). *Communicating health: A culture-centered approach.* Cambridge, MA: Polity Press.
- Zoller, H. M., & Dutta, M. J. (Eds.) (2008). *Emerging perspectives in health communication: Meaning, culture, and power.* New York: Routledge.
- Transcultural Nursing Society and the *Journal of Transcultural Nursing:* www.tcns.org
- Ethnomed: www.ethnomed.org (includes multilingual health information)
- Robert Wood Johnson Foundation on Vulnerable Populations: www.rwjf.org/vulnerable populations
- *Journal of Multicultural Counseling and Development:* www.multiculturalcenter.org/jmcd
- Guide to Choosing and Adapting Culturally and Linguistically Competent Health Promotion Materials: www11.georgetown.edu/research/gucchd/nccc/documents/Materials_Guide.pdf

that the man's condition exists "only in his head," although he vigorously denies any emotional upset (Kleinman, Eisenberg, & Good, 1978).

Examples such as this highlight the ways in which well-meaning people can trip over cultural gaps, sometimes with harmful consequences. There isn't room here to survey all the major cultures of the world, but I've done my best to integrate diverse information throughout the chapter and have chosen to spotlight three cultures to begin with—Asian and Pacific Island, Hispanic, and Arab. These are highly populous cultures whose members have migrated around the world. Perhaps this introduction will pique your interest in learning more (see Box 7.1).

Asian and Pacific Island

More than half the world's population (60.5%) lives in Asia (Population Reference Bureau, 2012), and in many respects, the widest cultural gap in the world is between Eastern and Western cultures, making it particularly interesting and challenging for people in those cultures to understand one another.

Asians and Pacific Islanders typically do not perceive the mind/body dualism popular in Western thought. They tend to see mind and body as an interwoven whole. And because they have historically put great stock in traditional holistic healing methods, they often seek Western medical care only if other methods have not worked. At that point, they may expect a quick alleviation of symptoms, and they may be disappointed if the doctor doesn't prescribe something that offers instant relief ("Reducing Health Disparities," 2005).

Although Americans may consider caregivers friendly when they are energetic and nonverbally immediate, Asians and Pacific Islanders typically prefer a quiet, unhurried demeanor that begins with nonthreatening information and moves very slowly into the arena of personal concerns (Purnell, 2008). Following are some other insights about Asian and Pacific Island cultures:

- Most people won't openly contradict or question another person, especially not an authority figure such as a physician. They may use the word "yes" to signal that they understand the speaker, not as a sign that they agree. If they have questions, they may not ask them, for this might be seen as criticizing the speaker.
- Because of their high regard for status, patients have traditionally declined to take part in treatment decisions, preferring that doctors make decisions on their behalf ("Reducing Health Disparities," 2005). That may be changing in some respects, however. Dana Lathan Alden and colleagues (2010) found that the majority of urban Vietnamese women they surveyed preferred that their doctors use a shared decision-making process with them regarding contraception use, perhaps because the women felt it was such a personal matter (Alden, Merz, & Thi, 2010).
- Physical touching and direct eye contact may be seen as overly personal and overly familiar.
- People from Asian cultures are typically not as emotionally expressive as Americans in public, and their nonverbal displays may mean different things. For example, in China it's common to smile when feeling sadness or discomfort ("Reducing Health Disparities," 2005).
- Asians and Pacific Islanders may be reluctant to say much about their health histories because

💬 IN YOUR EXPERIENCE

■ Do you have experience interacting with people from diverse cultures?

■ If so, what are the most important things you have learned?

■ Have you ever experienced health care in a different culture? If so, what was your experience like? How was it similar to the health care you experience at home? How was it different?

this information feels private to them. Caregivers may do well to get one bit of information at a time ("Reducing Health Disparities," 2005).
- Members of many Asian cultures consider that the dead continue to have influence and relationships with the living (Lassiter, 1998). This often makes the ideas of autopsies and organ donation distasteful to them.
- Another frequent cause of confusion is that people in many countries, including some Asian nations, calculate age differently from people in the West. For example, in Vietnam a person's age begins roughly when he or she is conceived and advances one year at every *Tet Nguyen Dan* (*Tet*), the Vietnamese New Year. That means that a child conceived shortly after Tet will be nearly 1 year old when born and will be considered 2 years old before the first anniversary of his or her birth (Purnell, 2008).

We will have a good deal more to say about Asian principles throughout the chapter, so let's turn now to health ideas in Hispanic cultures.

Hispanic

Hispanic (or *Latino*) is a broad term encompassing people (most of them Spanish-speaking) whose heritage is associated with Latin America, South America, Spain, and some African nations. As you can imagine, this is a particularly diverse culture, but its members tend to honor several key principles, which we will discuss here.

Among the highest of Hispanic values are the principles of ***personalismo*** (a preference for warm, friendly relationships rather than impersonal, institutional scenarios), ***respeto*** (embodied in respectful and deferential behavior toward people of greater age and social status), and ***confianza*** (the openness and trust among members of one's intimate circle) (Añez, Silva, Paris, & Bedregal, 2008). These values translate to a preference for well established, trusting relationships with caregivers, a general tendency to avoid conflict (especially with highly respected individuals), and sensitivity to displays of respect. Understanding these cultural expectations, it's easy to imagine how offensive and foreign it may seem for a doctor to walk in, address a Hispanic patient by his or her first name, and then launch directly into medical talk without first working to build a close, friendly, trusting relationship.

Another belief held by members of some traditional Latino communities is ***susto,*** the conviction that a "shocking, unpleasant, or frightening experience" may cause physical illness (Willies-Jacobo, 2007, para. 18). Willies-Jacobo describes a patient visit during which a Latina mother said her 15-year-old son was sick because of *susto*. Although the boy disclosed that the *susto* involved something his father said, he and his mother refused to say anything more, leaving the doctor in a quandary, trying to decide if she should respect the family's desire for privacy or investigate to see if abuse was involved. To caregivers in similar situations, Willies-Jacobo recommends the following:

• *Conduct a cultural awareness assessment.* Learn as much as possible about the patient's culture and incorporate that knowledge into assessment, diagnosis, and treatment considerations.
• *Assess family beliefs.* Keep in mind that overall culture doesn't tell the whole story. Every family has its own unique blend of beliefs and values.
• *Negotiate cultural conflicts.* Strive for ways to satisfy both patients' cultural expectations and the rigors of medical care. In this case, the doctor met with the son individually and asked the mother what treatments she would consider helpful. Since there was no further reason to suspect abuse, she resolved to keep an eye out for indications of maltreatment or emotional distress.

Cultural misunderstandings are one reason Hispanic Americans tend to underutilize health services. Language and citizenship status are additional barriers for some. About 25% of Hispanic Americans are not insured, a number that has grown in recent years (Rutledge & McLaughlin, 2008). Hispanic residents who are not citizens of the United States are particularly unlikely to have health insurance or to seek care. Hispanic Americans may also find mainstream health messages culturally unappealing and assume that such messages do not pertain to them. Partly as a result, Mexican American women are more likely to die from breast cancer than members of any other ethnic group.

Following are some suggestions for communicating effectively with Hispanic individuals:

• Learn *un poquito de Español* (a little bit of Spanish). Warren Ferguson (2008) reminds us that "language is the currency of health care" and that learning even a small amount of the patient's language is a valuable investment (para. 1).
• Begin with a warm and friendly greeting.
• Engage in friendly small talk and take time to build trusting relationships (*personalismo*).
• Show respect (*respeto*) through use of honorific titles such as Mr., Ms., Don, Señor, Señora, and Señorita. (It's okay to ask what title the person prefers.)
• Acknowledge and include family members and loved ones. Keep in mind that they're an important source of support and are often closely involved in making care decisions. "Family support is ever present," say Rick Zoucha and Barbara Broome (2008), adding that in Hispanic cultures, "family has meaning beyond blood or related connectedness. . . . Family may mean close friends of the family, known as 'compadres,' who may be present at times of health and illness" (p. 141). Health professionals should treat *compadres* with respect to avoid insulting the entire family.
• Keep in mind that religion is likely to be a source of great value and comfort to Hispanic individuals. It may also lead them to feel that health screenings and other measures are unnecessary because everything is in God's hands.
• If time matters, be specific. Time is typically a fluid concept in Hispanic cultures. Statements such as "Stop by after lunch" and "Take this medication first thing in the morning" may lead to misunderstandings.

- Traditional Hispanics may consult physicians only if care by a folk healer does not work. Be sensitive to this preference, and be aware that the patient may already be involved with folk treatments involving herbs, massage, prayer, and other remedies (Knoerl, 2007).

We turn now to a culture with origins in Africa and the Middle East.

Arab

The interdependence between Western countries and the Arab world is unmistakable. Yet much of what Westerners "know" about Arabs is based on stereotype and conjecture. Here we take a look at Arab culture as it pertains to health and health care.

The Arab world includes 22 diverse countries in the Middle East and North Africa, including Egypt, Libya, Iraq, Iran, Kuwait, Saudi Arabia, Lebanon, Palestine, Yemen, and the United Arab Emirates, among others. These nations are united by proximity and their common use of the Arab language. Although some Arabs are of Christian or Jewish faith, Arabs are predominantly (92%) Muslim (Arab American Institute, 2000).

It's hard to judge the number of Arab Americans, because the U.S. census groups them in the larger category of White Americans. And because many Arab Americans fear discrimination, they often don't self-identify their ethnicity in other surveys (Ahmad, 2004). About 1.7 million Americans are of Arab descent. Some of the most famous of them are Selma Hayek, Paula Abdul, Doug Flutie, Tony Shalhoub, and Shakira (Arab American Institute, 2012).

It is common for a traditional Arab household to include several generations as well as uncles, cousins, and others. Elders are deeply revered. Based on traditional gender roles, men are largely expected to provide for the family and women to raise the children and perform domestic tasks. Theirs is a collectivistic culture in which a dishonorable action by one member is considered to bring shame on the entire family. This means that some health conditions, such as mental illness and out-of-marriage pregnancies, may have powerful implications for the entire family. Health care professionals are encouraged to approach these matters delicately. Even when the issue is not a shameful one, many

> **?** **CAN YOU GUESS?**
>
> 1. What are the five most-spoken languages around the world?
>
> 2. In the Chinese culture, which one of the numbers 74, 8, 168, 58, and 22 is considered luckiest? Which one of the numbers 13, 666, 74, 169, and 0 is considered unluckiest?
>
> *Answers appear at the end of the chapter.*

traditional Arabs prefer that doctors not tell the patient directly about a serious and terminal illness, but instead give the news to the nearest relative or the male head of the family, who, in turn, will share it with the others (Ahmad, 2004).

Many Arabs have migrated due to war and violence in their homelands. Because of this experience and because they often face social isolation and relatively few professional opportunities in their new communities, Arab Americans are especially susceptible to depression, anxiety, and suicide. However, mental illness is considered so shameful in their culture that they often deny they are in distress and avoid seeking help (Douki, Zineb, Nacef, & Halbreich, 2007).

Arab immigrants are likely to find the American health system alien and perplexing. Since most Arab countries have universal coverage, the concepts of managed care, copayments, and insurance deductibles may be new to them. They may also be unaware of or reluctant to enroll in Medicare and Medicaid (Ahmad, 2004).

For the most part, Arabs are emotionally expressive and dedicated to being polite and agreeable, to such an extent that they may not disagree openly with their doctors. They enjoy getting to know health professionals and are typically put off by hurried transactions that don't involve a show of warmth and interest. They often show appreciation for health professionals with small gifts. To refuse these would be seen as a social rejection.

Because such a large percentage of Arabs are Muslim, let's turn now to the religious beliefs that influence the Arab culture and views of health.

Islam is the second largest religion in the world (behind Christianity). Worldwide, Muslims, comprise about one-fifth of the world's population. (About 20% of Muslims are of Arab descent. The majority are from south and southeast Asia.) Muslims consider their religion to be a synthesis of Christianity and Judaism. They honor a number of prophets, many of whom overlap with Jewish and Christian faiths, including Adam, Abraham, Moses, Solomon, and Jesus (Hammad, Kysia, Rabah, Hassoun, & Connelly, 1999). Muslims adhere to the Qur'an (also spelled *Koran*), the scripture of Muhammad, whom they consider the final prophet. According to the Muslim faith, the angel Jibr l (Gabriel) revealed the Qur'an to Muhammad as a set of universal, divine laws for human behavior. Thus, the Qur'an (Islam) is regarded as a way of life, including personal actions and spirituality as well as social structure, economy, politics, and so on (Hammad et al., 1999). Members of Muslim sects (e.g., Sunni, Shi'a, Sufism, Ahmadiyya) hold somewhat different beliefs, but most devout Muslims in every sect believe in Allah (God) and take part in ritualistic cleansing of the body, praying five times a day (preferably toward the east, the direction of the holy city Mecca, in Saudi Arabia), helping the poor, and fasting during daylight hours of Ramadan, an Islamic holy month. (Ramadan is based on the lunar calendar, so its dates differ from year to year.)

There are a number of implications relevant to health. For one, "Clinical staff should not be taken aback if a patient asks them, 'Which way is east?,'" note Adnan Hammad and colleagues (1999, p. 14). They should also be aware that Muslims' commitment to fasting—which they regard as a way to purify the body and maintain empathy for the poor and hungry—may at times dissuade them from taking oral and intravenous medications. During Ramadan they may even refuse critical, life-saving therapies. In such a case, say Hammad and colleagues, a health professional may appeal to a relative or family leader to convince the patient that it is permissible to take the medicine.

Health is important in the Muslim faith. Followers believe in free will, but they typically pray for good health, believing that Allah controls their ultimate destiny (Hamdan, 2007). Muslims may consider it presumptuous of a health professional to predict what will happen—be it death or a cure. They tend to perceive such predictions as overly bold and "as arrogant disrespect for God's will and an open invitation for disaster" (Hammad et al., 1999, p. 14). Adding the phrase "God willing" typically satisfies this concern.

Following are some other customs of which health professionals should be aware:

- In public, traditional Muslim women may cover their bodies and sometimes their faces to show modesty and out of recognition that a man who looks on a woman with interest is committing "the spiritual equivalent of adultery" (Hammad et al., 1999, p. 15). By the same token, commenting on the appearance of a woman or child may be seen as improper. Instead, Muslims appreciate such comments as "What a nice child" or "You have a very nice wife" (Hammad et al., 1999, p. 21).

- Part of the Muslim creed is caring for people in need. Therefore Muslims may be present at the bedside of Muslim community members, even if they did not previously know them.

- The traditional Muslim diet includes *halal* (permitted) foods, but forbids the consumption of pork or alcohol. This can make hospital food (including foods fried in animal lard) unacceptable and can be an issue with medications, such as some forms of insulin that are derived from pigs and cough syrup that includes alcohol.

- Traditional Muslims consider the left hand unsanitary (since it is presumably used for personal hygiene) and do not eat or drink with that hand. As a consequence, medical professionals should be careful not to put pills, drinking glasses, or food in the left hand.

- Muslim tradition largely dictates the separation of men and women, except in family interactions. This may mean a preference for same-sex doctors and female-only labor and delivery experiences.

- Some Muslims are uncomfortable shaking hands with someone of the opposite sex, although this varies a great deal. Hammad and associates (1999) recommend that doctors extend a hand in greeting but not take offense if a Muslim person doesn't reach for it.

- Direct eye contact is often regarded as a sign of disrespect.

- The Qur'an is typically interpreted as defining a subordinate role for women, who are granted fewer rights and opportunities than men in Arab countries (Douki et al., 2007).

- Children are honored and celebrated.

- Fertility is revered to such an extent that the

inability to bear children and even the onset of menopause can be seen as shameful (Douki et al., 2007).

- Premarital and extramarital sex are sources of profound disgrace, especially for females and their families. (Suicide over this disgrace is not uncommon in the Arab world [Douki et al., 2007].) Unmarried Muslim individuals may be insulted if physicians ask whether they are sexually active, believing this to be a judgment about their character.

- Muslims usually accept death without explanation as Allah's will, and custom dictates that they bury people very soon after death (on the same day, if possible). Autopsies are usually considered disrespectful and even horrifying, since traditional Muslims consider that the body feels pain until it is buried (Hammad et al., 1999).

Now let's turn to broader cultural perspectives about what it means to be healthy or ill.

> *Even without a doctor*
> *You have three doctors at hand*
> *Dr. Diet, Dr. Quiet, and Dr. Merryman*
>
> This proverb is a reminder that health often comes down to the basics—what we eat and drink, sleep and relaxation, and our ability to cultivate happiness (Sweet, 2012).

The Nature of Health and Illness

As we know by now, cultures conceptualize health in various ways. Some consider that disease is manifested differently within each person. Others see disease as something objective and independent, outside patients' control and beyond their understanding. This section establishes two basic ways of viewing health—as an organic phenomenon and as a harmonious balance.

Health as Organic

In many Western societies, germs and physical abnormalities are taken as signs of ill health. In the absence of these factors, a person is considered to be healthy. This perspective is consistent with the biomedical approach. The **organic perspective** assumes that health can be understood in terms of the presence (or absence) of physical indicators.

One strength of the organic perspective is its emphasis on scientific knowledge. Based on scientific principles, caregivers and researchers keep detailed patient records, conduct studies and experiments, identify risk factors, and link diseases to their causes (Marwick, 1997). This effort to learn and accumulate knowledge has led to remarkable advances in medicine, including pain remedies, diagnostic tests, vaccines, diverse treatment options, and numerous forms of medical technology.

Medical research has led to the development of **evidence-based medicine (EBM)**, the practice of making treatment decisions based on the results of scientific studies (Levin, 1998). EBM is used in many medical schools and hospitals as a strategy for avoiding medical waste and making effective decisions.

Physical evidence does not explain everything, however. A weakness of the organic model is its inability to account for conditions that cannot easily be verified. People who perceive illnesses that are not scientifically identifiable are often viewed with suspicion or are labeled hypochondriacs. Patients with undetectable conditions such as chronic fatigue syndrome sometimes say the worst part is that so many people regard their condition as "not real" (Komaroff & Fagioli, 1996). Western society's faith in the observable survives, despite evidence that science is imperfectly equipped to understand all aspects of the human body. Mental illnesses, long considered less real than physical illnesses, gained legitimacy in the 1950s as medicine began to recognize a chemical basis for them (Byck, 1986). The difference is science's ability, not the illnesses themselves.

One downside of the organic approach is that its definition of health is fairly narrow, largely excluding social, spiritual, and psychological factors that are sometimes relevant to illness episodes. Partly as a result, since the Industrial Revolution, many Western doctors have been reluctant to bring up spiritual concerns during medical visits, perhaps because it is time-consuming to be so inclusive or because patients have such diverse beliefs that it is difficult to understand or comment on them. But the organic approach can seem cold and impersonal, especially to people who are accustomed to a different style of care. African Americans have traditionally been dissatisfied with health care, partly because they feel snubbed by caregivers who seem disinterested in them as individuals. African American communities have traditionally placed great emphasis on community and religion. Compared to the personal concern of community members, clinical care can seem indifferent and unfeeling. Researchers led by Cheryl Holt (2008) found that African American women respond more favorably to breast cancer awareness booklets that feature spiritual beliefs and scripture than those that focus solely on medical information. The spiritual booklets in the study portrayed the body as a temple, recognized God's role in preparing doctors, and stressed the value of balancing mind, body, and spirit. Both the spiritual and the strictly factual versions of the booklet included the same advice and tips for early detection, but African American women in the study thought more carefully about the information when it was grounded in spirituality (Holt, Lee, & Wright, 2008).

Furthermore, although classifying people as either healthy or sick satisfies the logic and precision of scientific thought, such simplicity may be at odds with human experience. As Charles Rossiter (1975) points out, *sick* and *healthy* are inadequate to describe all aspects of the human condition. There are varying levels of sickness and varying levels of health. Moreover, some people seem to be unhealthy although they do not have specific diseases.

Another drawback is that organic explanations can be confusing for patients. Some doctors work hard to overcome this. In their (2005) case study, Timothy Edgar and colleagues describe how one doctor, Dr. Price, explained type 2 diabetes to a teenager just diagnosed with it. Dr. Price compared the boy's condition to a logjam on a river, explaining that his body was able to convert food into energy (logs) but that the receptor sites in the body (where the logs/energy were to be unloaded) weren't working properly. Therefore, she explained, they needed to put fewer logs (less starch and carbohydrates) into his system and to start an exercise program that would help "open" the receptor sites and help him feel more energetic (Edgar, Satterfield, & Whaley, 2005).

Finally, based on either/or thinking, people may assume that if they're not sick, they are perfectly healthy. Not so, argue some theorists. They propose that true health is not only physical, but reflects a harmonious balance between many aspects of life, a perspective that we turn to next.

Health as Harmony

As you may recall from Chapter 1, the idea of health as harmony is supported by the World Health Organization, which defines health as "a state of complete physical, mental, and social well-being and not merely the absence of disease or infirmity" (WHO, 1948). From this perspective, health is cultivated through personal beliefs, contact with other people, physical strength, and other factors. From the **harmony perspective**, health is not simply the absence of physical signs of disease; rather, it is a pleasing sense of overall well-being. This perspective is in keeping with the biopsychosocial perspective.

Members of traditional Navajo cultures believe that the best way to remain healthy is to maintain a balance between physical strength, social interactions, and spiritual beliefs (Bille, 1981). From their viewpoint, concentrating on only one factor can upset the delicate balance. For example, striving for physical strength without also seeking spiritual growth is not healthy, and a person may become ill because of the imbalance. This is not to say that Navajo deny the existence of germs. They accept that germs cause some diseases. But they also observe that some people are less vulnerable than others to germs. If several people are exposed to a contagious disease, some of them are likely to get sick, but others may not. Based on Navajo beliefs, people who live balanced lives are more likely to remain well, even when they are exposed to physical threats.

Members of the Odawa and Ojibway aboriginal communities in Canada believe that health is based on harmony with the environment, or Mother Earth (Wilson, 2003). As one member of the culture explained:

> She (Mother Earth) is something that heals you if you let it. You don't always feel it. You have to be thinking about it. You can't just go out for a walk and feel it. You have to be spiritually

connected to feel her. (Wilson, 2003, third section, para. 8)

In this belief system it is therapeutic to live in harmony with the environment.

Members of some Asian cultures think of health in terms of balanced energy (Uba, 1992). According to the Chinese Tao, **yin** and **yang** are polar energies whose cyclical forces define all living things. *Yin* is associated with coolness and reflection, and *yang* with brightness and warmth. Cycles and combinations of yin and yang define human life and are a common element uniting all forms of existence. Within this belief, one's central life energy is called **Qi** (pronounced *chee*, sometimes spelled "chi"). Illness and even death may result if *Qi* is wasted or if yin and yang are not balanced. Life energy is sustained and balanced by awareness, rhythmic breathing, physical regimens, and meditation. The concept is often difficult to grasp and to study. "One reason *Qi* can so easily be left out of scientific descriptions of TCM [traditional Chinese medicine] is because of its invisibility," writes Evelyn Ho (2006, p. 425). *Qi* is sensed rather than measured or directly observed. And unlike Western medicine, in which the practitioner and the patient are treated as distinctly separate entities, *Qi* is a force that flows through them both. As one acupuncturist described it to Ho, an acupuncturist is "the conduit between the heavenly and the earthly *Qi* and it comes through you and through your hands and into the needle and the point" (p. 426). Some highly experienced people are said to know what is wrong with a person by sensing the person's *Qi* visually or through touch.

Across cultures, folk healing is typically oriented toward lifeworld concerns. Usually, a folk healer's role is to integrate social support with spiritual faith and physical treatment. The *curanderos* of Mexican American cultures and the hand-tremblers of some Native American cultures are good examples. These folk healers are usually well-known members of their communities (Bille, 1981). As such, they are familiar and accessible, without institutional boundaries or technical jargon. *Curanderos* and hand-tremblers take extensive personal interest in their patients and preside over rituals that bring members of the community together. In this way, healing involves a show of moral support and a sense of peace and belonging.

IN YOUR EXPERIENCE

Can you think of times when your health was affected by organic factors? By issues of harmony? By both?

There is evidence that some people perceive more improvement when treated by folk practitioners than with conventional medicine (Kleinman et al., 1978). The discrepancy may amount to the distinction between healing and curing. McWhinney (1989, p. 29) calls *healing* a "restoration of wholeness," which includes spiritual and moral consideration, as opposed to purely physical *curing*, which he says may still leave a patient in "anguish of spirit" about the causes, effect, and fears associated with the illness.

One drawback of the harmony perspective is that it produces gradual and ambiguous results that can be difficult to measure. If immediate and measurable results are needed, the harmony perspective alone may seem insufficient. This is especially true for conditions such as cancer and broken bones, which have traditionally responded well to organic treatment.

A case in point is the rural community of Jharkhand, in eastern India, studied by Ambar Basu and Mohan Dutta (2007). After interviewing the impoverished residents of that region, Basu and Dutta noted that they live in a "twilight zone" between modernity and tradition. Many are no longer convinced of the power of traditional healers, *ojhas*, who may tell them that an illness is the result of someone's casting an "evil eye" on them, insufficient worship of the gods, or too few animal sacrifices. Residents say they often go to *ojhas* for minor illnesses because they are more affordable and accessible than doctors, who are often based in cities many miles from their village. However, most would prefer a doctor's care for serious illness, and they are acutely aware that distance and poverty preclude them from getting the care they sometimes want and feel they need (Basu & Dutta, 2007).

Another drawback is that people may be so concerned about maintaining harmony that they don't assert themselves. In Asian cultures, particularly, people may avoid saying "no" or giving answers they think will displease the other person because they want to preserve interpersonal harmony (Purnell, 2008).

In closing this section, it is important to note that organic and harmony perspectives are not necessarily at odds with each other. As mentioned, physical health is a significant component of both perspectives. Moreover, each model may be appropriate in different situations, and sometimes they are both appropriate. Depending on the nature of the illness, a person might seek an organic remedy, a harmonizing one, or both. In some cases, conventional practitioners team up with folk healers. Amos Deinard, a pediatrician at the University of Minnesota Hospital, says, "Our attitude is, you bring your shaman and we'll bring our surgeon and let's see if we can work on this problem together" (quoted by Goode, 1993, para. 7).

Social Implications of Disease

One function of culture is to make sense of the world. Cultural assumptions act as guides to interpretation, indicating why things happen and what significance we should attach to various events (Garfinkel, 1967). For instance, death might be interpreted as a glorious ascension to the afterlife or as a tragic and regrettable occurrence. Illness may be regarded as an unfair or random affliction or as a valuable opportunity for renewed awareness. (See Box 7.2 for a description of the theory of health as expanded consciousness.)

Joy Hart and Kandi Walker (2008) describe their work with isolated villagers in Belize. One 16-year-old girl they met left the local clinic before having a pap smear because she was confused by a nursing student's description of the procedure. But she returned to the clinic after her mother told her "a pap smear was part of the journey of being a woman" (p. 130). The researchers reflect that the mother's explanation calmed the girl's fears because it was "more cultural and familial" than the nurse's medical explanation.

It's often difficult to make sense of disease. Some cultures honor scientific explanations. But even in those cultures, scientific accounts sometimes seem inadequate. At different times in history, epilepsy, cancer, tuberculosis, mental illness, AIDS, and other ailments have been viewed so negatively that people with these conditions were shunned

or even imprisoned (H. S. Friedman & DiMatteo, 1979). Sick people may be regarded as a threat to the moral order because behaviors associated with their conditions are considered immoral or because their conditions seem contagious or frightening.

Many times, public reaction is not based on facts but on fears or cultural assumptions. Prior to 1950, people were so fearful of cancer that they typically avoided telling anyone outside the family if a loved one was diagnosed with it (Holland & Zittoun, 1990). They often chose not to tell the patient either. That has changed since the public has accepted that cancer is not contagious.

Social taboos have long surrounded the issue of mental illness as well. In sixteenth- and seventeenth-century England, public horror over insanity was so great that the mentally ill were incarcerated as criminals, after which they were treated brutally and denied the right to marry or own property (MacDonald, 1981). Still today, in many areas of the world, mental illness is considered God's punishment, and people make great efforts to deny and conceal it (Purnell, 2008).

Even cultures steeped in organic definitions of disease may react with fear and loathing when confronted with certain disorders. It's common to blame ill persons for their conditions. This section considers the social effects of diseases regarded as threatening to the moral order. It surveys a variety of ideas about illness, including the notion of disease as a curse, the social stigma of some illnesses, moral issues of prevention, and the implications of referring to patients as victims. These ideas represent different (sometimes overlapping) ways of considering health and illness within the context of cultural beliefs.

Disease as a Curse

Blaming someone is one way of making sense of frightening illnesses, write Dorothy Nelkin and Sander Gilman (1991) in a book about plagues. People may reason that disease is the result of curses inflicted by God or witches. It may be especially tempting to blame gods or witches when science and other explanatory models fail. White (1896/1925) proposes that, as long as people cannot explain illness by natural law, they attribute its cause and cure to the supernatural. As he puts it, "In those periods when man sees everywhere

BOX 7.2 THEORETICAL INSIGHTS

Theory of Health as Expanded Consciousness

The majority of us spend our lives trying to stay healthy, and when we get sick we want nothing more than to be well again. We may be missing the point. According to Margaret Newman's *theory of health as expanded consciousness*, a health crisis is not necessarily negative or undesirable (Newman, 2000). Instead, health events are integral parts of life that provide opportunities for growth and change.

Newman is inspired by the David Bohm's (1980) concept that our everyday life is influenced by underlying patterns that characterize who we are and what we experience. Bohm conceived of two types of order—the *explicate order*, made up of the tangible elements of our existence, and the *implicate order*, comprising patterns beneath the surface. Although the tangible elements of our lives may seem like the "real thing" because we can see, hear, taste, and feel them, the meaning of what we do often lies within the underlying, implicate order. Bohm compares the dual nature of life to waves on the ocean. We can see the waves, but we won't really understand what causes them unless we explore the underwater currents that give rise to them.

Within this metaphor, a health event makes waves. It disrupts what might otherwise seem to be a peaceful, unremarkable existence. As nurse and nurse educator Newman (2000) observes:

> The thing that brings people to the attention of a nurse is a situation that they do not know how to handle. They are at a choice point. Each of us at some time in our lives is brought to a point when the "old rules" do not work anymore, when what we have considered progress does not work anymore. We have done everything "right" but things still do not work. (p. 99)

You might ask: And this is a *good* thing? According to Newman, yes. In her view, life is a process of attaining greater levels of understanding and awareness. When things stop working well, we experience a sense of chaos. But, she says, if we "hang in there," the uncertainty and ambiguity of a health crisis may become a means of seeing underlying patterns and transcending previous limitations. This can be a richly rewarding and liberating experience (Newman, 2000).

Imagine a person who has worked throughout her life to support others. She has devoted her energy and time to doing well at work, caring for her family, running errands, serving on committees, cleaning the house and yard, and so on. She is lauded with thanks and awards. Meanwhile, she appears less physically fit than she used to be. Her hair and clothing are not carefully groomed and tended. But this is nothing compared to what is happening within her. In fulfilling so many outward "obligations," she neglects her own spiritual and emotional growth. Although she interacts frequently with people, she doesn't share much of herself or appreciate the uniqueness of the people around her.

Suddenly (or what appears to be suddenly), the woman comes down with the flu and must cancel her commitments for several days. Faced with this prospect, she might put all her energy into fighting the illness, frustrated that it has interrupted her life. Or she might look for a deeper level of meaning. What does the illness (an outward manifestation) suggest about what is happening within her? And at an even deeper level, what does this disruption signal about the underlying pattern of her life? Perhaps this is an opportunity to reevaluate a pattern that appears virtuous on the surface but is harmful to her and others in the larger scheme of things. Perhaps understanding the pattern will allow her to restructure her life in a way that is more functional and adaptive, allowing her to develop her inner self as well as perform helpful tasks in the tangible world. Or perhaps she will ignore the underlying currents until they give rise to a much bigger, harder to ignore "wave," such as a stroke or a heart attack.

Seen this way, health events are opportunities for developing higher levels of understanding and more effective interactions with our environments. Greater harmony between inner and outer levels of existence provides the means for seeing beyond one's self and transcending old habits and assumptions. As Newman learned from her mentor, Martha Rogers, "health and illness should be viewed equally as expressions of the life process in its totality" (Newman, 2000, p. 7).

Newman (2000) coaches nurses to help people find the meanings and patterns revealed by their health experiences, whether or not their diseases are eradicated. She writes:

> Transcendence of the limitations of the disease does not necessarily mean more freedom from the disease; it does mean more meaningful relationships and greater freedom in a spiritual sense. These factors are considered an expansion of consciousness. (p. 65)

Furthermore, a health crisis is not merely a senseless or regrettable circumstance. Newman (1986) writes that, since she began to regard health as the expansion of consciousness,

> illness and disease have lost their demoralizing power. . . . The expansion of consciousness never ends. In this way aging has lost its power. Death has lost its power. There is peace and meaning in suffering. We are free from the things we have feared—loss, death, dependency. We can let go of fear. (p. 3)

WHAT DO YOU THINK?

1. Have you ever learned something valuable about yourself as the result of a health crisis?
2. What can caregivers and loved ones do to help people evaluate their life circumstances when an illness occurs?
3. In what ways are your health and outward, everyday life (explicate order) influenced by underlying factors (implicate order)?

SUGGESTED SOURCES

Bohm, D. (1980). *Wholeness and the implicate order.* London: Routledge & Kegan Paul.

Coward, D. D. (1990, Fall). The lived experience of self-transcendence in women with advanced breast cancer. *Nursing Science Quarterly, 3*(3), 162–169.

du Pré, A., & Ray, E. B. (2008). Comforting episodes: Transcendent experiences of cancer survivors. In L. Sparks, H. D. O'Hair, & G. L. Kreps (Eds.), *Cancer, communication and aging* (pp. 99–114). Cresskill, NJ: Hampton Press.

Malinski, V. M. (Ed.). (1986). *Explorations on Martha Rogers' science of unitary human beings.* Norwalk, CT: Appleton-Century-Crofts.

Newman, M. A. (1995). *A developing discipline: Selected works of Margaret Newman.* New York: National League for Nursing Press.

Newman, M. A. (2000). *Health as expanding consciousness* (2nd ed.). Boston: Jones & Bartlett.

Rogers, M. E. (1986). Science of unitary human beings. In V. M. Malinski (Ed.), *Explorations of Martha Rogers' science of unitary human beings* (pp. 3–14). Norwalk, CT: Appleton-Century-Crofts.

miracle and nowhere law . . . he naturally ascribes his diseases either to the wrath of a good being or to the malice of an evil being" (p. 1).

During the bubonic plague of the fourteenth century, more than one-third of the European population died (Slack, 1991). Struggling to make sense of this devastating epidemic, people killed tens of thousands of women, accusing them of using witchcraft to make their neighbors ill (Nelkin & Gilman, 1991). Others attributed the plague to God's wrath over women's fashions, blasphemy, drunkenness, improper religious observances, and other behaviors (Slack, 1991).

Members of some African tribes attribute AIDS to the work of witches. Many of the Goba, who live in a rural area of Zambia, Africa, believe that death occurs naturally only in old age (Yamba, 1997). In all other cases, it is attributed to the work of witches in the community. (According to Goba beliefs, a person may be a witch and not know it.) The Goba use the same word (*ng'anga*) to refer both to healers and to witch finders. When a young person dies, suffers an injury, or is unable to conceive children, the family is expected to hire a witch finder to identify and often to kill the witch believed to be responsible. Supposed witches are publicly challenged to survive impossible feats such as drinking poison. If they don't survive, their guilt is assumed. Yamba reports that the tribe members maintain their belief in witches partly because they are unsatisfied with biomedical explanations of illness. If witchcraft is not involved in sexually transmitted diseases, then "why else, they argue, would two men be exposed to the same woman and yet one would become infected while the other would not?" (Yamba, 1997, para. 8).

All in all, people may suspect that supernatural forces are at work when rational explanations fail to make sense. One result of treating illness as a punishment or curse is that ill persons may be shunned and supposed witches accused and even killed. In light of this, people may not admit they are ill, and treatment may be withheld in the name of religion. In Europe in the late 1700s, some people refused the smallpox vaccination because it was regarded as interference with God's way (Nelkin & Gilman, 1991). For similar reasons, some Southeast Asians regard medical care as fruitless or a sign of weakness (Uba, 1992). Likewise, Kashmiri men in India, although at high risk for diabetes, frequently decline treatment or lifestyle changes because they feel that the disease is Allah's will and that they should enjoy life (including eating what they want) until it is their fate to die (Naeem, 2003).

Stigma of Disease

Even when illness is not regarded as a supernatural curse, it may be culturally prescribed to consider people with certain diseases corrupt or immoral. As Erving Goffman (1963) uses the term, **stigma** refers to a type of social rejection in which the stigmatized person is treated as dishonorable or is ignored altogether.

Social theorists compare HIV and AIDS to a plague, in that infected persons are often avoided and seen as dangerous and unprincipled. Numerous studies tell of HIV and AIDS survivors who have been fired from their jobs and abandoned by their families and friends (M. B. Adelman & Frey, 1997; Cawyer & Smith-du Pré, 1995). Stigmatized in this way, people with HIV or AIDS must often choose between two forms of isolation. Either they keep the diagnosis a secret (eschewing potential support), or they tell others and risk being shunned and avoided by them (Cline & Boyd, 1993).

 WHAT DO YOU THINK?

■ Why might members of a society stigmatize ill individuals?

■ Some people feel that smoking and obesity have become stigmatized in the United States. Do you agree or disagree? Why?

One effect of social stigma is that people's individuality, even their humanity, is overshadowed by the discrediting characteristic. A participant in Rebecca Cline and M. Faye Boyd's (1993) study of HIV survivors says:

> I am finding it harder and harder to get away from AIDS. . . . I am angry at people, society, for not looking at me as a normal person with a normal disease, putting labels on me and trying to isolate me, putting shame and guilt on me. (pp. 137, 139)

For those whose conditions stir society's fears and prejudices, disease is clearly more than a physical phenomenon. Some people literally die of embarrassment, too afraid or ashamed to seek care for medical conditions stigmatized by society. Others may keep their diagnoses secret for fear of retribution.

Sometimes people avoid medical evaluations because they are afraid of being stigmatized by the results. For example, although they are predisposed to breast cancer, highly religious Jewish women in Israel are less likely than others to seek genetic testing (Bowen, Singal, Eng, Crystal, & Burke, 2003). Given the history of persecution against Jewish people, these women are especially wary of being stigmatized as genetically "different" or "at risk" (Bowen et al., 2003). As the following section shows, moral issues are often applied to illness, even when health is regarded as an organic phenomenon.

The Morality of Prevention

It seemed for a time that reframing disease in scientific terms would shield sufferers from moral judgment. Ironically, Western society has attributed a moral quality to science, with the effect that people who get sick are often considered to be lazy or ignorant. The news is filled with health warnings and risk factors. Such information enables people to make healthy choices, enhancing their own well-being and assuring themselves of long, healthy lives. At least that's one implication: Take care of yourself and there is no reason you should become ill. Prevention information is enabling to an extent, but taken too far it may lead to prejudice against ill persons. One backlash of the prevention movement is that people may have so much confidence in prevention that they believe illness always results from laziness or indifference. The rationale is that, if illness can be prevented, ill people have not tried very hard to stay healthy.

"Why isn't it possible to just get sick without it also being your fault?" asks physician/essayist Paul Marantz (1990, p. 1186). Marantz describes the smug comments surrounding a young friend's unexpected death from heart failure. A medical resident minimized the man's death by dubbing him "a real couch potato" (Marantz, 1990, p. 1186). Marantz was angry that onlookers would judge his friend, even to the extent of making his premature death seem okay or deserved.

The fallacy that only the lazy or indifferent get sick compounds the hardship of being ill. People fall ill for reasons that are hard to explain, even though they have worked hard to stay healthy. Marantz (1990) and others propose that suffering is often made worse by the assumption that ill persons engineer their own misfortunes.

One alternative to blaming ill persons is to see them as victims of circumstances beyond their control. As you will see, however, there are social implications, as well, to playing the role of the victim.

Victimization

As the average life span has increased, so has the duration of chronic diseases. Many people with serious diseases survive and lead relatively normal lives. This has created a semantic dilemma. These people are not accurately described as "patients." So what do you call a person with AIDS or cancer or emphysema? A common practice is to call them victims, as in "AIDS victims" or "cancer victims." However, many people so described resent the implications of that characterization.

A participant in Cline and Boyd's (1993) study declared: "I'm HIV positive but I'm not a victim! I'm a *survivor!*" (p. 144). Another participant in the same study concurred: "I hate that word. I'm not a victim because I'm not allowing AIDS to victimize me. The word 'victim' really ticks me off. And 'innocent victims' implies that there are 'guilty victims'" (p. 145). These people's reactions attest to the power of cultural metaphors. Words and images imply values and judgments, with serious implications for those involved.

The following section examines different ways of conceptualizing patients' and caregivers' roles.

Patient and Caregiver Roles

Culturally speaking, there are right and wrong ways to "do" and to "treat" illness. That is, some behaviors are rewarded, whereas others bring social penalties. For example, members of Arab cultures expect women to cry out in pain during labor and delivery (Ahmad, 2004). But in some other cultures, the same behavior is considered weak and unseemly, even a sign that the patient has been evil in the past. For example, members of traditional Hispanic cultures typically believe pain should be endured stoically because it is God's wish (Duggleby, 2003).

Likewise, people might be expected to remain "respectfully" quiet in medical encounters or to take a "responsible" role by sharing their thoughts. The rules for being a good patient and a good caregiver may be contradictory and confusing. Nevertheless, with people's health hanging in the balance, health care participants may fervently wish to behave correctly. (See Box 7.3 for more about Thai customs regarding family members' role as health advocates.)

This section examines different roles patients and caregivers are expected to play. A **role** is a set of expectations that applies to people performing various functions in the culture. For example, people may play the roles of patient, doctor, sister, friend, employee, and parent. Each role is guided by a set of culturally approved rules. Typically, one role exists in relation to another: patient–caregiver, student–teacher, parent–child, and so on. A role may lose meaning without its counterpart (e.g., a teacher is not a teacher without students).

BOX 7.3 PERSPECTIVES

Thai Customs and a Son's Duty

Absolutely nothing in Thai culture is as important as a son's duty to take care of his elderly parents. My paternal grandmother came to live with my family when I was 15 years old. She left Chonburi, a small city in the eastern part of Thailand, and moved to Bangkok after my grandfather died of a heart attack. Grandmother Kim had been paralyzed for 20 years because of a bad fall, so my father insisted she must come to live with us so we could take proper care of her and so she wouldn't be lonely.

Grandmother Kim was 91 years old then, but she still had a great memory, especially about finances. Even though she had no expenses of her own, she insisted that my father give her a monthly allowance. She kept perfect mental notes on the status of her money so that she could distribute it as she pleased. For example, every day before I left for school, Grandmother gave me some money to give to the monk she watched on television each day. She was looking after her future by buying merit enough to go to heaven when she died. Grandmother also gave me money for myself each morning, and she gave other people money as well.

Although she required a lot of care and assistance, Grandmother was not depressed. Instead, she seemed happy and content with her financial projects and with providing advice to our family. Still, my mother and I watched over her constantly and we hired a private nurse to help take care of her. My mother was a very skillful and competent caregiver, since she had taken classes at the hospital to prepare her to take care of Grandmother Kim.

After I graduated from high school, I pursued a bachelor's degree at a university far from home. I would go back every weekend, however. When she was 95, Grandmother began to get weak. The doctor said she might have lung cancer. I didn't think she had any diseases; instead, I believed it was her time to go to heaven. My father didn't think she had lung cancer, either. He was convinced her lungs were perfect because she had no symptoms of any lung problem. No matter how strongly my father opposed the doctor's opinion, the doctor insisted on a lung biopsy as soon as possible. We agreed not to tell my grandmother about any suspicion of cancer, since we thought it might be too hard for her to know. We agreed only to tell her she had suffered a stroke. As we waited during the surgery, my father confided in me that he was unsure he had made the right decision to let the doctor do a biopsy.

When the results came back, my grandmother didn't have cancer. After she came home, everyone expected her to feel better. Unfortunately, Grandmother got worse. We took her to another doctor, who said that, since a biopsy could make an elderly patient weaker, it had been inappropriate to do the procedure. My father asked the doctor how much time his mother had left in this world. He told us that Grandmother could not be expected to live longer than one year. She died within several weeks.

Although I was away at the university when Grandmother died, I quickly returned. It is Thai custom that kin and family have to see the dead person before the body is placed in the coffin. Therefore I had a chance to see her for the last time in the mortuary. As my mother and I got her dressed and cut her hair, I noticed that Grandmother's body was small and cold. I told my mother that Grandmother had kissed me and told me to be a good girl the last time I saw her. Up to this day, I still remember every single word she told me. I think she knew her time to go was close. However, she didn't show any signs that she was afraid of death.

My father blamed the first doctor for his mother's death, but he blamed himself most of all. He thought that, if he had insisted the doctor not perform the biopsy, she would have stayed with us longer. My mother and I both tried to comfort father. I thought the best way to relieve him of some of his sorrow was to tell him that it was time for Grandmother to go. She had stayed longer than most other people could; also she had suffered from a stroke and had been paralyzed for a long time. However, I do understand my father's feeling because he is a son, and his responsibility is to do everything to keep his mother alive and healthy.

—PEM

Therefore, role-playing is a collaborative endeavor, and people usually adjust their performances to form meaningful combinations. This can be so compelling that people sometimes feel forced into roles they would rather not assume. For example, if your conversational partner adopts a parental role, you may feel like a child, and you may act that way even if you would rather not. To do otherwise might seem uncooperative and rude.

As you will see in this section, patients and caregivers often play complementary roles—as mechanics and machines, providers and consumers, parents and children, and so on. Keep in mind that these roles are collaborative achievements, supported by participants' mutual efforts. This doesn't mean the participants always like the roles they assume. They may be motivated by a sense of cultural appropriateness or the perceived need to "play the scene" as the other person is playing it.

Mechanics and Machines

From one perspective, caregivers are similar to mechanics and patients to machines. The implication is that the patient is relatively passive and the caregiver is expected to be analytical and capable of fixing the problems that are presented.

This perspective does not encourage emotional communication between patients and caregivers. The focus is more on identifying physical abnormalities and fixing them (Todd, 1989). When caregivers take on a mechanic role, they are typically more concerned with what they can observe and change than what the patient might be feeling.

Some people feel that scientific medicine is relatively mechanistic. That is, when caregivers take on the role of scientists, they are much like mechanics—concerned with the orderly physical functioning of the human body. As mechanics or scientists, caregivers are expected to be objective, value-neutral, and capable of collecting information, diagnosing a problem, and fixing it. From this perspective, it may seem inappropriate for caregivers to display emotions or to call into play such intangible notions as faith and spirituality. Eric Cassell (1991) puts it this way: "Adjectives like warm, tall, swollen, or painful exist only for persons but, ideally, science deals only with measurable quantities like temperature, vertical dimensions, diameters" (p. 18).

One advantage of the mechanic/scientist role is that it reduces the emotional drain on caregivers. If patients are like machines who simply need fixing, emotions need not become part of the process (Bonsteel, 1997). At the same time, the confidence that people can be fixed may seem comforting and neat.

Of course, patients may not appreciate being treated like machines. Some argue that ignoring patients' descriptions and considering them passive in their own care amounts to a mechanized form of medicine in which the patient is treated as little more than a set of parts. Richard Swiderski's (1976) analysis of medicine through the ages concludes that doctors have often considered patients less relevant than their pulse rates, blood, and urine. This is an image the public has embraced as well, as evidenced by patients' disappointment when their physicians do not run tests or prescribe medications. One reason for overuse of antibiotics is patients' insistence that treatment be embodied in some physical form, even when pharmacology suggests it will have no effect (Fisher, 1994).

Parents and Children

The popular expression "doctor's orders" suggests a relationship in which physicians issue directions that patients are expected to obey. This approach is referred to as **paternalism**, reflecting the idea that patients are like children and caregivers are like parents.

Members of some cultures carry this to an extreme. David Hufford (1997) tells of a tragic case in which a 14-year-old Asian immigrant to the United States felt ashamed for complaining about abdominal pain after her doctor said it was normal menstrual cramping. She refused further medical care for a year, until the liver cancer that had gone undiagnosed was so advanced that she died. Hufford points out the tragic consequences of stereotyping a young girl's condition, on the one hand, and adhering to cultural expectations that suffering be endured without complaint, on the other.

One implication of the paternalism model is that patients may be regarded as naive or incapable. There is a historical precedent for regarding patients as ineffectual, even as bungling intruders, in matters of their own health. In an 1871 commencement address at Bellevue Hospital College, the famous physician/poet/novelist Oliver Wendell Holmes (1891) warned graduates: "Your patient has no more right to all the truth you know than he has to all the medicine in your saddlebags. . . . He should only get so much as is good for him" (p. 388). Holmes advised the graduates to adopt the habit of "shrewd old doctors" who keep a few stock phrases to quiet "patients who insist on knowing the pathology of their complaints without the slightest capacity of understanding their scientific explanation" (p. 389).

Another implication is that doctors may be expected to know what is best for their patients. Some theorists (e.g., Emanuel & Emanuel, 1995)

believe this is a risky assumption because patients may have many feelings and desires unknown to their doctors. Expecting physicians to anticipate and act on patients' wishes may place an unrealistic burden on doctors and unfairly rob patients of opportunities to make their own decisions. (See Box 7.4 for more on this issue.)

Spiritualists and Believers

Caregivers also may be cast as spiritualists who use their powers on behalf of faithful patients. The image of caregivers as spiritual figures (and even

---

BOX 7.4 ETHICAL CONSIDERATIONS

Physician as Parent or Partner?

Medical ethicist Robert Veatch (1983) reflects that physicians are often criticized as being "aloof and unconcerned" rather than concerned and attentive, as people would like them to be. In short, physicians often act like strangers when patients wish they would act like friends or family members.

Paternalism (the idea that doctors are like parents) is a long-standing tradition. The Hippocratic oath, written approximately 2,500 years ago, beseeches physicians to use their best "ability and judgment" on each patient's behalf. This presumes that physicians are well acquainted with medicine *and* with the particular needs and preferences of each patient. Paternalism is also based on the belief that physicians are more capable of making medical decisions than patients are.

Some people feel that paternalism is outdated. Veatch (1983) points out that it is difficult to know patients well in the current age of large patient loads, specialization, and emergency and outpatient care. These factors make it unlikely that doctors will understand the unique needs and preferences of each patient. The paternalistic model is also criticized as inconsistent with patient empowerment, which presumes that patients are knowledgeable and active agents in their own health care (Emanuel & Emanuel, 1995).

WHAT DO YOU THINK?

1. Do you feel it is realistic or preferable for health caregivers to know their patients' feelings and values? If so, how might they accomplish this? If not, what alternatives would you suggest?
2. Can you think of circumstances in which you would want your physician to know your feelings and life circumstances?
3. Can you think of circumstances in which you would rather your physician did not know you well?
4. Do you feel patients are capable of making decisions about their own care?

SUGGESTED SOURCES

Emanuel, E. J., & Emanuel, L. L. (1995). Four models of the physician-patient relationship. In J. D. Arras & B. Steinbock (Eds.), *Ethical issues in modern medicine* (4th ed., pp. 67–76). Mountain View, CA: Mayfield.

Reilly, D. R. (2003, Winter). Not just a patient: The dangers of dual relationships. *Canadian Journal of Rural Medicine, 8*(1), np.

Veatch, R. M. (1983). The physician as stranger: The ethics of the anonymous patient–physician relationship. In E. E Shelp (Ed.), *The clinical encounter: The moral fabric of the patient–physician relationship* (pp. 187–207). Dordrecht, The Netherlands: D. Reidel.

as gods) was established thousands of years ago. As discussed in Chapter 2, the Egyptian physician Imhotep was eventually granted the status of a god. Jesus has been called "the great physician" and is revered for legendary acts of curing the sick (Moore, Van Arsdale, Glittenberg, & Aldrich, 1987). Throughout history, physicians have been described as "little gods," a celestial metaphor that extends to nurses, often portrayed as "angels of mercy" (Moore et al., 1987, p. 232).

Anthropologists have compared the doctor's role to that of a priest, a powerful and somewhat mysterious authority figure. This awe-inspiring image may be strengthened by patients' reverence and physicians' displays of power. Pendleton and colleagues (1984) point to doctors' laboratory coats, specialized vocabulary, and honorific titles as supporting props in this image. They also suggest that the image is bolstered by an information imbalance that makes physicians' knowledge seem all the more marvelous. They write: "Powerful rituals, such as examining and prescribing, are the more charismatic in the absence of adequate explanations" (p. 9).

Among the most well-known healer/spiritualists are the shamans of traditional Native American cultures. A shaman is believed to coax a patient's disease into his or her own body and then expel it through strength of will (Swiderski, 1976). The assumption is that illness is an invasion of magical or supernatural forces. The faithful believe shamans can communicate with beings beyond the physical world, an ability that gives them magical abilities and healing powers.

The success of a spiritual ceremony is often said to rely on the patient's faith in the healer and the greater spiritual force that has accepted the healer as a medium. One result of this assumption is that failure to recover may be construed as an indication of the patient's insufficient faith (Kearney, 1978). For this reason, patients may be particularly trusting and may benefit from the power of positive thinking. However, if their conditions do not improve, they may be loath to admit it.

Another spiritualist group is the Christian Science Church, whose members believe that conventional medicine is anti-Christian. "They are taught that 'illness is an illusion' and can be cured only through prayer," explains Andrew Skolnick (1990, para. 5). Christian Scientists believe that orthodox medical care makes illnesses worse. Thus,

they do not use drugs or surgery, and they refuse even simple home treatments such as heating pads, ice packs, and back rubs. Christian Scientists' refusal to allow medical care has raised controversy across the nation, especially when children's lives are involved (Skolnick, 1990). Some believe that denying children the medical care that might save their lives is a form of child abuse. For example, a Massachusetts couple, David and Ginger Twitchell, was convicted of involuntary manslaughter in 1990 after their 2-year-old son died from an obstructed bowel (Margolick, 1990). The couple had refused to allow doctors to treat the toddler, and medical experts considered his death preventable. Others feel that requiring medical care violates Christian Scientists' right to worship as they choose. The Twitchells were acquitted of the charges in 1993 on the grounds that a state law exempted people from child neglect charges if they were acting in accordance with their religious beliefs. Not long afterward, Massachusetts became the fifth state to revoke that law (Sanghavi, 2008).

A belief in the supernatural also characterizes the health beliefs of some southern Appalachians (Bille, 1981). In that culture, spiritual ceremonies involving faith healing and glossolalia (speaking in tongues) are believed to restore health. **Faith healers** are expected to channel the curative power of the Holy Spirit, which they pass to believers through ceremonies known as the laying on of hands. **Glossolalia** involves a trancelike state during which a worshipper seems to speak in a foreign language. It is believed that the language is known only to God or that it is a foreign tongue known to some but unknown to the worshipper, except through divine inspiration (Lippy & Williams, 1988).

Even scientists acknowledge the power of faith, although they are not likely to regard it as the central focus of their work. Evidence supports that people who expect to be cured sometimes are, even when the "treatment" is an inactive **placebo** such as flavored water or sugar. Placebo effects are so common that medical researchers routinely give some research participants an actual treatment and give other people a placebo. If the treatment group does not experience greater effects than the placebo group, the researchers cannot be sure that they are measuring anything more than the power of suggestion. Sometimes placebo effects are unintentional.

When thermometers were introduced in a British hospital in the 1800s, some patients assumed they were curative and seemed to recover spontaneously before the treatment could be administered (White, 1896/1925). The reverse is sometimes true as well. People who have no confidence in a treatment may be unaffected by it. These examples do not prove that all disease can be reduced to the effects of faith and emotions. However, they demonstrate that there's more to disease than meets the (microscopic) eye.

A religious-like faith in caregivers serves multiple goals. It inspires confidence (on the part of patient and caregiver), which may be an important part of healing. It also honors the extraordinary role caregivers play in managing life and health.

There is a downside, though, in dashed hopes and exorbitant malpractice claims. With the expectation that medicine can work miracles if done correctly, people may feel particularly angry when things don't go well, and they may rightly or wrongly charge that their caregivers are incompetent (Kreps, 1990).

Providers and Consumers

It has become popular to describe health care in terms of consumerism. Patients are regarded as shoppers or clients who pay caregivers primarily to provide information and carry out the patients' wishes (Roter et al., 1997). Consumerism is fueled in part by Internet resources. People can now look up extensive health information for themselves. Websites such as ConsumerReportsHealth.org, DoctorScorecard.com, and AngiesList.com now offer reviews of hospitals, treatments, products, and doctors—including consumer reviews of doctors' bedside manner, perceived quality of care, price, the cleanliness of their offices, the courteousness of their staff members, and more.

Competitiveness has made many caregivers especially mindful of patient satisfaction. However, some caregivers who see themselves as serving a higher purpose than profit margins find the marketplace metaphors disturbing. And analysts warn that consumer websites can have a backlash. For one, since anyone can file comments online but most people won't, the comments that appear may not represent most patients' opinions. For another, physicians who are worried about their stats may

be dissuaded from taking high-risk cases, which are more likely than others to result in lawsuits and disappointing outcomes. Thus, consumer reviews can inadvertently punish doctors for going out on a limb for patients with critical or rare conditions.

Years ago, Howard Friedman and M. Robin DiMatteo (1979) cautioned that consumerism may be a risky conceptualization for all involved. If the customer is always right, they wondered, will medical centers that respect patients' treatment decisions later be held liable if adverse outcomes result? Friedman and DiMatteo also worried that pleasing patients may sometimes be at odds with helping them. Considering that the most effective medical options are sometimes the most unpleasant, how far will caregivers go to avoid upsetting their patients?

Similarly, consumerism seems to place cost as a top priority. Richard Glass (1996) is concerned that physicians may choose less aggressive treatment options if they are forced to be more mindful of cost than care. A physician himself, Glass maintains that patients "rightly expect something different from their doctors than from consumer goods salespersons" (p. 148). He argues that a marketplace mentality may have "perverse effects" on medical care, and he beseeches health care managers not to interfere unduly in medical decision making.

There is some evidence that people who are well informed about health information don't view their doctors in quite the same way as before. Unlike generations past, we're unlikely to believe that doctors have all the answers (Lowrey & Anderson, 2006). This may diminish physicians' professional status. Or it may simply fuel a different kind of relationship, such as the one we will discuss next.

Partners

Only as partners do patients and caregivers assume roughly the same role. Of course, they each bring something different to the encounter in terms of experiences and expertise. But as partners, they are directed toward the same goals and they act as peers. The partner role is consistent with collaborative medical talk.

As partners, patients and caregivers ideally use a vocabulary they both understand, and they make decisions together. The success of health care managed in this way hinges largely on the

> **💬 IN YOUR EXPERIENCE**
>
> Which of the roles described in this section have you played as either a patient or a caregiver? Which appeal to you most? Why?

quality of patient–caregiver relationships. In 1996, the *Journal of the American Medical Association* introduced a column called "The Patient–Physician Relationship." In an article launching the new feature, Glass (1996, p. 148) proclaimed the doctor–patient link to be the "center of medicine," a covenant not to be compromised by impersonal reliance on technology or profit-oriented decisions. This emphasis underscores the importance of trusting communication between patients and caregivers.

Retired physician Francis Lombardo (1997) writes that he earned patients' trust and partnership by being a respectful listener. As he describes it: "Once a patient has sized you up as someone who won't hassle or ridicule him, he'll feel much freer to bring up those touchy topics himself, like the fact that he thinks he might be gay" (p. 121).

Some people find the partnership model appealing because it allows both patients and caregivers to have influence over medical decisions, as opposed to being strictly patient-centered or caregiver-centered (Beck, Ragan, & du Pré, 1997; Smith & Hoppe, 1991). Hufford (1997) attests that patients have important and relevant statements to make about their own health: "Sick people, it turns out, often do know exactly what has been happening to them, what it feels like, and when it happens, and there is nothing fictional about it" (p. 118).

One way to encourage patients' active participation is to follow the lead of Myra Skluth (2007) and create patient to-do lists. She and patients negotiate the terms of the to-do lists; then each keeps a copy. "This approach works very well," she says (p. 16). Because the to-do lists are in patients' charts, "if they call with questions, the nurses know exactly what I told them. I can also review the items with them at the beginning of the next visit—what they accomplished, and what they didn't and why. I find my patients really appreciate this" (p. 16).

Few people criticize the idea of patients and caregivers as partners. However, this may be a difficult transition to make. Patients and caregivers have traditionally upheld the expectation that caregivers will guide medical discussions and patients will be relatively quiet and passive in their presence. A shift is possible, and indeed we see some evidence of it, but it will require continued change and cooperation on both sides.

Implications

These interaction models characterize various aspects of medical discourse, yet they aren't as simple as they appear. Transactions often, perhaps always, involve elements of several models, even if one is dominant. Evelyn Ho and Carma Bylund (2008) make the point that holistic medicine such as acupuncture typically transcends and blends these models to such an extent that none of them provides an accurate description. One acupuncture intern in their study described holistic medicine this way: "It's about connecting yourself and your patients to the greater whole (the Tao, the yin-yang circle), and by doing so you both can rise to your highest potential" (p. 511). As Ho and Bylund observed, practitioners oriented to this goal were sometimes paternalistic, sometimes consensual, sometimes mechanistic. Mostly they invoked a blend of all the models.

After considering the many cultural viewpoints and options available to people, the challenge of communicating effectively is especially evident. Let's review some of the experts' tips.

Communication Skill Builder: Developing Cultural Competence

Although it is useful to be aware of overall cultural differences, be careful about assuming cultural beliefs based on people's appearance or ancestry. For example, Hispanic Americans may have roots in Central America, South America, or the Caribbean—all of which have different customs (Murquia, Peterson, & Zea, 2003). To recognize cultural and individual differences, Betty Pierce Dennis and Ernestine Small (2003) suggest that caregivers consider the following questions when getting to know people from other cultures:

- How do the client and family members identify themselves? For example, do they call themselves American, Jamaican, Puerto Rican, Russian American, or Ghanaian?
- Are the caregivers' questions answered by the client or by another family member?
- Is there a family member who always speaks first? Who makes decisions?
- Do the family members speak with the caregiver in English and to each other in another language?
- Will you need an interpreter? Is so, select one that fits the family structure. For example, if only men respond to interview questions, a child or a female would not be an appropriate interpreter.
- Determine how respect is shown. Ask what titles should be used. First names may be regarded as disrespectful.
- In some cultures, maintaining eye contact shows interest and involvement, but in others it is considered disrespectful. Which is true in the client's culture?
- Food is cultural. What are the food choices of the client? Are ethnic dishes preferred? Can arrangements be made with the family based on the medical needs of the client?

To conclude the chapter, we will look at two overarching issues relevant to the way that health is shaped by culture and exerts its own influence. We will start with holistic therapies, which have a great deal in common with many of the ideas about balance and health maintenance we have discussed here.

Holistic Care

Warm and softly lit, lovely music playing in the background, clean with white sheets on a massage table. So far so good. . . . Jing had me lay on my stomach. It was a great idea. I couldn't see the needles and it helped my breathing regulate. Thank goodness for yogic breathing! Jing's soft, calm voice continued to set the tone. Truth? I could barely feel the needles go in. . . . If I hadn't known that something was happening, I'm not quite sure what I would have thought the incredibly mild sensation was on my skin. There was the slightest of sensations, followed by a feeling of

energy flowing. . . . When they were all in, Jing asked me about my comfort, made sure I was okay, wrapped me up, and sweetly and comfortably allowed me to have the experience for about twenty minutes or so. The best way that I can describe the experience is to relate it to twinkling lights. . . . It was a lovely, subtle feeling. . . . The rest of the day I felt relaxed, calm and as serene as I feel after a restorative yoga class. . . . Allergies have been less of a problem than they have been in over twenty years. —Lisa, acupuncture client ("Fertility," 2012, np)

Such is the experience of one acupuncture client. In the United States, options such as acupuncture, meditation, and chiropractic, once derided as quackery, are gaining renewed acceptance. There are a number of reasons for this, including their emphasis on open communication. The following section describes holistic forms of medicine, factors fueling recent interest in them, and their advantages and drawbacks.

Definitions

The term *alternative medicine* has traditionally been applied to therapies that have not been scientifically researched and consequently approved by professional associations such as the AMA. However, "alternative" is not a particularly accurate description of these therapies. As Lisa Schreiber (2005) points out, it's not an either/or proposition. Many people use "alternative" therapies in conjunction with other treatments. For example, meditation, prayer, and yoga are not biomedical means of treating cancer, but most oncologists agree that, if they are useful in promoting emotional well-being, they are valuable components of a treatment regimen.

Some have adopted the term *complementary medicine* or *alternative and complementary medicine (CAM)*. But these are problematic as well, in that they define these therapies not by what they *are* but simply in terms of their (implicitly peripheral) relation to biomedicine. Another semantic alternative is the term *traditional medicine*, used in parts of the world such as Africa, Asia, and Latin America. However, this term seems to exclude recent innovations. At a preconference meeting at the National Communication Association some

---

BOX 7.5

Holistic Medicine at a Glance

Acupuncture is believed to stimulate and balance the body's energy flow (*Qi*) through the use of tiny needles inserted in the skin.

Ayurveda is based on ancient Indian practices, including yoga, diet, and meditation.

Biofeedback involves learning to recognize the body's physiological states (such as tension) and to control them.

Chiropractic medicine focuses on the physical alignment of the spine, muscles, and nerves.

Herbal therapies use plant extracts such as chamomile, licorice, and St. John's wort to treat ailments ranging from skin conditions to asthma and depression.

Holistic care emphasizes overall well-being (physical and emotional), with an emphasis on maintaining health, not just curing ailments.

Integrative medicine combines biomedical and naturopathic therapies.

Homeopathic medicine uses very small doses to escalate symptoms in an effort to stimulate the body's immune system. (In contrast, most mainstream medical care is *allopathic*, relying on remedies that counteract symptoms.) *Homeo* is derived from the Greek word meaning "same," and *allo* comes from the Greek word for "other."

Naturopathic medicine focuses on diet and the use of herbal therapies to help people maintain good health.

Osteopathic medicine is taught in traditional medical schools. This branch of medicine focuses on the muscular and skeletal system, treating the body as an integrated unit.

Reiki (pronounced RAY-kee) is based on the Japanese tradition of channeling energy through the healer's hands to increase the patient's spiritual strength.

Traditional Asian medicine includes therapies such as herbal remedies, acupuncture, and massage. It is based on establishing a healthy flow of energy through the body and achieving harmony between mind, body, spirit, and surroundings.

---

years ago, I was part of an extended conversation on this issue. In the end, I think none of the delegates was entirely satisfied with the vocabulary available so far. For lack of a better term, I take Schreiber's suggestion and use the term *holistic medicine* here, rather than *alternative* and/or *complementary medicine*. Some make a good point that not all methods that fall within this rubric are holistic; but, for the most part, their approach is more holistic than biomedical therapies, which are grounded to a large extent in identifying specific causes and cures of illness. A brief glossary that explains the wide variety of holistic therapies is available in Box 7.5.

Popularity

There are several reasons for the recent popularity of holistic medicine. For one, an increasing number of people are receptive to the idea. About 38% of adults in the United States and 12% of children use holistic therapies such as acupuncture, chiropractic, aruveyda, meditation, massage, yoga, and hypnosis (National Center for Complementary, 2012). Acceptance is even greater in some areas of the world. In some parts of Asia and Africa, 80% of citizens rely primarily on holistic care (WHO, 2008a).

💬 IN YOUR EXPERIENCE

■ Have you ever taken part in holistic treatment (e.g., meditation, herbal supplements, acupuncture, chiropractic)?

■ If so, what was your experience?

■ If you were the patient, did you tell your doctor about it? Why or why not?

Second, well-trained caregivers are becoming more plentiful. In the United States, chiropractic is one of the fastest-growing occupations. There are currently about 52,600 chiropractors in the United States, and the number is expected to rise 28% between 2010 and 2020 (U.S. Bureau of Labor Statistics, 2012c). More than 50 colleges in the United States are devoted to chiropractic, traditional Asian medicine, and/or naturopathic medicine.

Third, research dollars are more available than in the past. In 1997, the U.S. Congress voted to fund an Office of Alternative Medicine as part of the National Institutes of Health (NIH). This new NIH office offers funding for researchers interested in testing the efficacy of diverse therapies. For example, acupuncture has been shown in clinical trials to help some people lose weight, relieve chronic depression, diminish some forms of pain, and meet a range of other treatment goals, particularly when combined with other forms of care (Cho, Lee, Thabane, & Lee, 2009; Tough & White, 2011; Zhang, Chen, Yip, Ng, & Wong, 2010).

Finally, many insurance companies and physicians are now giving the go-ahead to nonbiomedical treatments, and Medicare and workers' compensation plans in all 50 states reimburse chiropractic care.

Advantages

There are several reasons for the growing popularity of holistic care. For one, such care typically involves low-cost and low-technology methods. If these are useful, they stand to reduce health care costs. That's good news for insurance companies and managed care if people simultaneously maintain their involvement in conventional care (which they seem inclined to do). WHO is supporting research to see if low-cost herbal remedies can effectively treat malaria, AIDS, diabetes, and other conditions in impoverished areas of the world.

Second, complementary methods are usually based on simple principles that may be more understandable and less frightening to patients than conventional medicine (Brown, Cassileth, Lewis, & Renner, 1994). Patients often feel they better understand and can even manage their own holistic care. Astin (1998) found that people who use holistic therapies often choose them because they

> **BOX 7.6   RESOURCES**
>
> ## Curricula on Holistic Medicine
>
> The Association of American Medical Colleges provides guiding principles and an annotated bibliography for faculty who wish to integrate information about holistic therapies. See Gaster, Unterborn, Scott, and Schneeweiss's article, "What Should Students Learn About Complementary and Alternative Medicine?" (October 2007, *Journal of the Association of American Medical Colleges*, pp. 934–938).

reflect their personal philosophy about health. For the most part, these people are not dissatisfied with biomedicine, which suggests that they will continue to see both physicians and holistic care specialists.

Third, holistic practitioners often spend more time with their patients and develop closer relationships with them than do biomedical practitioners. This may suit people who feel that most medical settings are too impersonal. As a Costa Rican practitioner in Geist-Martin and Bell's (2009) study expressed it, "The most important thing is to listen. If I listen to the patient I am able to know what worries him, what he needs, what bothers him, and from there I can better maneuver the process" (p. 636). Providers in their study also spoke about the need to honor the patient's language and perspective: "If he says he feels like an elephant is pressing down on his chest, then you write 'Patient feels like an elephant is pressing down on his chest'; then in parentheses you write down the medical term for that symptom" (Geist-Martin & Bell, 2009, p. 637). In that way, the holistic care providers privilege neither medical language nor the Voice of Lifeworld, but honor them both.

People often say that being heard and not being rushed are their favorite aspects of holistic care visits. In a study of homeopathy, Christine Hartog (2009) observed that the visits were typically longer than doctors' visits, and because the homeopathy visits did not usually involve a physical exam, the entire encounter was available for communication, not just part of it. Patients in her study frequently remarked on how gratifying it was to be treated as a "whole person."

WHAT DO YOU THINK?

Would you be interested in a career in holistic medicine? Why or why not?

See Box 7.7 at the end of this section for career resources.

Similarly, participants in a British study of homeopathic care said they appreciate how well the caregivers listen, the equality within the patient–caregiver relationship, the compassion of the staff, and being treated holistically (Mercer & Reilly, 2004). Said a 46-year-old participant in the study about the homeopathy practitioner she visited:

> That was the most amazing thing—that he asked about all of that history. Nobody has ever done that, and I just have gone to hospitals over the years and they've said, "Yeah, your bones, your knee joints are sort of joined together, and we need to do another op"—that sort of thing. No but somehow, the way he asked questions and so on, I thought "oh gosh, this guy knows what he's doing because he's looking at this, everything together." . . . that sort of gave me hope. (quoted by Mercer & Reilly, 2004, p. 16)

Fourth, holistic therapies are usually more directed to health maintenance than is biomedicine, which has traditionally focused on curing and treating. The new imperative to conserve health care resources and money makes prevention appealing.

Finally, people may turn to holistic therapies if other methods offer little or no help. For example, symptoms of anxiety that are not alleviated by medication may sometimes be managed with relaxation and biofeedback.

Drawbacks

Many holistic therapies are nonthreatening. Energy work, relaxation, and minute traces of natural substances (as in homeopathy) are unlikely to hurt anyone. However, some therapies involve the use of herbs and other natural products. Because they are considered dietary supplements rather than drugs, the U.S. Food and Drug Administration does not require manufacturers to register them or prove their safety before they go on the market. Consequently, many supplements are not thoroughly researched. This is worrisome, first, because significant health risks are associated with some natural therapies. Taken by the wrong person or in the wrong amount, they can be deadly. Some natural remedies have caused lead poisoning, hepatitis, and renal failure. The herb germander, often included in herbal teas and tablets, has been linked to acute nonviral hepatitis. Before it was banned, the herb ephedra, sold as a natural enhancement for bodybuilding, was linked to at least 17 deaths (Capriotti, 1999; WHO, 2003, Update 83).

Another concern is that people may be swindled into buying useless products. Cancer patients, for instance, are vulnerable to advertisers who claim to provide the latest life-saving serum. Shark cartilage sells for as much as $115 per bottle, although there is no convincing evidence that it diminishes cancer.

Third, endangered plant species may be wiped out in the zeal to provide health benefits (and reap the financial awards) associated with high-demand herbal remedies. Already, harvesters have endangered rain forests in Malaysia, Africa, and the Amazon. Environmentalists urge world citizens to consider regulations, herbal farming, and ocean-based cultivation to protect the planet's wildlife.

A final drawback is principally an issue of perception. People who use holistic medicine may be inclined not to tell their doctors about it, which can lead to dangerous drug interactions. Only about one-third of Americans who use holistic therapies tell their physicians about them (Kennedy, Chi-Chuan, & Wu, 2007). A study of 80 people with cancer in the United Kingdom revealed that, when doctors were dismissive or critical of holistic therapies, people were more likely either to abandon them or to avoid mentioning them to the doctor (Tovey & Broom, 2007). One woman described her doctors' reaction to acupuncture: "They didn't actually ridicule it, but they said, hmmm [frowns]. I felt like they didn't really want to talk about it" (p. 2556). In another study, physicians were more likely to suggest acupuncture and chiropractic if they knew the practitioner and felt confident that he or she was well trained (A.-F. Hsiao et al., 2006). However, they were unlikely to know holistic practitioners unless they were part of the same practice, as when physician/acupuncturists or physician/chiropractors were on staff.

Holistic Medicine

Acupuncturist
Chiropractor
Holistic nurse
Massage therapist
Midwife
Naturopathic physician
Nutritionist/dietician
Reiki practitioner
Yoga instructor

CAREER RESOURCES AND JOB LISTINGS

- Academy of Nutrition and Dietetics: http://www.eatright.org
- Accrediting Bureau of Health Education Schools: http://www.abhes.org
- American Association of Naturopathic Physicians: http://naturopathic.org/content.asp?contentid=60
- American Chiropractic Association: http://www.acatoday.org
- American College of Nurse Midwives: http://www.midwife.org
- American Council on Exercise: http://www.acefitness.org
- American Massage Therapy Association: http://www.amtamassage.org/index.html
- Associated Bodywork and Massage Professionals: http://www.abmp.com/home
- Association of Chiropractic Colleges: http://www.chirocolleges.org
- Commission on Dietetic Registration: http://www.cdrnet.org
- International Association of Reiki Professionals: http://www.iarp.org
- U.S. Bureau of Labor Statistics Occupational Outlook Handbook: http://www.bls.gov/ooh

We conclude the chapter on a contrasting note, with a review of Western medicine taken to extremes, largely, it would seem, for the sake of profits.

Viagra: Case Study in Health-Culture Overlap

You know the commercial. A man driving a vintage Mustang along an arid country road (think Marlboro country) pulls into an old-fashioned gas station after steam begins to rise from his car's engine. It looks like car trouble. But not to worry. A confident male announcer says: "You're at the age where you don't get thrown by curve balls. THIS IS THE AGE OF KNOWING HOW TO GET THINGS DONE" (these capitalized words appear on screen during the voice-over). The man calmly opens the hood, ducks inside the station for a cool bottle of water, which he sips while walking confidently past the (obviously older) male mechanic, who has stopped what he's doing to watch the man. As the announcer asks: "So why would you let something like erectile dysfunction get in your way?" the driver pours the water into his radiator and shuts the hood, ready to go again. The man resumes his drive as the announcer says: "With every age comes responsibility. Ask your doctor if your heart is healthy enough for sex. Side effects may include headache, flushing, upset stomach, and abnormal vision. . . . " Again in the Mustang, the man drives away, windows down, to the tune of bluesy guitar rifts.

For now, let's set aside the reality that the elderly mechanic is a far more likely candidate for erectile dysfunction than the younger Mustang driver. Although ED is most common among men age 65 and older, Pfizer is criticized for marketing the drug to younger men, with the result that the largest growing segment of Viagra users are men ages 18 to 55 (Delate, Simmons, & Motheral, 2004). Let's focus instead on the 1,824 deaths related to sildenafil, the active ingredient in Viagra, as well as 14,818 instances of other adverse effects (including heart attacks) that have been reported to the U.S. Food and Drug Administration in the last 10 years (Lowe & Costabile, 2012). Despite these, the potentially serious consequences of taking the drug are offset in commercials by words, music, and images that suggest the opposite. One blogger quipped that, in the content of what we know about Viagra, the Howlin' Wolf song behind the commercial "sounds like someone having a heart attack/stroke and an orgasm simultaneously."

The independent masculinity of the model in the commercial, supported by the ease and confidence with which he handles what might otherwise be a frustrating scenario, is underscored by the all-cap message that "THIS IS THE AGE OF KNOWING HOW TO GET THINGS DONE." The implication is clear—real men, the kind of men who drive muscle cars and cause other men to stop and stare—don't slow down or proceed cautiously if a little trouble occurs "under the hood." They take action right away.

One thing's for sure: Viagra has captured people's attention. It's second only to Coca-Cola in terms of brand-name fame (Baglia, 2005). In *The Viagra Ad Venture*, Jay Baglia (2005) explores the cultural impact of the Pfizer product that at least one reporter has dubbed "the national drug of choice." Baglia's analysis reveals a carefully constructed deep-pockets campaign to define (in the most lucrative terms possible) what it means to be a man. The persuasive pitch, observes Baglia, is supported by an adoring media and health officials' willingness to consider the male erection a medical necessity covered by insurance and military benefits—even when it threatens to break the bank. Let's look at a few of the most potent implications of the hype about the little blue pill.

Implication 1: To Be a Man You Have to Get It Up

Viagra commercials have gone through several incarnations. Before the "get things done series" was the *Viva Viagra!* theme. A typical spot in that series showed a rather awkward man taking dance lessons with a Latina instructor. Then the scene shifted to a wedding reception at which the man, now confident and in control, whirled a diamond-bejeweled blonde woman around the dance floor as a voice-over intoned: "Whatever steps you're taking to impress your partner, don't let erectile dysfunction get in the way." Clearly, part of "impressing your partner" involves getting an erection.

The *Viva Viagra!* ads showed instant relationship transformations. A woman overlooked her timid neighbor, a wife sat despondently at the other end of the sofa, and various other images of Dullsville until—Wow!—instant spark. The women seemed almost comically overjoyed to find that the men in their lives were suddenly Viagra-improved. (As we will soon discuss, gay men, although they are as likely as any other man to experience ED, are not part of the image Pfizer has created.)

The message is clear, says Baglia (2005): "Nothing tells a man he is masculine—not muscles, earning potential, an attractive partner, or even height—so much as his erection does" (p. 9). The "get things done" ads have gone even further. They don't hint at sex very much. The focus is on something deeper: masculinity itself. The implication is that one sort of man takes Viagra—a "real" man, in the sense of one who is sexy, youngish, self-reliant, and cool under pressure.

And if that's not reductive and intimidating enough, Pfizer has raised the bar on acceptable "male sexual performance" so high that men are nearly certain to feel inadequate. A man who scores 21 points or fewer on Pfizer's 25-point Sexual Health Inventory for Men is instructed to ask his doctor for help. In the tricky game of measuring up to social expectations, it seems Pfizer has defined *normal* and *masculine* to suit its own ends. Judging by the 25 million males who have secured a Viagra prescription so far (Viva Viagra, 2008), men are buying it—literally and figuratively.

Implication 2: To a Physical Ailment Let There Be a Physical Remedy

Following closely on the heels of a well-designed sucker punch to the ego, Pfizer offers this reassurance: Don't feel bad, men. It's not under your control. It's under *ours*. What used to be considered "male impotence"—a term that suggests no specific cause but conveys an "unmasculine" sense of powerlessness—is now referred to as *erectile dysfunction* (ED), a less emotional term that connotes a physical disorder (Baglia, 2005). Certainly there are physical conditions associated with some cases of impotence. But experts have long maintained that stress, emotions, relational health, and state of mind often play a part as well. The Viagra promise brushes those factors aside. The men who take Viagra, if we believe the commercials, have none of those problems.

You may have noticed the double standard. On one hand, a man is defined by his erectile function. On the other, ED is outside a man's control (Baglia, 2005). That's the conundrum that makes Viagra seem indispensable, even to many men who have no erectile dysfunction. Although ED is most common among men 65 and older, 1 in 5 healthy men ages 18 to 30 have taken some form of erectile dysfunction drug, usually, they say, to boost their "sexual confidence" or "sexual performance" (Bechara, Casabé, De Bonis, Hellen, & Bertolino, 2010). "You get the 24-year-old who thinks he has erectile dysfunction if they stay up all night and can't get up and do it five times the next morning," says Thomas Jarrett, MD, head of urology at George Washington University (quoted by S. James, 2011, para. 19). It's no coincidence, suggests Baglia (2005), that the actors in the commercials have gotten noticeably younger through the years.

It's a dangerous situation. Even when Viagra doesn't cause health problems of its own, it may mask them. Some health experts urge men to address underlying factors that may contribute to ED, such as depression, stress, diabetes, kidney disease, hypertension, obesity, prostate cancer, and cardiovascular disease, rather than risk their health even more with a pharmaceutical work-around. At one point, Pfizer boasted that underlying health concerns were coming to light in record numbers when men who wouldn't usually see their doctors made appointments to get Viagra. The prevalence of online subscription opportunities that don't require a medical exam seems to short-circuit that benefit, however.

Implication 3: Women Are Passive but Grateful Recipients of Male Attention

In influencing cultural ideas about masculinity, Pfizer simultaneously implicates women's identity. In the *Viva Viagra!* ads, it's the man's job to instigate intimacy and romance. He gives the meaningful look, takes dance lessons, presents the woman with flowers, buys a motorcycle, and so forth. Women seldom play a role except to respond, quite enthusiastically, to their men's sudden sexual interest. Women in the ads tend to embody passive, traditional roles. For example, Baglia (2005, p. 84) describes an article in *LifeDrive* (a Pfizer magazine dedicated to Viagra-related stories) that encourages men to demonstrate their "Casanova" potential by washing the dishes, explaining: "This is a gift she will truly love. Do some of *her* chores" (emphasis added).

Women are noticeably absent in the "getting things done" series, perhaps because the men in

WHAT DO YOU THINK?

■ Do you feel that Pfizer exploits men in the way it markets Viagra? Why or why not?

■ Do you think companies that advertise medical products should be sensitive to the ways they influence cultural ideas about masculinity, femininity, sex, and race? Why or why not?

them are portrayed as independent loners, not as the type who pal around with females, unless, presumably, they're cashing in on Viagra effects that have nothing to do with driving a GTO through the dessert.

Implication 4: Real Men are White and Straight

In the pervasive images that Pfizer presents, masculinity is portrayed in mostly White, relentlessly heterosexual ways. In this context, "other ways of being a socio/sexual human being don't exist" says Baglia (2005, p. 98). It's a rub with which women are all too familiar. Exploitive sales pitches that depict feminine attractiveness in Anglo terms spare women of color to some extent. For example, eating disorders have traditionally been less prevalent among Black women than among White women. However, being typecast as other, subordinate, or outright nonexistent is no better. In many ways, it's worse.

Implication 5: Intimacy Equals Vaginal Penetration

The suggestion that Viagra yields virility, confidence, and sexual fulfillment is so palpable that many men are surprised when they don't automatically feel aroused. "What happens when a man first takes a Viagra pill? Absolutely nothing," writes Tara Parker-Pope (2002, para. 10). She explains that the drug isn't an aphrodisiac. "Among several men interviewed who have used the drug, not one of them experienced any feeling or sensation after taking the pill," Parker-Pope says. "The nothingness is so intense that the most common reaction is a slight panic that the drug isn't going to work" (para. 11).

Just as Viagra doesn't produce sexual feelings in men, neither does it create instant intimacy between people. True intimacy, Baglia (2005) reminds us, doesn't come in a pill but through communication, closeness, trust, and mutual respect. And sex comes in many forms that do not require a rigid member, served up pronto.

R. V. Scheide—who despite having no actual ED symptoms conned his doctor into giving him a Viagra prescription but, to his credit, feels a little bad about it—asks with at least a modicum of sarcasm: In today's fast-paced life, who has *time* for true intimacy? Scheide (2006) invokes George Ritzer's idea of the McDonaldization of society to suggest that we tend to treat sex the same way (Ballantine, Roberts, & Ritzer, 2008; Ritzer, 1993). McSex, we might call it, is served up quickly, without much wait and with very little effort or forethought—à la Viagra. Or at least that's the sales pitch.

Is that what we want—a "Viagra utopia" of fast-food sex in which masculinity and intimacy are reduced to the likelihood of a penile erection? Are erections so essential to intimacy and happiness that it's worth risking men's health and sometimes their lives to attain them? These are important questions. But they're often lost in the hype. Most media accounts, far from challenging the shaky presumptions of Pfizer's campaign, have endorsed Viagra as "the new miracle drug," "the potency wonder drug," and "the new national drug of choice" (quoted by Baglia, 2005, p. 28). Granted, some writers *have* taken issue with the dangers and fallacies of the Viagra promise. Baglia quotes a *Newsweek* reporter who made the point that "a poor lover plus Viagra does not make a good lover, but merely a poor lover with an erection" (p. 37). But the risks of Viagra are typically downplayed, and most media professionals are not stepping up to include marginalized populations in the conversation. Of 52 Viagra-related news stories that Baglia studied, none of them mentioned gay men in reference to erectile dysfunction.

With an advertising budget of nearly $128 million a year, Viagra is unlikely to disappear from the media or the public conscience (Arnold, 2012). And the presence of similar drugs with similar advertisements is likely to compound the effect. Maybe, despite ourselves, we'll be humming Howlin' Wolf all day. But there is one thing we *can* do, says Baglia (2005). We can stop to consider the implications and think for ourselves. Recognizing that

More About Viagra, Health, and Culture

Baglia, J. (2005). *The Viagra adVenture*. New York: Peter Lang.

Friedman, D. M. (2003). *A mind of its own: A cultural history of the penis*. New York: Penguin.

Loe, M. (2004). *The rise of Viagra: How the little blue pill changed sex in America*. New York: New York University Press.

culture doesn't affect only health communication—that, sometimes, it's the other way around—we can be skeptical consumers of health information. We can recognize the marginalizing effects of narrow definitions of masculinity, femininity, intimacy, sex, race, ethnicity, gender, health, and so, and we can reject exclusionary images that cast some among us as less vital or important than others. (There's a great deal more to say about the Viagra phenomenon. For information about Baglia's book and other resources, see Box 7.8 above.)

SUMMARY

Social desirability and cultural modes of expression influence the way people think about health and illness. As we strive to become better communicators, it's important to understand cultural diversity.

People from traditionally Asian and Pacific Island, Hispanic, and Arab cultures are similar in that they tend to value trusting relationships and to prefer health care encounters in which caregivers take time to know their patients. They are also sensitive to status differences, sometimes to the extent of masking their disagreement or confusion so as not to offend the caregiver or create disharmony. People from Asian cultures may seem reserved to Westerners because they often avoid direct eye contact and emotional expressiveness except in close relationships. Traditionally, Hispanic individuals place a high value on warm, trusting relationships and respect. They typically consider that close friends and family members are integral in coping with hardship. Caregivers who do not realize this can cause offense and interfere with social support. On the other hand, learning even a bit of a patient's native language can help caregivers be more effective.

Traditional Arabs may be alarmed if their physicians make predictions, believing that only Allah controls the future and that humans invite disaster by making bold forecasts about what will happen. Like Asians, they are likely to consider mental illness shameful and to deny that they are in emotional distress. Islamic diet and customs can seem alien to Westerners, but they are understandable with a little effort.

From one perspective, disease is an organic phenomenon, and what shows up under a microscope may be more to the point than a patient's subjective experiences. Consistent with the biomedical model, this perspective considers undetectable conditions less real than physically verifiable ones. From another perspective, some people believe health is affected by harmony among such factors as relationships, spiritual forces, the environment, behavior, and energy fields within the body. The organic perspective lends itself to scientific and statistical analysis, whereas the harmony perspective recognizes illness as a phenomenon that occurs for different reasons in different people. Health is believed to reflect harmony among all aspects of a person's life. From this perspective, personal viewpoints, habits, and social networks are considered integral parts of the health equation.

The premises that underlie diverse beliefs may be more similar than they seem. Even staunch supporters of the organic approach admit that stress and attitude affect healing. And people in many cultures acknowledge an organic element as well as a spiritual element to disease. The theory of health as expanded consciousness proposes that a health disruption can be a valuable opportunity for reflection and change.

Diseases and their implications are open to cultural interpretation. Particularly when great uncertainty surrounds a disease or when medicine can do little to help, people are likely to assume that supernatural forces are at work. Society may also stigmatize people who have dread diseases as being menacing and contemptible. At the other extreme, people may regard ill individuals as helpless victims.

Cultural values and assumptions are embodied in the roles that patients and caregivers play. How one interprets illness has an effect on the type of healing process preferred. If disease is regarded as a physical phenomenon, patients may be like passive machines and caregivers like mechanics or scientists. Patients may be considered incapable if they are cast as children seeking the guidance of parent-like caregivers who know what is best.

Caregivers have been deified to varying extents. Even orthodox practitioners who pride themselves on science-based care are regarded with awe for their extraordinary ability to understand and treat illness. In some cultures, healers are spiritual leaders, expected to channel supernatural powers for the benefit of faithful patients. Considering patients and caregivers to be consumers and providers is more enabling for patients, but some people worry that medical care may suffer if it is forced to uphold the rules of the marketplace. Finally, as partners, patients and caregivers work to build mutually satisfying relationships and care plans.

Holistic care specialists focus primarily on lifestyle changes and natural remedies. These diverse therapies are gaining popularity based on public interest, an increase in trained care providers, new research, and increased acceptance by health plans and biomedical practitioners.

Some people seek holistic care when they're not satisfied with the results or nature of biomedicine. In the majority of cases, however, people continue to see physicians and other practitioners as well. The downsides are that some products are not well researched before they go on the market, people may be tricked into buying useless products, and large-scale harvest of natural remedies threatens the environment. Although individuals may assume that natural products are not harmful, they can be deadly. All in all, it's a good idea to become knowledgeable about herbs and supplements before trying them.

Sometimes health-related products and the way in which they are marketed have profound effects on cultural ideals. Viagra is one such product. Some analysts question marketing strategies that seem to downplay the risks of Viagra while exaggerating men's need for it. Especially worrisome is the degree to which Pfizer and some other advertisers create and escalate social insecurities in the interest of making money.

Key Terms and Theories

culture
personalismo
respeto
confianza
susto
halal
organic perspective
evidence-based medicine (EBM)
harmony perspective
yin and yang
Qi
theory of health as expanded consciousness
explicate order
implicate order
stigma
role
paternalism
faith healers
glossolalia
placebo

Discussion Questions

1. How do Easterners and Westerners typically regard health and wellness? What elements of each perspective appeal to you? Why?
2. In what ways does diverse cultural knowledge help us to be more effective concerning health communication?
3. Describe some of the cultural beliefs and practices of Asians and Pacific Islanders. How might these influence health communication?
4. Discuss the importance of *personalismo, respeto*, and *confianza* in traditional Hispanic cultures. How might these ideas influence health communication?
5. What is a *compadre?* What should health professionals know about Hispanic culture in regard to *compadres?*

6. Describe some of the cultural beliefs and practices of Arabs and Muslims. How might these influence health communication?
7. What are the strengths and weaknesses of the organic approach? What are the strengths and weaknesses of the harmony approach?
8. Describe the idea of yin, yang, and *Qi* and how they influence traditional Chinese ideas about health and health care.
9. Describe the principles of the theory of health as expanded consciousness. What is the role of the explicate order? The implicate order? What role do nurses (and other caregivers) play in helping people cope with health episodes?
10. What are the implications of regarding illness as a curse?
11. How can an emphasis on prevention lead to prejudice against ill people?
12. What are some of the expectations regarding care for family members in Thai culture?
13. Name and describe some of the role sets that patients and caregivers play. How is each role set you described likely to affect health communication?
14. What factors contribute to the popularity of holistic medicine? What are the potential advantages? Disadvantages?

Answers to *Can You Guess?*

1. In order, from the largest number of speakers to the least: Mandarin Chinese, Hindi (India), English, Spanish, and Bengali (India and Bangladesh) (Gordon, 2005).

2. The number 168 is the luckiest of those listed because it involves the lucky number 8 and, when said in Chinese, 168 sounds like "the success is rolling in" (Tse, 1999). The number 74 is unluckiest because it sounds similar to "will die" (Tse, 1999).

PART IV

Coping and Health Resources

We all need each other.

—LEO BUSCAGLIA

Two of the most powerful means we have for staying healthy and happy have little in common with each other on the surface.

One is the love and support of people around us. Research is overwhelming that people who have close and supportive relationships with others consider themselves healthier, cope with adversity better, and tend to live longer than others. Communication is the means through which we foster and maintain those ties. In Chapter 8, we will talk about the role of social support, including how we can be effective listeners and good friends and what it means to cope, together, with health crises and end-of-life experiences. We will also look at a few social-support disasters, when efforts that were meant to be helpful turned out to be hurtful instead. The lessons from those experiences can help us avoid the same outcomes.

The second resource is communication technology. At first glance, technology feels far removed from the warmth of companionship and social support. But we find that it can help us to establish and maintain supportive relationships, become well informed, and feel that we have the resources to cope with health issues. The possibilities are expanding faster than we ever imagined, as you will see in Chapter 9.

This unlikely combination of health resources reminds us that—in its many forms—communication is a powerful part of what allows us to be happy in good times and in the midst of life's great challenges.

CHAPTER EIGHT

Social Support, Family Caregiving, and End of Life

Struggling to be strong after the death of his young daughter, Alonzo is hurt and mystified when friends' first question is, "How is your wife?"

Margie misses the normal times, when people talked to her about the weather, boys, and school. Now they just hold doors for her and try not to stare at her wheelchair.

Everyone knows Drew's illness is very serious, but no one speaks of it to him. Drew wonders how he's supposed to cope with such an emotional topic in silence.

Lucy spends two hours each morning and three hours each evening caring for her three children and her elderly mother. In between, she maintains a full-time job outside the home. Lucy is glad she can help, but she wonders how many years it will be before she can take a vacation or spend a quiet day alone. Such thoughts make her feel sad and guilty.

Mario is pleased with life and himself. Things have not been easy, but he appreciates the pleasures of life like never before. Friends and loved ones are closer and he is at peace with himself. He marvels that dying has brought about some of the best days of his life.

As these scenarios suggest, the majority of communication about health does not occur in a doctor's office or hospital. It occurs at home, at the grocery store, on the telephone, and in other settings of everyday life. Spouses, children, friends, and coworkers often have as much influence as doctors and nurses.

Social support includes a broad range of activities, from comforting a friend after a romantic disappointment, to listening while a grieving father tells and retells his story, to performing an Internet data search, to acknowledging that a handicapped individual is a normal person.

Most people perform more supportive behaviors than they realize and, as a consequence, have positive effects on people's health and moods. Research shows that supportive communication can help speed healing, reduce loneliness, reduce symptoms and stress, lessen pain, and build self-esteem (see, e.g., Chia, 2009; Segrin & Domschke, 2011; Thomtén, Soares, & Sundin, 2011). And the benefits go both ways. People who provide social support often feel an enhanced sense of well-being themselves (Robinson & Tian, 2009).

This chapter begins with a conceptual overview of coping and social support, including the role that communication plays as we demonstrate caring for others, strive for a sense of control, and negotiate uncertainties. We will talk about the benefits of social support, but also what happens when well-intentioned efforts hurt more than they help. Then we will briefly explore the role of animal companions and the idea of health crises as transformative experiences before we examine social support in two contexts—family caregiving and end-of-life experiences.

Social support can help minimize the number of stressful events in our lives (a main effect) and help us cope when difficult circumstances arise (a buffering effect).

Conceptual Overview

In the simplest sense, **social support** is people helping people. Melanie Barnes and Steve Duck (1994) define social support as "behaviors that, whether directly or indirectly, communicate to an individual that she or he is valued and cared for by others" (p. 176). Some theorists (e.g., Albrecht & Adelman, 1987) consider that the central function of social support is increasing a person's sense of control. Their viewpoint is substantiated by research (covered in this chapter) that people cope best when they feel well informed and actively involved. This section describes different coping mechanisms and the role social support plays in helping people through crisis situations.

Theoretical Perspectives

The **buffering hypothesis** holds that social support is most important when we encounter potentially

stressful experiences, in which case knowing that other people are there for us can cushion (buffer) us from feeling overwhelmed or helpless (Cohen & Wills, 1985). For example, your ability to cope with bad news may be strengthened by the conviction that loved ones will stick by you no matter what, will be understanding listeners, will help with information and assistance, and so on. The buffering process is likely to be especially meaningful if the support offered matches the support you feel you need. A friend of mine says that, when he tore the anterior cruciate ligament (ACL) in his knee on vacation, he was relatively calm about it because his girlfriend, a physical therapy assistant, was by his side, telling him what to expect in terms of pain, treatment, and recovery. He says her presence and knowledge made the experience feel "doable."

In another sense, social support is like money in the bank. It's nice to know it's there, even if we don't spend it. The **direct-effect** or **main-effect model** proposes that social support is beneficial even when we aren't encountering notable stressors. A strong social network helps us feel valued every day and is a reassuring reminder that friends' support is always available (Barnes & Duck, 1994). When Joann Reinhardt and colleagues (2006) interviewed adults age 65 and older who were experiencing vision loss, they found that participants

After Patrick Swayze (shown here in younger days) was diagnosed with pancreatic cancer, he talked openly about his treatment experiences and his outlook on life and death. His narrative affected many people in similar circumstances. Have you ever felt a sense of connection with a famous person or someone else you didn't know personally? What effect did that have? (AP Photo)

were least likely to be depressed and most likely to adapt well to lifestyle changes if they perceived that they had strong emotional support. For them, actually receiving support was less important than knowing it was there if they needed it (Reinhardt, Boerner, & Horowitz, 2006).

Indeed, the main-effect model suggests that we may encounter fewer stressful episodes and enjoy greater overall health if we have strong social networks (Cohen & Wills, 1985). Older adults who are unsatisfied with the amount of emotional support they received from friends and family members are twice as likely to rate their health only "fair" or "poor" as their peers who feel emotionally supported (White, Philogene, Fine, & Sinha, 2009). They may even live longer. In an Australian study of people 70 and older, those with the most active social networks (in the top third as compared to their peers) were 22% more likely to live another 10 years than those with the least active networks (Giles, Glonek, Luszcz, & Andrews, 2005). This is no surprise to older adults who have experienced the death of a spouse. They typically say that the best coping strategy is to keep busy and interact with others, and the worst coping strategy is to isolate oneself at home (Bergstrom & Holmes, 2000).

There are several reasons for the link between social ties and good health. One is that we learn from others and develop confidence through interactions. Teens are most likely to negotiate safer-sex options with their partners (Troth & Peterson, 2000) and avoid eating disorders (Botta & Dumlao, 2002; Miller-Day & Marks, 2006) if they come from families that display a collaborative problem-solving orientation rather than a distant or conflict-avoidant orientation. Others' actions are informative guides to behavior, especially in intense and uncertain times. For example, when news

broke that Patrick Swayze had pancreatic cancer at about the same time health communication scholar Barbara Sharf learned that her childhood friend Rita had been diagnosed with the disease, Sharf says that Swayze's narrative became part of their experience as well. Sharf (2010) writes that she scanned newsstands for tidbits, enthralled by Swayze's resolve to keep working and his frank descriptions about both the tolerable and the "hellish" aspects of the disease. When she heard news of Swayze's death 4 months after Rita's, she said the news brought fresh waves of grief.

Second, physical benefits are associated with strong social ties. Resting blood pressure and blood glucose levels are lower (healthier) among people who express a great deal of affection compared to those who don't (Floyd, Hesse, & Haynes, 2007); shared humor boosts immunity and other health benefits (Alston, 2007; Wanzer, Sparks, & Frymier, 2009). In contrast, lonely individuals are more likely than others to sleep poorly, to feel stressed, and to have poor health (Hawkley, Masi, Berry, & Cacioppo, 2006; Segrin & Passalacqua, 2010).

Third, loved ones may support us in making healthy decisions. Teenagers are most likely to be effective when confronting their peers about alcohol abuse if both parties perceive that they are good friends and that the concern is legitimate (Malis & Roloff, 2007). Likewise, romantic partners with whom we share a high sense of intimacy are more likely than others to convince us to improve our diets and engage in other healthy behaviors (Dennis, 2006).

It is important to note that the quality of our relationships is more important than the quantity. Having a few close friends and loved ones is typically healthier than an active social life without much intimacy (Segrin & Passalacqua, 2010). And it matters why people support us. Friends' attention is flattering partly because it is freely given, whereas family members are more obliged. When individuals studied by Metts and Manns (1996) told loved ones they had HIV or AIDS, friends were typically more supportive than family, perhaps because the family members were more overwhelmed by their own emotions.

Friendship quality is especially important in later life. After age 70 or so, we're likely to put stock in a small number of very close friends and family members (Nussbaum, Baringer, Fisher, & Kundrat, 2008). These smaller, more intimate networks are well suited to situations in which we may have limited mobility, when close friends are likely to rely extensively on each other, and when changes in hearing and vision may impact our communication abilities (Nussbaum et al., 2008). (See Box 8.1 for more about the effects of communication impairments.)

In short, the buffering hypothesis and main-effects model suggest that social support is helpful during both major life events and the challenges of everyday life. For many reasons, in ways that change throughout our lives, having strong social ties is good for our health. Later in the chapter, we will discuss other theoretical perspectives, including dialectics and problematic integration theory. But to establish a basis for those, let's first shift to the more specific topic of coping.

Coping

To understand social support, it is useful to consider what it means to cope. As Sandra Metts and

---

BOX 8.1

When Communication Ability Is Compromised

Unfortunately, health concerns can interfere with social interaction and friendships, particularly when an individual's ability to communicate is affected. When researchers led by Jennifer Bute (2007) interviewed friends and loved ones of people with compromised communication abilities, they found that some of them continued to feel an easy and even improved camaraderie despite communication limits. But many experienced it as a profound loss, particularly if dementia was involved (Bute, Donovan-Kicken, & Martins, 2007). Said one woman in the study: "It is a different relationship. . . . I have lost the friend I used to have before" (p. 239).

WHAT DO YOU THINK?

1. Have you ever experienced difficulty communicating with someone because of a disability? If so, how did you handle the situation?

2. Has your ability to communicate ever been compromised, even temporarily? Did people respond to you differently? If so, how?

3. What would you do if a loved one could no longer communicate easily with you? Do you think it would change your relationship? If so, how?

Heather Manns (1996) define it, **coping** is "the process of managing stressful situations" (p. 356) that range from everyday hassles to life-threatening occurrences.

Coping usually involves two efforts: changing what can be changed (**problem solving**) and adapting to what cannot be changed (**emotional adjustment**) (Tardy, 1994). Of course, it's not always easy to know when to solve a problem and when to adjust to it. The options vary according to the people and the circumstances involved. Often, coping strategies depend on how much control people believe they have over their situation.

Sometimes attaining a sense of control requires reevaluating ideas about one's body. Canadian

WHAT DO YOU THINK?

■ In what ways do you perceive that you control your health?

■ What factors do you consider to be out of your control?

■ What has led you to these beliefs?

researchers Jennifer English and colleagues (2008) interviewed women about the strategies they used to heal emotionally and physically from the effects of breast cancer. From the respondents' stories, the researchers conceptualized the body as a "therapeutic landscape." Often, they say, that term is used to describe places and physical environments such as spas, gardens, and nature that foster a sense of peace and well-being. In this case, English and colleagues applied the same idea to the body, regarding it as a place of illness but also of healing and recovery.

Breast cancer is particularly relevant to the landscape image, of course, because mastectomies represent a physical redefinition of the body-physical. Although the women interviewed were unaware of the landscape concept, their stories naturally illustrated the concept. For example, one woman described her body as a damaged object:

> It was feeling like I had been broken. . . . My body was cut up and I took all these chemical drugs and I was radiated, and you know what I mean. I just sort of in my mind felt like I was coming from a not very good physical place. (p. 71)

Another described the realization that radiation was permeating the very cells of her body. She felt the experience was simultaneously taking her into the depths of her unconscious. The women also spoke of the physical changes in their bodies—hair loss, weight gain, and their new awareness of the food, air, and other elements that were affecting their bodies. In a therapeutic sense, they spoke about the healing properties of time spent with friends, exercising, and enjoying nature. Many said such pleasures were more intense because life had lost some of the taken-for-granted quality it used to have. The authors conclude:

> The body, being the smallest and most personal landscape, represents the embodiment of illness for women living with breast cancer. In other words, the body is both an everyday site of illness but also an everyday landscape of healing. (English, Wilson, & Keller-Olaman, 2008, p. 76)

In this way and many others, illness, coping, and healing occupy the same spaces in human experience.

Sense of Control

When people believe they can manage their health successfully, they are said to have **health self-efficacy** (Bandura, 1986). Efficacy is derived from the Latin term for "change-producing." People with high self-efficacy are more likely than others to maintain healthy lifestyles because they are confident in their ability to make changes that have positive consequences. A sense of self-efficacy may be fostered by positive experiences in the past, encouragement from others, and an **internal locus of control**, the belief that people control their own destinies. Locus of control is more general than health self-efficacy, although the two are often related. Many North Americans have an internal locus of control. As a result, they're change-oriented and hard working, but they may be frustrated by failure and may feel baffled and betrayed when things don't work out as they had planned. People who believe they control their own fate may be reluctant to ask for help and may believe they're responsible for what happens—both good and bad. Faced with ill health, they might ask, "What did I do to cause this?" Even assured that no one is to blame, these people may feel guilty and ineffectual.

Sometimes making sense of a health event involves comparing it to something familiar. In a study of American and Puerto Rican male veterans recovering from strokes, many of the men compared having a stroke to a crash or a hurricane because it was unexpected and destructive (Boylstein, Rittman, & Hinojosa, 2007). But the men typically chose a different metaphor—war—to describe their recovery. Like war, they said, recovery requires immense courage, determination, and active engagement. "I've always been a fighter," said one man (p. 284). Another said, "You quit, they're gonna win. Now where's the fight in you?" (p. 284).

The researchers note that, in the men's stories, the "enemy" was typically a body part (an arm, a leg, or a hand) that no longer worked like before and that required diligent therapy and exercise. The men's explanations revealed that, although their strokes seemed to have come from out of the blue, they considered themselves active agents in getting well again.

In contrast, people who don't believe they can change their health for the better have low health self-efficacy. This is common in cultures in which people have an **external locus of control**, that is, the belief that events are controlled mostly by outside forces. Because of their belief in fate, these people are sometimes characterized as **fatalistic**. They are likely to regard events as God's will or the natural order of things.

People with low health self-efficacy may not be motivated to take personal action regarding health matters. For example, even if they are aware of healthy dietary recommendations, they may not change their diets because they do not feel they have control over their health (Rimal, 2000). In fatalistic cultures, people may reason: "It makes no sense to change my lifestyle. I will die when it's my time, no sooner or later," or "I'm sick because God willed it. Therefore, it's not right to seek a medical cure."

People with a fatalistic worldview are significantly more likely than others to feel that cancer is unpreventable and to avoid seeking information about the subject (Ramanadhan & Viswanath, 2006). And, as you might expect, adolescents with an external locus of control are more apt to "follow the crowd" and smoke if their friends do (Booth-Butterfield, Anderson, & Booth-Butterfield, 2000).

Our locus of control may also influence how we interpret other people's actions and health. For example, do people become overweight because of behavioral choices or because of factors beyond their control? As information surfaces about a genetic tendency toward obesity in some people, the public is likely to feel more sympathetic toward overweight people (Jeong, 2007). But at the same time, people may become more lax about health behaviors, concluding that obesity either is or isn't their genetic destiny and there's not much they can do about it (Jeong, 2007).

As with most things, the extremes are typically dysfunctional. People at either end of the internal/external locus-of-control scale are likely to have trouble coping. One moderating effect, at least for fatalists, is a healthy dose of confidence. Some researchers have found that people are less likely to avoid threatening health messages if they are well informed and confident about prevention methods (Fry & Prentice-Dunn, 2005).

People with high self-efficacy are typically problem solvers, highly motivated to protect their own health. However, they may be at a loss when illness reduces their sense of control. In some situations, people are powerless to change their health status or to repay their caregivers' kindness. One man adapting to physical limitations after a stroke described his frustration this way: "It's hard to depend on other people to take you places. Because, you know, they have things they have to do, and they need to get done, and you don't want to interfere with their schedule" (Egbert, Koch, Coeling, & Ayers, 2006, p. 49). Forced dependence may be especially demoralizing for people who have always believed they can control their health. In these situations, a belief in fate may help people accept what they cannot change. All in all, effective coping seems to combine elements of both problem solving and acceptance.

Dialectics

Of course, no one perceives an entirely internal or external local of control. We occupy a perspective somewhere between the two, and we may shift perspectives over time. This is an observation well explained by **dialectics**, which describes the ongoing tension of meaning between coexisting but contradictory constructs such as hopeless and hopeful (Baxter, 1988; Rawlins, 1989). We continually navigate meaning within dialectic continua based on our circumstances, beliefs, and interactions with others. For example, family caregivers often describe ongoing efforts to balance the dialectic between *attending to their own needs* and *sacrificing themselves* to care for loved ones (Brann, Himes, Dillow, & Weber, 2010). In the same way, people may struggle to find a balance between *expressing their emotions openly* and *suppressing emotional displays* to avoid distressing others (Brann et al., 2010).

People also manage the dialectic between being *hopeful* and *realistic*. Hospice volunteers often report that their most difficult communication challenge is helping loved ones accept the inevitability of death instead of hoping against all odds for a last-minute turnaround (Planalp & Trost, 2008). Most Westerners consider it adaptive to be optimistic, and it sometimes is. But dialectics challenges the notion that there is one right or static way to think. Instead, meaning is adaptive and changing. For example, a man caring for his wife following a stroke said that, after several years of determined optimism, they began to accept that she would never use her arm and leg again. As he put it, "We backed off . . . We're not expecting miracles anymore" (Brann et al., 2010, p. 327). That sense of acceptance can sometimes bring peace and can lead to more effective, realistic coping strategies.

We cope with some degree of stress every day. But crises test our limits. Let's take a closer look at what's involved when that happens.

Crisis

At every crisis in one's life, it is absolute salvation to have some sympathetic friend to whom you can think aloud without restraint or misgiving.

WOODROW WILSON

A **crisis** is an occurrence that exceeds a person's normal coping ability. The first sign of crisis is usually a sense that events are out of control. This may

give rise to panic or denial. For example, the parent of a seriously ill child remembers: "I didn't want to talk about it because it was something I wanted to shut in the back of my mind and have go away" (Chesler & Barbarin, 1984, p. 123).

People in crisis are likely to feel that things have changed, perhaps forever. During difficult times, people often yearn for the simple routines that characterized everyday life (Wartik, 1996). It may seem that things will never be the same again. Following a death, for example, grieving loved ones may wonder how they will ever resume daily activities when they feel so sad and disconnected to the things that used to seem normal. It is common for people in intense grief to forget momentarily how to perform simple routines such as using an ATM and driving from one place to another (Wartik, 1996).

A major crisis may serve as a turning point or dividing line. People affected by serious illnesses often feel their life has two parts, before the diagnosis and after it (Buckman, Lipkin, Sourkes, Toole, & Talarico, 1997). Circumstances are so radically altered that nothing seems the same. The change is not always negative. People who learn to cope with terminal illnesses or near-death experiences sometimes say they are happier than before, appreciating pleasures they used to disregard. A cancer survivor interviewed by Jennifer Anderson and Patricia Geist Martin (2003) reflects on the strength and courage she has discovered while undergoing surgery and radiation treatments:

> I wear my scar as a badge of courage but I've never thought of myself as a courageous person. But I am, I am a courageous person. People notice the scar. But you know, I don't mind the scar. Years ago, I decided that I wanted to change my name, to pick out who I wanted to be. Ivy came to mind because I liked the plant. It's a vine, it is strong, you can cut it down and it comes back. There's a lot of strength in Ivy. (p. 138)

We will talk more about transformative health experiences later in the chapter.

Normalcy

A sense of crisis doesn't usually abate until it seems that life is normal again. **Normalcy** is essentially the sense that things are comfortable, predictable, and familiar. Being normal is not always as easy as it sounds. It requires the cooperation of other people, even strangers (Barnes & Duck, 1994). Consider the dilemma of individuals with physical disabilities. Often, their toughest challenge is not learning to use wheelchairs or other appliances. It's resuming a sense of life as usual. Without this, they are trapped in a crisis-like state, excluded from the comfortable give and take of everyday transactions with people (Braithwaite, 1996). Persons with disabilities may be inundated with people willing to help them but with very few who engage them in casual conversation or friendly debates over politics or sports. When people behave as if individuals with disabilities are unlike other people (even by being unusually kind or helpful toward them), they perpetuate a sense of crisis and alienation (Braithwaite, 1996).

While researching support groups, I heard a young woman who had recently become blind say she longed to do favors for friends again. As she put it: "You appreciate people's help, but it's not the way life really is. You want to help back and no one lets you do that." In short, it is hard to lead a normal life when everyone treats you as if you are abnormal.

We have talked about the value of social support and personal coping strategies. But how do the two intersect? Here are some of the communication strategies involved.

Following an automobile accident that left her paralyzed from the neck down, Samantha Rodzwicz was eager to return to college as soon as possible. Since then, she has helped to raise more than $40,000 to help others. Sam is shown here at her college graduation in 2010 with her sister Veronica. Sam is now completing a master's degree in communication.

Coping and Communication

Coping strategies and social support often look very much alike in that they tend to fall into two main categories: **action-facilitating,** performing tasks and collecting information; and **nurturing,** building self-esteem, acknowledging and expressing emotions, and providing companionship (Cutrona & Suhr, 1994). Here is an overview of communication strategies based on these categories.

Action-Facilitating Support

Two types of action-facilitating support are performing tasks and favors and providing information. For instance, people might support someone trying to lose weight by sharing fitness information, buying healthy foods, and serving as exercise companions.

Tasks and favors are called **instrumental support** (Cutrona & Suhr, 1994). Research shows that instrumental support is most appreciated when care receivers feel they are active participants and are involved in decision making (Bottorf, Gogag, & Engelberg-Lotzkar, 1995). **Informational support** might involve performing an Internet data search, sharing personal experiences, passing along news clips, and so on. Information can help people increase their understanding and make wise decisions.

Even when people cannot change their circumstances, those who are knowledgeable about what is happening usually feel more in control, experience less pain, and recover more quickly than others. Margo Charchuk describes the sense of hopelessness and impotence she felt as the mother of a seriously ill child (Connor) in a neonatal intensive care unit (NICU). "I felt that I was an outsider looking in with no voice in the care of my child," she writes (Charchuk & Simpson, 2005, p. 198). While uninformed, she felt hopeless. Charchuk urges health providers to foster hope, even when the outcome is uncertain:

> In my experience, health care providers can help parents to enjoy their child and find hope in the moment even if the child will not ultimately survive. . . . I hoped that he would live, but I also had hope that I was being a good mother and that I was doing all that I could to ensure his health and safety. When I was involved in his care, my hopes increased, as this enabled me to feel I was being a good parent. I did not lose hope when the information was bad; I only lost hope when I was given no information at all. (pp. 194–195)

Charchuk describes a dilemma that many people feel in health situations. She sensed that, if she showed emotion, Connor's caregivers would consider that she was incapable of hearing the hard truths and making important decisions, but if she didn't show emotion, they might overlook her fervent concern and desire to know more. One of the most hope-enhancing events of Charchuk's account occurred when a NICU nurse invited her to rub the baby's back to soothe him. "The importance of this small amount of control that I was able to take helped restore my hope," she remembers (p. 199).

Although most people, like Charchuk, say it feels better to be well informed, sometimes too much information can feel overwhelming and compromise our coping ability. The theory of problematic integration (see Box 8.2) describes how and why we manage ambiguous, contradictory, and complex information.

Nurturing Support

Nurturing typically involves three types of support: esteem support, emotional support, and social network support. These are not directly oriented to task goals but, rather, to helping people feel better about themselves and their situations.

Esteem support involves efforts to make another person feel valued and competent. Here's a beautiful example from a study by Maria Carpiac-Claver

and Lené Levy-Storms (2007) in a long-term care facility:

> A nurse aide stands next to the resident after delivering her tray of food and says in a soft and moderately pitched voice, *Hi [resident's name]. Okay. Want a spoon?* The resident, with laughter in her voice, says, *Thank you* and smiles broadly at the nurse aide. The nurse aide gives the resident a spoon and says, *Here you go.* The resident thanks the nurse aide while shaking her head and pulling the nurse aide down to give her a kiss on the cheek. (p. 61)

The researchers observed other nurse aides laughing and singing with residents and helping those with cognitive impairments keep their memories active. Carpiac-Claver and Levy-Storms identified four themes of the nurse aides' affective communication: *personal conversation*—pleasantries and talk not directed to any particular task, *addressing the resident*—using the person's name or a term of endearment, *checking in*—asking and looking to see if the resident is feeling okay or needs anything, and *emotional support/praise*—as in saying "You look beautiful today!" or "Congratulations!"

Encouraging words may ease feelings of helplessness and despair (Wills, 1985). People often report that unconditional approval is the most helpful form of support. Statements such as "We're behind you no matter what you decide" are comforting reminders that loved ones will not leave if the situation is difficult to handle. Listening is also important. Studies show that most distressed individuals are not looking for advice; they just want to talk and be heard (Lehman, Ellard, & Wortman, 1986). Following are some tips from the experts on listening well.

COMMUNICATION SKILL BUILDER: SUPPORTIVE LISTENING

Brant Burleson, a leading authority on social support, offered the following tips for being a supportive listener (based on Burleson, 1990, 1994).

- *Focus on the other person.* Give the person a chance to talk freely. Focus on what he or she is saying rather than on your own feelings and experiences.

BOX 8.2

Theory of Problematic Integration

Imagine that you will go through life knowing with relative certainty what to expect and how to feel. Perhaps you'll graduate, establish a rewarding career, stay healthy and fit until retirement, and enjoy your later years with the money you have wisely saved along the way. At least this is what you expect and what you hope will happen.

The theory of problematic integration is based on the idea that we orient to life in terms of *expectations* (what we think will probably happen) and *evaluations* (whether occurrences are good or bad) (Babrow, 2001). However, our expectations and values are challenged almost constantly in large and small ways. (Although this sounds regrettable, the challenges are actually opportunities for greater development, a point to be discussed presently.)

As defined by Austin Babrow and colleagues, the **theory of problematic integration** describes a process in which communication serves to establish a relatively stable orientation to the world but also to challenge and transform that orientation (Babrow, 1992; Brashers & Babrow, 1996; Ford, Babrow, & Stohl, 1996; Russell & Babrow, 2011). *Problematic integration* (PI) occurs when expectations and evaluations are at odds, uncertain, changing, or impossible to fulfill. The disruption may be relatively minor (perhaps a setback that delays graduation) or major (someone close to you is diagnosed with a life-changing illness). Whatever the case, communication will play a pivotal role at every stage of your experience. As Babrow (2001) puts it:

> Communication shapes conceptions of our world—both its composition and meaning, particularly its values. [Problematic integration theory] also suggests that communication shapes and reflects problematic formulations of these conceptions and orientations to experience. (p. 556)

In recognizing that communication helps to define, challenge, and transform our experiences, Babrow (2001) makes the point that uncertainty is not inherently bad or good, and we're not always able to extinguish uncertainty by dousing it with information. Sometimes uncertainty exists because we have

According to the theory of problematic integration, we continually construct and confront meaning as we evaluate, bracket, integrate, and compare information from many sources within what philosophers call the blooming, buzzing confusion of experience.

too little or too much information or because we are not sure what to make of the information presented to us.

We make sense of the world partly through the stories we tell and partly through our efforts to achieve coherence between our narratives and other accounts, or what Russell and Babrow (2011) call "preexisting narrative frames," such as media depictions of environmental hazards and terrorism. As we both construct and confront narrative themes, we assess risk by selectively evaluating, bracketing, integrating, and comparing information from many sources within what philosophers call the blooming, buzzing confusion of experience (Russell & Babrow, 2011).

Uncertainty and ambivalence may also be inherent in the information we receive about our health and threats to it. Scientific findings change, and every promise of relief is accompanied by some degree of risk and side affects (Gill & Babrow, 2007; Russell & Babrow, 2011). Furthermore, resolving one uncertainty may produce others. Babrow writes that "PI permeates human experience" (p. 564), although it's difficult to predict when and how uncertainties will arise. Going back to Babrow's first point, the notion of uncertainty is not necessarily undesirable. Indeed, he suggests that uncertainty presents an "opportunity for self-exploration" (p. 563).

Consider the example of advance-care planning provided by Stephen Hines (2001). Medical professionals have typically been disappointed by patients' disinclination to specify what care they wish to have (or forgo) should they become too ill to express their wishes. Hines suggests that people shy away from the issue because health care professionals, in their desire to reduce their own uncertainty in end-of-life situations, have not been very sensitive to the uncertainties experienced by prospective patients and their loved ones. In short, people may neglect to file advance-care directives, not because they are indifferent or stubborn, but because the uncertainty surrounding them feels unmanageable.

This brief review does not encompass all the facets of problematic integration theory, but hopefully it does illustrate something about the ways in which people constitute, challenge, and transform their understandings, particularly in health-related crises.

- *Remain neutral.* Resist the urge to label people and experiences as good or bad. Likewise, encourage the speaker to describe experiences rather than label them.
- *Concentrate on feelings.* Focus on feelings rather than events. It's usually more supportive to explore why someone feels a certain way than to focus on events themselves.
- *Legitimize the other person's emotions.* Statements such as "I understand how you might feel that way" are typically more helpful than telling the other person how to feel or how not to feel.
- *Summarize what you hear.* Calmly summarizing the speaker's statements can help clarify the situation and help the distressed individual understand what he or she is feeling. As Burleson (1994) explained: "Due to the intensity and immediacy of their feelings, distressed persons may lack understanding of these feelings" (p. 13).

Emotional support includes efforts to acknowledge and understand what another person is feeling. This support is particularly valuable when people must adapt to what they cannot change. In a health crisis it's common to feel angry, baffled, afraid, depressed, or even unexpectedly relieved or giddy.

Emotions are a natural part of coping with health crises, yet many people are not comfortable with emotional displays—theirs or others people's. They may be afraid to appear weak or may be reluctant to upset others. The result is that people tend to present the appearance that things are going well, even when they're not. In interviews with grieving parents, fathers were more likely than mothers to use work as a distractive coping mechanism, whereas the women were more likely than the men to talk about their feelings and stay close to family members. Partly as a result, the women reported feeling more in control of their grieving process than the men did 6 months after the loss of a child (Alam, Barrera, D'Agostino, Nicholas, & Schneiderman, 2012). Although it was probably not obvious to others, the men probably needed support as much as their wives did.

Problems may arise when people find themselves feigning a cheerfulness they do not feel or avoiding subjects they actually wish to discuss. Suppressing emotions commonly leads to depression, especially among men (Flynn, Hollenstein, & Mackey, 2010). When asked, people (patients, caregivers, and others) often say they avoid sensitive topics because they don't wish to distress the people around them (Gotcher, 1995). However, when interviewed individually, the same people usually express the private wish that those topics be brought into the open. In the long run, it's usually easier to cope when emotions can be expressed and discussed without trepidation. Following are some tips for accomplishing this.

COMMUNICATION SKILL BUILDER: ALLOWING EMOTIONAL EXPRESSION

- *Look for "affective moments."* Physician Frederic Platt (1995) encourages caregivers to stay tuned for signs of strong feelings such as anger, sadness, fear, and helplessness. These are opportunities to understand something important about the other person and his or her coping status, he says.

- *When necessary, give yourself a moment.* Emotions often flood out other thoughts, making it difficult to respond effectively. A helpful strategy is to say, "Let me stop and think about what you've been telling me for a moment" (Platt, 1995, p. 25).

- *Keep in mind that people usually benefit from opportunities to talk openly and honestly.* People with advanced cancer who feel they can talk about subjects like death and pain with their loved ones typically cope better than people who consider those topics taboo (Thomsen, Rydahl-Hansen, & Wagner, 2010).

- *People in grief often find it insensitive and unhelpful when others try to minimize their losses or get them to cheer up.* One cancer survivor put it this way: "The emotions went up and down, up and down. I talked to Jack and he listened. There was a point where Jack's optimism got to me. It was like stop, you're not listening to me. I could die, stop" (Anderson & Geist Martin, 2003, p. 137).

- *Acknowledge and respect emotions.* Branch, Levinson, and Platt (1996, para. 15) suggest the following communication tools for responding to emotions: (1) Acknowledge the emotion: "I can understand how upsetting it must be," (2) show respect: "You've been doing your best to cope," (3) reflect: "It sounds as though you are really feeling overwhelmed," and (4) support and partner: "Maybe we can work together on these things."

All in all, it's important to remember that emotions are a natural part of the coping process and that the person who displays strong and even conflicting emotions may be coping more effectively than the one who keeps a stiff upper lip.

SOCIAL NETWORKS

Common sources of social-network support include family members, friends, professionals, support groups, virtual communities, and self-help literature. Each source is likely to provide a somewhat different form of assistance. Since we have said a good deal already about the value of social networks, we will focus here on support groups.

Support groups are made up of people with similar concerns who meet regularly to discuss their feelings and experiences. As defined by Schopler and Galinsky (1993), support groups may utilize a range of formats, from informal self-help groups (with an emphasis on shared concerns and minimal intervention by a facilitator) to treatment groups (providing a form of psychological therapy with active guidance by a trained professional). In recent years, online support groups and virtual communities have joined the list. We will talk more about those in Chapter 9.

In their various forms, support groups are popular around the world. More than 24,000 Al-Anon/Alateen group meetings are conducted in 30 languages in 115 countries (Al-Anon.org). There are also support groups for people dealing with grief, codependence, an enormous variety of illnesses and addictions, and other concerns. The effort may be justified. Support group members tend to experience fewer symptoms and less stress, and they may even live longer than similar people who are not members ("Living With Cancer," 1997; Wright, 2002).

Support groups have several advantages. Being around similar others may help people feel that they're not alone or abnormal. Similar others can also give firsthand information on what to expect and how to behave. At the same time, support group members may feel better about themselves because they're able to both express empathy with others and receive empathic messages themselves (Ham et al., 2011). Another advantage is the convenience and low cost of support groups. Because they're made up mostly of laypersons, there are few or no fees, and for the most part, members can schedule meetings where and when they wish.

The greatest dangers are that support groups will become counterproductive gripe sessions or that members will develop an us-versus-them viewpoint. They may begin to feel that no one outside the group understands them as well as they understand each other, a form of oversupport we will discuss next.

When Social Support Goes Wrong

Considering the many benefits of social support, it may seem that such efforts are always beneficial. Actually, ineffective social support can hurt more than it helps, and even people with good intentions

Many of her friends didn't know how to respond when Suleika Jaouad (shown here) was diagnosed with leukemia. (Photo by Ashley Woo)

often grapple with the uncertainties of comforting. Here are a few examples.

Friends Disappear

When Suleika Jaouad was diagnosed with leukemia at age 22, everything in her life changed. She was forced to give up her new job in Paris and return to the United States to move back in with her parents, spend months in the hospital, and cope with treatments that were painful and frightening and will make it difficult for her to conceive children in the future. In the midst of all of this, she says, she was shocked that many of her friends suddenly disappeared from her life. She explains:

> I think another aspect of being a young adult with cancer is that most of your friends, hopefully, you know, have never had to experience life-threatening illnesses themselves. . . .

So a lot of my friends had no idea how to respond and found it really difficult not just to find the right words, but sometimes to find any words at all. ("Life Interrupted," On the Social Awkwardness, 2012, para.1)

Jaouad said was she was hurt and mystified by her friend's absence when she really needed them. (For more about her story, see *Check It Out!* below)

Hurtful Jests

Here's another example, shared by Sherianne Shuler, who learned a great deal about effective and ineffective social support efforts when her 15-month-old daughter Lily was hospitalized with a rare, life-threatening infection. In an article about the experience in the journal *Health Communication*, Shuler (2011) describes a visit to the hospital waiting room by an acquaintance who joked insensitively: "Nice hair, Shuler! . . . That's what you've got to love about Sheri Shuler, you don't care about things like that! If it were me, I'd be worried about my hair. But you just don't care!" Hurt, Shuler replied, "I think if you had a daughter in a coma and on a ventilator you wouldn't care." Inwardly, she says, she was silently screaming, "SHE'S SERIOUSLY STILL TALKING ABOUT HOW SHITTY I LOOK?" (p. 200). The comments made her self-conscious at a time when she already felt vulnerable and overwhelmed.

Shuler also remembers feeling overwhelmed by the number of phone calls and emails she received and grateful that she could post information on a blog since the process was therapeutic and took less energy than talking to everyone separately. Phone messages with offers such as "call if you need . . . " were also unhelpful. Although people meant well, the energy and temerity it took to make such requests during a difficult time were prohibitive. Shuler observes, "As we learned, there are plenty of ways to offer well-meaning but ineffective support" (p. 199).

On the other hand, Shuler says it was immensely comforting when friends sent cards, letters, snacks, and healthy meals without being asked and without expecting anything in return. And she was grateful

---

CHECK IT OUT!

■ Visit Suleika's blog, "Life Interrupted," at the *New York Times* website at http://well.blogs.nytimes.com/author/suleika-jaouad/.

■ Listen to an interview with her on NPR's "Talk of the Nation" at http://www.npr.org/2012/05/16/152840031/life-interrupted-by-cancer-diagnosis-at-22.

Sheri and Lily Shuler, age 6, today

for people who took turns being present with her in the hospital waiting room without expecting her to talk or play hostess in any way. Says Shuler, "I was floored by this thoughtful support my friends were providing. It was the gift of space and company simultaneously." (p. 199) Fortunately, Lily made a full recovery.

Too Much Support

Especially if "supportive" efforts are offered inappropriately or profusely, they can impair people's coping abilities. **Oversupport is** defined as excessive and unnecessary help (Edwards & Noller, 1998). Following is a discussion of three types of oversupport: overhelping, overinforming, and overempathizing.

Overhelping is providing too much instrumental assistance. This can make people feel like children or shield them from life experiences. People who

are overhelped may become needlessly dependent on others, feel left out of life activities, and begin to doubt their own abilities (Goldsmith, 1994). Helen Edwards and Patricia Noller (1998) found that some women's take-charge attitude led them to be overly domineering in caring for their elderly husbands. Couples in this situation reported high conflict and low morale. Their relationships and their attitudes suffered.

Forcing information on people when they are too distraught to understand it or accept it (**overinforming**) may only heighten their stress. Philip Muskin (1998) calls this "truth dumping" and warns people against it. Health-related information can be confusing and frightening. Facts change and outlooks vary. People may shy away from the truth, preferring to preserve hope or minimize their confusion.

Overempathizing is actually something of a misnomer, because it applies only to a particular type of empathy, called *emotional contagion*. In a general sense, **empathy** is the ability to show that you understand how someone else is feeling. Katherine Miller and colleagues (1995) identified two components of empathy: **empathic concern**, which is an intellectual appreciation of someone's feelings; and **emotional contagion**, which involves actually feeling emotions similar to the other person's. Research shows that the second kind, emotional contagion, can be overdone.

Taken to extremes, emotional contagion can be detrimental to both support providers and recipients. For example, support groups members sometimes empathize so much with each other that they perceive people outside the group to be ignorant and uncaring, which discourages them from developing social networks with diverse people (Fisher, Goff, Nadler, & Chinsky, 1988). Another danger is that people may hesitate to express themselves to listeners who are likely to become upset. In Eric Zook's (1993) case study, a man who cared for his dying partner at home remembers: "As long as I was kind of detached and logical about it, he would take it [his declining health] very well" (p. 117).

Finally, some people find emotional empathy overwhelming or belittling. They may avoid scenes in which others seem to pity them. Wayne Beach (2002) describes the "stoic orientation" adopted by a father and son discussing the news that the mother was diagnosed with cancer. The son received the news calmly. Rather than reacting emotionally, he initially responded with a series of "OK's" and technical questions such as "That's the one above her kidney?" (p. 279). Beach speculates that this factual, stoic orientation saved the father and son from immediately "flooding out." In this way, they were able both to maintain composure and to display that they were knowledgeable and capable of coping with the news.

A Note of Encouragement

Before you become too self-conscious about offering social support, consider that, although some of these examples were hurtful, the lessons behind them are fairly simple.

- *Don't overwhelm distressed individuals with requests for information.* If it's important for people to stay informed, appoint one person to convey news to the others.
- *Be careful with humor, and avoid making jokes at others' expense.* People may not feel like laughing during a tense situation, and joking put-downs can be devastating when people are already feeling vulnerable.
- *"Call me if you need me" is usually not helpful.* It puts the onus for action on the distressed individual at a time when he or she is probably not up to the effort.
- *It's okay if you don't know what to say; just say something gentle or be available to listen.*
- *Adopt a no-strings-attached approach.* When uncertain what to do, provide a quiet favor such as mowing the lawn, leaving a casserole, or simply being present without requiring anything from the distressed individual.

Here's a follow-up to the story about Suleika Jaouad, who was initially hurt by her friends' silence. Jaouad says their dilemma began to dawn on her when she remembered how she felt, just a few years before, when a friend phoned her to say that he had testicular cancer. She says:

> I remembered feeling so afraid when he called me and shared his diagnosis with me. And following that phone call, I, you know, I sat down and tried to compose an email, and I just didn't feel like I had the right words. I couldn't find the perfect words, so I said nothing. And I wasn't there for him at all during his cancer treatment. And I tried to remember that, and it's helped me forgive and understand the reactions of certain friends in my life and to realize that generally it's not that people don't care. It's that they're afraid or that they don't know what to say. (para. 3)

Jaouad's advice to people who want to offer comfort but aren't sure what to say is to forget about finding "the perfect words" and just say something. For her part, she says a highlight of her year was apologizing to the friend she had been unable to comfort several years before. "He understood, and he said, 'I know that you understand now,'" she says (para. 4).

On that note, let's turn to a form of love and comfort that communicates a great deal but requires no words at all.

Animals as Companions

At Sunrise Hospital in Las Vegas, Nevada, care sometimes comes with four legs and floppy ears. About 12 dogs visit the hospital every few days through Pet Partners (formerly the Delta Society), a nonprofit organization that provides training and coordination for more than 10,000 carefully trained animal-volunteer teams throughout the world. The animals serve as therapeutic companions to people with health concerns.

Pet Partners leaders say the animals (mostly dogs and cats, but also a few horses) provide stress relief, a break from boredom, inspiration, and health benefits. The furry friends have been known to inspire people to keep up difficult physical therapy routines and to distract and calm children undergoing medical procedures. The staff at Sunrise Hospital reports that the animals are some patients' only visitors and they are a fun pick-me-up for everyone who chooses to take part. "Often time, you'll see a patient who is really down in the dumps, and the dogs will show up in the room and their eyes light up," says Tracy Netherton, the hospital's volunteer coordinator (quoted by DeLucia, 2011, para. 4).

There is evidence that animal companions often have positive effects on people's anxiety levels (Barker & Dawson, 1998), blood pressure (Allen, Blascovich, & Mendes, 2002), recovery time (Allen et al., 2002), and survival rates after heart attacks (Friedmann & Thomas, 1995); and even that trained dogs can help with the diagnosis and treatment of conditions such as diabetes, cancer, and epilepsy (Wells, 2009).

Oncologist Edward Creagan of Mayo Clinic is a believer. He includes the names of people's pets in their medical history notes. In his experience, pets can be people's reason for living, and talking about pets is often calming for staff members as well as patients. Creagan attests, "None of us can speak about their pets without smiling" (Pet Partners video, nd). (See the *Check it Out!* sidebar for more about Pet Partners and a video link to Creagan's story.)

We turn now to a type of experience that may occur when you least expect it and may have profound consequences for coping.

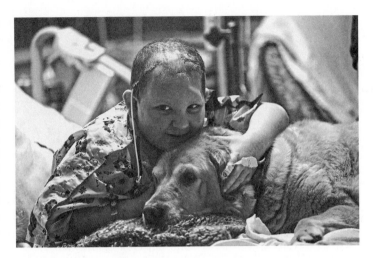

A pediatric patient cuddles with a furry visitor, courtesy of the Pet Partners program. (Photo Provided by Pet Partners)

IN YOUR EXPERIENCE

■ Have you ever felt that an animal was a good friend? Why or why not?

■ Do you think animal companionship affects your coping ability?

CHECK IT OUT!

■ Visit the Pet Partners website at http://www.pet-partners.org.

■ For footage of actual patient visits and background about Pet Partners, visit http://www.deltasociety.org/page.aspx?pid=659.

■ To view a brief video in which Edward Creagon, MD, talks about the therapeutic value of animal companionship, see http://www.deltasociety.org/page.aspx?pid=642.

Transformative Experiences

Carol Bishop Mills remembers the day her daughter Maren was born:

> Dr. Jacobs, the NICU doctor, approached my bed about 15 minutes later and handed me a gorgeous baby girl. He was very pleasant and smiled when he told us all about her. "Mr. and Mrs. Mills, your daughter is quite healthy. She seems to have a strong heart, and her kidneys will be fine. There was some fluid pooled, but it will eliminate itself naturally. Her APGAR scores [used to measure a newborn's health] were 8 and 9 [out of a possible 10]. She's a beautiful little girl. There are some preliminary indicators in her features that she might have trisomy 21, Down syndrome, but we need to run some blood work to confirm that." (Mills, 2005, p. 198)

The Mills were not surprised; they suspected that their baby might have special needs. But they *were* deeply grateful—grateful that the doctor had not said "I'm sorry" or labeled their daughter "abnormal." Instead he saw, as they did, a unique, perfect little girl in radiant good health with a condition not all children have.

Maren dressed as a fairy at her fifth birthday party

Good health is often defined in terms of what is "normal" or "expected." A deviation from that can feel like a tragedy—meaningless and unfair. In reality, however, what looks on the surface like a "bad outcome" can turn out to be one of life's most valuable and important gifts. Mills (2005) attests that, although no one hopes to have a child with Down syndrome, "it is simply a gift we were given that we would have never known to ask for and probably would never have understood before our Little Miss Magic captivated our hearts" (p. 196).

In this section we explore instances in which, in the midst of what might seem to be great hardship, people discover unexpected rewards. From the perspective of social constructivism (e.g., Berger & Luckmann, 1966), life is defined largely by a quest for meaning that is shaped both by our own experiences and by our interactions with others. To illustrate the powerful effect of social interaction, let's return to Mills' (2005) case study, but this time we will look through the eyes of Kate, another mother, who has just given birth to Joshua:

> We heard a cry, we saw our boy, and then heard the following from Dr. Lee, "I am so sorry to tell you this. This baby looks like a Down's. I'm so sorry. . . . In 20 years, I've never delivered a Down's. Didn't you have tests? . . . I'm sure it's a Down's. I am so, so sorry." (quoted by Mills, p. 199)

As you might imagine, Kate's experience was much different from the Mills'. "In my heart, I knew the Down syndrome was my fault, and it was clear the doctor was angry," Kate remembers thinking. "I didn't have a boy, in my mind, I had an 'it,' a Down's, one of those short, funny, retarded kids that work at grocery stores. My mind flooded with thoughts of drooling, retardation, the little yellow buses, the teasing, and the problems" (quoted by Mills, p. 199).

Mills (2005) reports that Kate and her husband Chris have come to realize that Down syndrome is only one feature—a relatively insignificant one—in the myriad qualities that make their son Joshua wonderful. But they have often had to overcome health professionals' hurtful comments in the process. Considering what people may learn from her experiences, Mills says, "I really hope that students realize that, often, it is not the diagnosis that is so scary, but the language we use to talk about it . . . is so embedded in cultural disdain that [it] taints our view. . . . "

We may all sometimes fall into the hurtful trap of believing, as Kate and Chris's doctor did, that there is a norm—a normal way to look, a normal life span, a normal reaction, and so on—and that what is "normal" is the "good" or "right" way to be. Most people who experience a crisis initially feel the same way, wondering: *Is this my fault? What did I do to deserve this? Why did this happen? Can I make it okay again?* In short, if the norm is right, a deviation means something has gone dreadfully wrong. This is a common assumption because the unknown is often frightening and because, as humans, we are continually involved in sense-making, and an unexpected occurrence can rob of us our sense of safety and meaning. For this reason, it is especially important to learn more about diverse ways of being (in other words, shrink our distrust of the unknown) and to remind ourselves continually that, although it takes courage to embrace them, some of life's most enriching gifts lie beyond the status quo.

You might be surprised how frequently people who have been part of health crises (even to the

Maren with brothers Jonah and Archie on vacation

extent of learning that they don't have long to live) ultimately consider themselves grateful for the experience. du Pré and Eileen Berlin Ray (2008) examined such episodes in a study of **transcendent experiences**, which they define as episodes in which people come to perceive an overarching meaning, or supra-meaning, within experiences that might otherwise seem senseless or unthinkable (p. 103). The term *supra-meaning* comes from psychologist Victor Frankl's (1959) reflections about life in a Nazi concentration camp during World War II. In the midst of suffering more horrific than most of us can imagine, Frankl observed that some of his fellow prisoners still found a reason to value life and to be optimistic about the future, largely because they perceived a meaning in life that was not bounded by the chain-link fences that kept them physically captive. Frankl came to believe that a quest for meaning is the primary motivation of human nature. From his perspective, write du Pré and Ray, "transcendence is not denial of one's circumstances, but an awareness that those circumstances exist within the framework of something

more meaningful than one might previously have imagined" (p. 103).

In a similar way, people who don't have long to live sometimes say life takes on a new, larger meaning that makes everyday concerns seem trivial. As one cancer survivor put it:

> I am no longer concerned that someone might see me in the same outfit and I no longer have to have the same sweater in every color. I can now not finish a book if I don't like it. Every day is a guessing game. But that's okay. I'm still here to talk about it. (Brett, 2003, p. B1).

Others say they have been able to lay old grievances to rest and have developed a heightened appreciation for nature and loved ones. Many people facing life-altering circumstances say they have found larger meaning in a spiritual quest that involves helping others, dedicating themselves to a cause larger than themselves, allowing themselves to be creative and have fun, and seeking to live up to their full awareness and potential (Egbert, Sparks, Kreps, & du Pré, 2008). Some people say the loss of a loved one was relieved in part by the knowledge that his or her organs helped save lives. (See Box 8.3 for more on this topic.)

This is not an easy or guaranteed process. Transcendence often happens when we least expect it. But being aware that what appears tragic on the surface may eventually yield something beautiful is a good start toward coping when things seem their darkest.

We turn next to two contexts with powerful implications for social support and coping: family caregiving and end of life.

Friends and Family as Caregivers

Carol Green rushes into the caregiver support group with her hair partly in curlers, her sweater buttoned crookedly, a smudge on her face, two different shoes, and a panicked look on her face. "I can't find my keys! We have an appointment, we're late, and I CAN'T FIND MY KEYS!" she exclaims, wildly tossing items from her overflowing handbag.

BOX 8.3

Organ Donations: The Nicholas Effect

Recently I strolled through a park in Rome with Andrea Mongiardo, a 23-year-old Italian whose heart once belonged to my own son.

With this comment, Reg Green (2003) introduces the Nicholas Green Foundation website, named in honor of 7-year-old Nicholas, who was killed near Naples by robbers who mistook the Greens' car for their own and fired into the vehicle. Even in their shock and grief over the sudden attack, Reg Green recalls, he and his wife agreed that Nicholas's organs should be donated to others. The family has since befriended the seven people whose lives were changed as a result. Reg Green remembers when he and his wife met these organ recipients for the first time:

> Our grief was still agonizingly raw. But that meeting, which both of us had to steel ourselves to attend, was explosive. A door opened and in came this mass of humanity, some smiling, some tearful, some ebullient, some bashful, a stunning demonstration of the momentous consequences every donation can have. We now think of them as an extended family. We've watched the children grow and leave school and get their driver's licenses and the adults go back to work. One of them, 19-year-old Maria Pia Pedala, in a coma with liver failure on the day Nicholas died, bounced back to good health, married and has since had a baby boy. And, yes, they have called him Nicholas. (para. 11)

Reg Green's (1999) book *The Nicholas Effect: A Boy's Gift to the World* and a video of the same title tell the family's story.

In the United States, an average of 19 people a day die waiting for organ transplants (OrganDonor.gov, 2008). The waiting list is more than 100,000 people long, and the greatest need is for kidneys (accounting for 76% of all transplants).

The issue of organ donation is an emotional one. Based on sensationalized accounts on TV and in the movies, people may fear that medical professionals will allow them to die so they can have their organs or that their organs will be sold on the underground market (Frates, Bohrer, & Thomas, 2006; Morgan, Harrison, Afifi, Long, & Stephenson, 2008).

In reality, physicians who care for a patient are not involved in decisions about his or her organ donation. That is handled by an entirely different staff and medical team. Moreover, strict U.S. laws prohibit the sale or purchase of organs as well as bribery for desired organs ("Organ Donation," 2008, para. 3). Another common myth is that organ donation will mar a deceased person's appearance such that the family cannot have an open casket at the funeral. This is not true. Physicians are able to maintain the person's appearance so that people cannot tell the difference ("Organ Donation," 2008).

WHAT DO YOU THINK?

1. What factors make you more (or less) inclined to register as an organ donor?
2. What is most fearful about the prospect? What is most appealing?
3. Unlike the Greens, who live in Italy, people in the United States are not usually given the opportunity to meet the people who receive a loved one's organs. Would you want to meet them? Why or why not?
4. Have you seen TV programs or movies in which people's organs are misused? Were the depictions realistic, in your opinion? Do you think such depictions affect people's attitudes about organ donation?

SUGGESTED RESOURCES

- *Journal of the American Medical Association* on Organ Donation: http://jama.ama-assn.org/cgi/reprint/299/2/244.pdf
- U.S. Department of Health and Human Services: OrganDonor.gov
- National Kidney Foundation Facts About Organ Donation and Transplant: www.kidney.org/news/newsroom/fs_new/25factsorgdon&trans.cfm
- Mayo Clinic: "Organ Donation: Don't Let These 10 Myths Confuse You": www.mayoclinic.com/health/organ-donation/FL00077
- The Nicholas Green Foundation: www.nicholas-green.org
- YouTube video The Nicholas Effect: see http://www.youtube.com/watch?v=SHBV-TcF1Ii

"The audience roars," Green says. "They recognize the situation. They are family caregivers." The scenario is a skit, but it's only partly satirical. The sense of being in disarray, trying to manage constantly changing situations involving medications, appointments, finances, companionship, insurance claims, bathing, dressing, food preparation, transportation, emotional support, organizing and apprising others, and so on, is real, she says.

Green and Kenny Holt are co-facilitators of family caregiver support groups and training opportunities offered by the Council on Aging of West Florida. At these and similar group meetings around the country, anyone interested may learn skills, share concerns, socialize, and take a breather from the everyday demands of family caregiving.

"At meetings, after we cover the essential information, I always say to people, 'If this is your only chance to get out this week, go now! Catch a movie, read a book, take some time for yourself,'" says Green. "Sometimes we need that permission to get away for a little while. My dream is I want to give something back to these people who give so much."

Green draws upon her years as a nurse and her personal experience caring long-distance for a parent who has dementia. She is among the 13% of family caregivers in the United States who coordinate services and travel frequently to take care of loved ones who live more than an hour's drive away ("Caregiving in the U.S.," 2009).

Holt created a 188-page booklet for family caregivers that includes information about local and state resources; the stages of caregiving; strategies to manage finances and avoid burnout; how to safely lift, bathe, and position a care recipient; wills and trusts; emergency preparedness; the grieving process; and more.

On the inside front cover are these words:

TAKE CARE OF THE BIG PRIORITIES FIRST . . . EVERYTHING ELSE WILL FIT IN AROUND. YOU AS CAREGIVER . . . ARE **YOUR** *BIGGEST PRIORITY!*

The comprehensive guide that Holt has created is a gold mine in a process that can otherwise feel baffling and overwhelming. As the authors of a report by the American Association of Retired Persons (AARP) point out, "individuals and their

> ●●● **IN YOUR EXPERIENCE**
> ■ Have you ever been involved in caring for a loved one at home?
> ■ If so, what did you find rewarding about the experience?
> ■ What was difficult about it? What might make it easier?

families generally view chronic illness and disability from the perspective of the 'whole person,' not as separate, discrete services or treatments;" however, health care services are often fragmented and specialized, creating a logistical nightmare for family caregivers (Feinberg, Reinhard, Houser, & Choula, 2011, p. 4).

The need for integrated support is rising along with the need for family caregivers. Reasons for the increase are manifold. For one, the number of people age 65 and older is expected to triple worldwide between 2009 and 2050 (U.S. Census Bureau, 2009). Already, 13% of Americans are at least 65, and experts predict the proportion to reach 20% by the year 2050 (U.S. Census Bureau, 2011a). The same trend is occurring in more than 100 other countries, notable among them Germany, Italy, China, and Japan (U.S. Census Bureau, 2009).

Another factor is that hospital stays are shorter than they used to be. As Donna Laframboise (1998) puts it: "Good news! You can go home from the hospital tomorrow. Bad news! You'll have to do everything yourself, even though you're still on crutches or full of stitches" (p. 26). A third reason that family caregiving is on the rise involves economic conditions. We will talk more about those in a minute.

As we review the rewards and challenges of family caregiving, keep in mind that loved ones are an important source of social support, but they also need support themselves. While the rewards of caregiving can be immensely gratifying, family caregivers experience grief, uncertainty, and exhaustion as well, and their needs are frequently overlooked in concern over the ill individuals. This section focuses on people who provide ongoing care for loved ones at home. Before we begin, note that we often speak in terms of *family caregivers,* and the vast majority

(86%) are indeed family members, but the rest are actually honorary family members—friends and neighbors who pitch in as well ("Caregiving in the U.S.," 2009).

Profile of the Family Caregiver

About 61.6 million people in the United States provide some amount of at-home care for a loved one during the year, and 42.1 million of them care for an adult loved one at home for an average of 20.4 hours per week (Feinberg et al., 2011; "Caregiving in the U.S.," 2009). That's the equivalent of squeezing two additional full-time work weeks into every month. According to the "Caregiving in the U.S." (2009) study:

- Some 66% of all family caregivers are women.
- The average age of a family caregiver is 49.
- At least 37% of people who care for an older adult also have children or grandchildren living with them.
- Most care recipients (62%) are female, with an average age of 69.3.

The challenge for family caregivers is to balance many factors at once, including the costs involved. Let's look at those next.

The Economics of Family Caregiving

The value of care offered for free by loved ones is estimated at $450 billion per year in the United States, a figure that increased $75 billion between 2007 and 2009, when the latest figures were released (Feinberg et al., 2011). (See Figure 8.1.) To put that in perspective, federal and state governments contributed a total of $361 billion to Medicaid long-term care provisions in 2009—$89 billion less than the value attributed to family caregivers. In fact, if we paid family caregivers, their salaries would total more than the annual revenue

Value of Family Caregivers' Contributions

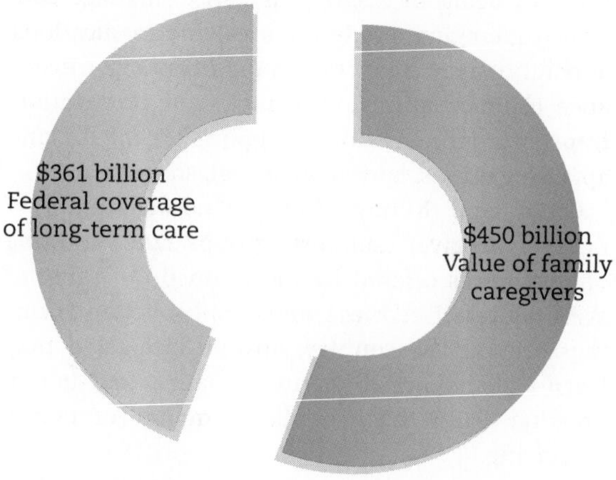

$361 billion Federal coverage of long-term care

$450 billion Value of family caregivers

FIGURE 8.1 The value of volunteer efforts by family caregivers in 2009 was significantly more than the federal government paid, through Medicaid, for long-term care expenses. Family caregivers save the country money, but they often sacrifice their own retirement funds and savings to make ends meet.

Sources: Feinberg et al. (2011)

of Wal-Mart, Toyota, Ford, and Daimler combined (Feinberg et al., 2011).

Family caregivers save taxpayers money, but the process can be financially devastating to them personally. According to a 2009 study by Evercare and the National Alliance for Caregiving, among families who provide care for loved ones at home:

- 47% have drained all or most of their savings to make ends meet;
- 60% have difficulty paying for basic needs and have cut back on retirement savings; and
- 43% have experienced a loss in wages or hours because of caregiving duties.

On the bright side, 76% say that these sacrifices have allowed them to maintain a steady quality of care for their loved ones ("Evercare Study," 2009).

As mentioned, the need for family caregiving has risen partly because of economic concerns. In the United States, the average cost of a private room

❓ CAN YOU GUESS?

What percentage of family caregivers say that dementia is their main concern?
The answer appears at the end of the chapter.

in a nursing home is $81,030 a year, and the average monthly cost of a one-bedroom assisted living apartment is $3,300, with additional costs of $1,000 per month or more if dementia-related care is required ("Genworth," 2012). Medicaid may cover some of the costs, but only if the nursing home resident is out of money. Most states require that people be down to their last $2,000 to qualify (R. W. Johnson, 2008).

Home care is typically less expensive than nursing homes and assisted living facilities, and professional assistance is available for family caregivers who can afford them or who qualify for free or subsidized services. Assistance might involve visits by licensed home health professionals, who provide therapy and medical assistance; home health aides, who typically help with nonmedical care such as bathing and changing bandages; or homemaker aides, who don't offer hands-on care but do help with household chores and errands. Adult day centers are emerging in many communities, where people can spend as many as 8 hours a day taking part in social and therapeutic activities at a central location. (To compare the costs of these options, see Figure 8.2.)

However, evidence suggests that home health resources are underutilized, either because of the costs involved or because people don't know about them. Currently, unpaid family caregivers provide *all* the at-home care for 2 out of 3 older adults with disabilities (Feinberg et al., 2011).

Cost Comparison

$7.25/hour
Adult Day Health
Center

$18/hour
Licensed Homemaker
Aide

$19/hour
Licensed Home
Health Aide

FIGURE 8.2 Adult care centers are becoming a popular, cost-effective way for older adults who need assistance to socialize and engage in activities while family caregivers are at work or engaged in other activities.

Sources: "Genworth 2012 Cost of Care Survey"

Stress and Burnout

Caregiving is no simple task. By some estimates, adults today will spend more time caring for their parents than they will raising their own children. In addition to providing medical care and assistance, family caregivers are frequently responsible for maintaining households and budgets, working at careers outside the home, and providing information and support to others.

Legislation passed in the 1990s helps career people provide care for needy family members. The **Family and Medical Leave Act of 1993** guarantees that people can take up to 12 weeks off work to care for ailing family members, seek medical care themselves, or bring new children into their families (through birth, adoption, or foster parenting). However, the act does not require that employers *pay* workers while they're on leave, and it doesn't apply to all companies or all employees. To be eligible, employees must have worked at the company at least 1 year for an average of 25 hours or more per week. Only companies with at least 50 employees are obligated to provide medical and family leave.

Although most people juggling careers and caregiving say they feel good about what they do overall, it's easy to feel stressed, exhausted, and resentful at times. Said a 31-year-old caring for her ill mother: "Your parents have given you so much that the last thing you're ever going to do is not help them out. But at the same time, it's so hard. I get resentful sometimes" (quoted by Laframboise, 1998, p. 26).

Part of the strain is emotional. Caregivers may grieve over future plans that no longer seem possible. A 76-year-old woman caring for her ailing husband lamented: "This isn't how we planned to spend our retirement years. . . . Why did this happen to us?" (quoted by Ruppert, 1996, p. 40).

It's also painful to see a loved one suffer or change. The progression of Alzheimer's disease is particularly heart wrenching. Caregivers may watch sadly as the individual's personality and awareness gradually change. Sometimes Alzheimer's patients become belligerent or unable to recognize the people around them (see Box 8.4). To make matters worse, caregivers may feel guilty about their own frustration and resentment. It may seem wrong to be angry with a person who is ill and needy.

BOX 8.4 PERSPECTIVES

A Long Goodbye to Grandmother

A few years ago, I lost my grandmother to Alzheimer's disease. Until she died, I saw my grandmother every week of my life. We had a very close relationship.

Alzheimer's is not a disease that just appears one day and kills you. It causes gradual deterioration of a person's memory and sense of being. Minutes and days and years all seem the same or don't exist at all. My grandmother's condition started about 1 year before her death.

Before Grandma got Alzheimer's, our extended family was fairly close. No one wanted to put Grandma in a nursing home, but caring for her was not going to be easy. Her three daughters (including my mother) decided Grandma would stay with each of them for one week at a time.

Grandma and I had always enjoyed playing Scrabble and working crossword puzzles together. She always tried to get me to use my thinking skills. My favorite times were when she would tell me stories about when she was a young girl or a teenager. She was a very flirty girl, although she had a prissy attitude as an elderly person.

As Grandma's forgetfulness worsened, she often forgot what year it was. She would also forget to eat. Soon she could no longer remember conversations we had had. I could answer a question and 5 minutes later, she'd ask it again. I would tell her every week why and where I was going to school. We would talk about the world now compared to the world in her day. Sometimes she would talk out loud to her parents, who had been dead 50 or 60 years.

Her worst times were at night. She stayed up most of the night talking to people she thought were there. As much as I loved Grandma, I would get aggravated with her during those nights of constant talking.

Several times a night, we'd go into her room to comfort her. She'd whine and cry like a child. It was difficult for me to deal with this. I started distancing myself from her during the day because she made me angry with the things she did at night. Even though I knew she had no idea what she was doing, it still aggravated me.

The stress started wearing on other family relationships as well. The daughters started finding fault with each other. No one said anything out loud, but the frustration was there under the surface. I was sad to see relationships start to disintegrate. I asked my grandmother to forgive me even if she didn't quite understand why.

Over the months, Grandma's condition deteriorated. She lost touch with reality and she lost trust in her family. One day she and I were home by ourselves and I got her a glass of water. When I gave it to her, she smelled it. Then she looked at me and said, "I never thought you would do this." I asked what she meant, and she said, "Of all people, I didn't think you would poison me. I expected the others, but not you." This hurt me very much. I took the glass of water and poured it down the sink and let her watch me pour a new glass. But she continued to believe I was trying to kill her.

By the time she died, Grandma weighed less than 95 pounds. The times that I could talk with her were over. She stayed with us for the last month of her life. She was in such bad condition we didn't want to move her. The night of her death my mom and dad left for church and I stayed behind. I read her the Bible and sang her some songs while I played my guitar. As I did this she began to cry a little. I didn't expect her to respond, but that was a special moment. About 5 hours later, she died in her bed, with her family in the room with her.

—NICHOLAS

Family caregivers may also feel unprepared to perform the tasks delegated to them. Although they now perform many services once carried out by health professionals, they often receive only minimal instruction on what to do and what to expect. As a result, they may feel overwhelmed and may worry that they will do something wrong or miss important warning signs. When a loved one's life is at stake, the pressure can be as exhausting as the physical demands of caregiving.

Family caregivers may jeopardize their own health if they overextend themselves. People are like elastic, says Geila Bar-David of the Caregiver Support Project in Toronto (Laframboise, 1998). If they are stretched too thin for too long, they will lose strength and may even snap. Caregivers who are reluctant to leave their posts may need reminding that they will be of no use unless they remain healthy (emotionally and physically) themselves.

Caring for Caregivers

We began this unit with information about a caregivers' support group. Family caregivers need time for themselves as well as assistance and education. They also need a break from the social isolation that can come with at-home caregiving. Friends and other family members are a promising source of support. In a meta-analysis of 50 studies about family caregiving, a prominent theme was that caregivers missed opportunities to socialize with others (Al-Janabi, Coast, & Flynn, 2008).

Communication plays a large role. In a study of 76 older adults and family caregivers, participants with high communication competence were less stressed and more satisfied than others (Query & Wright, 2003). And caregivers often say that a word of encouragement or thanks is their greatest reward. Said one man who cares for his wife at home:

> Sometimes she'll look up to me and give me such a priceless lovely smile, which says it all and then the other morning she laid down for a bit and looked up to me and said, "You're lovely. I love you." It came out clear as a bell. Well, you can't put a price on that, can you? (Al-Janabi et al., 2008, pp. 116–117)

All in all, supportive communication can sweeten the rewards of caregiving and lessen the demands.

CHECK IT OUT! For more resources and data about family caregivers see the following websites:

■ AARP Planning Guide for Families: http://assets. aarp.org/www.aarp.org_/articles/foundation/aa66r2_care.pdf

■ Family Caregiver Alliance: http://www.caregiver.org/caregiver/jsp/home.jsp

■ National Alliance for Caregiving: http://www.caregiving.org

■ National Association of Area Agencies on Aging: http://www.n4a.org

■ National Caregivers Library: http://www.caregiverslibrary.org/home.aspx

■ National Council on Aging: http://www.ncoa.org

■ National Family Caregivers Association: http://www.nfcacares.org

■ U.S. Administration on Aging National Family Caregiver Support Program: http://www.aoa.gov/AoA_programs/HCLTC/Caregiver/index.aspx

■ U.S. Department of Health and Human Services Caregiver Resources: http://www.adsa.dshs.wa.gov/caregiving

For a list of resources for family caregivers, see the *Check It Out!* box.

End-of-Life Experiences

It was not my first time at the Cleveland Clinic—I had visited my sister-in-law, Annie, there before. But as I walked in this time, I knew that things were going to be different. I knew that Annie was dying of ovarian cancer that she had been fighting for the past 2½ years and that we were going to be facing a whole host of new issues this time. (Teresa Thompson, 2011, p. 177)

With this statement, Thompson begins an examination of what she calls "a delicate balance" between hope and information at the end of life. She describes Annie's experiences managing the need for both hope and frank information. When the two seemed contradictory, Thompson says, the warmth of the caregiver's demeanor often made the difference in Annie's ability to cope effectively with the information. Thompson concludes that "hope is best engendered by a combination of honesty and empathy" that encompasses faith, dignity, peace, humor, and meaning, as well as treatment goals (p. 185).

In this section we explore the role of communication and social support at the end of life. Death is an unpleasant topic to people in many Western cultures. "Death is un-American. It doesn't square with our philosophy of optimism, of progress," wrote Herbert Kramer, a terminally ill cancer patient (Kramer & Kramer, 1993, para. 21). Nevertheless, dying is inevitable, and it marks a stage of life during which social support is crucial. End-of-life experiences also can be more meaningful and beautiful than many people realize.

To some people, the phrase "a good death" seems like an oxymoron. They don't believe there is such thing. However, many people argue that dying can be a special (albeit emotional) experience with many positive aspects. This section analyzes these two perspectives, which are characterized as "life at all costs" and "death with dignity." It also explains advance-care directives and offers experts' advice for dealing with death.

Life at All Costs

Have you ever walked past a hospital morgue? Probably not. Most hospitals locate the morgue in an out-of-the-way area where people will not chance upon it. Morgue staff members may be regarded as somewhat weird and eccentric based on their choice of occupation. This may seem perfectly understandable if you grew up in a society in which death was regarded as something gross and ghoulish.

Today's Grim Reaper is a modern-day version of Thanatos, the merciless and malicious Greek god born of "darkness" and "sleep." In Greek mythology, Thanatos is often depicted as a rival of Bios (Greek for "life"). The lessons of such tales are easy to divine: Death is the enemy of life. Life is victory, death a merciless and permanent defeat. In modern terms, medicine is associated with Bios. Health professionals are considered, quite literally, to be in *mortal* combat with the enemy, death. Hence we entertain such notions as "battling cancer" and "fighting for one's life." These conceptualizations thrive in an atmosphere in which death is considered taboo and unknown and medicine the ultimate savior.

If you are a caregiver pledged to maintain life, death may be more than creepy; it may represent failure. Caregivers have several incentives to keep patients from dying. For one, they are typically trained to preserve life, not allow it to end. Most physicians approach medicine as detectives and problem solvers—endeavors that are successful only if they solve the mystery and fix the problem (Ragan & Goldsmith, 2008). Moreover, death is frightening, even to professionals who have encountered it before (Hegedus, Zana, & Szabó, 2008). Saving a life is usually a rewarding experience, whereas a patient's death may bring feelings of guilt and grief. Finally, caregivers (doctors especially) may be harshly criticized or sued if a patient dies. Physicians' decisions are often intensely scrutinized by family members, lawyers, insurance companies, quality assurance and risk management personnel, administrators, and others. Jack McCue (1995) attests: "It is little wonder that physicians engage in inappropriately heroic battles against dying and death, even when it may be apparent to physician, patient, and family that a rapid, good death is the best outcome" (para. 2).

Medicine's dedication to preserving life has many benefits. Caregivers' devotion and talent, along with their access to medical technology, has helped to increase the average American's life expectancy from 47.3 to 78.3 years since 1900 (U.S. Census Bureau, 2012). But a "life at all costs" approach can rob people of the opportunity for a good death. Susan Block (2001) calls a good death "The Art of the Possible." The means of realizing this possibility, she says, lie in making people physically comfortable and helping them nurture caring relationships, maintain a sense of self, find meaning, feel a sense of control, and prepare for death. One man at the end of his life attested: "What this last year has provided me with

WHAT DO YOU THINK?

Cultural concepts of death vary widely, from the idea of a popping gently like a soap bubble, as in the Japanese concept of *pokkuri shinu,* to the ancient Greek depiction of Thanatos as the grim reaper. In your opinion, is there such thing as a good death? If so, how would you describe it?

is the occasion to be deliberately open to receiving other people's love and care . . . and I'm delighted when it happens" (quoted by Block, p. 2902).

Many caregivers who become comfortable with death say it's a privilege to be with people at the end of their lives. A physician Block (2001) interviewed said of one dying patient:

> I really like seeing him because no matter how distraught I am about that particular day or feeling overwhelmed . . . I feel so much better after each visit with him. It's almost like he's a doctor to me. (p. 2903)

Loved ones often feel the same way, that they have learned something precious by being present at the end of a cherished individual's life.

Conventional wisdom says we're likely to lose faith or be angry at God when someone close to us dies. But this occurs mostly when death is sudden or when people haven't accepted its inevitability. Participants in Maureen Keeley's (2004) study of "final conversations" say their loss was tempered by a renewed sense of comfort, meaning, and spirituality. Said one, "You can't go through this . . . witnessing death, without that awe of what life is. Where it comes from and where it goes" (quoted by Keeley, 2004, p. 95). In another episode, a survivor remembers asking a loved one, "When you get to heaven, you know, keep an eye out for my girls," and her reply, "I will, you know. I'll be their guardian angel" (p. 97). In these episodes, the dying individual was able to help others find peace and comfort.

Proponents of a good death remind us that it might *not* involve preserving life as long as possible. As McCue (1995) proposes, "a rapid, good death" is sometimes preferable to a prolonged, painful end. Prolonging life sometimes means prolonging death. And caregivers and others who perceive death to be a frightening enemy are not equipped to help with end-of-life care. Dying individuals sometimes feel forgotten and ignored because their caregivers are uncomfortable with death, reluctant to become emotionally involved with them, and uncertain how to act around dying people.

Unfortunately, the opportunity to die peacefully among loved ones is sometimes lost in a confusion of tubes, wires, monitors, and hospital restrictions. It may be comforting to have professionals on hand, but it's hard for loved ones to be present and difficult to maintain a sense of intimacy and individuality in an institutional setting such as a hospital. Communication scholar Sandra Ragan reflects on the difference between her father's death and her sister's:

> Dad's death was a conflicted one: He died in a hospital, connected to various machines, and in constant fear, until his last 48 hours, when he entered a morphine-induced semiconsciousness, that his doctors would not give him adequate medication. (Ragan, Wittenberg & Hall, 2003, p. 219)

In contrast, her sister died at home under hospice care:

> Sherry died peacefully in her own home with no medical intervention other than oxygen, a catheter, and the blessing of morphine and Ativan. Her family and loved ones surrounded her, and throughout her last night, she was cradled by her daughter and her beloved cocker spaniel. (Ragan et al., 2003, pp. 219–220)

Death with Dignity

In Japan, a metaphor for the ideal death is *pokkuri shinu*, which translates roughly into "popping like a bubble." People in many cultures share the same wish, of living fully and then dying without languishing slowly away. In the United States, a good death is often described as one in which people maintain dignity and die surrounded by loved ones and familiar, comforting surroundings.

The motto of death with dignity is attributable mostly to **hospice**, an organization that provides support and care for dying individuals and their families. Hospice provides **palliative care**, that is, care designed to keep a person as comfortable and fulfilled as possible at the end of life but not designed to cure the main illness once it has been determined that medical care will not improve it. More than 4 in 10 of all dying patients in the United States now receive hospice care, mostly at home during the last 3 weeks of their lives, and of those, 86.6% consider their care to be "excellent" ("Hospice Care," 2012).

Central to hospice's philosophy is the belief that death is a natural part of life, thus personal and unique. People are encouraged to die as they have lived, surrounded by the people and things they love most. Hospice volunteers and professional caregivers visit with terminally ill individuals and their loved ones to talk with them about death (if they wish), to make sure the dying person is not in pain, to encourage spiritual exploration (if they wish), and to provide many forms of assistance. In this effort, hospice is more oriented toward personal expression, emotions, spirituality, and social concerns than is conventional Western medicine. Loved ones are considered important participants in the dying process.

Beth Perry, a hospice nurse, recalls an especially rewarding experience helping a dying patient. "Roman, a handsome man in his mid-50s, seemed too well to be a **patient** on a palliative care unit," she remembers (Perry, 2002, para. 5). But Roman *was* dying, and he was bored and tired of the process—ready for the tedium to end. Although Roman's caregivers knew his death was near, they sought a way to rekindle his sense of purpose. Someone remembered that he and his wife had bought a new home just before he became ill, and the grounds were not yet landscaped. They suggested that the couple plan the garden and grounds together. "The result was amazing," writes Perry:

> The next time we visited the pair, gone was the stony silence, the painful watching of time tick by. Instead, we found the two of them with their noses in the same magazine, eagerly debating annuals versus perennials, tulips versus delphiniums. (para. 7)

Although Roman did not live to plant the garden, his last days were filled with enthusiasm rather than boredom. Julie, another nurse caring for Roman, says, "People can take almost anything, but they can't take being forgotten. They want to know that something they have done will live on after they die, and sometimes it is part of my role to help them" (quoted by Perry, 2002, para. 8).

Sometimes it is difficult to know what to say during end-of-life experiences. Sandra Sanchez-Reilly, MD, coauthor of *Communication as Comfort: Multiple Voices in Palliative Care,* told a dying patient in her care, "There are five things I tell my patients to say to everyone in their last day of their lives. Please forgive me; I forgive you; I love you; I will miss you. Goodbye." When the patient said he was not scared and wiped away a tear, Sanchez-Reilly said to him: "You have taught the team many things today,

Mr. _____. The team is here to learn. What else would you like to teach them?" (Ragan, Wittenberg-Lyles, Goldsmith, & Sanchez-Reilly, 2008, p. 80).

In another instance described in the same book, a husband helped his wife accept the need for hospice. Elaine Wittenberg-Lyles describes the hospital-room interaction, which she witnessed as a researcher. The patient expressed her fears about enrolling in hospice to a nurse who suggested the idea, until the patient's husband took his wife's hand in his and said to her through his tears: "I've been married to you for almost twenty-five years. I have never cheated on you. I have never lied to you. I'm not lying to you now. You need hospice. I need hospice. We need hospice" (Ragan et al., 2008, p. 146). Then the two leaned toward each other and cried.

Hospice volunteers also play a vital role. A beautiful account of this is available in Elissa Foster's (2007) book *Communicating at the End of Life: Finding Magic in the Mundane.* In the book, Foster chronicles her year as a hospice volunteer and shares the stories of other volunteers and the patients she meets along the way. Threaded throughout the narrative is Foster's relationship with Dorothy, a petite, energetic woman with "lively blue-green" eyes and white, close-cropped hair. Dorothy is under hospice care because doctors recognize that she is in the final stages of chronic obstructive pulmonary disease (COPD). Foster captures the confusion and concern she feels as Dorothy's condition seems, alternately, to deteriorate and improve over time. She also reveals the mutuality of their relationship. Dorothy is not simply the recipient of Foster's care; the caring goes both ways. When Dorothy dies, Foster visits her family, shares hugs and tears with them, and thanks them for "sharing" their mother with her. She later reflects: "My relationship with Dorothy taught me that I could connect with someone whom I hardly know, simply by being there and being willing to let it happen" (p. 210).

We turn next to the concept of slow medicine. Slow medicine does not necessarily involve palliative care, but the two have something in common—a commitment to taking our time and developing caring relationships.

Slow Medicine

As physician Dennis McCullough (2008) explains in *My Mother, Your Mother,* the "slow medicine" concept draws inspiration from Italy, where people in some communities have decided to resist the urge to eat, drive, talk, and live quickly. In some slow cities, cars are no longer allowed downtown. This permits people to walk more safely and leisurely and to visit with neighbors along the way. McCullough, a geriatrician, has adapted a similar philosophy of care that emphasizes deep, rich understanding, wisdom, patience, and flexibility. The central tenets of slow medicine include: (1) take time to understand older adults as individuals with rich histories, wisdom, and challenges; (2) work to develop a healthy, trusting balance between independence and assistance; (3) communicate with warmth, caring, and patience; (4) be a steadfast advocate for people who are in need; and (5), as McCullough puts it, exhibit "kindness, no matter what" (p. 12).

McCullough (2008) compares a slow medicine annual review to the traditional medical workup:

> Unlike the battery of lab tests and screenings a doctor might order for you at middle age, in late life it is rather an exercise in attentive listening. Most questions focus on medical problems certainly, but also include asking how an elderly man, say, spends his time, searching for clues about his emotional state, observing how his mind works, and inviting him to share his own insights about these important aspects of successful aging. (p. 23).

He encourages the families of older adults to adopt the same slow style. "Over the course of three full days, just go and be with your parent without escaping into your own preferred activities," McCullough encourages (p. 27). Observe your parent's routines and rituals. This intimate time is likely to be more enjoyable and more intimate than a jam-packed itinerary. It also better equips you to notice "slow slips" in health that might be reversed with early care and to differentiate between the preferences of youth and the pleasures of later life.

Advance-Care Directives

Advance-care directives describe in advance the medical care a person wishes to receive (or not receive) if he or she becomes too ill to communicate.

The idea behind slow medicine is not to compromise the quality of medical care, but to imbue it with warmth, patience, and gentleness.

These directives take some of the pressure off caregivers and loved ones who might otherwise be forced to make those decisions on their own.

Despite the advantages, the majority of U.S. residents have not written advance-care directives or even conveyed their wishes about end-of-life care to their physicians. By most estimates, fewer than 26% of U.S. residents have filed advance-care directives with their doctors. The percentage is as high as 70% among the nation's nursing home residents, but they constitute less than 10% of the population. That leaves an overwhelming number of people without written instructions about their end-of-life care, even though communicating one's preferences is central to the idea of a good death (Borreani et al., 2008). Confusion about advance directives is particularly prevalent among people with literacy challenges (Sudore, Schillinger, Knight, & Fried, 2010).

Advance-care directives have become more specific through the years. When they were first conceptualized as "living wills" in the 1960s, they typically referred in vague terms to "heroic" life-saving measures (Emanuel & Emanuel, 1998). This presented obvious difficulties in interpretation (e.g.: Is a feeding tube heroic? Is intravenous therapy heroic?). It's now common for advance-care directives to include a person's preferences regarding specific procedures and circumstances, to endow someone with decision-making authority, and to describe the person's philosophy of life and death to help guide decisions during unanticipated circumstances. (See Box 8.5 for a discussion of the right-to-die issue.)

BOX 8.5 ETHICAL CONSIDERATIONS

Do People Have a Right to Die?

Oregon made history in 1997 by legalizing physician-assisted suicide for terminally ill patients. Under the law, a doctor may help a person commit suicide if at least two physicians verify that the person has less than 6 months to live and the patient requests help with suicide at least once in writing and twice verbally, with at least 15 days between requests.

Physician-assisted suicide refers to instances in which, at the request of a terminally ill person, a doctor provides the means for that person to end his or her own life (Krug, 1998). The doctor does not actually kill the patient. This is different from **euthanasia** (also called *mercy killing*), in which a physician or family member intentionally kills the patient to end his or her suffering. The distinction lies in who does the killing—the patient or another person.

The person most commonly associated with physician-assisted suicide was Jack Kevorkian, a physician who, by his own estimate, assisted in the suicides of 130 people. Kevorkian was tried for murder five times, but he was not convicted until the fifth trial, which concluded in April 1999. Kevorkian was declared guilty of second-degree murder by a Michigan jury and sentenced to 10 to 25 years in prison. The conviction was based on an assisted suicide that Kevorkian videotaped and allowed to be broadcast on *60 Minutes* (Willing, 1999). Kevorkian, who was released on parole in 2007 and died in 2011, argued that he was motivated by compassion for people dying slow, painful deaths. His opponents charged that he was a medical "hitman" operating outside the law (Robertson, 1999).

Controversy over physician-assisted suicide is likely to continue for quite some time, with people vigorously arguing both sides of the issue. Proponents of physician-assisted suicide include Dax Cowart, who was badly burned in an explosion in 1973 (Cowart & Burt, 1998). Two-thirds of Cowart's body was burned in the accident, and he lost his eyesight and his fingers. For more than a year Cowart begged doctors to let him die. Despite his pleas, medical teams continued to treat his burns. The treatment kept Cowart alive and eventually helped him regain the ability to walk. But during that time he was in nearly unbearable agony. He recalls: "The pain was excruciating,

it was so far beyond any pain that I ever knew was possible, that I simply could not endure it" (para. 21). Cowart supports physician-assisted suicide. However, even if a law such as Oregon's had been in place when his accident occurred, he would not have qualified for lawful physician-assisted suicide because he was not dying.

Cowart is now an attorney in Corpus Christi, Texas, and describes himself as "happier than most people." But he maintains his conviction that people should not be forced to undergo treatment they do not wish, even if that treatment is needed to keep them alive (Cowart & Burt, 1998). Faced with the same ordeal again, he feels he would wish to die and should be allowed to do so. Cowart's views are captured in his videos *Please Let Me Die* and *Dax's Case*.

On the other side of the issue, some argue that people in intense pain and grief may not see things clearly enough to make life-ending decisions. They point out that Cowart has changed his mind about living with his disabilities. Although he initially felt life would be empty, he now is happy and successful (Cowart & Burt, 1998). Other critics say ill (even terminally ill) patients may request death for the wrong reasons. They may be afraid about the future, feel out of control and scared, or believe they are a burden to loved ones (Muskin, 1998). For these reasons, they feel it is wrong to help someone commit suicide, even if the person requests it.

WHAT DO YOU THINK?

1. Under what circumstances, if any, do you feel patients should be assisted in killing themselves?
2. Should it make a difference whether a patient is terminally ill or not?
3. If you were in Dax Cowart's place, do you feel you would want to die? What would you have done if you were Cowart's caregivers and loved ones?
4. What do you think of the argument that people who are scared and in pain may be not thinking clearly enough to make life-or-death decisions?
5. What do you think of the counterargument—that people should not second-guess the patient's wishes because they cannot fully understand the extent of his or her personal suffering?

BOX 8.6   CAREER OPPORTUNITIES

Social Services and Mental Health

Mental health counselor

Social worker

Psychologist

Social service manager

Hospice/palliative care provider

Home health aide

Senior citizen services providers

CAREER RESOURCES AND JOB LISTINGS

- American Mental Health Counselors Association: www.amhca.org
- Mental health counselor job profile: www.jobprofiles.org/heacounselor.htm
- American Psychological Association: www.apa.org
- National Association of School Psychologists: www.nasponline.org
- American Board of Professional Psychology: www.abpp.org
- National Organization for Human Services: www.nationalhumanservices.org
- Hospice: www.hospicenet.org
- Hospice careers: hospicechoices.com
- Center for Hospice and Palliative Care: www.centerforhospice.org/careers.cfm
- National Association for Home Care and Hospice: www.nahc.org
- Senior citizen services provider job profile: www.jobprofiles.org/heaelderlycaregiver.htm

Communication Skill Builder: Delivering Bad News

One of the most difficult communication challenges that anyone faces is sharing devastating news with another. Bad news is never easy to give or to receive. But there are a number of communication strategies that help optimize people's coping ability. Here are some suggestions from the experts on how to share bad news compassionately.

- *Build caring relationships from the beginning.* In a study of recently diagnosed cancer patients, Pär Salander (2002) found that patients did not describe one distinct event during which they learned of their diagnosis. They considered that it occurred within the context of ongoing relationships with the medical staff. Said one woman: "The kindness, the support, and the help I received from the entire staff when treatment started is what I appreciate the most" (p. 724).
- *Foreshadow the disclosure.* A simple statement such as "The news isn't as good as we hoped" may help prepare people for what's to come.
- *Invite the recipient to bring along supportive others.*
- *Talk in a quiet, private place.* Resist the temptation to deliver bad news in a hallway or semi-private space. Likewise, avoid delivering bad news over the phone whenever possible (Sparks, Villagran, Parker-Raley, & Cunningham, 2007).
- *Tell the truth.* People typically cope better when they know what's happening and what to expect. This is true even when death is expected. A participant in Thomas McCormick and Becky Conley's (1995) study said, "That's one of the things that I like my doctor for, because he was plain with me that I was incurable" (para. 38). She explained that people who don't know they are dying cannot prepare for it emotionally or practically. They lose the chance to settle financial affairs, communicate with loved ones, set new priorities for their limited time, and adjust emotionally to what's occurring.
- *Be clear about your meaning.* Patients often interpret hedge terms such as "possible" to mean that the news giver is attempting to soften the blow of bad news rather than convey actual uncertainty (Pighin & Bonnefon, 2011). Asked to interpret comments such as "It is possible the pain will increase," most patients felt the caregiver was really saying that the pain would "probably" or "certainly" increase (Pighin & Bonnefon, 2011, p. 171).
- *Avoid medical jargon.*
- *Acknowledge and legitimize emotions.* Emotions are a natural part of the coping process. Ignoring them may make the news recipient feel foolish or inappropriate. Instead, acknowledge emotions with statements such as "I know this is very hard

to hear," "I understand this can feel overwhelming," and "It's natural to feel a range of emotions when you learn something like this."

• *Take your cues from the recipient.* Don't be surprised if people seem stoic or distant on hearing bad news, whereas others are tearful or even angry. It's hard for any of us to say how we will react in such circumstances. Patients typically say it's unhelpful when someone attempts to impose a particular agenda or set of emotions on them (Maynard & Frankel, 2006). One patient whom Salander (2002) interviewed wondered: "Why did they have to be so dramatic? Suddenly, everybody looked so grave and became so low-voiced. It gave me a feeling of unreality" (p. 725).

• *Show genuine caring.* As one woman put it: "A hug or supportive word in passing worked miracles" (quoted by Salander, 2002, p. 727).

• *Inform and empathize.* Research shows that, no matter how bad the news, patients want both high-quality information and empathy, and one does not compensate for the other. In other words, lots of information doesn't make up for a lack of emotional supportiveness or vice versa. Patients want both (Sastre, Sorum, & Mullet, 2011).

• *Be aware of personal and cultural preferences for bad news delivery.* Some people, such as members of traditional Native American cultures, prefer that bad news be delivered indirectly through metaphors and storytelling (Thompson & Gillotti, 2005). In some other cultures, speaking bad news aloud is considered unlucky.

• *Offer support.* Indicate your own support and offer other resources to help people learn, adjust, and cope.

• *Be ready with options and a plan of action.* Although some people may need time to take in the bad news before they make decisions, most say that having a specified next step helped them funnel their energy and emotion in positive ways and feel less like helpless victims.

• *Schedule an information follow-up.* Keep in mind that few people can absorb and remember many details when they are feeling intense emotions. Written materials may help, as will a follow-up visit to talk about the details once the news has sunk in.

For career resources relevant to mental health and coping, see Box 8.6.

Communication Skill Builder: Coping With Death

One positive aspect of death is that it draws people together. Loved ones who may not have seen each other in years unite again with a common concern. Death also provides an occasion for contemplating life and the purpose of living. A sense of insight and spirituality often surrounds death (McCormick & Conley, 1995). Moreover, by sharing in loved ones' deaths, people may become less fearful of death themselves. Joyce Dyer, who wrote *In a Tangled Wood* (1996) about her mother's 9-year experience with Alzheimer's disease, reflected after her death:

> I want to remember every moment I had with my mother, including every second of the last nine years. I want to remember her toothless grin, her screams, her growing fondness for sweets and then for nothing at all, the bouquets of uprooted flowers she picked for me from her unit's patio, the way she tried to fold her bib, the rare pats on my cheek that meant everything, her last words, her last party, her last dance. And I want to remember what I learned from aides and nurses, from volunteers and cleaning staff, from my mother's own sick friends. I don't want to forget a single thing. (Dyer, 1996, p. 136)

People may be surprised by the mixture of emotions they feel about death. Most of us are not sure what to expect, and consequently we are often uncertain how to act around dying individuals. Based on news reports and movies, people typically imagine death as violent and scary. However, the majority of deaths are nothing like that. Colin Parkes (1998) describes the typical death as a "quiet slipping away" without pain or horror.

One nurse described her initial discomfort when a young man in her care joked that he had to live quickly because he would not live long (Erdman, 1993). The nurse was eventually able to laugh with the young man when he quipped that he was watching movies on fast-forward and bathing his dog in the drive-through carwash to save time. Writes Erdman: "The nurse was at first caught off guard by the patient's comments, but the humor opened the door to further communication about death" (p. 59).

Three themes emerge in the narratives of older adults reflecting on the death of loved ones: loss, feelings, coping. The feelings are mixed, but not as negative as you might expect. In Caplan, Haslett, and Burleson's (2005) study of older adult bereavement narratives, 36% of the feelings were negative (fear, loneliness, sadness), but 43% were positive (optimism, thankfulness for time spent together, and so on). Said one woman, whose husband died in 1993: "I don't dwell on the sickness and problems of what happened then, but my thoughts and memories instead, think of all the good and wonderful life we had together with the six children" (p. 244).

In her book *On Death and Dying*, Elisabeth Kübler-Ross (1969) describes the process of coping with death in five stages: denial and isolation, anger, bargaining, depression, and acceptance. Not everyone experiences all five stages or in the order given, but dying individuals and the people around them are likely to experience many of these phases. Although with enough time and support many people eventually feel peaceful about death, they may at times refuse to believe what is told them, or they may feel angry, overwhelmed, sad, or hopeless. Often, people feel their God has let them down, and they react by showing anger or attempting to bargain for mercy. It may be reassuring to remember that these stages are common and legitimate components of the coping process.

Summary

A diverse number of behaviors make up social support. Support is useful in everyday life and in times of crisis. What is most supportive depends on the nature of the situation, the people involved, and their perception of health self-efficacy. Sometimes problem solving is the most effective coping strategy. In those instances, instrumental and informative support are likely to be appreciated. When the situation calls for emotional adjustment, nurturing support may be a useful way to help people feel better about themselves, express their emotions, and feel that others will stand by them in times of trouble.

Even a relatively minor health event can constitute a crisis if the people involved don't have

IN YOUR EXPERIENCE

How much experience have you had with death? How comfortable are you with talking about death and dying?

adequate skills or resources to cope with it. Often, the difference between thriving and declining involves the amount of social support that we perceive is available to us.

Being normal sounds easy, but to members of society viewed as abnormal, achieving a sense of normalcy can seem as impossible as it is desirable. People do well to remember that individuals who have disabilities or are ill do not usually benefit from being treated as if they are childlike or helpless.

People usually cope more effectively when they can discuss sensitive topics than when they feel compelled to feign cheerfulness. Don't assume that individuals are coping well because they are quiet or do not display much emotion. Research suggests that these people often receive less support than others, although they probably need it just as much. Communication is most supportive when it allows distressed individuals to express themselves as they wish and to set the pace for talk and action. Supportive listeners are attentive, nonjudgmental, and able to help people understand their own emotions.

Information is often useful in coping, but as the theory of problematic integration points out, information sometimes creates as many uncertainties and contradictions as it does certainties. Sometimes it can be overwhelming.

The quality of our relationships (with family members, friends, and even animals) has a powerful effect on our health. Strong networks, including social support group membership, are often life enhancing. Likewise, what seems like a crisis is sometimes revealed as a transcendent experience in which people come to perceive an overarching meaning that makes sense of situations that initially seemed tragic or pointless.

Although social support is invaluable, inappropriate or excessive amounts of it can be counterproductive. Too little assistance can make people feel abandoned. Too much can cause a sense of helplessness and dependence. Likewise, too much information or ill-timed disclosures can tax people's coping ability, and emotional contagion can be exhausting and can discourage people from describing their feelings. A few simple guidelines can help to ensure that supportive efforts are comforting rather than hurtful.

As the need for family caregivers has risen, the demands on their time have increased as well. Loved ones are an important source of social support, but they, too, need support. Support groups, skills-training programs, and the assistance of family and friends are key.

Medicine has traditionally considered death a failure, to be avoided at all costs, but groups such as hospice promote the philosophy that there is such a thing as a good death. For the most part, a good death unites people in a sense of peace and comfort. When people are able to cope effectively, death may bring people together and help them overcome their fears.

Key Terms and Theories

social support
buffering hypothesis
direct-effect or main-effect model
coping
problem solving
emotional adjustment
health self-efficacy
internal locus of control
external locus of control
fatalistic
dialectics
crisis
normalcy
action-facilitating support
instrumental support
informational support
nurturing support
esteem support
emotional support
support groups
theory of problematic integration
oversupport
overhelping
overinforming
overempathizing

empathy
empathic concern
emotional contagion
transcendent experiences
Family and Medical Leave Act of 1993
hospice
palliative care
advance-care directives
physician-assisted suicide
euthanasia

Discussion Questions

1. How is social support linked to health and longevity? What are some reasons for the link between social support and health?
2. How are our social networks likely to change as we age? Why?
3. How is a sense of normalcy related to social support?
4. What are two types of action-facilitating support? Give an example of each from your own experience.
5. Describe forms of nurturing support and give an example of each from your own experience.
6. What are some communication strategies for supportive listening? For allowing emotional expression?
7. In what ways can people be oversupportive? What are the likely outcomes of different types of oversupport. Name five tips for assuring that sure social support efforts are effective.
8. Have you ever felt that an animal was a good friend? Why or why not? Do you think animal companionship affects your coping ability?
9. Compare the birth experiences of Carol Bishop Mills and her husband with those of Kate and Chris. What do you learn from these examples?
10. What does the term *transcendent experience* mean? Can you think of examples from movies or your own experiences?
11. Describe the provisions of the Family and Medical Leave Act of 1993.
12. Have you experienced the death of a loved one? How did it compare to the process de scribed in "A Long Goodbye to Grandmother" (Box 8.4)?
13. In your opinion, is there such a thing as a good death? If so, how would you describe it?

14. Why might caregivers adopt a life-at-all-costs perspective? What are the potential disadvantages of such a perspective?
15. What role does hospice play?
16. Do you have an advance-care directive? Why or why not?
17. What is your opinion of the right-to-die issue (Box 8.5)? Why?

Answers to *Can You Guess?*

B. 10 years

The percentage of family caregivers who say dementia is their main concern doubled (from 6% to 12%) between 2004 and 2009 ("Caregiving in the U.S.," 2009).

eHealth, mHealth, and Telemedicine

Children in the cocoa farming region of Ghana are seen by a health professional. An mHealth program links the nation's limited number of doctors via mobile phone. (Photo by Kim Naylor/Divine Chocolate)

In Ghana there is 1 doctor for every 12,000 residents, compared to 1 in 300 in the United States. And Ghana residents are at substantially higher risk than Americans for tuberculosis, HIV/AIDS, malaria, and many other diseases. Clearly, it is critical to make the most of every physician. An innovative mHealth (mobile health) program is helping to do just that.

Mobile Doctors Network (MDNet) provides free texting and mobile-to-mobile service for physicians in Ghana and other parts of Africa so they can easily talk to each other no matter where they are (WHO, 2011a). As part of the program, physicians receive directories listing thousands of doctors and their specialties. The idea is that communication matters, and the evidence bears it out.

Since the MDNet program began in 2008, Ghanaian physicians have exchanged more than 1 million calls and texts during which they have helped each other with difficult cases, offered assistance in emergencies, and made patient referrals. Consequently, patients are now more likely to receive medical care, and physicians report that overall medical quality has improved (WHO, 2011b).

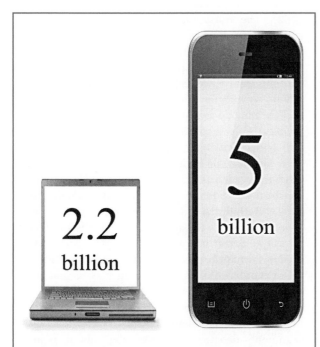

FIGURE 9.1 Worldwide, mobile technology is more than twice as prevalent as computer-based Internet usage, especially in developing countries, where people are more likely to have mobile technology than electricity.

CHECK IT OUT! For more on mHealth programs in Africa and around the world, visit the World Health Organization website at http://www.who.int/goe/mobile_health/en/index.html.

Here's another example. In 2007, a program to help children with cleft lips and palates in South Africa was languishing. Free care was available, but few people knew about it. In the first 6 weeks, print and radio ads revealed only 12 children who required surgery. Surgeons and facilities were available, and program sponsors knew the need was critical, but they couldn't reach the people who needed them. Then came Please Call Me, a text-messaging program. Sponsors sent a brief message to mobile phone users asking them to text back SMILE if they knew someone who needed cleft-related surgery. More than 355 people responded in the first 3 days, resulting in 42 free surgeries (Deign, 2011). Surgeries have now surpassed 320, another indication that mHealth can be a useful means of getting the word out and making the most of limited resources.

In this chapter we explore **eHealth**, the use of electronic means to transfer health information and resources; **mHealth**, which involves the use of devices such as mobile phones, tablet computers, and personal digital assistants (PDAs) to promote good health; and **telemedicine** (also called telehealth), which uses technology to span geographical barriers in the provision of health care (WHO, 2010a, 2011b). The overarching category of eHealth includes mhealth, telemedicine, and a variety of other activities such as communication between everyday people via blogs (short for *web logs*), Tweets, text messages, and other electronic means. Telemedicine is distinguished by efforts to facilitate and extend the provision of health services, which typically includes sharing diagnostic data, making treatment recommendations, and communicating with patients. Our increasing reliance on these technologies as both health citizens and professionals underscores the central role communication plays in health.

"Africa is poor in landlines and hospital beds but rich in cellphones," explains Justine Gerardy (2012, para. 6). Based on that, program sponsors scrapped their original plan to link doctors via the Internet, and chose to focus on mobile technology instead. Consider that approximately 2.2 billion people around the world access the Internet through desktop or laptop computers, and only 37% of them are in developing countries ("Information," 2011). These 2.2 billion people represent about 33% of the world, and the richest part of it at that. In contrast, more than 5 billion people worldwide use devices such as mobile phones and tablet computers, and more than 7 in 10 of them live in countries with low or middle incomes (WHO, 2011b). (See Figure 9.1.) Wireless signals now cover 85% of the world, making mobile access more prevalent than both electricity and non-mobile Internet service. You can see why mHealth (also called m-health) has emerged as a special field of interest.

WHAT DO YOU THINK?

Is a career in health information technology appealing to you? Why or why not?
See Box 9.2 at the end of the chapter for career resources.

eHealth

I had a question, you know? I didn't really feel comfortable asking my mom, 'cause she was the only one around. You know, I was like, I went on the Internet and I was like, "Can a girl get pregnant during her period?"

This statement by a 17-year-old high student in Rachel Jones and Ann Biddlecom's (2011, p. 115) study of teens' online communication illustrates one role the Internet plays in health-related behavior. Sometimes eHealth is an alternative to talking about topics that are embarrassing to discuss with another person. As you will see in this section, people have this and numerous other goals in mind when they utilize electronic health resources. We will explore these goals as we pursue answers to questions such as: *Why and under what circumstances do people seek electronic health information? Is eHealth information mostly helpful or counterproductive?* and *How does eHealth communication compare with face-to-face transactions?*

Theoretical Foundations

Before we begin, let's clarify the role that eHealth plays in shaping public discourse and establishing social ties.

THE THREE SPHERES

As social actors, we recognize that different rules of engagement apply to our interactions depending on the circumstances. G. Thomas Goodnight (1982) and Robert Cox (2010) have identified three spheres with powerful influence on the way we communicate with others: the personal, technical, and public.

The **personal sphere** involves communication between a small number of people that is usually not made part of the public record (Goodnight,

1982). The most common example is a casual conversation between friends or acquaintances. In today's environment, texts and emails to close friends also fall within this sphere. If, in personal communication, we seek to debate an issue, we usually do so with few formal rules of argumentation, and we may be swayed by the personalities of the people involved to either overstate or understate our claims (Goodnight, 1982).

In contrast, the **technical sphere** is governed by strict rules, such as agreed-upon standards for what constitutes evidence and causality (Goodnight, 1982). Rather than a conversation between two friends, think of a debate between scientists or trial attorneys. Scientific journals are replete with technical information, carefully vetted based on a strict set of standards. This information may or may not have a presence in everyday discourse.

The **public sphere** is more inclusive than the other two. It is created through "conversation, argument, debate, or questioning" about issues that concern people at a community or global level (Cox, 2010, p. 26). As Cox puts it, active discourse about subjects of mutual interest brings the public sphere into being. One way this occurs is when concerns previously treated as private become topics of shared interest with others. We will discuss this further later in the chapter. But first keep in mind Cox's assertion that the public sphere is not confined to official spaces such as courtrooms or Senate chambers, but occurs as well in restaurants and supermarkets, on radio call-in shows, and any other space in which people engage with each other. These days it also occurs via Facebook, Twitter feeds, blogs, websites, and other electronic venues. In short, the public sphere involves a diversity of perspectives in a discursive climate that invites participation.

Here's a health-related example. When Candace and Steve Lightner's 13-year-old daughter was killed by a drunk driver in 1980, it might have been treated as a personal tragedy. Their other two children had, at different times, also been injured by impaired drivers, but had survived. In all three cases, the drivers received little or no punishment. But by the third incident, this one even more tragic than the others, Candy Lightner had had enough. She felt that the issue of drunk driving was not a personal issue but a public one, and she launched a grassroots campaign that gave rise to Mothers

Against Drunk Driving (MADD) and new levels of public awareness and legislation.

As you can see in this example, the spheres are not always clearly distinct from each other at a glance. However, Goodnight (1982) maintained that an important difference is present beneath the surface, namely the discursive standards that establish what is appropriate and admissible within each sphere. Goodnight worried that the public sphere might be "eroded" by overreliance on personal evidence, which is subject to distortion by personality and other factors, and technical evidence, whose parameters are sometimes inadequate to admit diverse forms of reason and evidence.

We have only scratched the surface concerning the theoretical implications of spheres (to read more, see Box 9.1). But a basic understand will do for now in that it highlights a fascinating aspect of emerging communication technology—the widespread potential for people to introduce issues into the public sphere. As in the MADD case and many others, powerful implications emerge when health, often a deeply personal concern, becomes the topic of public communication. That has always been true, and grassroots efforts have always existed. What is changing is the ease and access with which people can place information in the public sphere. **Web 2.0**, a term used to describe Internet users' ability to create and share information online (via YouTube, blogs, wikis, and so on), has made it possible for everyday citizens to step beyond the role of information consumer into the shoes of message creators and publishers. Now, with a bit of basic training and access to a computer, nearly anyone can create messages and make them available worldwide. The extent to which those messages are adopted as topic of public discourse varies. The point is that the widespread ability to do this is unprecedented in history. This changes the nature of our relationships with others.

WEAK AND STRONG TIES

It's now relatively easy to communicate about personal matters with people you are never likely to meet in person. Rather than keeping a personal journal, you might create a blog or Twitter feed on which you post ideas and reflections that anyone can see. You might expect your friends to visit your blog but may be surprised by postings from

---

> ### BOX 9.1
>
> ## Resources
>
> Cox, R. (2010). *Environmental communication and the public sphere* (2nd ed.). Thousand Oaks, CA: Sage.
>
> Goodnight, T. G. (1982). The personal, technical, and public spheres of argument: A speculative inquiry into the art of public deliberation. *Journal of the American Forensic Association, 18*, 214–227.
>
> Habermas, J. (1989). *The structural transformation of the public sphere: An inquiry into a category of bourgeois society.* (T. Burger, Trans.). Cambridge, MA: MIT Press (originally published in 1962).

people you don't know who say your words moved them or they relate to what you are experiencing. In some ways, we're not as alone as we used to be. Our potential for social interaction and connection with diverse others (at least as far as we can take that electronically) is nearly infinite.

Relevant to this idea is Mark Granovetter's **social network theory**, which proposes that we experience **strong ties** with people whose social networks overlap ours a great deal (close friends and members of our inner circle) and **weak ties** (acquaintanceships) with people whose social networks do not overlap much with our own (Granovetter, 1973, 1983). We tend to interact with our close friends in what Granovetter (1983) refers to as a "closely knit clump" (p. 202). There are advantages to this in terms of stability, loyalty, and comfort. However, Granovetter asserts that weak ties are also important in that they help us avoid an isolated and insular perspective on the world.

It is often through weak ties that we learn new ideas, are exposed to opportunities beyond our current circumstances, and experience the flexibility of being different from the expectations of our close friends. In addition, people to whom we have strong ties tend to experience the same stressors that we do, so weak ties can be sources of support when our close friends feel as overwhelmed as we do. And the ties that bind sometimes change. If, for example, we learn we have diabetes, we may feel we suddenly have less in common with our old friends (who still engage in their customary ways of thinking, eating, and behaving) than we used to and more in common with people we don't know well but who have the same lifestyle/health concerns we do. For these reasons, Granovetter (1973, 1983) titled his seminal essays "The Strength of Weak Ties."

Health blogs make it possible to create a sense of community among people with weak ties. For example, blog coordinators at Wego Health, a social media company that encourages collaboration among health care activists, propose a question each month and invite people to post their thoughts about it. In April 2012, the question was: "If you had a superpower—what would it be? How would you use it?"

Tiffany Marie Peterson (2012), who identifies herself as a lupus ePatient, responded to the superpower question with her version of the Miranda Rights that police in the United States recite to crime suspects. Her version, Miranda Health Rights, is for a different sort of offender, those guilty of offering "ridiculous uneducated notions" such as:

> It's my fault I have lupus . . . a miracle herb can cure my disease . . . if only I just ate 10 vegetables a day lupus would disappear . . . how I should just quit while I'm ahead because there's no cure and so on. (para. 9)

BOX 9.2

Profile of an ePatient

In the broadest sense, ePatients are "Internet-savvy" people who "meet their own health needs using the Internet and other information and communication technology" (Kim & Kwon, 2010, p. 712). They typically find health-related information, share it with others, investigate treatment options and more, online. They tend to be comparatively young, well educated, and affluent, meaning they're probably already information rich (Koch-Weser, Bradshaw, Gualtieri, & Gallagher, 2010). Even though ePatients use online resources more than other people, most of them say their doctors are still their favorite source of health information. They just yearn for more detail than their physicians typically provide (Kim & Kwon, 2010).

The term *ePatient* is still evolving. Many people who look up health information online and share it with others aren't patients at all. For example, nearly 7 in 10 people who seek cancer information online don't have cancer (Kim & Kwon, 2010). Kyunghye Kim and Nahyun Kwon (2010) advocate a finer distinction by defining **ePatients** as "people with illness seeking information or help from the Internet to make informed health decisions" (p. 712).

No matter how you define the concept, electronic health information and ePatients are here to stay.

Peterson's "Miranda Health Rights" includes the following:

> I have the right to remain silent and refuse to comply shall you inflict any harm upon my health . . . You have the right to consult Dr. Google before speaking/approaching me with ignorance about my condition/and or health. If need be I can refer to you to an Epatient advocate and have them present during questioning now or in the future . . . If you cannot conduct a Google search, information will be selected for you before any uneducated responses or questioning. (para. 8)

She concludes: "These Miranda Health rights are my superpowers!" (para. 10). Peterson's post displays her experience with eHealth. She refers to herself as an ePatient and sees "Dr. Google" and "Epatient advocates" as superpower antidotes to the harm caused by people who offer uninformed advice. In her case, the Internet is a way to vent, share stories with others, and alleviate ignorance about a condition that many people do not understand. (For more on ePatients, see Box 9.2.)

Stephen Rains and David Keating (2011) found that bloggers with chronic health conditions perceive that people who visit their blogs offer them valuable social support, which correlates with an enhanced sense of well-being (Rains & Keating, 2011). "Blogging involves broadcasting one's concerns in a format that is public and mediated," the researchers write (p. 527). As a result, bloggers perceive support via strong ties with family and friends, but the researchers found that bloggers consider weak-tie support from people they don't know well to be just as powerful. They suggest that, especially when strong-tie support is inadequate, blogs may be a way of receiving support from people who would otherwise be unavailable to give it.

A few lessons emerge from considering eHealth communication from the perspective of spheres and social ties. One is that the options for health-related expression and social support (a topic we discussed in Chapter 8) are expansive at both the personal and public level. Another is that, with a proliferation of messages in the public sphere, there is some danger that we will mistake narratives, and even misconceptions, for scientific truths. As mentioned in Chapter 1, Raluca Cozma (2009), for one, worries

that inaccuracies may be perpetuated if people rely on folk wisdom rather than facts. She found knowledge differences between, on the one hand, people who rely heavily on personal-sphere sources such as blogs and, on the other, people who rely more on health organization websites (public sphere sources) and health news sites (technical sphere sources). People whose information came mostly from the personal sphere were more likely than the others to believe health myths, such as the common but unsupported notions that carrots improve eyesight, filtered cigarettes prevent cancer, and calcium-rich foods prevent tooth decay. Just as Goodnight worried that the public sphere would be eroded, others worry about unfortunate results if the technical sphere loses status as a source of reliable information.

With these issues in mind, let's take a closer look at people's motivation for using communication technology.

Why and When do We Seek Electronic Health Information?

My alarm clock went off hours before the sun began rising. I silenced it, slowly got out of bed and began getting ready for my morning gym session. Sill half-asleep, I turned on the bright lights of the bathroom and began brushing my teeth. What happened next is something I never imagined could happen and something I will remember for the rest of my life.

Health events, such as this one described by a university student, sometimes sneak up on us when expert care isn't readily available. Here's what happened next:

I had somehow managed to open my mouth too wide while brushing my teeth and it was stuck opened. My poor jaw was stuck opened with toothpaste dripping from the corners of my lips. At that moment, panic set it. Tears were rolling down my cheeks. I felt so helpless. I frantically got online and tried to find solutions.

In this case, the woman's first impulse was to seek information online. "It was so early I didn't want to wake up my roommate," she explains. "So I'm standing there with my mouth hanging open trying to Google 'how to fix your jaw' in my cell phone."

In this section we will examine the reasons people seek health information electronically. Earlier in the chapter we heard the perspective of a teenager who sought sex education online because she didn't want to ask her mother. In the case of the dislocated jaw, the motivations were to find information quickly, to avoid inconveniencing others, and hopefully, to solve an unexpected and urgent dilemma. As we explore theories of eHealth information-seeking, consider how well they describe your experiences.

One perspective is that uncertainty motivates information seeking, especially if we perceive an urgent need or risk. Theorists call it our **information sufficiency threshold**, the amount of information we need to feel capable of coping with and understanding a threatening issue (Chaiken, 1980; Chaiken, Giner-Sorolla, & Chen, 1996; Griffin, Dunwoody, & Neuwirth, 1999). In the story of the dislocated jaw, the young woman said her first reaction was to think, "I don't know what to do!" That sent her scrambling for information in the quickest way she could think of—a Google search on her phone. It was a clear case of information insufficiency, and she was highly motivated to learn quickly.

However, uncertainty isn't always the singular or deciding factor. For a variety of reasons, we might

not seek information even if we acknowledge that we don't know much about a health issue. Maybe we don't believe more knowledge will make a difference. The **health information acquisition model** established the basis for many theories that have followed it. The model proposes that we are motivated to seek information when something calls our attention to a concern, we don't perceive that we are well informed about it, it seems important to find out soon, and we think we will be able to find trustworthy and useful information (Freimuth, Stein, & Kean, 1989). Central to this theory is the idea that people first consider how much they already know and then weigh the costs and rewards of seeking additional information. The woman with the dislocated jaw said she felt sure she could fix the problem if she learned how to do it online. She had high self-efficacy (a term you may remember from Chapter 8 that describes the belief that we can make a difference in managing our own health).

Let's add some additional dimensions. The **Theory of Motivated Information Management** (TMIM) by Walid Afifi and Judith Weiner (2004) has several aspects in common with the health information acquisition model in that both presume that people seek information when they are anxious about something and feel it would be helpful to learn more about it. TMIM, however, also addresses coping confidence (*Am I ready to deal with what I might learn?*) and people's choice of information channels (*How might I get this information?*). According to TMIM, the likelihood that we will seek information depends on our perceived need for it, our coping ability, and the way in which the information is conveyed. Regarding information channels, TMIM addresses not just why we want information and what we hope to learn but *how* we seek that information. Afifi and Weiner propose that we seek information most readily from sources we believe to be relevant, accurate, and trustworthy.

If you think information is the same no matter how it's conveyed, consider how you would like to receive bad news about your health. Would a tweet or text message be as effective as a phone call? Would a phone call be as effective as a face-to-face conversation? Most people prefer that sensitive and important information be conveyed in emotionally immediate, information-rich ways (Salander, 2002). Especially when the stakes are high, we appreciate the presence of both verbal and non-verbal cues and indications that the other person cares and is willing to listen. (The exception is that some people prefer to receive emotional news at a distance so that they can avoid "flooding out" emotionally in front of other people [Beach, 2002].) Most of us prefer to hear serious news directly from an expert. In short, the source matters to us, and it affects how likely we are to believe what we read and hear.

It follows from TMIM that, when the stakes are high, we typically prefer interpersonal communication with people we highly trust. Partly for this reason, people who don't feel their doctors are empathic and patient-centered are more likely than satisfied patients to seek health information on the Internet (Tustin, 2010). Satisfied patients may already feel their needs have been met, whereas the others don't.

Yet another dimension is added by the **Integrative Model of Online Health Information Seeking**, which posits that social structures and inequities manifest in individual differences, which influence how able and motivated we are to seek eHealth information (Dutta, Bodie, & Basu, 2008). For example, if we believe health authorities don't care about people like us, we're unlikely to put much stock in their advice or to actively seek health information. Or perhaps our reading skill or access to computers is limited, or we have more pressing concerns than long-term health, such as satisfying our hunger or surviving day to day in a violent neighborhood. An important aspect of this theory is that it focuses on individual differences, but it recognizes that they don't happen by chance. Discrimination, hunger, violence, and other factors are often rooted in macro-level issues such that some groups of people have advantages that others don't. Mohan Dutta and colleagues (2008) explain:

> In the absence of health-enhancing structures within the minority community, young people are less likely to learn about the relevance of health behaviors, to have role models promoting health behaviors, and to value health-promoting behaviors owing to the lack of resources that would support such behaviors. As a consequence, they are more likely to focus on the daily struggles of survival. (p. 184)

WHAT DO YOU THINK?

If you think information is the same no matter how it's conveyed, consider how you would like to receive bad news about your health. Would a tweet or text message be as effective as a phone call? Would a phone call be as effective as a face-to-face conversation?

From this perspective, eHealth is not simply a matter of making information available, but of addressing social factors and access issues that influence, on a deeper level, how likely people are to seek and to trust health information.

In contrast to the youth whom Dutta and colleagues describe, people who feel they are proficient at finding health information online are more likely than others to be active Internet users (Rains, 2008a). In this way, one set of advantages (skill and confidence) heightens others (knowledge and its benefits). This is noteworthy because, unlike television, Internet navigation requires a certain level of confidence and a rather sophisticated set of skills. There is also a degree of social expectation. Our chances of going online are heightened if people who are important to us expect us to do so and if they support online information seeking as a valid effort (Smith-McLallen, Fishbein, & Hornik, 2011). This is another factor that may be lacking in underprivileged populations—the social expectation that people can use technology to improve their lives.

As you can see, theories about information seeking naturally overlap because they reflect similar phenomenon, but theorists add various nuances to the picture. Most theorists suggest (and research supports) that we are most likely to seek health information if we are confident that we can find information and use it affectively, we feel emotionally capable of dealing with what we find, and we expect that the results will be worth the effort. The Theory of Motivated Information Management focuses a great deal on interpersonal sources of information and reminds us that the source and channel sometimes matter as much as the content. As one of the first models to focus specifically on electronic modalities, the Integrative Model of Online Information Seeking calls attention to social structures and opportunities that constrain individual action. Unlike information that we may glean incidentally from TV or billboards, eHealth information usually comes to our attention because we actively seek it. One exception is information in pop-up advertisements or tangential hits that can sometimes be different from what we are seeking and can even contradict healthy advice. We will discuss this topic in more detail later in this chapter.

Is Online Health Information Useful?

As you might imagine, there are advantages and disadvantages to using eHealth resources. Let's start with the good news.

First, the Internet is typically engaging and in-depth, which gives it a leg up on TV news. People who rely on newspapers and Internet for cancer information are typically better informed than people who rely on local TV news, probably because information in writing is usually more detailed and precise than television content (Kealey & Berkman, 2010). People who rely on TV news for cancer information often underestimate their cancer risk because such programming most often focuses on ways to prevent cancer, which makes it seem an avoidable outcome (Kealey & Berkman, 2010).

Second, the Internet is a gratifying source of practical advice, available whenever we need it. Some evidence indicates that Internet information is most satisfying when it helps us accomplish a particular goal, such as choosing the foods we will eat, treating a minor injury, curing a headache, and so on. People who find practical information online are usually more satisfied with their experience than people who seek to increase their knowledge about a health concern without an action goal in mind (Lee, Park, & Widdows, 2009).

A third advantage is the potential for targeted messages. Text messages and tweets now offer regular tips, reminders, and encouragement. We will talk about these more in the section on mHealth.

Fourth, online resources offer a means to connect with other people to share information and social support, particularly for people who are short on time or transportation, have disabilities or responsibilities that prevent them from leaving home, or who find comfort in the relative anonymity of technology-mediated conversations. People with HIV/AIDS who make use of Internet information are found to have greater knowledge of the condition, more success coping, and larger support networks than similar people who do not go online (Kalichman et al., 2003). And evidence suggests that the advice peers offer each other is usually quite good. In one instance, a grieving man who shared his story online received dozens of immediate replies. People said they understood how he was feeling and advised him to continue therapy, find solace in his religious faith, be kind to his wife, accept others' help, and resist any temptation to abuse drugs. Therapists surveyed by T. Ferguson (1997) applauded the people's kind efforts, and most said they would not have been able to help the man in such an "immediate, compassionate, and practical way" themselves (para. 8).

But eHealth sources fall short in some ways. For one thing, it can be hard to find trustworthy information. One team of researchers found 41 inaccuracies in 18 cancer information websites (Bernstam et al., 2008). In light of how much bad information is available, media literacy is critical. University students asked to rate the quality of medical information rated it about the same, although some of them were informed that the source was the U.S. National Institutes of Health (an unbiased and scientific source) and some believed it was published online by Pfizer Pharmaceuticals (a commercial enterprise with an interest in promoting particular products) (Kim, 2011). As you will see in Chapter 11, one of the keys to media literacy is considering the sender's motive and whether the sponsor is likely to be biased.

Add to the list information that is accurate but counterproductive. Jones and Biddlecom (2011) point out that the Internet is not great at providing sex education. As one teenager in their study put it, you can find information about safer sex and abstinence online if you look for it, but along the way you're likely to find a lot more information leading you in the opposite direction:

> The Internet, it's pretty much just like a giant billboard for sex. It's really, it's not a good place to go if you are young, because being on Internet, because all the pop ups and things you could type in kind of makes you want to have sex. So it really doesn't enforce the abstinence

rule and birth control, safe sex anything. (quoted by Jones & Biddlecom, 2011, p. 118)

Like this teen, most of those in Jones and Biddlecom's study felt that the Internet was not a helpful resource for information about abstinence or contraception.

Another drawback is the challenge of sorting through voluminous information online, especially when the information is new to us, complex, or far outside the realm of common knowledge. A recent Google search for "breast cancer" yielded more than 276 million hits. Similarly, in a study of online resources for people with HIV or AIDS, Keith J. Horvath and colleagues (2010) found an extensive but potentially bewildering amount of information about the physical, emotional, and social aspects of those conditions. Information overload can be especially distressing for people who are newly diagnosed and may not yet have a good idea of what to expect or how to judge the timeliness and quality of the information they find. The researchers suggest that websites adopt a stepwise framework that begins with a general overview and allows readers to move in stages to more complex and varied information. Otherwise, they say, rather than serving as a source of comfort, online information can be frightening, confusing, and overwhelming.

A third drawback involves the irony that people most in need of health information are least likely to get it online, where such information is most plentiful. Although health risks tend to be highest among less-educated, low-income, and older people, people in those groups are less likely than others to learn about health online. Researcher Diane Smith (2011) found that college graduates are nearly 2½ times more likely to use the Internet for health information than people who didn't graduate from high school. Likewise, people earning $75,000 a year are more likely to rely on the Internet than people who make less than $25,000, and people ages 18 to 29 are 3 times more likely than people 60 and older to learn about health online.

For a variety of reasons, people differ in terms of the type and amount of information they seek and the information to which they are incidentally exposed. Jeff Niederdeppe and colleagues (2007) differentiate between **health information seeking,** which involves an active search for information,

and **health information scanning**, which includes information that comes up in conversation or in the media and sticks in the memory. They have found that information gained while health *seeking* is usually of greater depth and of more direct assistance in making medical decisions. However, people are exposed to far more information incidentally than purposefully, making health *scanning* important as well.

Another crucial element in becoming well informed is **health information efficacy**, confidence in our ability to get and understand health information. Health information efficacy is highest among people who are well educated, those who are active in their communities, and people who keep up with health stories in the news (Basu & Dutta, 2008). Women are typically more likely than men— and older adults more likely than younger ones—to have high health information efficacy and to be actively oriented to seeking health and prevention information (Basu & Dutta, 2008). These comparisons are important because confidence and health information-seeking can help with coping and decision making.

And finally, information isn't a cure-all. eHealth can help augment health efforts, but it's not a replacement for personal contact. Overreliance on technology-mediated communication may prevent people from developing relationships in their own communities, ultimately robbing them of the types of social support that cannot be transmitted via fiber optics. And information isn't always enough. In the case of the dislocated jaw, the young woman eventually woke her roommate and the two of them conducted a more thorough search on their computer. "I had to put a wash cloth in my mouth because I was drooling," the student now says, laughing. "We *had* to fix it!" But when nothing they read online worked, they went to a hospital emergency room, where a doctor was able to get her jaw in place again. Interestingly, when the same thing happened to the student several weeks later, she didn't go online. Instead, she went straight to the ER. Her sense of self-efficacy had vanished during the first experience. "I tried. It's too hard," she says.

As an aside to the story, the roommate's mother was a nurse, but they avoided calling her because it was so early in the morning. After a few *Communication Skill Builder* tips on using the

Internet effectively, we will consider: *How does online communication affect how we communication one person to another?*

Communication Skill Builder: Using the Internet

Because there is both reliable and unreliable health information on the Internet, experts offer the following suggestions.

- Don't trust information if there is no author or sponsor or if the source given isn't well known.
- Look for another source if the sponsors are trying to sell a product rather than offer free information. Plenty of websites make reliable health information available free.
- Don't rely on information if it is dated, references are missing, or references don't seem legitimate.
- Keep in mind that legitimate health practitioners don't speak in terms of "secret formulas" or "miraculous cures." Only con artists use such language (Kowalski, 1997). Other red-flag claims include such wording as "Treats all forms of cancer," "Cancer disappears," and "Nontoxic" ("Beware of Online," 2008, np).
- Don't be convinced by case studies of "actual" satisfied customers. An isolated case does not prove a product's effectiveness, and this may not be an actual customer.
- Do your own research. Read medical journal articles. Ask health professionals.
- Read the fine print carefully. Look for disclaimers and vague wording.
- Report suspicious claims to the Federal Trade Commission, Better Business Bureau, or state attorney general's office.

? **CAN YOU GUESS? Part 1**

Which group below is most likely to get health information on TV? From family and friends? From health care providers?

A. Black Americans

B. Hispanic Americans

C. Non-Hispanic White Americans

Answers appear at the end of the chapter.

How does eHealth Communication Compare?

With the best will in the world, unless your friends and family have been through it they just won't get it. . . . They won't understand the raw pain of not being able to have your own children. The only people who will understand that are other people who are in your place. And now the Internet is here, I mean what people did before the Internet I don't know.

This statement by a participant in Lisa Hinton and colleagues' (2010, p. 439) study of people undergoing fertility treatment brings up a good question: *How are things different since the Internet?*

A concern among many analysts is that, whereas before the Internet we relied almost exclusively on health professionals for medical information and advice, people may now rely on Internet sources instead. So far, research shows that the equation is a little more complicated and not quite as grim as that. People don't seem to pick one over the other. In fact, some evidence suggests that, when people pursue information online they are *more* likely, rather than less likely, to seek the care of a face-to-face care provider (C. J. Lee, 2008). This is true especially when people have low trust in physicians (C. J. Lee, 2009). Chul-Joo Lee (2009) explains:

> High-trust people already were visiting their physicians as much as they needed to. On the other hand . . . Internet exploration of a health topic may inform someone that a specific health concern is important, and thus drive even those who have little trust to seek out a physician. (pp. 74–75)

Overall, evidence suggests that we use online and interpersonal communication to varying degrees based on how accessible they are and how well each of them meets our needs.

By the same token, a disappointing medical encounter can be the impetus for an Internet search. People who are dissatisfied by communication with their health care providers are more likely than others to seek eHealth information (Hou & Shim, 2010). In these cases, the Internet may be a means to meet social and informational needs that are not satisfied in face-to-face communication.

This phenomenon is well expressed in **uses and gratifications theory**, which suggests that people engage with mediated messages in an active, goal-oriented way. The implication is that, far from being passive recipients of whatever comes our way, we are motivated to engage with media when doing so satisfies our need for information, cognitive exercise, social stimulation, escape, entertainment, or some other need (Katz, Blumler, & Gurevitch, 1974).

Consider the reasons you turn on the TV or boot up your computer after a long day. Maybe you hope to catch up on the day's news (information needs), relax and forget about your worries (escape and entertainment), watch a show about the history of the solar system (cognitive exercise), enjoy the familiar personalities of characters in your favorite sitcom (social stimulation), or catch up with friends via Facebook or other social media (social interaction). As media have changed, so have our habits. Today, the average college student spends nearly 3 hours a day on social networking sites, mostly catching up with friends (Raacke & Bonds-Raacke, 2008).

Conversely, perhaps you had a great day and just want to sit outside and watch the sunset in peace and quiet. This may a sign that, today at least, you don't need electronic media to satisfy needs. They have been met in other ways.

The same premise applies to health needs. The Internet seems to be most useful when it helps us meets needs we haven't been able to fulfill otherwise. For example, women newly diagnosed with breast cancer who have unmet needs for information or emotional support are more likely than others to use Internet sources and to gravitate to the type of online information that best meets their needs (Lee & Hawkins, 2010). In much the same way, television and Internet use are positively correlated with healthy behaviors among people with low or moderate levels of interpersonal communication, but the Internet does not significantly enhance healthy behaviors in people with active social networks, perhaps because they are already well informed (C. J. Lee, 2008). All in all, Internet and television may compensate to some extent for interpersonal communication deficits.

Of course, even when health providers we love give us a lot of attention and information, it's unlikely that they can satisfy all of our needs all of the time. We may wish to learn more after we have assimilated

? **CAN YOU GUESS? Part 2**

How many hours a day does the average college student spend on social networking sites?
Answers appear at the end of the chapter.

what they have told us in person. Or we may seek the validation that only similar others can provide.

When Hinton and colleagues (2010) interviewed people undergoing treatment for infertility, they discovered a pervasive sense of social isolation among them. Because conception is an intimate and emotional matter, difficulty conceiving a child is sometimes perceived as a personal failing, and because they were coping with treatment cycles and disappointments most people around them had never experienced, many of the people interviewed felt separate from the people around them—as if they were the "odd one out" or even a "leper" or "pariah" (Hinton, Kurinczuk, & Ziebland, 2010, p. 438). Many said the Internet was a "friend," a "lifeline," or even their "only friend" during the experience (p. 438). One woman interviewed for the study described her experience with an online forum this way:

> And you suddenly feel normal. You feel accepted. You can go on the forum and say, you know, "I've just walked past a pregnant woman in Sainsbury's and I found myself standing in the fruit and veg aisle bawling my eyes out." And everyone else would think, "Oh, that's a bit of an overreaction." The girls in the forum were just like, "No I'm with you, I've done that, I've been there." (p. 438)

In this way, Internet conversations were often a source of simultaneously personal and anonymous (weak-tie) support. This was true when people merely "lurked" (read without commenting) on sites and when they took an active role.

There is another link between eHealth and patient-caregiver relationships in that patients do not always disclose to their doctors that they use online resources, which can lead to misunderstandings and confusion. Rebecca Imes and colleagues (2008) found that patients are likely to stay quiet about online searches if they feel confident that they can judge the quality of online information for themselves, they are afraid their caregivers would think less of them, they don't feel there is enough time to work it into the conversation, and/or they don't want to give the impression of encroaching on the provider's "turf" (p. 545). The research team cautions that patient satisfaction and quality of care may be compromised if patients do not feel comfortable disclosing what they are thinking to their doctors or checking the veracity of information they have seen online (Imes, Bylund, Sabee, Routsong, & Sanford, 2008).

All in all, it seems we participate in eHealth (if we are motivated and able) to satisfy some of the same needs fulfilled by in-person health care. For the most part, one is a compliment to, not a substitute for, the other. Let's shift now to a particular type of eHealth.

mHealth

Imagine using your mobile phone to monitor the heart rate of an unborn child and transmit that information instantly to a database so that medical professionals can monitor pregnancy and labor even when they can't be there in person. Mercy Hospital Mount Lawley in Western Australia is testing equipment that does just that, with hopes that it will one day be used all over the world (WHO, 2011a). Computer scientists invented the mobile phone app (short for *application*) to serve as an easy-to-use, low-cost version of equipment usually found only in hospitals. They hope it will facilitate prenatal care for women in remote regions and for those with high-risk pregnancies.

Other apps are being developed to measure and monitor oxygen levels in the blood and more. Some apps involve little more than the camera in your smart phone, with which you might instantly send photos or video to a health professional to learn, for example, if the bite on your arm is from a poisonous spider or if a person is exhibiting signs of a stroke (WHO, 2011a). Or you might use an app to track depression, weight changes, drug reactions, and other health concerns.

A variety of **social entrepreneurs** (people who apply business principles to societal needs) are focused on health. Health-related mobile apps are expected to become a $52 billion-per-year industry within the new few years (Clancy, 2011). Communication technology experts working to develop mHealth resources have found that the best systems do not replace existing health services; they extend them beyond their current reach.

But mHealth is not without challenges. One is the lack of a standard operating platform among mobile devices. Partly as a result, most efforts are still small-scale and experimental (WHO, 2011a). Other challenges are the cost of technology, the need for public education about mHealth, and privacy concerns.

One area of mobile health with few barriers is the use of **short message services** (**SMS**) such as texts and tweets. Since health involves everyday choices, SMS options are emerging that offer regular tips and encouragement about diet, weight control, mental health, and more. Marketed in the right way, consumers seem receptive. When health promoters in San Francisco offered a free text-message service about sexual health for 15- to 19-year-olds, more than 4,500 people expressed an interest in signing up (Lefebvre, 2009). (See *Check It Out!* for more about free text-message reminders.)

So far we have talked mostly about the interface between information consumers and creators. Let's move to a different component of eHealth.

Telemedicine

From her living room, a physician looks in on patients in the hospital. They're able to see each

---

? **CAN YOU GUESS? Part 3**

Who relies on the Internet for health information more—people who are healthy or people who aren't?

The answer appears at the end of the chapter.

CHECK IT OUT!   Free text-message services provide health-related tips and reminders as frequently as you want them about issues you choose. Here are a few to consider:

■ Stickk: http://www.stickk.com

■ Mobile Health Interventions: http://www.healthtxts .com/pages/health-txts.php

■ Remember it Now: http://www.rememberitnow .com

other and converse through two-way interactive television. A small keyboard allows the doctor to check her email messages, review patient charts, order prescriptions, examine diagnostic information, and read the latest research. This isn't science fiction. It's David Bates and Anthony Komaroff's (1996) vision of telemedicine.

The technology has been available for some time to make Bates and Komaroff's vision come true. But in many ways telemedicine has lagged behind expectations. In this section we will consider gains in the field and some of the factors holding it back. First, here's a brief overview.

As the World Health Organization puts it, telemedicine is "healing at a distance" (WHO, 2010a, p. 8). (*Tele* is Greek for "far.") It may involve the use of smart telephones, computers, PDAs, email, social media, Internet links, interactive video, and more. Telemedicine is distinguished from eHealth and mHealth in that it serves primarily to improve communication between health professionals and patients. Here are a few examples of how telemedicine works.

A Doctor's Visit, Telemedicine Style

A classic example of telemedicine is the program at East Carolina University (ECU) School of Medicine. In the early 1990s, the ECU staff began offering long-distance medical consultations to inmates at Central Prison, 100 miles from campus (Whitten, Sypher, & Patterson, 2000). The patients and caregivers interact via a teleconference link that allows them to see and talk to each other. Medical personnel at the university and prison work together to conduct exams and discuss medical information. Digital cameras and digital stethoscopes transmit detailed information to the off-site physician. Since beginning the program, ECU has expanded it to serve people in rural communities where specialists are not available. The program has been recognized by *Telehealth Magazine* as one of the country's Top 10 Telemedicine Programs.

Another telemedicine program, this one in Mexico, is designed to reduce the incidence of breast cancer, the leading cause of death among women there. Prior to the program's implementation in 2007, only about 1 in 14 women underwent breast cancer screening. Five years later, the figure was closer to 1 in 5 (WHO, 2010a, p. 20). The program requires that skilled technicians be on site,

but physicians can interpret diagnostic images from central locations rather than traveling across the country. Operating expenses are low enough that affordable fees for mammograms should soon sustain it indefinitely (WHO, 2010a).

Telemedicine in the Future

We have already discussed the leaps being made in mHealth monitoring, but Glenn Forbes of the Mayo Clinic envisions an even more futuristic image of telemedicine, in which people have small microchips inserted under their skin or carry digitized medical information cards that allow medical personnel anywhere in the world to monitor their health. Forbes imagines how the process would work if he were traveling in another country:

> I feel fine, but I check in every once in a while. If I have a chip embedded, I might even be unknowingly "checking in." Every seven days Mayo checks my blood sugar and could send me a message about needing to cut back on the cookies because my sugar level went up from 116 to 124. This information and advice is part of my partnership—part of what I have decided to purchase for my personal benefit. (quoted by Berry & Seltman, 2008, p. 239)

Or, Forbes says, he might have a plastic card that he inserts into a "Health Maintenance ATM" anywhere in the world if he has a health concern, such as frequent headaches. The card transmits his health information and location to his home clinic, where the staff might respond, "Your genetics suggest that you are prone to headaches if you've been eating too much pasta" (p. 239). The clinic staff could also recommend a nearby clinic that is part of the network and has access to his online medical records.

Forbes says this futuristic model will not alleviate the need for face-to-face health communication, good listening skills, and sensitivity. Indeed, because patients' information will be so readily available, he says, patients and caregivers might have *more* time to talk about current concerns.

Telemedicine as Medical Outsourcing

Behind the scenes, telemedicine has made possible a degree of medical outsourcing that might surprise you. For example, if you undergo an x-ray, CT scan, MRI, ultrasound, or nuclear medicine scan, there's a good chance a radiologist across the world will evaluate the results—a process called *ghosting*. Some 60% of countries surveyed by WHO use teleradiology (WHO, 2010a). One of the largest medical outsourcing firms is NightHawk Radiology Service, which provides **teleradiology** (radiology analysis from an off-site location) for more than 1,400 health care organizations in the United States (Douglas, 2008). More than half of the firm's 100 radiologists live outside the United States. Because health professionals in the United States are licensed by individual states, some NightHawk radiologists have 38 state licenses and privileges to practice at more than 400 hospitals (Singh & Wachter, 2008). The company employees 35 people just to manage licensing and credentialing!

We examine the impacts of medical outsourcing and other forms of telemedicine more in the following section on the pros and cons of technology-based health communication.

Advantages for Consumers

The World Health Organization (WHO) lists the main advantages of telemedicine as "access, equity, quality, and cost-effectiveness" (WHO, 2010a, p. 8). Indeed, many people are optimistic that telemedicine will conserve money and resources. And communication technology offers a number of benefits to patients, especially those who don't live near major medical centers.

First, technology may enable patients and caregivers to communicate more often and more openly, which may improve the quality of care. For example, MyCareTeam.com offers software that allows people with diabetes to learn information, log their blood sugar levels, and talk to health care providers. "The communication in this virtual space removes the pressures of time and immediacy from the encounter and provides ongoing management of uncertainty for both participants," report James D. Robinson and colleagues (2011, p. 126) after studying nearly 1,000 person-to-person emails exchanged by participants and care providers in the program. Messages included helpful information about diet and current glucose levels, offers to provide assistance ("I can give you a ride"), social integration ("Stop by next time you are in"), emotional support ("It is really hard to lose weight"), esteem social support ("You are one of our best patients"), requests for health information, self-disclosure ("I am getting married"), and technical support ("Is the new monitor working?") (p. 129). The research team found that social integration messages were most common, constituting 41% of all messages, followed by information (21%) and requests for information (13%). By contrast, self-disclosure was rare, occurring in fewer than 1 message in 100. Advantages of the system include the ability to monitor and comment upon ongoing health indicators, patients' ability to pose questions within the context of daily life without the time constraints of a medical visit, and the opportunity for ongoing social support in many forms. Robinson and colleagues conclude that the interactions are "in some ways more patient-centered than a traditional office visit" (Robinson, Turner, & Levine, 2011, p. 132).

If health professionals are worried about numerous and rambling emails, the evidence suggests they can rest easy. In a review of 24 studies about emails between patients and health professionals, Jiali Ye and colleagues (2010) found that the emails were usually concise and medically relevant. This was true of patients' emails and doctors'. Patients typically addressed only one concern per email and avoided making urgent or inappropriate requests. In sum, patients who were invited to email seldom abused the privilege, but the knowledge that they *could* email their doctors made them feel significantly more satisfied about their care than patients without email access (Ye, Rust, Fry-Johnson, & Strothers, 2010).

Patients may also be willing to disclose information via long-distance technology (particularly through email) that they would be uncomfortable sharing face to face (Baur, 2000). There is encouraging evidence that email communication between

? CAN YOU GUESS? Part 4

■What percentage of U.S. residents say they would like to have online access to their doctors, their medical records, and their test results?

■What percentage would be willing to pay for more that type of access?

Answers appear at the end of the chapter.

patients and caregivers is as patient centered, or more so, than face-to-face transactions. Debra Roter, Susan Larson, and colleagues (2008) found that—in contrast to in-person visits, during which doctors do most of the talking—patients do most of the "talking" in emails, outnumbering physicians' comments 2 to 1. They also report that patients seem to feel more comfortable disclosing emotions and praising and thanking their doctors in emails than in person, perhaps because email communication is less intimidating and less constrained by time limits. And physician responses, although briefer than patients', are usually informative, confirming, and reassuring. Doctors displayed empathy and reassurance in 53% of the emails Roter and colleagues studied. For example, one doctor told a patient via email: "Please don't ever think of doing so [e-mailing me] as bothering me—I welcome your participation in these decisions!" (Roter, Larson, Sands, Ford, & Houston, 2008, p. 83). Overall, coders rated physicians' emails to be equally as friendly, respectful, and responsive as patients' emails.

Second, technology may allow people in underserved communities access to doctors and medical care usually reserved for big-city dwellers. Doctors, particularly specialists, are disproportionately located in densely populated areas and are relatively scarce in rural ones (Matusitz & Breen, 2007). With telemedicine, a person can conceivably contact a health professional anywhere in the world by phone, email, voice mail, or computer (Wright, 2008).

Third, better care can mean less expense. Telemedicine reduces the need for each small town to have its own set of medical specialists. Patients in smaller markets can stay close to home rather than transferring to major medical centers. Plus, easier access may mean identifying and treating illnesses before they become severe and more costly to treat (Whitten et al., 2000).

Fourth, patients may become better educated about health matters through long-distance consultations and access to computer databases. The online Medline database, updated daily by the National Library of Medicine, provides information from more than 19 million journal articles and includes links to health information presented in more than 39 languages. For many people with health concerns, such information is a way to feel

IN YOUR EXPERIENCE

Have you ever emailed personal information to a health care provider? Does your experience support the research findings?

more in control. The majority of participants in Alex Broom's (2008) study of men with prostate cancer say they appreciate the information they found online and feel it helped them manage the uncertainties of treatment decisions. Said one man in the study: "Knowledge is power. I like to be in control of my situation and the way I want to do that is by knowing what is going to happen. . . . I really need that information to feel ok" (p. 98).

Finally, electronic health records can prevent the hassle of repeating the same information (insurance company, emergency contact, and so on) at every provider's office. Online records can also help doctors share notes and guarantee that a patient's records won't be destroyed in a fire or natural disaster.

Advantages for Caregivers

Caregivers may benefit from telemedicine as well. First, being able to communicate with patients and colleagues in remote locations reduces travel time and the demands on office space and staff. There are even benefits closer to home. "E-mail is a timesaver," declares Shelly Reese (2008). A physician can email a patient when he or she has time, rather than playing phone tag. Email also allows doctors to think through patient questions and to research them before replying. One physician whom Reese interviewed said his staff is able to respond to about 80% of the emails he receives. Because emails are more detailed than the typical phone message, he can quickly scan the contents to see who should best respond to them. Furthermore, emails can reduce the number of unnecessary office visits and after-hours phone calls. Patients who are able to access their physicians via secure email require 7% to 10% fewer office visits and make 14% fewer after-hours calls to their doctors ("The E-Mail," 2007; Reese, 2008). Emails are also time savers for staff members, who can send out appointment reminders instantly rather than calling patients one by one (Reese, 2008).

Social media applications may also improve medicine. Between 60% and 80% of physicians either already communicate with patients online or predict that they will in the near future (Modahl, Tompsett, & Moorhead, 2011). Most believe it will make communication easier and more convenient and will provide innovative means to monitor patients' health. As one doctor put it, online applications have the potential for "better education, increased compliance, and better outcomes" (Modahl et al., 2011, p. 7).

Second, vital information can be transmitted from one location to another instantly or with only a brief delay, amplifying opportunities for immediate response and medical teamwork. A cardiologist, for example, can monitor a patient's heart activity and direct paramedics' efforts even before the patient arrives at the hospital. At least 64% of the caregivers in the ECU study say they have learned valuable skills and information while participating in exams with other doctors and specialists (Whitten et al., 2000). Additionally, most doctors now use handheld PDAs to look up prescription drug information and perform other tasks (Terry, 2007). Although telemedicine can be expensive and complicated, low-tech procedures are often quite helpful as well. "As long as you have a computer, Internet access, and a camera, you can do telemedicine," says Kathleen Fiamma, a technology consultant at a nonprofit agency that advocates for telemedicine in underserved areas (quoted by Eccles, 2012, para. 4).

Third, telemedicine may involve electronic images that can be enlarged, manipulated, and shown in vivid, 3-dimensional depictions. These are useful for diagnostics, and health professionals say the images help them show patients exactly what's happening in their bodies (Murray et al., 2011).

Fourth, diagnostic images and patient records can be electronically stored and quickly retrieved, even by people in different locations. Caregivers may be able to access the medical charts of patients they are seeing for the first time. This could save time in emergencies and allow medical teams to coordinate patient care more effectively. The ability to quickly and consistently share information also helps with routine decision making and teamwork. Says a radiology manager:

> The biggest advantage is having images available all the time to everyone. So as soon as I take a picture of you, somebody can see it. In fact, everybody can see it. So where, if you were to come in . . . and you've broken an arm and you have to be referred to the orthopaedic surgeons, there is no backwards and forwards of one piece of film following you around or not as the case may be. (quoted by Murray et al., 2011, p. 6)

If the systems are well designed, online medical records can also help physicians and researchers collect data on the usefulness of various drugs and therapies (Kush, Helton, Rockhold, & Hardison, 2008).

Disadvantages

With so many advantages it may seem puzzling that telemedicine is not more prevalent. Although the technology continues to improve, much of it has been available for years.

One reason for the slow beginning is cost. Technology is expensive and quickly outdated. A second concern involves scheduling. Nearly half of the ECU participants studied said it's a hassle to schedule two teams of medical caregivers (one on-site and one remote) to take part in telemedicine consultations (Whitten et al., 2000).

There are also concerns about legal liability, especially concerning advice given online without the benefit of a full medical exam. In a study of more than 4,000 physicians in the United States, 73% said they worry they will be sued for malpractice if they offer advice online (Modahl et al., 2011). Legal experts caution doctors to include disclaimers such as the following if they offer guidance or assistance online, especially if they have not treated the patient personally: "This is not an official medical opinion because I haven't performed an examination. If you need specific medical advice, make an appointment with me or with a physician in the

 WHAT DO YOU THINK?

Can you think of other ways telemedicine could improve medicine?

appropriate specialty in your area" (Johnson, 2007, p. 30).

A fourth reservation concerns privacy. Some people worry about electronic eavesdropping and the possibility that hackers could gain access to confidential patient records. Some 71% of physician surveyed said they are worried about privacy violations (Modahl et al., 2011). To restrict access, medical networks now rely on encryption (secret coding) and electronic "firewalls" designed to stop unauthorized users from reaching confidential data. Secure email systems endorsed by the AMA and many private insurers are also available (Reese, 2008). By most accounts, these systems are good, although not perfect. But the human component is worrisome as well. Online access means more people would have the chance to view patients' private information than ever before. That worry is compounded in light of international medical outsourcing. Privacy laws apply to people in the United States, but it's less clear if, say, teleradiologists in other countries (some of them with widely different laws and cultural expectations about privacy) can legally be held to those standards.

Fifth, information in patients' electronic health records can be restrictive and hard to use if the formats are not well designed and if physicians are not careful about what they include. One problem is that some online forms require caregivers to fill in lengthy amounts of patient information. For example, a pediatrician may be required to ask every patient a time-consuming list of safety questions (use of bike helmets, seatbelts, etc.). This leaves less time to focus on the patient's immediate concerns (Hartzband & Groopman, 2008). Physicians Pamela Hartzband and Jerome Groopman (2008) describe an additional concern, namely, their frustration with doctors who include inappropriate or too much information in patients' online health records. In some cases, doctors plagiarize. "We have seen portions of our own notes inserted verbatim into another doctor's note," say Hartzband and Groopman (p. 1656). In addition to being unethical, this practice results in repetitive, too-long medical records that fail to present each physician's thoughtful analysis of the patient's condition. Another factor that bogs down medical records is a lengthy hodgepodge of test results. If such information is not well organized, more is not better—it's just overwhelming. Write Hartzband and Groopman:

A colleague at a major cancer center that recently switched to electronic medical records said that chart review during rounds has become nearly worthless. He bemoaned the vain search through meaningless repetition in multiple notes for the single line that represented a new development. "It's like 'Where's Waldo?'" he said bitterly. Ironically, he has started to handwrite a list of new developments on index cards so that he can refer to them at the bedside. (p. 1656)

Sixth, it's still somewhat unclear how caregivers can or should be compensated for services rendered long distance. Should they charge for phone conversations, email correspondence, and the like? If so, how should those rates compare to the cost of face-to-face visits? Reservations about this issue and the fear of being inundated by patient messages and questions have made some caregivers leery of opening up new lines of communication. The issue is becoming clearer, however, as reimbursement agencies—mindful that a phone call or email can prevent a more expensive outcome—are increasingly willing to reimburse providers for technology-assisted communication. In 2008, a group of health insurance companies launched a pilot project in Pennsylvania in which they pay doctors to keep close tabs on patients using email and websites. Another part of the agreement is that participating physicians will keep a percentage of office hours open so that sick patients can schedule appointments within 48 hours (Goldstein, 2008). The hypothesis is that technology and quick-response protocols will save money in the long run.

Seventh, it's unclear how medical licensing and malpractice laws (both of which vary by state and country) will apply to medical care that spans state and national boundaries. As mentioned, many teleradiologists are licensed in multiple states. Most physicians are not, so it remains to be determined exactly how state laws will apply to "virtual visits" across borders.

Eighth, as we have discussed, greater use of technology may widen the gap between the well served and the underserved. The cost and complexity of technology suggests that it will proliferate in the households of well-educated and affluent people first, increasing access to those already known to use health resources and systematically excluding underprivileged individuals.

WHAT DO YOU THINK?

Can you think of any other drawbacks or challenges of telemedicine?

Finally, some worry that telemedicine will become a less effective substitute for face-to-face communication. No one expects (or even wants) telemedicine to replace face-to-face medical visits entirely. Still, the limits of technology may restrict what patients and caregivers are able to convey to each other (Baur, 2000). Researchers in Japan found that patients who took part in both face-to-face interactions and telemedicine visits were equally satisfied with them, but doctors were less satisfied with the telemedicine visits, feeling that the technology limited communication (Lui et al., 2007). Considering the limitations, some people worry that medical decisions will be made on the basis of incomplete or misleading information. Chamberlain (1994) cautions that high-tech methods cannot make up for poor communication: "No amount of technology is going to compensate for an ill-conceived or ill-designed message. The buck stops there . . . with the communicator" (para. 4).

WHO urges the creation of international guidelines in regard to privacy, access, and liability (WHO, 2010a). The authors of the Global Observatory for eHealth report write:

> It is imperative that telemedicine be implemented equitably and to the highest ethical standards, to maintain the dignity of all individuals and ensure that differences in education, language, geographic location, physical and mental ability, age, and sex will not lead to marginalization of care. (WHO, 2010b, p. 11)

Summary

Cyberspace is occupied by a larger number of voices than we imagined even 10 years ago. The nature of those voices is still evolving. Whereas information in public media was once filtered through gatekeepers, for better or worse, the gates are open. Electronic resources allow us to

---

BOX 9.3 CAREER OPPORTUNITIES

Health Information Technology

Computer and Information Systems Manager
Health Information Administrator or Technician
Software developer

CAREER RESOURCES AND JOB LISTINGS
- American Health Information Management Association: http://www.ahima.org
- Association for Computing Machinery: http://www.acm.org
- Commission on Accreditation for Health Informatics and Information Management Education: http://www.cahiim.org
- Health Buzz by the U.S. Department of Health and Human Services: http://www.healthit.gov/buzz-blog/university-based-training/helping-students-launch-health-information-technology-careers-oregon-health-science-universitybased-training-program
- National Workflow Center for Emerging Technologies: http://www.nwcet.org
- U.S. Bureau of Labor Statistics Occupational Outlook Handbook: http://www.bls.gov/ooh

---

look up information quickly and easily and to engage with people we don't know personally, blurring the lines between information creator and information consumer as well as boundaries between the public, technical, and personal spheres. Some people worry that, with so much information at our disposal, it will be difficult to distinguish between reliable information and folk beliefs.

The proliferation of mobile devices represents a promising avenue. More than 5 billion people, many of them in developing countries, now have the ability to communicate across great distances and even to use their mobile phones to monitor health conditions and vital signs.

Rather than passively attending to messages that come our way, most of us tend to be relatively proactive in seeking information we believe will reduce our health risk and help manage our anxiety.

However, health-seeking behaviors may be muted by distrust, lack of confidence, and the belief that such messages don't apply to us.

All in all, the Internet has the potential to educate people in the greatest need of health information, but, overwhelmingly, the people who have Internet access and the ability to use it are already information rich. A knowledge gap exists because of access, information preference, perceived relevance, and reading ability. (We'll discuss the knowledge gap more in Chapter 13.)

We may happen upon electronic health information accidentally if it turns up in a Google search or a pop-up message, but unlike television, we mostly control the content of what we see online. A quick click can make something appear or disappear from our screen at will. This has given theorists something new to think about as they explore the reasons that we search for health information.

Telemedicine offers many opportunities, but issues of cost, access, privacy, and legal liability continue to hamper full-scale implementation. It's likely that we'll overcome many of these barriers as we re-negotiate what it means to be health professionals and patients.

Overall, technology expands the options and the challenges for health communication. Patients and caregivers may have access to more information and more means of message transmission than ever before, but the rules and expectations are still forming.

Key Terms and Theories

eHealth
mHealth
telemedicine
three spheres
personal
technical
public
Web 2.0
social network theory
strong ties
weak ties
ePatients
health information acquisition model
Theory of Motivated Information Management (TMIM)

Integrative Model of Online Health Information Seeking
health information seeking
health information scanning
health information efficacy
uses and gratifications theory
social entrepreneurs
short message services (SMS)
teleradiology

Discussion Questions

1. Why are many health advocates and social entrepreneurs adopting mobile technology rather than traditional Internet methods?

2. How are eHealth, mHealth, and telemedicine similar? How are they different?

3. Describe and contrast the three spheres of engagement. What opportunities does Web 2.0 present in light of these spheres? What potential disadvantages may result?

4. You decide to create a blog about your experience getting in shape for a triathlon. How might factors involved in social network theory influence what happens as a result?

5. Describe a typical ePatient. What's problematic about the term ePatient?

6. Describe some of the most common reasons people seek health information online and the factors that might discourage them from doing so. Your answer should integrate the following terms and theories: information sufficiency threshold, the health information acquisition model, the Theory of Motivated Information Management, and the Integrative Model of Online Health Information Seeking.

7. Describe four potential advantages of using eHealth resources and four disadvantages.

8. Explain the difference between health information seeking and health information scanning. How does the quality of information typically differ?

9. How does the uses and gratifications theory help to explain our eHealth behavior? Give an example from your own experience.

10. What advantages does telemedicine offer to consumers? To caregivers?

11. What are the potential disadvantages of telemedicine?

Answers to *Can You Guess?*

PART 1

A. Black Americans—Most likely to rely on TV

B. Hispanic Americans—Most likely to rely on family and friends

C. Non-Hispanic White Americans—Most likely to rely on health care providers

(Smith, 2011)

PART 2

The average college students spends about 3 hours a day on social networking sites.

PART 3

People in good to excellent health use the Internet more and trust it more than people in fair to poor health, who are more likely to rely on TV (Smith, 2011).

PART 4

Some 60% of U.S. residents surveyed said they would like to have online access to their doctors, their medical records, and their test results ("Online Usage," 2008). And 25% said they would be willing to pay more for it.

PART V

Communication in Health Organizations

Good leaders make people feel that they're at the very heart of things, not at the periphery. Everyone feels that he or she makes a difference to the success of the organization. When that happens people feel centered and that gives their work meaning.

—WARREN BENNIS

People who devote their lives to serving others deserve excellent leaders who support their efforts and remove obstacles that might limit their effectiveness. In this section, which consists of one very important chapter, we look at what it takes to be a great leader in health care. As you will see, leaders have the potential to transform how health care is provided. They don't call all the shots. Instead, they bring out the best in people and enable them to create powerful systems designed to succeed. Leadership involves health care administrators, but also the work of human resources, marketing, and public relationships professionals, whose job it is to build great teams, support outstanding service, and serve the community. Ultimately, the communication abilities of people in these diverse roles help to determine how health care happens, who is involved, how people regard health care organizations, and whether work is a joy or a daily exercise in frustration.

CHAPTER TEN

Health Care Administration, Human Resources, Marketing, and PR

The call came in: "The helicopters are having a hard time identifying the hospital with all the power out in the city." They said, "Find the biggest American flag you can find." When you're in marketing and public relations, you do all sorts of things!"

—KENDRICK DOIDGE

As vice president of marketing and public relations at West Florida Hospital, Kendrick Doidge[1] (pronounced *dodge*) is no stranger to the unexpected demands of crisis management. Less than a year before Hurricane Katrina, he was marketing and public relations coordinator at another hospital when Ivan, a Category 3 hurricane, hit closer to home in Pensacola, Florida.

During Ivan, 4,000 members of the community took refuge in the hospital, joining patients and staff members who were there as well. "The storm raged all night," Doidge remembers,

> At one point, when we had over 2,000 people camped out in the lobby of the hospital, the winds were blowing so hard the windows were starting to bow inward. Staff members physically held the front doors shut while we evacuated everyone to the basement. . . . Then the basement began taking in water during the night.

---

1. Unless otherwise indicated, all quotes attributed to Doidge are from a personal interview conducted by the author.

Meanwhile, personnel caring for patients worried about their own homes and families. (Indeed, more than 30 hospital employees lost their homes and nearly everything they owned that night.) Touched by their selflessness, Doidge worked hard to keep everyone well informed. All the while, he helped supervise an emergency contact center in the hospital, monitored communication with the National Guard and other emergency personnel, stayed in touch with the media, and kept tabs on conditions in the hospital. The team's meticulously rehearsed crisis management plan was in full operation.

As a marketing and public relations professional at a large hospital, Kendrick Doidge stays in touch with internal and external stakeholders.

But that wasn't all. Doidge's motto is "be willing to do anything, and don't mind doing the little things" (Outzen, 2005, para. 16). So he also helped with the innumerable tasks that emerge without warning in a crisis. For example, Doidge joined colleagues in hauling 50-pound oxygen tanks up several flights of stairs.

"That's one thing I learned about crisis management," he says, laughing, "move the oxygen tanks out of the basement before the electricity goes out and the elevators stop working!" Like most of the region, the hospital was without electricity and running water during the storm and for days afterward. In the thick of things, the staff wheeled patients into hallways so they wouldn't be near windows. They even delivered five babies during the overnight storm, sometimes by flashlight.

For weeks after the storm, Doidge handled media inquiries from around the country, publicized the hospital's makeshift triage unit for people hurt during the hurricane and recovery effort, and organized assistance for staff members who had lost their homes. "You do everything you can to prepare for a crisis, and you keep learning while you're in the middle of one and ever afterward," he says, adding, "We learned a lot during Ivan that helped us 9 months later when Dennis, a Category 2 storm, hit the area."

Now, just a few months after Dennis, Pensacola was safe, but Tulane Medical Center in New Orleans, a sister institution to West Florida Hospital, was in trouble. In the tense days before and after Katrina, choppers evacuated as many patients as possible from New Orleans to the Pensacola facility.

"After the helicopters landed here and unloaded patients, the staff at our hospital would fill them up with supplies to take back to New Orleans," Doidge says. Now his task was to find an American flag quickly enough to make the next return flight. "I started calling around and found that the biggest flag around was flying over Joe Patti's Seafood across town. I called and asked if we could have it. They immediately said yes," he says. "Then I got in the car and realized, 'I didn't tell them my name. They won't know who I am.'" But, as a testament to community spirit, the flag was folded and ready for him when he walked in the door. "They said, 'Are you the one who called about the flag? Here it is,' and I rushed back to the hospital with it," Doidge says.

In New Orleans, crews draped the flag over the edge of the roof and down the exterior wall of the Tulane Medical Center. It became a recognizable symbol of the rescue effort. "That flag had a life of its own," Doidge says. "There were rumors that it was from the World Trade Towers, that it had flown in Iraq—you name it. There's a book about Katrina, and a part in the middle is devoted to that flag."

Doidge, who has a bachelor's degree in political science and a master's degree in health communication leadership, is lauded for his skill in marketing, public relations, and crisis management. As a health care administrator, he is also involved in long-term planning and staffing decisions. He has a reputation for being honest and compassionate, even in tough situations.

We will hear more about Doidge's experiences as well as others' in this chapter, which focuses on the work of health care administrators, human resource specialists, marketing and public relations professionals, and crisis management experts. We will explore some of the key issues and goals within each profession and will learn from the experts which communication strategies are most effective. We cannot cover the full range of activities these professionals accomplish, but hopefully your curiosity will be piqued to learn more. A *Career Opportunities* box later in the chapter will guide you in the right direction for that. The chapter culminates with strategies for offering outstanding service to patients and their loved ones.

As you read, notice how central communication is in each profession. Also keep in mind the overlap between job responsibilities. Some of us will serve as specialists in these areas, but everyone in health care is involved with them. As we discussed in Chapter 5, systems are interrelated collections of people and ideas. What happens in one part of the system affects what happens everywhere else within it. In health care, leadership, human resources, public relations, and crisis management are part of everyone's job.

Health Care Administration

Irving S. Shapiro, the legendary CEO of DuPont and long-time trustee of the Howard Hughes Medical Center, was fond of saying that leaders are "first and foremost in the human relations and communication business" (1984, p. 157). He expanded on the idea this way:

> One important day-to-day task for the CEO is communication, digesting information and shaping ideas, yes, but even more centrally, the business of listening and explaining. . . . One of the first lessons a manager learns while climbing the corporate ladder is how little he [or she] can accomplish by relying on his [or her] own brains alone. (Shapiro, 1984, pp. 157–158)

Health care administrators range from CEOs and vice presidents to clinical managers and directors of admissions, medical records, education, business affairs, and many other units. Success in the field usually requires a graduate degree in a field such as health care administration, public health, business administration, or health communication. People seldom go straight into administrative roles, but instead work their way up the ladder ("Career," 2012). Candidates for administrative positions have usually gained experience in any number of health care agencies such as nonprofit organizations, clinics, nursing homes, mental health facilities, clinics, hospitals, and more. Experience in other fields may also be relevant.

As a case in point, Doidge's first job after college was at a visitor information and convention center, where he says he "learned to treat people how you would want someone to treat you or a member of your family." "We assisted several hundred people a day, and I really learned the importance of customer service," Doidge says of that experience. He then further honed his skills working in membership development for the Chamber of Commerce before he applied for a job in hospital marketing and public relations.

"I didn't know anything about health care when I got that job," he says. "I knew about strategic communication, and I set out to learn everything I could about health care." Part of his education involved enrolling in a graduate program in health communication. "Never assume you know it all," he advises others. "You have to keep learning."

Part of the learning curve in health care is becoming acquainted with changing conditions that shape the market. Let's examine some of the current issues that influence the work administrators do.

We will focus here on consumerism, competition, consolidation, and the need to develop quicker, more responsive systems than in the past. Then we will examine relevant communication strategies recommended by the experts.

Changing Market

Health care has changed dramatically in the last few decades, primarily because of efforts to control costs. As you may recall from Chapter 2, in the 1970s, insurance and governmental agencies began to limit the amounts they would pay for medical services in the United States. Subsequently, health organizations have been faced with deficits unless they cut their own costs. Organizations unable to adapt quickly or efficiently enough have closed their doors. Some 949 U.S. hospitals closed between 1980 and 1993 (American Hospital Association [AHA], 1994). Hospitals in minority neighborhoods were especially hard hit. A staggering 70% of hospitals in predominantly African American or Hispanic neighborhoods closed between 1990 and 1997 (Robert Wood Johnson Foundation, 2001).

Closures have tapered off, but many hospitals have stayed afloat only by closing expensive service lines such as trauma units and emergency departments. The number of emergency departments in the United States plummeted 27% between 1990 and 2009 (Hsia, Kellerman, & Shen, 2011). This has officials worried about the country's ability to respond to disasters and epidemics. And many existing hospitals, especially in rural areas, still face uncertain futures. Based on the latest numbers, more than half of the nation's hospitals are losing money (Fox, 2009).

Consumerism

"Being a patient is about the least amount of fun anyone can have as a consumer," point out Leonard Berry and Kent Seltman (2008, p. 167). Even more than in other industries, every customer/patient in health care wants and deserves to be treated as an individual with unique needs and perceptions. And patients have choices—a reality underlined by highly visible advertising and marketing efforts and by an unprecedented amount of health information available in the news media and on the Internet. In this context, patients are well-informed consumers

? CAN YOU GUESS? Part 2

In what year did *Time* magazine run the following pronouncement?

"High prices have hit hospitals with such a staggering blow that many may have to close their doors. . . . In the past year, hospital payrolls jumped 40%, food more than 43%, drugs 38.9%. Meanwhile, the hospitals had an unprecedented horde of patients."

The answer appears at the end of the chapter.

who are asked to choose between different health services vying for their business.

People in health organizations realize like never before the value of consumer satisfaction, and many are taking steps to eliminate unnecessary irritants. For example, some hospital staffs have redesigned the admissions process. Rather than fill out lengthy paperwork the day of admission, they now obtain information over the phone in advance so people feel less hassled when they arrive for treatment. Others have authorized employees to reimburse patients for lost items (dentures, eyeglasses, pillows, clothing, and so on) and to award gift certificates and coupons when they see fit. A nurse once told me, "It's amazing how much good will you can inspire with a free lunch!" After employees at the hospital where she worked were given cafeteria coupons to pass along to others, patient satisfaction increased considerably. Says the nurse:

Now, when we see a patient's family that has been waiting around for results or a procedure, we can say, "I'm sorry you have had to wait so long. Please have lunch on us. We'll have everything ready by the time you get back." There's no amount of advertising that can outmatch a free meal when you are hungry, tired, and frustrated! And it makes us feel good to help. We're not the bad guys. We're the ones who understand and help, not just the patients, but their families, too.

Consolidation

In an effort to control costs, many health organizations that once operated independently are

"We went from 2,000 employees to 5,000 employees in 2 years. We didn't know each other. We didn't like each other. We didn't have a common vision. We didn't even have a common mission." — Eleanor McGee, health care executive (pictured here)

now part of larger enterprises. By the mid-1990s, more than half the hospitals in the United States had been bought by large corporations (Shortell, Gillies, & Devers, 1995). Many others merged with competitors or formed alliances with other health organizations. **Integrated health systems** offer a spectrum of health services that may include hospitals, outpatient surgery centers, doctors' offices, fitness centers, nursing homes, rehabilitation centers, hospices, and more (Slusarz, 1996).

The idea is that, by sharing resources, integrated health systems can reduce operating costs and be more competitive. Takeovers, mergers, and alliances present communication challenges, however. For one, long-standing competitors may suddenly find themselves working together. Health care executive Eleanor McGee recalls a

consolidation in the late 1990s this way: "We went from 2,000 employees to 5,000 employees in 2 years. We didn't know each other. We didn't like each other. We didn't have a common vision. We didn't even have a common mission" (quoted by du Pré, 2005, p. 312). In circumstances such as this, organizational members may struggle to form new relationships and to find ways to integrate their ideas, or they may do as people in many health systems have done and continue to operate as separate entities under one (rather invisible) umbrella. Partitioning is understandable, but it hampers people's ability to share resources and coordinate patient care.

Another challenge of integration is that, as organizations become more complex, it's difficult to manage them by the old rules. In *Good to Great,* Jim Collins (2001b) summarizes the challenge:

> Entrepreneurial success is fueled by creativity, imagination, bold moves into unchartered waters, and visionary zeal. As a company grows and becomes more complex, it begins to trip over its own success—too many new people, too many new customers, too many new orders, too many new products. What was once great becomes an unwieldy ball of disorganized stuff. (p. 121)

It's hard to maintain clarity as an organization grows. Rapid change can feel disorienting and overwhelming. And whereas people in small organizations often perceive themselves to be one cohesive team, factions and division are common in larger ones.

Leaders often react to these forces by establishing hierarchies and complex chains of command. This may help team members feel more organized, but it can also suppress creativity and make it seem that upper level leaders, not frontline employees, are in charge of the organization's design and destiny. In Collins' terms, an "executive class" with most of the power and perks begins to emerge, distinctly separate from others in the organization. As this happens, "the creative magic begins to wane as some of the most innovative people leave, disgusted by the burgeoning bureaucracy and hierarchy" (Collins, 2001b, p. 121). In short, centralized, bureaucratic decision making is an effort to keep everyone marching in the same direction, but it can be sluggish and inhibiting. We will talk more about these challenges and opportunities throughout the chapter.

Efficiency and Six Sigma

In the new market there will be two kinds of organizations—quick and dead.

—ANN L. HENDRICH, NURSE EXECUTIVE

Hendrich's prediction (quoted by Porter-O'Grady and colleagues, 1997, para. 10), points to another effort to succeed in a competitive market—rethinking processes that waste time and money. People in some health organizations are using techniques including Six Sigma to analyze the efficiency of everyday procedures such as sharing information, ordering lab tests, delivering meal trays, dispensing medication, and responding to patient requests.

Six Sigma is a process in which analysts chart each stage in a workplace routine, time how long it takes, and then consider the various outcomes. The goal is to determine which actions add value and which contribute to waste and errors. These considerations are particularly important in health care because of the high costs involved and because even a small error can have drastic consequences. Carolyn Pexton (nd) explains:

> In terms of impact to the patient, a defect in the delivery of health care can range from relatively minor, such as food on a tray that doesn't match the doctor's orders, to significant, such as operating on the wrong limb. In a worst-case scenario, the defect can be fatal, as when a medication error results in the patient's death. (para. 5)

Experts estimate that avoidable errors cost about $17.1 billion and cause about 98,000 deaths per year in the United States (Pham et al., 2012; Van Den Bos et al., 2011). Even errors that don't harm a patient's health, such as waiting an extra day in the hospital for lab results, are costly.

As you might expect, analysts often find that procedures don't always work according to original design, so people adapt **workarounds**, that is, alternative ways of accomplishing tasks. Over time, people may adopt so many workarounds that immense variations and holes in the system develop.

For example, consider discharge procedures in a hospital nursing unit. Using a Six Sigma process at one hospital, DeBusk and Rangel (nd) found that it took an average of 3 hours to discharge a patient—give or take 2 hours. In other words, some patients left in 1 hour and some waited 5 hours. That's a problem, because while one patient is waiting to vacate a bed, very often staff members elsewhere are waiting to transfer another patient (or soon-to-be-patient) into that bed. Bottlenecks in the process mean long wait times, discomfort, compromised care, heightened frustration, and wasted time and money. Imagine waiting around 5 hours for your loved one to be discharged. Now double that, considering that somewhere else in the same hospital a family is waiting 5 hours to get *into* that room.

DeBusk and Rangel soon realized why discharge times varied so widely: Every nurse on the unit followed a slightly different procedure. Some placed paperwork awaiting signatures in a bin for others to pick up (usually about 73 minutes later). Other nurses didn't use the bin but went directly to people for their signatures (which usually required about 9 minutes). Because staff members at the nurses' desk couldn't accurately predict how long it would take to get signatures, they typically waited until all signatures were collected to call a social worker to educate a patient about aftercare procedures, resulting in delays as long as 2½ hours. And even when all discharge procedures were final, there wasn't a standard way to alert transport personnel of that, so patients sometimes waited around until someone happened to notice that their paperwork was complete and initiate the final step.

The Six Sigma analysts were able to work with the nurses to create what they call a lean process map, a streamlined procedure that shaved more than 2 hours off the average discharge time, with very little variation. The new process reduced patients' average wait to a consistent 48 minutes (shorter than the quickest time previously), made everyone's job easier, and minimized the chances of error and oversight (DeBusk & Rangel, nd). (For more resources about Six Sigma, see Box 10.1.)

Next we move on to some of the skills that help health care administrators inspire the best in people. As you will see, while it's important that leaders require everyone's best efforts, it's inadvisable for leaders to make all the decisions.

Six Sigma and Other Efficiency Process Models

Arthur, J. (2011). *Lean Six Sigma for hospitals: Simple steps to fast, affordable, and flawless healthcare*. New York: McGraw-Hill.

Duffy, G. L., Moran, J. W., & Riley, W. J. (2010). *Quality function deployment and Lean Six Sigma applications in public health*. Milwaukee, WI: Quality Press.

Pexton, C. (nd). Framing the need to improve healthcare using Six Sigma methodologies. iSixSigma. Retrieved from http://healthcare.isixsigma.com/library/content/c030513a.asp

Rooney, J. J., & Vanden Heuvel, L. N. (2004, July). Root cause analysis for beginners. *Quality Progress, 37*(7), 45.

Vanden Heuvel, L., & Robinson, C. (2005, Summer). How many causes should you pursue? *Journal for Quality and Participation, 28*(2), 22–23.

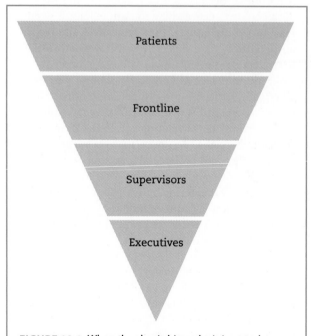

FIGURE 10.1 When the classic hierarchy is inverted, executives act as servant leaders by listening to and supporting the frontline and holding everyone accountable for excellence.

Communication Skill Builder: Shared Vision and Dispersed Leadership

Profitability is a necessary condition for existence and a means to more important ends, but it is not the end in itself.

—JAMES COLLINS AND JERRY PORRAS (1997, P. 57)

It may seem counterintuitive, but decisions made solely in the interest of making money usually don't, at least not in the long run. Evidence that we will cover more fully later in the chapter suggests that a single-minded focus on profits often leads to questionable judgment and short-term success at best. The more inspiring and more lucrative option is to place the emphasis on people, principles, and sustainability. Following are some tips from the experts on doing that.

Invert the pyramid. In a classic bureaucratic hierarchy, the people at the top make most of the decisions, get the biggest perks, reap the greatest financial rewards—and seldom see or talk to service-line employees or clients. The inherent tension and lack of communication are problematic. Moreover, whereas everyone in the organization typically tries to please the bosses, patients aren't even in the hierarchy.

Some theorists advocate turning the pyramid upside down. In a health care organization, the largest and highest tier is then devoted to patients and customers. Everyone in the organization is oriented to serving *them,* either directly or indirectly. The next-highest tier is made up of frontline service providers—a diverse assortment of everyone who has direct contact with people the organization is designed to serve (patients, families, community members, and so on). In health care, the frontline includes clinicians, volunteers, cafeteria staff, housekeepers, valets, event coordinators, and so on. Subsequent layers are devoted to mid-level supervisors.

In servant-leadership style, CEOs and other executives are on the bottom. From this perspective, their job is to listen, encourage, support, and remove barriers so people throughout the organization can do what they do best. A classic example of a servant leader was Ken Iverson, former CEO of Nucor Steel. Iverson eliminated executive perks, cut his own salary to be more closely in line with others', reduced the staff at corporate headquarters

"We Hate the Rules"

"We hate rules," says James F. Nordstrom, former co-chair of the Nordstrom department store, adding, "the minute you come up with a rule you give an employee a reason to say no to a customer."

There is only one rule in the Nordstrom employee handbook: *Use good judgment in all situations.* Consequently, when a Nordstrom associate learned about a woman who had arrived in the area in the midst of a medical crisis (her husband was about to have emergency brain surgery) and didn't have a car or clothing appropriate for the climate, she personally picked the woman up at the hospital, brought her to the store, helped her select clothing, and drove her back to the hospital. The associate knew that in extending this kindness she would be fulfilling Nordstrom's mission of serving customers, and she wouldn't be breaking any rules to do it.

For more about Nordstrom, see Spector and McCarthy (2005). Direct quotes presented here appear on p. 141.

to 25 people (in a company with 7,000 employees), and put frontline employees' needs first. Nucor—which was nearly bankrupt when Iverson assumed leadership—became a $3.5 billion Fortune 500 company. In his book *Plain Talk*, Iverson (1997) summarizes his philosophy this way:

> The people at the top of the corporate hierarchy grant themselves privilege after privilege, flaunt those privileges before the men and women who do the real work, then wonder why employees are unmoved by management's invocations to cut costs and boost profitability. . . . When I think of the millions of dollars spent by people at the top of the management hierarchy on efforts to motivate people who are continually put down *by* that hierarchy, I can only shake my head in wonder. (pp. 58–59)

Lest this sound too critical of executives, who usually work very hard and bear immense pressure, it's important to note that an inverted pyramid serves

them well, too. They are spared the overwhelming burden of being responsible for decisions at all levels. Instead, accountability is dispersed throughout the organization. Leaders in a supportive role are more a part of the overall team and typically enjoy unprecedented appreciation and loyalty from the people they serve.

Empowerment allows teams to create systems and work environments that are tailor-made for success. People with adequate training, authority, and resources don't usually need much supervision, particularly if everyone is responsible for meeting clear goals. The typical result is higher morale among both employees and customers. The "We Hate the Rules" feature (Box 10.2) about the Nordstrom department store presents a powerful example of this.

Build relationships by listening. Health care leadership expert Quint Studer (2003) maintains that feedback is as crucial as oxygen. As a hospital administrator, he borrowed a technique from physicians and began "rounding" everyday—visiting units throughout the hospital to talk to patients, families, and employees. He typically introduced himself to employees this way: "Hi, I'm Quint Studer. I work for you." After a few questions about the person's experiences and the positive things going on in his or her unit, Studer made it a point to ask, "Do you have the tools and equipment to do your job?" or "What can I do to make your job easier?" And, even more remarkably, he followed through. At one hospital, stories are still told about Studer's influence more than 15 years ago. People continue to marvel that he made hot water reliably available in the ICU, had lights added in the parking lot, provided cleaning supplies in nursing units, and much more—usually within 24 hours of learning about a need. Even changes that seem small on the surface resulted in greater efficiency and happier employees and patients (du Pré, 2005).

Doidge adopted a similar strategy when he signed on at West Florida Hospital. He set out to meet everyone he could. "It would sort of surprise people at first when I asked if I could sit with them in the hospital cafeteria," he says. But people soon got used to his friendly manner and willingness to listen. Doidge recalls one nurse who said:

> Here's what you can do to make my job easier: You can get us different printer paper. The holes

"Health care administration is all about people. No matter what you are in charge of—it all comes down to people. It's nonstop communication." — Kendrick Doidge

in the paper don't match up to the prongs in our patient binders, so we have to fold and bend every page we add to a patient's chart.

It turned out that the same problem was plaguing nurses units throughout the hospital. The paper was frustrating everyone, and it had been for some time. With a quick visit to the supply-chain office, Doidge identified the problem. "Who knows how long ago, someone had apparently bumped the hole-puncher by accident and changed the alignment," says Doidge. With a simple adjustment, a long-standing problem was solved. "You wouldn't believe the response," Doidge recalls, describing the scene:

It was the same week we announced a pay raise, but everyone was talking about the *hole punches.* The nurse who suggested it was hero. That just shows you, our job is to listen to the people caring for our patients. They'll tell you if you ask.

But they don't have time to go looking for the source of problems like that.

When leaders listen, they send the message that team members matter and are valued. And listening yields valuable information. Frontline employees are typically more familiar than anyone about clients' wishes and the organization's daily routines. Steve Miller, a worldwide manager at Shell Oil Company, emphasizes the need to treat members at every level as intelligent change agents:

In the past, the leader was the guy with the answers. Today if you're going to have a successful company, you have to recognize that no leader can possibly have all the answers. The leader may have a vision. But the actual solutions about how best to meet the challenges of the moment have to be made by the people closest to the action. (quoted by Pascale, 1999, p. 210)

With a similar belief, Mayo Clinic staff members attribute a great deal of their success to team spirit and their respect for each other. "I know by name the custodians that work in the emergency department, and I appreciate them as much as I appreciate my physician colleagues," says Anne Sadosty, an emergency care physician with Mayo Clinic (quoted by Berry & Seltman, 2008, p. 58).

Push decision making to the lowest level possible. A shared vision is nothing if it has not been integrated into everyday ways of doing things. One strategy is for leaders to tell team members what to say, what to do, and how to behave. This is effective in fairly predictable and straightforward situations. There are medical protocols for conducting tests and administering medications, and sometimes communication protocols are effective as well. At one hospital I know of, staff members make it a point to say: "Is there anything else that I may do for you? I have the time." That's a script that seems to work well. Staff members say patients are more forthcoming about their concerns because of it. This ultimately saves time and leads to a better experience. Partly as a consequence, patients' satisfaction scores at that hospital are some of the highest in the country.

Determining who should be involved in decisions can be tricky. Leadership theorist Wayne Hoy observes that, if you ask human relations theorists if team members should be involved in decision making, they say, "Of course!" Ask people from the scientific management camp and they answer, "Only if they have expertise." Open-systems social scientists usually say, "It depends" (Hoy, 2003, slide 2). The **Hoy-Tarter Model of Shared Decision Making** (Hoy & Tarter, 2008) proposes that leaders consider two main questions when determining whom to include in decision making: *Does the team member have a personal stake in the outcome?* (In other words, is the topic relevant to her or him?) and *Does the team member have expertise on the topic?* If the answer is yes to both, the basic foundations are present for shared decision making. Layered on top of that are other considerations such as: *Is it likely that this person will agree with the decision even without being personally involved in it? Does he or she have the skills to participate effectively in decision making?* and *Do the people involved trust each other?*

One interesting application of the Hoy-Tarter model is that we can apply it to leaders as well as to frontline team members. Compared to the frontline, executive-level leaders often have less personal stake in workplace procedures and less personal knowledge about them, partly because they are not on the frontline as much and partly because people are typically hesitant to be candid with leaders they don't know well. The result, says health care satisfaction expert Irwin Press, can be a lot of top-down rules that don't serve anyone very well.

When assessing employee satisfaction in health care organizations, Press begins by asking employees to list the "really stupid rules" that hamper them from doing a good job. "This is fun and focuses analytical attention on the often arbitrary nature of regulations," says Press (2002, p. 42). Next, he asks people to examine rules that serve a purpose but do not work well. For example, Press asks, is it necessary that nurses deliver meal trays? Could other staff members perform this task and free nurses to respond more quickly to patients' requests?

Press (2002) also advises that, if the rules and paperwork are important, leaders must allow team members the time and space to complete them. For example, it's unrealistic to expect an employee to answer the phone, file reports, and respond to others' needs in the same small space or in brief amounts of time. Frustration and poor service are likely to result. If the regulations are important, Press declares, make fulfilling them part of the job.

WHAT DO YOU THINK?

■ If your boss asked you to list the "really stupid rules," what would you include on the list?

■ Would you be comfortable making suggestions? Why or why not?

CHECK IT OUT!   "How could central dispatch, 20 miles away, have a better understanding of the situation than the officer at the scene? Any information about the problem would be coming from the officer anyway."—Free Lee

For more about this episode and others, see If Disney Ran Your Hospital (2004) by Fred Lee.

Another drawback of centralized decision making is the time it takes. Opportunities for change are often lost or delayed before top-level leaders know about them or can act upon them. This can be fatal in today's fast-moving market. And when service breakdowns occur, frontline team members may have to wait for authorization from "higher-ups" before they can resolve the issues. The result is often a frustrating delay on top of an already disappointing situation.

Health care consultant Fred Lee offers a frustrating example of centralized decision making (Lee, 2004). He arrived at a hospital one morning to conduct a training session, only to find that the classroom was locked. A security officer arrived, but even though he had a key, he was required to get permission from his supervisors across town to open the door, and they were not available. "I'm really sorry," said the security officer while the entire class waited in the hall. Lee reflects: "How could central dispatch, 20 miles away, have a better understanding of the situation than the officer at the scene? Any information about the problem would be coming from the officer anyway." Lee sympathizes with the employee who was rendered powerless (and no doubt embarrassed) because supervisors did not trust employees to act on their own judgment.

Considerations such as these have led health care experts Thom Mayer and Robert Cates (2004) to advise: "Make no decision at a higher level that can be made at a lower level" (p. 58). They point out that health care is a personal service offered at an individual level, therefore "the people responsible for the service delivery must be entrusted with the power to make service meaningful" (p. 58).

Hold people accountable. A key component of empowerment is holding people at every level of the organization responsible for goals they help to set and regularly measuring progress to help team members gauge what's working and what isn't (Chang, Shih, & Lin, 2010; Donahue, Piazza, Griffin, Dykes, & Fitzpatrick, 2008).

To make the process effective, experts suggest that measurement not be used to punish team members. If so, they will have an incentive to set goals too low or to enhance the results artificially, as in asking patients to give them perfect scores rather than constructive ideas. Feedback mechanisms should be based on what team members *themselves* want to know in the interest of continual self-improvement. In Mayer and Cates' (2004) terms, measurement should be a tool, not a club.

Here's a great example. Lynn Pierce was a nurse manager in a hospital when the staff decided to post the results of weekly patient satisfaction surveys throughout the hospital. That meant that everyone (staff members, patients, visitors, VIPs, and anyone else in the hospital) could see the scores, as well as charts that compared patient satisfaction scores in various departments. There was no punishment involved, but the numbers were hard to ignore. Pierce says that, although she frequently made excuses for her unit's scores when they were kept private, having them posted changed her point of view. "I started thinking, 'My numbers are going to come up! I won't be left behind,'" she says. Pierce says she began seeing patient requests, not as time-consuming chores, but as opportunities. She laughs, "'You want a Coke?' I'd call Dietary and say, *'Send 'em a six-pack!'*" (quoted by du Pré, 2005, p. 317).

Celebrate successes. One benefit of measuring performance is the opportunity to celebrate when things go well. Experts suggest sending handwritten thank-you letters to employees and their families, posting thank-you letters from patients, holding celebrations when the organization reaches key goals, informally praising people who do good

work, and developing formal recognition programs to honor heroic efforts.

In closing this section, it bears emphasizing that leaders are not obsolete once they empower team members. As James Pepicello and Emmett Murphy (1996) point out, empowerment "does not relieve leadership of its responsibility to lead" (para.17). It does mean that leaders' role is different. No longer is leadership defined by one's position or title. Instead, it is characterized by interpersonal skills, including the ability to inspire, recognize, and reward others (Jobes & Steinbinder, 1996, para. 23).

If it seems overwhelming to contemplate all that health care administrators do, keep in mind that they don't do it alone. Success relies on the integrated efforts of many people. In the next section we will explore how human resources specialists contribute.

Human Resources

Nothing beats being part of a team that is expected to produce great results. . . . If you have the wrong people on the bus, nothing else matters. You may be headed in the right direction, but you still won't achieve greatness. Great vision with mediocre people still produces mediocre results. —JIM COLLINS (2001A, DISCIPLINED PEOPLE, PARA. 7)

After studying consistently top-performing companies in the United States, Collins (2001b) debunked the idea that people are a company's most important asset. "People are *not* your most important asset," he clarified, "the *right* people are" (p. 13). Indeed, as we all know, the wrong people, or people who are not well prepared, can be your worst nightmare—damaging trust, running off great team members, causing mistakes, and damaging morale.

In a book with the provocative title *The No Asshole Rule,* Stanford University professor Robert Sutton (2007) presents empirical evidence that people who treat others badly are bad for business, no matter how good they seem to be at some aspects of the job. Sutton calculated what he dubs the TCA (total cost per asshole) of workers in a wide variety of fields and concluded that the disadvantages of people who insult, belittle, and bully others far outweigh the advantages. Even bullies

BOX 10.3 CAREER OPPORTUNITIES

HEALTH CARE ADMINISTRATION
President or CEO
Chief operating officer
Chief financial officer
Health information manager
Director of human resources
Strategic planning director
Medical director
Nursing director
Departmental director (e.g., Department of Nursing, Surgery, Medical Records, Human Resources, Marketing, Public Relations, Education, Information Technology, Billing, Risk Management)
Medical office manager

CAREER RESOURCES AND JOB LISTINGS
- U. S. Bureau of Labor Statistics: http://www.bls.gov/ooh/Management/Medical-and-health-services-managers.htm
- Association of University Programs in Health Administration: www.aupha.org
- American College of Health Care Administrators: www.achca.org
- American College of Health Care Executives: www.healthmanagementcareers.org

HEALTH CARE HUMAN RESOURCES
Human resource manager
Recruiter
Training and development specialist
Compensation and benefits manager
Customer service representative

CAREER RESOURCES AND JOB LISTINGS
- American Society for Healthcare Human Resources Administration: http://www.ashhra.org/

- Society of Human Resource Management: http://www.shrm.org/Pages/default.aspx
- U.S. Bureau of Labor Statistics: http://www.bls.gov/ooh/Business-and-Financial/Human-resources-specialists.htm
- Workforce HR Jobs: http://www.workforce hrjobs.com/a/all-jobs/list

HEALTH CARE MARKETING AND PUBLIC RELATIONS
Public relations professional
Strategic planning manager
Marketing professional
Advertising designer
Physician marketing coordinator
Community services director
In-house communication director
Pharmaceutical sales representative

CAREER RESOURCES AND JOB LISTINGS
- Society for Health care Strategy & Market Development: www.shsmd.org/shsmd_app/index.jsp
- International Association of Business Communicators: www.iabc.com
- Public Relations Society of America: www.prsa.org
- Public Relations Society of America Health Academy: www.healthacademy.prsa.org
- American Association of Advertising Agencies: www.aaaa.org
- American Advertising Federation: www.aaf.org
- Strategic Health Care Communication (job listings): www.strategichealthcare.com/career
- U.S. Bureau of Labor Statistics: http://www.bls.gov/ooh/Management/Public-relations-managers-and-specialists.htm
- PharmaceuticalSales.com

considered to be "top" salespeople, he says, cost companies more than they bring in because of lawsuits, staff turnover, angry clients, and so on. Moreover, their attitudes tend to be contagious, such that the people around them offer poorer service as well. Sutton advises: "Avoid pompous jerks whenever possible. They not only can make you feel bad about yourself, chances are you will eventually start acting like them" ("Work Matters" blog post, nd, np). Just for fun, see *Check It Out!* on the next page for a chance to test your own bully quotient.

In my experience facilitating leadership workshops, Sutton's advice evokes a chuckle, but also plenty of nods and knowing looks. Nearly all of us have worked with people who evoke fear and anxiety in those around them. Typically, even their bosses would rather not deal with them, so the bullies often remain where they are, running off clients and colleagues. The challenge of working with hostile team members is unacceptable anywhere, but particularly in health care organizations, where leaders struggle to attract and keep qualified personnel in already stressful environments. Health care staffing shortages (see Box 10.4) make it imperative for leaders to do whatever they can to attract and keep qualified personnel. This includes listening closely to employees' needs, responding to their ideas, and involving them in collaborative efforts to create satisfying environments.

In this section we look at the contributions of human resource personnel and others who cultivate talent and vision and, ideally, give us the luxury of working with ethical, dedicated people. Human resource specialists are involved in recruiting, hiring, and training staff members; overseeing employee benefits and compensation; mediating employee concerns; providing for mentoring, counseling, and assistance; recognizing outstanding achievements; and monitoring team member satisfaction and retention. Qualifications typically include at least a bachelor's degree in human resources, personnel, communication, psychology, or another field related to human dynamics ("Becoming," 2011).

BOX 10.4

Staffing Shortages in Health Care

Experts estimate that the United States will be short-staffed by nearly 1 million nurses, 124,000 physicians, and 706,00 home health aides by the year 2025 (AHA, 2008; Dill & Salsberg, 2008; U.S. Bureau of Labor Statistics, 2012a, 2012b). There are numerous reasons for the shortfall.

One involves population shifts. A growing elderly population is placing increasing demands on the health care system. The number of people over age 85 will triple between 2008 and 2050, reaching an unprecedented 19 million, increasing the overall need for health services by at least 40% (U.S. Census Bureau News, 2008).

A second factor is the Patient Protection and Affordable Care Act, passed in 2010. By creating provisions for nearly all Americans to be insured and receive regular health care, it will increase the need for qualified caregivers. (The act also includes billions of dollars in grants and training opportunities to prepare new caregivers.)

Third, at the same time health care needs are increasing, the number of trained caregivers, which is already insufficient, is expected to *decrease*. This is partly because many caregivers are at retirement age themselves. About 1 in 3 practicing male physicians in the United States is 55 or older, and 4 in 10 registered nurses are 50 or older ("Registered Nurse," 2007; U.S. DHHS, 2006b).

The physician shortage is slightly less extensive than the nursing shortage, partly because some women who might previously have pursued nursing careers are now going to medical school instead. Whereas nursing was once one of the few career paths available to women, the number of first-year college students aspiring to become nurses dropped by 75% between 1974 and 1986, as women began to choose other career options (Green, 1988). As a result of that fairly recent shift, female physicians are younger, on average, than their male counterparts. Only 1 in 8 female doctors is 55 or older (U.S. DHHS, 2007). However, men have not joined nursing at the rate once expected. Today, only about 7% of registered nurses in the United States are male ("Male Nurses," 2011).

A fourth factor is insufficient funding for colleges and universities. U.S. nursing schools turn away as many as 40,283 qualified applicants a year because they don't have the budgets or facilities necessary to accept more students (American Association of Colleges of Nursing, 2008). (As mentioned, provisions of the Affordable Care Act may help with that somewhat. We'll talk more about that in Chapter 12.)

Finally, many health professionals are changing careers. Nearly 1 in 5 registered nurses in the United States is not employed as a nurse. That equates to about 490,000 qualified people who have opted out of the nursing workforce (U.S. DHHS, 2006b). The most common reason is burnout from working in understaffed units. Because of the nursing shortage, and to save money, many hospitals and residential care facilities have fewer staff members than before. This includes nurses, nurse aids, technicians, housekeeping staff, and so on. Nurses are often called on to fill the gaps (Apker, 2001). Stress is also elevated by the demands of caring for sicker patients. Because of reimbursements limits, hospital patients today are "quicker and sicker" than in the past. Rather than a patient load in which some patients are quietly recovering and others are really sick, *everyone* is really sick.

Hospital nurses in Hendrich and colleagues' (2008) study walked an average of 3 miles per 10-hour shift. The researchers conclude: "A picture emerges of the professional nurse who is constantly moving from patient room to room, nurse station to supply closet and back to room, spending a minority of time on patient care activities" (p. 31). The researchers note that it's no surprise that nurses leave the profession. Hendrich and colleagues urge health care leaders to consider ways to make nurses' jobs more efficient and less demanding.

The nursing shortage affects health care professionals. It also hurts patients. An extensive study of 799 hospitals by the U.S. Department of Health and Human Services revealed that patients in understaffed units are significantly more likely than others to have urinary tract infections, pneumonia, shock, and upper gastrointestinal bleeding—conditions that can often be averted or minimized with careful attention ("HHS Study Finds," 2001). Patients in understaffed units were also more likely to have extended hospital stays and less likely to be successfully resuscitated after cardiac arrest. Jack Needleman and associates (2006) found that hospitals can actually save money by hiring more RNs because nurses in well-staffed units have fewer emergencies, patient deaths, and mistakes to manage.

Theoretical Foundations

Before exploring the research and strategies relevant to human resources, let's consider some of the foundational theories in the field. As you will see, theorists have examined issues such as: *What ethical principles should we consider concerning the treatment of people on our teams? How are people different from other types of resources?* and *What brings out the best in team members so that, together, we have the greatest chance of success?*

Richard de Charms laid the groundwork for many current theories of motivation and workplace dynamics. His (1968) **theory of personal causation** proposes that people naturally resist being treated as **pawns** who are required to relinquish control and blindly follow orders, but people typically respond enthusiastically and with

dedication when they are treated as **origins**, that is, active participants in designing and carrying out worthwhile tasks. de Charms' work was as much about ethics as productivity. He felt that people deserve to be treated as something more than cogs in a machine, and he observed that people make their greatest contributions when they are actively engaged. Consequently, de Charms (1977) advocated a participatory model that he called "plan-choose-act-take responsibility" in which people work together to make decisions, carry them out, and continually analyze and improve their own performance.

A similar idea is available in Douglas McGregor's (1960) **Theory X and Theory Y** model, which proposes that managers tend to fall into one of two basic camps—those who believe people are naturally lazy and must be prodded and supervised to be productive (Theory X managers) and those who believe people enjoy the inherent rewards of work and are motivated to make a positive difference (Theory Y managers). McGregor observed that managers' attitudes are influential in bringing out either the worst or the best in people. People treated as if they are lazy and untrustworthy are likely to act that way and visa versa. This theory and relevant research lend further credence to the notion that it is both ethical and expedient to empower team members.

Frederick Herzberg conceived of a more complicated interplay between factors. His **motivation-hygiene theory** suggests that a different set of factors engender satisfaction versus dissatisfaction (Herzberg, 1968; Herzberg, Mausner, & Snyderman, 1959). According to the theory, people are typically satisfied with their work if they believe they are making an important difference, are respected, and are learning and improving. Herzberg called these factors **motivators**. However, dissatisfaction typically arises over a different set of issues, which he called **hygiene factors**. These include feeling underpaid, forced to work in unhealthy or unproductive conditions, and frustrated by unfair rules and policies. Herzberg found that, in the absence of such factors, people are typically not dissatisfied. However, it doesn't follow that they are satisfied, either. To be satisfied, if you recall, we must feel that our work is important and we are respected. The lesson here is that dissatisfaction typically arises from factors (such as pay) that are extrinsic to our work, and motivation arises from the inherent satisfaction of making a difference. Managers who focus on only one or the other are unlikely to create the conditions in which people are both satisfied and highly motivated.

In health care, it is particularly important to recruit outstanding people and to make sure they feel rewarded and valued. Although human resource personnel typically do not work directly with patients, their have immense influence on the quality of those interactions.

Communication Skill Builder: Building Great Teams

A critically ill patient was admitted to Mayo's hospital in Phoenix shortly before her daughter was to be married, and she was unlikely to live to see the wedding. The bride told the hospital chaplain how much she wanted her mother to see her get married, and he conveyed this to the critical care manager. Within hours, the hospital atrium was transformed for a wedding service, complete with flowers, balloons, and confetti. Staff members provided a cake and a pianist, and nurses arranged the patient's hair and makeup, dressed her, and wheeled her bed to the atrium. The chaplain performed the service. On every floor, hospital staff members, other patients, and visiting family and friends ringed the atrium balconies "like angels from above," to quote the bride. The wedding scene provided not only evidence of caring to the patient and her family but also a strong reminder to the staff that the patient's needs come first. The event reflects the clinic's spirit of volunteerism at its best. (Berry & Seltman, 2008, p. 57)

This moving story is evidence of Mayo Clinic's simple vision, known to every employee and used as the basis for all decisions: *The needs of the patient come first* (Berry & Seltman, p. 24). Volunteerism refers to employees' willingness to do more than they have to do because they want to make a difference and they know organizational leaders will back them up.

This level of commitment and compassion doesn't happen automatically, but results from a concerted effort on many levels. The process begins with selecting the right people, then training them well and weaving the mission into every aspect of daily work. Following are strategies for creating and building outstanding teams from a human resources perspective.

HIRE CAREFULLY

The first step toward success, says Collins (2001b), is getting the "right people on the bus." Mayer and Cates (2004) wholeheartedly concur. They ask: "Are there days when you come to work and see the people you are working with and think to yourself, 'Bring it on! Whatever we've got to do today, this team of people can make it happen!'?" (p. 7). If so, they say, you are surrounded by **A-team players**, the type who love a challenge, have a positive attitude, and inspire everyone around them. But if you said no, you understand the concept of B-team players. They inspire a different internal dialogue on the way to work, one that sounds more like this: "Shoot me, shoot me, shoot me! I can't work with him—I worked with him yesterday!" (Mayer & Cates, p. 7).

Mayer and Cates describe **B-team players** as negative, lazy, late, confused, and always surprised by the demands of the job. B-team players are "fundamentally toxic" and quite potent, in that it just takes one to poison things for everyone. A major part of a leader's job, maintain Mayer and Cates, is getting B-team members either to reform (which might involve moving them to positions more in line with their talents and passions) or to leave. An even better strategy, they say, is to hire the right people in the first place.

Linda Minton of Parkwest Medical Center in Knoxville, Tennessee, describes how she knew that a new nurse, Paul, would be an A-team member. A woman in her 80s with Alzheimer's was admitted for a blood transfusion under Paul's supervision. When the woman became afraid and pulled out her IVs, her daughter was tearful and distraught. The patient repeatedly requested to be left alone and allowed to go home, but Paul knew that she needed the life-saving treatment. Minton recalls:

> Paul again quietly explained that she could not go home, but he also asked if there were anything else she might like to do. Quickly she responded, with a big smile on her face, "I would like to dance." Paul, who is not a dancer, said, "You will have to lead." She agreed, and so—they danced. What a wonderful sight, seeing this lovely lady calmed by the impromptu dance. It was at that moment that we all knew Paul had a place at Parkwest Medical Center. (*What's Right in Health Care*, 2007, p. 666)

Human resource personnel can be influential in recruiting and selecting A-team players. Experts remind us that it is important to find people with the right attitude and passion as well as the right credentials. Before making hiring decisions, members of highly successful organizations typically conduct multiple interviews with candidates, invite input from people with whom they would work, and consider candidates' intangible qualifications such as patience, appreciation for diversity, and interpersonal skills.

TEACH THE CULTURE AND VALUES

This section began with an example of the volunteer spirit of Mayo Clinic. By helping to teach the organization's culture and values, human resource personnel are involved in making such remarkable encounters possible. At Mayo, employees hear the clinic's motto, "The needs of the patient come first," within the first 5 minutes of new-employee orientation and several times a day ever after. As one employee said, "Mayo becomes part of your DNA" (quoted by Berry & Seltman, 2008, p. 26). Having a strong, clear purpose provides unity, even among diverse people and departments. Team members contribute in different ways, but because they are united by a clear mission, they all know and agree on what they are trying to achieve together.

CONTINUALLY RECRUIT INTERNAL TALENT

By most estimates, it costs about $75,000 to replace an employee who earns $50,000 and even more for people in higher pay grades (Bliss, 2012). Expenses involve lost productivity and the cost of recruiting, interviewing, training, and so on. That doesn't even include the frustration of disrupted relationships and being short-staffed in the meantime. It is to everyone's benefit to keep great team members on board. Human resources personnel can help retain talented people in the following ways:

- *Provide ongoing leadership training.* Ideally, leadership training and development do not begin or end when people become designated leaders. The process begins long before that and continues throughout a person's career.
- *Keep no secrets.* If people are to be accountable, they must know where they stand and how the organization is performing. One strategy is to make financial records and satisfaction survey reports available to all employees so they can chart their success and receive immediate market feedback on what works well and what does not (Studer, 2003).
- *Make organizational leaders accessible.* Avoid placing administrative officers in far-off or segregated areas. Encourage leaders to interact freely throughout the organization and to share conversations, praise, and ideas.

- *Reward people for sharing ideas.* Develop a program that invites employees' suggestions and rewards them for submitting workable ideas that improve services, save money, and increase employee morale.
- *Respond to ideas.* Even when the ideas cannot be implemented, people want to know they have been heard. Designate committees to review ideas, respond to them all, and initiate implementation whenever possible. (See Box 10.5 for more on innovative, inclusive leadership.)
- *Prepare people to participate actively.* In the previous section, we explored reasons to invest in dispersed leadership. The advantages are numerous, but success is not guaranteed. Participative decision making is typically good for morale and effective at yielding high-quality decisions (Bucknall & Thomas, 1996; McNeese-Smith, 1996). Human resource personnel can help people build the skills to effectively engage in shared governance.

Based on the theories we have reviewed, encouraging people to use and develop their talents is productive for health care organizations and enriching for the people who comprise them. Recruitment is the first step, but it also pays to continually re-recruit talented team members and hire from within when the talent is available. In a way, point out Berry and Seltman (2008), employment is a job interview "that lasts for years" (p. 29).

Now let's look at the contributions of marketing and public relations professionals, who work both internally and externally to help health care organizations succeed.

Marketing and Public Relations

We began this chapter with Kendrick Doidge's observation that, "When you're in marketing and public relations, you do all sorts of things!" As you can see from the examples of his work so far, that is certainly true. In this section we will talk more about health care marketing and public relations, two career fields that, while not the same, are often interrelated.

Traditionally, health care marketing has been concerned mostly with promoting business and profitability, and public relations has focused on

---

BOX 10.5

A Model for Innovative Leadership

When writers for the *Harvard Business Review* interviewed 100 innovative business leaders, they identified some common characteristics among them (Davenport, Prusak, & Wilson, 2003). For one, innovators are *idea scouts*, always looking for new ideas within the organization and outside it. They talk to people and really listen. They are also *tailors* who modify new ideas to suit the organization's needs, while inviting frequent and candid input from others. As the process continues, the best innovators are *promoters* who sell their ideas to people throughout the organization, communicating effectively and enthusiastically with top and middle management as well as frontline employees and clients. Finally, innovators are *experimenters*. They pilot and test new ideas on a small scale to prepare them for wider adoption. Importantly, innovators are *not* do-it-all-myself types. When an innovation has been tested and refined, they "get out of the way and let others execute" (Davenport, Prusak, & Wilson, 2003, p. 58). The implications for communication are clear: Observe, listen, invite feedback, sell your ideas, experiment, and enable others.

WHAT DO YOU THINK?

1. In what ways are you an idea scout? Think of the best idea scout you know. How does he or she do it?
2. What steps might you follow to tailor ideas to a particular organization or group of people?
3. What skills are needed to promote new ideas?
4. Have you ever been part of (or coordinated) a pilot study or experimental program? Did you feel it was worthwhile? What did you learn during the process?
5. Why are skillful innovators not "do-it-myself" types when it comes to implementing widespread changes?

---

enhancing an organization's image and larger mission. Marketing professionals are likely to be involved with stakeholder groups who are central to business development. This may include marketing directly to physicians who might make patient referrals, conducting market research, helping develop new services to meet market needs, branding and promoting an organization through advertising and other means, communicating internally, and engaging in strategic planning. Results are often measured in terms of financial success and organizational growth. (See Box 10.6 to explore the ethical considerations of advertising health services.)

BOX 10.6   ETHICAL CONSIDERATIONS

Should Health Organizations Advertise?

Health organizations have traditionally relied on word-of-mouth promotion, but competition has led to more diverse marketing strategies. The AMA, which banned physician advertising in 1914, lifted the ban in 1975 under pressure from the U.S. Supreme Court, which felt that the ban restricted public information and physicians' livelihood (Kotler & Clarke, 1987). Although doctors have been somewhat reluctant to advertise aggressively themselves, many insurance companies and managed care organizations are avid advertisers, as are pharmaceutical companies, which spend more than $2 billion a year to advertise prescription drugs (Kane, 2003). (You'll read more about this in Chapter 11.)

Although competition is fierce, "selling" medical services remains a controversial subject. Many types of health care organizations (hospitals, managed care organizations, nursing homes, and so on) do advertise. However, physicians have typically limited themselves to simple ads, such as those that announce the opening of a new practice.

Some people object to advertising medical services and products. Robert Boyd (1997), for one, argues that "media hype" has no place in health. He warns that it's confusing enough to keep up with medical research without being bombarded by sales pitches promoting various health products and services.

A related worry is that claims made by health organizations (such as "Best cancer care") are hard to evaluate, and patients don't typically have the expertise to know when advertisers are making exaggerated or inaccurate claims. Moreover, seriously ill patients and their loved ones may be particularly vulnerable to advertising claims because they so badly want to believe that a cure is possible (Irvine, 1991).

Others fear that health advertisements will alarm people and make them needlessly preoccupied with health issues. Alison Bass (1990) describes a hospital advertisement that shows a woman examining her breasts for lumps. The headline reads: "This woman just missed the cancer that will kill her" (p. 1). Bass concludes: "People who provide health care have begun playing on the very fears and anxieties they are supposed to alleviate" (p. 1).

There is also concern that advertising will damage the professional image of caregivers. Critics cringe at sales ploys that make health professionals seem silly or greedy. For example, some clinics have offered money-back guarantees if patients are not satisfied with the care they receive. Health ethicist John La Puma (1998) wonders if free toasters will be the next marketing strategy.

People who support health advertising have a simple but compelling case as well. They feel that advertising is a useful way to let the public know about service providers and services (Bass, 1990). Proponents of health-related advertisements maintain that consumers are wise enough to be skeptical about advertisers' claims and to avoid being taken in by misleading promises.

WHAT DO YOU THINK?

1. Should doctors advertise their services? Why or why not?
2. Some physicians feel that lawyers' professional image has been tarnished since they have begun to advertise on television. Do you agree? Why or why not? Do you think it would be the same for physicians?
3. Should other providers (e.g., hospitals, drug companies, rehabilitation centers, managed care organizations) advertise? Why or why not?
4. If advertising is allowed, should there be any restrictions on what the ads may (or must) contain?

Public relations professionals in health care are usually involved in such activities as media relations and publicity, publication design, internal communication, strategic planning, special events, health education and promotion, fundraising, volunteer recruitment, and crisis management. The most coveted public relations professionals are those who work in an integrated fashion both within an organization and with external stakeholders. "Long gone are the days when public relations practitioners could claim they were successful after getting their organization positive publicity in the local newspaper," says PR theorist and researcher Kurt Wise (2007), pointing out that "CEOs now expect public relations professionals to demonstrate they can contribute to the bottom-line success of an organization" (p. 162).

Although marketing and public relations are not the same, if they are done well they complement each other. An organization that is not financially sustainable will accomplish very little. At the same time, an organization without a strong reputation and mission is unlikely to be financially successful. It's common in health care for marketing and public relations professionals to work closely together. And sometimes people do both.

Foundations for Theory and Practice

Following are communication best practices from marketing and public relations experts, as well as the theories behind them. As a foundation for the rest, we will spend the most time on cultivating mutually beneficial relationships.

FOCUS ON RELATIONSHIPS

Relationship management and relationship marketing emerged in the late 1980s and have been received with particular enthusiasm in health care. They reflect the idea that transactions don't always (or even, usually) have a distinct beginning, middle, and end (Dwyer, Schurr, & Oh, 1987). For example, if we undergo surgery, our impression of the hospital probably does not begin when we walk in the door. It began much earlier. And what happens while we are a patient is likely to influence our willingness to seek care there in the future. Considering this, marketing and public relations professionals who focus on ongoing relationships are more

---

BOX 10.7 RESOURCES

Journals in the Field

HEALTH CARE ADMINISTRATION
 Advances in Developing Human Resources
 The Health Care Manager
 Health Care Management Review
 Health Care Management Science
 Health Sciences Management Research
 International Journal for Quality in Health Care
 International Journal of Integrated Care
 Journal of the American Medical Directors Association
 Journal of Health Administration Education
 Journal of Health Management
 Journal of Health, Organisation and Management
 Journal of Healthcare Management
 Journal for Healthcare Quality
 Journal of Public Health Management & Practice
 Managed Health Care Executive

HEALTH CARE HUMAN RESOURCES
 Human Resources Development Journal
 Human Resources for Health
 Journal of Health & Human Resources
 Journal of Health & Human Services Administration

HEALTH CARE MARKETING AND PUBLIC RELATIONS
 Cases in Public Health Communication & Marketing
 Health Marketing Quarterly
 International Journal of Pharmaceutical and Healthcare Marketing
 Journal of Health Care Marketing
 Journal of Hospital Marketing and Public Relations
 Journal of Management and Marketing in Healthcare
 Marketing Health Services
 Public Relations Journal
 Public Relations Review

---

effective than others in attracting and sustaining not only consumers and partners, but loyal fans of the organization.

Relationships of all types matter. Coworker relationships influence organizational culture and set the tone for consumer interactions. And organizational boundaries matter little. Relationships with external stakeholders can be the difference between building a new wing and going without. As Berkowitz (2007) points out, "it is extremely difficult to seek donations to build a cancer center, heart center, or women's health program, and ask for a donation from any individual before the organization has a relationship with that donor" (p. 128). In health care, even supposed competitors often team up to fund community clinics for the uninsured, host health fairs, coordinate care in crisis situations, and more. "The demands on and responsibilities of today's health care organizations are too difficult and overwhelming to accomplish without the assistance of strategic partners and other publics," attest Guy, Williams, Aldridge, and Roggenkamp (2007, p. 2).

Many people feel that relationship development is not only good business but is also the key to improving health care and lowering costs. As marketing theorist Lawrence Crosby (2011) puts it:

> Quality and cost issues are not about healthy individuals collapsing on the street and being rushed to the hospital for a sophisticated diagnosis by TV's Dr. House. They are about chronic problems that have been simmering for years that eventually boil over into far bigger problems. Managing the prevention/treatment/follow-up life cycle requires a relationship approach. (p. 13)

Crosby posits that today's often-fragmented approach to health care encourages treatment overlaps, inconsistencies, distrust, and neglect that could be overcome with stronger, more trusting relationships.

Robert Morgan and Shelby Hunt's (1994) **commitment-trust theory of relationships** proposes that people make relatively enduring judgments between alternatives based on trust, shared values, loyalty, and commitment—and that, of these, *commitment* and *trust* are the greatest predictors of relationship strength. The theory further posits that, once enduring relationships are formed, we (as consumers, providers, or colleagues) benefit from a sense of stability, uncertainty reduction, and enhanced identity, and we're likely to remain invested in those relationships as long as the benefits outweigh the relational costs, which may include conflict and a sense that other alternatives

have emerged that are even more rewarding. This means it's important to foster relationships, to continually nurture them, and to work through relationship threats.

Relationship management has dispelled the notion that marketing and public relations professionals can be effective engaging in only one-way communication with the public (Berkowitz, 2007). Actually, that notion was never very satisfying, particularly in health care. As early as 1939, Alden Brewster Mills prescribed that health care public relations should be, more than anything else, an effort to develop "mutual understanding, good will and respect" (Mills, 1939, p. 3). With the same conviction, James Grunig and colleagues advocate **two-way symmetrical communication**, meaning ongoing, open dialogue between members of an organization and the larger publics it serves (see, e.g., Grunig, 1992; Grunig, Grunig, & Dozier, 2002). The lesson is that, as in any relationship, listening is as important as talking.

In sum, many people believe that relationship management—with its focus on enduring, mutual benefits for everyone involved—is the most important focus of public relations and marketing. As you might imagine, communication is central to relationship management, being the mechanism by which we convey trust and commitment and manage conflict. And it's not enough for only marketing and public relations professionals to engage in relationship development. Everyone must be involved. We focus next on efforts to integrate marketing and public relations throughout an organization.

INTEGRATE

"Selling is trying to get people to want what you have. Marketing is trying to have what people want," says health care consultant Terrance Rynn (quoted by Lee, 2004. p. 5).

One mistake professionals make is trying to boost business by promoting substandard services. Not only will that not work, says Fred Lee (2004), it will make matters worse. He advises: If a service is subpar, don't promote it. "The worst thing you can do for a poorly delivered service is to get more physicians or patients to try it and find out how bad it is" (p. 6). For this reason, it is important not to consider marketing and public relations as "add-ons" to a health care system, but as integral

"I get my bagels from a bagel guy in one of those movable stands on the sidewalk. One day I didn't have enough money with me to cover what I'd just ordered. He said, 'don't worry, pay me next time.' When a new vendor set up his cart much closer to my apartment, to my surprise I found I didn't go to him. . . . My loyalty goes to the bagel guy who trusted me." —Kevin Jackson, *Building Reputational Capital* (p. 8)

emergency department. The researchers observed and interviewed staff members, most of whom felt they were "under bombardment" (p. 131), unprepared for the communication challenges they faced every day and discouraged by the hostile attitudes of their coworkers. Worst of all, perhaps, the staff largely perceived that administrators were indifferent to their concerns, thus they were helpless in a bad situation. The researchers observed that the personnel who were confused, frustrated, and anxious were hampered in their ability to do a good job and were poor ambassadors for the organization. They encouraged leaders to focus on employee concerns, recognizing that public relations is as much an internal function as an external one.

DEVELOP REPUTATION, NOT ONLY IMAGE

An organization's greatest competitive advantage is not its size, location, or prices. The greatest predictor of success is its character and the constancy of its reputation (Jackson, 2004). In the book *Building Reputational Capital,* Jackson (2004) presents compelling evidence supporting a simple but powerful idea: *Organizations flourish when people are loyal to them.* The *Lesson of the Bagels* (at left) is a great example of customer loyalty. And the principle applies to employee loyalty as well. Jackson found that the best employees—the kind with strong integrity, lasting commitment, and good will themselves—flock to companies that make them feel proud to work there.

In contrast, organizations that defy public trust, no matter how large they are (think Enron, Rupert Murdoch's media empire, and Tyco) are often eventually toppled by scandal. These companies experience what Jackson calls "relational bankruptcy," which no amount of marketing or public relations can undo. Jackson proposes that "the things that matter most to your business, that enable it to work, to be productive—trust, integrity, fair dealing—exist beyond conventional measurements of the firm's value" (p. 2).

This is particularly true in health care. It's difficult to judge a clinic, hospital, or nonprofit organization except on the basis of its reputation. No matter how high-tech or beautiful a medical center is, it's unlikely people will trust their lives or their donations to people they don't trust.

components in strategic planning and organizational design.

Because marketing and PR professionals are continually involved in scanning the larger environment and listening to what people want and need, they can be valuable players in internal decision making. Besides, the more they know about services, the better and more authentically they can promote them to others.

An interesting example of internal public relations is provided in Trent Seltzer and colleagues' (2012) article "PR in the ER" in which they describe communication in a busy, university-affiliated

Jackson (2004) distinguishes between corporate **identity** (what makes an organization recognizable in comparison to others), **image** (an overall but sometimes fleeting feeling about a company based on its "personality"), and **reputation** (a long-term assessment by a range of constituencies about the "character, conscience, and credibility" of an organization) (p. 43). He presents a model of three different types of companies, described here.

People in what we might call **Point-A-to-Point-B companies** are motivated primarily by profits and are willing to engage in questionable means to reach profitable ends. Although the bottom line might look healthy for a while, people in these companies usually experience short-term success at best. They engender little loyalty from customers or employees, and in the end, they may expend a great deal of time and money dealing with legal troubles and scandals, if the company survives at all.

People in the second type of company, which we'll call **superficially image-based**, realize the value of a positive image, but they seek it through advertising campaigns and slogans that sound good but don't necessarily reflect the true nature of the company. In this company, principles are espoused, but they aren't always enacted. This approach is unlikely to engender long-term success.

The third company is **reputation-based**, meaning that it has a positive image, but more important, people throughout the organization consistently embody high principles in all that they do. This is possible largely because people know the principles and because leaders and policies support those principles, even when it takes a little more time and money to live up to them. Jackson (2004) demonstrates that only in this type of organization can people afford to engage in transparent decision making, which is important because transparency is the key to lasting trust. His research suggests that reputation-based companies are the only ones that experience long-term success.

In summary, Jackson (2004) makes the point that image can be superficial, but an organization's reputation—good or bad—is based on how its members treat people every day in every situation.

So far we have been talking mostly about guiding principles. We will close this section with a skill-builder about one of the many communication tools marketing and public relations professionals use.

> **CHECK IT OUT!**   For a comprehensive guide to using social media for crisis communication see Special Report: Crisis Communication and Social Media (Currie, 2009) at http://www.boozallen.com/insights/insight-detail/42420696.

Communication Skill Builder: Two-Way Communication and Social Media

Throughout much of the past 100 years, marketing and public relations professionals have worked in concert with journalists to educate and inform the public. That's still an important part of what they do, but, as you know, technologies such as the Internet, Facebook, and Twitter now make it possible to disseminate messages without going through formal media channels, and it's relatively inexpensive to do so. That doesn't mean social media campaigns are always easy or effective.

For the most part, the jury is still out on social media. We know people are using the technology. We just don't always know if their efforts yield results. Among 1,500 health care administrators surveyed, 82% say that their marketing efforts include social media. However only 4% of them feel it's very effective, and only 32% rate it as effective ("Industry Survey," 2011). Most people in health care who use social media say it represents less than 10% of their total marketing effort.

As we continue to experiment with social media, here are some suggestions by the experts.

- **Be interactive.** Health journalist Carrie Vaughan (2012) describes a hospital that had only 80 "friends" (most of them employees) on Facebook until the PR and marketing staff hosted an online cute baby contest in conjunction with an upcoming event. The number of friends quickly soared to 1,153.
- **Link messages to key services.** To make the most of high readership numbers, link social media messages to services you'd like to promote. Vaughan (2012) gives the example of a "What Do You Heart?" online contest linked to publicity about cardiac services.
- **Be educational.** Social media can allow people to watch medical procedures and receive other

health-related information not previously available. The staff at Henry Ford Hospital in Detroit now uses Twitter to tape and broadcast some surgeries, along with the surgeons' comments. "Doing this removes a real communication barrier," says health care technology expert Charles Parks. "It helps make something scary much more comprehendable" (quoted by Cohen, 2009, para. 12). (If you're comfortable viewing surgery, enter search terms Henry Ford Hospital and Twitter surgery at YouTube.com to see samples for yourself.)

- **Integrate a range of channels.** The most effective campaigns involve a range of media such as Facebook, Twitter, and blogs, and link one to the others (Vaughan, 2012).

- **Update people during a crisis.** Social media offer a quick and inexpensive way to keep people abreast of developments in a crisis. For example, when a broken water main left 2 million people near Boston without water, experts at Tufts University and the Boston Public Health Commission used brief text messages, emails, and Twitter feeds to notify people about water outages and to warn them to boil water that might have been contaminated by the breach. City officials also used computerized phone messages and megaphones to alert residents without access to social media (Gualtieri, 2011). Based on experiences such as these, experts recommend that organizations planning to use social media in crises enlist volunteers and train them in advance, keep messages succinct, monitor incoming messages, avoid sending inconsistent messages, and have a back-up plan in case technology or connections fail (Currie, 2009).

- **Don't forget the "worried well."** Nathan Huebner of the CDC urges crisis managers to consider people who are not directly affected by a crisis but are distressed by it or anxious about loved ones. The "worried well" typically outnumber the people who are directly affected, Huebner points out, and keeping them well informed prevents undue anxiety and may keep them out of harm's way themselves (Currie,

When 8 people died and 55 people became ill after eating infected cantaloupe in 2011, the CDC issued Twitter feeds, Facebook messages, emails, blog posts, and other social media messages, in addition to using more traditional media channels. For more examples of CDC's extensive social media efforts, go to http://www.cdc.gov/socialmedia.

2009). For more on this topic, see Chapter 13 on public health and crisis communication.

- **Maintain relationships.** As we have discussed, strong relationships may enhance patient outcomes, build loyalty, and help with fundraising. Social media can help. A surgical weight loss center in Las Vegas regularly sends Facebook messages with encouraging words and links to healthy information to friends of the site. More than 300 people have given the site "likes" (Patterson, 2012).

- **Develop a social media policy.** The downside of social media is that it's quick, accessible, and inexpensive for *everybody*. Comments posted on an employee's personal Facebook page can violate patient confidentiality or endanger partnerships with other organizations. Consequently, many organizations are educating employees about social media practices and establishing policies such as the following: be respectful (avoid offensive, profane, embarrassing, or slanderous statements), uphold copyright laws, obtain approval before linking to the company website, maintain confidentiality concerning patients and proprietary information about the company, and do not speak as a member of the organization without getting approval to do so. For a copy of Kaiser Permanente's social media manual and others, see *Check It Out!*

CHECK IT OUT! To see the Kaiser Permanente social media policy and approximately 100 others, enter search term Social Media Employee Policy Examples at socialmediatoday.com.

Crisis Management

Time magazine proclaimed it the "Summer of the Shark" in July 2001. One of the lead stories was about Jessie Arbogast, an 8-year-old who was bitten by a 7-foot shark while he waded knee-deep in the Gulf of Mexico. Shark attacks are rare enough to be newsworthy no matter what, but this one was especially spellbinding. While the shark still had the boy's arm in its jaws, Jessie's uncle and another man grabbed the enormous animal by the tail and prevented it from dragging Jessie into deeper water. They were able to save the boy, but not his arm, which was severed by the shark's teeth. Remarkably, the men managed to wrestle the 200-pound shark onto the beach while others carried Jessie to shore. Then, after medics loaded the boy onto an airmed helicopter, a park ranger and a lifeguard/firefighter recovered the boy's arm from the shark's mouth and sent it to the hospital via an ambulance. Jessie Arbogast suffered massive injuries and brain damage, but he lived, and surgeons were able to reattach his arm during a 12-hour surgery. (For more on this story, see Roche, 2001.)

The remarkable story was covered by media outlets around the world, including CNN, ABC, NBC, CBS, and Fox News. Kendrick Doidge remembers because they were camped out in his parking lot. Soon after the shark attack occurred, Arbogast was a patient at Sacred Heart Hospital in Pensacola, where Doidge was marketing and public relations coordinator. "I received over 300 calls in 24 hours," he remembers. "As soon as Jessie Arbogast was transferred to our hospital, the parking lot filled with media live-remote trucks."

One of the crucial components of crisis management, says Doidge, is communicating well with everyone involved. After quickly securing permission to have the media trucks move to a shopping mall across the street so patients and their families would not be inconvenienced, Doidge and a diverse team of hospital personnel convened to put their crisis management plan into action.

"You have the most thorough crisis management plan you can, but every crisis is different," he says. "We got everyone together to organize how we would handle this one." During that meeting someone made a comment that set the tenor for the entire experience. Doidge explains:

> The thing about a crisis is that it gets a lot of attention, but you still have other responsibilities you can't neglect. At that first meeting, someone said, "We're going to give Jessie Arbogast the best care possible. But we have 30 other children in that same unit. We can't lose sight of that either."

From that point on, says Doidge, everyone thought in those terms.

> When the makers of Snicker Bars asked to send Snicker Bars to Jessie because they heard that was his favorite candy, we said, "Only if you send enough for all the kids on that unit." They did. The governor of Florida and the governor of Alabama wanted to come visit Jessie in the hospital. We said, "Okay, if you visit with *all* the patients and all their families." And they did. When we had press conferences, we stressed to people, "This is a team effort. This is what we do. We're doing everything possible for Jessie Arbogast, the same as we do for every child in our care."

A cool head has earned Doidge accolades in crisis management. "I've learned you take your time, you listen to people, and you do the right thing," he says. "I'm a parent, and I know if my child were in the hospital, I wouldn't want to think that anything distracted the staff from providing the best care possible. That's what it comes down to, even in a crisis."

By their very nature, health organizations are likely to be part of crises. As Kathleen Fearn-Banks (1996) defines it, from an organizational perspective, a **crisis** is "a major occurrence with a potentially negative outcome affecting an organization, company, or industry, as well as its publics, products, services, or good name" (p. 1). In health care, the crisis usually has an external origin: a natural disaster, an accident, or an outbreak of contagious disease. In such cases, health care organizations (especially hospitals and health departments) may be called on to explain the crisis and to keep the public informed about it. In some cases, the crisis originates within the organization—a fire, a baby kidnapped from the nursery, charges of extortion. In any case, it's important to have a well-developed plan for handling crises, collecting information, and making information available to members of the organization, the media, and the public.

In Chapter 12 we will talk extensively about handling public health crises, and many of the same principles apply, so we will keep this overview brief. But it's worth mentioning that crises have implications not just for the public. There's an organizational component as well. Crisis management is a job for communication specialists, especially those in public relations. Here are some helpful tips for preparing a crisis plan and managing publicity during a crisis, based on Fearn-Banks' (1996) book *Crisis Communication.*

- Let people within the organization know what constitutes a crisis and whom to contact at the first sign of crisis.
- Designate a primary spokesperson for the organization (usually the CEO or public relations director), and help that person decide what information to release and how.
- Develop good relationships with media professionals before a crisis occurs, and don't play favorites during a crisis.
- Educate people in the organization about how to handle a crisis and how to get information.
- Keep up-to-date contact information for designated spokespersons, media professionals, stakeholders, and emergency management professionals.
- Maintain supplies that will be necessary if electricity or Web access is unavailable.
- Plan ahead how you will accommodate members of the media on site.

As you can see, none of the strategies outlined in this chapter occurs in isolation. Public relations specialists usually head crisis management teams, but they are the first to admit that outstanding team members make it possible to offer excellent service on an everyday basis and in extraordinary times. Leaders, human resource personnel, and others make that possible. Let's conclude the chapter with advice from service excellence.

Service Excellence is Everyone's Job

Many of the ideas in this chapter are oriented to service excellence. Based on decades of experience conducting patient satisfaction surveys, Press (2002) presents five reasons to focus on patient satisfaction:

1. High satisfaction is linked to patient cooperation with treatment protocols, even when they are frightening or uncomfortable.
2. Satisfied patients experience less stress than others.
3. Highly satisfied patients actually *feel* better than others and recover more quickly.
4. Patients who have positive experiences become "apostles" for the organization, promoting it to others.
5. There is a high correlation between satisfied patients and satisfied employees.

All of these add up to competitive strength and bottom-line gains. As much as 30% of profits are based on patient satisfaction (Press, 2002). And there's another reason not to be overlooked. In their book *Leadership for Great Customer Service,* Mayer and Cates (2004) suggest:

6. The number-one reason "to get customer service right in health care is . . . it makes the job easier" (p. 5).

Mayer and Cates observe that team members *like* coming to work when they feel they are making a difference rather than swimming upstream, when they enjoy the work they do and are able to have creative input, and when they feel valued and supported by coworkers and supervisors. Here are some tips from the experts on building cultures that sustain these ideals. You will see that much of the emphasis is on employee satisfaction. As many have observed, it's unlikely that dissatisfied employees will lead to happy customers, but happy employees will go far beyond the job description to do a good job.

Blow their minds. Doing the job right isn't enough. People expect that. Inspiring customer loyalty requires giving people *more* than they expect. Mayer and Cates (2004) put it this way:

> How much credit do we give airlines for getting us from point A to point B and not killing us? How about *none*—we expect that. Your patients expect excellent clinical care (the destination). But they also expect excellence service (the journey). (p. 26)

The team at the Nordstrom department store calls it "fabled service"—the kind that people tell their friends about for years to come. By most estimates, customers who indicate they are "satisfied" (4 on a 5-point scale) may or may not come back to the organization. People *expect* to be satisfied. Only those who rate themselves "very satisfied" (5 on a 5-point scale) are likely to be loyal customers. Some organizations miss this distinction when they combine scores and conclude that, say, "95% of our customers are satisfied or very satisfied." Cognizant of the immense difference between "satisfied" and "very satisfied," for example, Disney considers anything less than a 5 to be a failing score (Lee, 2004).

Recognize and create moments of truth. Jan Carlzon, the highly successful CEO of Scandinavian Airlines, titled his 1987 memoir *Moments of Truth.* In the book Carlzon advances the idea that satisfaction and loyalty are made or broken during 50,000 moments of truth every day. These occur any time people develop an impression of the organization based on how they are treated. The Mayo Clinic staff encountered a moment of truth when a woman seeking care in the emergency department declined to be admitted although she was quite ill. In encouraging her to share her concerns, the staff learned that she was from out of town and had left her dog in her truck, parked in the hospital lot. The staff might have discharged her as she requested. Instead, a nurse volunteered to take care of the woman's truck and her dog. The nurse wasn't even dissuaded when he realized the truck was an 18-wheeler. He got permission to park the truck at

a local shopping mall for a few days and recruited a fellow nurse with a commercial license and truck-driving experience to move it there. Then the nurse looked after the woman's dog until she was well enough to leave the hospital.

Use service failures as a springboard. A few years ago I conducted a series of service-excellence workshops for the staff of a large hospital. Over several days' time, as each new group of participants came through, I asked them to think of times they had received excellent customer service. Their answers were inspiring.

One woman ordered a dress from a department store to attend her niece's wedding out of town. First, the store's tailor made a mistake with the alterations. Then the dress wasn't ready when it was promised. Eventually, it was the day before she was to fly out for the wedding and the woman still didn't have her dress. She was frustrated and ready to buy something off the rack at another store and never do business with the original store again. But then a gracious sales associate called her to apologize and say that she would personally drive to the tailor's, retrieve the dress, and deliver it to the woman's home that evening. The associate arrived on her doorstep with the dress as promised, and the woman was so touched by her apologies and extra effort that she has been a loyal customer ever since.

Another workshop participant said she bought a new car, but two days later it died on her way to work. Frustrated and fearing that she had just invested in a lemon, the woman called the dealership. An associate answered immediately, apologized, and said he would be there (on the roadside where she was stranded) in 10 minutes. To her astonishment, he arrived even sooner, handed her the keys to a new loaner car, and encouraged her to be on her way. He waited for the tow truck, had the woman's car fixed (a minor adjustment to the computer), and delivered it to her driveway a few days later. She proclaims herself a lifelong customer.

As I listened to these stories and many more like them, it occurred to me that they were service-recovery stories. Things certainly did not go perfectly. Indeed, in nearly every instance the customer was ready to walk away forever—frustrated and inclined to tell everyone he or she knew about the poor treatment. But in each case, an associate (who was often not to blame for the service failure) turned the situation around by apologizing and giving far-better-than-expected service. The moral is that service recovery is often an opportunity to turn a customer into a loyal fan.

Mayer and Cates (2004) offer the following tips for service recovery:

- Address the issue immediately. Denying or ignoring a complaint is the worst thing you can do.
- Listen without interrupting, acknowledge the problem or mistake, and apologize for it.
- Ask for another chance to get it right.
- Ask how you can fix the problem, and tell the customer what to expect next.
- Fix it—and then some!
- Follow up, and let the person know what you have done to ensure that such mistakes don't happen in the future.

Tell stories and honor heroes. Stories such as the ones in this chapter become guiding principles for others. They portray what is best and most noble in the things we do. One of the most effective ways to support a culture is to encourage its stories. Good leaders appreciate their value and share them often. Here's one more, from Lafayette General Hospital, where I used to work. While I was there, this true story was told every Christmas, in departments all across the hospital:

An ambulance arrived late in the evening on Christmas Eve with a woman and her two young children, who had been involved in an automobile accident. The children were okay, but the woman died soon after arriving at the hospital. Her husband was working on an offshore oil rig, and police were unable to reach him. The emergency department staff was devastated for these two children who had just lost their mother and were stranded in a hospital with no family on Christmas Eve. The nurses, doctors, and unit receptionist tried to comfort and entertain the children as best they could until their shift change. The stores were closed, so they took turns driving to their homes to get supplies and gifts to create a makeshift holiday for the children. Sacrificing time they might have spent relaxing with their own families, the nurses worked into the night so that, when the children awoke on Christmas morning, the room was decorated with a tree surrounded by presents. Many staff members had brought their families to the hospital to share Christmas morning with the children. "The employees' kids were amazing," remembers one nurse. "Here they were, in a hospital on Christmas morning, watching children they didn't know open gifts that had been under *their* trees with *their* names on them the day before. And they were just so happy to share. There wasn't a dry eye in the place, I can tell you!"

Summary

Health care administrators play a key role in monitoring market conditions, uniting diverse people toward a common mission, and enabling team members to do their best. Well-designed systems can also reduce stress and minimize errors. Processes such as Six Sigma are designed to analyze workplace procedures carefully so that people can avoid wasting time and money. True empowerment means that administrators are servant leaders who are open to the ideas and concerns of team members who are encouraged to be decisive and accountable. In many health care organizations, employees are increasingly encouraged to think of ways to please customers, solve problems, work together in teams, and come up with innovative methods to improve care and conserve resources.

There is a strong incentive for people in health care organizations to create appealing work environments and to retain and develop the talent they have. Human resource personnel play an important role by helping to recruit, train, support, and retain outstanding team members. Informed by evidence that people perform best when they are actively engaged, human resource personnel can help people develop the skills and confidence to participate in decision making and leadership. To navigate the challenges ahead and offset staffing shortages, we must help health care professionals do their jobs without burning out. This means giving them the freedom to create pleasant work environments that foster teamwork and relieve stress, resisting the temptation to overwork staff members, and providing frequent breaks and replenishment.

With health care dollars limited and competition steep, people in health organizations have an incentive to anticipate as accurately as possible what health services people are likely to need and to tailor their services accordingly. Marketing and public relations professionals can help with this. They work to build trusting relationships with internal and external stakeholders to promote business, encourage healthy habits, and attract loyal patients and benefactors. Social media is emerging as a tool in the effort to maintain relationships, promote key services, educate people, and manage crisis communication.

Public relations professionals are often in charge of creating crisis communication plans on which they rely during natural disasters, image-threatening events, high-profile events, health scares, and other situations that put health care organizations in the limelight. Handling crises well requires communication skills, preparation, a commitment to key values, and a willingness to handle unexpected demands.

Finally, excellence is everyone's job. People throughout health care organizations are called upon to offer legendary service, recognize moments of truth, overcome service obstacles, and honor the noble spirit of helping other people.

Key Terms and Theories

integrated health systems
Six Sigma
workarounds
Hoy-Tarter Model of Shared Decision Making
theory of personal causation
pawns
origins
Theory X and Theory Y managers
motivation-hygiene theory
motivators
hygiene factors
A-team and B-team players
commitment-trust theory of relationships
two-way symmetrical communication
corporate identity, image, and reputation
Point-A-to-Point-B companies
superficially image-based companies
reputation-based companies
crisis

Discussion Questions

1. What is involved in a Six Sigma analysis?
2. What are some techniques suggested for visionary and dispersed leadership?
3. What functions do human resource personnel fulfill in health care?
4. Describe the factors that have contributed to staffing shortages in health care.
5. Describe the significance of pawns and origins in de Charms's theory of personal causation. Give an example from your own experience in which you felt like a pawn and an example in which you were treated as an origin.
6. You have been promoted to supervisor. If you adopt a Theory X approach, how will you treat team members? How will you treat them if you adopt a Theory Y approach? Which do you think will be more effective? Why?
7. You don't make a lot of money, but you feel good every evening thinking about the lives you changed as a result of the work you do. Describe these factors based on motivation-hygiene theory.
8. Describe at least four communication strategies involved in building great teams.
9. What are the qualities exhibited by innovative leaders in Davenport and colleagues' (2003) study (Box 10.5)?
10. In health care, how are marketing and public relations similar? How are they different?
11. In your opinion, should physicians advertise? If not, why not? If so, should their ads adhere to particular regulations or ethical guidelines?
12. Explain the concept of relationship marketing and relationship management. What are some of the main ideas that support a relationship approach to marketing and public relations? Include a description of the commitment-trust theory of relationships and two-way symmetrical communication in your answer.
13. What is the "lesson of the bagels?" Have you ever had a similar experience? If so, what happened?
14. Describe at least three strategies for successful health care marketing and public relations.
15. What are the differences between identity, image, and reputation? How do these concepts characterize Point-A-to-Point-B companies, superficially image-based companies, and reputation-based companies?
16. Describe at least six tips for using social media effectively in health care public relations.
17. How did Kendrick Doidge and the rest of the crisis management team respond when the hospital was besieged with media attention after a

shark-attack patient was admitted? Do you agree with the way they handled the situation? Why or why not?

18. What are some suggestions for improving service excellence? Which are your favorites among the ones listed in this chapter?

19. Describe at least five reasons to focus on patient satisfaction and four techniques for providing outstanding service.

Answers to *Can You Guess?*

PART 1

1. There are about 303,000 health care administrators in the United States.

2. They make an average of $84,270 per year ($40.52 per hour).

3. Employment prospects are expected to increase 22% between 2010 and 2020.

Source: U.S. Department of Labor, 2012

PART 2

The notice about hospital closures appeared in 1947, soon after the end of World War II ("Hospitals in the Red"). It doesn't make current challenges any less real, but sometimes it's nice to know we're not the first to face such a crisis, isn't it?

PART VI

Media, Public Policy, and Health Promotion

How wonderful it is that nobody need wait a single moment before starting to improve the world.

—ANNE FRANK

In this section we look at people and events that change the world. We explore the role of mass media in shaping cultural and global ideas about what it means to be healthy and successful. We will also look at the efforts of public health experts and consider how we might apply the lessons from AIDS, SARS, and terrorism to our own efforts. We will follow the process of health care reform in the United States, including passage of the Patient Protection and Affordable Care Act (sometimes called Obamacare), and what it might mean for health communication at every level. In the final two chapters, we will use theory and expert advice to create a hypothetical public health campaign.

As you end this unit, I hope you'll feel that your understanding of health communication has deepened and broadened. Keep an eye on the news. Health care is ever changing, and perhaps with the insights and examples we have discussed, you can take an active role yourself in shaping the future of health and health communication.

CHAPTER ELEVEN

Health Images in the Media

DO WHAT HUBBY TELLS YOU?

When a group of British researchers found that submissive women were slightly less likely to have heart attacks than other women, they prepared a media release they felt was accurate, interesting, and readable. Many media organizations ran the release or suitable portions of it. However, others misconstrued the study to mean that women should return to being housewives. Headlines about the study admonished, "Put Down That Rolling Pin Darling, It's Bad For Your Heart" and "Do What Hubby Says and You'll Live Longer. Professor's Shock Advice to Women." The researchers were discouraged by journalists' handling of the story, calling the supposed link between submissiveness and housewifery "bewildering" (Deary, Whiteman, & Fowkes, 1998).

The researchers in this example report that they learned a valuable lesson: Where health is concerned, the mass media is both friend and foe. The publicity helped the scientists share valuable knowledge and promote their work. However, inaccuracies and exaggerations made them wonder if some of the stories did more harm than good.

In this chapter we examine health's presence in mass communication. **Mass communication** is the dissemination of messages from one person (or one group of persons) to large numbers of people via media, including television, radio, computers, newspapers, magazines, billboards, video games, and other means of sharing information with large audiences (Biagi, 1999). As you will see, there is evidence that media messages encourage people to overeat, doubt their attractiveness, drink alcohol, smoke, and neglect physical activity. However, mass communication is also irreplaceable for getting health information to large numbers of people. Such information may enable them to better understand their own health and experience more control over their lives.

As we explore the ways that mass media messages shape our ideas about health, we will begin with health images in advertising, news, and entertainment. As you will see, research often shows a link between media use and various behaviors, such as overeating and drinking. Remember that this doesn't prove that the media, or the media alone, *cause* these behaviors. Mass-mediated messages are only one of many influences on health. Their effects are likely to be lessened or exaggerated by a range of other factors, including personal preferences, culture, social networks, and health status. The chapter concludes with information about <u>media literacy</u>—a systematic process of becoming more skeptical and more informed mass-media consumers so we don't unwittingly buy into harmful and unrealistic ideas.

Most of us feel that we're not personally susceptible to persuasive messages in the media, but we think other people are. W. Phillips Davison (1983) coined the term **third-person effect** to describe this perception. For example, teens often believe their peers will be more likely to smoke if they see pro-smoking messages in the media, but they tend to feel immune from media effects themselves (Gunther, Bolt, Borzekowski, Liebhart, & Dillard, 2006). Here's a look at some theories behind media effects, following by some examples of the health-related messages we encounter every day.

Theoretical Foundations

In a video about sexist images in advertising, *Killing Us Softly 3*, Jean Kilbourne (2000) observes that people frequently tell her they are not affected by the media. "Of course, they are usually standing there in their Gap t-shirt while they say this," she laughs.

In reality, we are all affected by the media to varying extents, and the impact is greatest if we spend a lot of time with media and have limited personal experience with the phenomena we see depicted. The two theories described here—cultivation theory and social comparison theory—consider how media messages influence our attitudes and expectations about the world. Before we look at them, let's review the figures on media use among children and teens today.

What used to be considered heavy media use is now the norm. According to an extensive study by the Henry J. Kaiser Family Foundation (2010), U.S. children ages 8 to 18 spend slightly more than 7½ hours a day (about 2,786 hours a year) engaged with

CAN YOU GUESS? Part 1

1. What percentage of U.S. youth ages 8 to 18 have a mobile phone?

2. How long, on average, do 8- to 18-year-olds spend using their phones every day?

3. How long do they spend talking on their phones versus performing other activities on them?

Answers appear at the end of the chapter.

WHAT DO YOU THINK?

■ How much time, per day, do you spend watching television? Playing video games? Texting? Talking on the phone? Listening to music? Reading books, magazines, or newspapers?

■ Are you influenced by media messages? If so, how?

■ Do you assume that other people are influenced by media messages? Why or why not?

entertainment media devices such as smart phones, MP3 players, computer tablets, and television—sometimes several of them at once. The average is lower (about 4½ hours per day) among children whose parents have set time limits on media use, but only about 30% of youth fall into that category. And the average is much higher (about 13 hours a day) among heavy users, who tend to make poor grades, experience more sadness, and get into more trouble than their peers. (See Figure 11.1.) Black and Hispanic children tend to fall disproportionately in the range of heavy media use, especially TV watching.

Cultivation theory helps to explain why children may be especially vulnerable to advertising messages. According to the theory, people develop beliefs about the world based on a complex array of influences, including the media. Media's influence is not uniform or automatic, but it is likely to be most profound if (a) media images are highly consistent, (b) people are exposed to large amounts of media, and (c) these people have a limited basis for evaluating what they see and hear (Gerbner, Gross, Morgan, & Signorielli, 1994). To clarify, consider that children have fewer experiences and less knowledge than adults. Because of this, they're less

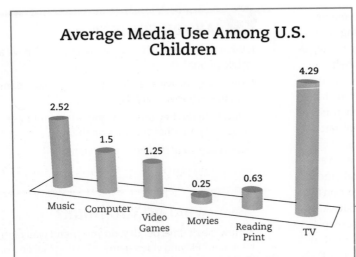

FIGURE 11.1 On average, children in the United States spend about 7½ hours a day using entertainment media and about 38 minutes a day reading books, magazines, and newspapers. Daily media use is higher (about 13 hours a day) among 1 in 5 children. Children are engaged with more than one medium 29% of the time (thus the total here exceeds 7½ hours).

Source: Henry J. Kaiser Family Foundation, 2010

able to perceive that media images may be wrong or unrealistic. The same principle would hold true if you watched a documentary about a faraway land about which you knew very little. People familiar with that land might see inaccuracies in the documentary that you would be unable to identify.

The effect is compounded among high media users because not only is their exposure high, but the more time they spend tuned into mass media, the less opportunity they have to experience activities that might provide a basis for comparison. Researchers in Thailand found that children who watched TV more than their peers were more likely to think that television portrayals were realistic and to want to be part of TV families (Jantarakolica, Komolsevin, & Speece, 2002).

Social comparison theory helps to explain why people yearn to emulate the models they see in the media. Proposed by Leon Festinger (1957), **social comparison theory** suggests that people judge themselves largely in comparison to others. Want to know if you are attractive, popular, healthy, or smart? The only answer may lie in how you stack

up to the people around you. Social comparisons can be useful when they enhance self-esteem or serve as the basis for reasonable self-improvement. However, they become dysfunctional when the comparison establishes an unrealistic standard (like being supermodel thin or weight-lifter strong).

Next, let's look at deliberate attempts to influence people's behavior through advertisements for health-related products.

Advertising

Direct-to-Consumer Advertising

This product may cause headaches, drowsiness, stomach upset, liver problems, heartbeat irregularities . . .

In 1985, the U.S. Food and Drug Administration (FDA) ruled that pharmaceutical companies could advertise product categories to the public. But the most dramatic change came later, in 1997, when the FDA relaxed the rules even more to make the United States one of only two countries (the other is New Zealand) to allow brand-name prescription drug advertising. Selling prescription drugs in public venues such as the mass media is called **direct-to-consumer** (**DTC**) advertising, as compared to *physician marketing*, in which drugs are marketed to doctors, who, in turn, make patients aware of them as they perceive a need to do so.

Since 1997, names such as Claritin, Lipitor, and Viagra have become as familiar as Coca-Cola and Tide. And along with the ads have come a now-familiar list of disclaimers—so familiar that one guest on an online medical site asked the doctor: "Do *all* prescription drugs cause diarrhea and dry mouth?" These *are* common side effects, but you hear about them so much because of a rather nebulous FDA guideline known as "fair balance," which states that, if advertisers present the potential benefits of a drug, they must also report potentially harmful side effects. In the name of fairness (sort of), for every promise of relief you're likely to hear a list of disagreeable outcomes you might also experience. The "sort of" means that the guideline is only loosely and rather lopsidedly upheld. For quick evidence of this, compare the lengthy information in a magazine pharmaceutical ad to the brief disclaimer you hear on a TV or radio commercial for the same drug.

The "fair balance" guideline also explains why some prescription drug ads make no claims at all. The announcer might just say, "Ask your doctor about Zertec." Based on FDA guidelines, an ad that doesn't make a *positive* claim doesn't have to provide cautionary information either. In the case of no-claim ads, sponsors apparently believe that you will recognize the drug and its purpose by name, that the disclaimers, if mentioned, would scare you away, or that you'll be curious enough to ask about or research the drug.

ADVANTAGES OF DTC ADVERTISING

From one standpoint, advertisements for needed products are beneficial. Without them, consumers might not know that treatment options exist for indigestion, asthma, allergies, depression, restless legs, and the like (Beltramini, 2010).

It's hard to say how many people actually ask their doctors and pharmacists about advertised drugs. Soontae An (2007) found that people are mostly likely to bring up advertised medicines when they consider themselves to be knowledgeable about health matters. This may be a small percentage of the public. In one U.S. study, only 1 in 10 people reported making drug-specific requests at the doctor's office (DeLorne, Huh, & Reid, 2006). And patient surveys in New Zealand yield similarly low numbers (Dens, Eagle, & De Pelsmacker, 2008). But doctors tend to report a higher frequency of requests. In a *Consumer Reports* study of American physicians, 78% said patients occasionally ask them for drugs they have seen advertised on TV ("Finally," 2007).

The discrepancy in numbers may arise because doctors perceive implied requests even when patients don't ask for advertised drugs outright. As you might expect, people in fair or poor health are more likely to ask about specific drugs than people in good or excellent health (A. Lee, 2009). However, this doesn't apply to people over age 75. Although they tend to see health care providers more frequently than others and have more

WHAT DO YOU THINK?

■ Researchers have found that some people suffer low self-esteem because they regularly compare themselves to unrealistic standards such as supermodels or bodybuilders. Do you find yourself doing that? Why or why not?

■ If you are around children, what reactions do you observe as they are exposed to messages in the media?

■ How do you think we can minimize the effects of media images that establish unrealistic standards of attractiveness?

IN YOUR EXPERIENCE

■ Have you ever become interested in a drug because you saw it advertised? If so, why?

■ Have you done research or asked your doctor or pharmacist about a particular drug? Why or why not?

chronic health concerns, people in that age group are less inclined than younger patients to make requests of their doctors, probably because they consider it inappropriate or disrespectful (A. Lee, 2009).

People who do ask health professionals about specific drugs most often talk to their doctors (43% of the time) and to pharmacists (25%), and less often to nurses and other physicians (A. Lee,

2010). Although people consult pharmacists less frequently, they tend to put more stock in their opinions, even to the extent of switching doctors if they are unreceptive to pharmacists' advice (A. Lee, 2010). Lee observed that there are multiple opinion leaders when it comes to selecting prescription drugs.

Another advantage of DTC advertising is that active competition can inspire product development. We presumably benefit when drug companies strive to offer the most appealing and useful products. For example, high interest in cholesterol-reducing drugs spurred research and development efforts in the 1990s (Calfee, 2002). By targeting people at moderate risk for heart attacks, drug companies expanded their markets and motivated consumers to visit their doctors for preventive treatment before their conditions worsened. Marketplace stimulation has not lived up to its full potential, however. A substantial number of "new" drugs are actually what Marcia Angell (2004) calls "me too" drugs—close copycats of already existing products.

DISADVANTAGES OF DTC ADVERTISING

Although health information is beneficial within limits, it also has drawbacks. For one, expensive advertising drives up the price of health products. Americans spent $320 billion a year on prescription drugs in 2011 (Johnson, 2012). Prescription drug prices rose 26% between 2005 and 2009 for the brand-name drugs used the most by older Americans (Thomas, 2012). That's double the average price hike on consumer goods during that time. Part of the price goes to marketing. Pharmaceutical companies spend about $58 billion a year to sell their products (Fiore, 2011). Especially worrisome is that pharmaceutical companies pay physicians more than $761 million per year in consulting fees, speaking honoraria, research fees, and other expenses. Whereas some of the expenses are justified, the amounts are often exorbitant, and analysts feel that, in many cases, the money is an incentive for doctors to prescribe more of the drugs the company sells (Ngyuen, Ornstein, & Weber, 2011). The $761 million figure reflects only the amount that a dozen or so companies have voluntarily disclosed so far. Based on new legislation, all drug companies must make public the amount they pay doctors, so

---

BOX 11.1 ETHICAL CONSIDERATIONS

Do More, Feel Better . . . Make More Money?

The slogan of GlaxoSmithKline pharmaceutical company is "do more, feel better, live longer." But in 2012, the company agreed on the largest health care fraud settlement in history, volunteering to pay $3 billion in response to charges that it promoted the use of Paxil for teenagers, even though the drug has been shown to increase suicidal tendencies in teens, and promoted Wellbutrin as a weight-loss drug and remedy for sexual dysfunction, although the drug is only approved to treat severe depression. The company was also accused of squelching medical evidence about its products.

---

we're likely to see the reported dollar amounts rise. "Hundreds of thousands of doctors receive money, meals and educational items," say Charles Ornstein and Tracy Weber, who have been researching the issue for ProPublica, a nonprofit agency that investigates issues of public interest (Allen, 2012, para. 5).

Second, health professionals worry that—based on the dazzling scenarios in prescription-drug commercials—people may believe that high-priced designer drugs are better than others and that drugs will not only cure anything that ails them, but will yield increased happiness and excitement as well. Consider a few examples from Rebecca Cline and Henry Young's (2004) content analysis of pharmaceutical ads:

- 93% of the models in arthritis drug ads were shown engaging in physical activity,
- 100% of the models in ads for HIV treatments appeared healthy, and
- 85.7% of models in cancer-related ads appeared healthy.

"The message is obvious," the researchers conclude. "With treatment by prescription drugs, the consumer with the associated condition can be attractively healthy looking and lively" (Cline & Young, 2004, p. 151). As a result of such unrealistic expectations, consumers may squander money on unnecessary medications, seek prescriptions for the wrong reasons, feel disappointed when their doctors don't prescribe the drugs they see in the media, and feel let down when the results are less dramatic than advertisers have led them to believe.

Concerns about DTC advertising have intensified as advertisers have become bolder, promoting not only drugs but devices used in complex medical procedures. For example, when the makers of a stent involved in coronary angioplasty launched their "Life Wide Open" advertising series, the ads show models enjoying a range of sporting and outdoor activities, presumably after having their clogged arteries cleared by angioplasty. However, there is little mention of how dangerous angioplasty actually is. And critics worry that ads promising "quick and easy" cures will dissuade people from taking care of themselves in the first place. The authors of an article in the *New England Journal of Medicine* wrote:

> A specialized medical device such as a stent can be selected and implanted only by someone with a very sophisticated medical understanding that no member of the lay public could realistically expect to gain from a DTCA campaign. (Boden & Diamond, 2008, p. 2197)

Boden and Diamond (both physicians) wonder: Is it responsible to "sell" a specialized and risky medical procedure in a 60-second time slot?

That question becomes even more significant when we consider evidence that drug companies sometimes downplay their products' risks. When Wendy Macias and colleagues studied 106 pharmaceutical TV commercials, they found that 2 violated the FDA's "fair balance" requirement and another 10 were borderline. The rest gave customary, but minimal, amounts of information about potential side effects (Macias, Pashupati, & Lewis, 2007). Even more frightening is evidence that the side effects drug companies report often come from research they have funded and overseen themselves. The FDA requires research evidence that drugs are safe and useful before they are put on the market. The problem is that drug companies now pay for much of this research themselves, and they have an interest in seeing the drugs released as quickly as possible, with as few documented side effects as

? CAN YOU GUESS? Part 2

What celebrity chef (not famous for making healthy dishes) announced that she had been diagnosed with diabetes in 2012 and soon after accepted a multimillion-dollar contract to promote a diabetes drug in Novo Nordisk television commercials?

The answer appears at the end of the chapter.

possible. There are reports of drug company executives firing researchers, refusing to release adverse research findings, denying research funding when methods are not expected to yield the desired results, and so on. Sergio Sismondo (2008) concluded that pharmaceutical companies "not only fund clinical trials but also routinely design and shape them" (para. 5). He reports that drug companies often have their staff statisticians perform data analyses and then hire people to write the research reports and corral them through the publication process.

A tragic example is the Merck Pharmaceutical Vioxx case. After years of denying that its top-selling pain medication (Vioxx) posed significant health risks, Merck officials finally withdrew the drug in 2004. By that time, between 27,000 and 60,000 people had died from the drug's side effects (Lyon, 2007). In studying Merck documents and communiqués, researcher Alexander Lyon found that a pervasive "market mentality" led Merck decision makers to suppress and minimize information about Vioxx's harmful side effects. Lyon recommends that pharmaceutical companies be prohibited from involvement in research about the products they sell.

Third, some experts worry that Americans are developing an unhealthy preoccupation with their own health, based largely on the amount of health care products and information now surrounding them. "We're not exactly a nation of hypochondriacs. But we're close," writes Jennifer Harper (1997, p. 40).

Finally, while some people are overrepresented in DTC images, others are left out of the picture, reinforcing health disparities. For example, although heart disease is the leading cause of death among both men and women, nearly two in three ads show only men (Cline & Young, 2004). And African

American and Hispanic models almost always play minor roles in general-audience DTC advertising, if they are pictured at all (Ball, Liang, & Wei-Na, 2009; Cline & Young, 2004; Mastin, Andsager, Choi, & Lee, 2007).

There are exceptions to the mostly White rule, but you have to look in Black-oriented publications to find most of them. According to Teresa Mastin and colleagues (2007), about 75% of the pharmaceutical ads in Black-oriented magazines feature only Black models. But even these ads present a distorted picture of what African Americans need. For example, there are four times as many heart-care ads in magazines targeted to women in general than in magazines targeted specifically to African American women, although African Americans are at higher risk for heart disease than other groups. And 80% of the ads directed to Black females are for birth control pills, a bias that isn't present in general-readership women's magazines. Mastin and colleagues conclude that direct-to-consumer ads are not educating *all* consumers about health risks and treatment options (Mastin et al., 2007).

COMMUNICATION SKILL BUILDER: EVALUATING MEDICAL CLAIMS

As you've seen, consumers who rely on advertisements for health information don't always (or even often) get a clear picture. Here are some tips for evaluating the claims in medication ads.

- *Don't put too much stock in the wording.* Joel Davis (2007) found that people were most optimistic about drugs when the side effects were presented in language that downplayed their severity, such as "Side effects were mild and might include . . . ," "Side effects tend to be mild and often go away," and "Few people were bothered enough to stop taking the drug." Keep in mind that reassuring word choices don't necessarily mean these drugs are safer than others.
- *Look to print sources for detailed information.* Broadcast commercials mention potential side effects only briefly. Magazine ads include a great deal more information (Boden & Diamond, 2008).
- *"Newer" doesn't necessarily mean better.* Pharmaceutical companies vie for the public's attention by advertising the "newest" and

"latest" therapies. But the rush to the marketplace doesn't actually mean the medication is "improved," or even that it's safe (Lyon, 2007).

Even advertisements that seem unrelated to health care often affect our health by influencing social expectations about how we should behave, what we should eat and drink, and how we should look. The remainder of this section discusses advertising's impact on nutrition, alcohol, and body image.

Nutrition

It's been called the "coach potato physique," characterized by soft bulges where muscle ought to be. Heavy television viewing is consistently linked to obesity, partly because TV offers a triple punch to good nutrition. People usually burn few calories while watching, they have a tendency to snack while viewing, and the commercials usually encourage consumption of non-nutritious foods. In addition, commercials sometimes distort people's knowledge of nutrition and influence their food preferences for the worse. As the researchers in one study concluded, in the content of television commercials, "fruits and vegetables are virtually nonexistent" (Kotz & Story, 1994, para. 11).

OBESITY

The prevalence of TV commercials for fatty and sugary foods may have serious implications for health, considering that overweight people are at elevated risk for heart disease, cancer, diabetes, and sudden death. African American women are at especially high risk for obesity and related concerns. This may be partly because of advertisements. When Linda Godbold Kean and Laura Prividera (2007) compared ads in *Essence* (aimed mostly at female African Americans) and *Cosmopolitan* (targeted to women in general), they found that 13% of the ads in *Essence* were for fast food, compared to 1% of the ads in *Cosmopolitan*. Furthermore, *Cosmopolitan* readers were exposed to more weight-loss products and claims (mentioned in 41% of the ads) than were *Essence* readers (12% of ads). (While these messages may be helpful to *Cosmopolitan* readers trying to maintain a healthy weight, it should also be noted that many of the weight-loss claims—such as those for low-carbohydrate whiskey—were not exactly health conscious.)

The editorial content in magazines is not making up the difference. Articles in general-audience women's magazines such as *Ladies Home Journal* and *Good Housekeeping* offer twice as many recommendations to cut back on fast food as the articles in *Ebony, Essence,* and *Jet* (Campo & Mastin, 2007). The general-audience magazines placed more emphasis on small portions and whole-grain and high-protein foods. In contrast, the African American magazines were more likely to present fad diets and to encourage women to rely on God and religious faith to help them lose weight (Campo & Mastin, 2007).

Another media distortion, in the United States and abroad, is that media messages often cast obesity as a beauty issue rather than a serious health concern. Swedish researcher Helena Sandberg (2007) argues that this trivializes weight's importance and leads people to think that a healthy size is more important for women than for men. Indeed, males are typically less concerned about their weight than women, even though male obesity rates are nearly equivalent to women's ("New CDC Study," 2007). And when overweight men do want to lose a few pounds, the majority do not aim low enough. Researchers report that about 59% of overweight men envisioned an ideal weight for themselves that was still overweight by medical standards (Neighbors & Sobal, 2007).

As the next section shows, weight and nutrition issues begin in childhood.

EFFECTS ON CHILDREN

Since 1988 the incidence of childhood obesity in the United States has doubled among children ages 6 to 11 and has tripled among 12- to 19-year-olds ("Childhood," 2008). These youth are at risk for heart disease, diabetes, sleep apnea, joint problems, and high blood pressure.

Part of the problem is that children are exposed to an average of 5,500 televised food commercials pear year (Desrochers & Holt, 2007), and the commercials often misrepresent what healthy food is all about. For example, no matter how much TV they watched at home, first- through third-graders in Kristin Harrison's (2005) study were

WHAT DO YOU THINK?

■ Do you think fast food ads influence your eating habits?

■ Why do you think women tend to overestimate how much weight they should lose, whereas men tend to underestimate their own need to lose weight?

IN YOUR EXPERIENCE

■ How often do you think about your weight?

■ Do you envision an ideal weight for yourself?

■ How does your ideal compare to medical standards?

roughly equivalent in their nutritional knowledge of products, such as fruit and dairy, that are not heavily advertised. But when Harrison asked the children to choose the more nutritional option between cottage cheese and fat-free ice cream and between orange juice and Diet Coke®, those who watched a lot of television were more likely to consider (incorrectly) that the highly advertised diet products were better for them. The chances are high, Harrison concluded, that children exposed to a lot of commercials will assume that diet products are, by nature, more nutritious than other foods.

When researchers showed preschoolers in the Netherlands fresh banana slices and banana candy, the children preferred the candy. But when they packaged the fresh fruit in packages decorated with the popular cartoon characters SpongeBog SquarePants or Dora the Explorer, the children considered the fruit to be just as appealing as the candy (de Droog, Valkenburg, & Buijzen, 2011). The researchers propose that pairing fruit with images that children already view favorably may increase its appeal.

The distortion continues in the supermarket. A Canadian study of 367 products marketed to children revealed that 89% of them were unhealthy (Elliott, 2007). Fruits and vegetables constituted less than 1% of the products aimed at kids. And beware: 62% of the unhealthy products—despite having high levels of sugar, fat, and sodium—came in packages that touted their "nutritional value."

? CAN YOU GUESS? Part 3

1. Worldwide, how does the number of people who are obese today compare with the number classified as obese in 1980?

2. What percentage of children in the United States are obese today?

Answers appear at the end of the chapter.

ACTIVITY LEVELS

It should be noted that advertising is not entirely to blame for the obesity linked to TV viewing. Some researchers suggest that the sedentary nature of heavy viewing is as unhealthy as the content. Children and teens with televisions in their bedroom are heavier, on average, than their peers, even when they are otherwise physically active (Rey-Lopez et al., 2012). And heavy television viewing may lead to other unhealthy behaviors. For example, youngsters who watch a lot of television are more likely than their peers to smoke (Gidwani, Sobol, DeJong, Perrin, & Gortmaker, 2002). Researchers speculate that extensive viewing substitutes for physical activities and social development that might otherwise help teens avoid peer pressure.

High media use is also linked to sleep deprivation. Children today sleep an average of 2 hours less per night than children in the early 1980s (Zimmerman, 2008). Authorities blame TV, video, the Internet, and computer games. They say these activities sometimes cut into sleep time and leave children too excited to sleep when the lights go out. Children may also feel less sleepy because they aren't getting much exercise and because the glow from TV and computer screens inhibits melatonin secretion, an important chemical in sleep functioning (Zimmerman, 2008).

If media messages influence the way we eat, they're also likely to influence the way we drink and whether we use tobacco. Particularly worrisome are appeals to youthful audiences, as we will discuss next.

Tobacco

In 1994, some 46 states entered an agreement with the tobacco industry that included restrictions on

A Lucky Strike ad in 1935 shows Santa Claus—in full beard, red suit, and pack on his back—smoking a cigarette above the caption "Luckies are easy on my throat." (Copyright Bettmann/Corbis/ AP Images)

the number and placement of tobacco advertisements. The Master Settlement Agreement (MSA), as it is called, bans tobacco advertising in public transit systems, on television, and in the movies, and it severely limits the placement of tobacco billboards near sports stadiums, shopping malls, arcades, and other places that youth frequent. The MSA is meant to restrict tobacco marketing overall, but in particular, to shield youthful audiences from it. Beyond requiring a warning label, the rules don't restrict the content of tobacco ads or packaging, however.

To see how content may have changed since the 2003 settlement, Tae Hyun Baek and Mark Mayer (2010) compared tobacco ads in *Cosmopolitan, Sports Illustrated,* and *Rolling Stone* in 1994 with those that ran nearly 10 years later. The researchers found that the ads have become more sexually suggestive since 1994 and more, rather than less, directed to youthful audiences. Most notably, the ads show an increase in sexually suggestive messages and in the presence of young, scantily clad women. "This use of models, especially women, as sexual objects or decoration in advertisement is not a new phenomenon," the researchers reflect, but it's disappointing, they say, that companies continue to depict smokers as young and sexy.

There is further evidence that tobacco companies have stepped up their implicit marketing efforts since the MSA in 1994. When Hye-Jin Paek and colleagues (2010) studied nearly 50 years of cigarette advertising in U.S. magazines, they identified a trend. Beginning in the 1930s, tobacco companies often touted the "health benefits" of smoking, such as soothing the throat, preventing coughs, and enhancing relaxation. (Yes, they actually claimed that cigarettes *prevent* coughs and throat irritation.) Those false claims ended in the 1950s under pressure from the Federal Trade Commission (FTC). After that, tobacco ads and packages included implicit, rather than outright, claims in favor of smoking. For example, marketers began relying on visual cues suggesting that smokers are popular, attractive, healthy, and relaxed, and that smoking is natural and soothing (associated with pleasant scenes from nature). Paek and collaborators found that pleasing images (such attractive models interacting socially while smoking) are even more prevalent after the MSA than before it (Paek, Reid, Choi, & Jeong, 2010).

Alcohol

Beer commercials often show drinkers surrounded by beautiful women, fun-loving friends, and exotic locales. But the reality isn't nearly so glamorous. Alcohol-related accidents kill 5,000 underage drinkers per year in the United States, and the risk of drinking problems later in life is 5 times greater for people who begin drinking before age 15 than for those who wait until they are 21 ("Underage Drinking," 2012). Heavy drinkers risk liver damage, hypertension, and strokes, and they are more likely than their peers to hurt others (and to be hurt) in accidents and acts of violence (Nestle, 1997). Considering these risks, beer companies are sometimes criticized for portraying drinking episodes as fun and sexy.

Health warnings all but drown in the ocean of pro-alcohol messages. Alcoholic beverage ads outnumber responsible drinking PSAs at least 22 to 1 ("Youth Exposure," 2010). And the alcohol ads are designed to appeal. When market researchers asked teens to name their five favorite Super Bowl commercials, three of them were for beer ("Beer Commercials," 2009). Young people may remember and like these commercials so much because the spots are designed for them. Consider the following:

- Youth ages 21 and younger were exposed to 71% more alcohol advertising in 2009 than were youth of the same age in 2001 ("Youth Exposure," 2010).
- More alcoholic beverage commercials air before 9 p.m.—when you might expect young viewers to be watching—than later in the evening. Additionally, there is a spike in the number of commercials on weekdays from 3 to 5 p.m. Researchers speculate that these commercials are intentionally aimed at schoolchildren since "it would be a reasonable assumption that most people in employment will not have returned home until after 5 p.m." (Alcohol Concern, 2007, p. 13).
- Nearly one-third of radio ads for alcoholic beverages are aired when the listening audience is mostly teens rather than adults ("Youth Exposure," 2011).
- Promotional efforts for alcopops (alcoholic beverages mixed with fruit juice or other flavoring) and wine are broadcast on the radio when teenage girls are most likely to be listening ("Youth Exposure," 2011).
- African American youth see about 42% more ads for distilled spirits than youth in general ("African-American," 2012).

 CAN YOU GUESS? Part 4

1. What percent of 8th graders in the United States have drunk alcohol in the last 30 days?

2. Kids are more likely to see alcohol ads than adults are. How many more ads are they likely to see than their parents in a typical year?

Answers appear at the end of the chapter.

Alcoholic beverage companies buy heavily in magazines aimed at young, minority audiences and employ rappers and youthful-appearing spokespersons designed to catch the attention of young people. Says the director of an alcohol and drug recovery center in San Francisco: "The models they use in the ads have to be 21, but they're the youngest 21-year-olds you'll ever see" (quoted by F. Green, 2003, p. 1C).

This early exposure seems to make a significant difference. Peter Anderson and colleagues (2009) reviewed 13 longitudinal studies about alcohol use. They found that 12 of the 13 studies provided evidence that teens who are regularly exposed to positive messages about drinking (either in movies or advertisements) are more likely than their peers to drink heavily and to start drinking at an early age (Anderson, de Bruijn, Angus, Gordon, & Hastings, 2009). Altogether, the studies involved more than 38,000 youth in Europe and the United States.

The good news is that, despite the odds, responsible drinking messages may have some influence. Itzhak Yanovitzky and Jo Stryker (2001) observed that, over time, binge drinking among youth decreased in the midst of news coverage about its harmful effects. The downturn is not likely to continue, however, unless media professionals keep the dangers of binge drinking on the public agenda.

Body Image

Consumers are repeatedly warned that their skin, weight, hair, breath, clothing, and teeth are "problem areas" requiring vigorous and immediate attention—at a price. Theorists call this **pathologizing the human body**, making natural functions seem weird and unnatural (Wood, 1999). In short, advertisers are accused of making people feel bad about themselves so they will be willing to pay for "needed" changes.

Adolescents are particularly susceptible to these messages. With the physical and social changes of adolescence comes a heightened self-consciousness that makes it easy to escalate (and capitalize on) teens' insecurity. Advertisers often encourage an obsessive concern with physical appearance, sometimes to the detriment of people's health and self-esteem. "Advertisers realize that having your period is the grossest thing in the world, and they want to help," quips Ann Hodgman (1998, p. 38), adding: "As long as Procter & Gamble can scare a teen into thinking that [a boy] can see her bulky maxi through her dress, she'll buy Always. . . . If a teen wasn't obsessing about it before, Tampax wants her to start."

Teens are encouraged to buy (or convince their parents to buy) skin care creams, lotions, powders, perfume, makeup, shaving cream, shampoo, bath oil, mouthwash, toothpaste, and more. Aside from making teens feel unattractive without them, these products can be health risks when they cause rashes, hives, eye irritation, or other reactions.

One problem is that media images are inherently unrealistic. Whether these images are fashion spreads in Singapore and Taiwan that focus mostly on facial beauty, or American images that emphasize sex appeal, clothing, and the body, fashion designers and other advertisers establish alluring but unattainable standards and then rake in profits as people strive to measure up (Frith, Shaw, & Cheng, 2005). For example, researchers calculate that, to attain the proportions of a Barbie doll, a woman would have to be more than 7 feet tall, with a bust 5 inches larger than normal and a waist 6 inches smaller (Duewald, 2003). The same contrast is evident between the average-size woman, who wears a size 12 to 14 ("plus" sizes by fashion-industry standards) and fashion models, who typically wear sizes 0 or 2 (Betts, 2002). Model Coca Rocha remembers fashion moguls' advice when she began modeling at age 15. "They said, 'You need to lose more weight. The look this year is anorexia. We don't want you to be anorexic, but that's what you need to look like'" (quoted by Scott, 2008, para. 12).

After a number of fashion models died from malnutrition, fashion leaders in some countries began to crack down. The Council of Fashion Designers of America has urged designers to inch up the average size of models in their shows. So far, the increase is barely perceptible—models who wear sizes 2 and 4 rather than 0 (Scott, 2008). In bolder efforts, fashion leaders in Spain now deny runway jobs to models with a body mass index below 18 (the recommended range is 18.5 to 25), and fashion leaders in London require models to show doctors' certificates that they are healthy or, if they have eating disorders, that they are being treated for them (Cartner-Morley, 2007).

HEALTH EFFECTS

Unrealistic standards can have serious health consequences. About 90% of American women within a normal weight range wish they were thinner, and more than 50% of underweight women either like their weight or wish they were thinner (Neighbors & Sobal, 2007). Men typically express less dissatisfaction with their bodies, but 20% of men in Neighbors and Sobal's study wanted to gain weight, and 48% wanted to lose.

Although obesity is a serious health threat, extreme efforts to change one's body can be dangerous or even deadly. About 11 million Americans (the majority of them female) suffer from eating disorders, which may damage their hearts and livers, make their bones brittle, and even kill them ("Facts About," 2011). Although eating disorders often start in adolescence, they don't end there. In fact, children are likely to feel that their bodies are inferior partly because their parents are preoccupied about their own weight and appearance (Maynard, 1998). Abusing anabolic steroids to become more muscular is another problem. More than 1 million Americans have abused steroids (National Institute on Drug Abuse [NIDA], 2007). The risks include cardiovascular disease, liver damage, hair loss, sterility, aggressiveness, and depression. Nearly 30% of teenagers in the United States say that illegal steroids are readily available to them (NIDA, 2007), but the profile of the average steroid abuser will probably surprise you. He is 30 years old, Caucasian, highly educated, and well employed, and although not active in sports, he's interested in developing a more muscular appearance (Cohen, Collins, Darkes, & Gwartney, 2007). Researchers observe that, for most steroid users, the goal is to measure up to Western ideals of masculine attractiveness rather than to excel at sports.

ETERNAL HOPE

Why do people keep buying what the media sells? There is evidence that people are hopeful when they

? CAN YOU GUESS? Part 5

1. How many minutes per hour does the typical TV station devote to public service announcements (PSAs)?

2. By the time a person is 65, how much time has he or she probably spent watching television?

Answers appear at the end of the chapter.

see idealized models and are optimistic that they can attain the same look. Philip Myers and Frank Biocca (1992) were surprised when female college students in their study reacted favorably to television programs and commercials featuring slender women. Immediately after viewing these images, most viewers were more elated than depressed, and they tended to consider *themselves* to be thinner than usual. The researchers concluded that media images make idealized body shapes seem attainable, causing an optimism that may later turn to disappointment because it's infeasible for most people to look like that.

Let's turn, now, to a different type of programming that often includes health-related messages.

News Coverage

When a spokesperson announced that America's Health Network would show a live Internet broadcast of a woman giving birth in June 1998, more than 50,000 curious viewers logged on to witness the event (Charski, 1998). Now live births can be viewed most days on cable TV, as can plastic surgeries and a host of other medical procedures. Additionally, health is the topic of special-interest television channels, magazines, books, and radio advice programs. About 1 in 12 stories on local TV news focuses on health (Wang & Gantz, 2010). Americans have access to more health information than ever before, in the form of websites and news, entertainment, and educational programming.

Madge Kaplan, a health news reporter on the public radio program *Marketplace,* states that covering health issues is "a rich, exciting and suspenseful journey" (Kaplan, 2003, para. 4). "My hope is that health care reporting stay closely tied to the central purpose of health care—service to patients. . . . This means we need to do a better job

CHECK IT OUT! Go to healthnewsreview. org to see how experts rate the accuracy of health news in specific TV programs, networks, magazines, and newspapers. You can also access a list of 5-star health stories selected by experts on the basis of their accuracy and usefulness.

illustrating our story subjects' multidimensional character" (para. 13).

The main criticism of health news is that, in the rush to provide the latest information, media professionals sometimes oversell scientific findings and overlook ongoing, everyday concerns. This section examines health news in terms of accuracy and sensationalism and discusses the advantages of media coverage. It concludes with a discussion of interactive technology, which is revolutionizing the way people get health information.

Accuracy and Fairness

Although many media professionals do an admirable job of informing the public about health issues, a sizable number of health stories are misleading and exaggerated. When researchers compared 25 scientific studies to 60 newspaper and magazine articles about them, they found numerous inaccuracies and no stories that they considered to be excellent reflections of the research (Motl, Timpe, & Eichner, 2005). The most common errors occurred when writers overgeneralized the results of medical studies. For instance, a study of older women might be reported simply as a study about women or older adults, although the heath concerns of these populations may be significantly different. Such inaccuracies are particularly troubling since it's often difficult for readers to verify scientific information for themselves.

One worry is that overly optimistic news about medical research will give people false hope. As early as 1997, headlines in major publications suggested an imminent cure for AIDS ("When AIDS Ends" in the *New York Times Magazine* and "The End of AIDS?" in *Newsweek*). Jon Cohen (1997) cautioned: "If treatments don't live up to unrealistic expectations, researchers fear a public backlash against medical science" (para. 2). Premature reports about cures for cancer raise the same fear.

(See *Check It Out!* for more on the accuracy of health news sources.)

Sometimes the concept of "accuracy" is problematic in itself. For example, Raul Reis (2008) reports that Brazilian and U.S. newspapers cover the issue of stem cell research differently. Brazilian papers tend to focus on it as a scientific matter, whereas American journalists more often focus on the ethical implications. Where health is concerned, there are more than two sides to any coin.

Sensationalism

Media professionals are also criticized for favoring sensational health news rather than useful information about everyday concerns. For example, SARS and West Nile virus (characterized in such terms as "mysterious" and "deadly") get far more coverage than heart disease, which is the world's leading cause of death (Berry, Wharf-Higgins, & Naylor, 2007). And reporters forecasting a potential bird flu pandemic rely largely on sensational stories that do not provide enough information for the public to feel prepared and confident if the crisis arises (Dudo, Dahlstrom, & Broussard, 2007). When researchers compared cancer news coverage to actual incidence of cancers, they found that newspapers in the United States overreported information on breast cancer, leukemia, pancreatic cancer, and bone/muscle cancer, especially when someone famous had been diagnosed with them. However, the papers underreported information about male reproductive cancer, lymphatic/Hodgkin's disease, and thyroid cancer (Jensen, Moriarty, Hurley, & Stryker, 2010). Likewise, although HIV and AIDS get a great deal of attention, less than 1% of the stories address their incidence in older adults, which may be one reason that people over age 50 know less about the subject than younger people do and tend to feel particularly shocked and ashamed if they become infected (LaVail, 2010).

In some instances, snappy headlines have little to do with conclusive evidence. In the United States, news coverage (especially TV news coverage) of cancer often highlights potential causes of cancer that have not yet been substantiated, such as dry cleaning chemicals, excessive exercise, and deodorant (Niederdeppe, Fowler, Goldstein, & Pribble, 2010). Partly for that reason, people who rely on TV news coverage a great deal are likely to think that cancer is unavoidable (Niederdeppe et al., 2010).

Advantages of Health News

Despite the criticisms, health news does offer several advantages. Media organizations are credited with increasing people's awareness about health. And even when medical news is not what scientists would wish, its presence keeps health on the public agenda and (they hope) garners support for medical science (Deary et al., 1998). For example, coverage of breast cancer has substantially increased since the 1970s and has focused mostly on new treatment methods and scientific breakthroughs (S. Cho, 2006). That's good, except that some other forms of cancer receive only minimal coverage (T. R. Berry et al., 2007).

It should also be said that news writers are not entirely to blame for misleading health coverage. The fault lies partly with the nature of news and the nature of science. News, especially TV news, is brief. About 74.5% of TV news stories last less than 60 seconds (Wang & Gantz, 2010). Furthermore, it's the nature of news to be unusual and recent (Taubes, 1998). The public is hungry for current and interesting information, and media professionals strive to provide it. However, it's the nature of science to be meticulous and cautious, weighing diverse evidence over long periods of time (Taubes, 1998). Consequently, news writers are at a disadvantage in trying to cover scientific news accurately. The latest groundbreaking study may reach different conclusions from the study before it or after it. Science is full of reliable accounts that, for one reason or another, arrive at different conclusions, so even the experts don't agree (Vardeman & Aldoory, 2008). For example, gastroenterologist Tadataka Yamada (2008) owns up to being in the "Acid Mafia," his humorous term for physicians who initially refused to believe evidence that gastric ulcers are caused by bacteria rather than stress. Finally, to convince the skeptics, one of the medical researchers actually drank a solution containing the bacterium and became ill because of it. Yamada eventually came around, and the medical researchers who discovered the bacteria-ulcer link won a Nobel Prize in 2005. "New ideas should not have to fight so hard for oxygen," Yamada (2008, p. 1324) now preaches. Even so, health news writers trying to report up-to-date information are likely to find themselves with considerable ambiguity on their hands.

Furthermore, reporters may be ill prepared to meet the extraordinary challenges that health

The Dr. Oz Show, featuring physician/professor Mehmet Oz, presents information about a range of health topics, such as weight control, your body's warning signs, cancer, pain management, healthy foods, and more. The syndicated program has won multiple Emmys in the Informative Talk Show category. (AP Photo/Arthur Mola)

coverage presents. Medical terminology and statistical analyses make medical science difficult to understand and interpret, and comparatively few reporters are trained to do so. On the bright side, with many sources of health news available, the chances are greater that people can evaluate and compare information, judging for themselves what is credible and useful (Eng et al., 1998).

Communication Skill Builder: Presenting Health News

Here are some suggestions offered by Melissa Ludtke and Cathy Trost (1998) to help media news writers present fair coverage.

- *Favor the factual over the sensational and trendy.*
- *Don't allow ongoing issues to fade from coverage.* "Put a fresh face on coverage of long-standing health issues like asthma, lead poisoning and infant mortality" (para. 20).
- *Never rely on just one source.* Consult a number of experts; read a variety of reliable literature.
- *Set the record straight.* If a health news item is revealed to be untrue or misleading, update the public.

Also see Box 11.2 for career opportunities in health journalism.

BOX 11.2 CAREER OPPORTUNITIES

Health Journalism

Print or broadcast health news reporter
Health news editor
Media relations specialist
Nonprofit organization publicity manager
Health publication editor
Journal or magazine editor

CAREER RESOURCES AND JOB LISTINGS

- Association of Health Care Journalists: www.healthjournalism.org/prof-dev-jobs.php
- Association for Education in Journalism and Mass Communication (includes job listings): aejmc.org
- Broadcast Education Association (includes job listings): www.beaweb.org
- Foundation for American Communications: www.facsnet.org
- Henry J. Kaiser Media Fellowships for Health: kff.org/mediafellows/index.cfm
- National Association of Broadcasters (includes job listings): www.nab.org
- National Press Foundation: www.nationalpress.org
- U.S. Department of Labor Occupational Outlook for News Analysts, Reporters, and Correspondents: www.bls.gov/oco/ocos088.htm

---

Entertainment

Medical settings have long been popular in entertainment programs. Shows such as *Marcus Welby* and *General Hospital* were forerunners of today's medical dramas. In this section we will examine how medical care and health issues are portrayed in entertainment programming. As Webb and colleagues (2007) point out, "in today's media-saturated world, education has become indistinguishable from entertainment and . . . popular films have an impact on beliefs, behaviors, attitudes, and knowledge" (p. e1226). Even programs designed entirely to entertain can have important implications for health.

Portrayals of Health-Related Behaviors

The mad scientists cackles as he prepares his next victim. The music rises, the lights dim . . .

Characterizations like this are fun, but they are also suggestive. People base their perceptions of mental illness and other health concerns partly on fictional portrayals, whether they're realistic or not.

MENTAL ILLNESS AND DEMENTIA

One media distortion is the traditional portrayal of mentally ill persons as violent and dangerous. That characterization has never reflected reality. For one thing, only about 2% of actual hospital patients in the United States have mental illnesses, compared to 8.5% of the patients in TV medical dramas (Hetsroni, 2009). For another, only about 11% of people with mental illnesses are violent, which is roughly equal to the proportion of violent people in the overall population. James Willwerth (1993) attests: "In reality, most mentally ill patients are withdrawn, frightened and passive" (para. 6).

The incidence of violence among characters with mental illness has decreased in recent years. And for better or worse, some forms of mental illness have become popular topics in entertainment programming. One example is *Monk*, a USA Network program about a quirky, brilliant detective with obsessive-compulsive disorder. During its 7 years on the air, the series and cast won numerous awards, including six Emmys and a Golden Globe, and it was honored by the U.S. Substance Abuse and

Mental Health Services Administration (SAMHSA) and the Anxiety Disorders Association of America. In the show, Monk is fond of saying that his obsessive attention to detail is "a blessing—and a curse." In some ways, it makes him extraordinarily good at what he does. In other ways, it limits and frightens him. A viewer poll on the *Monk* website asked guests to vote for Monk's weirdest phobia from a list that included puppets, slime, driving, milk, monkeys, and more. However eccentric, such generally likable media portrayals make a difference, according to SAMHSA administrator Charles G Curie. "The entertainment industry is a powerful vehicle for helping shape public opinion," says Curie, adding that "positive portrayals show the nation that people with mental health problems do live, learn, work, and fully participate in the American community" (SAMSHA, 2005, para. 5). Some applaud *Monk* for showing an appealing character who, although affected by a serious mental illness, is a brilliant and much-admired professional. Others are less comfortable with the show, pointing out that Adrian Monk is portrayed simultaneously as "needy, emotional, and plagued by self-doubts" (D. A. Johnson, 2008, para. 8).

DISABILITIES

Television tends to perpetuate unrealistic stereotypes about people with physical disabilities. "The one-dimensional victim often portrayed in popular media accounts bears little resemblance to the actual lives of individuals with intellectual disabilities," writes researcher Carol Pardun (2005), who studied 3,900 media portrayals and newspaper articles about people with disabilities. Pardun found that 50% of media depictions show people with disabilities working in careers, whereas only about 32% of people with disabilities are actually employed, and 60% live in poverty, a condition not usually reflected in media portrayals. Pardun found that people with disabilities are disproportionately depicted as victims to be pitied and that persons with intellectual disabilities are nearly invisible in the media.

One effort to give people with disabilities a voice is *Ouch,* a website sponsored by the British Broadcasting Corporation (BBC). *Ouch* is an open forum in which people with disabilities can share views and read columns, calendars, and news items of interest. The website provides a safe place for readers to talk about episodes that others might not understand. For example, Thoreau (2006) describes a funny and revealing article, "Holiday Diary: A White Man Abroad," in which a man with albinism reflects on a vacation with his friends. In his online posts, the man wonders if he should color his hair before the trip to look a "wee bit more 'normal'" and worries about too much sun exposure, quipping, "I'm a white cap, for crissakes, and I'm gonna fry like a sausage in the sun" (quoted by Thoreau, 2006, p. 458). He also describes his relief that, once the vacation begins, he seems to "be topping the score" in terms of attracting women (p. 458). Thoreau reflects that the man's witty self-commentary finds an appreciative audience on the website but that an underlying theme of the article is the writer's sense of being, in many ways, isolated from and different from his friends.

SEX

You're likely to see a lot of sex on TV, but exactly how much depends on when you watch. Sex in prime-time programs has steadily but modestly decreased since 1975 (Hetsroni, 2007b). But other programs, such as reality shows, have made up the difference. Overall, the proportion of programs that depict or imply sexual intercourse has doubled (from 7% to 14%) since 1997/1998 (Kunkel et al., 2007). In programs that include sexual references, characters *talk* about sex about 4.6 times per hour and *have* sex (usually implied rather than shown explicitly) about 2 times per hour (Kunkel, Eyal, Finnerty, Biely, & Donnerstein, 2005). Kunkel and associates (2005) write: "If the topic of sex on television was frequent in the past, it is now nearly ubiquitous" (Conclusion, para. 8).

A few other trends are notable as well:

- More same-sex couples than ever before are having sex on the small screen (Hetsroni, 2007b). Whereas TV references to homosexual sex were virtually nonexistent in 1975, the topic is now raised once every 3 or 4 viewing hours during prime time (Hetsroni).
- There has been a dramatic decrease in the amount of teen sex portrayed on TV (Kunkel et al., 2005). TV sex is now more likely to occur between married partners (Hetsroni, 2007b).

• There are slightly fewer acts of sexual aggression on TV than in the past (Hetsroni, 2007b).

In terms of safer-sex references, the numbers are higher than they used to be but still quite low. About 1 in 25 TV sex scenes includes verbal or visual reference to safer sex methods (Kunkel et al., 2005). But such references are far more scarce (about 1 in 200 episodes) when you figure in music, magazines, and movies aimed at teen audiences (Hust, Brown, & L'Engle, 2008). Stacey Hust and colleagues surveyed more than 3,000 middle school students about their favorite programs, magazines, songs, and recording artists and then content-analyzed the most popular choices. They found that, across formats aimed at teen audiences, safer sex is still depicted as "humiliating and humorous" (p. 14), boys are portrayed as sexually ravenous, and sexual protection is considered the responsibility of girls. The researchers report: "In the rare instances when condoms were discussed or depicted, boys had condoms as a kind of toy, whereas girls were more knowledgeable and more likely to have a condom when it was needed" (p. 17). Even when condoms were present, they were usually treated comically rather than as topics of serious discussion with health consequences.

There is mixed evidence about a supposed link between viewing sex in the media and having sex at a young age. Steinberg and Monahan (2010) found little evidence that media was the deciding factor in spurring early sexual experiences. But some research suggests that it might be influential. In one study, researchers compared 12- to 17-year-olds in the 90th percentile of TV-sex viewing with same-age peers in the 10th percentile or lower. Heavy viewers were significantly more likely to have sex within a year of the study (Collins et al., 2004). Other research suggests that it's not just how *much* sex adolescents view, but how realistic they consider it to be. In a study of Dutch teens, Peter & Valkenburg (2006) found that adolescents (particularly boys) who viewed what they considered to be realistic online sex typically considered it instructional about how to have sex in real life. They were subsequently more likely than their peers to consider having sex in the near future and to approve of sex in casual relationships.

Of course, we can't assume that media sex causes interest in real-life sex. It may be the other way

around—that people who are already interested in sex more readily seek out media depictions of it. Either way, the issue is important, considering that sexually active adolescents are at higher risk than adults for contracting sexually transmitted infections (STIs), including HIV ("Sexual Health," 2008). Nearly 46,000 adolescents in the United States have already contracted HIV, and about 9.1 million are infected with other STIs every year. Additionally, about 42 in 1,000 female teens give birth in the United States each year ("Sexual Health").

VIOLENCE

Contrary to popular opinion, primetime television is not more violent than it used to be. Based on Amir Hetsroni's (2007a) meta-analysis of 40 years of related research, the incidence of prime-time violence peaked in the late 1970s and the mid-1990s, when viewers were likely to see between 5.5 and 7.3 assaults per hour. By 2002, murders in prime-time television were half as numerous as in 1997. Violence may be down, but there's still a lot of it. No matter what time you watch TV, you're likely to see violence in 2 out of 3 programs (Smith, Nathanson, & Wilson, 2002). And the movies are no better. Even the previews are violent. About 75.7% of movie previews include violence, and 56% show sexuality (Oliver & Kalyanaraman, 2002).

One criticism of media violence is that the effects are unrealistic. People run through machine gun fire unscathed. They're shot or stabbed but continue to perform like athletes. Evil characters die, but heroes seldom do. George Gerbner (1996) calls it happy violence: "'Happy violence' is cool, swift, painless, and always leads to a happy ending, so as to deliver the audience to the next commercial in a receptive mood" (para. 10). In a study of PG-13 movies, Theresa Webb and colleagues (2007) report that, although violence was prevalent, enduring harm to victims was "either nonexistent or largely unrealistic" (p. e1226). In the fast-paced world of entertainment, it seems that violence is popular, but lengthy recoveries are boring. The result is an on-screen world in which violence lacks serious consequences.

Most researchers agree that there is an association between violence in the media and violence in real life. Evidence suggests that children exposed to media violence are more likely than others to engage in violent behavior themselves (Huesmann, Moise-Titus, Podolski, & Eron, 2003; Wartella, 1996). Graphic violence in video games has also been linked to aggression among children (Eastin & Griffiths, 2006; Pesky & Blascovich, 2007). In one study, youth who played a video game with "blood on" (an option that displays gory depictions of characters' wounds) were slightly but significantly more likely than "blood-off" players to indicate feelings of anger and to say they would react violently if someone ran into them on the sidewalk (Farrar, Krcmar, & Nowak, 2006).

Of course, not everyone reacts to media violence in the same way, and it's difficult to isolate media effects among the many factors that influence people (Haridakis, 2006). Women tend to use the media to moderate their mood when they feel angry, whereas males are more likely to choose programs that mirror their anger (Knobloch-Westerwick & Alter, 2006). For some people, violence in the media is a substitute for acting out. For others, media images tend to escalate their sense of aggression. One prevalent effect of media violence, even when people don't feel more aggressive themselves, is that high media users tend to feel afraid and to overestimate the threat of violence in their environment (Nabi & Sullivan, 2001; Romer, Jamieson, & Aday, 2003).

Portrayals of Health Care Situations

Medical dramas seem to offer a backstage pass to medicine. What most people "know" about the interior of a surgery unit or a doctor's lounge they learned from television. Areas usually off limits to the public are open for inspection, or at least it seems that way. In some ways, medical dramas are likely to give people mistaken impressions about the way medical work is done.

Based on television portrayals, it may seem that the extremes are the norm. A greater percentage of TV patients die than in real life and a greater number of them experience miraculous recoveries. The reality, of course, is somewhere in the middle. Let's look at how medical dramas tend to distort what really happens.

Kimberly A. Neuendorf (1990) dubbed the tendency to portray doctors as "all-powerful and all-good" as the "Marcus Welby syndrome." Health

crises arise and are resolved on TV in 30-minute or 1-hour segments, compared to the weeks or months often required to resolve real-life medical conditions. In a classic study, researchers examined instances of CPR (cardiopulmonary resuscitation) in TV episodes (Diem, Lantos, & Tulsky, 1996). They found that CPR was usually administered to children and young adults, and most of them recovered fully and quickly. Some even regained full health in a matter of minutes. In everyday life, however, CPR is most often used to help older adults having heart attacks, and it only saves 2% to 30% of actual patients, many of whom suffer lasting disabilities. Susan Diem and coauthors conclude that television medical dramas encourage people to believe in miracles that aren't likely to occur.

At the same time, medical dramas rely on death as a dramatic element. The mortality rate among TV patients is nearly 9 times greater than the norm, promoting the researcher who discovered the disparity to quip, "if you must be hospitalized, television is not the place" (Hetsroni, 2009, p. 311). Dying is a quick and dramatic ending with a great deal of entertainment value, but don't let it fool you. In actual hospitals, most people survive, but recovery takes a while.

We might also be fooled by the way people look on TV. In real life, about 4 in 10 hospital patients are male. On TV, however, 7 in 10 are male (Hetsroni, 2009). And, whereas men are overrepresented in medical dramas, Hispanic Americans and older adults are under-represented (Hetsroni, 2009).

Entertainment programming also presents dramatic but untrue information about organ donation. In their study of network television programs, Susan Morgan and colleagues (2007) found numerous story lines about organs sold illegally, people murdered for their organs, doctors giving preferential treatment to their favorite organ recipients, and people allowed to die prematurely so that others could have their organs. The researchers also found fictional accounts of organ recipients who behave criminally or irresponsibly, squandering the life-sustaining gift they have received. On television, donors are often depicted as "good people," but a corrupt system sometimes treats them as nothing more than "spare parts" (Morgan, Harrison, Chewning, Davis, & DiCorcia, p. 148). All of these depictions—though the stuff of exciting drama—are grossly unrealistic. "We often wonder where members of the public get 'crazy ideas' about organ donation like the existence of the black market, the corruption of the organ allocation system, and the untrustworthiness of doctors," the authors reflect. "The answer may have been quite literally in front of us for years" (Morgan et al., 2007, p. 149).

Entertainment and Commercialism

It's usually easy to tell the difference between a commercial and a television program or movie. But what if a commercial looks like entertainment or commercial messages are subtly embedded in entertainment programming?

ENTERTAINOMERCIALS

Journalists have coined the term **entertainomercials** to characterize sales pitches that resemble entertainment programming ("Entertainomercials," 1996). A classic example involved Joe Camel, the former cartoon-like mascot of Camel cigarettes. R. J. Reynolds Tobacco Company introduced the colorful, sunglass-wearing camel in 1988 advertising. Although company officials insisted that the animated character was not meant to capture children's interest, it had that effect. Sales of Camel cigarettes to children rose from $6 million per year to $476 million per year (DiFranza et al., 1991). Within a few years, children were as familiar with Joe Camel as with Mickey Mouse (Fischer, Schwartz, Richards, & Goldstein, 1991). Under public and legal pressure, Reynolds ceased using images of Joe Camel in 1997, after a 10-year run (Vest, 1997).

PRODUCT PLACEMENT

The tobacco industry is also involved in another type of commercial/entertainment blend called product placement. **Product placement** means that a sponsor pays (with cash, props, services, or so on) to have a product or brand name included in a movie, a television program, a video game, or some other form of entertainment. Subtle product placements (sometimes called *stealth ads*) can be considered a form of subliminal advertising, in that the viewer may not be consciously aware of seeing items displayed but may develop an impression about them based on their association with other elements of the drama (Erdelyi & Zizak, 2004). At the very least, critics argue, when viewers suspend disbelief to enjoy the reality of an entertainment program, they shouldn't have to worry that they are being exposed to embedded commercial messages all the while.

For a time, the Federal Communication Commission (FCC) forbade paid product placements within television programs. The rule was only loosely enforced, however, and it went out the window in a culture filled with online pop-up ads anyway. Now, television shows are required to make it known (usually in the closing credits) if products have been provided. The Nielsen Company, famous for establishing viewership ratings, now has its own product placement division and keeps tabs on several hundred thousand placements per year (Moss, 2008). *American Idol* usually has the most product placements, with upwards of 600 product placements annually, followed by *The Biggest Loser, Celebrity Apprentice,* and others ("Primetime Shows," 2011). A number of reality shows, such as *Survivor* and *Big Brother*, also make the top 10.

Product placements have always been allowed in movies, and the numbers are increasing. Steven Spielberg earned $25 million for placing 15 brand-name products in the movie *Minority Report*, leading at least one reviewer to comment on the irony of the characters' on-screen resistance to a mind-controlling regime (King, 2002). Other notable examples include Reese's Pieces in *E.T.*, the Dr. Pepper can that Peter Parker uses for target practice in *Spider-Man*, and the FedEx trucks and planes in *Castaway*.

Product placements become health communication when they concern the way people think or behave concerning health issues. This may range from an emphasis on fast food and cigarettes to athletic gear. A particular concern arises when product placements are used to dodge restrictions

WHAT DO YOU THINK?

■ Do you think viewers are affected by product placements in the movies and on television? If so, how?

■ Do you agree or disagree with the argument that people should be able to enjoy entertainment programming without being wary of embedded sales pitches? Why?

on conventional advertising. Tobacco industry documents obtained in the 1990s show that companies secretly rewarded actors and producers to display their cigarettes prominently in the movies (Basil, 1997). Stars, including Sean Connery, Sylvester Stallone, Paul Newman, and Clint Eastwood, have allegedly accepted expensive cars and jewelry in return for smoking brand-name cigarettes on the big screen. Promoting cigarettes in this way violates several restrictions: (1) the prohibition on advertising tobacco on radio, TV, or in the movies; (2) the ban on celebrity endorsements; and (3) federal law requiring health warnings on all tobacco packages and advertisements (Basil, 1997). These restrictions, initiated in the 1960s and furthered by the Master Settlement Agreement in 1994, are based on medical evidence that tobacco products are serious health hazards to tobacco users and the people around them.

As the next section shows, some people have decided to fight fire with fire, using the product placement strategy to promote recommended health behaviors. See Box 11.3 for ethical issues related to health images in entertainment programs.

BOX 11.3   ETHICAL CONSIDERATIONS

Is the Entertainment Industry Responsible for Health Images?

Does the entertainment industry have a responsibility to promote healthy behaviors? Some claim that entertainment writers and producers behave irresponsibly when they consistently portray unhealthy and unrealistic images of life and health.

One way that the media distort reality is by showing unhealthy and violent behaviors without the natural consequences (Gerbner, 1996). People are shot with guns but continue to run and fight. Others overeat but appear to be slender and healthy nevertheless (Brown & Walsh-Childers, 1994). Another way that media messages often misrepresent health is by depicting ill (especially mentally ill) individuals as dangerous, corrupt, and antisocial (Signorielli, 1993).

There's a gray zone where health and entertainment overlap. Even programs presented as healthy sometimes aren't. For example, *The Biggest Loser* and similar reality shows chronicle people involved in multiweek, boot-campish efforts to shed 50, 60, or even 100 pounds. Their experiences can be inspirational, but are they realistic or even healthy? Fitness guru/physician Pamela Peeke (2011) reflects on the show *Heavy*:

The people who were chosen are severely obese, with average weights in the range of 400–600 pounds. . . . There are frequent moments of what seems to be embarrassing over exposure of the participants, with numerous half-naked shots revealing enormous rolls of fat. If the producers wanted shock value, they achieved their goal. (para. 5)

Even worse, she reflects, is the producers' insistence that all the participants need is discipline and sweat, prescribed in a merciless fashion by trainers (always thin) who show the participants little understanding or compassion. The people featured "repeatedly noted that they felt addicted to food, and that food had become the default for life's stresses as well as pleasures. Yet, despite their pleading for help, all they seemed to experience was a grueling workout schedule," Peeke says (para. 6). It's no wonder, she asserts, that most people regain the weight when they leave the show. The routines aren't sustainable, and "biceps curls, although integral to physical health, don't help to change eating behavior" (para. 6).

Some people argue that the entertainment industry need not offer shocking or distorted views of reality. They challenge Hollywood to create engrossing yet realistic programming. Going one step further, some people advocate pro-social programming to educate people while they are entertained.

On the other side of the issue, people argue that entertainment programming should not be harnessed to a social agenda. They feel that artistic creativity is compromised when writers and producers must adhere to social guidelines. Moreover, they say, it is difficult to know whose agenda should prevail.

When health professionals disagree about specific guidelines for healthy living, is it entertainers' job to decide which viewpoint should be represented? If the industry is held to a standard of realism, they wonder, what will become of fantasy themes and movies made famous by earlier generations, when different social expectations prevailed.

WHAT DO YOU THINK?

1. Do you think entertainment programming influences people's behavior? For instance, are people more likely to use condoms if they see their favorite characters talking about them in television programs or in the movies?

2. Should entertainers consider how their programs might influence audience members?

3. Do you think it is irresponsible of the entertainment industry to misrepresent the natural consequences of violent or otherwise unhealthy behavior?

4. Do you think it would diminish the entertainment value of your favorite movies and TV shows if they showed healthy behaviors or realistic consequences?

5. Do you believe programs designed specifically to promote healthy behaviors would be popular in the United States? Do you think such programs should be created? Why or why not

Entertainment-Education Programming

Producers may embed subtle messages in programs, not to sell products but to educate or persuade people regarding health matters. Efforts to benefit the public using an entertainment format are known as **entertainment-education** or pro-social programming. The idea, say Piotrow and colleagues, is that "no one enjoys being lectured to but everyone enjoys and often *learns* from entertainment, whether broadcast through radio or television, or performed in person" (Piotrow, Rimon, Merritt, & Saffitz, 2003, p. 5).

Entertainment producers today are likely to be lobbied by health advocates who urge them to incorporate health messages in their scripts, props, and story lines. The Hollywood, Health & Society and the Entertainment Industries Council encourage entertainment writers to portray health issues in accurate and informative ways. They provide websites with story ideas and scripts to incorporate health information in entertainment programming and information about topics ranging from AIDS to bat bites, car seats, suicide, and West Nile fever. For example, the Entertainment Industries Council urges writers not to use the term *hard drugs* because it implies incorrectly that drugs that are not "hard" are relatively harmless. It also recommends that characters be shown using seat belts and other safety devices.

In some countries, entire programs have been created to promote healthy behaviors. After *Nunl Dhuhyo!* (Open Your Eyes!) segments began airing on Korean television, the number of people who signed cornea-donation cards increased from just over 1,000 to nearly 14,000 (Bae & Kang, 2008). In the show, celebrity hosts conduct moving interviews with people who are hoping for cornea transplants to restore their sight.

A radio drama in Ethiopia, *Journal of Life*, depicted a main character who contracted HIV during an isolated sexual indiscretion and then unknowingly infected his wife. A random survey of the radio audience revealed that most listeners became emotionally involved in the storyline and that their resolve to engage in safer sex practices

CHECK IT OUT! For more about product placement and entertainment-education, see the following:

Greene, M. C., Strange, J. J., & Brock, T. C. (Eds.). (2002). *Narrative impact: Social and cognitive foundations.* Mahwah, NJ: Lawrence Erlbaum.

Shurn, L. J. (Ed.) (2004). *The psychology of entertainment media: Blurring the lines between entertainment and persuasion.* Mahwah, NJ: Lawrence Erlbaum.

Zillmann, D., & Vorderer, P. (Eds.) (2000). *Media entertainment: The psychology of its appeal.* Mahwah, NJ: Lawrence Erlbaum.

increased the more episodes they heard (Smith, Downs, & Witte, 2007).

For more on product placement and entertainment education, see *Check It Out!* on the previous page.

Impact of Persuasive Entertainment

Before you become too optimistic (or perturbed) about the prospects for incorporating messages within entertainment, it's important to ask: *Beyond the effects already mentioned, do messages in entertainment programs make much difference?*

Some theorists believe media images affect the way people view society, but not necessarily the way they view themselves personally. **Social adaptation theory** suggests that people evaluate messages by considering how useful the information is likely to be in their lives (Perse, Nathanson, & McLeod, 1996). In this regard, entertainment may have an edge over news. Leslie Snyder and Ruby Rouse (1995) found that people perceived entertainment portrayals to be more relevant to their lives than news items, because entertainment episodes tend to be more intimate and vivid. Snyder and Rouse's study revealed that movies and television programs increased people's perception of personal AIDS risk, while news coverage decreased their sense of being personally vulnerable. The researchers concluded that the dramatic nature of entertainment programming often makes it seem up-close and personal, whereas news coverage seems to depict what happens to "other people."

Concerning product placement, there are a few (but not many) striking success stories. After a character on *The Young & the Restless* saved a child using CPR techniques he "learned at the Red Cross," the Red Cross received thousands of calls from interested people (Drum, 1997). When a product placement deal put James Bond behind the wheel of a BMW Z3 roadster, the car maker had to put anxious buyers on waiting lists ("Let Us Put," 1996). Likewise, the sales of Reese's Pieces rose 65% after the release of *E.T.*, which depicted them as the favorite snack of a lovable outer-space creature (Babin & Carder, 1996).

Success stories aside, most product placements seem to do no more than increase brand-name recognition. College students who watched movie clips that included product placements were more inclined than others to say they would choose the brand from a range of similar alternatives (Moonhee & Roskos-Ewoldsen, 2007). But this depended largely on how prominently the product figured in the movie. Background depictions did not have much effect, but audiences were influenced by products that characters (especially likable characters) used actively, especially if they were integral to the plot.

One cause for concern is the underlying power dynamic of some education-entertainment programs. From a critical-cultural perspective, Dutta (2006) argues that education entertainment programs are typically designed to serve the goals, values, and priorities of the funding entity, rather than those of the target community. The result can be a form of cultural hegemony in which the values of the dominant culture are imposed on members of the marginalized community, without respect for (or even awareness of) the community's own values, culture, and circumstances. Another danger is that sponsors will focus on individual aspects of a problem—as in having fewer children per family—rather than tackling larger and more systemic issues such as the need to allocate resources fairly to all people (Dutta, 2006). These efforts tend to hurt more than they help, particularly considering that the philanthropic goal of a funding entity is often based on a deeper, more self-serving desire to create stable markets for its good and services, ensure tranquility in regions rich with natural resources, and so on. The tendency to impose the agenda of the powerful can be offset by involving community members in open dialogue and participation before, during, and after campaigns. But Dutta warns that many "participatory" efforts actually involve choosing between options preselected by campaign designers. In his view, only when social programming is created with an open and rich appreciation for the circumstances, culture, and needs of the focus community can we expect it to foster real and meaningful change. (We will talk more about the critical-cultural perspective in Chapter 14.)

Media Literacy

This chapter concludes where it began, with the reminder that the media's influence is by no means uniform. People are affected differently and to varying extents. Perhaps the best defense against excessive or negative media influence is the ability to analyze messages logically (Austin & Meili, 1994). That's a central tenet of media literacy.

Media literacy is defined as awareness and skills that allow a person to evaluate media content in terms of what is realistic and useful (adapted from Potter, 1998). According to Dorothy Singer and Jerome Singer's (1998) seminal overview, media-literate individuals are aware that advertisers are apt to highlight (and even exaggerate) the attractive aspects of their products and to downplay the disadvantages. They evaluate the creators' intent and try to figure out what is not being said and why. Media-literate individuals are also skillful at identifying portrayals that are unrealistic or have been enhanced by special effects. Overall, media-literate individuals tend to evaluate messages in terms of fairness and appropriateness, weighing ideas for themselves.

Teaching Media Literacy

Media literacy instruction usually involves an informative, an analytic, and an experiential stage. Arli Quesada and Sue Summers (1998) describe these stages well, and the discussion here is based on their work.

In the **informative stage,** participants in media literacy programs learn to identify different types of messages (persuasive, informative, and entertaining) and different types of media (television, radio, newspapers, and so on). They learn about the strengths and limitations of various media. For example, Internet resources are vast and accessible, but some sources are not trustworthy. Participants also learn about production techniques and special effects.

In the **analytic stage,** participants discuss their perceptions of media in general and of specific media messages. In this stage they typically deconstruct messages with guidance from a trained leader. **Deconstructing** a message means breaking it down into specific components, such as key points, purpose, implied messages, production techniques, and goals. For example, beer commercials often present a social reality in which drinking is fun and sexy. In deconstructing a beer commercial (or any other media message), participants try to identify the message's purpose, what information is missing from it, and how it compares to their own social reality. They might conclude that beer companies make drinking look fun to sell their products, but the reality is something more than or different from what the commercials show.

Finally, in the **experiential stage,** media literacy programs challenge participants to write their own news stories, design ads, perform skits, and participate in other creative efforts to help them understand the process and demystify the way media messages are created. Adolescents who have taken part in tobacco-related media literacy programs are more likely than others to think carefully about tobacco commercials and to decide not to smoke (Pinkleton, Austin, Cohen, Miller, & Fitzgerald, 2007). A particularly useful technique is to have them create their own antismoking messages (Banerjee & Greene, 2006). (See *Check It Out!* for resources about tobacco media literacy.)

Media literacy skills have been taught successfully to people of different ages. In one project, third graders watched a 28-minute video about advertising techniques and took part in guided discussions (Austin & Johnson, 1997). Following this brief exercise, they were more likely than other children to identify commercials as sales pitches, to see them as unrealistic, and to judge for themselves whether the behaviors depicted were appropriate or desirable.

A similar project helped college students critique fashion advertisements, noting how extremely thin or muscular the models were (Rabak-Wagener, Eickhoff-Shemek, & Kelly-Vance, 1998). The students were challenged to redesign the ads using models of different body sizes, ages, ethnicities, and

> **CHECK IT OUT!** For more tobacco and media literacy resources see the following:
> ■ Real Parents. Real Answers: www.realparentsrealanswers.com
> ■ Teens, Tobacco & the Media resource guide: depts.washington.edu/thmedia/view.cgi?section=tobacco&page=teenprojects
> ■ Center for Media Literacy: www.medialit.org/reading_room/article420.html
> ■ American Legacy Foundation: www.americanlegacy.org

physical abilities. They were consequently less likely to believe people should look like supermodels and were more satisfied with their own bodies.

Media literacy can be taught at home when parents help children understand aspects of the media messages they encounter. This is known as **parental mediation**. Adults are often able to make children aware of inaccuracies and discrepancies in media messages. For example, "Why does this program show thin people eating fattening foods?" (Austin, 1995) or "Is the violence shown in this program realistic?" (Nathanson & Yang, 2003). Research suggests that children get maximum benefits from media (while minimizing unfavorable influences) when their parents (1) limit media exposure; (2) choose programs with care; (3) watch, listen, or read alongside them; and (4) discuss program content with them (Austin, 1993; Austin, Roberts, & Nass, 1990; Singer & Singer, 1998).

Although the research about media literacy is encouraging overall, it doesn't suggest a cure-all. Some stereotypes persist, even when people have explicitly been told they are not valid. College students who watched a movie about a mentally ill murderer were more negative in their assessment of mentally ill persons than students who viewed an unrelated film (Wahl & Lefkowits, 1989). This was true even when the students saw a message stating that violence is not a characteristic of mental illness. The authors conclude that awareness and information campaigns will not be entirely successful at counteracting negative media portrayals.

Summary

Whether you regard the media as friend or foe, mass-mediated messages are an important component of health communication. The distinction in this chapter between advertising, news, and entertainment is useful for explanatory purposes, but do not forget that actual media exposure involves a great deal of blending and juxtaposing. For instance, a news story about eating disorders may be followed by an advertisement featuring unnaturally thin models. Such clashes are common, and contradictions of this nature may mitigate the effects of health-conscious messages.

Although it's difficult to say to what degree people's actions are affected by advertising, significant influence is suggested by the number of people who eat the unhealthy food advertisers promote, drink the beverages they sell, and strive to emulate supermodels. As Timothy Gibson (2007) puts it, "Our physical health depends, at least in part, upon the health of our media environment" (p. 125). Based on cultivation theory, children and adolescents may be especially susceptible to advertising messages because their frame of reference is limited. Social comparison theory suggests that people strive to measure up to "idealized" characters in the media, even when the ideals are far from attainable. Sometimes advertisers make natural conditions seem bad or unnatural (pathological) so that people will pay money to change them. Although advertising offers many advantages, it can be harmful if it encourages poor nutrition, drug and alcohol abuse, or an unhealthy reliance on cosmetics and fad diets. For example, the severity of mandated warning messages on tobacco packages is offset by other cues, such as soothing, relaxing colors and the word "light" in the product name.

As one of only two countries that allow direct-to-consumer advertising of pharmaceuticals, the United States is navigating relatively uncharted ground. DTC advertising offers advantages but presents a number of challenges and ethical dilemmas related to social justice, research objectivity, full disclosure, and market agendas versus altruism.

News coverage of health issues is important for sharing valuable knowledge. However, news audiences should remember that scientific findings are usually tentative, news stories tend to focus on unusual concerns, and coverage may be influenced by the desire to please advertisers or attract new audiences.

Entertainment portrayals may influence what people believe about medical care, risky behavior, and people with disabilities. Sex and violence are shown mostly for entertainment value, not as serious subjects with health consequences. In reality, medical miracles are less common than as shown on television, and people are more diverse.

Don't be surprised if the food, drinks, cigarettes, vehicles, and props in your favorite programs and movies were put in purposefully to please advertisers. Although product placements may not look like commercials, advertisers go to great expense, hoping that they will function like commercials. Health advocates sometimes use the same logic in inserting pro-health messages into entertainment programs, a practice known as education-entertainment programming.

Finally, media literacy allows people some control over how media messages affect them. Wise consumers learn to distinguish between reliable and unreliable information by critiquing media messages to determine their purposes, strengths, and limitations.

Key Terms and Theories

mass communication
third-person effect
cultivation theory
social comparison theory
direct-to-consumer (DTC) advertising
pathologizing the human body
entertainomercials
product placement
entertainment-education programming
social adaptation theory
media literacy
informative stage
analytic stage
deconstructing
experiential stage
parental mediation

Discussion Questions

1. Based on cultivation theory and social comparison theory, why and under what conditions are children particularly susceptible to media messages?
2. Describe the advantages and disadvantages of DTC advertising. In your opinion, do the advantages outweigh the disadvantages or not? Why?
3. Do you think it matters that some types of people aren't depicted in pharmaceutical ads as often as others? Why or why not?
4. What are some tips for being an effective consumer relevant to pharmaceutical advertisements?
5. In what ways does media consumption seem to affect body image? How does it affect children's eating habits and knowledge of nutrition?
6. How has tobacco advertising changed over time?

7. What evidence is there that alcoholic beverage makers target underage youth and racial groups? Have you seen experience of this yourself? If so, how? Do you think it has an effect?
8. In what ways do advertisers pathologize the human body? What are the health implications?
9. In what ways are health news items frequently distorted in the mass media? What are some reasons for this? What are the advantages and disadvantages of health news coverage in the mass media? What are some suggestions for reporters covering health topics?
10. What are some recent trends in how sex is portrayed in entertainment programming?
11. What did Gerbner mean by the term *happy violence*? Can you give some examples from your own media experience?
12. How might people be misled by TV medical dramas?
13. How does promoting cigarettes in the movies violate advertising regulations?
14. Describe some examples of entertainment-education programming.
15. When is entertainment-education most effective? What ethical considerations should be involved?
16. Describe the steps in teaching media literacy.

Answers to *Can You Guess?*

PART 1

1. Some 2 out of 3 (66%) U.S. youth ages 8 to 18 have a mobile phone.

2. Children and teens today spend about 1½ hours per day engaged with their mobile phones.

3. Youth spend nearly 1 hour per day listening to music and playing games on their phones—about twice as much time as they actually spend talking on them.

PART 2

1. Southern chef Paula Deen signed a multi-million-dollar deal with Novo Nordisk in 2012 soon after going public with a diabetes

diagnosis she had learned about 3 years earlier. Fellow chef Anthony Bourdain dubbed the deal hypocrisy, saying, "When your signature dish is hamburger in between a doughnut, and you've been cheerfully selling this stuff knowing all along that you've got Type 2 Diabetes . . . It's in bad taste if nothing else" (Conley, 2012, para. 6).

PART 3

1. The number of obese people in the world has nearly doubled since 1980 ("10 Facts," 2012).

2. About 33% (1 in 3) of U.S. children are obese.

PART 4

1. Approximately 14% of 8th graders in the United States have drunk alcohol in the last 30 days.

2. Youth are likely to see about 67,656 more alcohol ads than adults do in a typical year.

(Center on Alcohol Marketing and Youth, 2012)

PART 5

1. On average, broadcast and cable TV stations devote less than one-third of a minute (17 seconds) per hour to PSAs. That's less than one-half of 1% of airtime. And 46% of PSAs run between midnight and 6 a.m. ("Study Finds," 2008).

2. In 65 years, the average person will spend a total of 11.3 years in front of a TV set ("Nielsen Reports," 2008).

CHAPTER TWELVE

Public Health Crises and Health Care Reform

In 1986, a strange malady began afflicting cattle in Great Britain. Affected animals stumbled and staggered, unable to walk normally. Some of them became paralyzed. All died within a year of displaying symptoms, their brains partially eaten away by a disease that came to be called bovine spongiform encephalopathy (BSE), or, more commonly, mad cow disease. . . .

This chapter focuses on the overlap of a number of perspectives—public health, risk communication, crisis communication, and health care reform. We could spend an entire book on any one of these topics, and I encourage you to pursue them in more depth. Resource boxes throughout the chapter will get you started. But for now, there's an advantage in focusing on the overlap. It gives us an opportunity to look at real-life episodes with a rich appreciation for the complexities that confront the people who experience them. Although public health, risk, and crisis communication are not synonymous, it's often difficult within any one experience to say where one stops and the other starts. Likewise, an emphatic lesson of public health communication is that it does no good, it fact it often does harm, to encourage healthy behaviors when people lack the support and resources to carry them out. Consequently, we will conclude this chapter with a discussion of health care reform, especially the Affordable Care Act of 2010, which is changing the landscape of health care in the United States with powerful implications for health communication, prevention efforts, health disparities, and much more.

First, let's return to the mad cow disease saga to see what lessons it holds for us.

Mad Cow Disease

Scientists were unable to explain how the cattle got the debilitating disease, but it was similar in some respects to a neurological disease, scrapie, that had long affected sheep. Affected sheep would compulsively scratch themselves on fence posts and other materials. They, too, would inevitably wither and die, their brains full of spongy holes.

The similarity between scrapie and BSE was apparent, but scientists and public health experts lacked definitive answers to some important questions: *Through what means was the disease being transmitted from sheep to cattle, if that was indeed the source?* and *Could the disease jump to humans next?*

The stakes were high. On the one hand, there was no evidence, only conjecture, that the disease could be communicated to humans. Alerting the public might cause widespread fear. And there were economic concerns. Short of exterminating all the cattle in Great Britain, authorities were unsure how to stop BSE. On the other hand, silence would rob people of the opportunity to avoid exposure to what was, potentially, a deadly, incurable disease. British officials reassured the public that there was no known risk.

All the while, following a procedure common at the time, many of the deceased animals were being ground up and their bones and tissue (which are potent and inexpensive sources of protein) incorporated into feed for livestock, including other cows. In the early 1980s, to cut costs, farmers had altered the process to allow fatty and nerve tissue to remain in the mixture. By the time researchers realized that the disease was spread through contact with infected brain and nerve tissue, it was too late. Farmers had literally fed the disease to surviving members of their herds and perhaps to humans as well.

In 1988, officials banned the use of animal products in livestock feed, but the ban was not strictly enforced for several more years (Henahan, 1996). They also called for the slaughter of infected cattle and those behaving suspiciously. But, because the government initially compensated farmers at only about 50% of market value for sacrificed animals, farmers had little economic incentive to be vigilant (Dora, 2006).

In the meantime, British officials continued to insist publicly that there was no cause for alarm. In 1990, the minister of agriculture, John Gummer, staged a public photo opportunity during which he fed his 4-year-old daughter a hamburger (Lyall, 2000).

The public was not reassured. By 1993 more than 1,000 cases of BSE were surfacing every

💬 IN YOUR EXPERIENCE

■ Have you ever been frightened by a health scare in the news?

■ If so, how did you respond?

week (Henahan, 1996). To make matters worse, it emerged that the incubation period was as long as 7 years. Cattle are typically slaughtered when they are 3 to 5 years old, meaning that untold numbers of infected (but as yet asymptomatic) animals were being allowed into the animal and human food supply.

British authorities were still telling people not to worry. But the numbers kept escalating. Ultimately, 200,000 cattle in Great Britain were diagnosed with BSE, and 3.7 million were destroyed in precautionary efforts, causing the "near destruction of Great Britain's cattle industry" (Adams & Osho, nd, p. 1).

In 1995 and 1996, two teenagers died in Great Britain from a variant of Creutzfeldt-Jakob disease (vCJD), a fatal neurological disorder that causes brain damage similar to that of BSE. Researchers speculated that BSE might be involved. Other cases followed, and vCJD was definitively linked to beef consumption.

Finally, 10 years after they became aware of BSE, British officials publicly admitted the risk to humans. The authors of the book *Mad Cows and Mothers' Milk* lament that it took so long. They assert that officials' eagerness to downplay the issue resulted in "years of mismanagement, political bravado, and a gross underestimation of the public's capacity to deal with risk" (Leiss, Powell, & Whitfield, 2004, pp. 3–4).

Investigators for national and worldwide agencies have reviewed the mad cow disease saga, seeking lessons and identifying factors that led British officials to suppress this public health threat even as evidence of its severity mounted. They speculate that the following factors played a role:

• In Great Britain, as in many countries, agency boundaries made it unclear who had ultimate jurisdiction and whose interests should prevail. Involved were agencies in charge of food safety, agriculture, public health, international commerce, and more.

- Economic concerns discouraged aggressive action. Alarming the public might mean a drop in beef consumption; bankruptcy for farmers, meat packers, and others; food shortages; and so on. (Ultimately, inaction proved more costly. Not only did domestic consumption plummet, but at one point, British beef was banned worldwide.)
- Officials were wary of creating panic.
- Decision makers were hesitant to make judgment calls without scientific data.
- Officials were overwhelmed when the public and media urgently desired information, but the information available was changing and incomplete. Spokespersons often deemed it preferable to deliver words of comfort rather than to admit how much they didn't know.
- Because vCJD mimicked some of the symptoms of other neurological disorders, it was difficult to know exactly when, or if, BSE had affected humans.
- Officials were reassured by patterns of the past. Scrapie had been plaguing sheep for about 200 years with no known transmission to humans. It was tempting to assume that BSE would be the same (Ashraf, 2000).
- National leaders assumed that precautionary measures (e.g., changing livestock food and slaughtering infected herds) would be enough to halt the disease trajectory.

These factors underscore the complexity of public health and risk communication. It's easy to judge harshly from a distance and with the advantage of hindsight, and certainly we all want public health professionals to be honest with the public. But perhaps the greatest lesson is that handling a public health crisis is anything but easy. Dissecting past experiences is not meant to condemn the perpetrators so much as to help us avoid making the same mistakes again.

The BSE saga has calmed in recent years. Because researchers were able to ascertain how the disease was spread and regulators took action (albeit slowly), about 95% of BSE cases have been confined to Great Britain, and the numbers have decreased dramatically. However, boundaries are porous in our world economy. Cattle have been diagnosed with BSE in 24 countries (World Organisation for Animal Health, 2008). As of this writing, isolated cases are still being reported.

The greatest failure was one of communication. The public was kept in the dark about a lethal health threat. If people had been warned earlier of a danger—even a danger about which little was known—they could have chosen for themselves whether to eat beef. To date, 176 people have died from vCJD (Creutzfeldt-Jakob Disease Statistics, 2012). The numbers have tapered off since 2004, but one fact has scientists worried: The disease can take more than 25 years to incubate in humans. It's possible that people are infected and don't yet know it.

The complexity and importance of public health require us to be especially vigilant, principled, and well prepared. Keep the challenges of dealing with mad cow disease in mind as we consider what, exactly, is involved in public health efforts.

What Is Public Health?

As the vCJD crisis illustrates, public health involves the well-being of entire communities. Mary-Jane Schneider (2006) describes it this way:

> Just as a doctor monitors the health of a patient by taking vital signs—blood pressure, heart rate, and so forth—public health workers monitor the health of a community by collecting and analyzing health data. (p. 121)

And public health doesn't stop there. In the same way that physicians and other caregivers are devoted to keeping people well, public health professionals are concerned with maintaining the good health of the entire population (Schneider, 2006). They seek to accomplish this through education, community partnerships, health campaigns, immunizations, and other medical care by maintaining healthy standards in restaurants, day care centers, schools, and much more. There are more than 2,700 local health departments in the United States (National Association of City & County, 2012). (See Box 12.1 for more on career opportunities in public health.)

BOX 12.1   CAREER OPPORTUNITIES

Public Health

Epidemiologist
Health educator
Health researcher
Communication specialist
Media relations professional
Health campaign designer
Environmentalist
Health inspector
Nutritionist
Nurse
Physician
Risk/crisis communication specialist
Nonprofit organization director
Fundraiser
Professor/educator
Public policy advisor
Health department administrator
Business or billing manager
Patient advocate or navigator
Social worker
Emergency management director

CAREER RESOURCES AND JOB LISTINGS

- Pfizer Guide to Careers in Public Health: www.whatispublichealth.org/careers/index.html
- American Public Health Association CareerMart: www.apha.org/about/careers
- Partners in Information Access for the Public Health Workforce: phpartners.org/jobs.html
- Public Health Jobs Worldwide: www.jobspublichealth.com
- U.S. Department of Health & Human Services Careers: www.hhs.gov/careers/
- Association of Schools in Public Health: www.asph.org
- World Health Organization: www.who.int/employment/vacancies/en
- Centers for Disease Control and Prevention (CDC): www.cdc.gov/about/opportunities.htm

Also check the websites of your local hospitals and health departments.

CHECK IT OUT!   Following are a few online resources relevant to public health:
- Flu Wiki, a collaborative website about managing the threat of a flu pandemic: http://www.fluwiki.info/
- CDC's Public Health Information Network: http://www.cdc.gov/phin/
- CDC's Whyville virtual world involving community health issues: http://www.whyville.net/smmk/nice

In the classic definition presented by Charles-Edward A. Winslow (1923), **public health** is:

> the science and art of preventing disease, prolonging life, and promoting physical health and efficiency through organized community efforts for the sanitation of the environment, the control of community infections, the education of the individual in principles of personal hygiene, the organization of medical and nursing service for the early diagnosis and preventive treatment of disease, and the development of the social machinery which will ensure to every individual in the community a standard of living adequate for the maintenance of health. (originally published in Winslow's *The Evolution and Significance of the Modern Public Health Campaign*, 1923, reprinted in the "History of Public Health," 2002, np)

This definition prescribes that public health professionals be both proactive—seeking to avoid unhealthy conditions, illnesses, and injuries—and diligent about monitoring and responding to health needs that arise.

Modern thinking about public health recognizes that one-way communication hasn't worked very well. As Piotrow and colleagues (2003) put it, health communication is "no longer simply repeating untested slogans like 'A small family is a happy family'" (p. 2) or distributing how-to guides on contraceptive methods. Instead, professionals are oriented more toward **social mobilization**, large-scale efforts in which community members and professionals work interactively to define goals, raise awareness, and create hospitable environments for healthy behaviors. Social mobilization relies on teamwork, diversity, shared leadership, and active involvement (Patel, 2005). For

How effective do you think the "Don't Text While Driving" campaign is for mobilizing the public? Would seeing this sign change your behavior?

example, in an effort to stop the spread of leprosy in Bihar, India, World Health Organization (WHO) officials met with experts and citizens in the region. They realized that it was uncommon for local residents to check themselves for early signs of leprosy because they had very few full-length mirrors, they typically showered outdoors while partly clothed, and even married couples did not often see each other naked (Renganathan et al., 2005). More than a catchy slogan would be needed for people to establish the habit of checking their skin for subtle changes. Community members would willingly have to alter their lifestyles and customs. Changes of this sort are usually most successful when they are promoted by community opinion leaders rather than by outsiders.

Public health involves an array of health concerns. Traditionally, ongoing concerns such as diabetes, cancer, and heart disease fall within the rubric of *health promotion,* a topic we will cover more thoroughly in Chapters 13 and 14. *Risk communication* usually refers to health concerns that occur in a particular time and place, such as exposure to harmful substances, workplace dangers, and so on (Glik, 2007).

Risk and Crisis Communication

The National Research Council (1989, p. 21) defines **risk communication** as an ongoing process that involves, not just one message, but many diverse messages about risk factors as well as interactive discussions about how people perceive these factors, how they judge the risks, and how they feel about the risk messages themselves.

With mad cow disease, the officials chose largely to downplay the risk and to discourage open discussion about the danger BSE might pose to humans. A full six years before officials went public about the risk, the British journal *Nature* chided authorities for keeping people in the dark:

Never say that there is not danger (risk). Instead, say that there is always a danger (risk), and that the problem is to calculate what it is. And never say that the risk is negligible unless you are sure that your listeners share your own philosophy of life. ("Mad Cows and the Minister," 1990, p. 278)

The author of the article stressed that that the minister of agriculture "should be obliged to tell it like it is" (p. 278) and admonished that the cost of false reassurance was fear, distrust, and economic instability. "The British will not eat beef for fear that it will kill them, and the price has fallen ever further" (p. 278).

Downplaying the risk of eating beef ultimately created a sense of public distrust that made it difficult to believe anything the government said. Although risk communication professionals are sometimes in the business of soothing fears, in this case, health officials violated an important tenet of risk and crisis communication: *Be open about what you know, even if you don't have all the answers.* False reassurance—what Peter Sandman (2006a) calls "optimism masquerading as information" (para. 9)—can actually heighten fears and mistrust. This is supported by a second lesson that belies conventional wisdom: *Citizens rarely panic when they are well-informed.* Reporting on 50 years of research about people's behavior during disasters, Lee Clarke (2002) observes that, despite the "panic myth," people rarely act irrationally or selfishly in crisis situations. Instead, emergencies usually bring out the best in people. "When danger arises, the rule—as in normal situations—is for people to help those next to them before they help themselves" (Clarke, 2002, p. 24).

Sandman (2006b) describes three "risk communication traditions": (1) helping people who are *insufficiently concerned* appreciate that a serious risk exists; (2) reassuring and calming people who are *excessively concerned*; and (3) working with people who are *appropriately concerned* (those who are "genuinely endangered and rightly upset") to help them cope and function effectively (p. 257).

In its broadest sense, crisis communication can involve any number of events—a natural disaster, a scandal that rocks a political campaign, an epidemic, a chemical spill, and so on. In this chapter, we focus on communication about crises that involve public health. The Centers for Disease Control and Prevention (CDC, 2008) define health-related **crisis communication** as:

> An approach used by scientists and public health professionals to provide information that allows an individual, stakeholders, or an entire community to make the best possible decisions about their well-being, under nearly impossible time constraints, while accepting the imperfect nature of their choices. (para. 2)

The definition is telling in that it acknowledges "the nearly impossible" demands and the inherently "imperfect" nature of crisis management. Public health expert Deborah Glik (2007) observes that a crisis involves "unexpectedness, high levels of threat, an aroused and stressed population, and media looking for breaking news stories" (p. 35). Practitioners work hard to lay solid groundwork and learn everything they can, but overwhelming demands and emotions can challenge even the most experienced professionals.

Managing Perceptions

In her review of risk communication research, Katherine McComas (2006) observes that people tend to perceive some risks, such as being attacked by a shark while swimming at the beach, to be greater than they actually are, whereas people tend to have "optimistic biases" or "illusions of invulnerability" about other, statistically more threatening, risks, such as smoking and sun exposure (p. 78). This is particularly true when the risky behavior has pleasant or socially rewarding implications. For example, despite warning messages that we have heard, we may tell ourselves that we're too young to

CAN YOU GUESS? Part 1

1. Which state in the United States has the highest percentage of insured residents? Which state has the lowest percentage?

2. If you were buying health insurance for your family in the Philippines, how much would you pay per year?

3. If you were buying health insurance for your family in the United States, how much would you pay per year?

Answers appear at the end of the chapter.

IN YOUR EXPERIENCE

What has your experience been in crisis situations?

get skin cancer, that we'll put on sunscreen later, or that having a suntan is worth the risk.

Ratzan and Meltzer (2005) point out that consumers are not wrong when they see things differently from experts; they just have a different vantage point. "These two audiences receive different information, process it in unique ways, and respond to conclusions based on their own set of circumstances and concerns" (Ratzan & Meltzer, 2005, p. 324). It's complicated, of course, because members of the public are not uniform in their perceptions. For example, you may have felt your anxiety rise while reading about mad cow disease, perhaps because you've been to England, have seen news footage of infected cows struggling to walk, or you know how devastating a debilitating disease can be. Meanwhile, some readers may feel insulated from the issue and wonder what all the fuss is about. There's no right way to feel. Instead, we must remember as health communication practitioners that belittling or ignoring diverse perspectives is typically ineffective and even unethical.

How Scared Is Scared Enough?

While interacting with the public about health risks and crises, it's sometimes difficult to judge how much fear is productive and how much is disabling. It sometimes seems that public health advocates want people to be afraid of something nearly all of the time. As Dawn Hillier (2006) puts it, well-meaning health promoters sometimes feed the public "a steady diet of fearful programmes about impending calamities" (p. 30). After a while, people may be either too fearful to make effective choices or so weary of "fear appeals" that they discount them altogether. However, a *rational* fear of horrible outcomes is healthy and motivational. It's a fine line to walk. Sandman (2006b) captured the dilemma well when he wrote:

> The Holy Grail of crisis communicators is to get people to take precautions without frightening them. This is like trying to write a novel without using the letter "e"; it may be possible, but it's certainly a handicap. (p. 258)

By way of example, Sandman quotes a *New York Times* headline that read "Fear Is Spreading Faster Than SARS." He retorts: "As if it weren't supposed to. . . . If the purpose of fear is to motivate precautions, after all, then the fear must come before the precautions are needed" (p. 259). We will talk more about fear appeals in Chapter 14.

In the Heat of the Moment

An assortment of "lessons learned" appear in italics throughout this chapter. As I alluded to earlier, one of the lessons is that *crisis communication looks easier on paper than it feels in reality.* Vicki Freimuth (2006) recalls the challenges that health communication specialists at the CDC faced after the 2001 anthrax attacks:

> Health communicators have a particularly difficult time with speed, as they are accustomed to conducting formative research, carefully segmenting audiences, planning messages, and pretesting before releasing them. [In a crisis] all of these activities have to occur in hours, not days, weeks, or months. Theory and research are still critical, but must be internalized by the communicators so they are available to use on the spot. (p. 144)

And a cool-headed commitment to safety can be even more difficult at the actual site of an emergency. Dave Johnson (2006) recalls the chaos at the World Trade Centers when they were attacked in 2001:

> A violent explosion rips through your office complex. Multiple fires are burning. An ominous plume of heat, fire, dust, debris and an unknowable mixture of perhaps asbestos, silica, lead and other metals floats into the atmosphere. . . .

Firefighters and police and EMTs, over which you have no authority, arrive on the scene. The fire chief says "Get out of our way." His guys, and the police, don't wear proper protection. . . . Your own workforce is shocked. Some rush past the fires and debris, into the plume, searching for comrades. . . . It's chaotic. You're operating in a fog of disaster. . . . What do you say to your own workforce? To those outside your control, such as the firefighters? To the crowd of reporters? To threatened residents and business owners? And to your CEO, who won't wear a hard hat or respirator or safety glasses because, "We don't want to scare people"? (p. 58)

Johnson, who is editor of *Industrial Safety & Hygiene News,* presents some of the lessons learned about risk communication at ground zero.

- *"Beware of overly optimistic risk assessments,"* as when an EPA administrator prematurely announced one week after the disaster that the air in New York City was "safe to breathe" (p. 58). False reassurance can undermine experts' credibility and put people in danger.
- *Understand the different information needs of various stakeholders.* The ground-zero team found that, after workers heard officials reassure the public that the site was safe, supervisors had a hard time convincing the workers to use proper safety gear and caution.
- *"Understand the emotions and fears you are dealing with"* (p. 60). People who are worried, anxious, angry, or grief-stricken are likely to brush aside safety concerns, then be sorry later.
- *"Expect resistance to your message"* and don't give up (p. 60). Use a range of methods if necessary. When even New York City mayor Rudy Giuliani balked about wearing a hardhat, the ground-zero team presented him with one that said "VIP—Mayor" on the front. "It worked," said Stewart Burkhammer, an environmental safety and health consultant working at ground zero. At other times, Burkhammer said, bluntness worked better than subtlety. He once told the crew at a morning safety meeting, "I'm not going to be the one to tell the mayor we just killed somebody, so clean up your act" (quoted by Johnson, 2006, p. 62).
- *Foster relationships and open communication with partners (media, emergency personnel, and so on) before, during, and after a crisis.*

BOX 12.2 THEORETICAL INSIGHTS

Risk Management/ Communication Framework

Imagine that, after eating lunch in their school cafeteria, 125 local children have become ill, some of them requiring hospitalization. As the health education supervisor at the health department, you are expected to help manage the crisis. Your staff has received 25 calls from worried parents and 15 calls from media professionals, and the issue hasn't even hit the news yet. What do you do first?

You might start by refreshing your knowledge of Scott Ratzan and Wendy Meltzer's (2005) **risk management/communication framework** (RMCF). Drawing on extensive experience in crisis and risk communication, Ratzan and Meltzer developed their model to be an elegant and useful synthesis of guidelines presented in the WHO Maxims for Effective Health and Risk Communication, the U.S. Food and Drug Administration (FDA) Model for Risk Management, Covello's (2003) Best Practices in Public Health Risks and Crisis Communication, and other trusted models.

ESTABLISHING THE FOUNDATIONS

If you're wise, the first step in managing the crisis actually began long before it occurred. Experts recommend developing interactive and trusting relationships with stakeholders when things are calm. They also recommend creating teams and crisis management plans and practicing what to do when a crisis occurs. Another precaution is to collect information that will be helpful, quick at hand, and tailored to different audiences. Ratzan and Meltzer (2005) point out that there isn't always time in a crisis to construct and pretest new messages carefully. In your case, having ready access to good information about food-borne illnesses will make your job a great deal easier.

PARTNERING WITH STAKEHOLDERS

Stakeholders are important before, during, and after a crisis. Ratzan and Meltzer (2005) embrace a broad definition of *stakeholders* as "anyone and everyone touched by the event" (p. 325). In your case, this might mean parents, children, school employees, reporters, public officials, health professionals, food distribution and preparation personnel, state agencies, and

more. Ratzan and Meltzer observe that there are several benefits of engaging stakeholders: (1) they give you valuable, diverse input; (2) they can be (should be) active partners in achieving shared goals; and (3) mutual trust will allow you to be honest and open with each other.

In the current crisis, you might not know all of the stakeholders personally, but if you have made it a point to interact with at least a few key people in each group, you will be more effective in this crisis. In addition, you can activate your network to extend outreach to stakeholder groups. For example, if the health department supplies local schools with nurses, you might enlist the nurses' help in communicating with stakeholders. In the same way, you might call on health inspectors, media relations staff, PTA presidents, and others. If you have laid good groundwork and are open and trustworthy with stakeholders, a crisis can renew and strengthen relationships rather than damage them (Ratzan & Meltzer, 2005; Ulmer, Seeger, & Sellnow, 2007).

COMMUNICATING WITH THE PUBLIC

The majority of what you want conveyed will be passed along through mass media. Understanding media professionals' goals will help you work as partners rather than as adversaries. Be mindful that reporters have a stake in presenting immediate, accurate, and interesting information to the public. They look as foolish as you do if they pass along inaccurate information. But this doesn't mean you should keep them waiting until you know everything. "Today's media have a need for constant information updates to fill 24-hour broadcasts," Ratzan and Meltzer (2005) advise, adding: "Crisis communicators need to be aware that if they do not supply information, the media will report what they have" (p. 328).

In communicating with the public (either in person or through media channels), Ratzan and Meltzer (2005) recommend, be "clear, honest and compassionate" (p. 330). Being clear requires that you consider the different needs and literacy levels of stakeholders. Information that might make sense to researchers and clinicians can bewilder and frighten members of the public. All the while, show that you care and are feeling emotions. "This is the exact reason Mayor

Giuliani was so successful at managing a citywide crisis" after the 9/11 terrorist attacks, say Ratzan and Meltzer (p. 331). City residents believed that he genuinely cared. However, be sure that you don't allow your emotions to exaggerate or minimize the severity of the crisis. Your words and demeanor convey to the public how they should think and feel about the crisis. Always "think before you speak," urge Ratzan and Meltzer (p. 331).

INTERNAL COMMUNICATION STRATEGIES

In the general rush to meet public and media demands, it's easy to neglect teamwork in a crisis. But this oversight can lead to devastating mistakes. Ratzan and Meltzer (2005) underscore the importance of communicating regularly with members of your team. Depending on the duration of the crisis, you might call daily or twice-a-day briefings at which everyone can compare notes and impressions.

With these principles in mind, RMCF presents five stages of risk management (quoted verbatim from Ratzan & Meltzer, 2005, p. 335):

1. *Risk assessment:* Estimation and evaluation of risk
2. *Risk confrontation:* Determining acceptable level of risk in a larger context
3. *Risk intervention:* Risk control action
4. *Risk communication:* Interactive process of exchanging risk information
5. *Risk management evaluation:* Measure and ensure effectiveness or risk management efforts

As indicated, each of these stages involves partnering with stakeholders (members of the public, experts, media professionals, and others), making decisions, creating messages and communication strategies, and continually monitoring and refining your strategies.

WHAT DO YOU THINK?

With regard to the "sick schoolchildren" crisis described at the opening of this box:

1. Where would you begin? What would you do first?
2. What stakeholders might you involve, and why? What questions would you ask each stakeholder group?
3. How would you enlist the stakeholders as active partners in the process?
4. How will you get (and convey) answers to reporters' questions such as the following: How sick are the children? Could this be deadly? Can you arrange interviews with some of the children or parents? How likely is it that other children will come down sick? Have you definitively linked the illness to food served at school? If so, what food was it? Who is responsible for food at school? Is there a chance that the tainted food was distributed to other schools as well? To restaurants? To grocery stores?
5. What will you do when your staff can't keep up with all the phone calls, much less research the issue and contact stakeholders?
6. When the crisis has passed, how will you evaluate the success or failure of your efforts?
7. What might you do to prepare for future risks and crises?

SUGGESTED SOURCES

Covello, V. (2003). Best practices in public health risk and crisis communication. *Journal of Health Communication, 8*(1S), 5–8.

Ratzan, S., & Meltzer, W. (2005). (2005). State of the art in crisis communication: Past lessons and principles of practice. In M. Haider (Ed.), *Global public health communication: Challenges, perspectives, and strategies* (pp. 321–347). Boston: Jones and Bartlett.

Sixth Futures Forum on Crisis Communication. (2004, May). Reykjavik, Iceland. World Health Organization. Available online at www.euro.who.int/document/E85056.pdf

---

• *Be proactive rather than reactive.* "Communicate and instruct as much as possible in advance of an emergency," recommends Burkhammer. "We spent a lot of time being great reactors. . . . A lot of things were done by feel and guess. I think we were very poor proactors" (p. 62).

Box 12.2 presents a framework to help guide your efforts as you prepare for and manage a health crisis. With these lessons in mind, let's examine a few case studies involving risk and crisis communication around the globe.

Case Studies: A Global Perspective

In the past it was largely feasible to contain contagious illnesses such as smallpox and yellow fever to geographic sectors. Now, because more than 2 billion people a day fly to locations it would have taken days, weeks, or months to reach in the past, "an outbreak or epidemic in any one part of the world is only a few hours away from becoming an imminent threat somewhere else" (World Health Report, 2007, p. x). (See Box 12.3 for a profile of famous disease carriers and some tough considerations about personal liberties and public welfare.)

BOX 12.3   PERSPECTIVES

Typhoid Mary and TB Andy

Andrew Speaker, an Atlanta resident with drug-resistant tuberculosis (TB), traveled by plane to Europe and back in 2007, even though doctors say they told him not to fly because of the risk to others. Tuberculosis is dangerous and highly contagious, particularly in the recirculated air of an airplane cabin. Nearly 2 million people a year die from TB, mostly in developing countries (Global Health, 2008). The disease has made a deadly comeback in recent years because new strains have emerged that do not respond to drug therapy, and people with immune deficiencies such as HIV and AIDS are particularly susceptible to TB whether they have been immunized or not.

In Speaker's case, authorities in Italy were alerted to his health status and they refused to allow him to board a flight back to the United States. So Speaker and his wife (they were on their honeymoon) flew to Canada instead, where his status went unnoticed, and they were able to fly back to Atlanta. Many fellow airline passengers, angry that Speaker knowingly exposed them to a dangerous disease, later filed charges against him ("Plane Passengers Sue," 2007).

Some journalists nicknamed Speaker "TB Andy," referencing another famous figure in history, Typhoid Mary. In the years preceding 1906, Mary Mallon was a cook for wealthy families in New York. Authorities began to notice that, in the homes where she worked, an extraordinary number of people contracted typhoid fever. At the time, about 10% of people who got typhoid died from it. Mallon resisted being tested or being taken into custody. Indeed, she "brandished a meat fork and threats" so vociferously that it took five police officers to bring her in ("TV Program," 2004, para. 6).

Tests showed that Mallon was a typhoid carrier, although she manifested no symptoms herself. She was forcibly quarantined in a hospital on an island in New York City's East River. Her distraught letters from the time relate that she felt like a kidnap victim and a "peep show" ("In Her Own Words," 2004, last paragraph). Mallon was released after about 6 years. But when she disobeyed orders and returned to cooking professionally, she was taken into custody for the rest of her life. Historians have mixed feelings about whether Mallon was treated fairly or not.

WHAT DO YOU THINK?

1. Should the state take people into custody if they refuse to take actions (such as wearing gloves or face masks, agreeing not to fly, and so on) that would protect others from catching their illnesses? Does it matter what illness it is? Do colds and flu count? What about illnesses that are somewhat, but not highly, contagious?

2. Should airlines beef up their "no fly" lists so that people with highly contagious diseases are not permitted aboard? Why or why not?

3. If a person knowingly exposes others to a contagious disease, should the people who are exposed have the right to sue? Would you? Why or why not?

4. Historians have noted that Mary Mallon had little means of earning a living besides being a cook. If protecting others means changing careers, should the government help pay for new vocational training or education?

5. People whose immune systems are compromised by illness, chemotherapy, or other conditions are particularly susceptible to diseases that wouldn't endanger others. Should we exercise greater-than-usual precautions knowing

that such people are in our communities? Why or why not? What precautions would you consider reasonable?

6. In some countries, people who have colds wear disposable face masks (like surgical masks) in public to protect others. Should other countries adopt this practice as well? Why or why not? Would you wear a mask when you had a cold? Why or why not?

7. Many illnesses could be prevented if people washed their hands before eating. In Japan, even fast-food restaurants provide moist towelettes with every meal. Do you think other countries should adopt this practice? Why or why not?

8. A common means of transmitting illness is shaking hands with others and then touching food. Some people suggest that we'd be healthier (and perhaps avert epidemics) if we bowed or waved in greeting instead of shaking hands. What do you think?

For an excellent video about Mary Mallon, as well as discussion guides and ethical analyses, see www.pbs .org/wgbh/nova/typhoid.

Another problem is that diseases—and their resistance to known drugs—are multiplying. Margaret Chan, director-general of WHO, cautions that, since 1970, about one new disease has surfaced every year, contributing to the incidence of thousands of epidemics around the world ("World Health Report," 2007).

Contact with other people, especially a *lot* of other people, can be hazardous to your health. But health risks involve more than communicable diseases. They also encompass environmental issues, safety practices, exposure to hazardous substances, contaminated food and water, natural disasters, and more. The good news is that globalization has also improved worldwide awareness of public health. After a catastrophic earthquake and tsunami hit Japan in 2011, people around the world contributed more than $6.3 billion to the region ("One Year Since," 2012).

We could fill volumes with descriptions of public health issues around the world. Instead, let's look at a few case studies that illustrate some key principles, challenges, and lessons. The following discussion focuses on AIDS, bioterrorism, SARS, and avian flu.

Children in Sub-Saharan Africa can only hope for a brighter future than current conditions predict. That region now has the highest concentration of HIV infection in the world. (Photo provided by UNAIDS/A. Gutman)

AIDS

AIDS has been called the greatest public health challenge of the last half century. It has killed more than 30 million people since 1981, and about 33.3 million people are now living with HIV or AIDS. The death rate is close to 2 million people per year. And the crisis is particularly bad in Africa, where about 75% of those deaths occur ("Global AIDS Epidemic," 2010).

One challenge of AIDS is that related behaviors are sometimes considered taboo, immoral, or too personal to be discussed. Cultural rules about these behaviors vary widely from culture to culture. For example, although members of Western cultures mean well, their Judeo-Christian worldview can be baffling to others. Americans missed the mark when they designed public health messages urging people in Namibia, Africa, to prevent HIV by abstaining from premarital sex and by being faithful to their spouses. These concepts are not meaningful to most Namibian citizens, who are accustomed to polygamy and who tend to define marriage very loosely (Hillier, 2006). Hillier concludes: "Prevention campaigns have been silent about polygamous sexual cultures. . . . [They have] elevated the Christian monogamous marriage to the most desirable norm but it is not the only or most common form of sexual union" (p. 18). As a result, many foreign efforts are culturally unacceptable and are therefore ineffective at changing people's behavior.

Another difficulty is that HIV and AIDS cannot yet be prevented with a pill or a shot. The only way to prevent transmission is by changing people's behavior (Schneider, 2006). That's a tremendous challenge. And the issue can't wait. The average age of Sub-Saharan African residents has already plummeted from 62 to 47, mostly because of premature deaths from AIDS (AVERT, 2008).

Some health communication specialists have concluded that it's naive to assume that most people *won't* have sex. The trick, they feel, is to make safer sex sexier. The Pleasure Project, based in Oxford, England, is a cooperative effort to emphasize the erotic appeal of safer sex. The project's website explains:

> While most safer sex and HIV prevention programs are negative and disease-focused, The Pleasure Project is different: We take a positive, liberating, and sexy approach to safer sex. Think of it is as sex education . . . with the emphasis on "sex."

Project coordinators present condoms and alternatives to sexual intercourse as exciting and erotically stimulating. The website includes a racy directory of related organizations and programs, erotic tips for safer sex, and links to organizations that sell condoms and sex toys and donate the proceeds to the safer sex campaign.

The safer-sex-is-better-sex effort has been applauded by a range of public health experts. After reviewing relevant research, the authors of a Viewpoint article in *The Lancet* concur:

> Since pursuit of pleasure is one of the main reasons that people have sex, this factor must be

CHECK IT OUT!   You can access the Pleasure Project website at www.thepleasureproject.org. (A word of warning: The website is sexually explicit.)

addressed when motivating people to use condoms and participate in safer sexual behaviour. (Philpott, Knerr, & Maher, 2006, p. 3)

These are just a few of the many approaches to preventing HIV and AIDS. The good news is that, although the crisis is still very real, the rate of infection has dropped 19% since it peaked in 1999, largely because of public health efforts ("AIDS Score Cards," 2010, p. 5). Some lessons learned include the following.

- *Listen and learn.* Knowing what the public believes and is willing to do is just as important, sometimes more important, than knowing what experts think people *should* do (Covello, 2003).
- *Vary your approach.* Fear appeals can be highly motivational, but particularly for frightening and long-term crises such as AIDS, people may tune out fear messages because they are overwhelming or overly familiar. Innovative, culturally sensitive appeals may regain people's attention.

SARS

One of the great success stories in managing a public health crisis arose from worldwide efforts to contain severe acute respiratory syndrome (SARS). The issue first drew attention in February 2003, when a man in Vietnam was admitted to a hospital with a respiratory disorder. His condition deteriorated, and, although he was transferred to a Hong Kong medical center, he died within four days. Soon, seven caregivers who had been involved with the patient became sick as well. The disorder spread so quickly that, in slightly more a month, there were 150 cases of SARS in eight countries (WHO, 2003, March 16).

By May 2003, SARS had become a pandemic. New cases were emerging at the rate of 200 a day. The disease had spread to every continent. A total

of 8,000 people in 28 countries were infected (WHO, 2003, June 18). SARS was especially hard to contain because it was easily spread from person to person, it was infectious for more than a week before symptoms appeared, and it was hard to diagnose because the initial symptoms were similar to those of many other illnesses. Worst of all, SARS was deadly. About 10% of people who were infected (many of them hospital personnel) died.

The authors of the World Health Report (2007) recall:

> SARS incited a degree of public anxiety that virtually halted travel to affected areas and drained billions of dollars from economies across entire regions. . . . It showed that the danger arising from emerging diseases is universal. No country, rich or poor, is adequately protected from either the arrival of a new disease on its territory or the subsequent disruption this can cause. (p. xix)

However, it might have been worse. Remarkably, just 100 days into the crisis (June 18, 2003), spokespersons for WHO announced that the pandemic was under control and that new cases had dwindled to a handful a day. The crisis was over by July. How was that possible? Lessons from the experience illustrate how it happened.

- *Develop strong teams.* WHO credits "monumental efforts" by governments, health professionals, and public health agencies. Because officials around the world reported cases promptly, WHO and other agencies were able to monitor and contain new outbreaks as much as possible. WHO dubbed it "solidarity" and "interdependence" on a global scale never seen before (WHO, 2003, June 18, para. 8).

- *Don't forget the basics.* One of the world's oldest methods of limiting contagion, quarantines, worked. Officials worked internationally to limit travel that might expose people to SARS. At the same time, hospitals designated isolated SARS wards to keep those patients away from others.

- *Make the most of communication technology.* Communication technology allowed researchers and health experts to share data and new developments quickly and accurately. Because of this, they figured out how SARS was transmitted "in record time" (WHO, 2003, June 18, para. 11).

- *Keep everyone informed.* Although experts did a good job communicating with each other, members of some affected populations were out of the loop. In China, because of tight government controls on media content, many people were frustrated by the lack of SARS news coverage. People in China who were desperate for news used the Internet to seek and share information about SARS that they couldn't get otherwise (Tai & Sun, 2007).

- *Stop it at the source.* Once officials knew that SARS was transmitted via droplets spread during coughing and sneezing, they were able to educate health care workers about how to minimize the risk of infection.

In just a few months, SARS took a heavy toll. By the time it was contained, 8,098 people had been infected and 774 of those had died (CDC, 2005). However, containing the disease so quickly saved millions of lives. The SARS case is regarded as a model response to a nearly unthinkable public health threat.

Anthrax

Some public health crises are the result of intentional acts. The CDC (2007) defines **bioterrorism** as "the deliberate release of viruses, bacteria, or other germs (agents) used to cause illness or death in people, animals, or plants" (para. 1). Bioterrorism is not new. Schneider (2006) points out that when European settlers purposely gave Native Americans blankets used by people with smallpox, they were engaging in (tragically effective) germ warfare. Today, dense population centers are especially vulnerable to bioterrorism. Since 2001, the U.S. government has spent $635 billion on homeland security, yet hospital personnel warn that a widespread attack could easily overwhelm the health care system (Stone, 2011; "Threat," 2008). Bioterrorism, understandably, incites a great deal of fear.

One act of bioterrorism on American soil occurred in 2001, when 22 people were sickened and 5 died after contact with letters containing anthrax spores. Anthrax is a potentially deadly disease that people can get by breathing in, touching, or digesting a rare bacterium. In September and October 2001, someone sent four envelopes containing anthrax spores to media professionals and government officials. In doing so, the terrorist put many people, including postal workers and mailroom employees, at grave risk.

Because the anthrax attacks occurred soon after the terrorist attacks of September 11, public anxiety was particularly high. And because the attacks occurred through the mail, it was difficult to know who had been or might be exposed to anthrax. Potentially, anyone in the country might be next. As Haider and Aravindakshan (2005) put it: "The threat turned junk mail into potential parcels of danger" (p. 393). In contrast to a typical illness, which begins in one place and then may spread, this one was immediately a nationwide concern (Gursky, Inglesby, & O'Toole, 2003). At one point, health officials put 32,000 people on antibiotics, a preemptive move that experts speculate saved many lives.

In the article "Order Out of Chaos," Freimuth (2006) describes how the CDC Office of Communication (of which she was director) functioned in the high-pressure weeks following the anthrax attacks. The CDC is the arm of the U.S. Department of Health and Human Services in charge of public health efforts, education, information, and more. Staff members in the media relations office, which is one component of the communication division, usually field about 55 calls a week. But they received an average of 1,283 calls

WHAT DO YOU THINK?

■ Given the opportunity, would you like to be part of a crisis management team such as the CDC communication team? Why or why not?
■ What aspects of the job appeal to you most?
■ What do you think would be most difficult?
See Career Opportunities (Box 12.1) for resources.

a week in the 6 weeks following the anthrax attacks (Freimuth, 2006). In addition, the staff coordinated a total of 373 press briefings, press statements, and broadcast interviews in that time. "It was common in a single day to have interview requests from every network morning show, every network evening news hours, and the *Larry King Hour*," recalls Freimuth (p. 144). Since there was no way the 10-person media relations staff could meet the demands on their own, Freimuth oversaw a temporary reorganization in which the staff was tripled to 30 people who each worked four days a week, overlapping one day in the middle.

As with many public health crises, one of the greatest hurdles was managing uncertainty. Scientific evidence about inhalable anthrax was scant, and information that emerged was sometimes incomplete and inaccurate. As new information was released, media professionals sometimes treated the old information as "mistakes" (Freimuth, 2006, p. 142). And, in their eagerness to get information, some reporters turned to untrustworthy sources who were willing to offer speculative and self-serving information. The CDC staff, which prides itself on a "slow, thoughtful scientific" process, was forced to work quickly and with less deliberation than usual (Freimuth, 2006, p. 142). Friction sometimes resulted when scientists were concerned that their research might be oversimplified, but it was necessary to summarize scientific findings quickly and make them easy to understand. All the while, the FBI (which was officially in charge of the case) wanted some details kept secret to avoid compromising the investigation.

To keep up with demands and to ensure that stakeholder groups were not overlooked, members of the CDC communication staff organized themselves into teams. One team communicated with clinicians, another with concerned citizens, still others with media professionals, policy-makers, and the like. As in most crises, success was defined largely by communication. "Not all of these staff had to be communication specialists, but they needed to be managed by communication staff so that messages could be consistent across the agency and delivered in a timely manner," writes Freimuth (2006, p. 146).

Another challenge was to identify and prepare spokespeople. Freimuth (2006) reflects that the public naturally looks to political leaders for information and updates. But those leaders are often not well informed about scientific details, and they tend to comfort audiences rather than level with them. Scientists, although more knowledgeable, often err in the other direction, coming off as "logical and unemotional" (Freimuth, 2006, p. 142). The process of choosing and preparing spokespeople was difficult, but it was worth the extra effort. Kristen Swain's (2007) study of news coverage during the anthrax crisis shows that audiences responded most favorably when information was specific and was clearly linked to trustworthy sources.

The anthrax case involved people from many agencies and organizations. At the height of the crisis, when a suspicious substance was reported in the western United States, Freimuth was awakened at 3 a.m. to take part in a conference call involving nearly 15 people from a wide range of agencies. "It was impossible to sort out who was with what organization and what position they held," she says, "yet in that phone call, decisions had to be reached" (Freimuth, 2006, p. 143).

Many of the same confounders emerged in the anthrax case as in the mad cow disease saga: uncertainty, tension between agencies, the temptation to comfort, reluctance to frighten the public unduly, and so on. The anthrax case occurred over a shorter, more intense interval, however. And, although the anthrax case revealed serious deficits in the government's preparedness for a bioterrorist attack, the CDC Office of Communication was lauded as doing an admirable job during extremely trying circumstances.

The following lessons about public health and risk/crisis communication emerge from the anthrax case:

- *Crisis is a matter of perception.* In the same year that anthrax killed 5 people, 30,000 others died from influenza (Lovett, 2003). It's a phenomenon that risk and crisis communicators know well: Fear and uncertainty elevate some health concerns to crisis status, while far more prevalent killers, such as the flu and diabetes, often fail to make headlines.
- *Even if you don't specialize in crisis management, learn as much as you can about it and be prepared to take part.* The media relations restructuring was possible because the CDC staff pulled communication experts from a range of other duties and partnered them with content experts. Freimuth (2006) advises: "Health communicators working in any public health context need to add risk communication and crisis management skills to their repertoire" (p. 148).
- *Even in the midst of a crisis, don't be afraid to restructure the system if it helps you respond to stakeholders more effectively.*
- *Show genuine compassion.* Empathize with people's fears, sadness, and frustration. Crisis communication expert Vincent Covello (2003) advises: "Avoid using distant, unfeeling language when discussing harm, deaths, injuries, and illness" (p. 7).
- *Speaking with many voices is sometimes okay.* This lesson runs counter to crisis management advice for companies, individuals, and political campaigns. In those instances, it's important to deliver a clear, consistent message to the public. But a public health campaign is usually far more complex, and evidence suggests that allowing a range of viewpoints is sometimes effective and even preferable. After studying the anthrax case, L. Clarke and colleagues (2006) concluded that the situation was "naturally given to the expression of many voices" and that "a single voice with a single message would have been so discordant with actual circumstances that it could only misrepresent the risks that people might face" (p.

 WHAT DO YOU THINK?

■ If an incident of bioterrorism occurs in your state or community, what spokespeople will you trust most? Why?

■ What type of information will you want?

■ Through what channels are you most likely to seek information?

167). Experience shows that, even in a crisis, people expect and can cope with a range of expert viewpoints on complex issues. One caveat is that audiences who are already distrustful of public health messages may assume sources are being dishonest if they provide inconsistent information (Meredith, Eisenman, Rhodes, Ryan, & Long, 2007). For this reason, it is important not to hide inconsistencies, but to acknowledge and explain why they exist (Seeger, 2006).

- *Don't go it alone.* Covello (2003) advises organizations to "coordinate, collaborate, and partner with other credible sources" (p. 6). Such teamwork can help offset overwhelming demands on any one organization and can demonstrate to the public that multiple sources agree on key issues.

- *Don't overlook "forgotten publics."* In the anthrax case, postal workers were particularly sensitive to any implication that their safety was less important than the people to whom the dangerous letters were addressed. Similar tensions arose on a greater scale during the Hurricane Katrina crisis, when government agencies were accused of devaluing New Orleans residents on the basis of race and socioeconomic status (Fisher, 2007; Littlefield & Quenette, 2007; Waymer & Heath, 2007).

Next we turn to an issue that, as of this writing, is still in the pre-crisis phase.

Avian Flu

If you vowed never to eat another hamburger after reading the mad cow disease saga, take a deep breath. Like mad cow disease, avian flu has been passed from animals (in this case, birds) to people. But the effects are far more devastating. Compared to 10% of infected people who died from SARS, some 65% of people who get this version of bird flu (known so far as H5N1) die from it. In serious cases, there's nothing doctors can do. Within days, lung tissue dies, and so does the patient.

The first documented case of H5N1 occurred in Hong Kong in 1997. After that, the government oversaw the killing of every chicken in Hong Kong (about 1.5 million birds) (Appenzeller, 2005). The disease seemed to go away. But it resurfaced in 2003, killing millions of birds and affecting some humans. By 2007, more than 350 human cases had

CHECK IT OUT! Following are links to some risk/crisis communication centers:

■ Center for Risk Communication: www.centerforrisk-communication.com/home.htm

■ The Communication Initiative Network: www.com-minit.com

■ Peter Sandman's interactive blog about crisis and risk communication: www.psandman.com/gst2006.htm

Also check university websites. Many schools have developed centers for risk and crisis communication as well as degree programs in the field.

been diagnosed, and 230 people had died from it (WHO, 2007d).

The virus often kills birds in a matter of hours by destroying their lungs, brains, muscles, and intestines (Appenzeller, 2005). So far, people with H5N1 seem to have caught it from animals. Although scientists are not certain how the disease jumps to humans, they caution people to cook poultry fully, to use gloves and masks when handling live or dead birds, and not to use bird-dropping fertilizer.

But the real danger—and one that has public health officials around the world on high alert—is that this virus or a similar one will mutate so that it can spread from human to human. Flu viruses in the past have been remarkably adept at doing that. "It's bound to happen," predicts Jeremy Farrar, an Oxford University physician who specializes in avian flu, "and when it does, the world is going to face a truly horrible pandemic" (quoted by Appenzeller, 2005, para. 11).

If H5N1 becomes a pandemic, millions of people could die. It has happened before. During World War I, some 50 million people died from Spanish flu. That's more than three times the number of soldiers who died in the war (Appenzeller, 2005). Like avian flu, Spanish flu probably jumped from animals to people. That type of mutation is extremely dangerous because humans have few antibodies to protect them from the novel virus.

And if you're thinking that you rarely get the flu or that you get over it quickly when you do, beware. This version of the flu is especially dangerous for people who have well-functioning immune systems.

In serious cases, avian flu so overstimulates the body's immune system that the lungs become grossly inflamed with white blood cells, and life-sustaining tissues die (Appenzeller, 2005).

It's difficult to imagine overplanning for a crisis such as avian flu. As Barbara Reynolds (2006) points out, in any health crisis, "the devil is most certainly in the details" (p. 249). WHO (2007c) has released rapid-response guidelines for containing a deadly flu pandemic. Public health personnel in your community are probably already working on the local plan. WHO guidelines include the following: (1) Create a geographic "containment zone" when the first cases surface in order to separate people who have the disease, as well as those who have been exposed to it, from other people; (2)

create a "buffer zone" around the containment zone to reduce further the risk of contagion; and (3) communicate effectively with the public to maintain barriers, keep people informed, ensure that people within the containment zone have adequate care and supplies, and minimize stigmatization of people with the disease.

How will this work exactly? It sounds a bit frightening, but it's not as scary as the alternative. Imagine your community partitioned with roadblocks, warning signs, and guarded screening stations. No one except essential personnel will go in or out of containment zones for at least 20 days. It sounds like something from a movie, but it's no exaggeration. Health officials realize that the only way to save lives is to limit the spread of the virus. Inside the containment zone—which could be your neighborhood or a portion of your hometown—health officials will monitor people's health, care for and quarantine (in a hospital or at home) people who are infected, watch for new outbreaks, and help distribute antiviral medication to those who are still healthy. (See Box 12.4 for more about ethical dilemmas concerning who should receive the limited number of vaccines available.)

WHAT DO YOU THINK?

■ Would you be frightened if a containment zone were declared in your area? Why or why not?

■ Do you feel adequately informed about, and prepared for, such a crisis?

BOX 12.4 ETHICAL CONSIDERATIONS

Who Should Be Vaccinated?

The good news is that researchers have created a vaccine for H5N1. It's not perfect because they don't know exactly how the virus will mutate. And researchers must still make sure there are no harmful side effects. But even if the vaccine is approved, there won't be enough for everyone. So public health experts face a dilemma. After reading about bird flu in this chapter, consider what you would do in their shoes.

1. If you had to choose, which of the following populations would you vaccinate and why? (a) people who are most likely to die from the disease if they get it; (b) service providers such as health care professionals, fire fighters, and police officers; or (c) another population of your choosing.

2. Would you first vaccinate people in communities in which avian flu cases have already been diagnosed? Why or why not? If those citizens or their governments are unable to afford the vaccine, do you believe people in other countries should help pay for it? Why or why not?

3. Viruses such as the flu often spread quickly among children. Would you vaccinate them early on? Why or why not?

4. Are you in favor of *requiring* people at high risk for avian flu (such as those who regularly handle birds) to get vaccinated? Why or why not?

5. Depending on how the virus mutates, the vaccine might not be especially effective. Do you think governments should invest in it anyway? Why or why not?

6. Given the opportunity, would you choose to be vaccinated? Why or why not?

This means that, if a person in your household becomes ill, you may all be confined to your home until officials can be sure you are not contagious. And even if everyone in your household is healthy, if an outbreak occurs in your area, it would be advisable to remain in your home. Public health experts recommend that everyone maintain a 2-week supply of food, water, and needed medications just in case. They also recommend that people wash their hands frequently and cover their mouths when sneezing or coughing.

Because we are currently in a pre-crisis, planning phase concerning the next pandemic flu, it is difficult to know what lessons will emerge. But it's interesting to note that health officials are consciously building on what worked well in the SARS case. A visit to the WHO, CDC, or PandemicFlu.gov website reveals an extensive collection of materials, including health-tracking software, government agency contact lists, brochures and checklists for a wide range of stakeholder groups, and more. (See *Check It Out!*)

As with many other components of public health and risk/crisis management, success depends largely on effective communication (Seeger, 2006). It is no longer defensible to think of avian flu as an Asian crisis or a future scenario. Sandman (2006b) advises crisis communicators to imagine "that the crisis has just begun and to make a list of things they wish the public had already learned or already done" (p. 259). As members of the public, we might ask ourselves: *Are we aware and prepared for a deadly flu pandemic? If containment zones were created in our community next week or next month, would we understand what was happening? Are we (and our neighbors) prepared to stay in our homes for 2 weeks or longer?* Ideally, the public should answer yes to these questions well in advance of the crisis.

Wrapping It Up

Public health can feel overwhelming at the best of times. Add a crisis, and the demands are even greater. Sometimes it helps to remember that challenges are happening all the time, but so are victories. In his article "Still a Privilege to Be a Doctor," pediatrician Lawrence Rifkin (2008) pauses to reflect on the small miracles that health advocates accomplish every day:

Ashley's in Room 3, with a positive rapid strep. It doesn't get more commonplace than that.

CHECK IT OUT!   Here are some links to pandemic response plans:

■ To view WHO's 6-minute video *Global Alert, Global Response,* go to www.who.int/csr/en.

■ The official U.S. government pandemic response plan is available at pandemicflu.gov.

■ CDC resources are available at cdc.gov/flu/pandemic-resources.

Then, with a sense of wonder, I remember: A century ago, rheumatic fever complications from strep were the No. 1 cause of death in school-age children. Now, we hardly see rheumatic fever in this country; a few generations ago, Ashley may have been one of the victims. As I write out yet another prescription for amoxicillin, I think maybe I just saved a life. (Rifkin, p. 28)

On that note, let's shift to another zone of opportunity in the quest for public health.

Health Care Reform

Many Americans assume that the U.S. health care system is the best in the world. And it is, in some respects. It is the most responsive health system on the planet, meaning that it's the quickest to adapt to changing health needs (Commonwealth Fund, 2008c). However, it is also the leader in terms of spending. In this section we will examine the pros and cons of the system and what lies ahead.

Despite spending more than any other nation, per capita, on health care, the United States falls far short in terms of keeping people alive and healthy (ranked 72 among 191 industrialized nations), charging a fair amount for health services relative to other life expenses (ranked 54/55 in a tie with Fiji), and providing equitable treatment for everyone (ranked 32 in terms of health distribution). Compared to health care in other countries, the United States health system doesn't make the Top 5 list. Not even the Top 20. It comes in 37th.

These are the conclusions of the *World Health Report 2000*, created by WHO. It is the latest— and, for most purposes, the only—worldwide ranking of health systems. In Table 12.1 you can see that the United States is ranked far behind France,

Table 12.1 **World Health Systems Performance Ranking**

RANKING AMONG WORLD HEALTH SYSTEMS		TYPE OF HEALTH COVERAGE
1	France	Universal
2	Italy	Universal
3	San Marino	Universal
4	Andorra	Universal
5	Malta	Universal
6	Singapore	Universal
7	Spain	Universal
8	Oman	Universal
9	Austria	Universal
10	Japan	Universal
11	Norway	Universal
12	Portugal	Universal
13	Monaco	Universal
14	Greece	Universal
15	Iceland	Universal
16	Luxembourg	Universal
17	Netherlands	Universal
18	United Kingdom	Universal
19	Ireland	Universal
20	Switzerland	Universal
21	Belgium	Universal
22	Colombia	Universal
23	Sweden	Universal
24	Cyprus	Universal
25	Germany	Universal
26	Saudi Arabia	Universal
27	United Arab Emirates	Universal
28	Israel	Universal
29	Morocco	
30	Canada	Universal
31	Finland	Universal
32	Australia	Universal
33	Chile	Universal
34	Denmark	Universal
36	Costa Rica	Universal
37	United States	*
38	Slovenia	Universal
39	Cuba	Universal
40	Brunei	Universal

SOURCE: World Health Organization World Health Report, 2000

*The United States did not have universal coverage when this report was issued but has since passed legislation to implement it

Italy, Japan, the United Kingdom, and even some lesser known nations such as Andorra in southwest Europe.

And WHO isn't alone in its assessment. When researchers at The Commonwealth Fund—a New York–based foundation dedicated to improving health care—issued their *National Scorecard on U.S. Health Systems Performance,* they gave the United States a D (65%) on overall health, quality of care, access to care, efficiency, and equity (Commonwealth Fund, 2008c). The report's authors concluded: "The U.S. health system is on the wrong track" (para. 3).

Something different may lie ahead as a consequence of health care reform legislation in the United States. We will discuss this in more detail. But first, let's look at the system prior to national reform and what some cities and states did even earlier.

Spending

If health equaled wealth, U.S. citizens would live longer than anyone else. The United States spends eight times the worldwide average, per capita, on health care. (See Figure 12.1.) Yet 28 countries have longer life expectancies (WHO, 2008b). Despite how much the United States spends, it has fewer physicians per citizen than many industrialized nations. (See Figure 12.2.) And many countries that spend less than the United States offer health care to all their citizens, whereas, prior to health care reform measures passed in 2010, 45 to 50 million Americans were without health insurance.

Waste

There is a disconnect in the United States between spending and overall health outcomes. Many experts feel that's because of waste and because a large portion of U.S. expenditures have benefitted people who are already well served, while leaving out citizens in the greatest need.

Part of the waste results from excessive bureaucracy. "Lowering insurance administrative costs

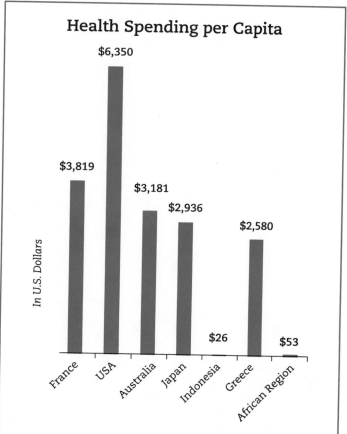

FIGURE 12.1 The United States spends more than any other nation, per capita, on health care.

Source: WHO, 2008b

alone could save up to $100 billion a year," according to the *National Scorecard* (Commonwealth Fund, 2008c, para. 6). The report's authors gave the United States an F (53%) on overall efficiency.

Waste also results from hospital visits and other care that could be avoided with better prevention efforts, more effective communication, and more equitable access to health care. Judged against prevention programs in 19 other industrialized nations, the United States came in last (Commonwealth Fund, 2008c). That's because Americans receive recommended levels of preventive care only about 55% of the time. Partly as a result, Americans suffer disproportionately from conditions that might

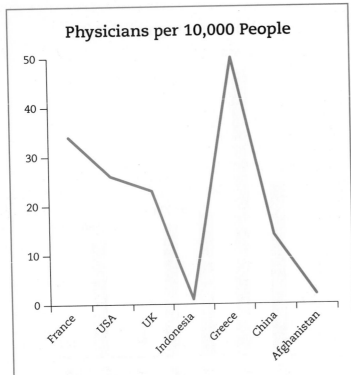

FIGURE 12.2 The United States has fewer physicians, per capita, than many countries, but far more than the poorest areas of the world. In Sierra Leone, there is only 1 doctor for every 36,574 people. If the doctor saw 15 patients a day and worked 7 days a week, it would still take more than 6½ years to see them all.

Source: WHO, 2008b

Moreover, money is squandered on duplications and inefficiencies. Americans are 3 to 4 times more likely than residents of other countries to report that their doctors order duplicate tests and don't have test results when they show up for appointments (Commonwealth Fund, 2008c). We have to ask: If doctors order duplicate tests because they have no good way of knowing if those tests have been done before or what they indicated, is it the doctors' fault or the system's fault? It's probably the system's fault.

A major culprit is the lack of medical information technology. In contrast to countries such as the Netherlands and New Zealand, in which nearly all physicians (98% and 92%, respectively) use **electronic medical records (EMRs)**, only about 57% of U.S. physicians utilize them (Hsiao, Hing, Socey, & Cal, 2012). EMRs (also called *EHRs*, for electronic health records) are similar to traditional patient records in that they chronicle medical visits, concerns, diagnoses, treatments, prescribed drugs, and so on. But because EMRs can be viewed and shared by a number of health professionals in different locations, they allow caregivers to more easily avoid treatment overlaps and drug interactions and to track patients' overall progress. EMRs are also invaluable in emergencies, when paper records might be unavailable or when waiting for them would waste precious time. As a result, EMTs save time, money, and lives. (On the bright side, only 17% of U.S. doctors used EMRs in 2001, so the figure is rising.)

Inequities and Oversights

Although the United States is the wealthiest nation on earth, the gap between *haves* and *have nots* is large, and that gap often determines who gets care. About 26% of families who earned at least $84,000 in 2007 said they would have sought more medical care if they could have afforded it. That's alarming enough. But among families that made half that much, most of them (61%) went without needed care (Commonwealth Fund, 2008a).

be prevented or minimized, such as obesity, diabetes, and cardiovascular disease, which affect about 150 million Americans (American College of Physicians, 2008, p. 55). Ignoring these conditions diminishes people's quality of life and productivity. It also wastes money, because preventing chronic conditions is typically less expensive than treating them once they have become serious.

💬 **IN YOUR EXPERIENCE**

Have you ever witnessed treatment duplications or health care practices that wasted time or money? If so, explain how.

In contrast, citizens of countries such as Canada, the Netherlands, and the United Kingdom seldom report that money is a concern when seeking care because their governments guarantee medical services for everyone (Commonwealth Fund, 2007).

In the United States, access to health care worsened for many decades. Health insurance premiums rose 10 times faster than wages between 2001 and 2008 (Robert Wood Johnson Foundation, 2008). Unable to afford coverage, an additional 14 million people joined the ranks of the uninsured, bringing the total to 49.9 million by the end of the decade (How, Fryer, McCarthy, Schoen, & Schor, 2011). Put another way, 4 in 10 adults under age 63 in the United States were uninsured or underinsured in 2008 (Commonwealth Fund, 2008c).

Quality of care varies by region. If you grew up in Massachusetts, for example, there's a 93% chance that you got all of the recommended vaccines when you were a toddler. But your odds are lower if you grew up in Nevada, where only 66.7% of youngsters get all their shots (State Scorecard, 2007, Table 3.4). The inequities begin at birth and last until death. In Maine, about 4.3 out of 1,000 babies die each year, compared to 10 infant deaths per 1,000 births in Mississippi (State Scorecard, 2007, Table 6.3). In North Dakota nursing homes, fewer than 8 in 100 high-risk residents get pressure sores, but in the District of Columbia, more than twice that many (19 out of 100) suffer from them (State Scorecard, 2007, Table 3.14). To find out how your state and country compare to others, see *Check It Out!*

Less Costs More

You might think that serving fewer people saves money. But the opposite is true. In the long run, it costs less to provide ongoing care than to wait until people's health deteriorates. In states with the lowest number of insured residents, the cost of health care is as much as 5 times greater than in well-insured states (Cantor, Schoen, Belloff, How, & McCarthy, 2007).

Many countries that outrank the United States in terms of health and longevity have devoted a greater percentage of their health care dollars to prevention and early detection. When I was in Japan studying their health system a few years ago, I was surprised to learn that most Japanese citizens see a doctor at least once month. The visits are often brief—just a

WHAT DO YOU THINK?

■ Are you surprised that the United States health system ranks 37th in the world? Why or why not?

■ What factors, if improved, might move the United States higher on the list?

CHECK IT OUT! To see how your state ranks in terms of health coverage, see the Henry J. Kaiser Family Foundation report at http://www.statehealth-facts.org/comparecat.jsp?cat=3.

few minutes long. But regular contact keeps lines of communication open and allows caregivers to monitor changes in people's health very closely. (This is a built-in feature of the Japanese system because doctors dispense prescription medication, usually in 2- or 4-week increments.)

As further evidence of Japan's commitment to prevention, consider this: Japan spends less than $3,000, per capita, on health care, which is the least of any industrialized nation. The United States spends the most—about $8,000 per person ("Health Expenditures," 2009; Mahon & Weymouth, 2012). However, Japan's system is ranked 10th in the world, whereas the United States' is ranked 37th, and people in Japan live an average of 5 years longer than Americans do ("World Health Statistics," 2012). (See Figure 12.3.) The discrepancy is largely because the United States spends big on technology but small on prevention. When conditions such as diabetes, obesity, and asthma are inadequately unaddressed, they drive up both health care costs and premature mortality rates (Mahon & Weymouth, 2012).

So far, we've been talking about overall dollars spent, but how does that translate to a household level? Let's examine the financial impact of health care on a personal scale.

Out of Pocket, Out of Luck

Even paying a fraction of personal medical costs can be financially devastating. Worldwide, 100 million people a year sink into poverty because of out-of-pocket medical bills (WHO, 2008b). The problem is worst in countries that require citizens to pay more than 15% of medical costs out of pocket. (The U.S. has been dangerously close to that at 13% [American College of Physicians, 2008].)

About half of U.S. residents who file for bankruptcy do so because of medical bills (Himmelstein, Warren, Thorne, & Woolhandler, 2005). And 3 in 4 of them were insured when their health crises began. One dilemma of employer-sponsored health insurance is that, if illness or injuries prevent people from maintaining their jobs, they lose health benefits when they most need them. From there, the downward spiral occurs quickly. And it doesn't take much. The average out-of-pocket medical debt for those who go bankrupt is $11,854 (Himmelstein et al., 2005).

Hope

There is hope. A range of successful health care models exists around the world and within the United States. Policy analysts for the Commonwealth Fund (Cantor et al., 2007; How, Fryer, McCarthy, Schoen, & Schor, 2011; "Rising to the Challenge," 2007) calculate that, if every U.S. state matched the national best, we could:

- Save 90,000 people a year who otherwise die from avoidable medical errors;
- Diminish the number of avoidable hospitalizations by 1.5 million;
- Provide dental and medical care to about 10 million children who currently go without;

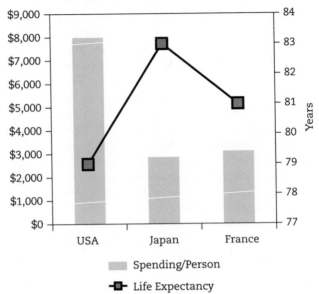

FIGURE 12.3 Although the United States spends more than twice as much as Japan and France on health care, per capita, the other countries have longer life expectancies, partly because they focus more on affordable access to care and on prevention.

Source: "Health Expenditures," 2009; Mahon & Weymouth, 2012; "World Health Statistics," 2012.

- Prevent 4 million people with diabetes from facing catastrophic outcomes such as kidney failure and limb amputation; and
- Save between $22 billion and $38 billion a year on Medicare.

Exemplars include Rhode Island—which leads the nation in quality of care, thanks partly to its initiative to build quality incentives into the state Medicaid plan; Hawaii—which has a low percentage of uninsured residents (8%), even though many of them work seasonal and part-time jobs, largely because citizens took the lead in 1974 to pass the first laws requiring employers to offer health plans; and Massachusetts—which recently set a new state record (only 5% uninsured) after implementing health care reform measures in 2007. Successes such as these have inspired nationwide health care reform.

? **CAN YOU GUESS? Part 2**

Massachusetts is the most-insured state in the union. But several other states are close. Which states come in second and third?

Answers appear at the end of the chapter.

The American Model

It may be tempting to blame health professionals for the problems in the U.S. system. But, as we mentioned with EMRs, the real issue runs deeper than that. Management theorist Peter Senge (2006) reminds us that "when placed in the same system, people, however different, tend to produce similar results" (p. 42). Health care is filled with highly talented, highly skilled, and compassionate people who want nothing more than to see better health outcomes. Indeed, they are often the most vocal of anyone about the need for improvements. But accomplishing real change requires more than individual action. We must rethink the system itself. So let's get a feel for the features of the U.S. system, then we'll talk about changes ahead.

MULTI-PAYER VERSUS SINGLE-PAYER

The first thing to know is that the United States is a **multi-payer** (also known as a *pluralistic*) **system**. That means that when someone receives medical care, the bill may be paid by a number of sources, including government-sponsored programs, private insurance companies, and individuals. If you grew up in the United States, Australia, Belgium, the Netherlands, France, Germany, or Switzerland (to name just a few), this mixture of public and private programs probably feels familiar to you. But if you're tuned into debates over health care reform or if you grew up in, for instance, Canada, the United Kingdom, or Japan, you're probably familiar with the alternative, a single-payer system.

As the name suggests, in **single-payer systems,** one source—often the government, although it can be another source, such as a national health insurance company—pays all the bills. This can be accomplished through taxes or by collecting subscription fees from individuals and/or employers.

In the Philippines, a national health insurance corporation, PhilHealth, covers all sectors of the population, including people who are employed, unemployed, retired, rich, or poor. Employers help fund the system for workers, and unemployed families can get coverage for about 100 Filipino pesos per month (about $2.26 in American currency). The system is not perfect. Enrollment is voluntary, hospital access in some rural areas is still quite

? CAN YOU GUESS? Part 3

Publicly funded programs such as Medicare, Medicaid, and the State Children's Health Insurance Program are known as the safety net, meant to help vulnerable and underserved populations. But holes in the net are rather large. In 2012, how many people in the US didn't qualify for its benefits except in life-threatening situations?

A. 5 million

B. 10 million

C. 20 million

D. 50 million

Answer appears at the end of the chapter.

limited, and residents may find themselves billed for "surpluses," which are portions of their medical bills not covered by PhilHealth. But at least 70% of the nation's residents are enrolled, no small feat in a country of 82 million people—many of them poor, rural residents—spread across more than 7,000 islands (Obermann, Jowett, Alcantara, Banzon, & Bodard, 2006). The program is regarded as a model for developing countries, proof that a nation need not wait for economic prosperity to begin offering health care to all citizens.

Some reformers in the United States advocate switching to a single-payer system. This idea is sometimes referred to as "Medicare for all." Although Medicare has some faults (most notably, gaps and complexities in its drug coverage policy), it has been quite successful overall. It covers 99% of people above retirement age, a group that, prior the 1960s, was largely out in the cold where health insurance was concerned. Research suggests that the health of many older adults improves once they are on Medicare (Anderson, 2008).

Here are some advantages of a single-payer system:

- *Large, diverse risk pool.* People pay into the system for most of their lives, even while they are healthy. This provides more money to cover people when they need care.
- *Wellness incentive.* When system administrators know they will care for a person all of his or her life, they have a vested interest in maintaining

that person's health from an early age. In multi-payer systems, knowing that subscribers may change insurers at any time, there is less incentive to invest in their long-term health.

• *Less need for expensive advertising.*
• *Less likelihood that health care dollars will fund extravagant salaries for CEOs and other corporate leaders.*
• *Clearer benefits.* If you have ever asked your doctor if a procedure is covered by your insurance plan, you may realize that the answer isn't always easy or foolproof. Some providers say they can't answer the question, and no wonder. They often deal with a mind-boggling number of plans and providers, each with its own parameters.
• *Lower administrative costs.* It costs less to administer one system than many. Additionally, it saves time and money when health care providers can follow one approval and billing procedure rather than dozens of different ones designed by a wide array of insurers. Multiply the savings by the number of doctors' offices, hospitals, rehab centers, pharmacies, diagnostic centers, and so on, and you get a sense of the impact.
• *Fewer coverage interruptions because of job changes or retirement.*
• *Easier-to-maintain national standards for health coverage.*

Those are the good points. There are some disadvantages of a single-payer system, however.

• *May involve a higher tax burden.* It may seem that health care is free in some states and countries, but the money to pay for it comes from somewhere, most often from taxes. The trade-off is usually favorable. That is, people pay less in taxes than they would for medical bills. But for some people, the idea of higher taxes is alarming.
• *May result in longer waits for elective and nonemergency procedures.* This is a common argument against single-payer systems. The data is actually mixed, though. In a number of countries with single-payer models, patients are able to schedule doctor visits and surgeries more quickly than in the United States (Commonwealth, 2007).
• *Less consumer choice than in free-market systems.*
• *Fewer luxuries.* In a free-market system, hospitals and medical centers often vie for patients who can pay top dollar by offering lavish amenities and surroundings. If everyone's care is funded at the same level, some of the amenities may disappear.
• *Lower payments.* If one entity sets reimbursement rates, the amount paid to health providers may be lower than it would otherwise be. One way Japan limits health care spending is by paying doctors and hospitals less than they are paid in the United States (Arnquist, 2009). This is, understandably, a concern for many providers.

Now that you understand the fundamental differences between multi- and single-payer systems, let's consider another concept that is central to current health care reform efforts.

UNIVERSAL COVERAGE MODELS

Imagine knowing that, from the moment you are born until you die, you can get health care any time you need it. **Universal coverage** means that all citizens (and, in some countries, all temporary residents and visitors as well) are assured of health care. Universal coverage is based on a commitment to offer health services to everyone who needs them, regardless of age, ability to pay, or any other factor. For example, Italy has universal coverage. When my friend Andrea was visiting there a few years ago, her son got food poisoning. Local residents escorted them to the emergency room of a Roman hospital. "They immediately gave him a stretcher," Andrea recalls. "He had two rounds of antibiotics, several liters of IV fluids, an ultrasound, and three blood tests, and he spent a night in the ER." There was no charge for the visit.

In some countries, universal coverage means that everyone is required to buy health insurance. In others, health care is funded through taxes. Either way, (1) the financial burden is distributed throughout people's lives, not imposed when they need care,

WHAT DO YOU THINK?

■ Do you prefer multi-payer or single-payer models? Why?

which means people can always get care and no one goes bankrupt over medical bills (WHO, 2010b); and (2) people are required to pay insurance premiums or taxes commensurate with their income levels. In short, everyone pays something, but not everyone pays the same amount. Health care costs for low-income citizens are subsidized so that everyone can afford coverage.

One idea behind universal coverage is that it makes sense, financially, to provide preventive care for all citizens, rather than paying for expensive treatment of avoidable illnesses. Another is that healthy citizens add to a nation's prosperity and productivity. And some argue, as well, that providing health care for everyone is a moral obligation. Physician Joseph Swedish (2008) puts it this way:

> We know firsthand what happens when an uninsured diabetic postpones treatment and ends up in the emergency room, or is hospitalized for a preventable complication. We treat the cancer patient who convinced himself to ignore early warning signs, fearing the expense associated with the lack of insurance coverage. These are human tragedies as well as avoidable costs. (p. 22)

Others join Swedish in arguing that financial considerations are well and good, but people come first. Churchill (1994) argues for universal coverage on moral grounds:

> Questions of reform should be seen as ethical choices, as political options for what sort of society we seek to have, and not primarily as issues of economic or organizational adjustments. . . . Health care reforms must be comprehensive morally and not just economically. Health policy must engage us in terms of common civic purpose, not only as individual consumers of health services. (p. 3).

Indeed, in many regions of the world, health care is considered an inalienable right. As you may have noticed in Table 12.1, nearly all of the top 40 health systems offer universal coverage. In fact, until the Affordable Care Act of 2010, the United States was the only wealthy industrialized nation that didn't.

It's not that Americans hadn't considered universal coverage before. Proposals to implement it date as far back as 1915 (Dranove, 2008). However,

WHAT DO YOU THINK?

Are you in favor of universal coverage? Why or why not?

there has not been widespread support for it until recent years. A 2002 survey revealed that 49% of physicians favored national health insurance (Ackermann & Carroll, 2003). Within five years, the majority of physicians (63%) and Americans (81%) said they were in favor of offering pubic health insurance in addition to private insurance so that everyone could have coverage (Commonwealth Fund, 2008b; Keyhani & Federman, 2009). Health care industry leaders—frustrated by insurance practices they feel are unfair to patients and by waste, fraud, and inefficiencies—are adamant as well. Some 86% of health care administrators surveyed say they favor insurance reform, and 78% support the option to buy affordable, state-sponsored insurance ("Health Spending," 2011).

Furthermore, the United States hasn't been entirely without universal coverage. In the past few years, some cities and states have launched their own plans. Notable among them are San Francisco, Massachusetts, and Vermont. It is useful to look at Massachusetts and Vermont, in part because they have already tried out provisions that are now being implemented nationwide. Let's see what we can learn from them.

MASSACHUSETTS AND VERMONT

If you live in Massachusetts or Vermont, you have a number of options for buying health insurance. Here's what they look like:

- You can enroll in a public program for people in financial need who are not eligible for employer-based health insurance. MassHealth is such a program. The most anyone pays is $105 per month for single coverage (Kaiser Commission, 2008, p. 9).
- Or you can apply for subsidies that help pay the cost of your insurance premiums. The amount of your subsidy depends on your income as it compares to the federal poverty line. For example, after subsidies, Vermont families whose annual

? CAN YOU GUESS? Part 2

In 2012, what was the Federal Poverty Line for a family of four?

A. $40,050 per year

B. $32,050 per year

C. $23,050 per year

D. $18,050 per year

2012). With 95% of the population now insured, Massachusetts is the best-insured state in the country (Long, 2008).

With this background, you know just about everything you need to understand national health care reform efforts. Nearly everyone agrees that it would be advantageous for all U.S. citizens to have health coverage. As you will see, the disagreements arise over how to go about it and how to pay for it.

National Health Care Reform

In March 2010, the Patient Protection and Affordable Care Act (Affordable Care Act, for short) was signed into law, setting the stage for dramatic changes in health care, including, for the first time, nationwide universal coverage in the United States. Because this act has such powerful implications for health and health communication, let's take a closer look at it. Here are a few key points:

- *Multi-payer model.* People who like their current insurance can keep it. Conversely, those who are dissatisfied with their coverage, don't qualify for private coverage, or can't afford private coverage can enroll instead in public programs. Refunds and tax credits are available to low-income citizens (roughly those who earn $92,000 or less for a family of four).
- *Public option.* Affordable, government-sponsored insurance will be offered through a cooperative effort between states and the federal government. A new Health Benefit Exchange is available at HealthCare.gov to help people choose from a variety of insurance options that meet designated standards for coverage.
- *Play or pay.* Employers must either offer their workers health benefits or contribute to the government-sponsored health care fund. (Tax incentives are provided for small businesses and nonprofit organizations to offset these costs.)
- *Consumer rights.* The act guarantees people the right to appeal insurance companies' decisions and to be insured through employee health plans (federally funded) if they retire before they are eligible for Medicare.
- *Services for older adults.* Older adults qualify for federal assistance paying for prescription drugs, more free preventive services than before, and more at-home care than before.

incomes are 200% of the federal poverty line pay about $60 per month for insurance.

- Or the state will help you find an affordable private insurance plan.

It's called a **public option** (short for *public health insurance option*) when the government offers an insurance plan such as MassHealth for people who cannot, or choose not to, buy insurance through a private company. For decades, state and federal governments helped pay medical costs for people in need (though Medicaid, Medicare, or so on), but only recently have they begun to offer health insurance to subscribers. Mostly, people subscribe to the public option because they cannot afford the cost of private insurance or they don't have access to employer-sponsored insurance.

In Vermont and Massachusetts, companies with 11 or more employees are required to **play or pay**. That is, they must either provide company-sponsored health plans that meet state regulations for minimum coverage or contribute to the state health insurance program. In Massachusetts, contributions equate roughly to $295 per employee per year, in Vermont $365 per employee per year. Rates are set to increase over time; but even so, the state contribution is typically less than a small company would pay for health benefits on its own.

The Massachusetts plan also includes an **individual mandate**, meaning that all residents of the state (with a few exceptions for religious reasons and other factors) are required to maintain health insurance. State residents must either submit proof of insurance with their annual income tax returns or pay a fine. The fines help pay for participation in the state system. So far, only 1% of state residents have incurred the fine ("Massachusetts,"

- *Health care resources.* The Affordable Care Act designates funding for (1) scholarships and student-loan-forgiveness programs for people who wish to become health professionals; (2) free and low-cost preventive care and early detection procedures ($15 billion); and (3) the creation of new public health centers to serve 20 million people.
- *Insurance reform.* Insurance companies are required to (1) offer coverage to grown children up to age 26 on their parents' plans; (2) offer preventive care procedures such as mammograms and colonoscopies without deductibles or copays; (3) submit proposed rate hikes for review, and (4) spend 85% of what they collect in premiums to pay for health benefits and quality improvements. Insurance companies are prohibited from denying coverage or charging higher-than-normal rates to people with preexisting health conditions and are prohibited from imposing lifetime limits on insurance benefits.
- *State partnerships.* The act also provides federal funds to help states (1) expand their Medicaid rosters; (2) compensate primary care doctors at rates no less than 100% of what Medicare would pay them; and (3) fund children's health insurance programs.

Other provisions are designed to improve quality of care, spur innovation, reduce fraud, and so on.

ADVANTAGES

Now that you know the basic provisions and evolution of the Affordable Care Act, let's look at some of the pros and cons.

- *Greater number of insured citizens.* One main goal of the Affordable Care Act is to insure 30 million additional Americans. It's still unclear when that figure will be reached, but analysts except dramatic gains in the next few years.
- *An alternative to job lock.* A weakness of employer-sponsored coverage is that people who switch or lose their jobs have had few affordable options for health insurance. The public option should diminish what economist David Dranove (2008) calls **job lock,** the tendency to stay with less-than-desirable jobs just to keep one's health

WHAT DO YOU THINK?

What is Obamacare? The Affordable Care Act *is* Obamacare. By some accounts, Hillary Clinton first adopted the nickname. Then it was embraced by people who opposed the Affordable Care Act. Beginning in 2011, President Obama began to publicly support and use the term himself. Do you have a favorable or unfavorable reaction to the term *Obamacare*? Why?

coverage. Additionally, people with preexisting concerns can now switch jobs without fear of being denied coverage.

- *Broader buy-in.* Requiring people to be insured throughout their lives spreads out the cost of health care and ensures that everyone pays into the system.
- *Minimal disruption.* People who are happy with their insurance need not change it.
- *Less emergency-room abuse.* Until now, hospitals have born a large and costly portion of the burden for caring for people without insurance. Obligated to provide care for people in critical need, regardless of the patients' ability to pay, hospital emergency rooms have become expensive safety nets for people without insurance or regular access to care. Universal coverage reduces the drain on hospitals by making other, less expensive, options available to people who need care.
- *More equitable employer contributions.* New tax breaks are designed to help small businesses, which have long been at a disadvantage because, with fewer employees, they have less bargaining power with insurance companies.
- *Job creation.* The need for qualified health professionals and health care administrative personnel is expected to rise precipitously (U.S. Bureau of Labor Statistics, 2012a, 2012b).
- *Healthier people.* As pointed out earlier, many feel that the most important reason to implement universal coverage is to boost the quality of life and the health of society overall.
- *Social commitment to healthy environments.* The authors of the 2010 World Health Report (WHO, 2010b) address the question "Why Universal Coverage?" by pointing out that societies that devote themselves to the good health of all their citizens don't merely invest in health care resources, but even more important, in

creating conditions and opportunities that support good health in the first place.

CHALLENGES AND DISADVANTAGES

It's also important to note that universal coverage is not perfect. Here are a few potential disadvantages:

• *Strain on resources.* Offering care to tens of millions of people who have largely gone without it might overload the current infrastructure. Although the Affordable Care Act includes funding to build new community health centers and train additional health professionals, some people are worried that the costs will be hard to bear (Murdock, 2012).

• *Inequitable coverage.* Even though a larger portion of Americans will be insured, their coverage and out-of-pocket burdens may differ because of differences in commercial insurance plans. Even in some "cradle to grave" health systems, there are out-of-pocket expenses. In the United Kingdom, these average about 1,200 pounds a year (about $2,200 in American currency) in addition to 3,850 pounds (about $7,000) in annual taxes to support the National Health

Table 12.2 Strengths and Weaknesses of the U.S. Health Care System

Prior to the Affordable Care Act (ACA)		After ACA
STRENGTHS	**WEAKNESSES**	**CHANGES**
• High-quality care available for those who can afford it	• Limited care available for 49.9 million uninsured Americans	• Affordable insurance available • New rules govern what insurance companies must cover • Individual mandate requires that people be insured
• Wide range of services, including elective procedures, available to those who can afford them	• Limited access contributes to health disparities by age, race, income, and literacy level	• Some groups, such as undocumented immigrants, are not covered
• Well-trained medical workforce	• Critical shortage of nurses and primary care physicians	• Staffing needs will increase • Additional funding available for caregiver training
• Highly responsive to emerging health concerns	• Minimal emphasis on prevention and health maintenance	• Increased funding for prevention and early detection
• Willing to make huge expenditures on health care	• Waste and inefficiencies limit return on investment • Rise in health care spending means less to spend on education, roads, housing, and other concerns	• Additional measures implemented to curb fraud and waste and reward good health outcomes (some analysts wonder if they will be enough) • Economic stimulus and job growth expected • Unclear how/if reimbursement rates for health providers will be affected
• Known for investing in expensive treatment technology	• Sluggish about adopting communication technology such as electronic medical records	• EMR will probably continue to expand as a means of tracking higher numbers of patients and enhancing overall efficiency • Unclear how or if spending on technology will be affected

System (Donnelly, 2008). That's less than most U.S. citizens pay for premiums and deductibles, but it does remind us that the playing field is rarely entirely level.

- *Continued disparities.* Documented immigrants are required to have health insurance, but they don't qualify for Medicaid or similar services for as many as 5 years. Undocumented immigrants are not eligible for public-option insurance (Siskin, 2011). Some critics charge that these omissions leave a vulnerable population at great risk (Doctors for Global Health, nd.)
- *Not far enough.* Some people believe that the Affordable Care Act doesn't do enough to eliminate fraud and waste, two of the biggest causes of high medical bills.

Table 12.2 lists the strengths and weaknesses of the American system prior to reform and the changes expected as a result of reform. So far, it's a tough call whether to put "cost" in the plus or minus column. On the one hand, the Affordable Care Act is designed to stop run-away expenditures, reward efficiency, and put greater emphasis on cost-saving prevention and early intervention. On the other hand, it will be costly, at least in the short run, to ramp up the health care system to provide services for the tens of millions who can soon take advantage of them. The Congressional Budget Office (an independent, nonpartisan agency) estimates that the cost of boosting insurance coverage will be about $1.1 trillion between 2012 and 2021 (Congressional, 2012). However, changes are expected to decrease the national deficit by $138 billion in the same time frame. Keep watching to see how it plays out.

All in all, we are living in a historic time. The future of health care is being crafted now, and it's safe to say that you will be involved in it, one way or another. To communicate competently about any aspect of health care, it's important to know the terminology and the basic issues. Hopefully what you have learned here will make you a more active participant in the process, whatever role you play.

Summary

A collection of case studies illustrates the complexities and interrelatedness of public health, risk communication, crisis communication, and health care reform. From the mad cow disease saga we learn that, even when scientists cannot provide definitive answers, it's dangerous and unethical to keep the public in the dark about a potential health threat. Public officials naturally worry about creating panic, but there is little to suggest that people do panic in crises. The majority of evidence suggests just the opposite: People try to help each other. This desire to help others can actually make it difficult to convince citizens and rescue workers to use safety precautions, as we saw following the 9/11 terrorist attacks. Although people seldom panic, public health experts are advised to use fear appeals with sensitivity. Overloading the public with frightening messages can cause undue worry. Conversely, offering false reassurance can mislead people and damage their trust in public officials. A different challenge is keeping an ongoing health crisis such as AIDS on the public agenda. Prevention efforts are complicated by the sensitive nature of transmission-related behaviors and the wide diversity of cultures affected. The AIDS case reminds us to listen to, respect, and understand the people we are trying to help.

The global nature of commerce and travel makes it imperative that health advocates around the world work together to monitor emerging concerns, track their incidence, and stop the spread of contagious illnesses as quickly as possible. The SARS case represents a successful effort to do just that. Efforts are already under way to respond to an avian fly pandemic if it occurs.

Although these lessons look easy on paper, the stress and demands of an actual crisis make them difficult to follow. The risk management/communication framework reminds us that the best crisis communicators lay solid groundwork before a crisis emerges so they have information at hand, trusting and open relationships with stakeholders, and well-developed and well-rehearsed plans in place. The anthrax case reminds us that a wide range of professionals is likely to be enlisted for help, making crisis management skills an important part of anyone's professional portfolio. At the same time, ethical dimensions of risk and crisis communication are everyone's businesses. In this chapter, we debated the question: Who should receive the limited number of vaccines in the case of a deadly pandemic?

Health care reform efforts are designed to create structures and processes that nurture good health among the population. The United States—despite spending more than other countries and despite its reputation for offering highly skilled, high-tech care—has not led the world on most health indicators, mostly because tens of millions of people have gone largely without health care. The Affordable Care Act, passed in 2010 suggests that universal coverage will become the norm in the United States. However, the issue is still evolving. Follow the developments in the years to come.

Key Terms and Theories

public health
social mobilization
risk communication
crisis communication
risk management/communication framework (RMCF)
bioterrorism
electronic medical records (EMRs)
multi-payer system
single-payer system
universal coverage
public option
play or pay
individual mandate
job lock

Discussion Questions

1. What lessons can we learn from the case study about mad cow disease?
2. What is public health? How does it compare to individual medical care?
3. What advice do you have for health crisis communicators who are worried about creating panic?
4. What is risk communication? What are the three risk communication traditions presented by Peter Sandman? Which is most descriptive of risk communication? Of crisis communication?
5. What factors should health communicators consider when using fear appeals?
6. Describe the risk management/communication framework (RMCF) that Scott Ratzan and Wendy Meltzer present.
7. Discuss the ethical implications raised by the Andrew Speaker and Mary Mallon (Typhoid Mary) cases. Why might such public health risks be even more salient today than in Mallon's time? What do you think we should do to protect individual liberties while preserving the public's health interest?
8. Describe the Pleasure Project's approach to preventing HIV transmission. Do you find this approach appealing or offensive? Why?
9. Give a basic timeline of events in the SARS case. How were the officials able to contain the disease so quickly?
10. Describe how the CDC staff handled the anthrax crisis and what we can learn from the experience.
11. This chapter contains about 27 lessons for risk and crisis communication. Name at least 15 of them. Try to think of examples from the book as well as examples that don't appear in the book.
12. Trace the development of the H5N1 avian flu case so far. Would you be frightened if a containment zone is declared in your area? Why or why not? Do you feel adequately informed about and prepared for such a crisis? Why or why not?
13. Discuss the ethical implications of administering to a limited number of people a vaccine against a deadly epidemic. Who do you think should be vaccinated first? Why?
14. How does the United States compare to other countries in terms of equitable care, health care spending, life expectancy, physician–citizen ratio, and use of electronic medical records?
15. In what ways are health care dollars wasted in the United States?
16. What is an electronic medical record? Why are EMRs valuable?
17. Describe the typical chain of events that leads a family in the United States to go bankrupt because of medical bills.
18. What are the advantages of a multi-payer universal coverage plan with an individual mandate and "play or pay" requirements for employers? What are the disadvantages?
19. What are the advantages and disadvantages of a single-payer program?
20. Explain the main provisions of the Affordable Care Act of 2010. What are the advantages and disadvantages? Which is your opinion, and why?
21. Outline at least five strengths and five weaknesses of the U.S. health care system. Which of these are most important to you? Why?

Answers to *Can You Guess?*

PART 1

1. Massachusetts has the highest percentage (95%) of insured residents. Texas has the lowest at 75% ("Health Insurance," 2012). In some parts of Texas, more than half the residents are uninsured ("Rising to the Challenge," 2012).

2. Insurance premiums for a family in the Philippines total about 1,200 Filipino pesos per year (equivalent to about $27 in the United States).

3. Insured families in the United States pay about $10,728 in premiums per year (Robert Wood Johnson Foundation, 2008).

PART 2

Hawaii is the second most-insured state, with only 8% of its residents uninsured. Vermont, Minnesota, Wisconsin, and Maine are tied for third, with 9% uninsured in each state ("Health Insurance").

PART 3

In 2012, nearly 5 million people didn't qualify for publicly funded programs known as the health safety net except in life-threatening situations.

PART 4

D. $23,050

Each year, the U.S. Census Bureau calculates a federal poverty line. In 2012, the poverty line for a family of four was $23,050 per year. Poverty thresholds are often expressed in percentages, as in "200% of the federal poverty line." This means that the family earns two times the poverty-line income.

CHAPTER THIRTEEN

Planning Health Promotion Campaigns

We love smokers. Heck, we love everybody. Our philosophy isn't anti-smoker or pro-smoker. It's not even about smoking. It's about the tobacco industry manipulating their products, research and advertising to secure replacements for the 1,200 customers they "lose" every day in America. You know, because they die.

This message is from truth®, the nation's largest youth smoking-prevention campaign. Messages like it appear in advertising campaigns and on the truth® website, which is loaded with interactive games, downloads, and videos. It's a campaign designed for a highly specific target market—youth ages 12 to 17. As the website proclaims:

> truth® is hard for someone over the age of 30 to understand. The adult world is very different from a teen's. The values are different. The goals are different. If adults don't get what we're saying and how we choose to say it, then it's probably okay.

It's more than okay. It's ingenious. And the campaign gets results. Teens' awareness of antitobacco messages nearly doubled in the first 10 months of the truth® campaign (Farrelly, Healton, Davis, Messeri, & Haviland, 2002). And 4 years after it began, 450,000 adolescents who were expected to start smoking hadn't, saving the country as much as $5.4 billion in medical costs over time (Farrelly, Nonnemaker, Davis, & Hussin, 2009; Holtgrave, Wunderink, Vallone, & Healton, 2009).

If you're over 17, you'll want to visit thetruth.com anyway. For one thing, it's a lot of fun. For another, you'd be hard-pressed to find a better showcase for health promotion. The campaign directors know what they're all about, they know their audience, and you never get the sense that they're faking it. Their goal is to be as up-front and honest as the tobacco companies are deceitful. Following are some tenets of the campaign's "secret sauce"—which is deliberately not secret at all. The following appears in big letters alongside bold graphics on the website.

Don't Say Don't

Tell someone not to do something and they will. Don't read the next sentence. See what we mean? We're not here to tell people not to smoke, because, well, it doesn't work.

Quality Providers of the Truth

We don't have money or influence—our power comes from facts and trust. Being an honest and dependable source of information is our bread and butter, because the minute we start bending and manipulating the truth, we're no better than the tobacco industry. Bottom line: Make it interesting, don't twist the truth.

The Problem with Immortality

When you're young, you think you're immortal. That can be a problem for a health message. The idea isn't to tell teens they're gonna die, but to show how tobacco companies exploit this illusion for their own benefit. ("About Us," 2012, para. 2, 3, & 5)

The campaign encourages teen involvement by sponsoring rock concerts, sporting events (including a skateboard junket with Tony Hawk), video games, videos, invitations to post original videos, and more.

The truth® campaign is sponsored by the American Legacy Foundation®, a national public health organization designed to prevent smoking among youth and to help smokers of all ages quit. The foundation launched truth® in 2000 with funding from the 1998 Master Settlement Agreement (see Chapter 11) between the tobacco industry and 46 states and 5 U.S. territories.

Analysts say truth® has been successful largely because its creators take time to understand and engage with the target audience. Whereas health promoters have long been frustrated by teens' tendency to do the opposite of what they're told, the truth® campaign honors their rebellious nature (Farrelly et al., 2002). Exposed to the deceit and manipulation behind tobacco companies' efforts, the people behind truth® wager—and they seem

> **CHECK IT OUT!**   Visit the truth® website at www.thetruth.com. You'll find videos, games, concert dates, actual tobacco-industry memos, and more.
>
> For a brief overview of how researchers measured the effects of the truth® campaign, see http://www.youtube.com/watch?v=GMSpLAFGbRo.

to be right—that teens will rebel against corporate greed by *not* smoking. As it says on the truth® website:

Rebellion Is Not A Bad Word

Rebellion is powerful stuff. And for years the tobacco industry used that power for their gain by making smoking an act of defiance. But the reality is this: If teens think they're being rebellious by smoking, they're really just following orders. And last time we checked, rebellion is about not doing what you're told all the time. ("About Us," 2012, para. 6)

All in all, truth® promises teens, "we're not here to blow sunshine up your nether regions. We're not out to preach. Our only goal is to make sure everyone gets the unfiltered, unadulterated facts about tobacco" ("About Us," para. 9). The campaign is an exemplar in how to partner with the target audience in ways that are respectful, collaborative, and transparent.

In this chapter we will talk about the first steps in creating an effective health-promotion campaign. In Chapter 12, we discussed the overlap between public health and crisis communication. Here we turn our attention to another side of the same coin—efforts to help people protect themselves from more chronic health threats such as cancer, obesity, diabetes, and accidents. Whereas crisis communicators typically try to assuage people's fears, the goal in health promotion is usually to alert people that they may be more vulnerable than they think. Keeping health issues on the public agenda and working with people to change their everyday behaviors can be as challenging as managing a crisis.

Health-promoting behaviors are those that "enhance health and well-being, reduce health risks, and prevent disease" (Brennan & Fink, 1997, p. 157). These behaviors include lifestyle choices, medical care, prevention efforts, and activities that foster an overall sense of well-being.

Health promotion campaigns are systematic efforts to influence people to engage in health-enhancing behaviors (Backer & Rogers, 1993). These efforts may involve the use of many communication channels, from face-to-face communication to mass media. The term **health promoter** includes anyone involved in the process of creating and distributing health promotion messages. This includes volunteers in the community, employees of nonprofit health agencies, public relations and community relations professionals, production artists, media decision makers, and more. As this list suggests, health promotion offers diverse career opportunities for communication specialists. (See Box 13.1.)

In this chapter we consider the challenges of promoting health behaviors among diverse members of the population. We begin with a brief overview of health campaigns, describing some particularly notable ones. Then we will follow the first four stages of designing a health promotion campaign:

Step 1: Defining the situation and potential benefits

Step 2: Analyzing and segmenting the audience

Step 3: Establishing campaign goals and objectives

Step 4: Selecting channels of communication

Steps 5 through 7, on designing and implementing a campaign, are covered in the next chapter. Keep in mind that it's important to know all the steps before you actually begin. Although evaluating and refining the campaign is the final step, you must consider from the beginning how you will accomplish those goals later on. The steps in these chapters are based on recommendations by J. D. Brown and E. R. Einsiedel (1990) and reflect an abbreviated version of the steps recommended by the CDC and the National Cancer Institute.

BOX 13.1   CAREER OPPORTUNITIES

Health Promotion and Education

Hospital-based health educator
School-based health educator
Community health educator
Director of nonprofit organization
Patient advocate or patient navigator
Professor/educator
Health information publication designer
Corporate wellness director
Fitness instructor

CAREER RESOURCES AND JOB LISTINGS

- American Association for Health Education: aahperd.org/aahe
- Society for Public Health Education: sophe.org
- Area Health Education Centers: http://www.nationalahec.org
- National Commission for Health Education Credentialing (NCHEC): nchec.org
- U.S. Bureau of Labor Statistics Occupational Outlook: bls.gov/oco/ocos063.htm
- Chronicle of Higher Education: chronicle.com/jobs
- Center for Disease Prevention and Control Division of Health Communication: http://www.cdc.gov/healthcommunication
- National Institutes of Health: nih.gov
- World Health Organization: who.int/employment/vacancies/en

Background on Health Campaigns

"Live long and prosper," the Vulcan salutation on *Star Trek*, seems to say it all. A long and healthy existence—isn't that what life is all about? You might think so. But it turns out that Vulcan logic isn't always able to explain human behavior, as Mr. Spock discovered.

Early health campaigns were designed with the confidence that, as humans, we want nothing so much as our own health and longevity. From that viewpoint it follows that, if we know a behavior is unhealthy, we won't act that way. In fact, we should go to great lengths to pursue health-enhancing outcomes. Seen this way, persuasion is not an issue. People only need reliable information. The motivation to comply with it is presumably already there, as innate as the animal instinct for survival.

Motivating Factors

It turns out that influencing human behavior isn't that simple. We are motivated by a number of factors that make us more or less receptive to health information and more or less motivated to change our behavior. Sometimes we do things we know to be unhealthy because the behavior is inexpensive, convenient, socially rewarding, or fun (Brown & Einsiedel, 1990). For instance, research indicates that people may drink alcoholic beverages even though they believe them to be unhealthy because they are reluctant to give up the social ritual of drinking with friends. Conversely, we sometimes change our behavior without knowing much about the change or the reasons for it. We may try a behavior (like taking vitamins) simply because someone in authority tells us to or because the change seems interesting, easy, fashionable, or so on. In these instances, knowledge may *follow* behavior change.

Research has not always been encouraging about health campaigns' actual effects. Campaigns have been criticized for naively seeking to change people's behavior without changing their circumstances (Green, 1996) and for assuming that knowledge reaches and affects all people equally (Brown & Walsh-Childers, 1994).

In reality, campaigns may raise awareness, but, unless the recommended behaviors are compatible with people's beliefs and are supported within their social networks, campaigns are unlikely to change much. Health promoters have discovered that we can't simply educate people about health and presume they will adjust their lifestyles accordingly. We must take a range of factors into account. We must know the audience and must consider not just how they might benefit from certain behaviors, but whether they would find that change difficult or unacceptable.

Exemplary Campaigns

This section describes five exemplary health promotion campaigns. Each provides an inspiring

? CAN YOU GUESS? Part 1

Which kills more people in the United States— tobacco or illegal drugs?

The answer appears at the end of the chapter.

lesson for promoters. Together, these examples illustrate that, as health promoters, we must often do more than simply give out information if we are to succeed. Sensitivity to audience needs, problem-solving skills, assessment, and careful planning and follow-through are required as well.

GO TO THE AUDIENCE

A health promoter interviewed by a student of mine once said, "You can't talk to people where you wish they were. You have to talk to them where they really are." His words characterize one quality of good campaigners: *They know their audiences well and design campaigns to suit those audiences.*

We've already talked about truth* as an excellent example of this. Another was a campaign designed to reach elderly African American women, who are at high risk for breast cancer but are often unable to afford cancer screening and are hard to reach via traditional media. Campaigner designers noted that the women they most wanted to reach had a favorite place for swapping stories and sharing information—the beauty salon (Forte, 1995). With this in mind, they arranged for salons in Los Angeles to show an educational video about breast cancer throughout the day. The video featured African American women and emphasized that they are at high risk for cancer. Salon clients were also given pamphlets about breast cancer and were offered free mammograms at a local clinic or in a mobile unit scheduled to visit the salon on a regular basis. According to Deirdra Forte, the beauty of this program was that "by showing the video where African American women already exchange information and socialize, they are more likely to understand and accept the benefit of mammography" (para. 22). The campaign was honored as one of the year's best by the U.S. Department of Health and Human Services. Similar programs have since been launched in numerous locations around the country (Linnan & Ferguson, 2007).

TAKE ACTION

Another lesson is that health promotion comes in many forms, and *sometimes actions are as important as words*. When the leaders of an extensive heart health campaign in New York City realized that preschoolers in the area received 40% of their daily saturated fat from whole milk served at school, they put down their pens for a while and rolled up their sleeves (Shea, Basch, Wechsler, & Lantigua, 1996; Wechsler & Wernick, 1992). In addition to public education, community involvement, and a multimedia campaign, the health promoters convinced school officials to serve low-fat milk. The program won awards for its open-eyed, innovative approach.

No-smoking laws and policies are another example. People who work in smoke-free organizations are nearly twice as likely to quit as other smokers, and employees who don't quit usually decrease their cigarette consumption by about 2.5 cigarettes a day (Bauer, Hyland, Li, Steger, & Cummings, 2005). It's unlikely that an information-only campaign could accomplish the same results.

MEASURE YOUR SUCCESS

The value of combining media exposure, community outreach, and scientific research was demonstrated by the Minnesota Heart Health Program (MHHP), which was one the most extensive health campaigns in American history (Luepker et al., 1994). It was conducted for 13 years (1980–1993) and involved nearly half a million people in the upper Midwest (Luepker et al., 1994). The goal of MHHP was to lower heart-disease risk factors (cholesterol, high blood pressure, and smoking) and increase heart-healthy behaviors such as exercise. It included an extensive mass media campaign, educational programs in schools, and the involvement of local organizations.

What made MHHP extraordinary was its dedication to charting the health outcomes of people exposed to campaign messages. It's a good example of how to *establish goals and measure your success*. Researchers monitored people's behavior over a period of years and compared people touched by the campaign to people in other communities. Over time, they found modest but significant decreases in high blood pressure, high cholesterol, and smoking in communities involved in the program (Luepker et al., 1994). There was also a notable increase in physical activity among female schoolchildren involved in the heart-healthy education programs (Kelder, Perry, & Klepp, 1993).

ENCOURAGE SOCIAL SUPPORT

An award-winning program called the 90-Second Intervention is being used in some places to lower Americans' risk of high blood pressure (Fishman, 1995). The intervention program is based on the principle that *recruiting social support for healthy behaviors increases the likelihood that people will stick to them*. The 90-Second Intervention was designed considering that many Americans (about 50 million) are at risk for high blood pressure, but compliance with medical advice is notoriously low, mostly because people with high blood pressure feel fine most of the time, so they don't perceive a reason to change their lifestyle or continue medication. (Despite the lack of symptoms, high blood pressure can lead to strokes, heart disease, and kidney disease.)

The campaign planners reasoned that people would be more likely to follow medical advice if their doctors were not the only ones imploring them to eat right, exercise, and stay on medication and if they receive daily encouragement. Therefore, they designed a simple intervention program that takes place in the doctor's office. During a checkup,

? **CAN YOU GUESS? Part 2**

People often don't know the nutritional value of the foods they eat (Lin, Mou, & Lagoe, 2011). How many calories and how many milligrams of sodium are in each of the following?

■ An Egg McMuffin and a latte with 2% milk

■ Two glazed doughnuts

■ A quarter-pound cheeseburger and cola,

■ Two slides of thick-crust pepperoni pizza and an 8-ounce sports drink.

Answers appear at the end of the chapter.

the doctor asks the patient to call a loved one and ask that person to commit to becoming a "health partner." The partner's role is to exercise with the patient, help maintain a healthy diet, and so on. The genius of the plan is that it makes healthy behaviors socially rewarding. The health partner and patient both benefit from the healthy activities they enjoy together, and the doctor is no longer the only one concerned about the problem. The 90-second phone call is presumably well worth the effort.

Next let's consider how we would create our own health campaign.

Step 1: Defining the Situation and Potential Benefits

To illustrate the steps in planning a health campaign, imagine that staff members of a university sports recreation department have asked us to help recruit new participants. Specifically, they would like to increase the number of people who go to the campus fitness center in their free time. The recreation department will not benefit financially from the added enrollment, but the staff wishes to increase participation because physical activity improves people's health. The rest of the chapter guides us through the initial steps of creating a campaign. The hypothetical sports recreation campaign is admittedly a small-scale effort, but many influential campaigns are aimed at limited audiences, and improving health habits among even a small group is a momentous goal. Furthermore, the steps given apply well to large and small campaigns.

If you're like many people, your first instinct is to post fliers and to send a story about the recreation program to the campus newspaper. Those may be effective steps, but before we begin, let's take the advice of professional campaign planners and do some preliminary research to assess potential benefits and the current situation (Nowak & Siska, 1995).

Benefits

At this stage, we should be interested in learning what benefits (if any) our efforts might achieve. Following are some questions we might research.

- Would exercising at the fitness center actually improve people's health?
- Would everybody benefit?
- Are there some people who would not benefit?
- Are there alternative ways to get the same benefits?

Answers to these questions can be obtained by reading published literature and talking with experts in the field. Such preliminary research will prepare us to share useful knowledge with others and may help us decide if the project is worthwhile.

Current Situation

Assuming that we find reasonable evidence to believe that people might benefit from exercising at the gym, the next step is to assess the current situation. Following are some questions to guide our preliminary research. The same questions will be useful later in guiding audience analysis. Remember that experts, program leaders, current participants, and nonparticipants are all valuable sources of information. In addition to these general questions, we may want to add some specific questions relevant to the campaign.

- How many people currently participate in the recommended behavior?
- What types of people participate and for what reasons? (Of interest is demographic information, such as age, sex, and income, as well as cultural, personal, social, or personality variables that might be relevant.)
- What are the strengths and weaknesses of the program (from the perspective of participants and nonparticipants)?
- What types of people do not participate?
- What are their reasons for not participating?
- What factors are most important to participants and nonparticipants (e.g., cost, convenience, social interaction)?
- Do people consider the potential benefits of this behavior important? Why or why not?
- Are there any conditions under which nonparticipants might participate?
- How do the people in the audience usually receive information (i.e., fliers, newspaper, radio, e-mail, etc.)?

- Through what channels do they prefer to get information?
- What information sources do they trust?

Preliminary answers to our questions may be surprising. We may find, for instance, that current sports recreation participants are not primarily concerned about health benefits. They go to the fitness center because their friends are there and they enjoy the social interaction. Or we might find that some people will not participate no matter how healthy physical activity is because they're afraid of looking foolish on the basketball court or out of shape in aerobics classes. Perhaps recreational programs are scheduled when many people cannot attend them. If these factors are important, simply educating people about the health benefits of exercise may not do much good.

Diverse Motivations

Keep in mind that health concerns are not people's only motivation. We are all most receptive to options that satisfy us on many levels (intellectual, emotional, personal, social, etc.). In assessing the situation, it's important not to assume that everyone is motivated in the same way we are. Consider (and ask about) the diversity among people who might participate in the sports recreation program. Our audience is probably not just traditional college students (a diverse group in itself), but international students, people with disabilities, middle-aged and older adults, experienced students and newcomers, university faculty and staff members, and maybe even community members and children.

In Step 2, we will attempt to learn about our audience and choose a portion of it to target. Being sensitive to diverse beliefs and motivations can help us understand why people behave as they do. This understanding is crucial to our success as health promoters.

Step 2: Analyzing and Segmenting The Audience

After assessing the health benefits and the current situation at the sports recreation department, we're ready to analyze the audience. This will involve asking a larger number of people many of the questions we asked in preliminary research.

Audience research may seem an unnecessary step, but experienced campaign planners know better. Audience analysis allows us to collect important data about people's behaviors and preferences. It pays to know, in advance, what sources target audience members use and trust, how they view their overall health, what their main concerns are, and more (Ledlow, Johnson, & Hakoyama, 2008). Edward Maibach and Roxanne Parrott (1995) applaud promoters for considering the audience's needs before they determine campaign goals. As they put it, audience-centered analysis "means that health messages are designed primarily to respond to the needs and situation of the target audience, rather than to the needs and situation of the message designers or sponsoring organizations" (p. 167).

Data Collection

There are several ways to learn about potential audience members. Preexisting databases are a good place to start (Salmon & Atkin, 2003). For example, we might request demographics about the student body and usage statistics from the campus recreation department. We should also seek more specific information about the target audience's beliefs, values, and habits.

This section describes how to get started, including how and when to get ethics-board approval for our study and the comparative advantages of using interviews, questionnaires, and focus groups to learn about the people we hope to help.

ETHICAL COMMITMENTS

Before we discuss the research phase, keep in mind that, to uphold the highest standards of ethics, we must get an official go-ahead to implement the research procedure we design. Usually, this means submitting the research plan to an **institutional review board (IRB),** an ethics panel that reviews and monitors research efforts to ensure that participants are treated fairly. Universities have IRBs, as do many organizations, especially in health care. If our research involves people from more than one organization, it may be necessary to get IRB approval from each of them.

The IRB will be interested to know how we will secure informed consent from participants (see Chapter 4), maintain their anonymity or keep their identities confidential, avoid causing unnecessary distress, and why the results we are likely to get are worth any risk or commitment we require from participants. We will need to make special efforts to protect the needs and rights of vulnerable populations if they are involved in our study, including children, people with cognitive disabilities, people recovering from abuse, seriously ill people, and so on. It's advisable to check IRB guidelines and timelines early on so that ethics will be first on our minds and we can avoid unexpected delays. (See *Check It Out!* for more resources.)

DATA-GATHERING OPTIONS

There are a number of ways we might learn more about the audiences involved in our campaign effort. Approach this with avid curiosity and a respect for multiple viewpoints. Here's a quick overview of some information-gathering methods we might consider.

Interviews. You'd be surprised what you can learn from asking and listening. Here are different interview strategies and the advantages and limitations of each (based on Frey, Botan, Friedman, & Kreps, 1991).

- **Highly scheduled interviews**. Interviewers are given specific questions to ask and are not allowed to make comments or ask additional questions. This helps minimize the interviewers' influence on respondents' answers, but it doesn't allow for follow-up questions or clarifications. Answers are typically brief but easy to tally and compare.
- **Moderately scheduled interviews**. Interviewers are given a set of questions but are allowed to ask for clarification and additional information as they see fit. These interviews are more relaxed and conversational, but less precise, than highly scheduled interviews.
- **Unscheduled interviews**. Interviewers are given a list of topics but are encouraged to phrase questions as they wish and to probe for more information when it seems useful and appropriate. These interviews are useful for collecting

CHECK IT OUT!

■ The National Institutes of Health offers a free, online instructional session about research ethics at http://phrp.nihtraining.com/users/login.php.

■ Check out the IRB approval procedures at your university. They are usually available through a department of sponsored research.

■ An IRB Guidebook is available through the Office for Human Research Protections: http://www.hhs.gov/ohrp/archive/irb/irb_guidebook.htm.

information about respondents' feelings, but they don't yield answers that can easily be compared or tallied.

Questionnaires. Because they can be administered to large numbers of people in less time than it would take to interview them, questionnaires are a popular way to collect audience information. A **questionnaire** asks respondents to write down their answers to a list of questions. In general, written responses are more limited than interview responses, but people may be more willing to answer sensitive questions in writing or online, especially if surveys are conducted anonymously.

Here are some guidelines for designing an effective questionnaire (based on Arnold & McClure, 1989, and Frey et al., 1991).

- *Keep it brief.* People are unlikely to complete surveys that take more than 10 minutes.
- *Seek immediate response.* If people take time to complete the survey right away, the response rate will be higher.
- *Collect demographic information.* This includes age, sex, income, college major, occupation, and the like. Ask respondents to select the appropriate responses from a list of all possibilities. (These are called **fixed-alternative questions**.) This makes it easy for them to answer and easy for us to count and compare answers.
- *Ask about knowledge and behaviors.* A mixture of open and closed questions will yield the most useful information. **Open-ended questions** allow respondents to express ideas in their own words (e.g., *How do you feel about basketball*

and aerobics?). **Close-ended questions** require very brief answers (*e.g., Do you prefer to work out with free weights or weight machines?*).

- *Pilot (pretest) the questionnaire.* We will test the questionnaire on a few people before administering it to everyone in our sample and ask the respondents to indicate if any questions are confusing or leading, if the fixed-alternative questions include all possible answers, and if they can think of other questions we should add.
- *Allow for anonymity.* Whether the questionnaire is on paper or online, it's ideal if people can respond anonymously.

Focus Groups. A third option for collecting information is the use of focus groups. A **focus group** involves a small number of people who respond to questions posed by a moderator (Berko, Wolvin, & Curtis, 1993). The moderator tries to encourage the group members to speak openly on topics relevant to the campaign. Members' comments are usually recorded so that they can be studied later. Focus groups are useful for learning the target audience's feelings about an issue. A research team led by Rose Clark-Hitt conducted focus groups with military members to see how they reacted to campaign materials, gauging their reaction to messages that encouraged them to "help a buddy take a knee," that is, to support their comrades in seeking mental health counseling without shame (Clark-Hitt, Smith, & Broderick, 2012).

Whether we use surveys, questionnaires, or focus groups, it's important to think carefully about whom to include. Choosing people to include is called **sampling** the population. Interviews and surveys allow us to collect information from people who reflect the diversity in the population we're considering. In contrast, focus group participants are members of a target group such as nontraditional students or freshmen. Too much diversity can make it hard to develop a focused discussion. For example, when Mary Frances Casper and colleagues (2006) conducted focus groups about coed drinking patterns, they had student participants fill out questionnaires in advance. Then they assigned students to one of three focus groups. The students didn't know it, but the groups reflected their typical drinking levels—nondrinkers, moderate, and more-than-average drinkers (Casper, Child, Gilmour, McIntyre, & Pearson, 2006). The researchers knew that participants were more likely to engage in open discussion if it emerged that other people in the room had similar feelings.

In our case, we might conduct separate focus groups with people who use the workout facilities and those who don't. Too much diversity among participants in any one group makes it difficult to develop key ideas and may discourage some people from participating. But we must be careful not to assume that one group speaks for the others or for the population overall.

Experts offer the following tips for conducting effective focus groups (based mostly on Greenbaum, 1991, and Katcher, 1997):

- Determine what type of information you most want to collect. Bruce Katcher (1997) advises: "You must be clear from the outset what you really want to learn from the participants and how you will use the information" (p. 222). For example, are we more interested in the opinions of people who already use the fitness center or people who are not yet involved?
- Design a list of open questions to get the information you most want.
- Appoint (or hire) a facilitator to lead the focus group discussion. A good facilitator helps people feel comfortable expressing their opinions, allows everyone to contribute to the discussion, and doesn't influence members' responses. Many experts recommend using a facilitator not associated with the promotion effort because focus group members may feel more comfortable voicing criticisms and because the facilitator may be more objective.

Creating Electronic Surveys

Here are some tips from the experts on creating online surveys ("Internet Surveys," 2008):

■ *Keep it quick, and keep it simple.*

■ *Go easy on formatting.* Complex graphics can make surveys difficult to open and to read.

■ *Avoid overkill.* We all probably receive more online survey requests than we can fulfill. Respect people's time by sending surveys only to the target audience.

■ *Be clear and honest* about whether responses will be anonymous (we don't know the respondent's identity) or confidential (we know, but we won't divulge, his or her identity).

- Choose 7 to 10 people from the target audience to make up each focus group.
- Arrange to conduct the focus group in a conference room or other comfortable area. (It's customary to provide refreshments for focus group participants.)
- Arrange to audiotape and videotape the session unobtrusively (with participants' permission). Review the information collected.
- Consider conducting multiple focus groups with different members of the target audience.

Choosing a Target Audience

It's not only effective to identify the group that we most want to reach and to make every effort to understand that audience, it's part of our ethical responsibility as health promoters. In this section we talk about the vulnerabilities and needs of various groups we might target. We'll start by examining the irony that the people who are easiest to reach and who are most receptive are probably already aware of what we'd like to tell them. Often, a more worthwhile challenge is to connect with people who are not already information rich.

THEORETICAL FOUNDATIONS

The **knowledge gap hypothesis** proposes that people with plentiful information resources (such as newspapers, televisions, computers, and well-informed friends and advisors) are likely to know more and to continue learning more than people with fewer information resources (Tichenor, Donohue, & Olien, 1970). Income and education are highly linked to resource availability and media habits. Consequently, people of high socioeconomic status tend to be knowledge rich, and people of low status tend to be knowledge poor. New information often increases the knowledge gap rather than diminishing it. In other words, the people who already know a lot learn more, and the others fall farther behind.

Unfortunately, people who are information poor are often most in need of health information. Here are just a few examples.

- Three years after a state medical assistance program for the uninsured was implemented in their community, 50% of low-income families

were still unaware of it (Rucinski, 2004).
- Mexican American women in rural areas more frequently die from breast cancer than other women, but they often know little about breast self-exams and the severity of the disease (Hubbell, 2006).
- Although members of minority cultures in the United States are at highest risk for contracting AIDS, African Americans and Hispanic Americans are typically less informed than others about AIDS (Ebrahim, Anderson, Weidle, & Purcell, 2003).

These knowledge gaps typically reflect socioeconomic status. The knowledge gap narrows or disappears for members of racial and cultural minorities who are affluent and well educated (Ebrahim et al., 2003).

There are several reasons that underprivileged persons are hard to reach with health messages. One barrier is ethnic. Underprivileged audiences tend disproportionately to be people from minority cultures. They may be skeptical about mainstream messages, either because they seem irrelevant (aimed at Whites rather than Blacks, for example) or because they mistrust the sources (Matthews, Sellergren, Manfredi, & Williams, 2002). Researchers note that African American men, although at higher-than-normal risk for prostate cancer, are relatively uninformed about the symptoms and risk factors. Men in one study said they largely distrust doctors, are unable to get much preventive care, and are culturally averse to being tested for or diagnosed with a disease, such as prostate cancer, that they consider emasculating (Allen, Kennedy, Wilson-Glover, & Gilligan, 2007).

Second, underprivileged people are more likely than others to rely on television than on more detailed sources, such as newspapers and online medical information. A so-called **digital divide** separates the information rich, who have easy access to the Internet (predominantly young, well-educated city dwellers) and the information poor, who are often rural residents with limited or no online access (Rains, 2008b). As you might expect, people with quick, convenient access to online sources are more likely to use them to access health information (Rains, 2008b). Thus, underprivileged persons' media habits often put them at a disadvantage.

Third, although they may watch television, members of ethnic co-cultures are more likely to trust interpersonal sources (such as friends and health professionals) than the mainstream media (Cheong, 2007). That's fine if they have ready access to health experts, but many don't. Female African American and Latina adolescents in one study were familiar with breast and lung cancer because they knew of people with those diseases. However, most of the girls had never heard of cervical cancer, even though it was receiving abundant media attention in connection with a new human papillomavirus (HPV) vaccine (Mosavel & El-Shaarawi, 2007). Their lack of knowledge is especially unfortunate because the vaccine is designed primarily for girls their age (Mosavel & El-Shaarawi, 2007).

Fourth, people may filter out new information because it doesn't mesh with what they know or believe. "Individuals selectively orient their attention to those stimuli in their environments that match their existing predispositions, values, and behaviors," explains Dutta-Bergman (2005, p. 112), adding that "campaign materials that propose to alter the belief structure of the receiver of the message are not likely to be adhered to. Instead, those individuals who are already interested in the issue end up learning more from the message."

Finally, underprivileged audiences may have different priorities. People who are worried about violence and hunger may feel that long-term health issues are the least of their worries (Holtgrave, Tinsley, & Kay, 1995).

REACHING UNDER-INFORMED AUDIENCES

In their article "Lessons From the Field," three noted health promotion specialists urge campaign designers not to overlook marginalized members of society. They write:

> Conducting communication research within diverse ethnic/racial/underserved communities will be especially important in the future. Attention to these audiences is a necessity, not a nicety. . . . Working with an audience for the first time inevitably brings frustrations as one discovers that principles applied successfully in the past with other populations do not necessarily fit in other contexts. Our experience has been that the potential payoff is worth the initial

frustration. (Edgar, Freimuth, & Hammond, 2003, p. 627)

It's not enough to encourage people to engage more with media. We must think, as well, about the subtext, values, and trust issues involved. For example, we know that, as a general rule, frequent mass-media consumption correlates with being well informed and resource rich. But media exposure benefits some groups more than others. Christopher Beaudoin and Esther Thorson (2006) found that, in terms of social capital, watching television news benefits European Americans significantly more than African Americans. They define **social capital** as the benefits possible when members of a community build positive social connections and a mutual sense of trust. Beaudoin and Thorson observe that members of African American communities often experience negative or less-than-optimal benefits from media use because they are so often portrayed negatively in the news and entertainment media. For them, media images may strengthen prejudice and powerlessness rather than provide information they feel they can trust and use. This may be true even when the messages are well intentioned. For example, highlighting the high incidence of HIV among African Americans and among gay men may get their attention, but it may also strengthen prejudice against them.

The challenge for us as health promoters is to earn trust, respond to community needs, and inform and enable people, at the same time being careful to avoid stigmatizing communities at risk (Smith, 2007). Here are a few suggestions.

- *Focus on social capital.* Recognize that health is not merely a matter of individual control. Prejudice, trust, community resources, social networks, and confidence have profound affects as well. (We'll cover this idea more thoroughly in Chapter 14.)
- *Tailor materials to audiences' literacy levels.* For example, Satya Krishnan (1996) recommends that clinics educate people with low reading skills by showing instructional health videos in medical waiting rooms.
- *Help build online skills and confidence.* For some people, access to health information is limited because they lack a computer or online capability. Even for those with access, a sense of self-efficacy is often missing (Rains, 2008a).

Evidence suggests that members of under-informed audiences benefit when they are coached to use the Web knowledgeably and confidently. The National Cancer Institute has helped fund a number of projects to "narrow the digital divide" by designing websites tailored to the needs of underserved populations and offering community workshops to teach people how to use them (Kreps, 2005).

With these issues in mind, let's turn to the important task of determining exactly whom to target with our campaign.

Segmenting the Audience

As we consider who should receive information about the sports recreation program, it may be tempting to target everyone possible. However, research suggests that appealing to an entire population at one time usually doesn't pay off. Because people tend to evaluate information based on its relevance to them, a broad message may seem too general for anyone to take personally (Slater, 1995). Furthermore, tastes differ, and what appeals to one group doesn't necessarily appeal to others. Messages that try to satisfy everyone often become so generic that they don't interest anyone. The odds are that, even on small campuses, the population is varied enough to make audience segmentation preferable.

Segmenting an audience means identifying specific groups who are alike in important ways and whose involvement is important to the purpose of the campaign (Slater, 1995). As we attempt to segment the audience, we must avoid grouping people based on superficial attributes. Characteristics such as race and income are not reliable indicators of how people think and behave (Williams & Flora, 1995). People within those categories may have very divergent viewpoints. Identifying groups on the basis of similar goals and experiences is harder to do, but it's more productive. Following are some questions to consider:

- Who is currently involved (and not involved) in the recommended activity?
- What are people's reasons for participating (or not)?
- Who stands to benefit from the recommended behaviors?

- Who is in most need of these benefits?
- Who might reasonably be expected to adopt these behaviors?
- Is there anyone who should *not* be encouraged to participate?

Remember that some campaigns do more harm than good by recommending behaviors inappropriate for the audience. For example, vigorous exercise is not right for everybody.

Keep in mind that indirect approaches sometimes work well for hard-to-reach audiences. People who plan campus lectures often ask professors to publicize them in class and to consider offering students extra credit for attendance. They recognize that students might be more influenced by their professors' encouragement than by flyers or word-of-mouth. A similar effect seems to hold true for teenagers and drug use. Parents with authoritative communication styles are more likely than others to be effective in discouraging their teenagers from using illegal drugs (Quick & Stephenson, 2007; Stephenson, Quick, Atkinson, & Tschida, 2005). This knowledge underscores the importance of including parents in antidrug campaigns.

Also be open to unexpected combinations. For instance, freshmen and university staff members may be alike in feeling out of place at the campus gym. Where our campaign is concerned, this similarity may be more important than the differences between these groups. Based on these similarities, we might decide that both freshman and staff members would respond more enthusiastically to personal invitations than to bulletin board notices.

It's sometimes difficult to decide where to draw the line in segmenting an audience. The choice may be to target a small audience of high-need individuals or a large audience whose needs are less severe. Sometimes campaign designers overlook great opportunities to help small audiences. For example, tobacco harvesters are a relatively isolated and overlooked community within the overall population. But they have serious health concerns. For one, they often suffer from nausea, dizziness, and heart rate disruptions caused by exposure to green tobacco leaves (Parrott & Polonec, 2008). They can minimize their risk simply by wearing thicker clothing and changing into dry clothes when moisture from the plants soaks them, but little effort has been devoted to educating farmers about this

WHAT DO YOU THINK?

Evidence suggests that young people are more receptive to messages that focus on social implications, such as offending others with second-hand smoke, than on personal consequences, such as getting lung cancer (Keller & Lehmann, 2008). Why do you think this is the case?

(Parrott & Polonec, 2008). This health concern might not be as widespread as some others, but it's a serious issue for the people involved, and results are readily attainable. All in all, there's no definitive rule for choosing between highly focused and more generalized approaches, but health promoters who are sensitive to audience needs and health benefits are most likely to make reasonable judgments.

Based on our audience analysis, we might decide to target our sports recreation campaign toward people new on campus (students, staff, or both), to community members, or to nontraditional students. We might find that current participants do not reflect the racial and ethnic diversity on campus, or that the current membership is mostly men or women, or that people with disabilities are not as involved as they could be. Consequently, we might direct the campaign toward groups that are currently underutilizing the sports recreation program or those people who have the greatest need of the benefits it offers. And don't forget the current participants. Maybe their involvement can be improved. The possibilities are numerous, making it especially important to know the audience well before choosing a segment of it to target.

Audience as a Person

Once a target focus community has been identified, imagine the audience as a single person, complete "with name, gender, occupation, and lifestyle" (Lefebvre et al., 1995, p. 221). With this "person" in mind, Lefebvre and colleagues (1995) pose the following questions for consideration.

- What's important to this person?
- What are the person's feelings, attitudes, and beliefs about the behavior change (including perceived benefits and barriers)?
- What are his or her media habits?

Imagining the audience as a person is useful in focusing the campaign and in creating messages that seem personal and immediate.

Every audience and every audience member is unique, but some overall characteristics may help guide our efforts. Here's some information that may be useful to us as we attempt to understand our focus community.

Young Audiences

Age may have some effect on how members perceive health messages. Although it's difficult to make generalizations about adult audiences, the developmental stages of youth often have relatively predictable effects.

Children are an important audience. As Erica Weintraub Austin (1995) points out, it's easier to prevent bad habits than to break them. Sending consistent messages to children early on may prevent them from developing unhealthy behaviors later. Evidence supports that children are strongly influenced by adults. On the bright side, young people tend to follow their parents' advice (Henriksen & Jackson, 1998). However, children often seek to emulate adult behaviors—even the unhealthy ones. Portraying behaviors such as smoking as "adult-only" may actually make them seem more appealing to youngsters.

Adolescents often believe they are unlike other people and that others do not understand them (this is called **personal fable**). Consequently, they are likely to assume that health warnings don't apply to them (K. Greene, Rubin, Hale, & Walters, 1996). Teenagers also tend to be extremely self-conscious and to feel that people are scrutinizing their appearance and behavior (this is called **imaginary audience**). This makes them sensitive to peer pressure and social approval, which can work for or against health promotion efforts (K. Greene et al., 1996). A third factor, called **psychological reactance**, characterizes adolescents' desire to assert their independence and sense of personal control (Brehm, 1966). They often resent the sense that other people are telling them what to do, and they may rebel just to avoid feeling controlled.

Despite the challenges, there is some promising research about reaching children and adolescents.

- *Focus on immediate concerns.* Austin (1995) reminds health promoters that teens' immediate social concerns may outweigh their long-term health considerations. In Austin's words, adolescents may "care more that smoking will make their breath smell bad than that they could develop cancer" (p. 115).

- *Emphasize personal choice.* Adolescents tend to react negatively to messages that restrict their freedom of choice (Rains & Turner, 2007; M. J. Lee, 2010). Claude Miller and colleagues (2007) found that adolescents responded favorably when health messages included a "restoration of freedom" passage at the end, emphasizing their right to make healthy choices for themselves. The restoration postscript the researchers used included the following: "You've probably heard a lot of messages telling you to exercise for good health. . . . You know what is best for yourself. . . . Everybody is different. We all make our own decisions and act as we choose to act. Obviously, you make your own decisions too. The choice is yours. You're free to decide for yourself" (Miller, Lane, Deatrick, Young, & Potts, 2007, p. 240).

- *Remember, there are many stages of youth.* A few years can make a big difference in how youth audiences respond. Hye-Jin Paek's (2008) data indicate that younger children respond well to school-based programs, whereas older teens benefit more from high-sensation appeals and truth-based information such as the truth campaign's presentation of tobacco-related statistics and tobacco-industry memos.

Sensation-Seekers

The **activation model for information exposure** supports two premises: that persuasive messages are most effective when they stimulate an optimal amount of arousal in the reader/viewer, and that what is "optimal" for one person may be boring or too intense for another (Donohew, Palmgreen, & Duncan, 1980). Here's a case in point. In the 1990s, *Rolling Stone* magazine ran an advertisement that proclaimed, "Why Women Find a Little Prick Attractive." Beside the headline was a photograph of a beautiful woman in black lingerie. Smaller wording explained that "the prick" in question was a small mark on a man's finger where he had drawn blood to verify that he was not HIV-positive

IN YOUR EXPERIENCE

Humor can be effective in avoiding the boomerang effect of psychological reactance. In one study, university students were more attentive to humorous PSAs about alcohol abuse than to serious ones (Skalski, Tamborini, Glazer, & Smith, 2009). Can you think of a health campaign that effectively uses humor?

(Ivinski, 1997). The advertisement was for an at-home HIV test. It concluded: "And if the woman in your life is having any doubts—don't worry. That little prick is sure to satisfy her."

As you might imagine, "The Little Prick" ad drew considerable comment. At least one critic considered it irresponsible to portray a serious subject such as HIV in such a whimsical (some would say tasteless) manner. As Pamela Ivinski (1997) expressed it:

Using sex to sell a test that determines whether someone has contracted a virus that's often transmitted during sex, and then subtly implying in the copy that the user shouldn't worry because he'll probably test negative, and he can use that fact to attract women for more sex, is a little bit creepy, not to mention misleading and even cynical. (para. 8)

The advertisement's creators acknowledged that the ad was not for everyone, but they argued that it was shocking and sexy enough to make young men pay attention to an important topic.

The activation model can apply to audiences of any age or description. So far, researchers and campaign designers have used it most extensively for adolescent and young-adult audiences, who are more likely than others to be high **sensation-seekers**, meaning that they enjoy new and intense experiences (Everett & Palmgreen, 1995; Zuckerman, 1994). The danger with high sensation-seekers is that risky behaviors appeal to them. Not only are they less likely than others to take precautions, they are more apt to be in dangerous situations in the first place. For instance, compared to their peers, high sensation-seekers are more likely to think smoking is appealing (Paek, 2008). They are typically more impulsive about having sex, yet less willing than others to use condoms (Noar, Zimmerman,

Palmgreen, Lustria, & Horosewski, 2006). And they tend to associate with other high sensation-seekers, which can make their behaviors seem normal rather than dangerous or extreme (Yanovitzky, 2006). These factors may be challenging for health promoters. But also keep in mind that, because high sensation-seekers are receptive to novel situations, they typically welcome diversity and intercultural communication (Arasaratnam & Banerjee, 2011). This makes them less ethnocentric and more open-minded than normal, which may make them receptive to a range of health-related messages and spokespeople.

Here are a few promising lines of research about appealing to high sensation-seekers:

- *Make messages varied and intense.* Messages that have quick and vivid visual edits and loud and fast music typically have the most impact on high sensation-seekers, teens, and tweens (9- to 12-year-olds) (Lang, Schwartz, Lee, & Angelini, 2007; Niederdeppe, Davis, Farrelly, & Yarsevich, 2007).
- *Make the most of low-distraction environments.* Donald Helme and colleagues (2007) successfully influenced middle-school students' attitudes about smoking when they used laptop computers in the classroom to expose students to three episodes of *Friends* in which the researchers had interspersed antismoking PSAs (Helme, Donohew, Baier, & Zittleman, 2007). Interestingly, both intense and mild-content PSAs made an impact on high sensation-seekers in the sample, perhaps because the PSAs were embedded in entertainment programming and the classroom offered relatively few distractions.
- *Run PSAs during popular programs.* High sensation-seekers who watch a lot of television don't necessarily remember a lot about the PSAs they see. But they do typically remember the PSAs that appear during their favorite programs (typically sports, comedy, and cartoons for 16- to 25-year-olds) (D'Silva & Palmgreen, 2007).

Part of the dilemma, of course, is that the intense messages that sensation seekers enjoy may be too much for most audiences, making it difficult to target high-risk individuals without offending others. (For ethical considerations about health promotion, see Box 13.2.)

As we complete Step 2 in creating a health campaign, it may seem that, although we've already done a lot of work, we still don't know what the campaign will involve. Our efforts will not go to waste. Research shows that campaigns launched without a clear understanding of the audience, current situation, and potential benefits are often frustrating to create and ineffective at reaching their goals. With a focus community in mind, we're ready for Step 3.

Step 3: Establishing Campaign Goals and Objectives

By this point we should have a fairly clear impression of the sports recreation department, its potential benefits, and the people we most want to reach with our campaign. Collecting and analyzing data have prepared us to establish specific objectives for our campaign. **Objectives** state in clear, measurable terms exactly what we hope to achieve with the campaign. We might consider the following questions.

- What exactly do we want people to start/stop/continue doing?
- If we hope to encourage a particular behavior, when (and for how long) should it occur to be of benefit?
- How will we know if our campaign has been successful?

Relevant to the sports recreation campaign, we may decide that signing up 40 freshmen in 3 months would constitute success. Or perhaps we've decided to focus on students with disabilities or on newcomers. Our objective may be to get at least 20 current participants to bring an individual from one of those groups to an event.

We must make sure our objectives are oriented to the overall purpose of the campaign. For instance, if people participate in only one climbing-wall session, will there be health benefits? If not, it may be important to aim for continued participation—perhaps attendance once a week for at least 2 months.

Let's think ahead about exactly how we will measure the effects of the campaign. This may involve

BOX 13.2 ETHICAL CONSIDERATIONS

The Politics of Prevention—Who Should Pay?

Health promotion may seem like a win–win situation. If people can be encouraged to prevent disease and injuries, they will enjoy better health and the nation's health costs will be minimized. How far should we carry this line of reasoning? Should people who work hard to be healthy get discount prices on health care and insurance? Should they be given advantages when competing for jobs? If people knowingly engage in unhealthy behaviors, should society help pay for their medical bills?

About 75 cents of every dollar spent on health care in the United States goes to treating chronic illnesses, many of which could have been avoided with healthier diets, more exercise, and abstention from tobacco use ("Interview," 2007). And that figure doesn't even include the cost of treating preventable *injuries*. The added expense eats up tax money and leads to hikes in health insurance rates. As Daniel Wikler (1987) puts it, "The person who takes risks with his [or her] own health gambles with resources which belong to others" (p. 14). Some theorists argue that people who continue risky behavior (like smoking, overeating, or driving without seatbelts) when they know it is bad for them should pay from their own pockets when their behavior leads to medical expenses.

In a related issue, some feel that companies that profit from selling unhealthy products should pay part of the health bill. State governments have successfully sued tobacco companies for damages, charging that it's unfair for them to make huge profits while others foot the enormous bill of treating tobacco-related illnesses. The numbers are staggering. At least 50 chemicals in tobacco smoke are known to cause cancer (WHO, 2007b). Around the world, more than 5 million people a year die from tobacco-related illnesses, including 600,000 who are killed by the effects of secondhand smoke (WHO, "Tobacco," 2012). Experts estimate that smoking costs Americans $193 billion a year in medical expenses and lost productivity (CDC, "Tobacco-Related Mortality," 2011).

Some companies now refuse to hire smokers or people who are extremely overweight because they are at greater health risk, and thus are likely to cost

the company more money than others in terms of health benefits and sick leave. Similarly, some insurance companies offer a discount to people who don't smoke and those who remain accident-free or who complete informational programs such as defensive-driving courses.

On the other side of the issue, some worry that governments and employers are becoming too involved in people's lifestyle decisions. Some charge that groups like Mothers Against Drunk Driving (MADD) are taking a good thing too far by seeking to punish people for drinking even small amounts of alcohol (DiLorenzo & Bennett, 1998). Similarly, policy analyst Will Crawford (1997) warns that the government may soon be telling people what to eat in the name of controlling obesity. Some people say that increasing the "sin taxes" on alcohol and tobacco will hurt consumers, not companies, and they're afraid the taxes will be extended to cover snack foods and other not-so-healthy items. A third argument is that health concerns such as obesity are not always matters of individual control. Obesity has many causes, including social norms and heredity. People may gain weight because of medications or other health conditions. However, media coverage tends to sway the public toward considering obesity as either an individualistic or a societal issue (Kim & Willis, 2007). All in all, opponents of tighter health requirements say you cannot assume people are fully in control of their health, and you cannot control the risks people take without controlling their freedom of choice.

WHAT DO YOU THINK?

1. Should people who knowingly take health risks pay more than others for health insurance? Should they be denied insurance? Should they be denied health services?

2. Should people be required by law to engage in healthy practices such as being immunized and exercising regularly?

3. Should it be against the law to sell or advertise products known to have a high health risk? Does it matter if such products are addictive?

4. Do you agree with the rationale behind many states' seatbelt and motorcycle helmet laws—that people who neglect safety precautions not

only endanger their own lives but increase the trauma and expense for everybody?

5. How do you weigh the argument that some people are not well informed about health issues (perhaps because they cannot read or cannot afford a computer) and that it's unfair to expect them to follow health guidelines about which they know little or nothing?

6. In your opinion, which of the following behaviors (if any) should be grounds for denying or limiting health benefits? On what criteria do you make your judgments?

Smoking
Engaging in unprotected sex
Exceeding the speed limit
Snow skiing
Neglecting to exercise regularly
Overeating
Playing football
Rescuing accident victims

7. If a person has a family history of a disease, should he or she be required by society to take extra health precautions?

❓ CAN YOU GUESS? Part 2

One challenge of health promotion is monitoring which diseases are most prevalent and most deadly. Take a stab at ranking the following from highest (1) to lowest (10) in terms of annual deaths around the world.

_____ lower respiratory infections
_____ lung cancer
_____ dementia
_____ stomach cancer
_____ colon and rectal cancers
_____ AIDS
_____ diabetes
_____ heart disease
_____ stroke
_____ chronic obstructive pulmonary artery disease (COPD)
_____ breast cancer

Answers appear at the end of the chapter.

follow-up surveys or sign-up sheets to keep track of participation. Setting measurable goals will allow us (and others) to determine if the campaign has been a success.

Health promoters are increasingly being held accountable for their efforts. **Accountability** means demonstrating how the results of a project compare to the money and time invested in it. For example, a hospital reorganized its marketing and public relations department because patient surveys showed that people chose the hospital based on their doctor's advice, not on advertising. The hospital didn't discontinue advertisements completely. (The same study revealed that billboards, while they didn't bring in new patients, significantly raised workplace morale.) But the public relations staff redirected part of their effort into marketing services directly to physicians.

In the larger population, a useful means of tracking health risks and changes is the use of **disease maps**, which look like regular maps but are color-coded to show the incidence of disease in geographical areas. These maps present a great deal of information in a way that's clear and visually appealing (Parrott, Hopfer, Ghetian, & Lengerich, 2007). (See *Check It Out!* for links to online disease maps.) For example, you might look up a cancer map of the United States and feel alarmed that your state is shaded in a color that, according to the map key, signifies high cancer incidence. With some maps, you can click on regions and get more detailed information, such as cancer rates in your hometown or neighborhood, links to charts and graphs, even relevant photographs. If they are accurate and up to date, disease maps have an advantage over complex reports. Imagine scanning tables of disease statistics about every area of your community and state. It might take you hours and many volumes of paperwork to show what a simple map can convey in a few minutes. And even if you carefully reviewed the data in table format, it would be easy to overlook health patterns that show up vividly on a disease map—like cancer rates that are particularly high around an industrial plant or river. This information is useful in accomplishing what some researchers call *environmental justice* or *environmental equity*, meaning that attention is given to demographically situated populations that lag behind others or require more resources than they currently have to ensure citizens' health (Waller, Carlin, Xia, & Gelfand, 1997).

Keeping in mind the factors involved in understanding a target audience, let's consider how we might appeal to the people we chose to target with our campaign.

Step 4: Selecting Channels of Communication

A **channel** is a means of communicating information, either directly (in person) or indirectly (through media such as TV or radio or computers). To select the best channels for our campaign, let's consider which channels our target audience uses and trusts most.

Sometimes channel selection is limited by time or money. Our sports recreation enrollment effort will probably not involve full-color magazine ads or sophisticated television commercials. Nevertheless, as health promoters, we should be familiar with all types of channels. Moreover, let's not assume too quickly that a channel is out of our reach. For example, we may not produce television commercials, but we might book appearances on campus or community television talk shows.

Channel Characteristics

Let's consider the advantages and limitations of different channels. Experts suggest that channels for a health campaign be evaluated in terms of reach, specificity, and impact (Schooler, Chaffee, Flora, & Roser, 1998). **Reach** refers to the number of people who will be exposed to a message via a particular channel. **Specificity** refers to how accurately the message can be targeted to a specific group of people. **Impact** is how influential a message is likely to be.

Television and the Internet usually have larger and more diverse audiences than other media. As such, they have immense reach. However, when audiences are large and diverse, it can be hard to tailor messages to particular people. Television, especially, has low specificity, although that has

> **CHECK IT OUT!** Disease maps are available at:
> - CDC Map Gallery: cdc.gov/gis/gallery.htm
> - U.S. Department of the Interior: diseasemaps.usgs.gov/index.html

changed somewhat with the creation of special-interest cable and satellite programs. The Internet can be more specific, if we put the effort into selecting people within the target audience and/or posting information with specific identifiers that will lead interested people to it.

Although it may be tempting to aim for the broadest reach possible, it's advisable to focus on our target audience. Exposure that is broader than necessary can waste resources and contribute to information overload, making it difficult for people to identify which messages are most important and relevant to them (Lang, 2006).

Impact is usually related to arousal and involvement. **Arousal** refers to how emotionally stimulating and exciting a message is (Schooler et al., 1998). When we view words and images about risky products, such as condoms, liquor bottles, and cigarettes, we typically experience greater emotional and physical arousal than with more innocuous products, such as soda cans and juice bottles (Lang, Chung, Lee, & Zhao, 2005). We tend to identify the risky products more quickly and remember them longer (Lang et al., 2005). This can make it difficult for healthy campaign messages (especially if they are sedate) to compete with advertisements for unhealthy products.

Interactive computer programs are a good example of high-arousal messages that can be used to promote healthy behaviors. Interactive, on-screen messages are often very engrossing, with colorful graphics, moving images, and sound (Street & Rimal, 1997). Roberto and colleagues (2007) report success using an interactive computer program to involve high school students in safer sex and pregnancy-prevention efforts. Compared to other students, those who took part in the online program were more knowledgeable about STDs, more aware of their personal risk, more reluctant to have sex, and more confident about their ability to use safer sex practices if they did have sex.

Involvement is the amount of mental effort required to understand a message (Parrott, 1995). Interpersonal communication is high involvement. It requires a great deal of thought and action. Thus, health professionals, family members, and friends tend to have high impact. Newspapers are also high-involvement channels, because people must read and use their imaginations. Television is low involvement, because viewers passively observe the sounds and sights displayed for them.

The **elaboration likelihood model** proposes that when we are highly involved with a message, we pay close attention to details and evaluate the message thoroughly. As a consequence, we remember high-involvement messages longer than others and are more likely to act on them (Briñol & Petty, 2006; Petty & Cacioppo, 1981). In short, people usually pay closer attention when using high-involvement channels, such as reading and talking, and this affects how much they are influenced by the information. Surveys show that people who use high-involvement channels are usually better informed about health than people who rely on low-involvement channels such as television.

Communication Technology: Using Computers to Narrowcast Messages

We often speak of *broadcasting* messages to large audiences. Messages in the mass media draw people's attention to health topics. However, there are advantages to *narrowcasting* as well. Evidence suggests that, no matter what form a message takes, our primary considerations are: *Does this apply to me?* and *Can I trust the source?* (Ko, Campbell, Lewis, Earp, & DeVellis, 2011).

💬 IN YOUR EXPERIENCE

Audiences in positive moods—as when they're watching comedies—are more receptive than others to detection messages (e.g., breast self-exam, cancer screening, and so on). Audiences in negative moods—when, say, they're watching dramas or news shows—are more receptive to prevention messages such as using sunscreen (Anghelcev & Sar, 2011). Can you compare two different experiences when you were given the same health advice but your mood was different? What about your experience was different?

Narrowcasting, or tailored communication, is designed to meet the specific needs of individual consumers. That is, it's designed to be highly relevant. Matthew Kreuter and colleagues (1999) employ the example of a doctor's visit to treat high cholesterol. As usual, the physician offers advice on diet and exercise, but this time the doctor also provides a printout tailor-made for the patient:

> It seems like the cold weather has been keeping you from walking every day like you had hoped to in your physical activity plan. Did you know that many of the local malls open early in the winter for walkers? Crestwood Mall is the one closest to your house, and it opens for walkers at 6:30 every morning. Mall walking might also help with your recent lack of motivation. You've been struggling with exercise because your walking partner moved away, and this might be a way for you to meet some new people, and not feel like you're exercising alone. (Kreuter, Farrell, Olevitch, & Brennan, 1999, p. 2)

The information might also include healthy recipes suited to your family's preferences and tips for finding healthy food in the local supermarket.

Before receiving tailored health messages from a physician, people typically fill out questionnaires about their health, habits, preferences, and environments. The questions go beyond simple demographics such as age and sex (Rimal & Adkins, 2003). For example, if the goal is to help older adults avoid harmful falls, the questions may ask about the presence of stairs, handrails, and rugs and the need to do lawn work and home repairs (Kreuter et al., 1999). This information is entered into computer databanks (either online or in the doctor's office) that produce individualized profiles and suggestions. For example, the tailored response might suggest ways to reorganize one's home to minimize the chance of falling and community resources to help with riskier activities, such as house painting and snow shoveling (Kreuter et al., 1999). It is also possible to key in information about an individual's education and literacy level so that the resulting printout is usable and comprehensible, perhaps showing mostly pictures and diagrams if the client is not proficient at reading (Bernhardt & Cameron, 2003).

The idea is that people are more likely to act on customized information than to sift through data that may or may not apply to them or that may exceed their comprehension level. Kreuter and colleagues (1999) compare tailored health messages to a realtor who provides a list of homes that meet a client's wishes rather than a realtor who says, "Here's a street map of our entire city. By going up and down all the streets, you're sure to find something that meets your needs" (p. 4).

Health promoters in charge of large campaigns may not have license to be quite so specific. But they can still tailor messages to some extent. For example, Valerie Pilling and Laura Brannon (2007) took a tailored approach in creating a responsible-drinking website for college students. Some students in the study viewed a version of the website tailored to suit their personalities (either responsible, communicative, logical, or adventuresome), while others viewed more general messages about the danger of binge drinking. Students who viewed the tailored messages were significantly more likely than the others to consider the website interesting, to predict that it would be effective, and to say that the materials affected their attitudes about drinking. In their review of the literature, Barbara Rimer and Matthew Kreuter (2006) applaud such efforts and encourage health promoters to continue refining tailored messages to suit recipients' cultural and motivational preferences. In tailored-information websites, a spokesperson of the same race as the reader might present the information, artwork and graphics might vary, and information might be more or less complex, based on the recipient's preference.

Unfortunately, many health websites have not realized the full potential for narrowcasting. A review of 21 safer sex websites revealed that most of them were moderately targeted at best (Noar, Clark, Cole, & Lustria, 2006). Noar and coauthors suggest that health-oriented web developers might invite users to complete a brief questionnaire when they register and then use that information to highlight key health information throughout the rest of the site.

Multichannel Campaigns

As you've seen, broadcasting and narrowcasting have advantages. Many times, the best chance of making a difference is to reach people through several

> **CHECK IT OUT!** For a personalized assessment of your diet, try out Food-A-Pedia, a free, interactive website at which you can see the sugar, sodium, fat, and caloric content of the foods you eat, track what you eat, create your own plan, and so on. The site is sponsored the U.S. Department of Agriculture. Access it at https://www.choosemyplate.gov/SuperTracker/foodapedia.aspx.

channels (Flay & Burton, 1990). Multichannel efforts are important because people have different communication patterns and preferences. What appeals to some people may not appeal to others. For example, when researchers studied the impact of campaign messages in Hawaii encouraging people to eat healthy foods and walk regularly, they found that television PSAs were seen about equally by all members of the population (Buchthal et al., 2011). However, residents with low incomes and literacy challenges benefited less than others from printed messages. On the bright side, they benefited more than others from radio PSAs and campaign posters in supermarkets. The researchers suggest that reaching members of the target audience where they are (as in the fruit and vegetable aisle), with messages they can easily understand, is critical to minimizing knowledge gaps.

Mass-mediated and interpersonal channels are also complementary, in that the media messages typically influence what people think about and talk about (see Rogers & Dearing, 1988), but people do not simply buy into everything the media says. They are also likely to be influenced by discussions with neighbors and family members. **Diffusion of innovations** theory refers to the process through which new information is filtered and passed along throughout a community (Rogers, 1983). Research shows that some community members are opinion leaders who have credibility by virtue of their expertise or social standing. They often pass along new ideas and information from the media to other people. In this way, media messages may influence people indirectly whether they use the media or not. The process by which people relay media messages to others is called **two-step flow** (Brosius & Weimann, 1996; Lazarsfeld, Burleson, & Gaudet, 1948). When Uriyoan Colon-Ramos and colleagues studied survey responses from nearly 13,000 adults in the United States, they found that about 2 in 100 had extensive social networks of 75 people or more, to whom they regularly offered guidance about a range of matters, including health. It seems like a small proportion of people, but the effects may be significant both ways. Most of the highly networked opinion leaders were eager to learn health information, were tuned into a variety of health information sources, and were likely to engage in healthy behaviors themselves (Colon-Ramos et al., 2009).

Summary

Successful health promotion recognizes that people don't necessarily change their behaviors because they have been presented with new health information. As campaign designers, we must take into account the concerns, habits, and preferences of the people we wish to influence. Campaigns with the best chance of succeeding talk to people where they are, whether it is the beauty salon, the athletic field, or the doctor's office. They make it practical for people to adopt healthy behaviors, even if it means changing public policy or offering free treatment. Good health campaigns are thorough and are backed by long-term commitment. The best campaigns involve members of the focus population as active participants and recruit social support for healthy behaviors. Furthermore, they speak with many voices, including the concerned tones of loved ones, the calm assurance of experts, and the printed and recorded messages of mass media.

Because people are inclined to pay more attention to messages that seem relevant to them, campaigns directed at "everyone" may not pique the interest of anyone. Health campaign success stories show that it's important to know the audience well, take positive action, establish clear goals, measure success, and make behaviors socially rewarding.

Whereas illness and disease prevention seem to benefit everyone, ethical dilemmas are involved, such as: Should people be rewarded or penalized based on their health-related behavior? How should we balance people's right to choose for themselves with society's interest in keeping costs down? Where do we draw the line between healthy and unhealthy behaviors?

The first step in creating a health campaign is to research potential benefits of the campaign. Find out who stands to gain, who is already behaving according to campaign recommendations, and what alternatives exist.

The second step is to choose a target audience. Interviews, questionnaires, and focus groups are useful ways to learn about potential audience members—what they like, what they know, how they typically behave, what they consider important, and more. We may wish to target people in great need or those who are most likely to respond to the campaign. At the same time, keep in mind audience characteristics such as self-consciousness, sensation hunger, confidence, need for independence, and psychological reactance. It's often challenging to reach audiences who are culturally different from the mainstream. However, considering the knowledge gap hypothesis, these audiences are often the most in need of health information and assistance.

With a target audience in mind, the third step in creating a health campaign is to establish clear and measurable objectives so we can accurately assess a campaign's effects. Fourth, we select channels through which to communicate campaign messages. Channels typically differ in terms of reach, specificity, and impact. Sometimes narrowcasting is more effective than broadcasting, in that it helps message recipients focus on information that is tailored to their interests, abilities, and resources. Often, the best campaigns make use of several channels. All in all, the media play an important role in promoting health issues, but media impact is limited without interpersonal reinforcement.

Key Terms and Theories

health-promoting behaviors
health promotion campaigns
health promoter
institutional review board (IRB)
highly scheduled interviews
moderately scheduled interviews
unscheduled interviews
questionnaire
fixed-alternative questions
open-ended questions
close-ended questions

focus group
sampling
knowledge gap hypothesis
digital divide
social capital
segmenting an audience
personal fable
imaginary audience
psychological reactance
activation model for information exposure
sensation-seekers
objectives
accountability
disease maps
channel
reach
specificity
impact
arousal
involvement
elaboration likelihood model
narrowcasting
diffusion of innovations
two-step flow

Discussion Questions

1. Describe the strategy and principles of the truth® campaign. How do they relate to the principles suggested throughout the chapter?
2. Name some of the factors that influence people's behavior.
3. Name and describe the first four steps in creating a health promotion campaign.
4. What are four qualities of good campaigns, as illustrated by the exemplary campaigns in this chapter?
5. What are three types of interviews? How do they compare?
6. Provide some guidelines for designing an effective questionnaire.
7. What is the difference between an open-ended question and a closed-ended question?
8. Give some guidelines for conducting effective focus groups.
9. Using the knowledge gap hypothesis, explain why people of low socioeconomic status are often under-informed about health issues. How

does the digital divide figure in? What are some tips for reaching under-informed audiences?
10. Why is it important to select a specific target audience? What are some questions to consider when segmenting an audience?
11. What are some factors to keep in mind if the target audience includes children? If it includes adolescents?
12. Explain the activation model for information exposure. Link it to the concept of sensation seeking.
13. Do you believe people should pay more for health insurance if they engage in risky or unhealthy behaviors? Why or why not?
14. What are some questions to consider when determining campaign goals?
15. Explain how channels differ in terms of reach, specificity, and impact. Explain how these apply to an actual campaign of your choosing.
16. Describe the process of creating narrowcast messages. What are the advantages of narrowcasting?
17. Why are multichannel efforts recommended?

Answers to *Can You Guess?*

PART 1

Tobacco kills more people. Indeed, more people die from tobacco-related illnesses than from motor vehicle accidents, HIV, murder, illegal drug use, and suicide *combined* (CDC, "Tobacco-Related Mortality," 2011).

PART 2

An Egg McMuffin and latte with 2% milk contain 438 calories and 1014 mg of sodium; two glazed doughnuts contain 452 calories and 602 mg of sodium; a quarter-pound cheeseburger and cola contain 785 calories and 1298 mg of sodium; two slices of thick-crust pepperoni pizza and an 8-oz sports drink contain 666 calories and 1165 mg of sodium. Total: 2341 calories and 4079 mg of sodium.

Note: The total recommended daily allowance is 1,400 calories for women, 2,000 calories for men, and 2,399 mg of sodium (Food Tracker at *https://www.choosemyplate.gov/SuperTracker/ foodtracker.aspx*).

PART 3

1—heart disease, 2—stroke, 3—lung cancer, 4—lower respiratory infections, 5—COPD, 6—colon and rectal cancer, 7—dementia, 8—diabetes, 9—breast cancer, 10—stomach cancer, 11—AIDS (WHO, 2007a).

Note: AIDS is expected to be the third leading cause of death, worldwide, by the year 2031.

CHAPTER FOURTEEN

Designing and Implementing Health Campaigns

2/3 of RUTGERS students stop at 3 or fewer

almost 1 in 5 don't drink at all

(Provided by Lea Stewart, Rutgers University)

One of the most famous and most widely emulated campaigns on college campuses is the RU SURE campaign, developed in the 1990s at Rutgers University to curb the incidence of dangerous alcohol consumption. The campaign is based on evidence that college students usually overestimate the amount their peers drink. By providing students with more accurate statistics, campaign sponsors try to clarify that the norm is less extreme than students think. Thus, students need not drink excessively to fit in with their peers (Lederman & Stewart, 2005; Lederman, Stewart, Barr, Powell, Laitman, & Goodhart, 2001; Menegatos, Lederman, & Hess, 2010).

The RU SURE campaign is famous for its high level of student involvement and its novel ways of integrating campaign messages into everyday campus life. Through the years, campaign designers have distributed free T-shirts featuring a "Top Ten Misperceptions" list about life at Rutgers, including three misperceptions about drinking as well as humorous myths such as "You don't need shower shoes for the dorms." They have also engaged students in RU SURE Bingo games, developed

CHECK IT OUT! To see video elements of the RU Sure campaign, check out the following:

■ http://www.youtube.com/watch?v=jZJ5RbcUjCo
■ http://www.youtube.com/watch?v=E0hMG0yFNCw
■ http://www.youtube.com/watch?v=BY66eqVvjdl

curricula supplements for campus courses, and developed partnerships with community leaders and others.

Evidence on the Rutgers campus indicates that student estimates of peer drinking have dropped considerably since the RU SURE campaign began (Stewart, Lederman, Golubow, Cattafesta, Godhart, Powell & Laitman, 2002). "Communication majors are involved in all aspects of this campaign, from designing ways to deliver campaign messages to gathering evaluation data," says Lea Stewart, professor and director of the Rutgers Center for Communication and Health Issues. "Since no one works on the campaign without first learning about the scope and consequences of dangerous drinking among college students, we reach two audiences: our target audience of first-year students and a secondary audience of upper-level students."

Like many health-promotion efforts, the RU Sure campaign is based partly on social marketing. **Social marketing** means that campaign designers apply the principles of commercial advertising to pro-social campaigns, such as health-promotion efforts (Lefebvre & Flora, 1988). The rationale is that many of the techniques used to sell goods and services work equally well when promoting healthy lifestyles. From a social marketing perspective, health-related behaviors have a price tag of sorts. They "cost" something in terms of money, time,

IN YOUR EXPERIENCE

■ Have you noticed social-norm campaigns similar to RU Sure on your campus?

■ If so, what do you think of them?

■ In your experience, how much alcohol do most college students drink? How often?

■ If you learned that your estimates were inaccurate, would it influence the way you behave?

energy, or some other investment. Although the cost doesn't translate into profits for the health promoter, the promoter is a type of salesperson who tries to keep the costs as low as possible and convince people that the "price" of the recommended behavior is worth paying.

Because the concern in social marketing is primarily with what the "consumer" needs, health promoters make a great effort to understand the audience, assess its needs, and target specific people. Social marketing also involves using multiple channels and conducting follow-up research to measure the success of campaign efforts.

We will talk more about campaign strategies in this chapter. But first let's recap. Chapter 13 provided a guide to the first four stages of creating a health campaign:

Step 1: Defining the situation and potential benefits
Step 2: Analyzing and segmenting the audience
Step 3: Establishing campaign goals and objectives
Step 4: Selecting channels of communication

The process continues in this chapter with a description of key theories and techniques to create health-promotion campaigns. The hypothetical sports recreation campaign we began in Chapter 13 helps illustrate how a health-promotion effort comes together. We will continue it in this chapter. Keep in mind that the same steps apply to campaigns of various sizes on any number of health topics.

This chapter begins by introducing five influential models of behavior change: the health belief model, social cognitive theory, the embedded behaviors model, the theory of reasoned action, and the transtheoretical model. We will then explore the critical-cultural approach and describe the three final stages in campaign development:

Step 5: Designing campaign messages
Step 6: Piloting and implementing the campaign
Step 7: Evaluating and maintaining the campaign

Along the way, we will touch on a number of message-design perspectives, including the role of affect, social norms theory, the theory of normative social behavior, and the extended parallel process model.

Theories of Behavior Change

The theories described here emphasize that people make lifestyle decisions based on a complex array of factors, including personal perceptions, skills, social pressure, convenience, and more. Each of these theories has earned considerable respect among health communication scholars and health promoters. Space is not available to discuss each model in great detail, but this introduction should help orient you to the rich scholarship behind health campaign efforts and provide opportunities for further investigation. Applying these theories to health campaigns can have a positive effect—at least sometimes. Keep in mind that theories are only guiding principles, not magic formulas. No one theory works all of the time or with every audience.

Health Belief Model

The **health belief model** proposes that we base our behavior choices on five primary considerations (Rosenstock, 1960; Stretcher & Rosenstock, 1997). Namely, we're most motivated to change our behaviors if we believe that:

- We will be adversely affected if we don't change;
- The adverse effects will be considerable;
- Behavior change will be effective in preventing the undesired outcome;
- The effort and cost of preventive behavior is worthwhile; and
- We are moved to action by a novel or eye-opening occurrence, such as a brush with danger, a compelling warning message, or an alluring incentive.

In short, motivation is based on an individual's perception of personal susceptibility, serious consequences, worthwhile benefits, justifiable costs, and cues to actions.

The health belief model is used widely for assessing audiences and organizing campaigns. For example, Kami Silk and colleagues (2006) used components of the model to guide focus groups with female adolescents and adults prior

WHAT DO YOU THINK?

■ What's the first health-related PSA or campaign that comes to your mind? Why do you think it's so memorable?

■ What's your favorite PSA or campaign? Why?

■ Do you think health campaigns influence the choices you make? Why or why not?

to developing breast cancer prevention materials. They found that participants of all ages understood the severity of breast cancer, but they defined the consequences somewhat differently. The adolescents tended to emphasize the appearance-altering effects of the disease, such as hair loss during chemotherapy. The adults were more likely to know someone with breast cancer, to know a lot about the disease, and to feel personally susceptible.

The health belief model also reminds us to keep renewing our familiarity with target audiences. Jon Krosnick and coauthors report that, although the adverse affects of smoking are well known to many, about 34% of the public are still unaware that smoking causes or worsens oral cancer, and 35% are not aware that smoking increases one's risk for stroke (Krosnick, Chang, Sherman, Chassin, & Presson, 2006). Campaign designers who overlook these knowledge gaps may miss important opportunities.

Considering all of these factors, it seems naive to assume people will change simply because someone tells them to do so. A campaign message may be a cue to action, but unless someone has reason

IN YOUR EXPERIENCE

In a meta-analysis of 18 studies, Christopher Carpenter (2010) found that, of the factors included in the health believe model, *perceived barriers to behavior change* seem to have the most powerful effect on people's decisions, followed by how much people *expect to benefit* from behavior change and how *severe* they believe the repercussions will be if they don't. Compare a time when you successfully changed your behavior to a time when you were unsuccessful. Do these three factors explain the difference?

💬 **IN YOUR EXPERIENCE**

■ Can you think of a time when an event or message spurred you to action?

■ If so, why do you think it had that effect?

to believe that the recommended behavior is useful and worthwhile and that it will prevent an outcome that's otherwise likely to occur, the recommendation will probably not be motivation enough.

If we're trying to increase participation in our university's sports recreation program, we might consider how strongly members of our target audience believe the benefits we propose would actually help them. Let's say audience analysis reveals a number of statements such as "I know exercise is good for people. But I'm young and healthy. I don't have to worry about that yet." According to the health belief model, people who feel this way won't be motivated to seek the benefits proposed because they don't believe they need them. Our job as health promoters might be to show them more compelling evidence or to appeal to them on the basis of other goals, such as looking good, meeting people, and winning awards. Conversely, if people don't know about the benefits of exercise, the model advocates educating them. Knowledge doesn't ensure behavior change, but it's an important foundation for it. Research shows that people sometimes change their behavior without being well informed. However, these people are less likely to maintain the new behavior than others, especially if the change requires effort or discomfort (Valente, Paredes, & Poppe, 1998).

Social Cognitive Theory

Returning to the sports recreation campaign, imagine that everything seems to be in our favor. People are aware of the recreation program. They know

💬 **IN YOUR EXPERIENCE**

■ What behaviors are embedded in your lifestyle? Which of them are healthy? Unhealthy?

■ What would it take to change those behaviors?

about the benefits. They even feel they would benefit personally. Yet they don't plan to participate. This may seem very puzzling. What's a health promoter to do?

A promoter familiar with social cognitive theory would consider the environment. **Social cognitive theory** holds that we make decisions by considering the interplay of internal and environmental factors (Bandura, 1986, 1994). **Internal factors** include knowledge, skills, emotions, habits, and so on. **Environmental factors** include social approval, physical environment, institutional rules, and the like. According to the theory, we're most comfortable when internal and environmental factors are in sync. This may explain why changing people's minds doesn't necessarily change their behavior (Maibach & Cotton, 1995). Environments are persuasive as well. In our campaign, for example, people may not participate in recreational activities because they perceive that others will laugh at them, the hours are not convenient, or they don't know anyone at the gym.

Social concerns sometimes outweigh personal concerns, even if the behavior in question is particularly risky. When Donna Rouner and Rebecca Lindsey (2006) interviewed female college students, the researchers were impressed by how poised the women seemed. The students rated their knowledge of STDs highly, but they were still uncomfortable talking about condoms. The gap between knowing and doing is consistent with previous evidence that people sometimes wish to use condoms during sex, even plan to use them, but abandon their intentions because they're too embarrassed to bring up the subject. Especially for new partners who don't know each other well, it may seem more socially acceptable for sex "just to happen" than to talk about it in advance (Dennis, 2006). Significantly, people who *do* insist on condom use are typically good communicators—skillful at asserting themselves, understanding other people's feelings, self-disclosing, and managing conflict (Edgar, 1992; Monohan, Miller, & Rothspan, 1997). The implications are that communication skills and well-developed relationships can sometimes help people overcome environmental challenges.

Let's apply social cognitive theory to our sports recreation campaign. The theory suggests that, as health promoters, we must do more than make people aware of health risks. We must make healthy behaviors practical and socially acceptable. If we find that people in our target audience want to participate in recreational activities but are reluctant to do so, our job may be to help them develop new skills, improve the social atmosphere at the fitness center, suggest different hours, or make other changes that build their confidence and reduce the risks of participating.

Embedded Behaviors Model

The embedded behaviors model (Booth-Butterfield, 2003) is similar to social cognitive theory in that it recognizes internal and external influences on health-related behavior. However, the embedded behaviors model also includes consideration of the behavior itself: its frequency, complexity, familiarity or novelty, and links to other behaviors. In short, the **embedded behaviors model** suggests that behaviors are enduring to the extent that they are an integral part of our lifestyle or self-image and are supported by internal and external factors.

Some behaviors, such as switching to a salt substitute, are relatively easy to make because the change doesn't dramatically alter our lifestyle and because equally desirable alternatives are available. However, other behaviors (such as tobacco use) may be extremely difficult to give up. After studying teen smoking, Melanie Booth-Butterfield (2003) reported that "smoking is much more complex than simply buying cigarettes and smoking them" (p. 179). Some teen smokers say they feel a sense of belonging around others who smoke (although they typically insist that peer pressure hasn't influenced them). They report that cigarettes become like friends who are "always there" (p. 178) and that smoking is a way to manage their moods by relieving boredom and either soothing or energizing them.

Theory of Reasoned Action

The **theory of reasoned action** (**TRA**) is based on the assumption that we are rational decision makers. We don't just *happen* to behave one way or another. Instead, we make decisions and deliberate choices based on two primary considerations: (1) how strongly we believe a behavior will lead to positive outcomes, and (2) the perceived social implications of performing that behavior (Ajzen & Fishbein, 1980).

? CAN YOU GUESS?

1. People who smoke tend to die at a younger age than others. How many years of their lives do smokers usually lose?

2. How much does the tobacco industry spend every day to advertise its products?

3. The World Health Organization has named tobacco one of the most severe health threats of modern times. In what percentage of the world is tobacco advertising banned?

Answers appear at the end of the chapter.

TRA is similar to social cognitive theory in that both consider personal and social influences. However, TRA is more global in focus. Its predictive power lies in assessing the attitudes and behaviors of large numbers of people (Ajzen & Fishbein, 1980). Because TRA is designed to make generalizations, its founders don't consider it necessary (or even helpful) to focus on specifics such as personality, rules, and emotions. The effects of these variables tend to even out over large populations. By the same token, TRA doesn't assume that small changes will make much difference overall. As Ajzen and Fishbein put it, "Changing one or more beliefs may not be sufficient to bring about change in the overall attitude" (p. 81).

Icek Ajzen, one of the cofounders of TRA, extended the theory several years after its inception with the Theory of Planned Behavior (Ajzen, 1985, 1991), which addresses circumstances in which the conditions set forth in TRA are met—that is, we believe strongly in a behavior and perceive it to be socially supported—but we encounter circumstances in which it's difficult to follow through. For example, maybe we have said for months that we're going to start a new diet, but something always seems to prevent us from doing it. According to the **theory of planned behavior**, the difference between wanting to do something and actually doing it may lie partly in the strength of our intentions, which are shaped by three main factors: our attitudes about the issue and behaviors (*maybe we're not sure which diet to choose*), how socially rewarding and acceptable we consider it to be (*it might be easier if our friends weren't always eating hamburgers and French fries*), and the extent to which we feel—all things considered—that we can carry out the behavior (*we mean to make healthy dishes but it seems there's never time to buy and prepare them*). The theory is empowering in that it sensitizes us to some of the factors that underlie our choices. Without thinking about it too carefully, maybe we've been putting off a diet because no one around us is on one. Perhaps we can change that or make a choice to overcome it. The theory also reminds us that our intentions often affect the people around us. When Kyle Andrews and collaborators studied the link between parental behavior and childhood obesity, they found that parents are least likely to proactively guide their children's eating and TV-watching habits if (1) they don't feel strongly that those behaviors are important; (2) they don't see other parents they admire doing so; and/or (3) they're not sure those behaviors make much difference anyway—perhaps, the authors point out, because the parents have been frustrated by their attempts to manage their own weight (Andrews, Silk, & Eneli, 2010). The researchers suggest that health promoters keep in mind that knowledge is part of the equation, but attitudes, role models, and confidence are also significant factors in achieving long-lasting change.

It may seem that the macro focus of TRA is not very helpful in planning our sports recreation campaign. Indeed, our target audience may be too small

to make broad generalizations very useful. But TRA is of interest theoretically because it suggests that people make behavior changes based on their *overall* beliefs and perceptions. Small changes may not have much effect if they are outweighed by larger concerns. For example, imagine that a new study suggests that it's healthy for men to wear pantyhose. Do you suppose you could get the men on your campus to do so? Probably not. Their belief in the health benefits of pantyhose is probably outweighed by their desire to be socially acceptable. Luckily for us, physical exercise *is* widely accepted. What we propose is already in line with most people's overall intentions.

Transtheoretical Model

In analyzing the audience for our sports recreation campaign, imagine that we find some people *want* to exercise but that many of them are not doing so. We may even find that people *plan* to go to the gym but don't make it there. This is an important finding because it helps us understand our audience's state of mind. According to the **transtheoretical model**, we may not proceed directly from thinking about a problem to changing our behavior (Holtgrave, Tinsley, & Kay, 1995; Prochaska & DiClemente, 1983; Prochaska, DiClemente, & Norcross, 1992). Instead, we tend to change in stages. According to the model, change typically involves the following five stages:

> *Precontemplation:* Not aware of a problem
> *Contemplation:* Thinking about a problem
> *Preparation:* Deciding to take action
> *Action:* Making a change
> *Maintenance:* Sticking to the change for 6 months or more

The implication is that we react differently to health-promotion efforts depending on our current stage. Attention-getting information is called for when we are unaware of a problem. But skills training and encouragement may be more useful if we are already prepared to make a change. Furthermore, if we have already adopted the recommended behavior, we should be encouraged to continue it.

Hyunyi Cho and Charles Salmon (2006) found support for this concept when they exposed students to a variety of messages about skin cancer. Participants in precontemplation stages who viewed highly threatening messages were highly motivated to protect themselves, but they also reported higher-than-average feelings of hopelessness and fatalism. The authors concluded that fear appeals can call attention to previously unattended issues, but they may be counterproductive unless accompanied by clear and useful guidance.

From the perspective of the transtheoretical model, we choose options by weighing the relative pros and cons among a complex array of considerations. For example, Alan DeSantis (2002) described the camaraderie in a cigar shop where the regulars met to smoke and drink, seemingly impervious to the antismoking messages of loved ones and media campaigns and even to the smoking-related death of one of their own members.

> Within days, and sometimes hours, after wives and children have implored their husbands and fathers to quit smoking, the local press has reported on the "latest findings from the *New England Journal of Medicine*," or *20/20* has broadcasted its latest investigative report on the hazards of cigar smoking, the regulars at the cigar shop light back up, with only the smell of cigar smoke on their minds. (DeSantis, 2002, p. 169)

DeSantis described how cigar shop regulars justified their habit through collective arguments that cigar smoking was poorly understood by the medical establishment, was actually no more dangerous than mowing the lawn or driving on the freeway, and was beneficial, in that it relieved their stress. Members regularly talked about cigar smokers, such as George Burns and Milton Berle, who lived long lives and of health advocates who died young. Everyone in the shop knew the story of a heart surgeon who stopped by one day and reportedly asked, through a "relaxing" exhale, "Now how can that be bad for you?" (p. 185).

The cigar shop study illustrates the tenacity of behaviors embedded in social and environmental contexts. It also emphasizes that change is not automatic or linear. The stages described are only a general guide. People may remain in one stage indefinitely, lose interest, or skip steps.

Considering change as a stage-based process reveals some key challenges and opportunities for health campaign managers. One challenge is that we don't simply overhaul our behavior as soon

IN YOUR EXPERIENCE

- Can you think of behaviors you engage in even though you know they are unhealthy?
- What are the rewards of these behaviors?
- What would it take (if anything) to get you to quit?
- What advice do you have for health campaign designers trying to target this behavior?

as we hear new information (Maibach & Cotton, 1995). Change agents must be sensitive to barriers and motivations as well. Second, the transtheoretical model reveals why prevention efforts are particularly challenging. Inundating audience members with messages inappropriate to their stage of change may actually discourage them from proceeding. Rather than accelerate the change process, people may avoid the issue entirely.

The transtheoretical model presents opportunities for important contributions as well. Without motivational health campaigns, members of at-risk populations are likely to "remain stuck in the early stages" (Prochaska, Johnson, & Lee, 1998, p. 64). The model also suggests that changes, once made, must be supported. Effective campaigns are not simply one-shot affairs, but ongoing programs that support change and commitment.

Wrapping It Up

In closing our discussion of behavior change theories, it's important to point out that, as health promoters, we need not limit ourselves to any one model. The beauty of these theories is that they often overlap and call attention to different shades of meaning within the same process. Theories are like camera lenses, in that they help us achieve focus and clarity. This can be immensely helpful. But if we're not careful, a focus can be a limitation. In the next section we explore a different perspective.

Critical-Cultural Perspective

Return for a moment to the idea of a camera. When you look through the viewfinder you can

BOX 14.1 THEORETICAL INSIGHTS

Synopsis of Campaign-Related Theories

Cultural-critical perspective: Health is not simply a matter of personal agency, but is inextricably linked to larger issues of culture, power, control, identity, and social consciousness.

Embedded behaviors model: The likelihood for behavior change is related to the behavior itself—how frequent, complex, familiar, or novel it is and how interwoven it is with other valued behaviors.

Health belief model: People are more or less motivated to change their behavior based on their perception of personal susceptibility, serious consequences, worthwhile benefits, justifiable costs, and cues to actions.

Extended parallel process model: People evaluate threatening messages, first, to determine if they are personally at risk and, second, to judge whether they can prevent a harmful outcome. If they perceive a risk but do not feel they can avoid a bad outcome, they are likely to avoid the issue.

Normative social behavior theory: People are influenced by social norms to a greater or lesser degree, depending on how much they value the social approval to be gained by conforming, what outcomes they expect from the behavior, and how much they identify with the group.

Social cognitive theory: People make decisions by considering the interplay of internal factors, such as skills and knowledge, and environmental factors, such as environment and social approval.

Theory of planned behavior: The difference between wanting to do something and actually doing it lies partly in the strength of a person's intentions, which are shaped by attitudes about the issue and behaviors, how socially rewarding and acceptable the person considers the behavior to be, and the extent to which she or he feels able to carry out the behavior.

Theory of reasoned action: People make rational and deliberate choices based on how strongly they believe a behavior will lead to positive outcomes and the perceived social implications of performing that behavior.

Transtheoretical model: People tend to change in stages, ranging from precontemplation to contemplation, preparation, action, and maintenance.

---

zoom in on elements of the environment. But while you're focusing on one thing—even a very big thing like a sunset—there are other things you don't see. That's natural. The problem occurs when it begins to feel that what we see in the view-finder is all there is. No matter what our perspective, there's usually more there than meets the eye. In this spirit, critical theorists remind us that—for all the many contributions of the cognitive theories we have just discussed—they share a common focus: They treat health as primarily the product of choices we make as individuals (Dutta-Bergman, 2005). Granted, cognitive theories acknowledge that our choices are influenced by a range of factors. But the nexus is still individual thought and decision making. What if we assume that this is only part of the story and look at health issues through a wider angle lens?

Communication theorist Mohan J. Dutta has emerged as a leading advocate of the **critical-cultural approach**, which proposes that health is not merely the result of individual choices, but is intertwined with issues of culture, power, control, identity, and social consciousness. From this perspective, health-related behaviors are profoundly influenced by dynamics that are larger and more pervasive than any individual (Dutta-Bergman, 2005).

There is plentiful evidence to support the idea that health is, to a great extent, a socially enacted phenomenon. As you may remember from Chapter 6, health disparities typically observe social boundaries. The overall health of some groups is worse or better than the health of others, for a range of reasons that includes resources, prejudice and discrimination, trust, cultural mores, information, stress, living and working conditions, and more.

Assuming that people who are poor in information and resources have the same choices as other people requires that we overlook a host of factors that are very real to the people who experience them.

Moreover, it's not simply a question of having or not having. Cultural values and identities influence what is "good," "healthy," and "acceptable." The way a health expert views a particular behavior (such as smoking, drug use, driving fast, wearing a helmet, monogamy, and so on) may be very different from the way members of diverse cultures view it. Slater (2006) observes that health-related behaviors are often tied to issues of personal identity:

> Risk-taking teens may believe that alcohol or marijuana experimentation is part of what defines them as adventurous, fun party people. Farmers may believe that accepting risk of injury [as in deciding not to have roll-bars mounted on their tractors] in the interest of keeping costs low is part of what makes them farmers. (p. 155)

Conversely, scientific evidence suggests that these behaviors are dangerous. And health-related behaviors may also be attributed moral qualities such that they are considered bad, irresponsible, or evil. (This is especially true of issues such as drug use and sex.)

Considering these diverse viewpoints, a number of questions present themselves: Whose view is right? Who should decide how people ought to behave? And how is one's quality of life improved or diminished by the behaviors in question? These are difficult questions. The answers, say critical theorists, are not simple or universal. Rather than privileging one perspective over another, they advocate open and respectful dialogue about the issues—dialogues that involve the active participation of theorists, practitioners, and, most notably, members of the social group themselves (Dutta-Bergman, 2005).

Critical-cultural theorists observe that health promotion efforts that don't recognize the social contexts in which people live often fail to do much good. In fact, they often do harm—by reifying power differences, dominating the cultural landscape, and reinforcing the idea that people whose health is "poor" are not trying very hard or are like children who should be instructed by others. (See Box 14.2 for more on these ethical dilemmas.)

This is not to say that health promoters mindfully oppress the people they are trying to serve.

IN YOUR EXPERIENCE

■ What factors influence your own health-related behaviors (e.g., how often you visit a doctor, whether you exercise every day, eat right, and so on)?

■ In what ways are these behaviors affected by larger issues such as resources, culture, and social support?

It's more that their good intentions are often based on tacitly held assumptions about whose ideas are most valuable and who should be telling whom how to behave. You may say, "But they are only trying to teach people how to have better health." That's undoubtedly true. But let's unpack the baggage within that assertion. The idea of teaching implies that one person has knowledge or insight that he or she helps others comprehend. That's relatively unproblematic if we assume that the information is straightforward and value-free. One thing we know about health: It's never impersonal or value-free. So who defines what "better health" means? And who decides the best ways to accomplish that? When health promoters assume they have the answers to these questions, the result is often a paternalistic "I know what's best for you" mind-set. Actually, critical theorists argue, what is "best" is largely a matter of interpretation and value. Deborah Lupton (1998) asserts that health-promotion experts are often so confident about the importance of their scientific knowledge and worldview that the values and goals of the target community are "discounted as irrelevant and ignorant, as barriers to public health goals" (p. 4).

In the end, privileging one perspective, even if it seems to be "for people's own good," is an exercise

WHAT DO YOU THINK?

■ What do you think of the idea that health-promotion experts, although they mean well, often reinforce a group's marginal status by adopting a paternalistic "this is what you should do" mind-set?

■ Have you ever felt misunderstood or belittled by people who were trying to help you? If so, describe the experience.

BOX 14.2   ETHICAL CONSIDERATIONS

Three Issues for Health Promoters to Keep in Mind

Health promoters are faced with a number of ethical considerations. Among them is deciding how to warn audiences without needlessly frightening them. They must also be careful not to blame people for ill health, while at the same time encouraging people to prevent any illnesses and injuries they can. All the while, they must walk a fine line between making people concerned about illness and making them worried sick.

TIMING

When early evidence of a health risk surfaces, is it better to warn the public right away or to wait for more conclusive evidence? This question poses a dilemma for health promoters. On the one hand, researchers suggest that people are wary of premature announcements that are later shown to be inaccurate. Health news writer Alan Rees (1994) contends that "the average individual is caught in a withering crossfire of conflicting health messages and is inclined to disregard them all" (para. 7). For example, people were long urged to increase their exposure to sunlight to ensure sufficient amounts of vitamin D. Now people are encouraged to avoid sunlight to lower their risk of skin cancer. Conflicting messages such as these may confuse people and cause them to ignore health advisories.

On the other hand, it may take months or years to compile conclusive evidence. During that time, people may be exposed to health risks they might have avoided. People are likely to be angry if health officials are aware of potential risks yet do not warn the public.

SCAPEGOATING

It is difficult to know where the responsibility for personal health lies. For example, if children are not vaccinated, is it (1) the parents' fault for not bringing them to a doctor, (2) the government's fault for not providing neighborhood health services, (3) the city's fault for not providing better public transportation to the health unit, or (4) health officials' fault for not educating parents about the need for immunization? Although all of these factors probably contribute to the problem, part of a health promoter's job is to identify the conditions that most need improvement.

In doing so, however, it's easy to **scapegoat**, that is, to blame one person or group for the whole problem.

Scapegoating presents an ethical dilemma. It makes sense to focus attention on the condition or people with the greatest chance of making a difference. The typical health-promotion message cannot describe all the factors that contribute to a problem. However, focusing on one aspect or group of people may seem to place blame (Burdine, McLeroy, & Gottlieb, 1987). For example, a campaign that admonishes parents to bring their children in for vaccinations may alienate parents who don't have transportation to the public health unit and cannot afford private care. These parents may feel frustrated and criticized, and they may resent promoters' efforts. Second, people not held to blame may feel that the problem is no longer their responsibility. Ruth Faden (1987) asserts that government officials sometimes promote the idea that people are personally responsible for their health partly because this lets government off the hook. There's little imperative to make sweeping social changes or health care reform if it seems that health is solely the product of voluntary lifestyle changes.

Evidence fuels both sides of the debate, suggesting that personal choices and empowerment are important to health but that, at the same time, personal efforts are often constrained by environmental factors beyond individuals' control (such as money to afford medical care or sanitary living conditions). Health promoters may find themselves trying to identify key objectives without ignoring that every objective is intertwined with others.

STIGMATIZING

Prevention is the process of avoiding undesirable outcomes. People wear helmets to avoid head injuries, they are immunized to avoid diseases, and so on. Typically, the worse the potential outcome, the more people try to prevent it. Therefore health promoters try to motivate people by showing them how bad undesirable outcomes can be.

The dilemma is that, in portraying some *conditions* as undesirable, promoters may stigmatize some *people* as undesirable. Guttman (1997) warns that campaigners' good intentions sometimes backfire when they make people so frightened of diseases that they avoid the people who have them. For instance, an image of a child with a disability may be frightening enough to make children observe safety rules, but how are they likely to feel about children with disabilities? The same dilemma applies to AIDS publicity. People may become so frightened that they overprotect themselves by avoiding people who have AIDS.

WHAT DO YOU THINK?

1. Should health promoters release information about potential health risks immediately or wait for more conclusive evidence?

a. How long is it reasonable to wait?
b. What constitutes conclusive evidence?

2. Can you think of a way to promote public health without seeming to place the blame on certain people or groups?
3. Do you think it is possible to warn people about health hazards without stigmatizing people who have already been affected? Why or why not?

---

in power and often serves to marginalize and alienate people who see the world differently. Mohan Dutta and Rebecca de Souza (2008) trace the history of health-promotion efforts, showing that the tradition has largely been for those "in the center" to assist those "in the margins." They write:

> This position was based on the assumption of the expertise of those at the center, who could examine an underdeveloped community, evaluate its needs based on scientific instruments, and propose solutions that would supposedly propel the community toward development; the category of the "underdeveloped" was fixed in its position as the object of interventions, its people portrayed as the "primitive" receivers of campaign messages who were incapable of development without the helping hand of the interventionists. (p. 327)

Such efforts have often been experienced as insulting and naive, and, despite (and perhaps partly because of) widespread health-promotion campaigns, the gap between the health rich and the health poor around the world continues to widen at a staggering pace (Dutta & de Souza, 2008).

One approach recommended by the critical-cultural perspective involves embracing the notion of "many realities," none more correct or dominant than another (Dutta-Bergman, 2005, p. 117). This means shedding the notion that health promoters should set the agenda. Instead, it requires that they immerse themselves in the communities they serve, acting as facilitators who support community

members' efforts to decide for themselves what they consider important and how they can best attain their goals (Dutta-Bergman, 2005). Health experts can share what they know of science and theory, but it's important not to presume (or behave as if) that information is more right or important than participants' own perspectives. In other words, knowledge is one of many resources to be shared, not a tool to be used in the process of controlling others (Dutta, 2008). The goal is an interactive, ongoing process in which "problems are configured and reconfigured; solutions are generated and worked on based on the needs of the community as defined by community members" (Dutta-Bergman, 2005, p. 116). One objective is to build social consciousness about health and to engender a sense of **collective efficacy**, a communal sense that positive change can be accomplished. Dutta-Bergman (2005) also emphasizes the necessity of **community capacity**, the resources needed for good health, such as healthful food and water, safe shelter, and medical care. These basics are lacking in many parts of the country and the world.

Considering our campus campaign, we might choose to work with people who are frequently "in the margins" of fitness efforts. For example, we might focus on students and employees with physical disabilities. To accomplish this, we'll want to immerse ourselves, as best we can, in the concerns and viewpoints of the people in the focus community. (Even if you have a disability yourself, it's risky to make assumptions from your own perspective.) Perhaps there is an organization or support group at which people with disabilities openly discuss

WHAT DO YOU THINK?

You might be a member of the target audience for the sports recreation campaign. Take a moment to reflect on your own characteristics as an audience member.

■ Do you exercise frequently? Why or why not?

■ How do your considerations match up with the theories in this chapter?

their goals and concerns. With permission, we might attend meetings, or, if such a format doesn't already exist, we might organize a series of meetings. The process of encouraging people with disabilities to talk about fitness goals may be powerful in itself. There's likely to be great diversity among the people who participate, but we might learn that they share some common goals and face some common barriers they would like to overcome. Perhaps they're already involved in fitness efforts we don't know much about. We may find that, like many other people, they dread feeling conspicuous at the gym. Or perhaps they require specialized equipment or space that isn't currently available. It may be that health professionals focus mostly on their other concerns and don't encourage them to pursue fitness goals, so they don't feel confident about exercising. Already, you can probably imagine how issues of collective efficacy and community capacity might emerge and how you might help. Also keep in mind that—while it might seem patently audacious to tell people with disabilities how to behave if we don't understand their worldview—it can be equally as presumptuous to tell people from other cultures and communities how to think and act. Critical-cultural theory requires us to be respectful of "diverse realities" at every level.

The critical-cultural approach reminds us that nothing happens in isolation. What seem to be individual choices are often patterns of behavior shaped and reinforced by the systems in which they occur (Bohm, 1996; Senge, 2006). Ignoring the larger patterns can result in unproductive attempts at localized change. For example, health campaign designers frequently appeal to people to avoid or quit smoking, but they rarely tackle the larger issues of public policy and tobacco-industry standards (Dutta, 2008; Smith & Wakefield, 2006). Health promoters can help equalize disparities by advocating for community resources, public policies, and

issues of social justice to help communities overcome their marginalized status.

The medical director of a free, walk-in clinic I know is able to recite a long list of systems-level dilemmas. For one, the clinic received a grant to publicize its services to people who cannot afford medical care. But the grant doesn't cover operating expenses, and the staff is already overwhelmed. "It's kind of crazy to think publicity will solve the problem," he says. "Before we can serve more people, we need more staff." Another dilemma is that patients often cannot make scheduled appointments. "Maybe their boss won't let them off, or they don't have reliable transportation, or they work assorted day jobs and they can't afford to pass up an opportunity," explains the medical director, adding, "If we make appointments, the staff ends up sitting around when we could have been caring for other people." So the clinic maintains a come-anytime policy. But he says that's problematic as well: "You might get in right away, or you might have to wait for hours to see a doctor. People on hourly wages can't afford to do that. We're in a fix. We're here to serve, but limitations pop up every day." The issues the clinic faces are large ones. Health experts who are not aware of the systems, structures, and assumptions that relegate some people to "the margins" and others to "the center" risk being ineffective in accomplishing true change. And even worse, they may contribute to the very disparities they are trying to overcome.

Let's take this knowledge of theories and power differences back to our own campaign, as we discuss the three final stages: designing campaign messages, piloting and implementing the campaign, and evaluating and maintaining the effort.

Step 5: Designing Campaign Messages

As we discussed in Chapter 13, the first step in designing an effective campaign is to listen and ask questions. Experts recommend that campaign designers work closely with members of the focus community to determine what aspect of the problem is most important to them and then make that concern a focal point. Critical-cultural theory also behooves us to look at cultural values and the macro-level, systemic factors that affect the people we

Health Campaign Design and Management

Campaign director
Publication designer
Communication director
Media relations specialist
Public relations specialist
Director of nonprofit organization
Professor/educator

CAREER RESOURCES AND JOB LISTINGS

- Social Marketing Institute: social-marketing.org
- Chronicle of Philanthropy: philanthropy.com/jobs
- Wellness Council of America: welcoa.org
- American Journal of Health Promotion: health-promotionjournal.com
- National Institutes of Health: nih.gov
- World Health Organization: who.int/employment/vacancies/en

want to help.

It may turn out that our campaign doesn't involve the traditional step of creating messages that will be widely distributed to audience members. Instead, we might advocate for new hours at the fitness center, specialized fitness classes, more space or resources, skills training, or some other effort. Most campaigns, however, involve some degree of message creation and dissemination. Even if our principal effort is changing the structure, we'll want to get the word out somehow. In this section we focus on the central principles of message design.

Choosing a Voice

Campaign messages have a voice. The voice may seem masculine, feminine, young, old, friendly, casual, stern, or so on. Whatever its character, this voice embodies the mood and personality of the campaign. Here are some questions to consider in finding that voice.

- What is the campaign's personality and mood?

- Is it an authority figure or a friend?
- Is it a logical person or an emotional person?
- Is it the sort of person to whom the audience is likely to respond?

Even when words appear in print, the tone of the message gives the reader a sense of who is "talking" and what type of relationship the writer wishes to establish with the reader. Lefebvre and colleagues (1995) described how carefully decision makers at Nike considered the presentation of the "Just do it" advertising slogan. They decided not to use an exclamation mark after the statement and not to have an announcer say it aloud. "The concern was that the wrong voice, the wrong delivery, and the wrong inflection could have doomed the ads for many viewers" (Lefebvre et al., 1995, p. 224).

Of course, the source is even more apparent when the audience can see or hear a spokesperson deliver the message. Messages typically have more impact when the target audience trusts the spokesperson and thinks that he or she is capable and attractive. Celebrities can sometimes fill the bill. Michael J. Fox has been successful at calling attention to Parkinson's disease, raising money for research, and testifying before Congress (Beck, 2005). Basketball star Magic Johnson changed the public perception of HIV and AIDS when he announced in 1991 that he was HIV-positive. In the wake of his announcement, the National AIDS Hotline received 10 times as many calls as usual. New coverage and public knowledge about HIV transmission increased, especially among young people, and the number of people seeking HIV testing increased dramatically (Casey et al., 2003). After studying public reaction to Johnson's announcement, William Brown and Michael Basil (1995) concluded that people reacted so strongly because they felt they knew Magic Johnson.

There are drawbacks to using well-known spokespersons, however. Public role models sometimes behave in ways that contradict or cloud health campaign messages. For example, when Mark McGwire broke the major league home run record in 1998, even people who didn't follow baseball knew about it. Then it was revealed that McGwire had used androstenedione, a dietary supplement meant to speed muscle development. About 24% of the people who heard about his use of androstenedione wanted to learn more about it, and about

The Michael J. Fox Foundation for Parkinson's Research has raised nearly $300 million for research. Visit the website at https://www.michaeljfox.org.

22% said they would like to try it (Brown, Basil, & Bocarnea, 2003). This was certainly not a practice health experts wanted to promote. In another case, a pharmaceutical company in Australia paid a well-known soccer star the equivalent of $123,000 to stop smoking. He didn't. Fortunately for the promoters, the publicity surrounding the failed attempt nonetheless increased sales of nicotine-replacement therapies (Chapman & Leask, 2001). More recently, Tiger Woods, Kobe Bryant, and Michael Phelps have lost endorsement deals after they got in hot water for infidelity, rape charges, and illegal drug use, respectively.

There is also considerable evidence that audiences are most likely to believe people who are similar to them, an effect called **source homophily**

(Rogers, 1973). Not only do people pay more attention when the spokesperson is similar to them, they feel more personally vulnerable to the health risk (Rimal & Morrison, 2006). For example, African Americans typically prefer and are more likely to trust PSAs that feature African Americans rather than people of other races (Wang & Arpan, 2008). In a national survey, 50% of African Americans interviewed said they trust Black-oriented media, but only 34% trusted mainstream media sources (Brodie, Kjellson, Hoff, & Parker, 2008). This may be partly because 78% of the African American respondents felt that they are often left out of health-related news stories, and 76% felt they are overrepresented in stories about crime (Brodie et al., 2008).

Designing the Message

In designing an effective health campaign message, it's important to consider community expectations and the role of logic, emotion, and novelty. We begin by exploring the different ways that messages about the same health behavior can be framed. Then we'll talk about the art of matching messages to audience needs and emotions.

THEORETICAL FOUNDATIONS: MESSAGE FRAMING

You're walking through the mall with a friend when you come upon a booth proclaiming "Free Health Screening." The health professionals staffing the booth say they can give you a relatively accurate cholesterol score. They just need a drop or two of blood from your finger. And they can tell your body-fat percentage by gently pinching and measuring the skin on your upper arm. One of you says, "Sure! What do I have to lose?" and steps up to participate. The other says, "No thanks," and backs away quickly. Why do you and your friend respond so differently?

Message-frame theorists are interested in the way people interpret health-related behaviors and in health promoters' efforts to affect those interpretations (Slater, 2006). A famous example involves smoking. For years, health promoters tried to get people to quit because it was bad for their health. But the real turning point occurred when researchers proved the dangers of secondhand smoke. The issue was reframed from endangering self to endangering others. Whereas the personal risk seemed acceptable—even cool and rebellious to some—many people found it unacceptable to put others at risk. It was the same behavior, but framed differently. As Michael Slater (2006) puts it, relative to health, message framing "refers to the social priorities and the values with which a topic is implicitly associated" (p. 155). He proposes that it's unrealistic to expect people to adopt behaviors that are inconsistent with their personal or social identity.

As with most things health-related, effects are not simple or predictable. Men in the United States are still at particularly high risk for smoking. One reason may be that advertisers have done a good job framing smoking in culturally masculine terms. In a study of smoking references in men's magazines, Mohan Dutta and Josh Boyd (2007) found that smoking was consistently framed as a sensual pleasure, as independent and mysterious, and as occurring in places of power, in exotic lands, or in appealing outdoor locations. The researchers suggest that antismoking campaigns might turn around the masculine appeal of these themes by framing antismoking messages in similar ways.

Messages may be framed in respect to potential gains, losses, and risks (Rothman & Salovey, 1997). A **gain-frame appeal** illustrates the advantages of performing the recommended behavior. For example, people might be persuaded that eating a low-carbohydrate diet will keep their weight down and help prevent diabetes and heart disease. They gain something by following the diet. Conversely, a **loss-frame appeal** emphasizes the negative repercussions of not taking action, as in "People who eat a lot of processed carbohydrates are at risk for disease that can shorten their lives."

There is some evidence that gain-frame appeals are more effective than loss-frame appeals at getting people to engage in preventive behaviors (O'Keefe & Jensen, 2007; Rothman, Bartels, Wlaschin, & Salovey, 2006). For example, you might use sunscreen, brush your teeth twice a day, take vitamins, and so on. These are gain-related behaviors without much risk.

When Lance Armstrong confessed during an interview with Oprah Winfrey that he had used performance-enhancing drugs, many people felt the news coverage focused more on the loss of his cycling titles than on the harmful effects of illegal drugs. Researcher Brian Quick (2010) identified this as a common trend. Steroid abuse is more often portrayed as illegal rather than as unhealthy or deadly. (AP Photo/Courtesy of Harpo Studios, Inc., George Burns, File)

But it gets a little more complicated when the goal shifts from disease prevention to disease detection. For example, you may willingly stock your beach bag with sunscreen, but imagine that you notice a suspicious mole on your shoulder. If you're like most people, you'll feel a range of complicated emotions. Seeking a diagnosis is emotionally risky. You might learn that you have cancer and need treatment. It's emotionally self-protective to avoid what might be an anxiety-producing outcome. In fact, such avoidance can, and often does, last months or years.

But perhaps something else happens. You hear about someone who died of skin cancer or you see an alarming PSA. These are loss-frame messages, in that they highlight bad things that might happen if you don't take action. It's possible that you will become so frightened about what might be happening with your body that your anxiety will outweigh your desire to ignore the issue. Perhaps you'll make a doctor's appointment after all.

The rule of thumb is to promote disease *prevention* with gain-frame messages and disease *detection* behaviors (such as doctor visits and health screenings) with loss-frame messages. But actual evidence on the value of loss-frame messages is inconclusive (O'Keefe & Jensen, 2007). That's probably because

WHAT DO YOU THINK?

1. What factors might influence your decision to take part in a free health screening at the mall? What might you gain if you are tested? On the other hand, what unpleasant outcomes might result if you participate?

2. What if the stakes were higher? If you suspected that you had been exposed to HIV, what factors would influence whether you got tested or not? Why?

of the complex interplay of factors and emotions that surround health decisions. In our hypothetical example of the health booth at the mall, one of you is willing to be tested but the other isn't. Research is filled with such inconsistencies. In the suspicious mole scenario, maybe you wouldn't delay seeing a doctor if you noticed a suspicious mole. Perhaps you don't like uncertainty, you want to be sure it doesn't get any worse, you're pretty sure it's no big deal, or you have a checkup scheduled anyway so you'll mention the mole to avoid a second visit. In contrast, another person might see the same frightening PSA yet still put the issue off, perhaps reasoning that "If it hasn't killed me yet, it must not be too bad" or "I'll die when it's my time to die and there's not much I can do about it anyway." People are complicated, to say the least. Although we seem to share the basic desire to maximize gains and minimize losses, there are numerous reasons we might weigh these factors differently.

Some theorists argue that loss- and gain-framing is valid even though the evidence is mixed. They propose that aggregate-level trends are not apparent because the effects are felt on an individual level (Latimer, Salovey, & Rothman, 2007). In other words, what motivates you might not motivate the person next to you, so the overall numbers look like a wash even if some people benefited. The challenge, these theorists say, is for researchers and health promoters to focus on individuals and small groups who share common concerns rather than trying to reach large numbers of people with the same message.

COMMUNITY EXPECTATIONS

A message is effective only if people consider it relevant and meaningful. When she studied campaigns about prostate cancer screening, Juanne Nancarrow Clarke (1999) found that nearly all

the campaign messages embodied themes of male sexuality, machismo, and brotherhood. Although these messages may appeal to some men, others are probably turned off by an image that they don't feel applies to them. The same can be true of other audiences. A good deal of research has focused on college students' alcohol consumption. There is consistent evidence that students who drink typically believe that alcohol frees their inhibitions and makes them less shy and more socially engaging (Sopory, 2005). That's a tough perception to overcome. And it's one reason students and health advocates often disagree about how much drinking is too much. Although researchers tend to define five or more drinks as "binge drinking," students typically perceive that five drinks are within the normal range for their peers (Lederman, Stewart, Goodhart, & Laitman, 2008). They define a binge in more extreme terms. Consequently, researchers who survey students about "binge drinking" may be measuring something different from what they think. And students may feel that warnings about "binge drinking" don't apply to them because their behavior is within "normal" bounds (Lederman et al., 2008). (For more on social norms as the basis for safe-drinking campaigns, see Box 14.4.)

LOGICAL AND EMOTIONAL APPEALS

A **logical appeal** attempts to educate people and demonstrate a clear link between a behavior and a result. For example, it's logical to eat less if it will result in greater health and a longer life. An **emotional appeal** (also called an *affect appeal*) suggests that people should *feel* a certain way regarding their health or their behaviors. For example, they should be afraid to engage in unprotected sex, proud if they've quit smoking, or guilty if they're endangering others. Ellen Peters and colleagues (2006) propose that affect appeals serve four purposes: (1) they provide information, as when we think, "The people in that commercial look really happy; it must be a good product"; (2) they grab or hold our attention; (3) they motivate us to think carefully or take action; and (4) they link behaviors with community values, as when a message encourages us to recycle because it's good for the earth or to stop smoking because it puts our children in danger (Peters, Lipkus, & Diefenbach, 2006). Although emotions occur along a complex continuum, Peters

BOX 14.4   THEORETICAL INSIGHTS

What Does Science Say About Peer Pressure?

I think that alcohol is a huge part of adult life. It's like a rite of passage when you finally turn 21.

Every college student I know drinks.

College students love to party. It's tradition.

Thinking of your own undergraduate experience, you might find yourself nodding in agreement as you read these comments made by college students in Casper and colleagues' (2006) study (p. 295). Or you might shake your head in doubt. Experiences vary. And conventional wisdom suggests that your experience has a lot to do with the company you keep. It feels normal for partiers to party and nondrinkers not to drink. But in some instances, some people don't follow the crowd. What *does* science say about fitting in with the crowd?

On the one hand, there is ample evidence that people are more likely to engage in risky behaviors if their friends do. Having peers who smoke and approve of smoking is the single greatest predictor of a teen's decision to smoke cigarettes (Krosnick et al., 2006; Miller, Burgoon, Grandpre, & Alvaro, 2006). The same goes for kicking the habit. The overall decline in smoking hasn't occurred so much here and there as in distinct social clusters. In studying the issue, Nicholas Christakis and James Fowler (2008) found that smoking had persisted in some circles but that in others "whole groups of people were quitting in concert" (p. 2249).

One foundation for the RU SURE campaign that begins this chapter is **social norms theory**, which suggests that people base their behavior partly on what they consider appropriate and socially acceptable (Haines & Spear, 1996). The idea is that such campaigns may be especially influential in settings such as college campuses, where students are part of novel situations in which they are not immediately aware of cultural expectations. As you know, that campaign has had demonstrable success curbing student alcohol abuse.

But some social norm campaigns have been less successful. In a study of students at 37 colleges,

Wechsler and colleagues (2003) found that drinking was the same on campuses with social norm campaigns as on those without them. In another study, 72.6% of college students surveyed disbelieved the assertion that "most students drink 0 to 4 drinks when they party" (Polonec, Major, & Atwood, 2006, p. 23). And Shelly Campo and Kenzie Cameron (2006) found that, after viewing social-norming messages, light drinkers were even more determined to keep their drinking within healthy bounds, but heavier drinkers often went the other way. Their drinking intentions were *more* intense after viewing the normative messages. Another challenge to the power of social norms is that, in some cases, people find nonconformity appealing. People of varying ages who rank high on individualism or rebellious tendencies are likely to go *against* the norm (Lapinski, Rimal, DeVries, & Lee, 2007; Lee & Bichard, 2006).

Rajiv Rimal and Kevin Real (2005) have sought to make sense of the complexity with their **theory of normative social behavior (TNSB)**. The theory proposes that we *are* influenced by perceived social norms but that a variety of factors either strengthen or weaken how much those perceptions affect us. These include (1) how much we value the social approval to be gained from conforming, (2) the outcomes we expect from engaging in the behavior, and (3) the degree to which we identify with the group. In other words, if we like and value the group, we may want to "fit in" by acting in accordance with its norms, especially if the behavior offers rewards we like. However, our desire to fit in may be outweighed by other factors—as when the behavior seems inconsequential, we don't value or identify with the group very much, we enjoy being different, or we like the behavior so much we are willing to buck convention to do it. There's evidence that college students drink if/when they perceive that the rewards (such as loss of social inhibitions) outweigh the potential for negative repercussions, such as getting in trouble or getting hurt. And this is particularly true if they also perceive that drinking is accepted and approved by their friends (Rimal & Real, 2005).

So back to the initial question: *Does believing that "most people drink" or "drink a lot" mean we are likely to do the same?* So far, the best answer is that it depends. For one, it depends on how we define "most people."

The "norm" that researchers often use (as in "two of three college students stop at three or fewer drinks") is an aggregate statistic. It might change your mind about typical college student behavior. Or you might think, "They clearly haven't met *my* friends." Evidence suggests that, if the overall statistic seems different from what you perceive strongly within your own social network, you're likely to disbelieve or disregard it (Polonec, Major, & Atwood, 2006; Yanovitzky, Stewart, & Lederman, 2006). A second consideration concerns the perceived value of the behavior (Rimal, 2008). Whereas a **descriptive norm** describes "what most people do," an **injunctive norm** characterizes the perception that people *should* do it based on particular values (Boer & Westhoff, 2006; Rimal, 2008). For example, even if you believe that most of your friends occasionally drink and drive, you may refuse to do so yourself because you consider it wrong or irresponsible. Finally, TNSB suggests that norms affect us to the degree that it's socially and personally rewarding to live up to them. If any of a complex array of factors change (rewards, penalties, group membership, or so on), the power of the norm may change considerably.

Here are a few implications for health campaigns.

- *Correct misperceptions about descriptive norms.* Although descriptive norms don't tell the whole story, nearly everyone agrees that people who overestimate the prevalence of risky behaviors are more likely than others to feel that the behaviors are acceptable and even socially preferred.

- *Emphasize descriptive and injunctive norms.* For example, a sun-safety program was particularly effective when the health promoters presented both an injunctive norm (photos that showed undesirable skin damage) and a descriptive norm (information that most people now use sunscreen) (Mahler, Kulik, Butler, Gerrard, & Gibbons, 2008).

- *Don't rely solely on norming messages.* Norms sometimes take a backseat to other factors, such as personal enjoyment. College students in Cameron and Campo's (2006) study were most likely to smoke, exercise, and drink if they enjoyed those behaviors, even when there was no strong peer support for them. It may help to emphasize the negative repercussions of unhealthy behaviors as well as social norms.

- *Target social networks.* A common suggestion among social norm researchers is that campaigns address alcohol abuse as a social network issue. This often involves developing partnerships with sororities and fraternities, sports teams, student governments, and other groups.

The debate continues to be a lively and productive one. The success of RU SURE campaign at Rutgers may be based partly on its social norm foundation and partly on the integrated and multifaceted nature of the campaign itself. TNSB offers a rich, contextual understanding of the facets that figure into social norming, a concept that continues to evolve and to influence theorists as well as practitioners.

and colleagues observe that there are two basic "flavors"—positive and negative. For the most part, campaigns encourage people to strive for positive outcomes and avoid negative ones. Research discussed in this section describes the usefulness and the limitations of various emotional appeals.

Positive-Affect Appeals. Campaigns may promote positive emotional rewards in the form of popularity, a sense of accomplishment, honor, fun, or happiness. For example, after playing a fun and educational computer game named Right Way Café, university students scored higher than before the game on a nutrition quiz and rated themselves

more confident about food choices and more likely to make proactive choices about their diet (Peng, 2009).

Campaigns may also inspire positive affect because the messages themselves are pleasant or entertaining. Evidence suggests that relatively uninterested individuals are likely to judge information on a superficial level, perhaps based on the music, humor, or graphics or the attractiveness of the spokesperson (Petty & Cacioppo, 1986). If the announcement is not interesting or appealing, they may ignore it altogether. In contrast, people who are already concerned about an issue may want more detailed information. All in all, research shows that pleasant messages grab people's attention but that people may not take these messages as seriously as fearful ones (Monohan, 1995).

Negative-Affect Appeals. Some campaign designers attempt to motivate people by making them feel anxious, fearful, or guilty. There is evidence that fearful appeals are effective at convincing people to be tested for AIDS and to take other health precautions (Green & Witte, 2006; Hullett, 2006). But fearsome appeals can also inspire avoidant behaviors (Lang, 2006). In one study, women responding to a cancer screening campaign said they would not like to hear messages that escalated their fears about cancer or mammography (Marshall, Smith, & McKeon, 1995). They were already frightened by these topics, and they wanted clear information. Likewise, in a study involving Hispanic women, participants who believed that cancer was God's will didn't want information about the disease (Oetzel, DeVargas, Ginossar, & Sanchez, 2007). However, people who are not anxious about health risks often aren't very interested in prevention information (Millar & Millar, 1998). Intense messages might get their attention.

Communication theorist Kim Witte proposes that, if people are not at all anxious about a health topic, then they probably are not motivated to learn about it or to take action. However, if they are overly anxious, they may avoid the subject. Witte's **extended parallel process model** (EPPM) proposes that people evaluate a threatening message, first, to determine if they are personally at risk and, second, to judge whether they can prevent a harmful outcome. If they perceive a risk but don't feel they can avoid a bad outcome, they are likely to soothe their anxiety by avoiding the issue (Witte, 1997, 2008). For example, David Buller and colleagues (2000) found that parents of elementary school students responded favorably to a highly intense message about sun protection *if* the message presented an acceptable solution.

Simon-Arndt and associates (2006) used EPPM principles to test an interactive program for Marines. Marines in the study answered online questions about their alcohol consumption. Then they received online feedback about their risk levels and potential ways to prevent unhealthy outcomes (note the EPPM components). About 85% of the Marines who took part preferred this program

IN YOUR EXPERIENCE

Research shows that antitobacco messages that inspire neither fear nor disgust have little impact. However, we tend to avoid messages that are both fearful *and* disgusting. So be careful not to overdo it. For more, see Leshner, Bolls, and Thomas (2009) and Leshner, Vultee, Bolls, and Moore (2010). Can you recall images that were meant to illicit fear and disgust? If so, did you try to avoid them?

to other alcohol-use campaigns, perhaps because it seemed highly targeted to their own behaviors (Simon-Arndt, Hurtado, & Patriarca-Troyk, 2006).

Guilt, a feeling of remorse about having done something wrong, is a particularly strong emotion. Consequently, it's a useful tool for advertisers and health campaigners. Bruce Huhmann and Timothy Brotherton (1997) assert that people typically feel sorry or ashamed when they have behaved badly, especially when others are hurt by their actions. Advertisers who bring these feelings to the surface and offer a way to make retribution may find that people are willing to cooperate to soothe their consciences. Huhmann and Brotherton found that 1 in 20 magazine advertisements included a guilt appeal, ranging from "I wish I had started saving for my children's college education when they were young" (p. 36) to "Last night, 2 million children in the U.S. went to bed hungry" (p. 37). Guilt often seems to work. For example, people are more likely to sign up as organ donors if they think they will feel guilty for saying no (Wang, 2011).

Overall, negative affect is a popular component of persuasive messages, but it must be used carefully. Health promoters have overshot the mark in some cases. Women in the United States now consistently overestimate their risk of breast cancer (Jones, Denham, & Springston, 2007). And it isn't easy to reassure them. Amanda Dillard and colleagues found that it was just as difficult to reduce

WHAT DO YOU THINK?

How might the extended parallel process model apply to our hypothetical sports recreation campaign?

CHECK IT OUT! For guidance on creating your own health campaign, visit the following websites.

- The Community Tool Box: ctb.ku.edu
- The American Public Health Association: apha.org
- Global Dialogue for Effective Stop Smoking Campaigns: stopsmokingcampaigns.org/index.php?page=campaign_tool_kit
- *Making Health Communication Programs Work: A Planner's Guide* available at cancer.gov/pinkbook
- *Communication Planning with CDCynergy* available at cdc.gov/healthmarketing

women's sense of breast cancer danger as it was to *stimulate* their concern about other health risks (Dillard, McCaul, Kelso, & Klein, 2006).

Novel and Shocking Messages. Novel messages tend to catch people's attention and stick in their memory (Parrott, 1995). Some messages are novel (new or different) without being **shocking** (intense or improper). For instance, posting health warnings in public restrooms is an effort to use an unexpected format to reinforce the risks of smoking and drinking during pregnancy. It's a novel approach, but not particularly shocking. At other times, novel messages may be shocking because they deal with topics not usually discussed in public or because they are purposefully controversial to attract attention. One difficulty about using novel images to attract attention is that the novelty wears off (Walters, Walters, Kern-Foxworth, & Priest, 1997). Keeping novelty alive may mean becoming ever more risqué. It's sometimes difficult to balance decorum with the need for public awareness.

One difficulty surrounding AIDS awareness is that health promoters must deal with delicate issues like premarital sex and anal intercourse. Even when promoters don't mean to be shocking, they often are.

IN YOUR EXPERIENCE

- Have you ever seen a PSA you didn't like?
- If so, what made it unappealing?

Particularly when AIDS first became a health concern, condoms and gay sex were not socially acceptable topics for mass-media campaigns. In the 1990s, controversy arose concerning a poster campaign in New York City. The posters (which were hung in subway terminals) read "Young, Hot, Safe!" and showed images of homosexual couples kissing while holding condoms, gloves, and spermicide ("Controversy Heats Up," 1994). Some people felt the posters were indecent, while others argued that they communicated an important message to a high-risk group. (The poster campaign was discontinued soon thereafter.)

Lessons About Emotional Appeals. Here are a few guidelines, suggested by theorists and researchers, about using emotional appeals.

- *Match the emotion to the goal.* Emotional appeals are most persuasive when they are appropriate to the desired response. For example, fear appeals can alert people to danger, disgust appeals can make unhealthy behaviors unappealing, hope appeals can convince people it is worth taking action, and so on (Dillard & Nabi, 2006).
- *Build empathy.* "It won't happen to me" is a common response to health messages, even when they are highly arousing. For example, we may feel concerned about intravenous drug users because they are at risk for AIDS but perceive our own risk to be negligible because we aren't part of that group. We usually feel a sense of personal relevance only if we understand the message cognitively, the speaker effectively conveys his or her feelings of vulnerability, and we perceive that those feelings are relevant to our own situation (Campbell & Babrow, 2004).
- *Don't overdo it.* Too much affect can be counterproductive and cause people to avoid the issue or to worry unnecessarily (Peters et al., 2006, p. S155).

Step 6: Piloting and Implementing the Campaign

It's important to pilot (pretest) a campaign before launching it full-scale. **Piloting** usually involves selecting members from the target audience to review the campaign materials and comment on them. Salmon and Atkin (2003) state that early feedback is crucial:

> The feedback from the audience can reveal whether the tone is too righteous (admonishing unhealthy people about their incorrect behavior), the recommendations too extremist (rigidly advocating unpalatable ideas of healthy behavior), the execution too politically correct (staying within tightly prescribed boundaries of propriety to avoid offending overly sensitive authorities and interest groups), and the execution too self-indulgent (letting creativity and style overwhelm substance and substantive content). (p. 453)

Some questions to consider include these (adapted from Donohew, 1990):

- Are written messages easy to read and understand?
- Are recorded messages easy to understand?
- Do messages seem relevant and important?
- Are the messages appealing? Why or why not?
- Is the spokesperson effective?
- Does the information seem controversial or offensive?

It may be useful to survey people before and after they are exposed to campaign materials to see if there's any change in their knowledge, attitudes, and intentions. When possible, it's also advisable to survey people a week or a month after they were initially exposed to campaign materials to see how much they remember and whether message effects are still present. Remember to allow time to refine campaign messages based on the results of pretesting. Planning ahead will improve the campaign's likelihood of success.

Once campaign messages have been created, piloted, and refined, it's time to distribute them through chosen channels. In some cases (as with one-on-one communication, community presentations, and to some extent, online messages), health promoters have direct contact with community members and thus have control over what is conveyed. With the majority of channels, however, health promoters must rely on others to share, and sometimes to edit, their messages. For instance, editors and news directors choose what PSAs to publicize and when, and what topics to cover in the news. On a social level, community opinion leaders focus on some issues more than others, affecting what the people around

CHECK IT OUT! The following sources offer excellent advice about measuring the effect of your campaign.

Hornik, R. C. (Ed.). (2002). *Public health communication: Evidence for behavior change.* Mahwah, NJ: Lawrence Erlbaum.

Murray-Johnson, L., & Witte, K. (2003). Looking toward the future: Health message design strategies. In T. L. Thompson, A. M. Dorsey, K. I. Miller, & R. Parrott (Eds.), *Handbook of health communication* (pp. 473–495). Mahwah, NJ: Lawrence Erlbaum.

them think and believe. People in the media and the community who decide what information will be publicized and how are known as **gatekeepers**.

Good campaign designers employ a variety of communication channels to help ensure that messages make it to focus community members through one gate or another. Wise health promoters realize the importance of gatekeepers, include them in campaign planning, and consider their points of view. John McGrath (1995) observes that media gatekeepers are bound by multiple pressures (e.g., operating budgets, community demands, and time constraints). The promoter who gets to know gatekeepers personally and makes it easy for them to pass along information has a better chance of getting through to a community.

Step 7: Evaluating and Maintaining the Campaign

A campaign isn't over when it has been released to the public. Effective health promotion requires that campaign managers evaluate the success of the project, help community members maintain any positive changes they may have made, and refine and develop future campaign messages.

Evaluation

The effects of a campaign may be evaluated in several ways. A **pretest–posttest design** means that campaigners survey people before the campaign is released and then survey them again afterward

(Wimmer & Dominick, 1997). You might go about this in two different ways—by exposing people to campaign materials in a controlled environment (an **efficacy study**) or by testing people in the context of everyday life (an **effectiveness study**) (Evans, Uhrig, Davis, & McCormack, 2009, p. 315). W. Douglas Evans and colleagues (2009) found that efficacy studies offer several advantages: (1) you can make sure the participants are exposed to your campaign messages before they respond to your questions, (2) you minimize the likelihood that responses will be affected by extraneous factors, and (3) you can expose members of the target audience to multiple messages and see how their responses to them differ. Of course, efficacy studies may not tell you how many people in the larger population are affected or how, so you may want to use both.

The survey may indicate if people's attitudes, knowledge, or actions have changed since the campaign. Keep in mind that if changes have occurred, they may or may not be the result of campaign exposure.

To evaluate the impact of the truth® campaign described in Chapter 13, researchers conducted telephone surveys with 6,897 youth ages 12 to 17 before the campaign began (Farrelly, Healton, Davis, Messeri, & Haviland, 2002). The survey participants were chosen to represent teens in different ethnic and racial groups, urban and nonurban areas, and areas with and without other antitobacco campaigns. Researchers asked the youth to indicate their level of agreement or disagreement with statements about the tobacco industry, the social acceptability of smoking, and their intention to smoke within the next year. In follow-up interviews after the campaign's release, researchers asked 10,692 youth if they remembered seeing any antitobacco campaigns and, if so, what they remembered about them. They also asked about perceptions of the tobacco industry, the social acceptability of smoking, and the youths' intention to smoke in the next year. To factor out as many intervening variables as possible, researchers statistically controlled for such factors as the number of parents in the household, amount of television viewing, the presence of smokers in the household, and parental messages about smoking. With the data collected, researchers were able (1) to gauge the extent to which community members saw and remembered the campaign;

and (2) to compare youth attitudes before and after the campaign.

Another way to evaluate a campaign's success is to study actual behavior changes, such as the number of people who sign up for basketball or the number of hospital admissions or calls to a hotline. These evaluation techniques are useful, but it's always difficult to know precisely what effects a campaign has had. For one thing, the campaign isn't the only factor influencing people's attitudes and behavior. They may be affected by personal experiences, news stories, or other occurrences. Imagine trying to evaluate the impact of an AIDS-awareness program that happened to coincide with Magic Johnson's public announcement that he had HIV. Second, campaigns often have indirect effects. For instance, the campaign may have reached influential members of the community, who in turn spread the word to others. Thus, people who were not exposed to campaign messages personally may still be affected by them. Third, sometimes the success of a health campaign is reflected in what does *not* occur over the long run. For example, the coordinators of a drug-free program in elementary schools may not know if they've been successful until the children involved are adolescents or adults, by which time they will have been influenced by many other factors as well. When undesired behaviors do not occur, it is difficult to know how many people might have adopted those behaviors if not for the campaign.

Sometimes health campaigns have unintended or undesirable consequences. Audiences may be so turned off by the message that they actively avoid the subject or lose trust in the sender. Here's an extreme example. When I was in college, the 1936 film *Reefer Madness* made a comeback, not as the frightening documentary it was originally designed to be, but as a comedy. College students flocked to the local midnight movie to see the jerky-action black-and-white film in which young people smoke what the narrator (a high school principal) calls "demon weed" and immediately become shaky, wild-eyed, and demented. The students subsequently listen to "evil jazz" music and become serial killers—threats so unbelievable that the movie dialogue was often drowned out by the audience's laughter. We can only imagine the extent to which the outdated movie damaged the credibility of anti-drug messages at the time.

For better or worse, sometimes the best that campaigners can do is evaluate the **reach** (number of people exposed to campaign messages) and **specificity** (the type of people exposed to the messages) of a campaign. For this purpose, promoters can survey community members and keep track of when and where campaign messages are publicized.

Maintenance

Maintaining behaviors that have been positively influenced by a campaign involves continued encouragement and skills training. Keep in mind that people are most likely to continue new behaviors if they fully understand the benefits of doing so (Valente et al., 1998). Because some people try new behaviors without first fully understanding them, don't assume that people who begin a behavior are fully educated about it. Encouragement, incentives, and continued skills training can help people overcome setbacks they are likely to encounter (Maibach & Cotton, 1995).

Summary

Social marketers conduct extensive audience analyses and strive to create messages with the same appeal as commercial messages. The results of social marketing are measured, not in sales figures or profit margins, but in public awareness and improved health. These outcomes are often realized in subtle ways over long periods of time, but social marketers work hard to gauge the success of their efforts and apply what they learn to future campaigns.

Theories of behavior change explain the conditions under which people are likely to make lifestyle changes. The overall message is that behavior is influenced by a complex array of factors, both internal and external. Failing to consider these can lead to health campaigns that look good but have very little social value. In addition, campaign designers who fail to consider and accommodate audience members' beliefs and opportunities can alienate the people they hope to influence and can actually make things worse by promoting behaviors that people find offensive, puzzling, or even impossible to carry out. One alternative is for health advocates to serve as facilitators and enablers who help

communities set their own agendas and build collective efficacy and social capacity.

In designing campaign messages, health promoters should consider ethical implications concerning timing, scapegoating, and stigmatizing, as well as audience needs, campaign goals, and benefits of the recommended behaviors.

Campaign messages have different voices, ranging from stern to casual and friendly. Often, the spokesperson influences how the message is perceived. Research suggests that people typically respond most favorably to spokespersons who are similar to them, likable, and attractive. A celebrity may be an effective spokesperson or a public liability.

The same behavior may be framed in a number of ways to emphasize potential gains, losses, or social implications. Campaign messages also appeal to our logic and emotions. Some campaigns motivate people through positive affect, such as the promise of pleasure and happiness or the desire to fit in with social norms. Negative-affect appeals may induce people to change by stirring up feelings of anxiety, fear, and guilt. According to the extended parallel process model, anxiety is a powerful motivator, except when the threat is so overwhelming that people would rather avoid the issue. Novel and shocking messages typically create interest, but they may be controversial and offensive to some people.

Experts recommend that health promoters pilot new campaigns before implementing them. Testing campaign messages on sample community members can reveal unanticipated reactions and ambiguities so messages can be improved before they are publicly released. Finally, health promoters should evaluate campaigns once they are released, apply what they have learned to future efforts, and compare the results with their goals.

Key Terms and Theories

social marketing
health belief model
social cognitive theory
internal factors
environmental factors
embedded behaviors model
theory of reasoned action (TRA)
theory of planned behavior

transtheoretical model
critical-cultural approach
scapegoat
collective efficacy
community capacity
source homophily
gain-frame appeal
loss-frame appeal
social norms theory
theory of normative social behavior (TNSB)
descriptive norm
injunctive norm
logical appeal
emotional appeal
extended parallel process model (EPPM)
guilt
novel messages
shocking messages
piloting
gatekeepers
pretest–posttest design
efficacy study
effectiveness study
reach
specificity

Discussion Questions

1. What does social marketing involve?
2. Summarize the critical-cultural perspective.
3. What are the implications of blaming (scapegoating) people for engaging in risky health behaviors (Box 14.3)?
4. What are some questions to consider when choosing a "voice" and "personality" for a campaign?
5. What factors should you keep in mind when choosing a spokesperson?

6. What is meant by source homophily?
7. What does it mean to frame a health message?
8. Describe the components of the theory of normative social behavior.
9. In what circumstances are positive-affect messages usually effective? Negative-affect appeals? Think of as many examples as you can. Which type of appeal do you typically prefer, and why?
10. Explain the extended parallel process model as it relates to negative-affect appeals. Give an example from your own experience.
11. What types of audiences are likely to respond favorably to shocking or intense messages?
12. What are some questions to consider when piloting campaign materials?
13. What role do gatekeepers play in health-promotion efforts?
14. Why is it often difficult to assess accurately the impact of a health campaign?

Answers to *Can You Guess?*

1. Smoking cuts an average of 15 years off a person's life (WHO, 2008a).

2. Tobacco companies spend $36 million a day on advertising—in the United States alone. Their *daily* budget is more than the *annual* budget of the truth® campaign, which is the largest antitobacco campaign in history ("New Research," 2008).

3. Only 5% of the world's population is shielded from tobacco advertising ("WHO Wants Total Ban," 2008).

References

About us. (2012). Washington, DC: American Legacy Foundation. truth* website. Retrieved from http://www.thetruth.com/about/

Accreditation Council to Graduate Medical Education (ACGME). (2006, April). Introduction to competency-based education. Facilitator's guide. Chicago: Author. Retrieved from http://www.acgme.org/outcome/e-learn/21M1_FacManual.pdf

Achterberg, J. (1991). *Woman as healer*. Boston: Shambhala.

Ackerknecht, E. H. (1968). *A short history of medicine*. New York: Ronald Press.

Ackermann, R. T., & Carroll, A. E. (2003). Support for national health insurance among U.S. physicians: A national survey. *Annals of Internal Medicine, 139*, 795–801.

Adams, M. O., & Osho, G. S. (nd). A comprehensive evaluation of mad-cow disease: Evidence from public administration perspective. El Cajon, CA: National Social Science Association. Retrieved from http://www.nssa.us/journals/2007-28-2/2007-28-2-01.htm

Adams, N., & Field, L. (2001). Pain management 1: Psychological and social aspects of pain. *British Journal of Nursing, 10*(14), 903–911.

Adams, R. J., & Parrott, R. (1994, February). Pediatric nurses' communication of role expectations to parents of hospitalized children. *Journal of Applied Communication Research, 22*, 36–47.

Adelman, M. B., & Frey, L. R. (1997). *The fragile community: Living together with AIDS*. Mahwah, NJ: Lawrence Erlbaum.

Adelman, S. A. (2008, January 4). Be careful what you promise. *Medical Economics, 85*(1), 14.

Afifi, W. A., & Weiner, J. L. (2004). Toward a theory of motivated information management. *Communication Theory, 14*, 167–190.

African-American youth and alcohol advertising. (2012). Center on Alcohol Marketing and Youth: Alexandria, VA. Retrieved from http://www.camy.org/factsheets/sheets/African_American_Youth_and_Alcohol_Advertising.html

Ahmad, N. N. (2004, April 15). Arab-American culture and health care. Online publication. Retrieved from http://www.cwru.edu/med/epidbio/mphp439/Arab-Americans.htm

Ahmed, A. T., Mohammed, S. A., & Williams, D. R. (2007). Racial discrimination & health: Pathways & evidence. *The Indian Journal of Medical Research, 126*(4), 318–327.

AIDS Score Cards. (2010). UNAIDS, a United Nations program. Geneva, Switzerland: Author. Retrieved from http://www.unaids.org/global report/AIDSScorecards.htm

Ajzen, I. (1985). From intentions to actions: A theory of planned behavior. In J. Kuhl & J. Beckman (Eds.), *Action control: From cognition to behavior* (pp. 11–39). Heidelberg: Springer.

Ajzen, I. (1991). The theory of planned behavior. *Organizational Behavior and Human Decision Processes, 50*, 179–211.

Ajzen, I., & Fishbein, M. (1980). *Understanding attitudes and predicting behavior*. Englewood Cliffs, NJ: Prentice Hall.

Alam, R., Barrera, M., D'Agostino, N., Nicholas, D. B., & Schneiderman, G. (2012). Bereavement experiences of mothers and fathers over time after the death of a child due to cancer. *Death Studies, 36*, 1–22. doi:10.1080/07481187.2011.553312

Albrecht, T. L., & Adelman, M. B. (1987). Communicating social support: A theoretical perspective. In T. L. Albrecht & M. B. Adelman (Eds.), *Communicating social support* (pp. 18–39). Newbury Park, CA: Sage.

Alcohol Concern. (2007, July). *Not in front of the children—child protection and advertising*. London: Author. Retrieved from http://www.alcoholpolicy.net/files/Not_in_front_of_the_children.pdf

Alden, D. L., Merz, M. Y., & Thi, L. M. (2010). Patient decision-making preference and physician decision-making style for contraceptive method choice in an Asian culture: Does concordance matter? *Health Communication, 25*, 718–725.

Al-Janabi, H., Coast, J., & Flynn, T. N. (2008). What do people value when they provide unpaid care for an older person? A meta-ethnography with interview follow-up. *Social Science & Medicine, 67*, 111–121.

Allen, J. D., Kennedy, M., Wilson-Glover, A, & Gilligan, T. D. (2007, June). African-American men's perceptions about prostate cancer: Implications for designing educational interventions. *Social Science & Medicine, 64*(11), 2189–2200.

Allen, K. A., Blascovich, J., & Mendes, W. B. (2002). Cardiovascular reactivity and the presence of pets, friends, and spouses: The truth about cats and dogs. *Psychosomatic Medicine, 64*, 727–739.

Allen, M. (2012, May 30). Chatting with the reporters behind Dollars for Docs. New York: ProPublica. Retrieved from http://www.propublica.org/article/chatting-with-the-reporters-behind-dollars-for-docs

Allman, J. (1998). Bearing the burden of baring the soul: Physician self-disclosures and boundary management regarding medical mistakes. *Health Communication, 10*, 175–197.

Alston, S. (2007). Nothing to laugh at: Humour as a means of coping with pain and stress. *Australian Journal of Communication, 34*(1), 77–89.

American Association of Colleges of Nursing. (2008, September). Nursing shortage. Washington, DC: Author. Retrieved from http://www.aacn.nche.edu/Media/FactSheets/NursingShortage.htm

American Association of Colleges of Nursing. (2012, March 22). New AACN data show an enrollment surge in baccalaureate and graduate programs amid calls for more highly educated nurses. Author: Washington, DC. Retrieved from http://www.aacn.nche.edu/news/articles/2012/enrollment-data

American Association of Colleges of Osteopathic Medicine. (2012). What is osteopathic medicine? Author: Chevy Chase, MD. Retrieved from http://www.aacom.org/about/osteomed/Pages/default.aspx

American College of Physicians. (2008, January). Achieving a high-performance health care system with universal access: What the United Sates can learn from other countries. *Annals of Internal Medicine, 148*(1), 55–75.

American Foundation for Suicide Prevention (AFSA). (2008). Struggling in silence: Physician depression and suicide. Fact sheet. New York: Author. Retrieved from http://www.afsp.org/index.cfm?fuseaction=home.viewPage&page_ID=9859BF59-CF1C-2465-128DAE02D3C9B309

American Hospital Association (AHA). (1994). *Hospital closures, 1980 through 1993, a statistical profile.* Chicago: Health Care Information Resources Group.

American Hospital Association (AHA). (2008, March). Hospital facts to know. Washington, DC: Author. Retrieved from http://www.aha.org/aha/content/2008/pdf/08-issue-facts-to-know-.pdf

American Marketing Association. (2007, December 17). AMA definition of marketing. Chicago: Author. Retrieved from http://www.marketingpower.com/Community/ARC/Pages/Additional/Definition/default.aspx

American Medical Association (AMA). (2003). Low literacy has a high impact on patients' ability to follow doctors' orders. American Medical Association. Retrieved from www.ama-assn.org/ama/pub/print/article/4197-7395.html

American Medical Association (AMA) Minority Affairs Consortium. (2008). Board of Trustees report 15, "Diversity in medical education." Chicago: Author. Retrieved from http://www.ama-assn.org/ama/pub/category/12938.html

Amundsen, D. W., & Ferngren, G. B. (1983). *The clinical encounter.* Dordrecht: D. Reidel.

An, S. (2007, September). Attitude toward direct-to-consumer advertising and drug inquiry intention: The moderate role of perceived knowledge. *Journal of Human Communication, 12*(6), 567–580.

Anderlink, M. R. (2001). *The ethics of managed care: A pragmatic approach.* Bloomington: Indiana University Press.

Anderson, J. O., & Geist-Martin, P. (2003). Narratives and healing: Exploring one family's stories of cancer survivorship. *Health Communication, 15*(2), 133–143.

Anderson, N. (2008, September 17). Product placement still huge as advertisers fight DVRs. *Ars Technica*, np. Retrieved from http://arstechnica.com/news.ars/post/20080917-product-placement-still-huge-as-advertisers-fight-dvrs.html

Anderson, P., de Bruijn, A., Angus, K., Gordon, R., & Hastings, G. (2009). Impact of alcohol advertising and media exposure on adolescent alcohol use: A systematic review of longitudinal studies. *Alcohol and Alcoholism, 44*, 229–243.

Andrews, K. R., Silk, K. S., & Eneli, I. U. (2010). Parents as health promoters: A theory of planned behavior perspective on the prevention of childhood obesity. *Journal of Health Communication, 15*, 95–107. doi:10.1080/10810730903460567

Añez, L. M., Silva, M. A., Paris, M., Jr., & Bedregal, L. E. (2008). Engaging Latinos through the integration of cultural values and motivational interviewing principles. *Professional Psychology: Research and Practice, 39*(2), 153–159.

Angell, M. (2004, July 15). The truth about drug companies. *The New York Review of Books, 51*(12), np. Retrieved from http://www.nybooks.com/articles/17244

Anghelcev, G., & Sar, S. (2011). The influence of pre-existing audience and message relevance on the effective of health PSAs: Differential effects by message type. *Journal and Mass Communication Quarterly, 88*, 481–501.

Apker, J. (2001). Role development in the managed care era: A case in hospital-based nursing. *Journal of Applied Communication Research, 29*(2), 117–136.

Appenzeller, T. (2005, October). Tracing the next killer flu. *National Geographic, 208*(4), 2–31. Retrieved through Academic OneFile via Gale.

Arab American Institute. (2012). Demographics. Washington, DC: Author. Retrieved from http://www.aaiusa.org/pages/demographics/

Arab American Institute Foundation. (2000). Arab American population highlights. Washington, DC: Author. Retrieved from http://aai.3cdn.net/9298c231f3a79e30c6_g7m6bx9hs.pdf

Arasaratnam, L. A., & Banerjee, S. C. (2011). Sensation seeking and intercultural communication competence: A model test. *International Journal of Intercultural Relations, 35*, 226–233. doi: 10.1016/j.ijintrel.2010.07.003.

Are you a certified asshole? (nd) Retrieved from http://electricpulp.com/guykawasaki/arse/

Armstrong, K., McMurphy, S., Dean, L. T., Micco, E., Putt, M., Halbert, C. H., Schwartz, J. S., Sankar, P., Pyeritz, R. E., Bernhardt, B., & Shea, J. A. (2008). Differences in the patterns of health care system distrust between blacks and whites. *Journal of General Internal Medicine, 23*(6), 827–833.

Arnold, M. (2012, April 1). DTC: Beyond the blockbuster. *Medical Marketing & Media* online. Retrieved from http://www.mmm-online.com/dtc-beyond-the-blockbuster/article/233377/

Arnold, W. E., & McClure, L. (1989). *Communication training and development.* Prospect Heights, IL: Waveland Press.

Arnquist, S. (2009, August 25). Health care abroad: Japan. *The New York Times* online. Retrieved from http://prescriptions.blogs.nytimes.com/2009/08/25/health-care-abroad-japan/

Arrington, M. I. (2003). "I don't want to be an artificial man": Narrative reconstruction of sexuality among prostate cancer survivors. *Sexuality & Culture, 7*(2), 30–58.

Arthur, J. (2011). *Lean Six Sigma for hospitals: Simple steps to fast, affordable, and flawless healthcare.* New York: McGraw-Hill.

Ashley, B. M., & O'Rourke, K. D. (1997). *Health care ethics: A theological analysis* (4th ed.). Washington, DC: Georgetown University Press.

Ashraf, H. (2000, November). BSE inquiry uncovers "a peculiarly British disaster." *The Lancet, 356*, 1579–1580.

Association of American Medical Colleges. (2011). Table 24: MCAT and GPA grid for applicants and acceptees to U.S. medical schools, 2009–2011. Washington, DC: Author. Retrieved from https://www.aamc.org/data/facts/applicant matriculant/

Astin, J. A. (1998). Why patients use alternative medicine: Results of a national study. *Journal of the American Medical Association, 279,* 2548–2553.

Atherly, A., Kane, R. L., & Smith, M. A. (2004). Older adults' satisfaction with integrated capitated health and long-term care. *The Gerontologist, 44*(3), 348–357.

Aulagnier, M., Verger, P., Ravaud, J. F., Souville, M., Lussault, P. Y., Garnier, J. P., & Paraponaris, A. (2005). General practitioners' attitudes towards patients with disabilities: The need for training and support. *Disability and Rehabilitation, 27*(22), 1343–1352.

Austin, E. W. (1993). Exploring the effects of active parental mediation of television content. *Journal of Broadcasting & Electronic Media, 37,* 147–158.

Austin, E. W. (1995). Reaching young audiences: Developmental considerations in designing health messages. In E. Maibach & R. L. Parrott (Eds.), *Designing health messages* (pp. 114–144). Thousand Oaks, CA: Sage.

Austin, E. W., & Johnson, K. K. (1997). Immediate and delayed effects of media literacy training on third graders' decision making for alcohol. *Health Communication, 9,* 323–350.

Austin, E. W., & Meili, H. K. (1994). Effects of interpretations of televised alcohol portrayals on children's alcohol beliefs. *Journal of Broadcasting & Electronic Media, 38,* 417–435.

Austin, E. W., Roberts, D. F., & Nass, C. I. (1990). Influences of family communication on children's television-interpretation process. *Communication Research, 17,* 545–564.

AVERT: Averting HIV and AIDS. (2008, July 30). HIV and AIDS in Africa. West Sussex, UK: Author. Retrieved from http://www.avert.org/aafrica.htm

Azevedo, D. (1996). Taking back health care: Doctors must work together. *Medical Economics, 73,* 156–162.

Babin, L. A., & Carder, S. T. (1996, May). Viewers' recognition of brands placed within a film. *International Journal of Advertising, 15,* 140–151.

Babrow, A. S. (1992). Communication and problematic integration: Understanding diverging probability and value, ambiguity, ambivalence, and impossibility. *Communication Theory, 2,* 95–130.

Babrow, A. S. (2001). Uncertainty, value, communication, and problematic integration. *Journal of Communication, 51*(3), 553–573.

Backer, T. E., & Rogers, E. M. (1993). Introduction. In T. E. Backer & E. M. Rogers (Eds.), *Organizational aspects of health communication campaigns: What works?* (pp. 1–9). Newbury Park, CA: Sage.

Bae, H.-S., & Kang, S. (2008). The influence of viewing an entertainment-education program on cornea donation intention: A test of the theory of planned behavior. *Health Communication, 23*(1), 87–95.

Baek, T., & Mayer, M. (2010). Sexual imagery in cigarette advertising before and after the Master Settlement Agreement. *Health Communication, 25,* 747–757. doi:10.1080/10410236.2010.521917

Baglia, J. (2005). *The Viagra ad venture.* New York: Peter Lang.

Baldwin, D. M. (2003). Disparities in health and health care: Focusing on efforts to eliminate unequal burdens. *Online Journal of Issues in Nursing, 8*(1), 2.

Balint, J., & Shelton, W. (1996). Regaining the initiative: Forging a new model of the patient–physician relationship. *Journal of the American Medical Association, 275,* 887–892.

Ball, J., Liang, A., & Wei-Na, L. (2009). Representation of African Americans in direct-to-consumer pharmaceutical commercials: A content analysis with implications for health disparities. *Health Marketing Quarterly, 26,* 372–390. doi:10.1080/07359680903304328

Ballantine, J. H., Roberts, K. A., & Ritzer, G. (2008). *Our social world + the McDonaldization of society.* Thousand Oaks, CA: Pine Forge Press.

Baltes, M. M., & Wahl, H.-W. (1996). Patterns of communication in old age: The dependence-support and independence-ignore script. *Health Communication, 8,* 217–231.

Bandura, A. (1986). *Social foundations of thought and action: A social cognitive approach.* Englewood Cliffs, NJ: Prentice Hall.

Bandura, A. (1994). Social cognitive theory of mass communication. In J. Bryant & D. Zillman (Eds.), *Media effects: Advances in theory and research* (pp. 61–90). Hillsdale, NJ: Lawrence Erlbaum.

Banerjee, S. C., & Greene, K. (2006). Analysis versus production: Adolescent cognitive and attitudinal responses to antismoking interventions. *Journal of Communication, 56,* 773–794.

Banja, J. D. (2005). *Medical errors and medical narcissism.* Boston: Jones and Bartlett.

Banja, J. D., & Amori, G. (2005). The empathic disclosure of medical error. In *Medical errors and medical narcissism* (pp. 173–192.). Boston: Jones and Bartlett.

Banks, J. S. (director and producer). (2011). Mothers for traumatic brain injury (video). Created by students at Douglas Anderson School of the Arts in Jacksonville, FL. Retrieved from http://www.800tbihope.org/Events_and_Photos.html

Bao, Y., Fox, S. A., & Escarce, J. J. (2007). Socioeconomic and racial/ethnic differences in the discussion of cancer screening: "Between-" versus "within-" physician differences. *Health Services Research, 42*(3), 950–970.

Barker, S. A., & Dawson, K. S. (1998). The effects of animal-assisted therapy on anxiety ratings of hospitalized psychiatric patients. *Psychiatric Services, 49,* 797–801.

Barnard, A. (2003, January 22). Doctors brace for changes on patient privacy. *Boston Globe,* National/Foreign, p. A1.

Barnes, M. K., & Duck, S. (1994). Everyday communicative contexts for social support. In B. R. Burleson, T. L. Albrecht, & I. G. Sarason (Eds.), *Communication of social support: Messages, interactions, relationships, and community* (pp. 175–194). Thousand Oaks, CA: Sage.

Basil, M. D. (1997). The danger of cigarette "special placements" in film and television. *Health Communication, 9,* 191–198.

Bass, A. (1990, November 25). Health care marketing seeks gain from pain. *Boston Globe,* National/Foreign section, p. 1.

Basu, A., & Dutta, M. J. (2007). Centralizing context and culture in the co-construction of health: Localizing and vocalizing health meanings in rural India. *Health Communication, 21*(2), 187–196.

Basu, A., & Dutta, M. J. (2008). The relationship between health information seeking and community participation: The roles of health information orientation and efficacy. *Health Communication, 23*(1), 70–79.

Bates, D. W., & Komaroff, A. L. (1996). A cyberday in the life. *Journal of the American Medical Association, 275*, 753–755.

Bauer, J. E., Hyland, A., Li, Q., Steger, C., & Cummings, K. (2005). A longitudinal assessment of the impact of smoke-free worksite policies on tobacco use. *American Journal of Public Health, 95*, 1024–1029.

Baur, C. (2000). Limiting factors on the transformative powers of e-mail in patient–physician relationships: A critical analysis. *Health Communication 12*(3), 239–259.

Baxter, L. A. (1988). A dialectic perspective of communication strategies in relationship development. In S. Duck (Ed.), *Handbook of personal relationships* (pp. 257–273). New York: Wiley.

Beach, W. A. (2002). Between dad and son: Initiating, delivering, and assimilating bad cancer news. *Health Communication, 14*(3), 271–298.

Beach, W. A., & Japp, P. (1983). Storyifying as time-traveling: The knowledgeable use of temporarily structured discourse. In R. N. Bostrom (Ed.), *Communication yearbook 7* (pp. 867–889). New Brunswick, NJ: Transaction Book.

Bean-Mayberry, B. A., Chang, C. C., McNeil, M. A., Whittle, J., Hayes, P. M., & Scholle, S. H. (2003). Patient satisfaction in women's clinic versus traditional primary care cares in the Veterans Administration. *Journal of General Internal Medicine, 18*(3), 175–181.

Beaudoin, C. E., & Thorson, E. (2006). The social capital of Blacks and Whites: Differing effects of the mass media in the United States. *Human Communication Research, 32*, 157–177.

Bechara, A., Casabé, A., De Bonis, W., Hellen, A., & Bertolino, M. V. (2010). Recreational use of phosphodiesterase type 5 inhibitors by healthy young men. *The Journal of Sexual Medicine, 7*, 3736–3742.

Beck, C. S. (2005). Personal stories and public activism: The implications of Michael J. Fox's public health narrative for policy and perspectives. In E. B. Ray (Ed.), *Health communication in practice: A case study approach* (pp. 335–345). Mahwah, NJ: Lawrence Erlbaum.

Beck, C. S., & Ragan, S. L. (1992). Negotiating interpersonal and medical talk: Frame shifts in the gynecologic exam. *Journal of Language and Social Psychology, 11*, 47–61.

Beck, C. S., Ragan, S. L., & du Pré, A. (1997). *Partnership for health: Building relationships between women and health caregivers.* Mahwah, NJ: Lawrence Erlbaum.

Becker, G., & Newsom, E. (2003). Socioeconomic status and dissatisfaction with health care among chronically ill African Americans. *American Journal of Public Health, 93*(5), 742–748.

Beckman, H. B., & Frankel, R. M. (1984). The effect of physician behavior on the collection of data. *Annals of Internal Medicine, 101*, 692–696.

Becoming a hospital human resource manager. (2011). HealthcareAdministration.com. Retrieved from http://www.healthcareadministration.com/what-is-the-function-of-hospital-human-resource-management/

Beer commercials among favorite Super Bowl ads for teens. (2009, February 5). Drug-Free Action Alliance: Alexandria, VA. Retrieved from http://www.cadca.org/resources/detail/beer-commercials-among-favorite-super-bowl-ads-teens

Bell, D. J., Bringman, J., Bush, A., & Phillips, O. P. (2006). Job satisfaction among obstetrician-gynecologists: A comparison between private practice physicians and academic physicians. *American Journal of Obstetrics and Gynecology, 195*(5), 1474–1478.

Beltramini, R. F. (2010). DTC advertising's programmatic research and its effect on health communication. *Health Communication, 25*, 574–575. doi:10.1080/10410236.2010.496770

Benjamin, R. (2010). Health literacy improvement as national priority. *Journal of Health Communication, 15*, 1–3.

Benzil, D. L., Abosch, A., Germano, I., Gilmer, H., Maraire, J. N., Muraszko, K., Pannullo, S., Rosseau, G., Schwartz, L., Todor, R., Ullman, J., & Zusman, E. (2008, September). The future of neurosurgery: A white paper on the recruitment and retention of women in neurosurgery. *Journal of Neurosurgery, 109*(3), 378–386.

Berger, P., & Luckmann, T. (1966). *The social construction of reality.* New York: Doubleday.

Bergstrom, M. J., & Holmes, M. E. (2000). Lay theories of successful aging after the death of a spouse: A network text analysis of bereavement advice. *Health Communication, 12*(4), 377–406.

Bergstrom, M. J., & Nussbaum, J. F. (1996). Cohort differences in interpersonal conflict: Implications for the older patient–younger care provider interaction. *Health Communication, 8*, 233–248.

Berko, R. M., Wolvin, A. D., & Curtis, R. (1993). *The business of communicating* (5th ed.). Madison, WI: Brown & Benchmark.

Berkowitz, E. N. (2007). The evolution of public relations and the use of the Internet: The implications for health care organizations. *Health Marketing Quarterly, 24*(3–4), 117–130.

Bernhardt, J. M., & Cameron, K. A. (2003). Accessing, understanding, and applying health communication messages: The challenge of health literacy. In T. L. Thompson, A. M. Dorsey, K. I. Miller, & R. Parrott (Eds.), *Handbook of health communication* (pp. 583–605). Mahwah, NJ: Lawrence Erlbaum.

Bernheim, S. M., Ross, J. S., Krumholz, H. M., & Bradley, E. H. (2008). Influence of patients' socioeconomic status on clinical management decisions: A qualitative study. *Annals of Family Medicine, 6*(1), 53–59.

Bernstam, E. V., Walji, M. F., Sagaram, S., Sagaram, D., Johnson, C. W., & Meric-Bernstam, F. (2008, March). Commonly cited website quality criteria are not effective at identifying inaccurate online information about breast cancer. *Cancer, 112*(6), 1206–1213.

Berry, L. L., & Seltman, K. D. (2008). *Management lessons from Mayo Clinic: Inside one of the world's most admired service organizations.* New York: McGraw-Hill.

Berry, T. R., Wharf-Higgins, J., & Naylor, P. J. (2007). SARS wars: An examination of the quantity and construction of health information in the news media. *Health Communication, 21*(1), 35–44.

Bethea, L. S., Travis, S. S., & Pecchioni, L. (2000). Family caregivers' use of humor in conveying information about caring for dependent older adults. *Health Communication, 12*(4), 361–376.

Betts, K. (2002, March 31). The tyranny of skinny, fashion's insider secret. *New York Times*, p. 1, section 9.

Beware of online cancer fraud. (2008, September 18). Washington, DC: U.S. Food and Drug Administration. Retrieved from http://www.fda.gov/consumer/updates/cancerfraud061708.html

Bhopal, P. (1998, June 27). Spectre of racism in health and health care: Lessons from history and the United States. *British Medical Journal*, *7149*, 1970–1973.

Biagi, S. (1999). *Media/impact: An introduction to mass media*. Belmont, CA: Wadsworth.

Bibace, R., & Walsh, M. E. (1981). Children's conceptualizations of illness. In R. Bibace & M. E. Walsh (Eds.), *Children's conceptualizations of health, illness, and bodily functions* (pp. 31–48). San Francisco: Jossey-Bass.

Bickmore, T. W., Pfeifer, L. M., Byron, D., Forsythe, S., Henault, L. E., Jack, B. W., & Paasche-Orlow, M. K. (2010). Usability of conversational agents by patients with inadequate health literacy: Evidence from two clinical Trials. *Journal of Health Communication*, *15*, 197–210. doi:10.1080/10810730.2010.499991

Bille, D. A. (1981). The approach to health care in three American minorities. In D. A. Bille (Ed.), *Practical approaches to patient teaching* (pp. 85–94). Boston: Little, Brown.

Black, L. L., Jensen, G. M., Mostrom, E., Perkins, J., Ritzline, P. D., Hayward, L., & Blackmer, B. (2010). The first year of practice: An investigation of the professional learning and development of promising novice physical therapists. *Physical Therapist*, *90*, 1758–1773.

Blanch, D. C., Hall, J. A., Roter, D. L., & Frankel, R. M. (2008, September). Medical student gender and issues of confidence. *Patient Education and Counseling*, *72*(3), 374–381.

Blavin, F., Buettgens, M., & Roth, J. (2012, January). State progress toward health reform implementation: Slower moving states have much to gain. Princeton, NJ: Robert Wood Johnson Foundation. Retrieved from http://www.rwjf.org/files/research/73855.5608.stateprogress.qs71..pdfhttp://www.rwjf.org/files/research/74428.quickstrike.veterans.052412.pdf

Bleustein, C., Valaitis, E., & Jones, R. (2010). Effect of wait room time on ambulatory patient satisfaction. *Otolaryngology—Head and Neck Surgery*, *143*, P38–P39.

Bliss, W. G. (2012, January 24). Cost of employee turnover. Small Business Advisor website. Retrieved from http://www.isquare.com/turnover.cfm

Block, S. D. (2001). Psychological considerations, growth, and transcendence at the end of life. *Journal of the American Medical Association*, *285*(22), 2898–2905.

Bochner, S. (1983). Doctors, patients and their cultures. In D. Pendleton & J. Hasler (Eds.), *Doctor-patient communication* (pp. 127–138). London: Academic Press.

Bock, B. C., Becker, B. M., Niaura, R. S., Partridge, R., Fava, J. L., & Trask, P. (2008). Smoking cessation among patients in an emergency chest pain observation unit: Outcomes of the Chest Pain Smoking Study (CPSS). *Nicotine & Tobacco Research*, *10*(10), 1523–1531.

Boden, W. E., & Diamond, G. A. (2008, May 22). DTCA for PTCA—crossing the line in consumer health education? *The New England Journal of Medicine*, *358*(21), 2197.

Boer, H., & Westhoff, Y. (2006, February). The role of positive and negative signaling communication by strong and weak ties in the shaping of safe sex subjective norms of adolescents in South Africa. *Communication Theory*, *16*(1), 75–90.

Bohm, D. (1980). *Wholeness and the implicate order*. London: Routledge & Kegan Paul.

Bohm, D. (1994). *Thought as a system*. New York: Routledge.

Bohm, D. (1996). *On dialogue*. L. Nichol (Ed.). London: Routledge & Kegan Paul.

Bondeson, W. B., and Jones, J. W. (Eds.) (2010). *The ethics of managed care: Professional integrity and patient rights*. Dordrecht, The Netherlands: Springer.

Bonner, T. N. (1992). *To the ends of the earth. Women's search for education in medicine*. Cambridge, MA: Harvard University Press.

Bonsteel, A. (1997, March–April). Behind the white coat. *The Humanist*, *57*, 15–19.

Boodman, S. (1997, February 25). Silent doctors more likely to be sued;

malpractice study suggests that physicians' manner affects patients' readiness to go to court. *Washington Post*, p. WH9.

Booth-Butterfield, M. (2003). Embedded health behaviors from adolescence to adulthood: The impact of tobacco. *Health Communication*, *15*(2), 171–184.

Booth-Butterfield, M., Anderson, R., & Booth-Butterfield, S. (2000). Adolescents' use of tobacco, health locus of control, and self-monitoring. *Health Communication*, *12*(2), 137–148.

Borreani, C., Brunelli, C., Miccinesi, G., Morino, P., Piazza, M., Piva, L., & Tamburini, M. (2008). Eliciting individual preferences about death: Development of the End-of-Life Preferences Interview. *Journal of Pain and Symptom Management*, *36*(4), 335–350.

Botta, R. A., & Dumlao, R. (2002). How do conflict and communication patterns between fathers and daughters contribute to or offset eating disorders? *Health Communication*, *14*(2), 199–219.

Bottorf, J. L., Gogag, M., & Engelberg-Lotzkar, M. (1995). Comforting exploring the work of cancer nurses. *Journal of Advanced Nursing*, *22*, 1077–1084.

Boukus, E. R., Cassil, A., & O'Malley, A. S. (2009, September). A snapshot of U.S. physicians: Key findings from the 2008 health tracking physician survey. Center for Studying Health System Change. Retrieved from http://www.hschange.com/CONTENT/1078/

Bowen, D. J., Singal, R., Eng, E., Crystal, S., & Burke, W. (2003). Jewish identity and intentions to obtain breast cancer screening. *Cultural Diversity and Ethnic Minority Psychology*, *9*(1), 78–87.

Boyd, R. S. (1997, June 21). Medical aids, media reports 'a flood of confusing advice': Marketing hype, thirst for the news among causes of bewilderment. *Houston Chronicle*, p. 7.

Boylstein, C., Rittman, M., & Hinojosa, R. (2007). Metaphor shifts in stroke recovery. *Health Communication*, *21*(3), 279–287.

Brady, M. J., & Cella, D. F. (1995, May 30). Helping patients live with their cancer. *Patient Care*, pp. 41–49.

Braithwaite, D. O. (1996). "Persons first": Expanding communicative choices by persons with disabilities. In E. B. Ray (Ed.), *Communication and disenfranchisement: Social health issues and implications* (pp. 449–464). Mahwah, NJ: Lawrence Erlbaum.

Braithwaite, D. O., & Harter, L. M. (2000). Communication and the management of dialectic tensions in the personal relationships of people with disabilities. In D. O. Braithwaite & T. L. Thompson (Eds.), *Handbook of communication and people with disabilities: Research and applications* (pp. 17–36). Mahwah, NJ: Lawrence Erlbaum.

Braithwaite, D. O., & Japp, P. (2005). "They make us miserable in the name of helping us": Communication of persons with visible and invisible disabilities. In E. B. Ray (Ed.), *Health communication in practice: A case study approach* (pp. 171–179). Mahwah, NJ: Lawrence Erlbaum.

Braithwaite, D. O., & Thompson, T. L. (Eds.). (2000). *Handbook of communication and people with disabilities: Research and applications.* Mahwah, NJ: Lawrence Erlbaum.

Branch, W. T., Jr., Levinson, W., & Platt, F. W. (1996). Diagnostic interviewing: Make the most of your time. *Patient Care, 30*(12), 68–76.

Branch, W. T., Jr., & Malik, T. K. (1993). Using "windows of opportunities" in brief interviews to understand patients' concerns. *Journal of the American Medical Association, 269,* 1667–1668.

Brann, M. (2007). Health care providers' confidentiality practices and perceptions: Expanding a typology of confidentiality breaches in health care communication. *Qualitative Research Reports in Communication, 8*(1), 45–52.

Brann, M., Himes, K. L., Dillow, M. R., & Weber, K. (2010). Dialectic tensions in stroke survivor relationships. *Health Communication, 25,* 323–332.

Brann, M., & Mattson, M. (2004). Toward a typology of confidentiality breaches in health care communication: An ethic of care analysis of provider practices and patient perceptions. *Health Communication, 16*(2), 229–251.

Brashers, D. E., & Babrow, A. S. (1996). Theorizing health communication. *Communication Studies, 47,* 237–251.

Brehm, J. W. (1966). *A theory of psychological reactance.* New York: Academic Press.

Brennan, P. F., & Fink, S. V. (1997). Health promotion, social support, and computer networks. In R. L. Street Jr., W. R. Gold, & T. Manning (Eds.), *Health promotion and interactive technology: Theoretical implications and future directions* (pp. 157–169). Mahwah, NJ: Lawrence Erlbaum.

Bresnahan, M., Lee, S. Y., Smith, S. W., Shearman, S., Nebashi, R., Park, C. Y., & Yoo, J. (2007a). A theory of planned behavior study of college students' intention to register as organ donors in Japan, Korea, and the United States. *Health Communication, 21*(3), 201–211.

Bresnahan, M., Lee, S. Y., Smith, S. W., Shearman, S., & Yoo, J. H. (2007b). Reservations of the spirit: The development of a culturally sensitive spiritual beliefs scale about organ donation. *Health Communication, 21*(1), 45–54.

Brett, R. (2003, February 21). Life's great, say area survivors. *The Plain Dealer,* p. B1.

Brice, J. H., Travers, D., Cowden, C. S., Young, M. D., Sanhueza, A., & Dunston, Y. (2008). Health literacy among Spanish-speaking patients in the emergency department. *Journal of the National Medical Association, 100*(11), 1326–1332.

Briñol, P., & Petty, R. E. (2006). Fundamental processes leading to attitude change: Implications for career prevention communications. *Journal of Communication, 56,* S81–S104.

Britton, P. C., Williams, G. C., & Conner, K. R. (2008). *Journal of Clinical Psychology, 64*(1), 52–66.

The broccoli argument. (2011, March 1). *The New York Times* online. Retrieved from http://schott.blogs.nytimes.com/2011/03/01/the-broccoli-argument/

Brodie, M., Kjellson, N., Hoff, T., & Parker, M. (2008). Perceptions of Latinos, African Americans, and Whites on media as a health information source. In L. C. Lederman (Ed.), *Beyond these walls: Readings in health communication* (pp. 378–394). New York: Oxford University Press.

Broom, A. (2008). Virtually healthy: The impact of Internet use on disease experience and the doctor–patient relationship. In L. C. Lederman (Ed.), *Beyond these walls: Readings in health communication* (pp. 92–109). New York: Oxford University Press.

Brosius, H., & Weimann, G. (1996). Who sets the agenda? Agenda-setting as a two-step flow. *Communication Research, 23,* 561–580.

Brotman, S., Ryan, B., & Cormier, R. (2003). The health and social service needs of gay and lesbian elders and their families in Canada. *Gerontologist, 43*(2), 192–202.

Brown, H., Cassileth, B. R., Lewis, J. P., & Renner, J. H. (1994). Alternative medicine—or quackery? *Patient Care, 28,* 80–90.

Brown, J., & Addington-Hall, J. (2007). How people with motor neuron disease talk about living with illness: A narrative study. *Journal of Advanced Nursing, 62*(2), 200–208.

Brown, J. D., & Einsiedel, E. R. (1990). Public health campaigns: Mass media strategies. In E. B. Ray & L. Donohew (Eds.), *Communication and health: Systems and applications* (pp. 153–170). Hillsdale, NJ: Lawrence Erlbaum.

Brown, J. D., & Walsh-Childers, K. (1994). Effects of media on personal and public health. In J. Bryant & D. Zillmann (Eds.), *Media effects: Advances on theory and research* (pp. 389–415). Hillsdale, NJ: Lawrence Erlbaum.

Brown, T. (2012, March 14). Hospitals aren't hotels. *The New York Times* online. Retrieved from http://www.nytimes.com/2012/03/15/opinion/hospitals-must-first-hurt-to-heal.html

Brown, T. N., Ueno, K., Smith, C. L., Austin, N. S., & Bickman, L. (2007). Communication patterns in medical encounters for the treatment of child psychosocial problems: Does pediatrician–parent concordance matter? *Health Communication, 21*(3), 247–256.

Brown, W. J., & Basil, M. D. (1995). Media celebrities and public health: Responses to "Magic" Johnson's HIV disclosure and its impact on AIDS risks and high-risk behaviors. *Health Communication, 7,* 345–370.

Brown, W. J., Basil, M. D., & Bocarnea, M. C. (2003). The influence of famous athletes on health beliefs and practices: Mark McGwire, child abuse prevention, and androstenedione. *Journal of Health Communication, 8*(1), 41–57.

Bruck, L. (1996, September). Today's issues in tax exemption. *Nursing Homes, 45,* 43–46.

Buchholz, B. (1992, January–February). Psyching yourself: How to prepare for medical procedures. *Arthritis Today, 6*(1), 20–24.

Buchthal, O., Doff, A. L., Hsu, L. A., Silbanuz, A., Heinrich, K. M., & Maddock, J. E. (2011). Avoiding a knowledge gap in a multiethnic statewide social marketing campaign: Is cultural tailoring sufficient? *Journal of Health Communication, 16,* 314–327. doi:10.1080/10810730 .2010.535111

Buckman, R., Lipkin, M., Jr., Sourkes, B. M., Toole, S. W., & Talarico, L. D. (1997). Strategies and skills for breaking bad news. *Patient Care, 31,* 61–78.

Bucknall, T., & Thomas, S. (1996). Critical care nurse satisfaction with level of involvement in clinical decisions. *Journal of Advanced Nursing, 23,* 571–577.

Buller, D. B., Burgoon, M., Hall, J. R., Levine, N., Taylor, A. M., Beach, B., Buller, M. K., & Melcher, C. (2000). Long-term effects of language intensity in preventive messages on planned family solar protection. *Health Communication, 12*(3), 261–275.

Buntin, M., Haviland, A. M., McDevitt, R., & Sood, N. (2011). Healthcare spending and preventive care in high-deductible and consumer-directed health plans. *American Journal of Managed Care, 17,* 222–230.

Burda, D. (2008, April 28). The perfection injection; not paying for "never events" is a slippery slope. *Modern Healthcare, 38*(17), 20.

Burdine, J. N., McLeroy, K. B., & Gottlieb, N. H. (1987). Ethical dilemmas in health promotion: An introduction. *Health Education Quarterly, 14,* 7–9.

Burgoon, M. H., & Burgoon, J. K. (1990). Compliance-gaining and health care. In J. P. Dillard (Ed.), *Seeking compliance: The production of interpersonal influence messages* (pp. 161–188). Scottsdale, AZ: Gorsuch Scarisbrick.

Burleson, B. R. (1990). Comforting as social support: Relational consequences of supportive behaviors. In S. Duck & R. C. Silver (Eds.), *Personal relationships and social support* (pp. 66–82). London: Sage.

Burleson, B. R. (1994). Comforting messages: Significance, approaches, and effects. In B. R. Burleson, T. L. Albrecht, & I. G. Sarason (Eds.), *Communication of social support: Messages, interactions, relationships, and community* (pp. 175–194). Thousand Oaks, CA: Sage.

Bute, J. J., Donovan-Kicken, E., & Martins, N. (2007). Effects of communication-debilitating illnesses and injuries on close relationships: A relational maintenance perspective. *Health communication, 21*(3), 235–246.

Byck, R. (1986). *The encyclopedia of psychoactive drugs: Treating mental illness.* New York: Chelsea House.

Bylund, C. L. (2005). Mothers' involvement in decision making during the birthing process: A quantitative analysis of women's online birth stories. *Health Communication, 18*(1), 23–39.

Bylund, C. L., D'Agostino, T. A., Ho, E. Y., & Chewning, B. A. (2010). Improving clinical communication and promoting health through concordance-based patient education. *Communication Education, 59,* 294–311.

Caldroney, R. D. (2008, March 21). Why we've never been sued: This doctor and his partners have stayed out of the courtroom for nearly 30 years. Learn how to follow their lead. *Medical Economics, 85*(6), 30–32.

Calfee, J. E. (2002, Fall). Direct-to-consumer advertising of prescription drugs: Evaluating regulatory policy in the United States and New Zealand. *Journal of Public Policy & Marketing, 21*(2), 174.

Cameron, K. A., & Campo, S. (2006). Stepping back from social norms campaigns: Comparing normative influences to other predictors of health behaviors. *Health Communication, 20*(3), 277–288.

Campbell, R. G., & Babrow, A. S. (2004). The role of empathy in responses to persuasive risk communication: Overcoming resistance to HIV prevention messages. *Health Communication, 16*(2), 159–182.

Campo, S., & Cameron, K. A. (2006). Differential effects of exposure to social norm campaigns: A cause for concern. *Health Communication, 19*(3), 209–219.

Campo, S., & Mastin, T. (2007). Placing the burden on the individual: Overweight and obesity in African American and mainstream women's magazines. *Health Communication, 22*(3), 229–240.

Candib, L. M. (1994). Reconsidering power in the clinical relationship. In E. S. More & M. A. Milligan (Eds.), *The empathic practitioner: Empathy, gender, and medicine* (pp. 135–155). New Brunswick, NJ: Rutgers University Press.

Cantor, J. C., Schoen, C., Belloff, D., How, S. K. H., & McCarthy, D. (2007, June). Aiming higher: Results from a State Scorecard on Health System Performance. New York: The Commonwealth Fund Commission on a High Performance Health System. Retrieved from www.commonwealthfund.org/ publications/publications_show .htm?doc_id=494551

Caplan, S. E., Haslett, B. J., & Burleson, B. R. (2005). Telling it like it is: The adaptive function of narratives in coping with loss in later life. *Health Communication, 17*(3), 233–251.

Capriotti, T. (1999, February 1). Exploring the "herbal jungle." *MedSurg Nursing, 8,* 53.

Career: Health care administrator. (2012). *The Princeton Review* online bulletin. Retrieved from http:// www.princetonreview.com/careers. aspx?cid=76

Caregiving in the U.S. (2009). National Alliance of Caregiving and the American Association of Retired Persons. Retrieved from http://www .caregiving.org/data/Caregiving_ in_the_US_2009_full_report.pdf

Carlzon, J. (1987). *Moments of truth: New strategies for today's customer-driven economy.* New York: Harper & Row.

Carpenter, C. J. (2010). A meta-analysis of the effectiveness of Health Belief Model variables in predicting behavior. *Health Communication, 25,* 661–669. doi:10.1080/1041023 6.2010.521906

Carpiac-Claver, M. L., & Levy-Storms, L. (2007). In a manner of speaking: Communication sbetween nurse aides and older adults in long-term care settings. *Health Communication, 22*(1), 59–67.

Cartner-Morley, J. (2007, September 15). Catwalk inquiry wants medicals for models: Investigation paints disturbing picture: Passport checks reinforce London ban on under-16s. *The Guardian* (London), Final Edition, p. 7.

Casey, M. K., Allen, M., Emmers-Sommer, T., Sahlstein, E., Degooyer, D., Winters, A. M., Wagner, A. E., & Dun, T. (2003). When a celebrity contracts a disease: The example of Earvin "Magic" Johnson's announcement that he was HIV positive. *Journal of Health Communication, 8*(1), 249–256.

Casper, M. F., Child, J. T., Gilmour, D., McIntyre, K. A., & Pearson, J. C. (2006). Healthy research perspectives: Incorporating college student experiences with alcohol. *Health Communication, 20*(3), 289–298.

Cassedy, J. H. (1991). *Medicine in America: A short history.* Baltimore: Johns Hopkins University Press.

Cassell, E. J. (1991). *The nature of suffering.* New York: Oxford University Press.

Catlin, A., Armigo, C., Volat, D., Vale, E., Hadley, M. A., Gong, W., Bassir, R., & Anderson, K. (2008). Conscientious objection: A potential neonatal nursing response to care orders that cause suffering at the end of life? Study of a concept. *Neonatal Network, 27*(2), 101–108.

Cawyer, C. S., & Smith-du Pré, A. (1995). Communicating social support: Identifying supportive episodes in an HIV/AIDS support group. *Communication Quarterly, 43*, 243–258.

Cegala, D. J., & Broz, S. L. (2003). Provider and patient communication skills training. In T. L. Thompson, A. M. Dorsey, K. I. Miller, & R. Parrot (Eds.), *Handbook of health communication* (pp. 95–119). Mahwah, NJ: Lawrence Erlbaum.

Cegala, D. J., Street, R. L., Jr., & Clinch, C. R. (2007). The impact of patient participation on physicians' information provision during a primary care medical interview. *Health Communication, 21*(2), 177–185.

Center on Alcohol Marketing and Youth website. (2012). Available at http://www.camy.org/

Centers for Disease Control and Prevention (CDC). (2005, May 3). Frequently asked questions about SARS. Atlanta: Author. Retrieved from http://www.cdc.gov/ncidod/sars/faq.htm

Centers for Disease Control and Prevention (CDC). (2007, February 12). What is bioterrorism? Atlanta:

Author. Retrieved from http://emergency.cdc.gov/bioterrorism/overview.asp

Centers for Disease Control and Prevention (CDC). (2008, July 1). Overview of crisis & emergency risk communication. Atlanta: Author. Retrieved from http://emergency.cdc.gov/cerc

Centers for Disease Control and Prevention (CDC). (2010). Traumatic brain injury in the United States. Atlanta: Author. Retrieved from http://www.cdc.gov/traumaticbraininjury/tbi_ed.html

Centers for Disease Control and Prevention (CDC). (2011, March 21). Tobacco-related mortality. Atlanta: Author. Retrieved from http://www.cdc.gov/tobacco/data_statistics/fact_sheets/health_effects/tobacco_related_mortality/

Chaiken, S. (1980). Heuristic versus systematic information processing and the use of source versus message cues in persuasion. *Journal of Personality and Social Psychology, 39*, 752–766.

Chaiken, S., Giner-Sorolla, R., & Chen, S. (1996). Beyond accuracy: Defense and impression motives in heuristic and systematic information processing. In P. M. Gollwitzer & J. A. Bargh (Eds.), *The psychology of action: Linking cognition and motivation to behavior* (pp. 553–578). New York: Guilford.

Chamberlain, M. A. (1994). New technologies in health communication: Progress or panacea? *American Behavioral Scientist, 38*, 271–285.

Chang, L.-C., Shih, C.-H., & Lin, S.-M. (2010). The mediating role of psychological empowerment and organizational commitment for school health nurses: A cross-sectional questionnaire survey. *International Journal on Nursing Studies, 47*, 427–433.

Chapman, S., & Leask, J. A. (2001, December). Paid celebrity endorsement in health promotion: A case study from Australia. *Health Promotion International, 16*(4), 333–338.

Charchuk, M., & Simpson, C. (2005). Hope, disclosure, and control in the neonatal intensive care unit. *Health Communication, 17*(2), 191–203.

Charlton, C. R., Dearing, K. S., Berry, J. A., & Johnson, M. J. (2008). Nurse practitioners' communication styles and their impact on patient

outcomes: An integrated literature review. *Journal of the American Academy of Nurse Practitioners. 20*(7), 382–388.

Charmaz, K. (1987). Struggling for a self: Identity levels of the chronically ill. In J. Roth & P. Conrad (Eds.), *Research in the sociology of health care* (pp. 283–321). Greenwich, CT: JAI Press.

Charon, R. (2006). *Narrative medicine: Honoring the stories of illness.* New York: Oxford University Press.

Charon, R. (2009a). Narrative medicine as witness for the self-telling body. *Journal of Applied Communication Research, 37*, 118–131.

Charon, R. (2009b). The polis of a discursive narrative medicine. *Journal of Applied Communication Research, 37*, 196–201.

Charski, M. (1998, June 29). Now on the Net: Live birth. Next: The operating room. *U. S. News & World Report, 124*, 36.

Cheong, P. H. (2007). Health communication resources for uninsured and insured Hispanics. *Health Communication, 21*(2), 153–163.

Chesler, M. A., & Barbarin, O. A. (1984). Difficulties of providing help in a crisis: Relationships between parents of children with cancer and their friends. *Journal of Social Issues, 40*, 113–134.

Chia, H. L. (2009). Exploring facets of a social network to explicate the status of social support and its effects on stress. *Social Behavior & Personality: An International Journal, 37*(5), 701–710.

Chieh, L. H., & Tan, J. (2007, August 24). Medical schools see an influx of women; more women are studying medicine here since the quota was lifted in 2002. *Straits Times* (Singapore), np.

Childhood obesity. (2008, August 20). Atlanta: Centers for Disease Control and Prevention. Retrieved from http://www.cdc.gov/HealthyYouth/obesity/

Cho, H., Hall, J. G., Kosmoski, C., Fox, R. L., & Mastin, T. (2010). Tanning, skin cancer risk, and prevention: A content analysis of eight popular magazines that target female readers, 1997–2006. *Health Communication, 25*, 1–10. doi:10.1080/10410230903265938

Cho, H., & Salmon, C. T. (2007). Unintended effects of health communication campaigns. *Journal of Communication, 57,* 293–317.

Cho, S. (2006). Network news coverage of breast cancer. *Journalism and Mass Communication, 83*(1), 116–130.

Cho, S.-H., Lee, J.-S., Thabane, L., & Lee, J. (2009). Acupuncture for obesity: A systematic review and meta-analysis. *International Journal of Obesity, 33,* 183–196.

Cho, Y., & Yoon, S. W. (2010). Theory development and convergence of human resource fields: Implications for human performance technology. *Performance Improvement Quarterly, 23*(3), 39–56.

Chou, W.-Y., Wang, L. C., Finney Rutten, L. J., Moser, R. P., & Hesse, B. W. (2010). Factors associated with Americans' ratings of health care quality: What do they tell us about the raters and health care systems? *Journal of Health Communication, 15,* 147–156.

Christakis, N. A., & Fowler, J. H. (2008, May 22). The collective dynamics of smoking in a large social network. *New England Journal of Medicine, 358*(21), 2249.

Christen, R. N., Alder, J., & Bitzer, J. (2008). Gender differences in physicians' communicative skills and their influence on patient satisfaction in gynecological outpatient consultations. *Social Science & Medicine, 66*(7), 1464–1483.

Christmas, C., Park, E., Schmaltz, H., Gozu, A., & Durso, S. C. (2008). A model intensive course in geriatric teaching for non-geriatric educators. *Journal of General Internal Medicine, 23*(7), 1048–1052.

Chung, S. (2008, April 18). When a balance makes patients avoid you. Letter to the editor. *Medical Economics, 85*(8), 17.

Churchill, L. R. (1994). *Self-interest and universal health care: Why well-insured Americans should support coverage for everyone.* Cambridge, MA: Harvard University Press.

Ciechanowski, P., & Katon, W. J. (2006). The interpersonal experience of health care through the eyes of patients with diabetes. *Social Science & Medicine, 63,* 3067–3079.

Cipher, D. J., Hooker, R. S., & Sekscenski, E. (2006). Are older patients satisfied with physician assistants and nurse practitioners? *Official Journal of the American Academy of Physician Assistants, 19*(1), 39–40, 42–44.

Clancy, H. (2011, August 8). How will mobile technology help in healthcare? Look to developing nations. Smartplanet blog. Retrieved from http://www.smartplanet.com/blog/business-brains/how-will-mobile-technology-help-in-healthcare-look-to-developing-nations/17778

Clarke, J. N. (1999). Prostate cancer's hegemonic masculinity in select print mass media depictions (1974–1995). *Health Communication, 11*(1), 59–74.

Clarke, J. N., & Binns, J. (2006). The portrayal of heart disease in mass print magazines, 1991–2001. *Health Communication, 19*(1), 39–48.

Clarke, L. (2002, Fall). Panic: Myth or reality? *Contexts, 1*(3), 21–26.

Clarke, L. Chess, C., Holmes, R., & O'Neill, K. M. (2006, September). Speaking with one voice: Risk communication lessons from the U.S. anthrax attacks. *Journal of Contingencies and Crisis Management, 14*(3), 160–169.

Clarke, L. H., & Griffin, M. (2008). Visible and invisible ageing: Beauty work as a response to ageism. *Aging & Society, 28*(5), 653–674.

Clark-Hitt, R., Smith, S. W., & Broderick, J. S. (2012). Help a buddy take a knee: Creating persuasive messages for military service members to encourage others to seek mental health help. *Health Communication, 27*(5), 429–438. doi:10.1080/10410236.2011.606525

Clements, B. (1996). Talk is cheaper than three extra office visits. *American Medical News, 39,* 17–20.

Cline, R. J. W., & Boyd, M. F. (1993). Communication as threat and therapy: Stigma, social support, and coping with HIV infection. In E. B. Ray (Ed.), *Case studies in health communication* (pp. 131–148). Hillsdale, NJ: Lawrence Erlbaum.

Cline, R. J. W., & Young, H. N. (2004). Marketing drugs, marketing health care relationships: A content analysis of visual cues in direct-to-consumer prescription drug advertising. *Health Communication, 16*(2), 131–157.

Cohen, C. (2009, February 17). Surgeons send 'tweets' from operating room. CNN.com/technology. Retrieved from http://www.cnn.com/2009/TECH/02/17/twitter.surgery/index.html

Cohen, J. (1997). The media's love affair with AIDS research: Hope vs. hype. *Science, 275,* 289–299.

Cohen, J., Collins, R., Darkes, J., & Gwartney, D. (2007). A league of their own: Demographics, motivations and patterns of use of 1,955 male adult non-medical anabolic steroid users in the United States. *Journal of the International Society of Sports Nutrition, 4*(12), 1–14.

Cohen, S., & Wills, T. A. (1985). Stress, social support, and buffering hypothesis. *Psychological Bulletin, 98,* 310–357.

Colarossi, L., Billowitz, M., & Breitbart, V. (2010). Developing culturally relevant educational materials about emergency contraception. *Journal of Health Communication, 15,* 502–515. doi:10.1080/10810730.2010.492561

Collins, J. C. (2001a). Good to great (article). *Fast Company* online. Retrieved from http://www.jimcollins.com/article_topics/articles/good-to-great.html

Collins, J. C. (2001b). *Good to great: Why some companies make the leap . . . and others don't.* New York: HarperCollins.

Collins, J. C., & Porras, J. I. (1997). *Built to last: Successful habits of visionary companies.* Harper Business.

Collins, R. L., Elliott, M. N., Berry, S. H., Kamouse, D. E., Kunkel, D., Hunter, S. B., & Miu, A. (2004). Watching sex on television predicts adolescent initiation of sexual behavior. *Pediatrics, 114,* e280–e289.

Collins, S. R., Garber, T., & Davis, K. (2011, September 13). Number of uninsured in United States grows to 49.9 million; young adults benefiting from the Affordable Care Act. Washington, DC: Commonwealth Fund. Retrieved from http://www.commonwealthfund.org/Blog/2011/Sep/Number-of-Uninsured-in-United-States-Grows.aspx

Colon-Ramos, U., Atienza, A. A., Weber, D., Taylor, M., Uy, C., & Yaroch, A. (2009). Practicing what they preach: Health behaviors of those who provide health advice to extensive social networks. *Journal of Health Communication, 14,* 119–130. doi:10.1080/10810730802659111

The Commonwealth Fund. (2007). International health policy survey in seven countries. New York: Author.

Retrieved from www.common-wealthfund.org/surveys/surveys_show.htm?doc_id=568326

The Commonwealth Fund. (2008a). Cost-related access problems, by race/ethnicity, income, and insurance status, 2007. New York: Author. Retrieved from http://www.commonwealthfund.org/chart cartcharts/chartcartcharts_show.htm?doc_id=694054 www.commonwealthfund.org/surveys/surveys_show.htm?doc_id=568326

The Commonwealth Fund. (2008b, January 15). National survey on public's health care reform views: Americans favor keeping employer role in paying for health insurance; believe covering all should be shared responsibility of employers, individuals, and government. New York: Author. Retrieved from http://www.commonwealthfund.org/newsroom/newsroom_show.htm?doc_id=646974

The Commonwealth Fund. (2008c, July). Why not the best? Results from the National Scorecard on U.S. Health System Performance, 2008. New York: Author. Retrieved from www.commonwealthfund.org/publications/publications_show.htm?doc_id=69268

Conan, N. (2002, April 12). Medical privacy. National Public Radio's *Talk of the Nation*. Retrieved through LexisNexis.

Congressional Budget Office. (2012, March 13). CBO releases updated estimates for the insurance coverage predictions of the Affordable Care Act. Washington, DC: Author. Retrieved from http://www.cbo.gov/publication/43080

Conley, M. (2012, January 17). Paul Deen teams up with diabetes drugmaker Novo Nordisk. ABC world news online. Retrieved from http://abcnews.go.com/Health/paula-deen-confirms-type-diabetes-teams-novo-nordisk/story?id=15378730#.T_w6oBzH-SCA

Conrad, P. (1988). Learning to doctor: Reflections on recent accounts of the medical school years. *Journal of Health and Social Behavior, 29,* 323–332.

Controversy heats up over subway's safer sex ads. (1994, February 7). *AIDS Weekly, 9,* 9–10.

Corbin, J., & Strauss, A. L. (1988). Experiencing body failure and a disrupted self image. In J. Corbin & A. L. Strauss (Eds.), *Unending work and care: Managing chronic illness at home* (pp. 49–67). San Francisco: Jossey-Bass.

Cortés, D. E., Drainoni, M.-L., Henault, L. E., & Paasche-Orlow, M. K. (2010). How to achieve informed consent for research from Spanish-speaking individuals with low literacy: A qualitative report. *Journal of Health Communication, 15,* 172–182.

Cottingham, H. (1992). Cartesian dualism: Theology, metaphysics, and science. In J. Cottingham (Ed.), *The Cambridge companion to Descartes* (pp. 236–257). Cambridge: Cambridge University Press.

Coupland, N., Coupland, J., & Giles, H. (1991). *Language, society & the elderly.* Oxford: Blackwell.

Cousin, G., Mast, M. S., Roter, D. L., & Hall, J. A. (2012). Concordance between physician communication style and patient attitudes predicts patient satisfaction. *Patient Education and Counseling, 87,* 193–197.

Covello, V. T. (2003). Best practices in public health risk and crisis communication. *Journal of Health Communication, 8,* 5–8.

Covert, B. (2012, July 5). GOP's rejection of Medicaid funds is one more ideologically driven bad idea. *The Nation* online. Retrieved from http://www.thenation.com/blog/168736/gops-rejection-medic-aid-funds-one-more-ideologically-driven-bad-idea#

Coward, D. D. (Fall 1990). The lived experience of self-transcendence in women with advanced breast cancer. *Nursing Science Quarterly, 3*(3), 162–169.

Cowart, D., & Burt, R. (1998). Confronting death: Who chooses, who controls? *The Hastings Center Report, 28,* 14–24.

Cox, R. (2010). *Environmental communication and the public sphere* (2nd ed.). Thousand Oaks, CA: Sage.

Cozma, R. (2009, Fall). Online health communication: Source or eliminator of health myths? *Southwestern Mass Communication Journal, 24*(2), 69–80.

Crandall, S. J., Volk, R. J., & Loemker, V. (1993). Medical students' attitudes toward providing care for the underserved: Are we training socially responsible physicians? *Journal of the American Medical Association, 269,* 2519–2523.

Crawford, W. (1997, October). Taxing for health? *Consumers' Research Magazine, 80,* 34.

Creutzfeldt-Jakob Disease (CJD) Statistics. (2012). National Creutzfeldt-Jakob Disease Surveillance Unit: Edinburgh, Scotland. Retrieved from http://www.cjd.ed.ac.uk/figures.htm

Croft, J. B., Giles, W. H., Pollard, R. A., Kennan, N. L., Casper, M. L., & Anda, R. F. (1999). Heart failure survival rate among older adults in the United States. *Archives of Internal Medicine, 159,* 505.

Crosby, L. A. (2011, Spring). Healthy relationships: Think relationship management when it comes to solving the health care crisis. *Marketing Management, 20*(1), 12–13.

Currie, D. (2009). Special report: Crisis communication and social media. Expert roundtable on social media and risk communication during times of crisis: Strategic challenges and opportunities. Sponsored by American Public Health Association, the George Washington University School of Public Health and Health Services, International Association of Emergency Managers, and National Association of Government Communicators. Retrieved from http://www.boozallen.com/insights/insight-detail/42420696

Curtin, R. B., Walters, B. A., Schatell, D., Pennell, P., Wise, M., & Klicko, K. (2008). Self-efficacy and self-management behaviors in patients with chronic kidney disease. *Advances in Chronic Kidney Disease, 15*(2), 191–205.

Cutrona, C. E., & Suhr, J. A. (1994). Social support communication in the context of marriage: An analysis of couples' supportive interactions. In B. R. Burleson, T. L. Albrecht, & I. G. Sarason (Eds.), *Communication of social support: Messages, interactions, relationships, and community* (pp. 113–135). Thousand Oaks, CA: Sage.

Daly, A., Jennings, J., Beckett, J. O., & Leashore, B. R. (1995). Effective coping strategies of African Americans. *Social Work, 40,* 240–248.

Davenport, T. H., Prusak, L., & Wilson, H. J. (2003). Who's bringing you hot ideas and how are you responding?

Harvard Business Review, 81(2), 58–64, 124.

Davis, J. (2007). The effect of qualifying language on perceptions of drug appeal, drug experience, and estimates of side-effect incidence in DTC advertising. *Journal of Health Communication, 12*(7), 617–622.

Davis, K., Schoen, C., & Stremikis, K. (2010, June 23). Mirror, mirror on the wall: How the performance of the U.S. health care system compares internationally, 2010 update. The Commonwealth Fund. Retrieved from http://www.commonwealthfund.org/Publications/Fund-Reports/2010/Jun/Mirror-Mirror-Update.aspx?page=all

Davis, R. M. (2008). Achieving racial harmony for the benefit of patients and communities: Contrition, reconciliation, and collaboration. *Journal of the American Medical Association, 3003*(3), 323–325.

Davison, W. P. (1983). The third-person effect in communication. *Public Opinion Quarterly, 47*, 1–13.

Deary, I. J., Whiteman, M. C., & Fowkes, F. G. R. (1998). Medical research and the popular media. *The Lancet, 351*, 1726–1727.

deBusk, C., & Rangle, A., Jr. (nd). Creating a lean Six Sigma hospital discharge process. An iSixSigma case study. iSix Sigma Healthcare. Retrieved from http://healthcare.isixsigma.com/library/content/c040915a.asp

de Charms, R. (1968). *Personal causation: The internal effective determinants of behavior*. New York: Academic Press.

de Charms, R. (1977). Students need not be pawns. *Theory into Practice, 16*(4), 296–301.

de Droog, S. M., Valkenburg, P. M., & Buijzen, M. (2011). Using brand characters to promote young children's liking of and purchase requests for fruit. *Journal of Health Communication, 16*, 79–89. doi:10.1080/10810730.2010.529487

Deign, J. (2011, January 24). African m-health: How mobiles save lives in developing world. *The network: Cisco's technology news site*. Retrieved from http://newsroom.cisco.com/feature-content?type=webcontent&articleId=5879120

Delate, T., Simmons, V., & Motheral, B. (2004). Patterns of use of sildenafil among commercially insured adults in the United States: 1998–2002.

International Journal of Impotence Research, 16(4), 305–312.

DeLorne, D. E., Huh, J., & Reid, L. N. (2006). Age differences in how consumers behave following exposure to DTC advertising. *Health Communication, 20*(3), 255–265.

DeLucia, M. (2011, December 14). Dogs offer patient care that cannot be matched. Fox5 News, Las Vegas, Nevada. Retrieved from http://www.fox5vegas.com/story/16157761/pets-overcome-adversity-to-help-sunrise-patients-dogs-vegas-sunrise-hospital

Dennis, B. P., & Small, E. B. (2003). Incorporating cultural diversity in nursing care: An action plan. *Association of Black Nursing Faculty Journal, 14*(1), 17–25.

Dennis, M. R. (2006). Compliance and intimacy: Young adults' attempts to motivate health-promoting behaviors for romantic partners. *Health Communication, 19*(3), 259–267.

Dens, N., Eagle, L. C., & De Pelsmacker, P. (2008). Attitudes and self-reported behaviors of patients, doctors, and pharmacists in New Zealand and Belgium toward direct-to-consumer advertising of medication. *Health Communication, 23*, 45–61.

de Ridder, D. T. D., Theunissen, N. C. M., & van Dulmen, S. M. (2007). Does training general practitioners to elicit patients' illness representations and action plans influence their communication as a whole? *Patient Education and Counseling, 66*(3), 327–336.

Dervin, B. (1999, May). Sense-making's theory of dialogue: A brief introduction. Paper presented at a nondivisional workshop held at the meeting of the International Communication Association, San Francisco.

Dervin, B., & Frenette, M. (2001). Sense-making methodology: Communicating communicatively with campaign audiences. In R. Rice, & C. Atkin (Eds.), *Public Communication Campaigns* (3rd ed., pp. 69–87). Thousand Oaks, CA: Sage Publications.

DeSantis, A. D. (2002). Smoke screen: An ethnographic study of a cigar shop's collective rationalization. *Health Communication, 14*(2), 167–198.

Desrochers, D. M., & Holt, D. J. (2007). Children's exposure to

television advertising: Implications for childhood obesity. *Journal of Public Policy & Marketing, 26*(2), 182–201.

Diem, S. J., Lantos, J. D., & Tulsky, J. A. (1996). Cardiopulmonary resuscitation on television: Miracles and misinformation. *New England Journal of Medicine, 334*, 1578–1582.

DiFranza, J. R., Richard, J. W., Paulman, P. M., Wolf-Gillespie, N., Fletcher, C., Jaffe, R. D., & Murray, D. (1991). RJR Nabisco's cartoon camel promotes Camel cigarettes to children. *Journal of the American Medical Association, 266*, 3149–3153.

Dill, M. J., & Salsberg, E. S. (2008, November). The complexities of physician supply and demand projections through 2025. Center for Workforce Studies, American Association of Medical Colleges. Retrieved from http://www.innovationlabs.com/pa_future/1/background_docs/AAMC%20Complexities%20of%20physician%20demand,%202008.pdf

Dillard, A. J., McCaul, K. D., Kelso, P. D., & Klein, W. M. P. (2006). Resisting good news: Reactions to breast cancer risk communication. *Health Communication, 19*(2), 115–123.

Dillard, J. P., Carson, C. L., Bernard, C. J., Laxova, A., & Farrell, P. M. (2004). An analysis of communication following newborn screening for cystic fibrosis. *Health Communication, 16*(2), 195–206.

Dillard, J. P., & Nabi, R. L. (2006). The persuasive influence of emotion in cancer prevention and detection messages. *Journal of Communication, 56*, S123–S139.

Dillard, J. P., Shen, L., Laxova, A., & Farrell, P. (2008). Potential threats to the effective communication of genetic risk information: The case of cystic fibrosis. *Health Communication, 23*(3), 234–244.

Dillon, P. J. (2012). Assessing the influence of patient participation in primary care medical interviews on recall of treatment recommendations. *Health Communication, 27*, 58–65.

DiLorenzo, T. J., & Bennett, J. T. (1998, May). The U.S. is becoming a nanny state. *USA Today Magazine, 126*, 12–15.

Diversity in medical education: Fact and figures. (2008). Association of American Medical Colleges. Retrieved from https://members.aamc.org/eweb/upload/Diversity%20in%20Medical%20Education%20Facts%20and%20Fig%202008.pdf

Do, T.-P., & Geist, P. (2000). Embodiment and disembodiment: Identity transformation and persons with physical disabilities. In D. O. Braithwaite & T. L. Thompson (Eds.), *Handbook of communication and people with disabilities: Research and applications* (pp. 49–65). Mahwah, NJ: Lawrence Erlbaum.

Doctor–patient communication by race/ethnicity, family income, insurance, and residence, 2004. (2008). Results of the National Scorecard on U.S. Health System Performance, 2008. New York: The Commonwealth Fund. Retrieved from http://www.commonwealthfund.org/chart cartcharts/chartcartcharts_show.htm?doc_id=694048

Doctors for Global Health. (nd). Review of U.S. health care law from a human right perspective. Decatur, GA: Author. Retrieved from http://www.dghonline.org/content/health-care-reform-us

Donahue, M. O., Piazza, I. M., Griffin, M. Q., Dykes, P. C., & Fitzpatrick, J. J. (2008). The relationship between nurses' perceptions of empowerment and patient satisfaction. *Applied Nursing Research, 21*, 2–7.

Donnelly, L. (2008, February 17). Families pay 1,200 pounds a year to supplement NHS medical care. *Sunday Telegraph* (London), News, p. 6. Retrieved through LexisNexis Academic.

Donohew, L. (1990). Public health campaigns: Individual message strategies. In E. B. Ray & L. Donohew (Eds.), *Communication and health: Systems and applications* (pp. 136–170). Hillsdale, NJ: Lawrence Erlbaum.

Donohew, L., Palmgreen, P., & Duncan, J. (1980). An activation model of information exposure. *Communication Monographs, 47*, 295–303.

Donovan-Kicken, E., Tollison, A. C., & Goins, E. S. (2011). A grounded theory of control over communication among individuals with cancer. *Journal of Applied Communication Research, 39*, 310–330.

Dora, C. (Ed.). (2006). *Health, hazards, and public debate: Lessons for risk communication from the BSE/CJD saga.* Copenhagen: World Health Organization Europe.

Dorsey, J. L., & Berwick, D. M. (2008, February 27). Dirty words in healthcare. *Boston Globe*, Op-Ed, p. A9.

Douglas, C. (1994). The barber trembles. *British Medical Journal, 68*, 184.

Douglas, J. E. (2008, May). NightHawk Teleradiology Services: A template for pathology? *Bnet*, np. Retrieved from http://findarticles.com/p/articles/mi_qa3725/is_200805/ai_n25500303

Douki, S., Zineb, S. B., Nacef, F., & Halbreich, U. (2007). Women's mental health in the Muslim world: Cultural, religious, and social issues. *Journal of Affective Disorders, 102*(1–3), 177–189.

Dowling, C. G. (1997, February). Through the ages, artists and doctors have confronted the mysteries of anatomy. *Life, 20*, 48–56.

Dranove, D. (2008). *Code red: An economist explains how to revive the healthcare system without destroying it.* Princeton: NJ: Princeton University Press.

Drucker, P. F. (1993). *Post-capitalistic society.* New York: HarperCollins.

Drum, D. (1997, November 17). Product placement matures into placement of nonprofit causes. *Variety, 369*, S27–S28.

D'Silva, M. U., & Palmgreen, P. (2007). Individual differences and context: Mediating recall of anti-drug public service announcements. *Health Communication, 21*(1), 65–71.

Dudo, A. D., Dahlstrom, M. F., & Broussard, D. (2007). Reporting a potential pandemic: A risk-related assessment of avian influenza coverage in U.S. newspapers. *Science Communication, 28*(4), 429–454.

Duewald, M. (2003, June 22). Body and image; one size definitely does not fit all. *The New York Times* online. Retrieved from http://query.nytimes.com/gst/fullpage.html?sec=health&res=9F0DE7DD1638F931A15755C0A9659C8B63

Duffy, G. L., Moran, J. W., & Riley, W. J. (2010). *Quality function deployment and Lean Six Sigma applications in public health.* Milwaukee, WI: Quality Press.

Duffy, J. (1979). *The healers: A history of American medicine.* Urbana: University of Illinois Press.

Duggan, A. (2006). Understanding interpersonal communication processes across health contexts: Advances in the last decade and challenges for the next decade. *Journal of Health Communication, 11*, 93–108.

Duggan, A., Bradshaw, Y. S., Carroll, S. E., Rattigan, S. H., & Altman, W. (2009). What can I learn from this interaction? A qualitative analysis of medical student self-reflection and learning in a standardized patient exercise about disability. *Journal of Health Communication, 14*, 797–811. doi:10.1080/10810730903295526

Duggleby, W. (2003). Helping Hispanic/Latino home health patients manage their pain. *Home Healthcare Nurse, 21*(3), 174–179.

du Pré, A. (1998). *Humor and the healing arts: Multimethod analysis of humor use in health care.* Mahwah, NJ: Lawrence Erlbaum.

du Pré, A. (2002). Accomplishing the impossible: Talking about body and soul and mind during a medical visit. *Health Communication, 14*(1), 1–22.

du Pré, A. (2005). Making empowerment work: Medical center soars in satisfaction ratings. In E. B. Ray (Ed.), *Health communication in practice: A case study approach* (pp. 311–322). Mahwah, NJ: Lawrence Erlbaum.

du Pré, A., & Beck, C. S. (1997). "How can I put this?" Exaggerated self-disparagement as alignment strategy during problematic disclosures by patients to doctors. *Qualitative Health Research, 7*, 487–503.

du Pré, A., & Ray, E. B. (2008). Comforting episodes: Transcendent experiences of cancer survivors. In L. Sparks, H. D. O'Hair, & G. L. Kreps (Eds.), *Cancer, communication and aging* (pp. 99–114). Cresskill, NJ: Hampton Press.

Dutta, M. J. (2006). Theoretical approaches to entertainment education campaigns: A subaltern critique. *Health Communication, 20*(3), 221–231.

Dutta, M. J. (2008). *Communicating health: A culture-centered approach.* Cambridge, MA: Polity Press.

Dutta, M. J., Bodie, G. D., & Basu, A. (2008). Health disparity and the racial divide among the nation's youth: Internet as a site for change? In A. Everett (Ed.), *Learning race and ethnicity: Youth and the digital media* (pp. 175–198). Cambridge, MA: MIT Press.

Dutta, M. J., & Boyd, J. (2007). Turning "smoking man" images around: Portrayals of smoking in men's magazines as a blueprint for smoking cessation campaigns. *Health Communication, 22*(3), 253–263.

Dutta, M. J., & de Souza, R. (2008). The past, present, and future of health development campaigns: Reflexivity and the critical-cultural approach. *Health Communication, 23*(4), 326–339.

Dutta-Bergman, M. J. (2005). Theory and practice in health communication campaigns: A critical interrogation. *Health Communication, 18*(2), 103–122.

Dwyer, F. R., Schurr, P. H., & Oh, S. (1987). Developing buyer-seller relationships. *Journal of Marketing, 51*(2), 11–27.

Dyche, L., & Swiderski, D. (2005). The effect of physician solicitation approaches on ability to identify patient concerns. *Journal of General Internal Medicine, 20*(3), 267–270.

Dyer, J. (1996). *In a tangled wood: An Alzheimer's journey.* Dallas: Southern Methodist University Press.

Dym, H. (2008). Risk management techniques for the general dentist and specialist. *Dental Clinics of North America, 52*(3), 563–577.

Eastin, M. S., & Griffiths, R. P. (2006). Beyond the shooter game: Examining presence and hostile outcomes among male game players. *Communication Research, 33,* 448–466.

Eastman, J. K., Eastman, K. L., & Tolson, M. A. (1997). The ethics of managed care: An initial look at physicians' perspectives. *Marketing Health Services, 17,* 26–40.

Ebrahim, S. H., Anderson, J., Weidle, P., & Purcell, D. W. (2003). Race-related knowledge gap about treatment for HIV/AIDS, United States, 2001. Paper presented at the National HIV Prevention Conference, Atlanta.

Eccles, N. (2012, February 1). Telemedicine in developing countries: Challenges and successes. *Harvard College Global Health Review* online. Retrieved from http://www.hcs.harvard.edu/hghr/2012/02/01/telemedicine-in-developing-countrieschallenges-and-successes/

Economic Research Initiative on the Uninsured. (2005, December). Rising health care costs frustrate efforts to reduce uninsured rate, No. 10. Retrieved from eriu.sph.umich.edu/pdf/highlight-chernew.pdf

Economic Research Institute. (2012). Top managed care executive salary survey data. Redmond, VA: Author. Retrieved from http://www.erieri.com/index.cfm?fuseaction=research.Top-Managed-Care-Executive-salary-data-details&PositionId=7545&CityId=300

Edelstein, L. (1967). *Ancient medicine.* Baltimore: Johns Hopkins University Press.

Edgar, T. (1992). A compliance-based approach to the study of condom use. In T. Edgar, M. A. Fitzpatrick, & V. S. Freimuth (Eds.), *AIDS: A communication perspective* (pp. 47–67). Hillsdale, NJ: Lawrence Erlbaum.

Edgar, T., Freimuth, V., & Hammond, S. L. (2003). Lessons learned from the field on prevention and health campaigns. In T. L. Thompson, A. M. Dorsey, K. I. Miller, & R. Parrott (Eds.), *Handbook of health communication* (pp. 625–636). Mahwah, NJ: Lawrence Erlbaum.

Edgar, T. M., Satterfield, D. W., & Whaley, B. B. (2005). Explanations of illness: A bridge to understanding. In E. B. Ray (Ed.), *Health communication in practice: A case study approach* (pp. 95–109). Mahwah, NJ: Lawrence Erlbaum.

Educational programs in U.S. medical schools, 2001–2002. (2002, September 4). *Journal of the American Medical Association, 288*(9), 1067–1072.

Edwards, H., & Noller, P. (1998). Factors influencing caregiver–care receiver communication and the impact on the well-being of older care receivers. *Health Communication, 10,* 317–342.

Egan, T. (1988, May 1). Rebuffed by Oregon, patients take their life-or-death cases public. *The New York Times,* online. Retrieved from http://query.nytimes.com/gst/fullpage.html?res=940DE4DC1638F932A35756C0A96E948260&sec=health&spon=&pagewanted=all

Egbert, N., Koch, L., Coeling, H., & Ayers, D. (2006). The role of social support in the family and community integration of right-hemisphere stroke survivors. *Health Communication, 20*(1), 45–55.

Egbert, N., Sparks, L., Kreps, G. L., & du Pré, A. (2008). Finding meaning in the journey: Methods of spiritual coping for aging patients with cancer. In L. Sparks, H. D. O'Hair, & G. L. Kreps (Eds.), *Cancer, communication and aging* (pp. 277–291). Cresskill, NJ: Hampton Press.

Egerton, J. (2007, September 21). 11 ways to keep your patients satisfied: Your front-desk staff can make the patient experience positive or turn them off. Here's how to make sure that all goes well. *Medical Economics, 84*(18), 50–52.

Eggly, S. (2002). Physician–patient co-construction of illness narratives in the medical interview. *Health Communication, 14*(3), 339–360.

Eisenberg, E. M., Baglia, J., & Pynes, J. E. (2006). Transforming emergency medicine through narrative: Qualitative action research at a community hospital. *Health Communication, 19*(3), 197–208.

Eisenberg, E., & Goodall, H., Jr. (2004). *Organizational communication: Balancing creativity and constraint.* New York: Bedford/St. Martin's.

Ellingson, L. L. (2007). The performance of dialysis care: Routinization and adaptation on the floor. *Health Communication, 22*(2), 103–114.

Ellingson, L. L. (2011). The poetics of professionalism among dialysis technicians. *Health Communication, 26,* 1–12.

Elliott, C. (2007). Assessing "fun foods": Nutritional content and analysis of supermarket foods targeted at children. *Obesity Reviews, 9*(4), 368–377.

Ellis, B. H., & Miller, K. I. (1993). The role of assertiveness, personal control, and participation in the prediction of nurse burnout. *Journal of Applied Communication, 17,* 327–342.

Ely, J. W., Levinson, W., Elder, N. C., Mainous, A. G., III, & Vinson, D. C. (1995). Perceived causes of family physicians' errors. *Journal of Family Practice, 40,* 337–344.

The e-mail advantage. (2007, September 7). *Medical Economics, 84*(17), 28.

Emanuel, E. J., & Emanuel, L. L. (1995). Four models of the

physician–patient relationship. In J. D. Arras & B. Steinbock (Eds.), *Ethical issues in modern medicine* (4th ed., pp. 67–76). Mountain View, CA: Mayfield.

Emanuel, E. J., & Emanuel, L. L. (1998, May 16). The promise of a good death. *The Lancet, 351*, S21–S29.

Eng, T. R., Maxfield, A., Patrick, K., Deering, M. J., Ratzan, S. C., & Gustafson, D. H. (1998). Access to health information and support. *Journal of the American Medical Association, 279*, 1371.

English, J., Wilson, K., & Keller-Olaman, S. (2008). Health, healing and recovery: Therapeutic landscapes and the everyday lives of breast cancer survivors. *Social Science & Medicine, 67*, 68–78.

Entertainomercials. (1996, November 4). *Forbes, 158*, 322–323.

Epstein, R. M., Fiscella, K., Lesser, C. S., & Stange, K. C. (2010). Why the nation needs a policy push on patient-centered health care. New York, NY: The Commonwealth Fund. Retrieved from http://www.commonwealthfund.org/Publications/In-the-Literature/2010/Aug/Why-the-Nation-Needs-a-Policy-Push.aspx

Erdelyi, M, H., & Zizak, D. M. (2004). Beyond gizmo subliminality. In L. J. Shrum (Ed.), *The psychology of entertainment media: Blurring the lines between entertainment and persuasion* (pp. 13–44). Mahwah, NJ: Lawrence Erlbaum.

Erdman, L. (1993). Laughter therapy for patients with cancer. *Journal of psychosocial oncology, 11*, 55–67.

Erickson, S. (2008, May 16). The day I received my final verdict: A lawsuit left the author with worries about his reputation, until a surprising visit took place. *Medical Economics, 85(10)*, 32–33.

Evans, W. D., Uhrig, J., Davis, K., & McCormack, L. (2009). Efficacy methods to evaluate health communication and marketing campaigns. *Journal of Health Communication, 14*, 315–330. doi:10.1080/10810730902872234

Evercare study of the economic downturn and its impact on family caregiving. (2009, March). Evercare by United Healthcare (Minnetonka, MN) and the National Alliance for Caregiving (Bethesda, MD). Retrieved from http://www.nfcacares.org/

who_are_family_caregivers/care_giving_statstics.cfm

Everett, M. W., & Palmgreen, P. (1995). Influences of sensation seeking, message sensation value, and program context on effectiveness of anticocaine public service announcement. *Health Communication, 7*, 225–248.

Exposure to stress: Occupational hazards in hospitals. (2008, July). Atlanta: Centers for Disease Control and Prevention (CDC). Retrieved from http://www.cdc.gov/niosh/docs/2008-136/default.html

Facts about eating disorders. (2011). Washington, DC: Eating Disorders Coalition. Retrieved from http://www.eatingdisorderscoalition.org/documents/TalkingpointsEatingDisordersFactSheetUpdated5-20-09.pdf

Faden, R. R. (1987). Ethical issues in government sponsored public health campaigns. *Health Education Quarterly, 14*, 27–37.

Fahey, K. F., Rao, S. M., Douglas, M. K., Thomas, M. L., Elliott, J. E., & Miaskowski, C. (2008). Nurse coaching to explore and modify patient attitudinal barriers interfering with effective cancer pain management. *Oncology Nursing Forum, 35(2)*, 234–240.

Fanning, M. M. (1997). A circular organization chart promotes a hospital-wide focus on teams. *Hospital & Health Services Administration, 42*, 243–264.

Farber, N. J., Novack, D. H., & O'Brien, M. K. (1997). Love, boundaries, and the patient–physician relationship. *Archives of Internal Medicine, 157*, 229–294.

Farrar, K. M., Krcmar, M., & Nowak, K. L. (2006). Contextual features of violent video games, mental models, and aggression. *Journal of Communication, 56*, 387–405.

Farrelly, M. C., Healton, C. G., Davis, K. C., Messeri, P., & Haviland, M. L. (2002, June). Getting to the truth: Evaluating national tobacco countermarketing campaigns. *American Journal of Public Health, 92(6)*, 901–907.

Farrelly, M. C., Nonnemaker, J., Davis, K. C., & Hussin, A. (2009). The influence of the national truth® campaign on smoking initiation. *American Journal of Preventive Medicine, 36*, 379–384. Doi: 10.1016/j.amepre.2009.01.019.

Fearn-Banks, K. (1996). *Crisis communication: A casebook approach.* Mahwah, NJ: Lawrence Erlbaum.

Feinberg, L., Reinhard, S. C., Houser, A., & Choula, R. (2011). Valuing the invaluable: 2011 update. The growing contributions and costs of family caregiving. American Association of Retired Persons (AARP) Policy Institute. Retrieved from http://assets.aarp.org/rgcenter/ppi/ltc/i51-caregiving.pdf

Feldman, S. (2008). 2007 Dr.Score.com annual report card on patient satisfaction in the U.S. DrScore.com. Retrieved from http://www.drscore.com/press/report/012508.pdf

Fenton, J. J., Jerant A. F., Bertakis, K. D., & Franks, P. (2012). The cost of satisfaction: A national study of patient satisfaction, health care utilization, expenditures, and mortality. *Archives of Internal Medicine, 172*, 405–411. doi:10.1001/archinternmed.2011.1662

Ferguson, B., Lowman, S. G., & DeWalt, D. A. (2011). Assessing literacy in clinical and community settings: The patient perspective. *Journal of Health Communication, 16*, 124–134. doi:10.1080/10810730.2010.535113

Ferguson, J. A., Weinberger, M., Westmoreland, G. R., Mamlin, L. A., Segar, D. S., Green, J. Y., Martin, D. K., & Tierney, W. M. (1998). Racial disparity in cardiac decision making: Results from patient focus groups. *Archives of Internal Medicine, 158*, 1450–1453.

Ferguson, T. (1997, November-December). Health care in cyberspace: Patients lead a revolution. *The Futurist, 31(6)*, 29–34.

Ferguson, W. J. (2008). Un poquito. *Health Affairs, 27(6)*, 1695–1700. Retrieved from http://content.healthaffairs.org/cgi/content/full/27/6/1695

Fertility acupuncture: Fear and discovery. (2012, May 23). Path to Fertility blog. Retrieved from http://fertility-news.rmact.com/Path-To-Fertility-Blog/bid/105392/Fertility-Acupuncture-My-Personal-Experience-with-RMACT-Experts

Festinger, L. (1957). *A theory of cognitive dissonance.* Stanford, CA: Stanford University Press.

Finally, an antidote to TV drug ads. (2007, November 1). Yonkers, NY: Consumer Reports. Retrieved from http://blogs.consumerreports.org/health/2007/11/finally-an-anti.html?resultPageIndex=1&resultIndex=2&searchTerm=patient%20requests%20for%20advertised%20drugs

Fiore, K. (2011, August 22). Drug ads skirt FDA regulations. *ABC news online*. Retrieved from http://abcnews.go.com/Health/drug-advertisements-skirt-fda-regulations-study/story?id=14355765#.T_w_sRzH-SCA

Fischer, P. M., Schwartz, M. P., Richards, J. W., & Goldstein, A. O. (1991). Brand logo recognition by children aged 3 to 6 years: Mickey Mouse and Old Joe the Camel. *Journal of the American Medical Association, 266*, 3154–3158.

Fisher, B. (2008, April 18). Hospitalists: Look a bit deeper. Letter to the editor. *Medical Economics, 85*(8), 17.

Fisher, J. A. (1994). *The plague makers*. New York: Simon & Schuster.

Fisher, J. D., Goff, B. A., Nadler, A., & Chinsky, J. M. (1988). Social psychological influences on help seeking and support from peers. In B. H. Gottlieb (Ed.), *Marshaling social support: Formats, processes, and effects* (pp. 267–304). Newbury Park, CA: Sage.

Fisher, L. B. (2007, March). President Bush's major post-Katrina speeches: Enhancing image repair. Discourse theory applied to the public sector. *Public Relations Review, 33*(1), 40–48.

Fisher, S. (1984). Institutional authority and the structure of discourse. *Discourse Processes, 7*, 201–224.

Fishman, T. (1995). The 90-second intervention: A patient compliance medical technique to improve and control hypertension. *Public Health Reports, 110*, 173–178.

Flay, B. R., & Burton, D. (1990). Effective mass communication strategies for health campaigns. In C. Atkin & L. Wallack (Eds.), *Mass communication and public health* (pp. 129–146). Newbury Park, CA: Sage.

Florida hospital surgeons mistakenly amputate wrong leg of patient. (1995, March 20). *Jet online*. Retrieved from http://findarticles.com/p/articles/mi_m1355/is_n19_v87/ai_16717100

Floyd, K., Hesse, C., & Haynes, M. T. (2007, January). Human affection exchange: SV. Metabolic and cardiovascular correlates of trait expressed affection. *Communication Quarterly, 55*(1), 79–94.

Flynn, J. J., Hollenstein, T., & Mackey, A. (2010). The effect of suppressing and not accepting emotions on depressive symptoms: Is suppression different for men and women? *Personality and Individual Differences, 49*, 49582–49586. doi:10.1016/j.paid.2010.05.022

Fonarow, G. C., Abraham, W. T., Albert, N. M., Stough, W. G., Gheorghiade, M., Greenberg, B. H., O'Connor, C. M., Pieper, K., Sun, J. L., Yancy, C. W., & Young, J. B. (2008). Factors identified as precipitating hospital admissions for heart failure and clinical outcomes: Findings from OPTIMIZE-HF. *Archives of Internal Medicine, 168*(8), 847–854.

Ford, L. A., Babrow, A. S., & Stohl, C. (1996). Social support messages and the management of uncertainty in the experience of breast cancer: An application of problematic integration theory. *Communication Monographs, 63*, 189–208.

Ford, L. A., & Christmon, B. C. (2005). "Every cancer is different": Illness narratives and the management of identity in breast cancer. In E. B. Ray (Ed.), *Health communication in practice: A case study approach* (pp. 157–170). Mahwah, NJ: Lawrence Erlbaum.

Ford, L. A., & Yep, G. A. (2003). Working along the margins: Developing community-based strategies for communicating about health with marginalized groups. In T. L. Thompson, A. M. Dorsey, K. I. Miller, & R. Parrott (Eds.), *Handbook of health communication* (pp. 241–261). Mahwah, NJ: Lawrence Erlbaum.

Former UCLA employee indicted for HIPAA violations over celebs. (2008, May 5). *Modern Healthcare, 38*(18), 4.

Forrest, C. B., Shadmi, E., Nutting, P. A., & Starfield, B. (2007). Specialty referral completion among primary care patients: Results from the ASPN referral study. *Annals of Family Medicine, 5*(4), 361–367.

Forte, D. A. (1995). Community-based breast cancer intervention programs for older African American women in beauty salons. *Public Health Reports, 110*, 179–183.

Foster, E. (2007). *Communicating at the end of life: Finding magic in the mundane*. Mahwah, NJ: Lawrence Erlbaum.

Foubister, V. (1997). Advisory panel encourages minority doctor involvement. *American Medical News, 40*, 24.

Fowler, B. A. (2006). Claiming health: Mammography screening decision making of African American women. *Oncology Nursing Forum, 33*(5), 969–975.

Fowler, C., & Nussbaum, J. (2008). Communicating with the aging patient. In K. B. Wright & S. D. Moore (Eds.), *Applied health communication* (pp. 159–178). Cresskill, NJ: Hampton Press.

Fox, M. (2009). U.S. hospital profits fall to zero: Thomson Reuters. *Reuters online*. Retrieved from http://www.reuters.com/article/2009/03/02/us-hospitals-usa-idUSTRE5216G320090302

Frampton, S., Gilpin, L., & Charmel, P. (Eds.) (2003). *Putting patients first: Designing and practicing patient-centered care*. San Francisco: Jossey-Bass.

Frank, E., Carrera, J. S., Stratton, T., Bickel, J., & Nora, L. M. (2006). Experiences of belittlement and harassment and their correlates among medical students in the United States: Longitudinal survey. *British Medical Journal, 333*, 682–684.

Frank, E., Modi, S., Elon L., & Coughlin, S. S. (2008). U.S. medical students' attitudes about patients' access to care. *Preventive Medicine, 47*(1), 140–145.

Frankel, R. M., & Beckman, H. B. (1989). Conversation and compliance with treatment recommendations: An application of micro-interactional analysis in medicine. In L. Grossberg, B. J. O'Keefe, & E. Wartella (Eds.), *Rethinking communication: Vol. 2. Paradigm exemplars* (pp. 60–74). Newbury Park, CA: Sage.

Frankl, V. E. (1959). *Man's search for meeting*. Boston: Beacon Press.

Frates, J., Bohrer, G. G., & Thomas, D. (2006). Promoting organ donation to Hispanics: The role of the media and medicine. *Journal of Health Communication, 11*(7), 683–698.

Freimuth, V. S. (2006). Order out of chaos: The self-organization of communication following the anthrax attacks. *Health Communication, 20*(2), 141–148.

Freimuth, V. S., Stein, J. A., & Kean, T. J. (1989). *Searching for health information: The cancer information service model.* Philadelphia: University of Pennsylvania Press.

Frey, L. R., Botan, C. H., Friedman, P. G., & Kreps, G. (1991). *Investigating communication: An introduction to research methods.* Englewood Cliffs, NJ: Prentice Hall.

Fried, L. P., Francomano, C. A., MacDonald, S. M., Wagener, E. M., Stokes, E. J., Carbone, K. M., Bias, W. B., Newman, M. M., & Stobo, J. D. (1996). Career development for women in academic medicine: Multiple interventions in a department of medicine. *Journal of the American Medical Association, 276,* 898–906.

Friedman, D. M. (2003). *A mind of its own: A cultural history of the penis.* New York: Penguin.

Friedman, H. S., & DiMatteo, M. R. (1979). Health care as an interpersonal process. *Journal of Social Issues, 35,* 1–11.

Friedmann, E., & Thomas, S. A. (1995). Pet ownership, social support, and one-year survival after acute myocardial infarction in the cardiac arrhythmia suppression trial. *American Journal of Cardiology, 76,* 1213–1217.

Friedrich, D. D. (2001). *Successful aging: Integrating contemporary ideas, research findings, and intervention strategies.* Springfield, IL: Charles C Thomas Publisher.

Frith, K., Shaw, P., & Cheng, H. (2005). The construction of beauty: A cross-cultural analysis of women's magazine advertising. *Journal of Communication, 55*(1), 56–70.

Fry, R. B., & Prentice-Dunn, S. (2005). Effects of coping information and value affirmation on responses to a perceived health threat. *Health Communication, 17*(2), 133–147.

Fuchs-Lacelle, S., Hadjistavropoulos, T., & Lix, L. (2008). Pain assessment as intervention: A study of older adults with severe dementia. *Clinical Journal of Pain, 24*(8), 697–707.

Gabbard-Alley, A. S. (1995). Health communication and gender: A review and critique. *Health Communication, 7,* 35–54.

Gabbard-Alley, A. S. (2000). Explaining illness: An examination of message strategies and gender. In B. B. Whaley (Ed.), *Explaining illness* (pp. 147–170). Mahwah, NJ: Lawrence Erlbaum.

Gade, C. J. (2007). Understanding and defining roles in the pharmacist-patient relationship. *Journal of Communication in Healthcare, 1,* 88–98.

Gallagher, S., Phillips, A. C., Ferraro, A. J., Drayson, M. T., & Carroll, D. (2008). Social communication is positively associated with the immunoglobulin M response to vaccination with pneumococcal polysaccharides. *Biological Psychology, 78*(2), 211–215.

Gallo, L. C., Smith, T. W., & Cox, C. M. (2006). Socioeconomic status, psychosocial processes, and perceived health: An interpersonal perspective. *Annals of Behavioral Medicine, 31*(2), 109–119.

Gamlin, R. (1999). Sexuality: A challenge for nursing practice. *Nursing Times, 95*(7), 48–50.

Gany, F., Kapelusznik, L., Prakash, K., Gonzalez, J., Orta, L. Y., Tseng, C.-H., & Changrani, J. (2007). The impact of medical interpretation method on time and errors. *Journal of Internal Medicine, 22,* Supplement 2, 319–323.

Gany, F., & Ngo-Metzger, Q. (2008, January 17). Language barriers in health care: Special supplement. *Journal of General Internal Medicine,* online. Retrieved from http://www.commonwealthfund.org/publications/publications_show.htm?doc_id=649185

Garfinkel, H. (1967). *Studies in ethnomethodology.* Cambridge, MA: Polity Press/Basil Blackwell.

Garrison, F. H. (1929). *An introduction to the history of medicine* (4th ed.). Philadelphia: W. B. Saunders.

Gaster, B., Unterborn, J. N., Scott, R. B., & Schneeweiss, R. (2007, October). What should students learn about complementary and alternative medicine? *Journal of the Association of American Medical Colleges, 82*(10), 934–938.

Gearon, C. J. (2002). Planetree (25 years older). *Hospitals & Health Networks, 76*(10), 40–43.

Geist, P., & Dreyer, J. (1993). The demise of dialogue: A critique of medical encounter dialogue. *Western Journal of Communication, 57,* 233–246.

Geist, P., & Gates, L. (1996). The poetics and politics of recovering identities in health communication. *Communication Studies, 47,* 218–228.

Geist-Martin, P., & Bell, K. K. (2009). "Open your heart first of all": Perspectives of holistic providers in Costa Rica about communication in the provision of health care. *Health Communication, 24,* 631–646. doi:10.1080/10410230903242234

Geller, G., Bernhardt, B. A., Carrese, J., Rushton, C. H., & Kolodner, K. (2008). What do clinicians derive from partnering with their patients? Reliable and valid measure of "personal meaning in patient care." *Patient Education and Counseling, 72,* 293–300.

Gelsema, T. I., van der Doef, M., Maes, S., Janssen, M., Akerboom, S., & Verhoeven, C. (2006). A longitudinal study of job stress in the nursing profession: Causes and consequences. *Journal of Nursing Management, 14*(4), 289–299.

Genworth 2012 cost of care survey. (2012, April 20). Genworth Life Insurance Company, New York. Retrieved from http://www.genworth.com/content/etc/medialib/genworth_v2/pdf/ltc_cost_of_care.Par.40001.File.dat/2012%20Cost%20of%20Care%20Survey%20Full%20Report.pdf

Gerardy, J. (2012). Africa turns to cellphone for better health. mhealth Alliance web post retrieved from http://www.mhealthalliance.org/news/africa-turns-cellphones-better-health

Gerbner, G. (1996, Fall). TV violence and what to do about it. *Nieman Reports, 50,* 10–12.

Gerbner, G., Gross, L., Morgan, M., & Signorelli, N. (1994). *Living with television: The dynamics of the cultivation process.* In J. Bryant & D. Zillmann (Eds.), *Perspectives on media effects* (pp. 17–40). Hillsdale, NJ: Lawrence Erlbaum.

Getting doctors out in the neighborhoods. (2002, June 17). Davis, CA: UC (University of California) Newsroom. Retrieved from http://www.universityofcalifornia.edu/news/article/4472

Getting old is a pain. (2003, August). *National Geographic* (unnumbered Geographica supplement).

Gibson, T. A. (2007, May). WARNING—the existing media system may be toxic to your health: Health communication and the politics of media reform. *Journal of Applied Communication Research, 35*(2), 125–132.

Gidwani, P. P., Sobol, A., DeJong, W., Perrin, J. M., & Gortmaker, S. L. (2002, September). Television viewing and initiation of smoking among youth. *Pediatrics, 110*(3), 505–508.

Giles, H., Ballard, D., & McCann, R. M. (2002). Perceptions of intergenerational communication across cultures: An Italian case. *Perceptual and Motor Skills, 95*, 583–591.

Giles, L. C., Glonek, G. F., Luszcz, M. A., & Andrews, G. R. (2005, July). Effect of social networks on 10-year survival in very old Australians: The Australian longitudinal study of aging. *Journal of Epidemiology & Community Health, 59*(7), 574–579.

Gill, E. A., & Babrow, A. S. (2007). To hope or to know: Coping with uncertainty and ambivalence in women's magazine breast cancer articles. *Journal of Applied Communication Research, 35*(2), 133–155.

Gillespie, S. R. (2001). The politics of breathing: Asthmatic Medicaid patients under managed care. *Journal of Applied Communication Research, 29*(2), 97–116.

Gillisen, A. (2007). Patient's adherence in asthma. *Journal of Physiology and Pharmacology, 58*, Supplement 5, 205–222.

Glass, R. M. (1996). The patient–physician relationship: JAMA focuses on the center of medicine. *Journal of the American Medical Association, 275*, 147–148.

Glik, D. C. (2007, April). Risk communication for public health emergencies. *Annual Review of Public Health, 28*, 33–54.

Global AIDS epidemic. Fact sheet. Global reports. (2010). UNAIDS, a United Nations program. Author: Geneva, Switzerland. Retrieved from http://www.unaids.org/documents/20101123_FS_Global_em_en.pdf

Goffman, E. (1963). *Stigma: Notes on the management of spoiled identity.* Englewood Cliffs, NJ: Prentice Hall.

Goffman, E. (1967). *Interaction rituals.* New York: Pantheon Books.

Goffman, E. (1974). *Frame analysis: An essay on the organization of experience.* New York: Harper Colophon.

Goldsmith, D. J. (1994). The role of facework in supportive communication. In B. R. Burleson, T. L. Albrecht, & I. G. Sarason (Eds.), *Communication of social support: Messages, interactions, relationships, and community* (pp. 29–49). Thousand Oaks, CA: Sage.

Goldstein, J. (2008, May 13). Insurers pay caregivers to track patients. *Philadelphia Inquirer,* Health Daily, p. A01.

Goode, E. E. (1993, February 15). The cultures of illness. *U.S. News & World Report, 114*, 74–76.

Goodnight, T. G. (1982). The personal, technical, and public spheres of argument: A speculative inquiry into the art of public deliberation. *Journal of the American Forensic Association, 18*, 214–227.

Gorawara-Bhat, R., Gallagher, T. H., & Levinson, W. (2003). Patient-provider discussions about conflicts of interest in managed care: Physicians' perceptions. *American Journal of Managed Care, 9*(8), 564–571.

Gordon, E. J., Leon, J. B., & Sehgal, A. R. (2003). Why are hemodialysis treatments shortened and skipped? Development of a taxonomy and relationship to patient subgroups. *Nephrology Nursing Journal, 30*(2), 209–217.

Gordon, R. G., Jr. (Ed.), 2005. *Ethnologue: Languages of the world* (15th ed.). Dallas, TX: SIL International. Retrieved from http://www.ethnologue.com

Gorter, R. C., Bleeker, J. C., & Freeman, R. (2006). Dental nurses on perceived gender differences in their dentist's communication and interaction style. *British Dental Journal. 201*(3), 159–164.

Gotcher, J. M. (1995). Well-adjusted and maladjusted cancer patients: An examination of communication variables. *Health Communication, 7*, 21–33.

Govindarajan, A., & Schull, M. (2003). Effect of socioeconomic status on out-of-hospital transport delays of patients with chest pain. *Annals of Emergency Medicine, 41*(4), 481–490.

Grady, M., & Edgar, T. (2003). Racial disparities in healthcare: Highlights from focus group findings. In B. D. Smedley, A. Y. Stith, & A. R. Nelson (Eds.), *Unequal treatment: Confronting racial and ethnic disparities in health care* (pp. 392–405). Board on Health Sciences Policy. Institute of Medicine. Retrieved December 3, 2008, from http://books.nap.edu/openbook.php?isbn=030908265X

Granovetter, M. S. (1973). The strength of weak ties. *American Journal of Sociology, 78*, 1360–1380.

Granovetter, M. S. (1983). The strength of weak ties: A network theory revisited. *Sociological Theory, 1*, 201–233.

Grant, C. J., III, Cissna, K. N., & Rosenfeld, L. B. (2000). Patients' perceptions of physicians' communication and outcomes of the accrual to trial process. *Health Communication, 12*(1), 23–39.

Green, E. C., & Witte, K. (2006). Can fear arousal in public health campaigns contribute to the decline of HIV prevalence? *Journal of Health Communication, 11*(3), 245–259.

Green, F. (2003, June 20). Booze ads target Black teens, report finds. *San Diego Union-Tribune,* p. C1.

Green, J. (1996, September 15). Flirting with suicide. *New York Times Magazine,* p. 39.

Green, K. C. (1988, January). Who wants to be a nurse? *American Demographics, 10*, 46–49.

Green, R. (1999). *The Nicholas Effect: A boy's gift to the world.* Cambridge, MA: O'Reilly.

Green, R. (2003). A child's legacy of love. The Nicholas Green Foundation. Retrieved from http://www.nicholasgreen.org/articles.html

Greenbaum, T. L. (1991, September). Outside moderators maximize focus group results. *Public Relations Journal, 47*, 31–33.

Greenberg, L. (2004, May). Addressing the Accreditation Council for Graduate Medical Education competencies: An opportunity to impact medical education and patient care. *Pediatrics, 113*(5), 1398–1400.

Greene, J. (2008, February 25). Turning the tables: Insurers win low marks in doc-satisfaction survey. *Modern Healthcare, 38*(8), 58.

Greene, K. (2009). An integrated model of health disclosure decision-making. In T. D. Afifi & W. A. Afifi (Eds.), *Uncertainty and information regulation in interpersonal contexts: Theories and applications* (pp. 226–253). New York: Routledge.

Greene, K., Magsamen-Conrad, K., Venetis, M. K., Checton, M. G., Bagdasarov, Z., & Banerjee, S. C.

(2012). Assessing health diagnosis disclosure decisions in relationships: Testing the disclosure decision-making model. *Health Communication, 27*, 356–368.

Greene, K., Rubin, D. L., Hale, J. L., & Walters, L. H. (1996). The utility of understanding adolescent egocentrism in designing health promotion messages. *Health Communication, 8*, 131–152.

Greene, M. C., Strange, J. J., & Brock, T. C. (Eds.). (2002). *Narrative impact: Social and cognitive foundations.* Mahwah, NJ: Lawrence Erlbaum.

Greene, M. G., Adelman, R. D., & Majerovitz, S. D. (1996). Physician and older patient support in the medical encounter. *Health Communication, 8*, 263–279.

Griffin, R. J., Dunwoody, S., & Neuwirth, K. (1999). Information insufficiency and risk communication. *Media Psychology, 6*, 23–61.

Groopman, J. (2007). *How doctors think.* Boston: Houghton Mifflin.

Gross, R., McNeill, R., Davis, P., Lay-Yee, R., Jatrana, S., & Crampton, P. (2008). The association of gender concordance and primary care physicians' perceptions of their patients. *Women & Health, 48*(2), 123–144.

Grunig, J. E. (Ed.) (1992). Excellence in public relations and communication management. Hillsdale, NJ: Lawrence Erlbaum.

Grunig, L. A., Grunig, J. E., & Dozier, D. M. (2002) *Excellent public relations and effective organizations: A study of communication management in three countries.* Mahwah, NJ: Lawrence Erlbaum.

Gualtieri, L. (2011). Social media in crisis management and public health emergencies. *Medpagetoday* online. Retrieved from http://www.kevinmd.com/blog/2010/06/social-media-crisis-management-public-health-emergencies.html

Gunther, A. C., Bolt, D., Borzekowski, D. L. G., Liebhart, J. L., & Dillard, J. P. (2006). Presumed influence on peer norms: How mass media indirectly affect adolescent smoking. *Journal of Communication, 56*, 52–68.

Gursky, E., Inglesby, T. V., & O'Toole, T. (2003). Anthrax 2001: Observations on the medical and public health response. *Biosecurity and Bioterrorism, 1*(2), online version, np. Retrieved from http://www.upmc-biosecurity.org/website/resources/publications/2003_orig-articles/2003-06-15-anthrax2001observations.html

Guttman, N. (1997). Ethical dilemmas in health campaigns. *Health Communication, 9*, 155–190.

Guy, B., Williams, D. R., Aldridge, A., & Roggenkamp, S. D. (2007). Approaches to organizing public relations functions in healthcare. *Health Marketing Quarterly, 24*(3–4), 1–18. doi: 10.1080/07359680802118969.

Haas, S. (2002). Social support as relationship maintenance in gay male couples coping with HIV or AIDS. *Journal of Social and Personal Relationships, 18*(1), 87–111.

Habermas, J. (1989). *The structural transformation of the public sphere: An inquiry into a category of bourgeois society.* (T. Burger, Trans.). Cambridge, MA: MIT Press (originally published in 1962).

Haider, M., & Aravindakshan, N. P. (2005). Content analysis of anthrax in the media. In M. Haider (Ed.), *Global public health communication: Challenges, perspectives, and strategies* (pp. 391–406). Boston: Jones and Bartlett.

Haines, M. P., & Spear, S. F. (1996). Changing the perceptions of the norm: A strategy to decrease binge drinking among college students. *Journal of American College Health, 45*, 134–140.

Halbesleben, J. R. (2006). Patient reciprocity and physician burn-out: What do patients bring to the patient–physician relationship? *Health Services Management Research, 19*(4), 215–222.

Halbesleben, J. R., & Rathert, C. (2008). Linking physician burnout and patient outcomes: Exploring the dyadic relationship between physicians and patients. *Health Care Management Review, 33*(1), 29–39.

Halkowski, T. (2006). Realizing the illness: Patients' narratives of symptom discovery. In J. Heritage & D. W. Maynard (Eds.), *Communication in medical care: Interactions between primary care physicians and patients* (pp. 86–114). Cambridge: Cambridge University Press.

Ham, J. Y., Shah, D. V., Kim, E., Namkoong, K., Lee, S.-Y., Moon, J., Cleland, R., Bu, Q. L., McTavish, F. M., & Gustafson, D. H. (2011). Empathic exchanges in online cancer support groups: Distinguishing message expression and reception effects. *Health Communication, 26*, 185–197.

Hamdan, A. (2007). A case study of a Muslim client: Incorporating religious beliefs and practices. *Multicultural Counseling and Development, 35*, 92–100.

Hammad, A., Kysia, R., Rabah, R., Hassoun, R., & Connelly, M. (1999). Guide to Arab culture: Health care delivery to the Arab American community. Dearborn, MI: Arab Community Center for Economic and Social Services. Retrieved from http://www.accesscommunity.org/site/DocServer/health_and_research_cente_21.pdf?docID=381

Hardey, M. (2008). e-Health: The Internet and the transformation of patients into consumers and producers of health knowledge. In L. C. Lederman (Ed.), *Beyond these walls: Readings in health communication* (pp. 154–164). New York: Oxford University Press.

Haridakis, P. M. (2006). Men, women, and televised violence: Predicting viewer aggression in malehari and female television viewers. *Communication Quarterly, 54*(2), 227–255.

Harper, J. (1997, September 15). Information overload may be making some Americans sick. *Insight on the News, 13*, 40–41.

Harres, A. (2008). "But basically you're feeling well, are you?" Tag questions in medical consultations. In L. C. Lederman (Ed.), *Beyond these walls: Readings in health communication* (pp. 49–57). New York: Oxford University Press.

Harrington, N. G., Norling, G. R., Witte, F. M., Taylor, J., & Andrews, J. E. (2007). The effects of communication skills training on pediatricians' and parents' communication during "sick child" visits. *Health Communication, 21*(2), 105–114.

Harris, S. R., & Templeton, E. (2001). Who's listening? Experiences of women with breast cancer in communicating with physicians. *The Breast Journal, 7*(6), 444–449.

Harris, T. M., Parrott, R., & Dorgan, K. A. (2004). Talking about human genetics within religious frameworks. *Health Communication, 16*(1), 105–116.

Harrison, K. (2005). Is "fat free" good for me? A panel study of television viewing and children's nutritional knowledge and reasoning. *Health Communication, 17*(2), 117–132.

Hart, C., & Chesson, R. (1998). Children as consumers. *British Medical Journal, 316*, 1600–1603.

Hart, C. N., Kelleher, K. J., Drotar, D., & Scholle, S. H. (2007). Parent–provider communication and parental satisfaction with care of children with psychosocial problems. *Parent Education and Counseling, 68*, 179–185.

Hart, J. L., & Walker, K. L. (2008). Communicating health beliefs and practices. In K. B. Wright & S. D. Moore (Eds.), *Applied health communication* (pp. 125–142). Cresskill, NJ: Hampton Press.

Harter, L. M. (2009). Narratives as dialogic, contested, and aesthetic performances. *Journal of Applied Communication Research, 37*, 140–150.

Hartog, C. S. (2009). Elements of effective communication: Rediscoveries from homeopathy. *Patient Education and Counseling, 77*, 172–178.

Hartzband, P., & Groopman, J. (2008). Off the record: Avoiding the pitfalls of going electronic. *New England Journal of Medicine, 358*(16), 1656.

Harwood, J., & Sparks, L. (2003). Social identity and health: An intergroup communication approach to cancer. *Health Communication, 15*(2), 145–159.

Haskard, K. B., Williams, S. L., DiMatteo, R., Rosenthal, R., White, M. K., & Goldstein, M. G. (2008). Physician and patient communication training in primary care: Effects on participation and satisfaction. *Health Psychology, 27*(5), 513–522.

Hatch, J., & Clinton, A. (2000). Job growth in the 1990s: A retrospect. *Monthly Labor Review* online. Retrieved from http://www.bls.gov/opub/mlr/2000/12/art1full.pdf

Hawkley, L. C., Masi, C. M., Berry, J. D., & Cacioppo, J. T. (2006). Loneliness is a unique predictor of age-related differences in systolic blood pressure. *Psychology and Aging, 21*(1), 152–164.

Health economics: Soaring healthcare premiums seen as threat to managed care. (2003, July 14). *Health & Medicine Week*, p. 56.

Health expenditures per capita. (2009). Menlo Park, CA: Henry J. Kaiser Family Foundation. Retrieved from http://www.globalhealthfacts.org/data/topic/map.aspx?ind=66

Health insurance coverage of the total population states (2009–2010), U.S. (2010). (2012). Menlo Park, CA: Henry J. Kaiser Family Foundation. Retrieved from http://www.statehealthfacts.org/comparetable.jsp?ind=125&cat=3

Health literacy overview. (2003). American Medical Association. Retrieved from www.ama-assn.org/ama/pub/printcat/8577.html

Health Privacy Project. (2003). Myths and facts about the HIPAA privacy rule. U.S. Department of Health and Human Services. Retrieved from www.healthprivacy.org

Health promotion glossary. (1998). World Health Organization. Retrieved from www.who.int/hpr/ncp/support.documents.shtml

Health spending and reform implementation. The Commonwealth Fund/Modern Health Care opinion leaders survey. (2011, October). New York: Author. Retrieved from http://www.commonwealthfund.org/Publications/Data-Briefs/2011/Nov/Views-on-Health-Spending-and-Reform.aspx

Heath, C. (2006). Body work: The collaborative production of the clinical object. In J. Heritage & D. W. Maynard (Eds.), *Communication in medical care: Interactions between primary care physicians and patients* (pp. 184–213). Cambridge: Cambridge University Press.

Hegedus, K., Zana, Á., & Szabó, B. (2008). Effect of end-of-life education on medical students' and health care workers' death attitude. *Palliative Medicine, 22*, 264–269.

Helme, D. W., Donohew, R. L., Baier, M., & Zittleman, L. (2007). A classroom-administered simulation of a television campaign on adolescent smoking: Testing an activation model of information exposure. *Journal of Health Communication, 12*, 399–415.

Henahan, S. (1996). Mad cow disease: The BSE epidemic in Great Britain. An interview with Dr. Frederick A. Murphy. Washington, DC: Access Excellence at the National Health Museum. Retrieved August 26, 2008, from http://www.accessexcellence.org/WN/NM/madcow96.php

Hendrich, A., Chow, M., Skierczynski, B. A., & Lu, Z. (2008). A 36-hospital time and motion study: How do medical-surgical nurses spend their time? *The Permanente Journal, 12*(3), 25–34.

Henriksen, L., & Jackson, C. (1998). Anti-smoking socialization: Relationship to parent and child smoking status. *Health Communication, 10*, 87–102.

Henry J. Kaiser Family Foundation. (2011). Employee health benefits. 2011 summary of findings. Author: Menlo Park, CA. Retrieved from http://ehbs.kff.org/

Hensel, D., & Stoelting-Gettelfinger, W. (2011). Changes in stress and nurse self-concept among baccalaureate nursing students. *Journal of Nursing Education, 50*, 290–293.

Henson, N. (2007). Mosquito-style communication. *Dental Assistant, 76*(3), 32–35.

Heritage, J., & Robinson, J. D. (2006). The structure of patients' presenting concerns: Physicians' opening questions. *Health Communication, 19*(2), 89–102.

Herman, A., & Jackson, P. (2010). Empowering low-income parents with skills to reduce excess pediatric emergency room and clinic visits through a tailored low literacy training intervention. *Journal of Health Communication, 15*, 895–910. doi:10.1080/10810730.2010.522228

Herzberg, F. (1968, January/February). One more time: How do you motivate employees again? *Harvard Business Review, 46*, 53–62.

Herzberg, F., Mausner, B., & Snyderman, B. B. (1959). *The motivation to work*. New York: Wiley.

Hetsroni, A. (2007a). Four decades of violent content on prime-time network programming: A longitudinal meta-analytic review. *Journal of Communication, 57*, 759–784.

Hetsroni, A. (2007b). Three decades of sexual content on prime-time network programming: A longitudinal meta-analytic review. *Journal of Communication, 57*, 318–348.

Hetsroni, A. (2009). If you must be hospitalized, television is not the place: Diagnoses, survival rates and demographic characteristics of patients in TV hospital dramas. *Communication Research Reports, 26*, 311–322.

HHS [Health and Human Services] study finds strong link between patient outcomes and nursing staffing in hospitals. (2001, April 20).

Washington, DC: U.S. Department of Health and Human Services. Retrieved from newsroom.hrsa.gov

Hickman, J. M., Caine, K. E., Pak, R., Stronge, A. J., Rogers, W. A., & Fisk, A. D. (2009). What factors lead to healthcare miscommunications with older patients? *Journal of Communication in Healthcare, 2,* 103–118.

Hillier, D. (2006). *Communicating health risks to the public: A global perspective.* Burlington, VT: Gower.

Himmelstein, D. U., Warren, E., Thorne, D., & Woolhandler, S. (2005, February 2). Market watch: Illness and injury as contributors to bankruptcy. *Health Affairs* Web Exclusive, w5–w73. Retrieved from http://content.healthaffairs.org/cgi/reprint/hlthaff.w5.63v1

Hines, S. C. (2001). Coping with uncertainties in advance care planning. *Journal of Communication, 51*(3), 498–513.

Hinton, Lisa, Kurinczuk, J. J., & Ziebland, S. (2010). Infertility; isolation and the Internet: A qualitative interview study. *Patient Education and Counseling, 81,* 436–441.

Hirschmann, K. (2008). Blood, vomit, and communication: The days and nights of an intern on call. In L. C. Lederman (Ed.), *Beyond these walls: Readings in health communication* (pp. 58–73). New York: Oxford University Press.

History of public health. (2002). *Encyclopedia of public health.* Farmington Hills, MI: Gale Cengage. Retrieved from <http://www.enotes.com/public-health-encyclopedia/

Ho, D. (2002, January 18). Eli Lilly settles charges of violating the privacy of Prozac patients. Associated Press, Business News. Retrieved from LexisNexis.

Ho, E. Y. (2006). Behold the power of *Qi*: The importance of *Qi* in the discourse of acupuncture. *Research on Language and Social Interaction, 39*(4), 411–440.

Ho, E. Y., & Bylund, C. L. (2008). Models of health and models of interaction in the practitioner–client relationship in acupuncture. *Health Communication, 23,* 506–515.

Hodgman, A. (1998, May 25). Burb's eye-view. *Brandweek, 39,* 38.

Holland, J. C., & Zittoun, R. (1990). Psychosocial issues in oncology: A historical perspective. In J. C. Holland & R. Zittoun (Eds.), *Psychosocial aspects of oncology* (pp. 1–10). New York: Springer-Verlag.

Holmes, G. N., Harrington, N., & Parrish, A. J. (2010). Exploring the relationship between pediatrician self-disclosure and parent satisfaction. *Communication Research Reports, 27,* 365–369. doi:10.1080/08824096.2010.518922

Holmes, O. W. (1891). *Medical essays: 1842–1882.* Boston: Houghton Mifflin.

Holohan, J., & Chen, V. (2011, December). Changes in health insurance coverage in the great recession, 2007–2010. Menlo Park, CA: Kaiser Commission on Medicaid and the Uninsured. Retrieved from http://www.kff.org/uninsured/upload/8264.pdf

Holt, C. L., Lee, C., & Wright, K. (2008). A spiritually based approach to breast cancer awareness: Cognitive response analysis of communication effectiveness. *Health Communication, 23,* 13–22.

Holtgrave, D. R., Tinsley, B. J., & Kay, L. S. (1995). Encouraging risk reduction: A decision-making approach to message design. In E. Maibach & R. L. Parrott (Eds.), *Designing health messages: Approaches from communication theory and public health practice* (pp. 24–40). Thousand Oaks, CA: Sage.

Holtgrave, D. R., Wunderink, K. A., Vallone, D. M., & Healton, C. G. (2009). Cost–utility analysis of the national truth® campaign to prevent youth smoking. *American Journal of Preventive Medicine, 36,* 385–388.

Hopkins, H. (2007, May 18). Analysis: Older people fastest growing online segment in the UK. *Digital Media Wire,* online. Retrieved from http://www.dmwmedia.com/news/2007/05/18/analysis-older-people-fastest-growing-online-segment-in-the-uk

Hornik, R. C. (Ed.). (2002). *Public health communication: Evidence for behavior change.* Mahwah, NJ: Lawrence Erlbaum.

Horvath, K. J., Harwood, E. M., Courtenay-Quirk, C., McFarlane, M., Fisher, H., Dickenson, T., Kachur, R., & Simon Rosser, B. R. (2010). Online resources for persons recently diagnosed with HIV/AIDS: An analysis of HIV-related webpages. *Journal of Health Communication, 15,* 516–531.

Hospice care in America. (2012). National Hospice and Palliative Care Organization. Alexandria, VA: Author. Retrieved from http://www.nhpco.org/files/public/statistics_research/2011_facts_figures.pdf

Hospitals in the red. (1947, November 24,). *Time, L*(21), nonpaginated online version. Retrieved from http://www.time.com/time/magazine/article/0,9171,887776,00.html

Hou, J., & Shim, M. (2010). The role of provider-patient communication and trust in online sources in Internet use of health-related activities. *Journal of Health Communication, 15,* 186–199.

How, S. K. H., Fryer, A.-K., McCarthy, D., Schoen, C., & Schor, E. L. (2011, February). Securing a healthy future: The Commonwealth Fund State Scorecard on Health System Performance. New York: The Commonwealth Fund. Retrieved from http://www.commonwealthfund.org/~/media/Files/Publications/Fund%20Report/2011/Feb/Child%20Health%20Scorecard/1468_How_securing_a_healthy_future_state_scorecard_child_hlt_sys_performance_2011_web_final_v8.pdf

Hoy, W. (2003). Shared decision making: The Hoy-Tarter Simplified Model. PowerPoint available at http://www.waynekhoy.com/shared_dm_model.html

Hoy, W. K., & Tarter, C. J. (2008). *Administrators solving the problems of practice: Decision-making cases, concepts, and consequence* (3rd ed). Boston: Allyn & Bacon.

Hsia, R. Y., Kellerman, A. L., & Shen, Y.-C. (2011). Factors associated with closures of emergency departments in the United States. *Journal of the American Medical Association, 305,* 1978–1985.

Hsiao, A.-F., Ryan, G. W., Hays, R. D., Coulter, I. D., Andersen, R. M., & Wenger, N. S. (2006). Variations in provider conceptions of integrative medicine. *Social Science & Medicine, 62,* 2973–2987.

Hsiao, C.-J., Hing, E., Socey, T. C., & Cal, B. (2012). Electronic health record systems and intent to apply for meaningful use incentives among office-based physician practices: United States, 2001–2011. Atlanta: Centers for Disease Control and Prevention. Retrieved from http://www.cdc.gov/nchs/data/databriefs/db79.htm

Hsieh, E. (2006). Understanding medical interpreters: Reconceptualizing bilingual health communication. *Health Communication, 20*(2), 177–186.

Hubbell, A. P. (2006). Mexican American women in a rural area and barriers to their ability to enact protective behaviors against breast cancer. *Health Communication, 20*(1), 35–44.

Hudson, K. L., Holohan, M. K., & Collins, F. S. (2008). Keeping pace with the times: The Genetic Information Nondiscrimination Act of 2008. *New England Journal of Medicine, 358*(25), 2661–2663.

Huesmann, L. R., Moise-Titus, J., Podolski, C., & Eron, L. D. (2003). Longitudinal relations between children's exposure to TV violence and their aggressive and violent behavior in young adulthood: 1977–1992. *Developmental Psychology, 39*(2), 201–221.

Hufford, D. J. (1997). Gender, culture and experience: A painful case. *Southern Folklore, 54*, 114–123.

Huhmann, B. A., & Brotherton, T. P. (1997, Summer). A content analysis of guilt appeals in popular magazine advertisements. *Journal of Advertising, 26*, 35–45.

Hullett, C. R. (2006). Using functional theory to promote HIV testing: The impact of value-expressive messages, uncertainty, and fear. *Health Communication, 20*(1), 57–67.

Human genome project information. (2008). Website sponsored by the U.S. Department of Energy Office of Science, Office of Biological and Environmental Research, & Human Genome Program. Retrieved from http://www.ornl.gov/sci/techresources/Human_Genome/home.shtml

Hummert, M. L., & Shaner, J. L. (1994). Patronizing speech to the elderly as a function of stereotyping. *Communication Studies, 45*, 145–158.

Hust, S. J. T., Brown, J. D., & L'Engle, K. L. (2008). Boys will be boys and girls better be prepared: An analysis of the rare sexual health messages in young adolescents' media. *Mass Communication and Society, 11*(1), 3–23.

Huvane, K. (2008, October). Quick check-in: Kiosks are emerging as a potentially "easy win" that can increase patient satisfaction and improve staff efficiency. *Healthcare Informatics, 25*(10), 22–29.

Imes, R. S., Bylund, C. L., Sabee, C. M., Routsong, T. R., & Sanford, A. A. (2008). Patients' reasons for refraining from discussing Internet health information with their healthcare providers. *Health Communication, 23*, 538–547.

In her own words. (2004). Commentary about *The most dangerous woman in America* [video documentary], Nancy Porter (Writer/Director). NOVA in association with WGBH/Boston. Retrieved from http://www.pbs.org/wgbh/nova/typhoid

Industry survey. Marketing leaders. (2011). Study conducted by HealthLeaders Media Council. Retrieved from http://www.healthleadersmedia.com/pdf/survey_project/2011/Mkt_press.pdf

Information and communication technology facts and figures. (2011, December). International Telecommunication Union / Information and Communication Technology database. Author: Geneva, Switzerland. Retrieved from http://www.itu.int/ITU-D/ict/statistics/

Internet surveys. (2008). In P. J. Lavrakas (Ed.), *Encyclopedia of survey research methods* (online version, np). Thousand Oaks, CA: Sage. Retrieved from http://www.credoreference.com.ezproxy.lib.uwf.edu/entry/sagesurveyr/internet_surveys.

Interview: Former U.S. Surgeon General Richard Carmona, MD. (2007, November 30). *WebMD*. Retrieved from http://blogs.webmd.com/election-2008-expert-view/2007/11/interview-former-us-surgeon-general.html

Investigating continued gender disparities in physician salaries. (2008, August 20). Chicago: American Medical Association. Retrieved from http://www.ama-assn.org/ama1/pub/upload/mm/377/cmerpt19.pdf

Irvine, D. H. (1991, March). The advertising of doctors' services. *Journal of Medical Ethics, 17*, 35–40.

Iverson, K. (1997). *Plain talk: Lessons from a business maverick.* Somerset, NJ: John Wiley & Sons.

Ivinski, P. A. (1997, September–October). Test case: Sex and humor in pharmaceutical advertising. *Print, 51*, 44–46.

J. D. Power and Associates. (2008, May 23). Satisfaction with health plans varies dramatically from region to region, largely due to poor communication from insurance providers. Retrieved from www.jdpower.com/corporate/news/releases/pressrelease.aspx?ID=2008045

Jackson, K. T. (2004). *Building reputational capital: Strategies for integrity and fair play that improve the bottom line.* Oxford: Oxford University Press.

Jadad, A. R., & Rizo, C. A. (2003). I am a good patient believe it or not. *British Medical Journal, 326*(7402), 1293–1294.

James, A. S., Hall, S., Greiner, K. A., Buckles, D., Born, W. K., & Ahluwalia, J. S. (2008). The impact of socioeconomic status on perceived barriers to colorectal cancer testing. *American Journal of Health Promotion, 23*(2), 97–100.

James, F. (2012). Barney Frank's two top goals: Protecting Wall St. reform, social spending. National Public Radio, Washington DC. Retrieved from http://www.npr.org/blogs/itsallpolitics/2011/11/29/142918342/barney-franks-two-top-goals-protecting-wall-st-reform-social-spending

James, S. D. (2011, June 9). Honeymoon with Viagra could be over. ABC News. Retrieved from http://abcnews.go.com/Health/viagra-prescription-sales-sexual-expectations/story?id=13794726#.T_by6BzHSCA

Jangland, E., Gunningberg, L., & Carlsson, M. (2009). Patients' and relatives' complaints about encounters and communication in health care: Evidence for quality improvement. *Patient Education and Counseling, 75*, 199–204.

Janis, I. (1972). *Victims of groupthink* (2nd ed.). Boston: Houghton Mifflin.

Jantarakolica, K., Komolsevin, R., & Speece, M. (2002). Children's perception of TV reality in Bangkok, Thailand. *Asian Journal of Communication, 12*(1), 77–99.

Jarrett, N., & Payne, S. (1995). A selective review of the literature on nurse–patient communication: Has the patient's contribution been neglected? *Journal of Advanced Nursing, 22*, 72–78.

Jauhar, S. (2008a, June 17). Eyes bloodshot, doctors vent their frustration. *New York Times*, Late Edition, Section F, Science Desk Essay, p. 5.

Jauhar, S. (2008b). *Intern: A doctor's initiation*. New York: Farrar, Straus and Giroux.

Jecker, N. S., Carrese, J. A., & Pearlman, R. A. (1995). Caring for patients in cross-cultural settings. *Hastings Center Report, 25*, 6–15.

Jenkins, H. S. (2008, February 15). Patients love my broken Spanish: This determined ER physician taught himself a second language so he could communicate with all his patients. *Medical Economics, 85*(4), 42–43.

Jensen, J. D., King, A. J., Guntzviller, L. M., & Davis, L. A. (2010). Patient–provider communication and low-income adults: Age, race, literacy, and optimism predict communication satisfaction. *Patient Education and Counseling, 79*, 30–35.

Jensen, J. D., Moriarty, C. M., Hurley, R. J., & Stryker, J. (2010). Making sense of cancer news coverage trends: A comparison of three comprehensive content analyses. *Journal of Health Communication, 15*, 136–151. doi:10.1080/10810730903528025

Jeong, S.-H. (2007). Effects of news about genetics and obesity on controllability attribution and helping behavior. *Health Communication, 22*(3), 221–228.

Jha, A. K., Orav, E. J., Zheng, J., & Epstein, A. M. (2008, October 30). Patients' perception of hospital care in the United States. *New England Journal of Medicine, 359*(18), 1921.

Jibaja-Weiss, M. L., & Volk, R. J. (2007). Utilizing computerized entertainment education in the development of decision aids for lower literate and naive computer users. *Journal of Health Communication, 12*(7), 681–697.

Jobes, M., & Steinbinder, A. (1996). Transitions in nursing leadership roles. *Nursing Administration Quarterly, 20*, 80–84.

Johnson, D. (2006, November.) Risk communication in the fog of disaster. Lessons from ground zero. *Industrial Safety & Hygiene News, 40*(11), 58, 60, 62.

Johnson, D. A. (2008). Managing Mr. Monk: Control and the politics of madness. *Critical Studies in Media Communication, 26*(1), 28–47.

Johnson, L. A. (2012, April 4). US prescription spending again nearly flat. Associated Press online, np. Retrieved from http://news.yahoo.com/us-prescription-spending-again-nearly-flat-152831253.html

Johnson, L. J. (2007, August 3). Patient e-mail perils. *Medical Economics, 84*(15), 30.

Johnson, R. W. (2008, June). The strains and drains of long-term care. *American Medical Association Journal of Ethics, 10*(6), 297–400.

Jones, D., Gill, P., Harrison, R., Meakin, R., & Wallace, P. (2003). An exploratory study of language interpretation services provided by videoconferencing. *Journal of Telemedicine and Telecare, 9*(1), 51–56.

Jones, K. O., Denham, B. E., & Springston, J. K. (2007). Differing effects of mass and interpersonal communication on breast cancer risk estimates: An exploratory study of college students and their mothers. *Health Communication, 21*(2), 165–175.

Jones, R. K., & Biddlecom, A. E. (2011). Is the Internet filling the sexual health information gap for teens? An exploratory study. *Journal of Health Communication, 16*, 112–123.

Joy, S. V. (2008). Clinical pearls and strategies to optimize patient outcomes. *The Diabetes Educator, 34*, 54S–59S.

Kai, J. (1996). Parents' difficulties and information needs in coping with acute illness in preschool children: A qualitative study. *British Medical Journal, 313*, 987–990.

The Kaiser Commission on Medicaid and the Uninsured. (2008). States moving toward comprehensive health care reform. Menlo Park, CA: Author. Retrieved from www.commonwealthfund.org/chart-cartcharts/chartcartcharts_show.htm?doc_id=694054&cat_id=2095www.kff.org/uninsured/upload/State%20Health%20Reform.pdf

Kaiser Family Foundation and Pew Research Center's Project for Excellence in Journalism. (2008, December). *Health news coverage in the U.S. media. January 2007-June 2008*. Retrieved from http://www.journalism.org/files/HealthNewsReportFinal.pdf

Kaiser poll: Early reaction to Supreme Court decision on ACA. (2012, July 2). Menlo Park, CA: Henry J. Kaiser Family Foundation. Retrieved from http://healthreform.kff.org/PublicOpinion.aspx

Kakai, H. (2002). A double standard in bioethical reasoning for disclosure of advanced cancer diagnosis in Japan. *Health Communication, 14*(3), 361–376.

Kakizoe, T. (2008, May 18). Insight into the world: Pro-market theory hurts health care. *The Daily Yomiuri* (Tokyo), p. 4. Retrieved through LexisNexis Academic.

Kalichman, S. C., Benotsch, E. G., Weinhardt, L., Austin, J., Luke, W., & Chauncey, C. (2003). Health-related Internet use, coping, social support, and health indicators in people living with HIV/AIDS. *Health Psychology, 22*(1), 111–116.

Kane, C. (2003, February 20). Advertising: BBDP worldwide enters the lucrative category of marketing prescription drugs to consumers. *The New York Times*, Section C, p. 4.

Kaplan, M. (2003). Reporting on the business of health care. *Nieman Reports, 57*(1), 24–25.

Kaplan, R. M. (1997). Health outcomes and communication research. *Health Communication, 9*, 75–82.

Katcher, B. (1997). Getting answers from a focus group: Focus groups must be well conceived and conducted if they are to yield useful data. *Folio: The Magazine for Magazine Management, 25*, 222.

Kathan, J., & Marikar, S. (2012). Dick Clark, entertainment icon nicknamed 'America's oldest teenager,' dies at 82. ABC news. Retrieved from http://abcnews.go.com/Entertainment/dick-clark-entertainment-icon-nick-named-americas-oldest-teenager/story?id=16076252#.T74-mhyYiCB

Katz, E., Blumler, J., & Gurevitch, M. (1974). Uses of mass communication by the individual. In J. G. Blumler & E. Katz (Eds.), *The uses of mass communication* (pp. 19–32). Newbury Park, CA: Sage.

Katz, J. (1984). *The silent world of doctor and patient*. New York: Free Press.

Katz, J. (1995). Informed consent: Ethical and legal issues. In J. D. Arras & B. Steinbock (Eds.), *Ethical issues in modern medicine* (4th ed., pp. 87–97). Mountain View, CA: Mayfield.

Kealey, E., & Berkman, C. S. (2010). The relationship between health information sources and mental models of cancer: Findings of the 2005 Health Information National Trends Survey. *Journal of Health Communication, 15,* 236–251.

Kean, L. G., & Prividera, L. C. (2007). Communicating about race and health: A content analysis of print advertisements in African American and general readership magazines. *Health Communication, 21*(3), 289–297.

Kearney, M. (1978). Spiritualistic healing in Mexico. In P. Morley & R. Wallis (Eds.), *Culture and curing* (pp. 19–39). Pittsburgh: University of Pittsburgh Press.

Keeley, M. P. (2004). Final conversations: Survivors' memorable messages concerning religious faith and spirituality. *Health Communication, 16*(1), 87–104.

Kelder, S. H., Perry, C. L., & Klepp, K. (1993). Community-wide youth exercise promotion: Long-term outcomes of the Minnesota Heart Health Program and the Class of 1989 study. *Journal of School Health, 63,* 218–223.

Keller, P. A., & Lehmann, D. R. (2008). Designing effective health communications: A meta-analysis. *American Marketing Association, 27,* 117–130.

Kennedy, J., Chi-Chuan, W., & Wu, C.-H. (2007, May 17). Patient disclosure about herb and supplement use and adults in the US. *eCam,* pp. 1–6.

Kenney, C. (2010). *Transforming health care: Virginia Mason Medical Center's pursuit of the perfect patient experience.* New York: Taylor & Francis.

Kenyon, L. (2006/2007). Questions haunt nursing student. *Nursing New Zealand, 12*(11), 4.

Keyhani, S., & Federman, A. (2009). Doctors on coverage—physicians' views on a new public insurance option and medicare expansion. *The New England Journal of Medicine, 361*(14), e24-e24. doi:10.1056/NEJMp0908239

Kilbourne, J. (2000). *Killing us softly 3: Advertising's image of women.* North Hampton, MA: Media Education Foundation.

Kim, H. (2011). Pharmaceutical companies as a source of health information: A pilot study of the effects of source, web site interactivity, and involvement. *Health Marketing Quarterly, 28,* 57–85.

Kim, K., & Kwon, N. (2010). Profile of e-patients: Analysis of their cancer information-seeking from a national survey. *Journal of Health Communication, 15,* 712–733.

Kim, S.-H., & Willis, L. A. (2007, June). Talking about obesity: News framing of who is responsible for causing and fixing the problem. *Journal of Health Communication, 12*(4), 359–376.

King, S. (2002, July 19). Media: *Minority Report*—an expert's view. If product placement works, as it does in *Minority Report,* it can benefit a brand. *Campaign,* np. Retrieved October 2, 2008, from http://www.brandrepublic.com/Campaign/News/151376/

King, S. (2010). Pink diplomacy: On the uses and abuses of breast cancer awareness. *Health Communication, 25,* 286–289.

Kisa, K., Kawabata, H., Itou, T., Nishimoto, N., & Maezawa, M. (2011). Survey of patient and physician satisfaction regarding patient-centered outpatient consultations in Japan. *Internal Medicine, 50*(13), 1403–1410.

Klass, P. (1987). *A not entirely benign procedure: Four years as a medical student.* New York: Penguin.

Kleinman, A., Eisenberg, L., & Good, B. (1978). Culture, illness, and care: Clinical lessons from anthropological and cross-cultural research. *Annals of Internal Medicine, 88,* 251–258.

Knobloch-Westerwick, S., & Alter, S. (2006). Mood adjustment to social situations through mass media use: How men ruminate and women dissipate angry moods. *Human Communication Research, 32*(1), 58–73.

Knoerl, A. M. (2007). Cultural considerations and the Hispanic cardiac client. *Home Healthcare Nurse, 25*(2), 83–86.

Ko, L. K., Campbell, M. K., Lewis, M. A., Earp, J. A., & DeVellis, B. (2011). Information processes mediate the effect of a health communication intervention on fruit and vegetable consumption. *Journal of Health Communication, 16,* 282–299.

Koch-Weser, S., Bradshaw, Y, S., Gualtieri, L., & Gallagher, S. S. (2010). The Internet as a health information source: Findings from the 2007 Health Information National Trends Survey and implications for health communication. *Journal of Health Communication, 15,* 279–293.

Koermer, C. D., & Kilbane, M. (2008). Physician sociality communication and its effect on patient satisfaction. *Communication Quarterly, 56,* 69–86.

Koh, G. C., Khoo, H. E., Wong, M. L., & Koh, D. (2008). The effects of problem-based learning during medical school on physician competency: A systematic review. *Canadian Medical Association Journal, 178*(1), 34–41.

Komaroff, A. L., & Fagioli, J. (1996). *Medical assessment of fatigue and chronic fatigue syndrome: An integrative approach to evaluation and treatment* (pp. 154–181). New York: Guilford Press.

Kopfman, J. E., & Ray, E. B. (2005). Talking to children about illness. In E. B. Ray (Ed.), *Health communication in practice: A case study approach* (pp. 111–119). Mahwah, NJ: Lawrence Erlbaum.

Korkki, P. (2008, February 10). Going global with concerns on health costs. *New York Times,* Late Edition, Section BU, Monday and Business/Financial Desk, p. 2.

Korsch, D. M., & Negrete, V. F. (1972). Doctor–patient communication. *Scientific American, 227,* 66–74.

Kotler, P., & Clarke, R. N. (1987). *Marketing for health care organizations.* Englewood Cliffs, NJ: Prentice Hall.

Kotz, K., & Story, M. (1994). Food advertisements during children's Saturday morning television programming: Are they consistent with dietary recommendations? *Journal of the American Dietetic Association, 94,* 1296–1300.

Koven, S. (2012, June 29). Marriage equality, in sickness and in health. BostonGlobe.com. Retrieved from http://www.boston.com/lifestyle/health/2012/06/24/marriage-equality-sickness-and-health/MwK6A6R0iQxTlT4iMdJ3sI/story.html

Kowalski, K. M. (1997, October). On guard against health rip-off. *Current Health, 24,* 6–11.

Kramer, H., & Kramer, K. (1993, March–April). *Psychology Today, 26,* 26–27.

Kreps, G. L. (1988). Relational communication in health care. *Southern Speech Communication Journal, 53,* 344–359.

Kreps, G. L. (1990). Applied health communication research. In D. O'Hair & G. L. Kreps (Eds.), *Applied communication theory and research* (pp. 313–330). Hillsdale, NJ: Lawrence Erlbaum.

Kreps, G. L. (2005). Narrowing the digital divide to overcome disparities in care. In E. B. Ray (Ed.), *Health communication in practice: A case study approach* (pp. 357–364). Mahwah, NJ: Lawrence Erlbaum.

Kreps, G. L., Query, J. L., Jr., & Bonaguro, E. W. (2008). In L. C. Lederman (Ed.), *Beyond these walls: Readings in health communication* (pp. 3–14). New York: Oxford University Press.

Kreps, G. L., & Thornton, B. C. (1992). *Health communication: Theory & practice* (2nd ed.). Prospect Heights, IL: Waveland Press.

Kreuter, M., Farrell, D., Olevitch, L., & Brennan, L. (1999). *Tailoring health messages: Customizing communication with computer technology.* Mahwah, NJ: Lawrence Erlbaum.

Krishnan, S. P. (1996). Health education at family planning clinics: Strategies for improving information about contraception and sexually transmitted diseases for low-income women. *Health Communication, 8,* 353–366.

Kroll, T., Beatty, P. W., & Bingham, S. (2003). Primary care satisfaction among adults with physical disabilities: The role of patient–provider communication. *Managed Care Quarterly, 11*(1), 11–19.

Krosnick, J. A., Chang, L., Sherman, S. J., Chassin, L., & Presson, C. (2006). The effects of beliefs about the health consequences of cigarette smoking on smoking onset. *Journal of Communication, 56,* S18–S37.

Krug, P. (1998). Where does physician-assisted suicide stand today? *Association of Operating Room Nurses Journal, 68,* 869.

Kübler-Ross, E. (1969). *On death and dying.* New York: Macmillan.

Kulich, K. R., Berggren, U., & Hallberg, I, R.-M. (2003). A qualitative analysis of patient-centered dentistry in consultations with dental phobic patients. *Journal of Health Communication, 8*(2), 171–187.

Kundrat, A. L., & Nussbaum, J. F. (2003). The impact of invisible illness on identity and contextual age. *Health Communication, 15*(3), 331–347.

Kunkel, D., Eyal, K., Donnerstein, E., Farrar, K. M., Biely, E., & Rideout, V. (2007). Sexual socialization messages on entertainment television: Comparing content trends 1997–2002. *Media Psychology, 9*(3), 595–622.

Kunkel, D., Eyal, K., Finnerty, K., Biely, E., & Donnerstein, E. (2005). Sex on TV4. Menlo Park, CA: Henry J. Kaiser Family Foundation. Retrieved from http://www.kff.org/entmedia/upload/Sex-on-TV-4-Full-Report.pdf

Kush, R. D., Helton, E., Rockhold, F. W., & Hardison, C. D. (2008). Electronic health records, medical research, and the Tower of Babel. *New England Journal of Medicine, 358*(16), 1738.

La Puma, J. (1998). *Managed care ethics: Essays on the impact of managed care on traditional medical ethics.* New York: Hatherleigh Press.

Laframboise, D. (1998). When home is the hospital. *Chatelaine, 71,* 26–31.

Laine, C., & Davidoff, F. (1996). Patient-centered medicine: A professional evolution. *Journal of the American Medical Association, 275,* 152–155.

Lambert, B. L., Street, R. L., Cegala, D. J., Smith, D. H., Kurtz, S., & Schofield, T. (1997). Provider–patient communication, patient-centered care, and the mangle of practice. *Health Communication, 9,* 27–43.

Landon, B. E., Reschovsky, J. D., Pham, H. H., & Blumenthal, D. (2006). Leaving medicine: The consequences of physician dissatisfaction. *Medical Care, 44*(3), 234–242.

Lang, A. (2006). Using the limited-capacity model of motivated mediated message processing to design effective cancer communication messages. *Journal of Communication, 56,* S57–S80.

Lang, A., Chung, Y., Lee, S., & Zhao, X. (2005). It's the product: Do risky products compel attention and elicit arousal in media users? *Health Communication, 17*(3), 283–300.

Lang, A., Schwartz, N., Lee, S., & Angelini, J. R. (2007, September). Processing radio PSAs: Production pacing, arousing content, and age. *Journal of Health Communication, 12*(6), 581–599.

Lansdale, D. (2002). Touching lives: Opening doors for elders in retirement communities through e-mail and the Internet. In R. W. Morrell (Ed.), *Older adults, health information, and the World Wide Web* (pp. 133–151). Mahwah, NJ: Lawrence Erlbaum.

Lapinski, M. K., Rimal, R. N., DeVries, R., & Lee, E. L. (2007). The role of group orientation and descriptive norms on water conservation attitudes and behaviors. *Health Communication, 22*(2), 133–142.

Lassiter, S. M. (1998). *Cultures of color in America: A guide to family, religion, and health.* Westport, CT: Greenwood.

Latimer, A. E., Salovey, P., & Rothman, A. J. (2007). The effectiveness of gain-framed messages for encouraging disease prevention behavior: Is all hope lost? *Journal of Health Communication, 12,* 645–649.

Lauer, C. S. (2008a, April 28). Rx for local economies; healthcare picks up where manufacturing left off. *Modern Healthcare, 38*(17), 25.

Lauer, C. S. (2008b, March 10). The unwritten curriculum. Writer: Medical students learn from elders' cynicism. *Modern Healthcare, 38*(10), 50.

Laurant, M. G., Hermens, R. P., Braspenning, J. C., Akkermans, R. P., Sibbald, B., & Grol, R. P. (2008). An overview of patients' preference for, and satisfaction with, care provided by general practitioners and nurse practitioners. *Journal of Clinical Nursing, 17*(20), 2690–2698.

LaVail, K. H. (2010). Coverage of older adults and HIV/AIDS: Risk information for an invisible population. *Communication Quarterly, 58,* 170–187.

Lazarsfeld, P., Burleson, B., & Gaudet, H. (1948). *The people's choice.* New York: Columbia University Press.

Leadley, J. (2009, November). Women in U.S. academic medicine: Statistics and benchmarking report 2008–2009. Washington, DC: American Association of Medical Colleges. Retrieved from https://www.aamc.org/download/53502/data/wimstatisticsreport2009.pdf

Lederman, L. C., & Stewart, L. P. (2005). *Changing the culture of college drinking: A socially situated health communication campaign.* Cresskill, NJ: Hampton Press.

Lederman, L. C., Stewart, L. P., Barr, S. L., Powell, R. L., Laitman, L., & Goodhart, F. W. (2001). Using communication theory to reduce dangerous drinking on a college campus. In R. E. Rice & C. K. Atkin (Eds.), *Public communication campaigns* (3rd ed., pp. 295–299). Thousand Oaks, CA: Sage.

Lederman, L. C., Stewart, L. P., Goodhart, F. W., & Laitman, L. (2008). A case against "binge" as the term of choice. In L. C. Lederman (Ed.), *Beyond these walls: Readings in health communication* (pp. 292–303). New York: Oxford University Press.

Ledlow, G. R., Johnson, J. A., & Hakoyama, M. (2008). Social marketing and organizational efficacy. In K. B. Wright & S. D. Moore (Eds.), *Applied health communication* (pp. 85–103). Cresskill, NJ: Hampton Press.

Lee, A. (2009). Changing effects of direct-to-consumer broadcast drug advertising information sources on prescription drug requests. *Health Communication, 24,* 361–376. doi:10.1080/10410230902889480

Lee, A. (2010). Who are the opinion leaders? The physicians, pharmacists, patients, and direct-to-consumer prescription drug advertising. *Journal of Health Communication, 15,* 629–655. doi:10.1080/1081073 0.2010.499594

Lee, C.-J. (2008). Does the Internet displace health professionals? *Journal of Health Communication, 13,* 450–464.

Lee, C.-J. (2009). Physician trust moderates the Internet use and physician visit relationship. *Journal of Health Communication, 14,* 70–76.

Lee, F. (2004). *If Disney ran your hospital: 9½ things you would do differently.* Bozeman, MT: Second River Healthcare Press.

Lee, M. J. (2010). The effects of self-efficacy statements in humorous anti-alcohol abuse messages targeting college students: Who is in charge? *Health Communication, 25,* 638–646. doi:10.1080/10410236.2 010.521908

Lee, M. J., & Bichard, S. L. (2006). Effective message design targeting college students for the prevention of binge-drinking: Basing design on rebellious risk-taking tendency.

Health Communication, 20(3), 299–308.

Lee, S. Y., & Hawkins, R. (2010). Why do patients seek an alternative channel? The effects of unmet needs on patients' health-related Internet use. *Journal of Health Communication, 15,* 152–166.

Lee, Y. J., Park, J., & Widdows, R. (2009). Exploring antecedents of consumer satisfaction and repeated search behavior on e-health information. *Journal of Health Communication, 14,* 160–173.

Leeman-Castillo, B. A., Corbett, K. K., Aagaard, E. M., Maselli, J. H., Gonzales, R., & MacKenzie, T. D. (2007). Acceptability of a bilingual interactive computerized educational module in a poor, medically underserved patient population. *Journal of Health Communication, 12*(1), 77–94.

Lefebvre, C. (2009, October). Integrating cell phones and mobile technologies into public health practice: A social marketing perspective. *Health Promotion Practice, 10,* 490–494.

Lefebvre, R. C., Doner, L., Johnston, D., Loughrey, K., Balch, G. I., & Sutton, S. M. (1995). Use of database marketing and consumer-based health communication in message design: An example for the Office of Cancer Communications' "5 a Day for Better Health" program. In E. Maibach & R. L. Parrott (Eds.), *Designing health messages: Approaches from communication theory and public health practice* (pp. 217–246). Thousand Oaks, CA: Sage.

Lefebvre, R. C., & Flora, J. A. (1988). Social marketing and public health intervention. *Health Education Quarterly, 15,* 299–315.

Lehman, D. R., Ellard, J. H., & Wortman, C. B. (1986). Social support for the bereaved: Recipients' and providers' perspectives on what is helpful. *Journal of Consulting and Clinical Psychology, 54,* 438–446.

Leiss, W., & Powell, D. (with Whitfield, A.). (2004). Mad cows or crazy communications? In L. William & P. Douglas (Authors), *Mad cows and mothers' milk: The perils of poor risk communication* (2nd ed., pp. 3–25). Montreal: McGill–Queen's University Press.

Leshner, G., Bolls, P., & Thomas, E. (2009). Scare 'em or disgust

'em: The effects of graphic health promotion messages. *Health Communication, 24,* 447–458. doi:10.1080/10410230903023493

Leshner, G., Vultee, F., Bolls, P. D., & Moore, J. (2010). When a fear appeal isn't just a fear appeal: The effects of graphic anti-tobacco messages. *Journal of Broadcasting & Electronic Media, 54,* 485–507. doi:1 0.1080/08838151.2010.498850

Let us put you in the movies. (1996, September 16). *Brandweek, 37,* S3–S9.

Levin, A. (1998). Evidence-based medicine gaining supporters. *Annals of Internal Medicine, 128,* 334–336.

Levinsky, N. (1995). The doctor's master. In J. D. Arras & B. Steinbock (Eds.), *Ethical issues in modern medicine* (4th ed., pp. 116–119). Mountain View, CA: Mayfield.

Levy, D. R. (1985). White doctors and Black patients: Influence of race on the doctor–patient relationship. *Pediatrics, 75,* 639–643.

Li, H. Z., Krysko, M., Desroches, N. G., & Deagle, G. (2004). Reconceptualizing interruptions in physician–patient interviews: Cooperative and intrusive. *Communication & Medicine, 1*(2), 145–157.

Lief, H. L., & Fox, R. C. (1963). Training for "detached concern" in medical students. In J. I. Lief, V. F. Lief, & N. R. Lief (Eds.), *The psychological basis of medical practice.* New York: Harper & Row.

'Life interrupted,' by cancer diagnosis at 22. (2012, May 15). National Public Radio. *Talk of the Nation* broadcast. Transcript retrieved at http://www.npr.org/2012/05/16/152840031/life-interrupted-by-cancer-diagnosis-at-22

Lin, C., Mou, Y., & Lagoe, C. (2011). Communicating nutrition information: Usability and usefulness of the interactive menus of national fast food chain restaurants. *Journal of Communication In Healthcare, 4*(3), 187–199. doi:10.1179/1753807 611Y.0000000002

Lindberg, D. A. B. (2002). Older Americans, health information, and the Internet. In R. W. Morrell (Ed.), *Older adults, health information, and the World Wide Web* (pp. 13–19). Mahwah, NJ: Lawrence Erlbaum.

Linnan, L. A., & Ferguson, Y. O. (2007). Beauty salons. *Health Education & Behavior, 34*(3), 517–530.

Lippy, C. H., & Williams, P. W. (1988). *Encyclopedia of the American religious experience.* New York: Charles Scribner's Sons.

Liptak, A. (2012, June 28). Supreme Court upholds health care law, 5–4, in Obama victory. *The New York Times* online, np. Retrieved from http://www.nytimes.com/2012/06/29/us/supreme-court-lets-health-law-largely-stand.html?pagewanted=all

Liselotte, N. D., Thomas, M. R., Massie, S., Power, D. V., Eacker, A., Harper, W., Durning, S., Moutier, C., Szydlo, D. W., Novotny, P. J., Sloan, J. A., & Shanafelt, T. D. (2008). Burnout and suicide ideation among U.S. medical students. *Annals of Internal Medicine, 149*, 334–341.

Littlefield, R. S., & Quenette, A. M. (2007, February). Crisis leadership and Hurricane Katrina: The portrayal of authority by the media in natural disasters. *Journal of Applied Communication Research, 35*(1), 26–47.

Living with cancer. (1997, September). *Harvard Health Letter, 22*, 4–5.

Loe, M. (2004). *The rise of Viagra: How the little blue pill changed sex in America.* New York: New York University Press.

Löffler, W., Kilian, R., Toumi, M., & Angermeyer, M.C. (2003). Schizophrenic patients' subjective reasons for compliance and noncompliance with neuroleptic treatment. *Pharmacopsychiatry, 36*(3), 105–112.

Lombardo, F. A. (1997). If you don't befriend your patients, your competitors will. *Medical Economics, 74*, 121–124.

Longino, C. F. (1997, December). Beyond the body: An emerging medical paradigm. *American Demographics, 19*, 14–18.

Lovell, B., Moss, M., & Wetherell, M. A. (2011). Perceived stress, common health complaints and diurnal patterns of cortisol secretion in young, otherwise healthy individuals. *Hormones and Behavior, 60*, 301–305.

Lovett, R. A. (2003, May–June). Fact versus fear: We worry too much about man-made catastrophe. *Psychology Today, 36*(3), 14.

Lowe, G., & Costabile, R. A. (2012). 10-year analysis of adverse event reports to the Food and Drug Administration for phosphodiesterase type-5 inhibitors. *Journal*

of Sexual Medicine, 9, 265–270. doi: 10.1111/j.1743-6109.2011.02537

Lowes, R. (2008a, May 2). The concierge model: Want to spend more time with your patients? Consider a retainer practice. *Medical Economics, 85*(9), 69–73.

Lowes, R. (2008b, May 2). Open access, extended hours: Seeing patients when they want to be seen helps you respond to their needs and stay competitive. *Medical Economics, 85*(9), 62–72.

Lowrey, W., & Anderson, W. B. (2006). The impact of Internet use on the public perception of physicians: A perspective from the sociology of professions literature. *Health Communication, 19*(2), 125–131.

Ludtke, M., & Trost, C. (1998). Covering children's health. *American Journalism Review, 20*, 81–88.

Luepker, R. V., Murray, D. M., Jacobs, D. R., Jr., Mittelmark, M. B., Bracht, N., Carlaw, R., Crow, R., Elmer, P., Finnegan, J., Folsom, A. R., Grimm, R., Hannan, P. J., Jeffrey, R., Lando, H., McGovern, P., Mullis, R., Perry, C. L., Pechacek, T., Pirie, P. Sprafka, J. M., Weisbrod, R., & Blackburn, H. (1994). Community education for cardiovascular disease prevention: Risk factor changes in the Minnesota Heart Health Program. *American Journal of Public Health, 84*, 1381–1393.

Lui, X., Sawada, Y., Takizawa, T., Sato, H., Sato, M., Sakamoto, H., Utsugi, T., Sato, K., Sumino, H., Okamura, S., & Sakamaki, T. (2007). Doctor-patient communication: A comparison between telemedicine consultation and face-to-face consulation. *Internal Medicine, 46*, 227–232.

Lumma-Sellenthin, A. (2009). Talking with patients and peers: Medical students' difficulties with learning communication skills. *Medical Teacher, 31*, 528–534.

Lumsdon, K. (1996, February 5). A kinder, gentler ER. *Hospitals & Health Networks, 70*, 43–45.

Lund, C. C. (1995). The doctor, the patient, and the truth. In J. D. Arras & B. Steinbock (Eds.), *Ethical issues in modern medicine* (pp. 55–57). Mountain View, CA: Mayfield.

Lundine, K., Buckley, R., Hutchinson, C., & Lockyer, J. (2008). Communication skills training in orthopedics. *Journal of Bone and Joint Surgery, 90*(6), 1393–1400.

Lupton, D. (1998). A postmodern public health? *Australian and New Zealand Journal of Public Health, 22*(1), 3–5.

Lyall, S. (2000, October 27). British wrongly lulled people on "mad cow," report finds. *New York Times*, online version, np. Retrieved from http://query.nytimes.com/gst/fullpage.html?res=9C06E7DB1E31F934A15753C1A9669C8B63&n=Top%2FNews%2FScience%2FTopics%2FAnimals

Lyon, A. (2007, November). "Putting patients first": Systematically distorted communication and Merck's marketing of Vioxx. *Journal of Applied Communication Research, 35*(4), 376–398.

MacDonald, M. (1981). *Mystical bedlam: Madness, anxiety, and healing in seventeenth-century England.* Cambridge: Cambridge University Press.

Macias, W., & McMillan, S. (2008). The return of the house call: The role of Internet-based interactivity in bringing health information home to older adults. *Health Communication, 23*(1), 34–44.

Macias, W., Pashupati, K., & Lewis, L. S. (2007). A wonderful life or diarrhea and dry mouth? Policy issues of direct-to-consumer drug advertising on television. *Health Communication, 22*(3), 241–252.

MacLellan, D. L., & Lordly, D. (2008). The socialization of dietetic students: Influence of the preceptor role. *Journal of Allied Health, 37*(2), E81–E92.

Mad cows and the minister. (1990, May 24). *Nature, 345*, 277–278. Retrieved August 26, 2008, through ProQuest.

Maeda, T. Hobbs, R. M., Marghoub, T., Guernah, I., Zelent, A., Cordon-Cardo, C., Teruya-Feldstein, J., & Pandolfi, P. P. (2005). Role of the proto-oncogene Pokémon in cellular transformation and ARF repression. *Nature, 433*(7023), 278–285.

Magee, M., & D'Antonio, M. (2003). *The best medicine: Stories of doctors and patients who care for each other* (2nd ed.). New York: Spencer Books.

Magrane, D., Lang, J., Alexander, H., Leadley, J., & Bongiovanni, C. (2007, November). Washington, DC: American Association of Medical Colleges. Retrieved from http://www.aamc.org/members/wim/statistics/stats07/start.htm

Mahler, H. I. M., Kulik, J. A., Butler, H. A., Gerrard, M., & Gibbons, F. X. (2008). Social norms information enhances the efficacy of an appearance-based sun protection intervention. *Social Science & Medicine, 67,* 321–329.

Mahon, M., & Weymouth, J. (2012, May 3). U.S. spends far more for health care than 12 industrialized nations, but quality varies. New York: The Commonwealth Fund. Retrieved from http://www.commonwealthfund.org/News/News-Releases/2012/May/US-Spends-Far-More-for-Health-Care-Than-12-Industrialized-Nations-but-Quality-Varies.aspx

Maibach, E. W., & Cotton, D. (1995). Moving people to behavior change: A stage social cognitive approach to message design. In E. Maibach & R. L. Parrott (Eds.), *Designing health messages: Approaches from communication theory and public health practice* (pp. 41–64). Thousand Oaks, CA: Sage.

Maibach, E. W., & Parrott, R. L. (Eds.). (1995). *Designing health messages.* Thousand Oaks, CA: Sage.

Male nurses break through barriers to diversify profession. (2001, September 28). Robert Wood Johnson Foundation. Retrieved from http://www.rwjf.org/humancapital/product.jsp?id=72856

Malinski, V. M. (Ed.). (1986). *Explorations on Martha Rogers' science of unitary human beings.* Norwalk, CT: Appleton-Century-Crofts.

Malis, R. S., & Roloff, M. E. (2007). The effect of legitimacy and intimacy on peer interventions into alcohol abuse. *Western Journal of Communication, 71*(1), 49–68.

Managed care change. (2006, August 7). *Modern Healthcare,* p. 20.

Manfredi, C., Kaiser, K., Matthews, A. K., & Johnson, T. P. (2010). Are racial differences in patient-physician cancer communication and information explained by background, predisposing, and enabling factors? *Journal of Health Communication, 15,* 272–292. doi: 10.1080/10810731003686598

Marantz, P. R. (1990). Blaming the victim: The negative consequences of preventive medicine. *American Journal of Public Health, 80,* 1186–1187.

Margolick, D. (1990, August 6). In child deaths, a test for Christian Science. *New York Times,* online. Retrieved from http://query.nytimes.com/gst/fullpage.html?sec=health&res=9C0CE0D61030F935A3575BC0A966958260

Marion, G. S., Hildebrandt, C. A., Davis, S. W., Marin, A. J., & Crandall, S. J. (2008). Working effectively with interpreters: A model curriculum for physician assistant students. *Medical Teacher, 30*(6), 612–617.

Marks, R., Ok, H., Joung, H., & Allegrante, J. P. (2010). Perceptions about collaborative decisions: Perceived provider effectiveness among 2033 and 2007 Health Information National Trends Survey (HINTS) respondents. *Journal of Health Communication, 15,* 135–146.

Mars, R. (producer). (2011, June 30). The blue yarn. 99% invisible [podcast]. Distributed by Public Radio Exchange.

Marshall, A. A., Smith, S. W., & McKeon, J. K. (1995). Persuading low-income women to engage in mammography screening: Source, message, and channel preferences. *Health Communication, 7,* 283–300.

Martin, L. R., Williams, S. L., Haskard, K. B., & Dimatteo, M. R. (2005). The challenge of patient adherence. *Therapeutics and Clinical Risk Management, 1*(3), 189–199.

Marwick, C. (1997). Proponents gather to discuss evidence-based medicine. *Journal of the American Medical Association, 278,* 531–532.

Maslach, C. (1982). *Burnout: The cost of caring.* Englewood Cliffs, NJ: Prentice Hall.

Massachusetts health care reform: Six years later. Focus on health reform. (2012, May). Menlo Park, CA: The Henry J. Kaiser Family Foundation. Retrieved from http://www.kff.org/healthreform/upload/8311.pdf

Mast, M. S. (2007). On the importance of nonverbal communication in the physician–patient interaction. *Patient Education and Counseling, 67*(3), 315–318.

Mastin, T., Andsager, J. L., Choi, J., & Lee, K. (2007). Health disparities and direct-to-consumer prescription drug advertising: A content analysis of targeted magazine genres, 1992–2002. *Health Communication, 22*(1), 49–58.

Matthews, A. K. (1998). Lesbians and cancer support: Clinical issues for cancer patients. *Health Care for Women International, 1993,* 193–203.

Matthews, A. K., Sellergren, S. A., Manfredi, C., & Williams, M. (2002). Factors influencing medical information seeking among African-American cancer patients. *Journal of Health Communication, 7*(3), 205–219.

Mattson, M. (2010). Health advocacy by accident and discipline. *Health Communication, 25,* 622–624.

Matusitz, J., & Breen, G.-M. (2007). Telemedicine: Its effects on health communication. *Health Communication, 21*(1), 73–83.

Mayer, T. A., & Cates, R. J. (2004). *Leadership for great customer service: Satisfied patients, satisfied employees.* Chicago: Health Administration Press.

Maynard, C. (1998, September). How to make peace with your body. *Current Health, 2,* 66–71.

Maynard, D. W., & Frankel, R. M. (2006). On diagnostic rationality: Bad news, good news, and the symptoms residue. In J. Heritage & D. W. Maynard (Eds.), *Communication in medical care: Interactions between primary care physicians and patients* (pp. 248–278). Cambridge: Cambridge University Press.

McBride, B., & Cantor, D. (2010). Factors in errors of omission on a self-administered paper questionnaire. *Journal of Health Communication, 15,* 102–116. doi:10.1080/10810730.2010.525690

McCague, J. J. (2001, May 21). On today's older patients. *Medical Economics, 78*(10), 104.

McComas, K. A. (2006). Defining moments in risk communication research: 1996–2005. *Journal of Health Communication, 11*(1), 75–91.

McConatha, D. (2002). Aging online: Toward a theory of e-equality. In R. W. Morrell (Ed.), *Older adults, health information, and the World Wide Web* (pp. 21–41). Mahwah, NJ: Lawrence Erlbaum.

McCormick, T. R., & Conley, B. J. (1995). Patients' perspectives on dying and the care of dying patients. *Western Journal of Medicine, 163,* 236–243.

McCue, J. D. (1995). The naturalness of dying. *Journal of the American Medical Association, 273,* 1039–1044.

McCullough, D. (2008). *My mother, your mother: Embracing "slow medicine"—the compassionate approach to caring for your aging loved ones.* New York: HarperCollins.

McDermott, J. (1995). The first step (universal coverage is foundation for health care reform). *Journal of the American Medical Association, 273,* 251–254.

McGowan, B. (2001). Self-reported stress and its effects on nurses. *Nursing Standard, 15*(42), 33–38.

McGrath, J. (1995). The gatekeeping process: The right combinations to unlock the gates. In E. Maibach & R. L. Parrott (Eds.), *Designing health messages: Approaches from communication theory and public health practice* (pp. 199–216). Thousand Oaks, CA: Sage.

McGregor, D. (1960). *The human side of organization.* New York: McGraw-Hill.

McNamara, M. (2009). A look at patient navigators. CBS Evening News online. Retrieved from http://www.cbsnews.com/2100-500823_162-2842544.html

McNeese-Smith, D. (1996). Increasing employee productivity. *Hospital & Health Services Administration, 41,* 160–175.

McWhinney, I. (1989). The need for a transformed clinical method. In M. Stewart & D. Roter (Eds.), *Communicating with medical patients: Vol. 9. Interpersonal communication* (pp. 25–40). Newbury Park, CA: Sage.

Mead, G. H. (1934). *Minds, self, and society.* Chicago: University of Chicago Press.

Medical records: The growing threat to patient privacy. (2001, November 28). *San Diego Union-Tribune,* p. B8.

Menegatos Mercer, S. W., & Reilly, D. (2004). A qualitative study of patients' views on the consultation at the Glasgow Homoeopathic Hospital, an NHS integrative complementary and orthodox medical care unit. *Patient Education and Counseling, 53,* 13–18.

Meredith, L. S., Eisenman, D. P., Rhodes, H., Ryan, G., & Long, A. (2007, April–May). Trust influences response to public health messages during a bioterrorist event. *Journal of Health Communication, 12*(3), 217–232.

Merriam-Webster WWWebster Dictionary. (1999). Merriam-Webster Inc. Retrieved from www.m-w.com/cgi-bin/dictionary

Metts, S., & Manns, H. (1996). Coping with HIV and AIDS: The social and personal challenges. In E. B. Ray (Ed.), *Communication and disenfranchisement: Social issues and implications* (pp. 347–364). Mahwah, NJ: Lawrence Erlbaum.

Micalizzi, D. A. (2008, March 3). The aftermath of a "never event": A child's unexplained death and a system seemingly designed to thwart justice. *Modern Healthcare, 38*(9), 24.

Milika, R. M., & Trorey, G. M. (2008). Patients' expectations of the maintenance of their dignity. *Journal of Clinical Nursing, 17,* 2709–2717.

Millar, M. G., & Millar, K. (1998). Processing messages about disease detection and health promotion behaviors: The effects of anxiety. *Health Communication, 10,* 211–226.

Miller, C. H., Burgoon, M., Grandpre, J. R., & Alvaro, E. M. (2006). Identifying principal risk factors for the initiation of adolescent smoking behaviors: The significance of psychological reactance. *Health Communication, 19*(3), 241–252.

Miller, C. H., Lane, L. T., Deatrick, L. M., Young, A. M., & Potts, K. A. (2007). Psychological reactance and promotional health messages: The effects of controlling language, lexical concreteness, and the restoration of freedom. *Human Communication Research, 33,* 219–240.

Miller, K. I., Birkholt, M., Scott, C., & Stage, C. (1995). Empathy and burnout in human service work: An extension of the communication model. *Communication Research, 22,* 123–147.

Miller, K. I., Stiff, J. B., & Ellis, B. H. (1988). Communication and empathy as precursors to burnout among human service workers. *Communication Monographs, 55,* 250–265.

Miller, W. R., & Rollnick, S. (2002). *Motivational interviewing: Preparing people for change.* New York: Guilford Press.

Miller-Day, M., & Marks, J. (2006). Perceptions of parental communication orientation, perfectionism, and disordered eating behaviors of sons and daughters. *Health Communication, 19*(2), 153–163.

Mills, A. W. (1939). *Hospital public relations.* Chicago: Physicians Record Company.

Mills, C. B. (2005). Catching up with Down syndrome: Parents' experiences in dealing with the medical and therapeutic communities. In E. B. Ray (Ed.), *Health communication in practice: A case study approach* (pp. 195–210). Mahwah, NJ: Lawrence Erlbaum.

Minorities in medical education: Facts and figures 2005. (2005). Washington, DC: American Association of Medical Colleges. Retrieved from https://services.aamc.org/Publications/showfile.cfm?file=version53.pdf&prd_id=133&prv_id=154&pdf_id=53

Minority nursing statistics. (2009). Minority Nurse. Retrieved from http://www.minoritynurse.com/minority-nursing-statistics

Mishler, E. G. (1981). The social construction of illness. In E. B. Mishler, L. R. Amarasingham, S. D. Osherson, S. T. Hauser, & R. Leim (Eds.), *Social contexts of health, illness, and patient care* (pp. 141–168). Cambridge: Cambridge University Press.

Mishler, E. G. (1984). *The discourse of medicine: Dialectics of medical interviews.* Norwood, NJ: Ablex.

Mitka, M. (1996, August 26). Coalition presses to preserve affirmative action in medicine. *American Medical News, 39,* 1–4.

Modahl, M., Tompsett, L., & Moorhead, T. (2011, September). Doctors, patients and social media. Study conducted by the Care Continuum Alliance. Retrieved from http://www.quantiamd.com/q-qcp/doctorspatientsocialmedia.pdf

Molina, M. A., Cheung, M. C., Perez, E. A., Byrne, M. M., Franceschi, D., Moffat, F. L., Livingstone, A. S., Goodwin, W. J., Gutierrez, J. C., & Koniaris, L. G. (2008). African American and poor patients have a dramatically worse prognosis for head and neck cancer: An examination of 20,915 patients. *Cancer, 113*(10), 2797–2806.

Monohan, J. L. (1995). Thinking positively: Using positive affect when designing health messages. In E. Maibach & R. L. Parrott (Eds.), *Designing health messages: Approaches from communication theory and public health practice* (pp. 81–98). Thousand Oaks, CA: Sage.

Monohan, J. L., Miller, L. C., & Rothspan, C. (1997). Power and intimacy: On the dynamics of risky sex. *Health Communication, 9,* 303–322.

Moonhee, Y., & Roskos-Ewoldsen, D. R. (2007). The effectiveness of brand placements in the movies: Levels of placements, explicit and implicit memory, and brand-choice behavior. *Journal of Communication, 57,* 469–489.

Moore, J. R., & Gilbert, D. A. (1995). Elderly residents: Perceptions of nurses' comforting touch. *Journal of Gerontological Nursing, 21*(6), 6–13.

Moore, L. G., Van Arsdale, P. W., Glittenberg, J. E., & Aldrich, R. A. (1987). *The biocultural basis of health: Expanding views of medical anthropology.* Prospect Heights, IL: Waveland Press.

Moore, L. W., & Miller, M. (2003). Older men's experiences of living with severe visual impairment. *Journal of Advanced Nursing, 43*(1), 10–18.

Morgan, R. M., & Hunt, S. D. (1994). The commitment-trust theory of relationship marketing. *Journal of Marketing, 58*(3), 20–38.

Morgan, S. E., Harrison, T. R., Afifi, W. A., Long, S. D., & Stephenson, M. T. (2008). In their own words: The reasons why people will (not) sign an organ donor card. *Health Communication, 23*(1), 23–33.

Morgan, S. E., Harrison, T. R., Chewning, L., Davis, L., & DiCorcia, M. (2007). Entertainment (mis) education: The framing of organ donation in entertainment television. *Health Communication, 22*(2), 143–151.

Morse, D. S., Edwardsen, E. A., & Gordon, H. S. (2008). Missed opportunities for interval empathy in lung cancer communication. *Archives of Internal Medicine, 168*(17), 1853–1858.

Mosavel, M., & El-Shaarawi, N. (2007, December). "I have never heard of that one": Young girls' knowledge and perception of cervical cancer. *Journal of Health Communication, 12*(8), 707–719.

Moss, L. (2008, September 15). Cable's product placements drop 20% in first half: Nielsen. *Multichannel News,* np. Retrieved from http://www.multichannel.com/article/CA6596200.html

Motl, S. E., Timpe, E. M., & Eichner, S. F. (2005). Evaluation of accuracy of health studies reported in mass media. *Journal of the American Pharmacists' Association, 45*(6), 720–725.

Mulac, A., & Giles, H. (1996). "You're only as old as you sound": Perceived vocal age and social meanings. *Health Communication, 8,* 199–215.

Muller, J. H., Jain, S., Loeser, H., & Irby, D. M. (2008). Lessons learned about integrating a medical school curriculum: Perceptions of students, faculty and curriculum leaders. *Medical Education, 42*(8), 778–785.

Murdock, D. (2012, March 16). The unaffordable care act. *National Review Online.* Retrieved from http://www.nationalreview.com/articles/293612/unaffordable-care-act-deroy-murdock

Murphy, S. L., Xu J., & Kochanek, K. D. (2012, January 11). Deaths: Preliminary Data of 2010. *National Vital Statistics Report, 60*(4), 1–69. Retrieved from http://www.cdc.gov/nchs/data/nvsr/nvsr60/nvsr60_04.pdf

Murquia, A., Peterson, R. A., & Zea, M. C. (2003). Use and implications of ethnomedical health care approaches among Central American immigrants. *Health & Social Work, 28*(1), 43–51.

Murray, D. (2007, November 2). Hospitals vow a better response. *Medical Economics, 85*(21), 18.

Murray, E., Burns, J., May, C., Finch, T., O'Donnell, C., Wallace, P., & Mair, F. (2011). Why is it difficult to implement e-health initiatives? A qualitative study. *Implementation Science, 6*(6), np. Retrieved from http://www.implementationscience.com/content/6/1/6

Murray-Johnson, L., & Witte, K. (2003). Looking toward the future: Health message design strategies. In T. L. Thompson, A. M. Dorsey, K. I. Miller, & R. Parrott (Eds.), *Handbook of health communication* (pp. 473–495). Mahwah, NJ: Lawrence Erlbaum.

Muskin, P. R. (1998). The request to die: Role for a psychodynamic perspective on physician-assisted suicide. *Journal of the American Medical Association, 279,* 323–328.

Myers, P. N., & Biocca, F. A. (1992, Summer). The elastic body images: The effect of television advertisement and programming on body image distortion of young women. *Journal of Communication, 42,* 108–133.

Nabi, R. L., & Sullivan, J. L. (2001). Does television viewing relate to engagement in protective action against crime?: A cultivation analysis from a theory of reasoned action perspective. *Communication Research, 28*(6), 802–825.

Naeem, A. G. (2003). The role of culture and religion in the management of diabetes: A study of Kashmiri men in Leeds. *Journal of the Royal Society of Health, 123*(2), 110–116.

Nathanson, A. I., & Yang, M.-S. (2003, January). The effects of mediation content and form on children's responses to violent television. *Human Communication research, 29*(1), 111–134.

National Association of City & County Health Officials. (2012). About us. Washington, DC: Author. Retrieved from http://www.naccho.org/about/

National Center for Complementary and Alternative Medicine at the National Institutes of Health. (2012). The use of complementary and alternative medicine in the United States. Washington, DC: Author. Retrieved from http://nccam.nih.gov/news/camstats/2007/camsurvey_fs1.htm#use

National Coalition on Health Care. (2008). Health insurance costs. Washington, DC: Author. Retrieved from http://www.nchc.org/facts/cost.shtml

National Commission on Adult Literacy. (2008, June). Reach higher, America. Overcoming the crisis in the U.S. workforce. New York: Author. Retrieved from http://www.nationalcommissiononadultliteracy.org/ReachHigherAmerica/ReachHigher.pdf

National health care expenditures. (2012, January). Washington, DC: Center for Medicare and Medicaid Services, Office of the Actuary. Retrieved from https://www.cms.gov/Research-Statistics-Data-and-Systems/Statistics-Trends-and-Reports/NationalHealthExpendData/downloads/tables.pdf

National healthcare quality report. (2011). U.S. Department of Health and Human Services Agency for Healthcare Research and Quality. Rockville, MD. Retrieved from http://www.ahrq.gov/qual/nhqr11/nhqr11.pdf

National health expenditure projections 2008–2018. (2011). Centers for Medicare & Medicaid Services. Baltimore, MD: Author. Retrieved from http://www.cms.gov/site-search/search-results.html?q=projection

National Institute on Drug Abuse (NIDA). (2007, December). InfoFacts: High school and youth trends. Bethesda, MD: Author. Retrieved from http://www.drugabuse.gov/infofacts/hsyouthtrends.html

National Research Council. (1989). *Improving risk communication*. Washington, DC: National Academy Press. Retrieved from http://www.nap.edu/openbook.php?isbn=0309039436

Needleman, J., Buerhaus, P. I., Stewart, M., Zelevinsky, K., & Marrke, S. (2006, February). Market watch. Nursing staffing in hospitals: Is there a business case for quality? *Health Affairs, 25*(1), 204–211.

Neighbors, L. A., & Sobal, J. (2007). Prevalence and magnitude of body weight and shape dissatisfaction among university students. *Eating Disorders, 8*, 429–439.

Nelkin, D., & Gilman, S. L. (1991). Placing blame for devastating disease. In A. Mack (Ed.), *In time of plague: The history and social consequences of lethal epidemic disease* (pp. 39–56). New York: New York University Press.

Nemeth, S. A. (2000). Society, sexuality, and disabled/able bodied romantic relationships. In D. O. Braithwaite & T. L. Thompson (Eds.), *Handbook of communication and people with disabilities: Research and applications* (pp. 37–48). Mahwah, NJ: Lawrence Erlbaum.

Nestle, M. (1997, March–April). Alcohol guidelines for chronic disease prevention: From prohibition to moderation. *Nutrition Today, 32*, 86–92.

Neuendorf, K. A. (1990). Health images in the mass media. In E. B. Ray & L. Donohew (Eds.), *Communication and health: Systems and applications* (pp. 111–135). Hillsdale, NJ: Lawrence Erlbaum.

New CDC study finds no increase in obesity among adults; but levels still high. (2007, November 28).

Hyattsville, MD: National Center for Health Statistics. Retrieved from http://www.cdc.gov/nchs/pressroom/07newsreleases/obesity.htm

New research shows the national truth: youth smoking prevention campaign offset negative effects of decreased state tobacco control funding. (2008, April 3). Washington, DC: American Legacy Foundation. Retrieved from http://www.americanlegacy.org/2343.aspx

Newbart, D., & Grossman, K. N. (2003, June 24). Court rules in the affirmative. *Chicago Sun-Times*, p. 6.

Newman, M. A. (1986). *Health as expanding consciousness*. St. Louis, MO: C. V. Mosby.

Newman, M. A. (1995). *A developing discipline: Selected works of Margaret Newman*. New York: National League for Nursing Press.

Newman, M. A. (2000). *Health as expanding consciousness* (2nd ed.). Boston: Jones & Bartlett.

Newton, B. W., Barber, L., Clardy, J., Cleveland, E., & O'Sullivan, P. (2008). Is there hardening of the heart during medical school? *Academic Medicine, 83*(3), 244–249.

Ngyuen, D., Ornstein, C., & Weber, T. (2011, September 7). Dollars for docs: How industry dollars reach your doctors. Propublica: New York City, NY. Retrieved from http://projects.propublica.org/docdollars/

Nicolai, J., Demmel, R., & Farsch, K. (2010). Effects of mode of presentation on ratings of empathic communication in medical interviews. *Patient Education and Counseling, 80*, 76–79.

Niederdeppe, J., Davis, K. C., Farrelly, M. C., & Yarsevich, J. (2007). Stylistic features, need for sensation, and confirmed recall of national smoking prevention advertisements. *Journal of Communication, 57*, 272–292.

Niederdeppe, J., Fowler, E. F., Goldstein, K., & Pribble, J. (2010). Does local television news coverage cultivate fatalistic beliefs about cancer prevention? *Journal of Communication, 60*, 230–253.

Niederdeppe, J., Hornick, R. C., Kelly, B. J., Frosch, D. L., Romantan, A., Stevens, R. S., Barg, F. K., Weiner, J. L., & Schwartz, J. S. (2007). Examining the dimensions of cancer-related information seeking and scanning

behavior. *Health Communication, 22*(2), 153–167.

Nielsen reports TV, Internet and mobile usage among Americans. (2008, July 8). New York: Nielson Company. Retrieved from http://www.nielsen.com/media/2008/pr_080708.html

Noar, S. M., Clark, A., Cole, C., & Lustria, M. L. A. (2006). Review of interactive safer sex web sites: Practice and potential. *Health Communication, 20*(3), 233–241.

Noar, S. M., Zimmerman, R. S., Palmgreen, P., Lustria, M., & Horosewski, M. L. (2006). Integrating personality and psychosocial theoretical approaches to understanding safer sexual behavior: Implications for message design. *Health Communication, 19*(2), 165–174.

Noland, C., & Walter, J. C. (2006). "It's not our ass": Medical resident sensemaking regarding lawsuits. *Health Communication, 20*(1), 81–89.

Norander, S., Bates, J. P., & Bates, B. R. (2011). "D.O. or die": Identity negotiation among osteopathic medical students. *Health Communication, 26*, 59–70.

Nordby, H., & Nøhr, O. N. (2011). Care and empathy in ambulance services: Paramedics' experiences of communicative challenges in transports of patients with prolonged cancer. *Journal of Communication in Healthcare, 4*, 215–226.

Norling, G. R. (2005). Developing a theoretical model of rapport building: Implications for medical education and the physician–patient relationship. In M. Haider (Ed.), *Global public health communication* (pp. 407–414). Boston: Jones and Bartlett.

Novack, D. H., Suchman, A. L., Clark, W., Epstein, R. M., Najberg, G. E., & Kaplan, C. (1997). Calibrating the physician: Personal awareness and effective patient care. *Journal of the American Medical Association, 278*, 502–510.

Nowak, G. L., & Siska, M. J. (1995). Using research to inform campaign development and message design. In E. Maibach & R. L. Parrot (Eds.), *Designing health messages: Approaches from communication theory and public health practice* (pp. 169–185). Thousand Oaks, CA: Sage.

Nursing homes say Medicare change will cost them $5 billion. (2008,

May 5). *Modern Healthcare, 38*(18), 4.

Nussbaum, J. F. (2007). Life span communication and quality of life. Presidential address. *Journal of Communication, 57*, 1–7.

Nussbaum, J. F., Baringer, D., Fisher, C. L., & Kundrat, A. L. (2008). Connecting health, communication, and aging. In L. Sparks, H. D. O'Hair, & G. L. Kreps (Eds.), *Cancer, communication and aging* (pp. 67–76). Cresskill, NJ: Hampton Press.

Nussbaum, J. F., Pecchioni, L., Grant, J. A., & Folwell, A. (2000). Explaining illness to older adults: The complexities of the provider-patient interaction as we age. In B. B. Whaley (Ed.), *Explaining illness* (pp. 171–194). Mahwah, NJ: Lawrence Erlbaum.

Nussbaum, J. F., Ragan, S., & Whaley, B. (2003). Children, older adults, and women: Impact on provider–patient interaction. In T. L. Thompson, A. M. Dorsey, K. I. Miller, & R. Parrott (Eds.), *Handbook of health communication* (pp. 183–204). Mahwah, NJ: Lawrence Erlbaum.

Obermann, K., Jowett, M. R., Alcantara, M. O. O., Banzon, E. P., & Bodard, C. (2006). Social health insurance in a developing country: The case of the Philippines. *Social Science & Medicine, 62*, 3177–3185.

O'Connell, B., Bailey, S., & Pearce, J. (2003). Straddling the pathway from pediatrician to mainstream health care: Transition issues experienced in disability care. *Australian Journal of Rural Health, 11*(2), 57–63.

Oetzel, J., DeVargas, F., Ginossar, T., & Sanchez, C. (2007). Hispanic women's preferences for breast health information: Subjective cultural influences on source, message, and channel. *Health Communication, 21*(3), 223–233.

O'Keefe, D. J., & Jensen, J. D. (2007, October). The relative persuasiveness of gain-framed loss-framed messages for encouraging disease prevention behaviors: A meta-analytic review. *Journal of Health Communication, 12*(7), 623–644.

Older adults' health and age-related changes: Reality versus myth. (nd). American Psychological Association. Retrieved from http://www.apa.org/pi/aging/resources/guides/older-adults.pdf

O'Leary, S. C. B., Federico, S., & Hampers, L. C. (2003). The truth about language barriers: One residency program's experience. *Pediatrics, 111*(5), 1100.

Oliver, M. B., & Kalyanaraman, S. (2002). Appropriate for all viewing audiences? An examination of violent and sexual portrayals in movie previews featured on video rentals. *Journal of Broadcasting & Electronic Media, 46*(2), 283–299.

Olson, A. L., Gaffney, C. A., Lee, P. W., & Starr, P. (2008). Changing adolescent health behaviors: The healthy teens counseling approach. *American Journal of Preventive Medicine. 35*(5), S359–S3564.

One year since . . . (2012). Small good things. Retrieved from http://www.small-good-things.com/archives/2464

Online usage: 2008 survey of health care consumers. (2008). Deloitte. Retrieved from http://www.deloitte.com/dtt/article/0,1002,cid%253D192702,00.html

Orbe, M. P., & King, G., III. (2000). Negotiating the tension between policy and reality: Exploring nurses' communication about organizational wrongdoing. *Health Communication, 12*(1), 41–61.

Organ donation: Don't let these 10 myths confuse you. (2008). Rochester, MN: Mayo Clinic. Retrieved from http://www.mayoclinic.com/health/organ-donation/FL00077

OrganDonor.Gov. (2008). Access to U.S. government information on organ & tissue donation and transplantation. Washington, DC: U.S. Department of Health and Human Services. Retrieved from http://www.organdonor.gov

Orr, R. D. (1996). Transcultural medical care. *American Family Physician, 53*, 2004–2007.

Ota, H., Giles, H., & Somera, L. P. (2007). Beliefs about intra- and intergenerational communication in Japan, the Philippines, and the United States: Implications for older adults' subjective well-being. *Communication Studies, 58*(2), 173–188.

Outzen, R. (2005, November 3). Rising stars. *Independent News, 5*(42), np. Retrieved from http://inweekly.net/article.asp?artID=2040

Paek, H.-J. (2008). Mechanisms through which adolescents attend and respond to antismoking media campaigns. *Journal of Communication, 58*, 84–105.

Paek, H.-J., Reid, L. N., Choi, H., & Jeong, H. J. (2010). Promoting health (implicitly)? A longitudinal content analysis of implicit health information in cigarette advertising, 1954–2003. *Journal of Health Communication, 15*, 769–787. doi: 10.1080/10810730.2010.514033

Pahal, J. S. (2006). The dynamics of resident-patient communication: Data from Canada. *Communication & Medicine, 3*(2), 161–170.

Pardun, C. J. (2005). Changing attitudes, changing the world. Media's portrayal of people with intellectual disabilities. Special Olympics Report. Retrieved from http://www.specialolympics.org/NR/rdonlyres/eptchdrhwvdflwsrgeuegszs3xcau26ggwblw7635ux2-ecg6iyahhrm6gtfxenwq7astcfh7dw2jklyfop6ksnzinkh/CACW_Media_A4.pdf

Paris, M., & Hoge, M. A. (2010). Burnout in the mental health workforce: A review. *Journal of Behavioral Health Services and Research, 37*, 519–528.

Parker-Pope, T. (2002, November 11). Viagra is misunderstood despite name recognition. *Wall Street Journal*, online. Retrieved December 23, 2008, from http://www.usrf.org/breakingnews/bn_111202_viagra/bn_111202_viagra.html

Parkes, C. M. (1998). The dying adult. *British Medical Journal, 316*, 1313–1315.

Parkinson, J. R., & Jaffe, M. (2011, February 18). What's in a word? The debate over "ObamaCare": The name & the law. ABC News. Retrieved from http://abcnews.go.com/blogs/politics/2011/02/whats-in-a-word-the-debate-over-obamacare-the-name-the-law/

Parrott, R. (1995). Motivation to attend to health messages: Presentation of content and linguistic considerations. In E. Maibach & R. L. Parrott (Eds.), *Designing health messages: Approaches from communication theory and public health practice* (pp. 7–23). Thousand Oaks, CA: Sage.

Parrott, R., Hopfer, S., Ghetian, C., & Lengerich, E. (2007). Mapping as a visual health communication tool: Promises and dilemmas. *Health Communication, 22*(1), 13–24.

Parrott, R., & Polonec, L. (2008). Preventing green tobacco sickness in farming youth: A behavioral adaptation to health communication in health campaigns. In K. B. Wright & S. D. Moore (Eds.), *Applied health communication* (pp. 341–359). Cresskill, NJ: Hampton Press.

Parrott, R., Silk, K., Krieger, J. R., Harris, T., & Condit, C. (2004). Behavioral health outcomes associated with religious faith and media exposure about human genetics. *Health Communication, 16*(1), 29–45.

Parry, R. (2008). Are interventions to enhance communication performance in allied health professionals effective, and how should they be delivered? Direct and indirect evidence. *Patient Education and Counseling, 73,* 186–195.

Pascale, R. T. (1999). Leading from a different place: Applying complexity theory to tap potential. In J. A. Conger, G. M. Spreitzer, & E. E. Lawler, III (Eds.), *The leader's change handbook: An essential guide to setting direction and taking action* (pp. 195–220). San Francisco: Jossey-Bass.

Pateet, J. R., Fremonta, L. M., & Miovic, M. K. (2011). Possibly impossible patients: Management of difficult behavior in oncology patients. *Journal of Oncology Practice, 7,* 242–246.

Patel, D. S. (2005). Social mobilization as a tool for outreach programs in the HIV/AIDS crisis. In M. Haider (Ed.), *Global public health communication: Challenges, perspectives, and strategies* (pp. 91–102). Boston: Jones and Bartlett.

Paterniti, D. A., Pan, R. J., Smith, L. F., Horan, N. M., & West, D. C. (2006). From physician-centered to community-centered perspectives on health care: Assessing the efficacy of community-based training. *Academic Medicine, 81*(4), 347–353.

Patient perceptions of physician interpersonal quality of care. (2006, December). The Commonwealth Fund. Retrieved from http://www.commonwealthfund.org/snapshotscharts/snapshotscharts_show.htm?doc_id=381936

Patient satisfaction planner: Unsatisfactory stay sparks Planetree care model. (2007, September 1). *Hospital Peer Review,* np.

Patterson, J. (2012, March 4). Social media linking Las Vegas doctors, patients. *Las Vegas Review-Journal.* Retrieved from http://www.lvrj.com/health/social-media-linking-las-vegas-doctors-patients-141389473.html

Pearson, J. C., & Nelson, P. E. (1991). *Understanding and sharing* (5th ed.). Dubuque, IA: Wm. C. Brown.

Peeke, P. (2011, March 29). Reality shows abut the obese: Empowering or exploitative? *Everyday Fitness* (blog). Retrieved from http://blogs.webmd.com/pamela-peeke-md/2011/03/reality-shows-about-the-obese-empowering-or-exploitative.html

Pendleton, D., Schofield, T., Tate, P., & Havelock, P. (1984). *The consultant: An approach to learning and teaching.* Oxford: Oxford University Press.

Peng, W. (2009). Design and evaluation of a computer game to promote a healthy diet for young adults. *Health Communication, 24,* 115–127. doi:10.1080/10410230802676490

Pepicello, J. A., & Murphy, E. C. (1996). Integrating medical and operational management. *Physician Executive, 22,* 4–9.

Perry, B. (2002, November). Growth and satisfaction: "I became a nurse because I wanted to help others." *Canadian Business and Current Affairs, 98*(10), np.

Perse, E. M., Nathanson, A. I., & McLeod, D. M. (1996). Effects of spokesperson sex, public announcement appeal, and involvement in safe-sex PSA's. *Health Communication, 8,* 171–189.

Pesky, S., & Blascovich, J. (2007). Immersive virtual environments versus traditional platforms: Effects of violent and nonviolent video game play. *Media Psychology, 10*(1), 135–156.

Pet Partners video: The health benefits of pets. (nd). Author: Bellevue, WA. Retrieved from http://www.deltasociety.org/page.aspx?pid=642

Peter, J., & Valkenburg, P. M. (2006). Adolescents' exposure to sexually explicit online material and recreational attitudes toward sex. *Journal of Communication, 56,* 639–660.

Peters, E., Lipkus, I., & Diefenbach, M. A. (2006). The functions of affect in health communications and in the construction of health preferences. *Journal of Communication, 56,* S140–S162.

Peterson, E. D., Shah, B. R., Parsons, L., Pollack, C .V., Jr., French, W. J., Canto, J. G., Gibson, C. M., & Rogers, W. J. (2008). Trends in quality of care for patients with acute myocardial infarction in the National Registry of Myocardial Infarction from 1990 to 2006. *American Heart Journal, 156*(6), 1045–1055.

Peterson, T. (2012, April 3). My Miranda "health" rights. Wego health blog submission. Retrieved from http://community.wegohealth.com/profiles/blogs/my-miranda-health-rights-3rd-hawmc-superpowers-post

Petty, R. E., & Cacioppo, J. T. (1981). *Attitudes and persuasion: Classic and contemporary approaches.* Dubuque, IA: Wm. C. Brown.

Petty, R. E., & Cacioppo, J. T. (1986). *Communication and persuasion: Central and peripheral routes to attitude change.* New York: Springer.

Pexton, C. (nd). Framing the need to improve health care using Six Sigma methodologies. iSixSigma. Retrieved from http://healthcare.isixsigma.com/library/content/c030513a.asp

Pham, J. C., Aswani, M. S., Rosen, M., Lee, H., Huddle, M., Weeks, K., & Pronovost, P. J. (2012). Reducing medical errors and adverse events. *Annual Review of Medicine, 63,* 447–463.

Philpott, A., Knerr, W., & Maher, D. (2006). Promoting protection and pleasure: Amplifying the effectiveness of barriers against sexually transmitted infections and pregnancy. Viewpoint. *The Lancet* (www.thelancet.com), *368,* pp. 1–4. Retrieved from http://www.thepleasureproject.org/content/File/Pleasure_Lancet_Dec06.pdf

Physicians and surgeons. (2008). Occupational outlook handbook, 2008–09 edition. Washington, DC: U.S. Department of Labor. Retrieved from http://www.bls.gov/oco/ocos074.htm

Physicians are becoming engaged in addressing disparities. (2005, April). Institute for Ethics at the American Medical Association. Retrieved from http://www.ama-assn.org/ama/pub/category/14969.html

Physicians report growing dissatisfaction with "business" of medicine. (2008). Locum Tenens. Retrieved from www.locumtenens.com/

physician-careers/Business-of-Medicine.aspx

Pickering, A. (1995). *The mangle of practice: Time, agency, and science.* Chicago: University of Chicago Press.

Pighin, S., & Bonnefon, J.-F. (2011). Facework and uncertain reasoning in health communication. *Patient Education and Counseling, 85,* 169–172.

Pilling, V. K., & Brannon, L. A. (2007). Assessing college students' attitudes toward responsible drinking messages to identify promising binge drinking intervention strategies. *Health Communication, 22*(3), 265–276.

Pincus, C. R. (1995). Why medicine is driving doctors crazy. *Medical Economics, 72,* 40–44.

Pinkleton, B. E., Austin, E. W., Cohen, M., Miller, A., & Fitzgerald, E. (2007). A statewide evaluation of the effectiveness of media literacy training to prevent tobacco use among adolescents. *Health Communication, 21*(1), 23–34.

Piotrow, P. T., Rimon, J. G., II, Payne Merritt, A., & Saffitz, G. (2003). Advancing health communication: The PCS experience in the field. Center Publication 103. Baltimore: Johns Hopkins Bloomberg School of Public Health/Center for Communication Programs. Retrieved from http://www.jhuccp.org/pubs/cp/103/103.pdf

Piper, I., Shvarts, S., & Lurie, S. (2008). Women's preferences for their gynecologist or obstetrician. *Patient Education and Counseling, 72*(1), 109–114.

Planalp, S., & Trost, M. R. (2008). Communication issues at the end of life: Reports from hospice volunteers. *Health Communication, 23,* 222–233.

Plane passengers sue TB patient. (2007, July 13). CNN.com/health. Retrieved from http://www.cnn.com/2007/HEALTH/conditions/07/12/tb.suit/index.html

Platt, F. W. (1992). *Conversational failure: Case studies in doctor-patient communication.* Tacoma, WA: Essential Science.

Platt, F. W. (1995). *Conversation repair: Case studies in doctor-patient communication.* Boston: Little, Brown.

Platt, F. W., & Gordon, G. H. (2004). *Field guide to the difficult patient interview* (2nd ed.). Philadelphia: Lippincott Williams & Wilkins.

Polonec, L. D., Major, A. M., & Atwood, L. E. (2006). Evaluating the believability and effectiveness of the social norms message "Most students drink 0 to 4 drinks when they party." *Health Communication, 20*(1), 23–34.

Population Reference Bureau. (2012). World population growth, 1950–2050. Author: Washington, DC. Retrieved from http://www.prb.org/educators/teachersguides/human-population/populationgrowth.aspx

Porter-O'Grady, T., Bradley, C., Crow, G., & Hendrich, A. L. (1997, Winter). After a merger: The dilemma of the best leadership approach for nursing. *Nursing Administration Quarterly, 21,* 8–19.

Potter, J. E. (2002). Do ask, do tell. *Annals of Internal Medicine, 137*(5), 341–343.

Potter, W. J. (1998). *Media literacy.* Thousand Oaks, CA: Sage.

Press, I. (2002). *Patient satisfaction: Defining, measuring, and improving the experience of care.* Chicago: Health Administration Press.

Primetime shows with most product placement. (2011) CNBC News online. Retrieved from http://www.cnbc.com/id/45884892/Primetime_Shows_With_the_Most_Product_Placement?slide=1

Prochaska, J. O., & DiClemente, C. C. (1983). Stages and processes of self-change of smoking: Toward an integrative model of change. *Journal of Consulting and Clinical Psychology, 51,* 390–395.

Prochaska, J. O., DiClemente, C. C., & Norcross, J. C. (1992). In search of how people change applications to the addictive behaviors. *American Psychologist, 47,* 1102–1114.

Prochaska, J. O., Johnson, S., & Lee, P. (1998). The transtheoretical model of behavior change. In S. A. Shumaker, E. B. Schron, J. K. Ockene, & W. L. McBee (Eds.), *The handbook of behavior change* (2nd ed., pp. 59–84). New York: Springer-Verlag.

Public Relations Society of America. (2012). What is public relations? PRSA's widely accepted definition. Author: New York, NY. Retrieved from http://www.prsa.org/AboutPRSA/PublicRelationsDefined

Purnell, L. D. (2008, February). Traditional Vietnamese health and healing. *Urologic Nursing, 28*(1), 63–67.

Query, J. L., Jr., & Kreps, G. L. (1996). Testing a relational model for health communication competence among caregivers for individuals with Alzheimer's Disease. *Journal of Health Psychology, 1,* 335–351.

Query, J. L., Jr., & Wright, K. (2003). Assessing communication competence in an online study: Toward informing subsequent interventions among older adults with cancer, their lay caregivers, and peers. *Health Communication, 15*(2), 203–218.

Quesada, A., & Summers, S. L. (1998, January). Literacy in the cyberage: Teaching kids to be media savvy. *Technology & Learning, 18,* 30–36.

Quick, B. L. (2010). Applying the health belief model to examine news coverage regarding steroids in sports by ABC, CBS, and NBC between March 1990 and May 2008. *Health Communication, 25,* 247–257. doi:10.1080/10410230103698929

Quick, B. L., & Stephenson, M. T. (2007). Authoritative parenting and issue involvement as indicators of ad recall: An empirical investigation of anti-drug ads for parents. *Health Communication, 22*(1), 25–35.

Raacke, J., & Bonds-Raacke, J. (2008). MySpace and Facebook: Applying the uses and gratifications theory to exploring friend-networking sites. *Cybepsychology & Behavior, 11,* 169–174.

Rabak-Wagener, J., Eickhoff-Shemek, J., & Kelly-Vance, L. (1998, July). The effect of media analysis on attitudes and behaviors regarding body images among college students. *Journal of American College Health, 47,* 29–35.

Raffel, M. W., & Raffel, N. K. (1989). *The U.S. health system: Origins and functions* (3rd ed.). New York: John Wiley & Sons.

Ragan, S. L. (1990). Verbal play and multiple goals in the gynecological exam interaction. *Journal of Language and Social Psychology, 9,* 67–84.

Ragan, S. L., & Goldsmith, J. (2008). End-of-life communication: The drama of pretense in the talk of dying patients and their M.D. In K. B. Wright & S. D. Moore (Eds.), *Applied health communication* (pp. 207–227). Cresskill, NJ: Hampton Press.

Ragan, S. L., Wittenberg, E., & Hall, H. T. (2003). The communication of palliative care for the elderly cancer patient. *Health Communication, 15*(2), 219–226.

Ragan, S. L., Wittenberg-Lyles, E. W., Goldsmith, J., & Sanchez-Reilly, S. (2008). *Communication as comfort: Multiple voices in palliative care.* New York: Routledge.

Rains, S. A. (2008a, January/March). Seeking health information in the information age: The role of Internet self-efficacy. *Western Journal of Communication, 72*(1), 1–18.

Rains, S. A. (2008b, June). Health at high speed: Broadband Internet access, health communication, and the digital divide. *Communication Research, 35*(3), 283–297.

Rains, S. A., & Keating, D. M. (2011, December). The social dimension of blogging about health: Health blogging, social support, and well-being. *Communication Monographs, 78*, 511–534.

Rains, S. A., & Turner, M. M. (2007). Psychological reactance and persuasive health communication: A test and extension of the intertwined model. *Human Communication Research, 33*(2), 241–269.

Ramanadhan, S., & Viswanath, K. (2006). Health and the information nonseeker: A profile. *Health Communication, 20*(2), 131–139.

Ramirez, A. J., Graham, J., Richards, M. A., Cull, A., & Gregory, W. M. (1996). Mental health of hospital consultants: The effects of stress and satisfaction at work. *The Lancet, 347*, 724–729.

Ratanawongsa, N., Roter, D., Beach, M. C., Laird, S. L., Larson, S. M., Carson, K. A., & Cooper, L. A. (2008). Physician burnout and patient–physician communication during primary care encounters. *Journal of General Internal Medicine, 23*(10), 1581–1588.

Ratzan, S., & Meltzer, W. (2005). (2005). State of the art in crisis communication: Past lessons and principles of practice. In M. Haider (Ed.), *Global public health communication: Challenges, perspectives, and strategies* (pp. 321–347). Boston: Jones and Bartlett.

Rawlins, W. K. (1989). A dialectical analysis of the tensions, functions, and strategic challenges of communication in young adult friendships. *Communication Yearbook, 12*, 157–189.

Rawlins, W. K. (1992). *Friendship matters: Communication, dialectics, and the life course.* New York: Aldine De Gruyter.

Rawlins, W. K. (2009). Narrative medicine and the stories of friends. *Journal of Applied Communication Research, 37*, 167–173.

Reality check: 2008 survey of health care consumers. (2008). Deloitte. Retrieved from http://www.deloitte.com/dtt/article/0,1002,cid=192468,00.html

Recovering hope, reclaiming daily life. (nd). Methodist Rehabilitation Hospital website. Retrieved from http://www.methodist-rehab.com/patient_success_stories/guillain_barre_syndrome_3_5_2009.aspx

Reducing health disparities in Asian American and Pacific Islander populations. (2005). Management Sciences of Health. Office of Minority Health and Bureau of Primary Health Care. Retrieved from http://erc.msh.org/aapi/ca6.html

Rees, A. M. (1994). Consumer enlightenment or consumer confusion? *Consumer Health Information Source Book, 4*, 10–11.

Reese, S. (2008, April 18). Pick up the mouse, put down the phone: Trading e-mails with patients is easier than playing phone tag, and you may even get paid for it. *Medical Economics, 85*(8), 24–28.

Regan-Smith, M. G., Obenshain, S. S., Woodward, C., Richards, B., Zeitz, H. J., & Parker, A. S., Jr. (1994). Rote learning in medical schools. *Journal of the American Medical Association, 272*, 1380–1381.

Registered nurse population: Findings from the 2004 national sample survey of registered nurses. (2007, March). Washington, DC: U.S. Department of Health and Human Services. Retrieved from http://bhpr.hrsa.gov/healthworkforce/rnsurvey04

Reilly, D. R. (2003, Winter). Not just a patient: The dangers of dual relationships. *Canadian Journal of Rural Medicine, 8*(1), np.

Reilly, P. (1987). *To do no harm: A journey through medical school.* Dover, MA: Auburn House.

Reinberg, S. (2008, October 29). U.S. hospitals lag in patient satisfaction. *Health Day* online. Retrieved from http://www.healthday.com/Article.asp?AID=620778

Reinhardt, J. P., Boerner, K., & Horowitz, A. (2006). Good to have but not to use: Differential impact of perceived and received support on well-being. *Journal of Social and Personal Relationships, 23*(1), 117–129.

Reis, R. (2008). How Brazilian and North American newspapers frame the stem cell research debate. *Science Communication, 29*(3), 316–334.

Reiser, S. J. (1978). *Medicine and the reign of technology.* Cambridge: Cambridge University Press.

Renganathan, E., Hosein, E., Parks, W., Lloyd, L., Suhaili, M. R., & Odugleh, A. (2005). Communication-for-behavioral-impact (COMB): A review of WHO's experiences with strategic social mobilization and communication in the prevention and control of communicable diseases. In M. Haider (Ed.), *Global public health communication: Challenges, perspectives, and strategies* (pp. 305–320). Boston: Jones and Bartlett.

Results of *The New York Times*/CBS News poll. (2012, March 21–25). *The New York Times* online. Retrieved from http://www.nytimes.com/interactive/2012/03/27/us/03272012_polling_doc.html?ref=us

Rey-Lopez, J. P., Ruiz, J. R., Vicente-Rodriguez. G., Gracia-Marco, L., Manios, Y., Sjostrom, M., De Bourdeaudhuij, I., & Moreno, L. A. (2012). Physical activity does not attenuate the obesity risk of TV viewing in youth. *Pediatric Obesity, 7*, 240–250.

Reynolds, B. (2006, August). Response to best practices. *Journal of Applied Communication Research, 34*(4), 249–252.

Rhodes, S. D., Yee, L. J., & Hergenrather, K. C. (2003). Hepatitis A vaccination among young African American men who have sex with men in the Deep South: Psychosocial predictors. *Journal of the American Medical Association, 95*(4), 31S–36S.

Rifkin, L. (2008, March 21). Still a privilege to be a doctor: Though not immune to the hassles and hardships of practice, this physician tells why he experiences the joy of medicine. *Medical Economics, 85*(6), 28–29.

Rimal, R. (2000). Closing the knowledge–behavior gap in health promotion: The mediating role of self-efficacy. *Health Communication, 12*(3), 219–238.

Rimal, R. N. (2008, March/April). Modeling the relationship between descriptive norms and behaviors: A test and extension of the theory of normative social behavior (TNSB). *Health Communication, 23*(2), 103–116.

Rimal, R. N., & Adkins, D. A. (2003). Using computers to narrowcast health messages: The role of audience segmentation, targeting, and tailoring in health promotion. In T. L. Thompson, A. M. Dorsey, K. I. Miller, & R. Parrott (Eds.), *Handbook of health communication* (pp. 497–513). Mahwah, NJ: Lawrence Erlbaum.

Rimal, R. N., & Morrison, D. (2006). A uniqueness to personal threat (UPT) hypothesis: How similarity affects perceptions of susceptibility and severity in risk assessment. *Health Communication, 20*(3), 209–219.

Rimal, R. N., Ratzan, S. C., Arnston, P., & Freimuth, V. S. (1997). Reconceptualizing the "patient": Health care promotion as increasing citizens' decision-making competencies. *Health Communication, 9*, 61–74.

Rimal, R. N., & Real, K. (2005, June). How behaviors are influenced by perceived norms: A test of the theory of normative social behavior. *Communication Research, 32*, 389–414.

Rimer, B. K., & Kreuter, M. W. (2006). Advancing tailored health communication: A persuasive and message effects perspective. *Journal of Communication, 56*, S184–S201.

Rising to the challenge. Results from a scorecard on local health system performance. (2012). New York: The Commonwealth Fund. Retrieved from http://www.commonwealthfund.org/~/media/Files/Publications/Fund%20Report/2012/Mar/Local%20Scorecard/1578_EXEC_SUMM_Commission_rising_to_challenge_local_scorecard_2012_FINAL.pdf

Ritzer, G. (1993). *The McDonaldization of society*. Thousand Oaks, CA: Pine Forge Press.

Robert Wood Johnson Foundation. (2001). National program project report on urban hospital closing, mergers, and other reconfigurations. Princeton, NJ: Author. Retrieved from www.rwjf.org/reports/grr/0208054.htm

Robert Wood Johnson Foundation. (2008, April 29). Cost of insurance far outpaces income. Princeton, NJ: Author. Retrieved August 14, 2008, from www.rwjf.org/programareas/resources/product.jsp?id=28698&pid=1132

Robert Wood Johnson Foundation. (2010). Report projects of to 66 million Americans could be uninsured by 2019 unless health reform is enacted. Princeton, NJ: Author. Retrieved from http://www.rwjf.org/healthpolicy/product.jsp?id=42970

Roberto, A. J., Zimmerman, R. S., Carlyle, K. E., Abner, E. L., Cupp, P. K., & Hansen, G. L. (2007). The effects of computer-based pregnancy, STD, and HIV prevention intervention: A nine-school trial. *Health Communication, 21*(2), 115–124.

Roberts, L., & Bucksey, S. J. (2007). Communicating with patients: What happens in practice? *Physical Therapy, 87*(5), 587–594.

Robertson, T. (1999, March 26). Michigan jury gets Kevorkian case: Defendant cites civil rights leaders. *Boston Globe*, p. A3.

Robinson, J. D. (2003). An interactional structure of medical activities during acute visits and its implications for patients' participation. *Health Communication, 15*(1), 27–58.

Robinson, J. D., & Tian, Y. (2009). Cancer patients and the provision of informational social support. *Health Communication, 24*(5), 381–390. doi:10.1080/10410230903023261

Robinson, J. D., Turner, J. W., & Levine, Y. (2011). Expanding the walls of the health care encounter: Support and outcomes for patients online. *Health Communication, 26*, 125–134.

Robinson, S. (2009, March 6). Government-funded health care? We're already two-thirds there. Campaign of America's Future. Washington, DC: Author. Retrieved from http://www.ourfuture.org/blog-entry/2009031006/government-funded-health-care-were-already-23-there

Robinson, T., Callister, M., Magoffin, D., & Moore, J. (2006). The portrayal of older characters in Disney animated films. *Journal of Aging Studies, 21*, 203–213.

Roche, T. (2001, July 30). Saving Jessie Arbogast. *Time, 158*(4), 40–41. Retrieved from http://www.time.com/time/magazine/article/0,9171,1000445-1,00.html

Rodriguez, H. P., Anastario, M. P., Frankel, R. M., Odigie, E. G., Rogers, W. H., von Glahn, T., & Safran, D. G. (2008). Can teaching agenda-setting skills to physicians improve clinical interaction quality? A controlled intervention. *BMC Medical Education, 8*, 3–7.

Rogers, E. M. (1973). *Communication strategies for family planning*. New York: Free Press.

Rogers, E. M. (1983). *Diffusion of innovations* (3rd ed.). New York: The Free Press.

Rogers, E. M., & Dearing, J. W. (1988). Agenda-setting research: Where has it been, where is it going? In J. A. Anderson (Ed.), *Communication yearbook* (11th ed., pp. 555–593). Newbury Park, CA: Sage.

Rogers, M. E. (1986). Science of unitary human beings. In V. M. Malinski (Ed.), *Explorations of Martha Rogers' science of unitary human beings* (pp. 3–14). Norwalk, CT: Appleton-Century-Crofts.

Rollnick, S., & Miller, W. (1995). What is motivational interviewing? *Behavioural and Cognitive Psychotherapy, 23*, 325–334. Reprinted online. Retrieved from http://www.motivationalinterview.org/clinical/whatismi.html

Romer, D., Jamieson, K. H., & Aday, S. (2003, March). Television news and the fear of crime. *Journal of Communication, 53*(1), NA.

Rooney, J. J., & Vanden Heuvel, L. N. (2004, July). Root cause analysis for beginners. *Quality Progress, 37*(7), 45.

Rosen, I. M., Gimotty, P. A., Shea, J. A., & Bellini, L. M. (2006). Evolution of sleep quantity, sleep deprivation, mood disturbances, empathy, and burnout among interns. *Academic Medicine, 81*(1), 82–85.

Rosenstein, A. H., & O'Daniel, M. (2008). Managing disruptive physician behavior: Impact on staff relationships and patient care. *Neurology, 70*(17), 1564–1570.

Rosenstock, I. M. (1960). What research in motivation suggests for public health. *American Journal of Public Health, 50,* 295–301.

Rosenthal, S. L., Lewis, L. M., Succop, P. A., Burklow, K. A., Nelson, P. R., Shedd, K. D., Heyman, R. B., & Biro, F. M. (1999). Adolescents' views regarding sexual history taking. *Clinical Pediatrics, 38*(4), 227–233.

Rossiter, C. M., Jr. (1975). Defining "therapeutic communication." *Journal of Communication, 25*(3), 127–130.

Roter, D. L., Larson, S., Sands, D. Z., Ford, D. E., & Houston, T. (2008). Can e-mail messages between patients and physicians be patient-centered? *Health Communication, 23*(1), 80–86.

Roter, D. L., Stewart, M., Putnam, S. M., Lipkin, J., Jr., Stiles, W., & Iniu, T. S. (1997). Communication patterns of primary care physicians. *Journal of the American Medical Association, 277,* 350–357.

Rothman, A. J., Bartels, R. D., Wlaschin, J. & Salovey, P. (2006). The strategic use of gain- and loss-framed messages to promote healthy behavior: How theory can inform practice. *Journal of Communication, 56,* S202–S220.

Rothman, A. J., & Salovey, P. (1997). Shaping perceptions to motivate healthy behavior: The role of message framing. *Psychological Bulletin, 121,* 3–19.

Rouner, D., & Lindsey, R. (2006). Female adolescent communication about sexually transmitted diseases. *Health Communication, 19*(1), 29–38.

Rucinski, D. (2004, August). Community boundedness, personal relevance, and the knowledge gap. *Communication Research, 31*(4), 472–495.

Rudman, A., & Gustavsson, J. P. (2012). Burnout during nursing education predicts lower occupational preparedness and future clinical performance: A longitudinal study. *International Journal of Nursing Studies, 49,* 988–1001.

Rudolph, J. (2008, March 7). Bonding with patients when time is scarce: Even the busiest physician can find time to convey caring and concern. *Medical Economics, 85*(5), 50–51.

Ruppert, R. A. (1996, March). Caring for the lay caregiver. *American Journal of Nursing, 96,* 40–46.

Russell, L. D., & Babrow, A. S. (2011). Risk in the making: Narrative, problematic integration, and the social construction of risk. *Communication Theory, 21*(3), 239–260. doi:10.1111/j.1468-2885-.2011.01386.x

Rutledge, M. S., & McLaughlin, C. G. (2008, October). Hispanics and health insurance coverage. Robert Wood Johnson Foundation. Retrieved from http://www.rwjf.org/pr/product.jsp?id=35728

Ryan, E. B., Anas, A. P., & Vuckovich, M. (2007). The effects of age, hearing loss, and communication difficulty on first impressions. *Communication Research Reports, 24*(1), 13–19.

Ryan, E. B., & Butler, R. N. (1996). Communication, aging, and health: Toward understanding health provider relationships with older clients. *Health Communication, 8,* 191–197.

Saha, S., Guiton, G., Wimmers, P. F., & Wilkerson, L. (2008). Student body racial and ethnic composition and diversity-related outcomes in U.S. medical schools. *Journal of the American Medical Association, 300*(10), 1135–1145.

Salamon, J. (2008, May 26). My year inside Maimonides: A hospital with a polyglot patient body learns the importance of communication. *Modern Healthcare, 38*(21), 24.

Salander, P. (2002). Bad news from the patient's perspective: An analysis of the written narratives of newly diagnosed cancer patients. *Social Science & Medicine, 55,* 721–732.

Salas, E., Wilson, K. A., Murphy, C. E., King, H., & Salisbury, M. (2008, June). Communicating, coordinating, and cooperating when lives depend on it: Tips for teamwork. *Joint Commission Journal on Quality and Patient Safety, 34,* 333–341.

Salmon, C. T., & Atkin, C. (2003). Using media campaigns for health promotion. In T. L. Thompson, A. M. Dorsey, K. I. Miller, & R. Parrott (Eds.), *Handbook of health communication* (pp. 449–472). Mahwah, NJ: Lawrence Erlbaum.

Sandberg, H. (2007). A matter of looks: The framing of obesity in four Swedish daily newspapers. *European Journal of Communication Research, 32*(4), 447–472.

Sanders, L. (2003). The ethics imperative. *Modern Healthcare, 33*(11), 46.

Sandman, P. M. (2006a). Telling 9/11 emergency responders to wear their masks. In Comments and questions (and some answers). The Peter Sandman Risk Communication Website. Retrieved from http://www.psandman.com/gst2006.htm

Sandman, P. M. (2006b, August). Crisis communication best practices: Some quibbles and additions. *Journal of Applied Communication Research, 34*(3), 257–262.

Sanghavi, D. (2008, March 9). When science meets the soul. Maria and Jose Azevedo had to choose: Allow their baby to die a preventable death or save him while acting against their religion. The doctor who helped guide them shares their story. *Boston Globe,* p. 28.

Sarkar, U., Karter, A. J., Liu, J. Y., Adler, N. E., Nguyen, R., Lopez, A., & Schillinger, D. (2010). The literacy divide: Health literacy and the use of an Internet-based patient portal in an integrated health system—results from the Diabetes Study of Northern California (DISTANCE). *Journal of Health Communication, 15,* 183–196. doi:10.1080/10810730.2010.499988

Sastre, M. T. M., Sorum, P. C., & Mullet, E. (2011). Breaking bad news: The patient's viewpoint. *Health Communication, 26,* 649–655.

Scheide, R. V. (2006, January 25). Viagra and the culture of manhood. *Creating Loafing,* online. Retrieved December 24, 2008, from http://charlotte.creativeloafing.com/gyrobase/Content?oid=oid%3A7280

Schein, E. H. (1986). *Organizational culture and leadership.* San Francisco: Jossey-Bass.

Schmid Mast, M., Hall, J. A., & Roter, D. (2007). Disentangling physician sex and physician communication style: Their effects on patient satisfaction in a virtual medical visit. *Patient Education and Counseling, 68,* 16–22.

Schmid Mast, M., Hall, J. A., & Roter, D. (2008). Caring and dominance affect participants' perceptions and behaviors during a virtual medical visit. *Journal of General Internal Medicine, 23*(5), 523–527.

Schneider, M-J. (2006). *Introduction to public health* (2nd ed.). Boston: Jones and Bartlett.

Scholl, J. C. (2007). The use of humor to promote patient-centered care. *Journal of Applied Communication Research, 35*(2), 156–176.

Schooler, C., Chaffee, S. H., Flora, J. A., & Roser, C. (1998). Health campaign channels: Tradeoffs among reach, specificity, and impact. *Health Communication Research, 24*, 410–432.

Schopler, J. H., & Galinsky, M. J. (1993). Support groups as open systems: A model for practice and research. *Health and Social Work, 18*, 195–207.

Schreiber, L. (2005). The importance of precision in language: Communication research and (so-called) alternative medicine. *Health Communication, 17*(2), 173–190.

Schulman, K. A., Berlin, J. A., Harless, W., Kerner, J. F., Sistrunk, S., Gersh, B. J., Dubé, R., Taleghani, C. K., Burke, J. E., William, S., Eisenberg, J. M., & Escarce, J. J. (1999). The effect of face and sex on physicians' recommendations for cardiac catheterization. *New England Journal of Medicine, 340*, 618–626.

Schur, L. (director and producer), & Thompson, L. (producer). (2008). *Greedy for life.* Arlington, VA: Schur Schot Productions.

Schur, L. (director and producer), & Thompson, L. (producer). (2012). *The beauty of aging.* Arlington, VA: Schur Schot Productions.

Schwade, S. (1994, December). Hospitals with the human touch. *Prevention, 46*, 96–99.

Scott, M. K. (2008, September 11). Not-quite-so-thin is in for models at Fashion Week. *Associated Press.* Retrieved from http://ap.google.com/article/ALeqM5iN3K5rOZKX2Oe-XcYhoqPZN5VimAD934LH9G0

Seeger, M. W. (2006, August). Best practices in crisis communication: An expert panel process. *Journal of Applied Communication Research, 34*(3), 232–244.

Segrin, C., & Domschke, T. (2011). Social support, loneliness, recuperative processes, and their direct and indirect effects on health. *Health Communication, 26*, 221–232. doi:10.1080/10410236.2010.546771

Segrin, C., & Passalacqua, S. A. (2010). Functions of loneliness, social support, health behaviors, and stress in association with poor health. *Health Communication, 25*, 312–322.

Seltzer, T., Gardner, E., Bichard, S., & Callison, C. (2012). PR in the ER: Managing internal organization-public relationships in a hospital emergency department. *Public Relations Review, 38*, 128–136.

Senge, P. M. (2006). *The fifth discipline: The art and practice of the learning organization.* New York: Doubleday/Currency.

Sexual health of adolescents and young adults in the United States. (2008, September). Menlo Park: CA: Henry J. Kaiser Family Foundation. Retrieved from http://www.kff.org/womenshealth/upload/3040_04.pdf

Shannon, C. K. (2006, November/December). A gender-based study of attitudes and practice characteristics of rural physicians in West Virginia. *West Virginia Medical Journal, 102*(6), 22–25.

Shapiro, I. S. (1984, Fall). Executive forum. Managerial communication: The view from the inside. *California Management Review, 27*, 157–172.

Shapiro, R. S., Tym, K. A., Eastwood, D., Derse, A. R., & Klein, J. P. (2003). Managed care, doctors, and patients: Focusing on relationships, not rights. *Cambridge Quarterly of Healthcare Ethics, 12*(3), 300–307.

Sharf, B. (2010). The day Patrick Swayze died. *Health Communication, 25*, 628–631.

Sharf, B. F., Haidet, P., & Kroll, T. L. (2005). "I want you to put me in the grave with all my limbs": The meaning of active health participation. In E. B. Ray (Ed.), *Health communication in practice: A case study approach* (pp. 39–51). Mahwah, NJ: Lawrence Erlbaum.

Shea, S., Basch, C. E., Wechsler, H., & Lantigua, R. (1996). The Washington Heights-Inwood Healthy Heart Program. A 6-year report from a disadvantaged urban setting. *American Journal of Public Health, 86*, 166–171.

Shortell, S. M., Gillies, R. R., & Devers, K. J. (1995). Reinventing the American hospital. *Millbank Quarterly, 73*, 131–160.

Shue, C. K., O'Hara, L. L. S., Marini, D., McKenzie, J., & Schreiner, M. (2010). Diabetes and low-health literacy: A preliminary outcome report of a mediated intervention to enhance patient-physician communication. *Communication Education, 59*, 360–373.

Shuler, S. (2011). Social support without strings attached. *Health Communication, 26*, 198–201.

Shurn, L. J. (Ed.). (2004). *The psychology of entertainment media: Blurring the lines between entertainment and persuasion.* Mahwah, NJ: Lawrence Erlbaum.

Signorielli, N. (1993). *Mass media images and impact on health.* Westport, CT: Greenwood Press.

Silk, K. J., Bigsby, E., Volkman, J., Kingsley, C., Atkin, C., Ferrara, M., & Goins, L.-A. (2006). Formative research on adolescent and adult perceptions of risk factors for breast cancer. *Social Science & Medicine, 63*, 3124–3136.

Silvester, J., Patterson, F., Koczwara, A., & Ferguson, E. (2007). "Trust me . . . ": Psychological and behavioral predictors or perceived physician empathy. *Journal of Applied Psychology, 92*(2), 519–527.

Simon-Arndt, C. M., Hurtado, S. L., & Patriarca-Troyk, L. A. (2006). Acceptance of Web-based personalized feedback: User ratings of an alcohol misuse prevention program targeting U.S. Marines. *Health Communication, 21*(1), 13–22.

Singer, D. G., & Singer, J. L. (1998). Developing critical viewing skills and media literacy in children. *Annals of the American Academy of Political and Social Science, 557*, 164–179.

Singh, S. N., & Wachter, R. M. (2008). Perspectives on medical outsourcing and telemedicine—rough edges in a flat world? *New England Journal of Medicine, 358*(15), 1622.

Siskin, A. (2011, March 11). Treatment of noncitizens under the patient protection and affordable care act. Washington, DC: Congressional Research Service. Retrieved from http://www.ciab.com/WorkArea/DownloadAsset.aspx?id=2189

Sismondo, S. (2008). How pharmaceutical industry funding affects trial outcomes: Causal structures and responses. *Social Science & Medicine, 66*(9), 1909–1914.

Sixth futures forum on crisis communication. (2004, May). Reykjavik, Iceland. World Health Organization. Retrieved from http://www.euro.who.int/document/E85056.pdf

Skalski, P., Tamborini, R., Glazer, E., & Smith, S. (2009). Effects of humor on presence and recall of persuasive messages. *Communication*

Quarterly, 57, 136–153. doi:10.1080/01463370902881619

Skluth, M. (2007, September 7). Get patients involved. *Medical Economics, 84*(17), 16.

Skolnick, A. (1990). Christian scientists claim healing efficacy equal if not superior to that of medicine. *Journal of the American Medical Association, 264,* 1379–1381.

Slack, P. (1991). Responses to plague in early modern Europe: The implications of public health. In A. Mack (Ed.), *In time of plague: The history and social consequences of lethal epidemic disease* (pp. 111–132). New York: New York University Press.

Slater, M. D. (1995). Choosing audience segmentation strategies and methods for health communication In E. Maibach & R. L. Parrot (Eds.), *Designing health messages: Approaches from communication theory and public health practice* (pp. 186–198). Thousand Oaks, CA: Sage.

Slater, M. D. (2006). Specification and misspecification of theoretical foundations and logic models for health communication campaigns. *Health Communication, 20*(2), 149–158.

Slusarz, M. (1996). From fried rice to sushi: To market an integrated delivery system throw out the old menu. *Journal of Health Care Marketing, 16,* 12–15.

Smedley, B. D., Stith, A. Y., & Nelson, A. R. (2003). Unequal treatment: Confronting racial and ethnic disparities in health care. Board on Health Sciences Policy. Institute of Medicine. Retrieved December 3, 2008, from http://books.nap.edu/openbook.php?isbn=030908265X

Smith, D. (2011). Health care consumer's use of trust and health information sources. *Journal of Communication in Healthcare, 4,* 200–209.

Smith, K. C., & Wakefield, M. (2006). Newspaper coverage of youth and tobacco: Implications for public health. *Health Communication, 19*(1), 19–28.

Smith, M., Droppleman, P., & Thomas, S. P. (1996, January–March). Under assault: The experience of work-related anger in female registered nurses. *Nursing Forum, 31,* 22–33.

Smith, R. (2007, April/May). Media depictions of health topics: Challenge and stigma formats.

Journal of Health Communication, 12(3), 233–249.

Smith, R. A., Downs, E., & Witte, K. (2007, June). Drama theory and entertainment education: Exploring the effects of a radio drama on behavioral intentions to limit HIV transmission in Ethiopia. *Communication Monographs, 74*(2), 133–153.

Smith, R. C., & Hoppe, R. B. (1991). The patient's story: Integrating the patient- and physician-centered approaches to interviewing. *Annals of Internal Medicine, 115,* 460–477.

Smith, S. L., Nathanson, A. I., & Wilson, B. J. (2002). Prime-time television: Assessing violence during the most popular viewing hours. *Journal of Communication, 52*(1), 84–111.

Smith, S. W., Kopfman, J. E., Lindsey, L. L. M., Yoo, J., & Morrison, K. (2004). Encouraging family discussion on the decision to donate organs: The role of the willingness to communicate scale. *Health Communication, 16*(3), 333–346.

Smith-du Pré, A., & Beck, C. S. (1996). Enabling patients and physicians to pursue multiple goals in health care encounters: A case study. *Health Communication, 8,* 73–90.

Smith-McLallen, A., Fishbein, M., & Hornik, R. C. (2011). Psychosocial determinants of cancer-related information seeking among cancer patients. *Journal of Health Communication, 16,* 212–225.

Snyder, L. B., & Rouse, R. A. (1995). The media can have more than an impersonal impact: The case of AIDS risk perceptions and behavior. *Health Communication, 7,* 125–145.

Sood, S., Shefner-Rogers, C. L., & Sengupta, M. (2006). The impact of a mass media campaign on HIV/AIDS knowledge and behavior change in North India: Results from a longitudinal study. *Asian Journal of Communication, 16*(3), 231–250.

Sopory, P. (2005). Metaphor in formative evaluation and message design: An application to relationship and alcohol use. *Health Communication, 17*(2), 149–172.

Soule, K. P, & Roloff, M. E. (2000). Help between persons with and without disabilities from a resource theory perspective. In D. O. Braithwaite & T. L. Thompson (Eds.), *Handbook of communication and people with disabilities: Research and*

applications (pp. 67–83). Mahwah, NJ: Lawrence Erlbaum.

South, D. (1997). All I really need to know about medicine I learned from my patients. *Patient Care, 31,* 238–240.

Sparks, L., Villagran, M. M., Parker-Raley, J., & Cunningham, C. B. (2007). A patient-centered approach to breaking bad news: Communication guidelines for health care providers. *Journal of Applied Communication, 35*(2), 177–196.

Spector, R., & McCarthy, P. (2005). *The Nordstrom way to costumer service excellence: A handbook for implementing great service in your organization.* Hoboken, NJ: John Wiley & Sons.

State Medicaid fact sheets. (2012). Menlo Park, CA: Henry J. Kaiser Family Foundation. Retrieved from http://www.statehealthfacts.org/medicaid.jsp

State scorecard data tables. (2007, June). Supplement to *Aiming Higher*: Results from a state scorecard on health system performance. New York: Commonwealth Fund. Retrieved from /www.commonwealthfund.org/usr_doc/State_data_tables.pdf?section=4039

Steinberg, L., & Monahan, K. C. (2010). Adolescents' exposure to sexy media does not hasten the initiation of sexual intercourse. *Developmental Psychology, 47,* 562–576.

Stephenson, M. T., Morgan, S. E., Roberts-Perez, S. D., Harrison, T., Afifi, W., & Long, S. D. (2008). The role of religiosity, religious norms, subjective norms, and bodily integrity in signing an organ donor card. *Health Communication, 23*(5), 436–447.

Stephenson, M. T., Quick, B. L., Atkinson, J., & Tschida, D. A. (2005). Authoritative parenting and drug-prevention practices: Implications for antidrug ads for parents. *Health Communication, 17*(3), 301–321.

Stewart, L. P., Lederman, L. C., Golubow, M., Cattafesta, J. L., Godhart, F. W., Powell, R. L., & Laitman, L. (2002, Winter). Applying communication theories to prevent dangerous drinking among college students: The RU SURE campaign. *Communication Studies, 53*(4), 381–399.

Stivers, T. (2002). Presenting the problem in pediatric encounters:

"symptoms only" versus "candidate diagnosis" presentations. *Health Communication, 14*(3), 299–338.

Stone, A. (2011, August 31). 10 years after 9/11: How far did $635 billion spent on homeland security go? *Emergency Management* online. Author: Folsom, CA. Retrieved from http://www.emergencymgmt.com/safety/10-Years-After-911-Homeland-Security-Funding.html

Stratton, T. D., Saunders, J. A., & Elam, C. L. (2008). Changes in medical students' emotional intelligence: an exploratory study. *Teaching and Learning in Medicine, 20*(3), 279–284.

Street, R. L., Jr., Gordon, H. S., Ward, M. M., Krupat, E., & Kravitz, R. L. (2005). Patient participation in medical consultations: Why some patients are more involved than others. *Medical Care, 43*(10), 960–969.

Street, R. L., Jr., & Millay, B. (2001). Analyzing patient participation in medical encounters. *Health Communication, 13*(1), 61–73.

Street, R. L., Jr., & Rimal, R. N. (1997). Health promotion and interactive technology: A conceptual foundation. In R. L. Street Jr., W. R. Gold, & T. Manning (Eds.), *Health promotion and interactive technology: Theoretical applications and future directions* (pp. 1–18). Mahwah, NJ: Lawrence Erlbaum.

Stretcher, V. J., & Rosenstock, I. M. (1997). The health belief model. In K. Glanz, F. M. Lewis, & B. K. Rimer (Eds.), *Health behavior and health education* (pp. 41–59). San Francisco: Jossey-Bass.

Struggling in silence: Physician depression and suicide. (nd). Website. Retrieved November 8, 2008, from www.doctorswithdepression.org/

Studer, Q. (2003). *Hardwiring excellence: Purpose, worthwhile work, making a difference.* Gulf Breeze, FL: Fire Starter.

Study finds television stations donate an average of 17 seconds an hour to public service advertising. (2008, January). Henry J. Kaiser Family Foundation. Retrieved from http://www.kff.org/entmedia/entmedia012408pkg.cfm

Substance Abuse & Mental Health Services Administration (SAMSHA). (2005, July/August). SAMSHA honors film, TV, radio portrayals of mental illness. Washington, DC:

Author. Retrieved from http://www.samhsa.gov/SAMHSA_NEWS/VolumeXIII_4/article8.htm

Suchman, A. L., Markakis, K., Beckman, H. B., & Frankel, R. (1997). A model of empathic communication in the medical interview. *Journal of the American Medical Association, 277,* 678–683.

Sudore, R. L., Schillinger, D., Knight, S. J., & Fried, T. R. (2010). Uncertainty about advance care planning treatment preferences among diverse older adults. *Journal of Health Communication, 15,* 159–171.

Sugai, W. J. (2008, June 20). Taking a hard line with compliant patients. Talk back. Letter to the editor. *Medical Economics, 85*(12), 14.

Sutton, R. L. (2007). *The no asshole rule: Building a civilized workplace and surviving one that isn't.* New York: Warner Business.

Swain, K. A. (2007, Summer). Outrage factors and explanations in news coverage of the anthrax attacks. *Journalism and Mass Communication Quarterly, 84*(2), 335–352.

Swedish, J. (April 28, 2008). Our carpe diem moment; execs, clinicians must help policymakers find the way to universal coverage (Opinions Commentary). *Modern Healthcare, 38*(17), 22.

Sweet, V. (2012). *God's hotel: A doctor, a hospital, and a pilgrimage to the heart of medicine.* New York: Riverhead Books, Penguin.

Swiderski, R. M. (1976). The idiom of diagnosis. *Communication Quarterly, 24,* 3–11.

Tai, Z., & Sun, T. (2007, December). Media dependencies in a changing media environment: The case of the 2003 SARS epidemic in China. *New Media & Society, 9*(6), 987–1009.

Tan, G., Jensen, M. P., Thornby, J. I., & Anderson, K. O. (2006). Are patient ratings of chronic pain services related to treatment outcome? *Journal of Rehabilitation Research and Development, 43*(4), 451–460.

Tardy, C. H. (1994). Counteracting task-induced stress: Studies of instrumental and emotional support in problem-solving contexts. In B. R. Burleson, T. L. Albrecht, & I. G. Sarason (Eds.), *Communication of social support: Messages, interactions, relationships, and community* (pp. 71–87). Thousand Oaks, CA: Sage.

Tarrant, C., Windridge, K., Boulton, J., Baker, R., & Freeman, G. (2003, June 14). How important is personal care in general practice? *British Medical Journal (Clinical Research Edition), 326,* 1310.

Taubes, G. (1998). Telling time by the second hand. *Technology Review, 101,* 76–78.

Taylor, D. (1999). *The writer's guide to everyday life in Colonial America: From 1607 to 1783.* Cincinnati, OH: Writer's Digest Books.

Tellis-Nayak, V. (2005). Who will care for the caregivers? *Health Progress, 86*(6), 37–43.

10 facts on obesity. (2012, May). Geneva, Switzerland: World Health Organization. Retrieved from http://www.who.int/features/factfiles/obesity/en/Terrell, G. E. (2007, September/October). "Can't get no (physician) satisfaction?" *Physician Executive,* pp. 12–15.

Terry, K. (2007, August 3). Doctors are now getting more tech savvy: While EHRs remain uncommon, physicians are taking advantage of many new devices and media, our survey shows. *Medical Economics, 84*(15), 52–55.

Thomas, E. J., Sexton, J. B., & Helmreich, R. L. (2003). Discrepant attitudes about teamwork among critical care nurses and physicians. *Critical Care Medicine, 31*(3), 956–959.

Thomas, K. (2012, March 6). AARP study says price of popular drugs rose 26%. *The New York Times* reprints online, np. Retrieved from http://www.nytimes.com/2012/03/07/business/aarp-study-says-price-of-popular-drugs-rose-26.html

Thompson, T. L. (1984). The invisible helping hand: The role of communication in the health and social service professions. *Communication Quarterly, 32,* 148–161.

Thompson, T. L. (1990). Patient health care: Issues in interpersonal communication in the health and social service professions. In E. B. Ray & L. Donohew (Eds.), *Communication and health: Systems and applications* (pp. 27–50). Hillsdale, NJ: Lawrence Erlbaum.

Thompson, T. L. (2011). Hope and the act of informed dialogue: A delicate balance at the end of life. *Journal of Language and Social Psychology, 30,* 177–192.

Thompson, T. L., Dorsey, A. M., Miller, K. I., & Parrott, R. (Eds.) (2003). *The handbook of health communication.* Mahwah, NJ: Lawrence Erlbaum.

Thompson, T. L., & Gillotti, C. (2005). Staying out of the line of fire: A medical student learns about bad news delivery. In E. B. Ray (Ed.), *Health communication in practice: A case study approach* (pp. 11–25). Mahwah, NJ: Lawrence Erlbaum.

Thompson, T. L., Parrott, R., & Nussbaum, J. F. (2011). *The Routledge handbook of health communication.* New York: Taylor & Francis.

Thomsen, T., Rydahl-Hansen, S., & Wagner, L. (2010). A review of potential factors relevant to coping in patients with advanced cancer. *Journal of Clinical Nursing, 19,* 3410–3426. doi:10.1111/j.1365-2702.2009.03154.x

Thomtén, J., Soares, J., & Sundin, Ö. (2011). The role of psychosocial factors in the course of pain: A 1-year follow-up study among women living in Sweden. *Archives of Women's Mental Health, 14,* 493–503. doi:10.1007/s00737-011-0244-0

Thoreau, E. (2006). Ouch!: An examination of the self-representation of disabled people on the Internet. *Journal of Computer-Mediated Communication, 11,* 442–468.

Thorwald, J. (1962). *Science and secrets of early medicine* (translated by R. Winston & C. Winston). New York: Harcourt, Brace & World.

Threat of bioterrorism: A frustrating and persistent security risk. (2008, August 7). *Government Security,* Online Exclusive, np. Retrieved from General OneFile via Gale.

Tichenor, P. J., Donohue, G. A., & Olien, C. N. (1970). Mass media flow and differential growth in knowledge. *Public Opinion Quarterly, 34,* 159–170.

Todd, A. D. (1984). The prescription of contraception: Negotiations between doctors and patients. *Discourse Processes, 7,* 171–200.

Todd, A. D. (1989). *Intimate adversaries: Cultural conflict between doctors and women patients.* Philadelphia: University of Philadelphia Press.

Tough, E. A., & White, A. R. (2011). Effectiveness of acupuncture/dry needling for myofascial trigger point pain. *Physical Therapy Reviews, 16,* 147–154.

Tourangeau, A. E., & Cranley, L. A. (2005). Nurse intention to remain employed: Understanding and strengthening determinants. *Journal of Advanced Nursing, 55*(4), 497–509.

Tovey, P., & Broom, A. (2007). Oncologists' and specialist cancer nurses' approaches to complementary and alternative medicine and their impact on patient action. *Social Science & Medicine, 64,* 2550–2564.

Transue, E. R. (2004). *On call: A doctor's days and nights in residency.* New York: St. Martin's Griffin.

Troth, A., & Peterson, C. C. (2000). Factors predicting safe-sex talk and condom use in early sexual relationships. *Health Communication, 12*(2), 195–218.

Tse, H. (1999). Test your Asian IQ. *Asian-Nation: The landscape of Asian America.* Retrieved from http://www.asian-nation.org/asian-iq-quiz.shtml

Trujillo, J. M., & Hardy, Y. (2009). A nutrition journal and diabetes shopping experience to improve pharmacy students' empathy and cultural competence. *American Journal of Pharmaceutical Education, 73*(2), 1–10.

Tu, H. T. (2005, June). Medicare seniors much less willing to limit physician-hospital choice for lower costs. Center for Studying Health System Change, Issue Brief No. 96, np. Retrieved from www.hschange.org/CONTENT/744

Tucker, C. M., Herman, K. C., Pedersen, T. R., Higley, B., Montrichard, M., & Ivery, P. (2003). Cultural sensitivity in physician–patient relationships: Perspectives of an ethnically diverse sample of low-income primary care patients. *Medical Care, 41*(7), 859–870.

Tuffrey-Wijne, I., Hollins, S., & Curfs, L. (2005). Supporting patients who have intellectual disabilities: A survey investigating staff training needs. *International Journal of Palliative Nursing, 11*(4), 182–188.

Tustin, N. (2010). The role of patient satisfaction in online health information seeking. *Journal of Health Communication, 15,* 3–17.

TV program description. (2004). *The most dangerous woman in America* [video documentary], Nancy Porter (Writer/Director). NOVA in association with WGBH/Boston. Retrieved from http://www.pbs.org/wgbh/nova/typhoid/about.html

Twaddle, A. C., & Hessler, R. M. (1987). *A sociology of health* (2nd ed.). New York: Macmillan.

Uba, L. (1992). Cultural barriers to health care for Southeast Asian refugees. *Public Health Reports, 107,* 544–548.

Ulmer, R. R., Seeger, M. W., & Sellnow, T. L. (2007, June). Post-crisis communication and renewal: Expanding the parameters of post-crisis discourse. *Public Relations Review, 33*(2), 130–134.

Ulrich, C. M., Soeken, K. L., & Miller, N. (2003). Ethical conflict associated with managed care: Views of nurse practitioners. *Nursing Research, 52*(3), 168–175.

The ultimate family tree. (2005, May). *National Geographic, 207*(5), np.

UNAIDS: Joint United Nations Programme on HIV/AIDS. (2008, August). Global facts and figures. Retrieved from http://data.unaids.org:80/pub/GlobalReport/2008/20080715_fs_global_en.pdf

Underage drinking. (2012). National Institute on Alcohol Abuse and Alcoholism. Retrieved from http://pubs.niaaa.nih.gov/publications/UnderageDrinking/Underage_Fact.pdf

UNESCO (United Nations Educational, Scientific, and Cultural Organization) Institute for Statistics. (2008). According to the most recent UIS data, there are an estimated 774 million illiterate adults in the world, about 64% of whom are women. Montreal: Author. Retrieved from http://www.uis.unesco.org/ev.php?URL_ID=6401&URL_DO=DO_TOPIC&URL_SECTION=201

Uninsured in America. Key facts. (2000, March). Menlo Park, CA: Kaiser Commission on Medicaid and the Uninsured. Retrieved from http://www.pbs.org/newshour/health/uninsured/kaiserstudy/kaiser_key_facts.pdf

Unsworth, C. (1996). Team decision-making in rehabilitation. *American Journal of Physical Medicine & Rehabilitation, 75,* 483–486.

Urba, S. (1998). Sometimes the best thing I do is listen. *Medical Economics, 75*(9), 167–170.

U.S. Bureau of Labor Statistics. (2012a, February 1). Employment projections 2010–2020. Author: Washington, D.C. Retrieved from http://bls.gov/news.release/ecopro.nr0.htm

U.S. Bureau of Labor Statistics. (2012b). Occupational outlook handbook. Author: Washington, DC. Retrieved from http://www.bls.gov/ooh/Healthcare/Registered-nurses.htm

U.S. Bureau of Labor Statistics. (2012c, February 1). Table 3. The 20 industries with the largest projected wage and salary employment growth, 2010–2020. Washington, DC: Author. Retrieved from http://bls.gov/news.release/ecopro.t03.htm

U.S. Census Bureau. (2007). Income, poverty, and health insurance coverage in the United States: 2006. Washington, DC: Author. Retrieved from www.census.gov/prod/2007pubs/p60-233.pdf

U.S. Census Bureau News. (2008, August 14). An older and more diverse nation by midcentury. Washington, DC: Author. Retrieved from http://www.census.gov/Press-Release/www/releases/archives/population/012496.html

U.S. Census Bureau. (2009, June 23). Census Bureau reports world's older population projected to triple by 2050. Washington, DC: Author. Retrieved from http://www.census.gov/newsroom/releases/archives/international_population/cb09-97.html

U.S. Census Bureau. (2010a). Health insurance. Highlights: 2010. Washington, DC: Author. Retrieved from http://www.census.gov/hhes/www/hlthins/data/incpovhlth/2010/highlights.html

U.S. Census Bureau. (2010b, May). The next four decades. Washington, DC: Author. Retrieved from http://www.census.gov/prod/2010pubs/p25-1138.pdf

U.S. Census Bureau. (2011a, November). The older population: 2010. Washington, DC: Author. Retrieved from http://www.census.gov/prod/cen2010/briefs/c2010br-09.pdf

U.S. Census Bureau. (2011b). State and county quick facts. Washington, DC: Author. Retrieved from http://quickfacts.census.gov/qfd/states/00000.html

U.S. Census Bureau. (2012). Table 104. Expectations of life at birth, 1970 to 2008, and projections, 2010 to 2020. Washington, DC: Author. Retrieved from http://www.census.gov/compendia/statab/2012/tables/12s0104.pdf

U.S. Department of Health and Human Services (DHHS), Health Resources and Services Administration. (2006a). The registered nurse population: Findings from the 2004 national sample survey of registered nurses. Washington, DC: Author. Retrieved from http://bhpr.hrsa.gov/healthworkforce/rnsurvey04/2.htm

U.S. Department of Health and Human Services (DHHS). (2006b, October). Physician supply and demand: Projections to 2020. Washington, DC: Author. Retrieved from http://www.achi.net/HCR%20Docs/2011HCRWorkforceResources/Physician%20Supply%2

U.S. Department of Health and Human Services (DHHS), Office of the Surgeon General. (2007). The surgeon general's call to action to prevent and reduce underage drinking. Washington, DC: U.S. Department of Health and Human Services. Retrieved from http://www.surgeongeneral.gov/topics/underagedrinking/calltoaction.pdf

U.S. Department of Labor. (2012, March 29). Occupational outlook handbook, 2012–13 edition. Medical and health services managers. Washington, DC: Author. Retrieved from http://www.bls.gov/ooh/management/medical-and-health-services-managers.htm

Valente, T. W., Paredes, P., & Poppe, P. R. (1998). Matching the message to the process: The relative ordering of knowledge, attitudes, and practices in behavior change research. *Human Communication Research, 24*, 366–385.

Van Den Bos, J., Rustagi, K., Gray, T., Halford, M., Ziemkiewicz, E., & Shreve, J. (2011). The $17.1 billion problem: The annual cost of measurable medical errors. *Health Affairs, 30*, 596–603.

Vanden Heuvel, L., & Robinson, C. (2005, Summer). How many causes should you pursue? *Journal for Quality and Participation, 28*(2), 22–23.

Vangeest, J. B., Welch, V. L., & Weiner, S. J. (2010). Patients' perceptions of screening for health literacy: Reactions to the newest vital sign. *Journal of Health Communication, 15*, 402–412.

van Zanten, M., Boulet, J. R., & McKinley, D. (2007). Using standardized patients to assess the interpersonal skills of physicians: Six years' experience with a high-stakes certification examination. *Health Communication, 22*(3), 195–205.

Vardeman, J. E., & Aldoory, L. (2008). A qualitative study of how women make meaning of contradictory media messages about the risks of eating fish. *Health Communication, 23*(3), 282–291.

Vaughan, C. (2012, March 8). 4 social media strategies to build patient loyalty. *HealthLeaders Media.* Retrieved from http://www.healthleadersmedia.com/page-1/MAR-277456/4-Social-Media-Strategies-to-Build-Patient-Loyalty

Veatch, R. M. (1983). The physician as stranger: The ethics of the anonymous patient–physician relationship. In E. E Shelp (Ed.), *The clinical encounter: The moral fabric of the patient–physician relationship* (pp. 187–207). Dordrecht, The Netherlands: D. Reidel.

Veatch, R. M. (1991). *The patient–physician relation: The patient as partner, Part 2.* Bloomington: Indiana University Press.

Vernon, J. A., Trujillo, A., Rosenbaum, S., & DeBuono, B. (2007). Low health literacy: Implications of national health policy. Retrieved from http://www.gwumc.edu/sphhs/departments/healthpolicy/chsrp/downloads/LowHealthLiteracyReport10_4_07.pdf

Vest, J. (1997, July 21). Joe Camel walks his last mile. *U.S. News & World Report, 123*, 56.

Vickers C., & Goble, R. (2011). Well, now, okey dokey: English discourse markers in Spanish-language medical consultations. *The Canadian Modern Language Review, 67*, 536–567.

Viva Viagra. (2008). TV spots. Pfizer. Retrieved from http://www.viagra.com/content/viva-viagra-music.jsp?setShowOn=../content/viva-viagra.jsp&setShowHighlightOn=../content/viva-viagra-music.jsp

Volpintesta, E. J., & Kanterman, L. H. (2008, March 21). Hospitalists: Pro and con. Letter to the editor. *Medical Economics, 85*(6), 10.

Waalen, J. (1997). Women in medicine: Bringing gender issues to the fore.

Journal of the American Medical Association, 277, 1404–1405.

Wahl, O. F., & Lefkowits, J. Y. (1989). Impact of a television film on attitude toward mental illness. *American Journal of Community Psychology, 17,* 521–528.

Waitzkin, H. (1991). *The politics of medical encounters: How patients and doctors deal with social problems.* New Haven, CT: Yale University Press.

Wakeman, S. (2007, April 24). What's the difference between marketing and public relations? Blog: SimonWakeman public sector communications and marketing. Retrieved from http://www.simonwakeman.com/2007/04/24/whats-the-difference-between-marketing-and-public-relations/

Walker, K. L., Arnold, C. L., Miller-Day, M., & Webb, L. M. (2002). Investigating the physician–patient relationship: Examining emerging themes. *Health Communication, 14*(1), 45–68.

Waller, M, L. A., Carlin, B. P., Xia, H., & Gelfand, A. E. (1997, June). Hierarchical spatio-temporal mapping of disease rates. *Journal of the American Statistical Association, 92*(438), 607–617.

Walsh, K., Jordan, Z., & Apolloni, L. (2009). The problematic art of conversation: Communication and health practice evolution. *Practice Development in Health Care, 8,* 166–179.

Walters, T. N., Walters, L. M. Kern-Foxworth, M., & Priest, S. H. (1997). The picture of health? Message standardization and recall of televised AIDS public service announcements. *Public Relations Review, 23,* 143–159.

Wang, X. (2011). The role of anticipated guilt in intentions to register as organ donors and to discuss organ donation with family. *Health Communication, 26,* 683–690. doi:10.1080/10410236.2011.563350

Wang, X., & Arpan, L. M. (2008, January/March). Effects of race and ethnic identity on audience evaluation of HIV public service announcements. *Howard Journal of Communications, 19*(1), 44–63.

Wang, Z., & Gantz, W. (2010). Health content in local television news: A current appraisal. *Health Communication, 25,* 230–237. doi:10.1080/10410231003698903

Wanzer, M. B., Booth-Butterfield, M., & Gruber, K. (2004). Perceptions of health care providers' communication: Relationships between patient-centered communication and satisfaction. *Health Communication, 16*(3), 363–384.

Wanzer, M. B., Sparks, L., & Frymier, A. B. (2009). Humorous communication within the lives of older adults: The relationships among humor, coping efficacy, age, and life satisfaction, *Health Communication, 24,* 128–136.

Wanzer, M. B., Wojtaszczyk, A. M., Schimert, J., Missert, L., Baker, S., Baker, R., & Dunkle, B. (2010). Enhancing the 'informed' in informed consent: A pilot test of a multimedia presentation. *Health Communication, 25,* 365–374.

Wartella, E. A. (1996). The context of television violence. Paper presented at the annual meeting of the Speech Communication Association in San Antonio.

Wartik, N. (1996). Learning to mourn. *American Health, 15,* 76–81.

Waseem, M., & Ryan, M. (2005). "Doctor" or "doctora": Do patients really care? *Pediatric Emergency Care, 21*(8), 515–517.

Watermeyer, J. (2011). "She will hear me": How a flexible interpreting style enables patients to manage the inclusion of interpreters in mediated pharmacy interactions. *Health Communication, 26,* 71–81.

Watzlawick, P., Beavin, J. H., & Jackson, D. D. (1967). *Pragmatics of human communication.* New York: W. W. Norton.

Waymer, D., & Heath, R. L. (2007, February). Emergent agents: The forgotten publics in crisis communication and issues management research. *Journal of Applied Communication Research, 35*(1), 88–108.

Webb, T., Jenkins, L., Browne, N., Abdelmonen, A. A., & Kraus, J. (2007). Violent entertainment pitched to adolescents: An analysis of PG-13 films. *Pediatrics, 119*(6), e1219–e1229.

Wechsler, H., Nelson, T. F., Lee, J. E., Seibring, M., Lewis, C., & Keeling, R. P. (2003, July). Perception and reality: A national evaluation of social norms marketing interventions to reduce college students' heavy alcohol use. *Journal of Studies on Alcohol, 64*(4), 484–494.

Wechsler, H., & Wernick, S. M. (1992). A social marketing campaign to promote low-fat milk consumption in an inner-city Latino community. *Public Health Reports, 107,* 202–207.

Weech-Maldonado, R., Morales, L. S., Elliott, M., Spritzer, K., Marshall, G., & Hays, R. D. (2003). Race/ethnicity, language, and patients' assessments of care in Medicaid managed care. *Health Services Research, 38*(3), 789–808.

Weinberg, D. (2011, May 2). U.S. hospital turns to Toyota for management inspiration. Voice of America. Retrieved from http://www.voanews.com/content/us-hospital-turns-to-toyota-for-management-inspiration--121165799/163553.html

Weinrich, S., Vijayakumar, S., Powell, I. J., Priest, J., Hamner, C. A., McCloud, L., & Pettaway, C. (2007). Knowledge of hereditary prostate cancer among high-risk African American men. *Oncology Nursing Forum, 34*(4), 854–860.

Weiss, G. G. (2008, June 20). The new doctor–patient paradigm: How the shift from the "physician as wise parent" model to one of more shared responsibility is playing out in the exam room. *Medical Economics, 85*(12), 48–52.

Welch, G., Rose, G., & Ernst, D. (2006). Motivational interviewing and diabetes: What is used, and does it work? *Diabetes Spectrum, 19*(1), 5–11.

Wells, D. L. (2009). The effects of animals on human health and well-being. *Journal of Social Issues, 65,* 1540–4560.

Weston, W. W., & Lipkin, M., Jr. (1989). Doctors learning communication skills: Developmental issues. In M. Stewart & D. Roter (Eds.), *Communicating with medical patients. Vol. 9. Interpersonal communication* (pp. 43–57). Newbury Park, CA: Sage.

Whaley, B. B. (1999). Explaining illness to children: Advancing theory and research by determining message content. *Health Communication, 11,* 185–193.

Whaley, B. B. (2000). Explaining illness to children: Theory, strategies, and future inquiry. In B. B. Whaley (Ed.), *Explaining Illness* (pp. 195–207). Mahwah, NJ: Lawrence Erlbaum.

Whaley, B. B., & Edgar, T. (2008). Explaining illness to children. In

K. B. Wright & S. D. Moore (Eds.), *Applied health communication* (pp. 145–158). Cresskill, NJ: Hampton Press.

What's right in health care: 365 stories of purpose, worthwhile work, and making a difference. (2007). Compiled by Studer Group. Gulf Breeze, FL: Fire Starter.

White, A., Philogene, G., Fine, L., & Sinha, S. (2009). Social support and self-reported health status of older adults in the United States. *American Journal of Public Health, 99*(10), 1872–1878.

White, A. D. (1925). *A history of the warfare of science with theology in Christendom* (vol. 2). New York: D. Appleton (originally published in 1896).

Whitla, D. K. Orfield, G., Silen, W., Teperow, C., Howard, C., & Reede, J. (2003). Educational benefits of diversity in medical school: A survey of students. *Academic Medicine, 78*(5), 460–466.

Whitten, P., Sypher, B. D., & Patterson, J. D., III. (2000). Transcending the technology of telemedicine: An analysis of telemedicine in North Carolina. *Health Communication, 12*(2), 109–135.

Wicks, R. J. (2008). *The resilient clinician.* Oxford: Oxford University Press.

Wikler, D. (1987). Who should be blamed for being sick? *Health Education Quarterly, 14,* 11–25.

Wilkinson, S., Perry, R., Blanchard, K., & Linsell, L. (2008). Effectiveness of a three-day communication skills course in changing nurses' communication skills with cancer/palliative care patients: A randomized controlled trial. *Palliative Medicine, 22*(4), 365–375.

Willems, S. J., Swinnen, W., & De Maeseneer, J. M. (2005). The GP's perception of poverty: A qualitative study. *Family Practice, 22*(2), 177–183.

Williams, J. E., & Flora, J. A. (1995). Health behavior segmentation and campaign planning to reduce cardiovascular disease risk among Hispanics. *Health Education Quarterly, 22,* 33–48.

Willies-Jacobo, L. (2007, August). Susto: Acknowledging patient's beliefs about illness. *Virtual Mentor, 9*(8), 532–536.

Willing, R. (1999, April 14). Kevorkian sentenced to 10–25 years. *USA Today,* p. 1A.

Wills, T. A. (1985). Supportive functions of interpersonal relationships. In S. Cohen & S. L. Syme (Eds.), *Social support and health* (pp. 61–82). Orlando, FL: Academic Press.

Willwerth, J. (1993, February 15). It hurts like crazy. *Time, 141,* 53.

Wilson, K. (2003). Therapeutic landscapes and the First Nations people: An exploration of culture, health and place. *Health & Place, 9*(2), 83–93.

Wiltshire, J., Cronin, K., Sarto, G. E., & Brown, R. (2006). Self-advocacy during the medical encounter: Use of health information and racial/ethnic differences. *Medical Care, 44*(2), 100–109.

Wimmer, R. D., & Dominick, J. R. (1997). *Mass communication research* (5th ed.). Belmont, CA: Wadsworth.

Winslow, C.-E. A. (1923). *The evolution and significance of the modern public health campaign.* New Haven, CT: Yale University Press.

Wise, K. (2007). The organization and implementation of relationship management. *Health Marketing Quarterly, 24*(3–4), 151–166.

Witte, K. (1997). Preventing teen pregnancy through persuasive communications: Realities, myths, and hard-fact truths. *Journal of Community Health, 22,* 137–154.

Witte, K. (2008). Putting the fear back into fear appeals: The extended parallel process model. In L. C. Lederman (Ed.), *Beyond these walls: Readings in health communication* (pp. 273–291). New York: Oxford University Press.

Wolf, M. S., Williams, M. V., Parker, R. M., Parikh, N. S., Nowlan, A. W., & Baker, D. W. (2007). Patients' shame and attitudes toward discussing the results of literacy screening. *Journal of Health Communication, 12*(8), 721–732.

Women most active online audience for health information. (2003). *Datamonitor, M2Presswire.* Retrieved through LexisNexis.

Wood, J. (1999). *Gendered lives* (3rd ed.). Belmont, CA: Wadsworth.

Woodbury, B. (2007, August 29). Health savings accounts and high-deductible health plans. The Bell Policy Center, Denver. Retrieved from www.thebell.org/PUBS/IssBrf/2007/08-HSAs.php

Work matters. Bob Sutton blog. (nd). Retrieved from http://bobsutton.typepad.com/

World-class health care, step by step: Extracts from Health Minister Khaw Boon Wan's replies to MPs on a range of issues, including elderly care and longevity. (2008, March 4). *Straits Times* (Singapore), np. Retrieved through LexisNexis Academic Universe.

World Health Organization (WHO). (1948). Preamble to the Constitution of the World Health Organization. Official records of the World Health Organization, no. 2, p. 100. Retrieved from www.who.int/about/definition/en

World Health Organization (WHO). (2003). Update 83—one hundred days into the outbreak. Retrieved from www.whoi.int/csr/don/2003_16_18/en

World Health Organization. (2003, March 16). Epidemic and pandemic alert and response (EPR). Severe acute respiratory syndrome (SARS). Multi-country Outbreak. Update. Geneva, Switzerland: Author. Retrieved from http://www.who.int/csr/don/2003_03_16/en/index.html

World Health Organization. (2003, June 18). Epidemic and pandemic alert and response (EPR). Update 83. One hundred days into the outbreak. Geneva, Switzerland: Author. Retrieved from http://www.who.int/csr/don/2003_06_18/en/index.html

World Health Organization. (2007a). Fact sheet. The top ten causes of death. Geneva, Switzerland: Author. Retrieved from http://www.who.int/mediacentre/factsheets/fs310.pdf

World Health Organization. (2007b). Why is smoking an issue for nonsmokers? Geneva, Switzerland: Author. Retrieved from http://www.who.int/features/qa/60/en/index.html

World Health Organization. (2007c, October). Interim protocol: Rapid operations to contain the initial emergence of pandemic influenza. Geneva, Switzerland: Author. Retrieved from http://www.who.int/csr/disease/avian_influenza/guidelines/RapidContProtOct15.pdf

World Health Organization. (2007d, October). Options for the use of human H5N1 influenza vaccines and the WHO H5N1 vaccine stockpile. Geneva, Switzerland: Author. Retrieved from http://www.who.int/csr/resources/publications/WHO_HSE_EPR_GIP_2008_1d.pdf

World Health Organization. (2008a). Traditional medicine. Geneva, Switzerland: Author. Retrieved from http://www.who.int/mediacentre/factsheets/fs134/en/

World Health Organization (WHO). (2008b). World health statistics. Part 2. Global health indicators. Global health indicators. Geneva, Switzerland: Author. Retrieved from www.who.int/whosis/whostat/EN_WHS08_Table4_HSR.pdf

World Health Organization. (2010a). Telemedicine: Opportunities and developments in member states. *Global Observatory for eHealth series. Volume 2.* Geneva, Switzerland: Author. Retrieved from http://www.who.int/goe/publications/ehealth_series_vol3/en/index.html

World Health Organization. (2010b). The world health report. Executive summary. Geneva, Switzerland: Author. Retrieved from http://www.who.int/whr/2010/10_summary_en.pdf

World Health Organization. (2011a). Compendium of new and emerging health technologies. Geneva, Switzerland: Author. Retrieved from http://www.who.int/goe/call2012/en/index.html

World Health Organization. (2011b). New horizons for health through mobile technologies. Based on the findings of the second global survey on eHealth. Global Observatory for eHealth series. Volume 3. Geneva, Switzerland: Author. Retrieved at http://www.who.int/goe/publications/ehealth_series_vol3/en/index.html

World Health Organization. (2012, May). Tobacco. Geneva, Switzerland: Author. Retrieved from http://www.who.int/mediacentre/factsheets/fs339/en/index.html

World Health Organization. (2012). World health statistics 2012. World health indicators. Geneva, Switzerland: Author. Retrieved from http://www.who.int/health-info/EN_WHS2012_Part3.pdf

World Health Report, 2000. Health systems: Improving performance. (2000). Geneva, Switzerland: World Health Organization. Retrieved from http://www.who.int/whr/2000/en/

World Health Report, 2007. (2007). A safer future: Global public health security in the 21st century. Geneva, Switzerland: World Health Organization. Retrieved from http://www.who.int/whr/2007/en/index.html

World Organisation for Animal Health (OIE). (2008, September 1). Annual incidence rate of bovine spongiform encephalopathy (BSE) in OIE member countries that have reported cases, excluding the United Kingdom. Paris, France: Author. Retrieved from http://www.oie.int/eng/info/en_esbincidence.htm

Wright, K. (2002). Social support within an on-line cancer community: An assessment of emotional support, perceptions of advantages and disadvantages, and motives for using the community from a communication perspective. *Journal of Applied Communication Research, 31*(3), 195–209.

Wright, K. B. (2008). New technologies and health communication. In K. B. Wright & S. D. Moore (Eds.), *Applied health communication* (pp. 63–84). Cresskill, NJ: Hampton Press.

Wright, K. B., Banas, J. A., Bessarabova, E., & Bernard, D. R. (2010). A communication competence approach to examining health care social support, stress, and job burnout. *Health Communication, 25*, 375–382.

www.thepleasureproject.org. (2004). Oxford: Pleasure Project.

Wynia, M. K., VanGeest, J. B., Cummins, D. S., & Wilson, I. B. (2003). Do physicians not offer useful services because of coverage restrictions? *Health Affairs, 22*(4), 190–197.

Yamada, T. (2008, March 27). In search of new ideas for global health. *New England Journal of Medicine, 358*(13), 1324–1325.

Yamba, C. B. (1997). Cosmologists in turmoil: Witchfinding and AIDS in Chiawa, Zambia. *Africa, 22*(4), 190–197.

Yanovitzky, I. (2006, April/May). Sensation seeking and alcohol use by college students: Examining multiple pathways of effects. *Journal of Health Communication, 11*(3), 269–280.

Yanovitzky, I., Stewart, L. P., & Lederman, L. C. (2006). Social distance, perceived drinking by peers, and alcohol use by college students. *Health Communication, 19*(1), 1–10.

Yanovitzky, I., & Stryker, J. (2001, April 2). Mass media, social norms, and health promotion efforts: A longitudinal study of media effects on youth binge drinking. *Communication Research, 28*(2), 208–239.

Ye, J., Rust, G., Fry-Johnson, Y., & Strothers, H. (2010). E-mail in patient-provider communication: A systematic review. *Patient Education and Counseling, 80*, 266–273.

Yee, A. M., Puntillo, K., Miaskowski, C., & Neighbor, M. L. (2006). What patients with abdominal pain expect about pain relief in the emergency department. *Journal of Emergency Nursing, 32*(4), 281–287.

Yost, K. J., Webster, K., Baker, D. W., Jacobs, E. A., Anderson, A., & Hahn, E. A. (2010). Acceptability of the talking touchscreen for health literacy assessment. *Journal of Health Communication, 15*, 80–92. doi:10.1080/10810730.2010.500713

Young, A. (2004). *What patients taught me: A medical student's journey.* Seattle: Sasquatch Books.

Young, A., & Flower, L. (2002). Patients as partners, patients as problem-solvers. *Health Communication, 14*(1), 69–97.

Young, A. J., & Rodriguez, K. L. (2006). The role of narrative in discussing end-of-life care: Eliciting values and goals from text, context, and subtext. *Health Communication, 19*(1), 49–59.

Youth exposure to alcohol advertising on television. (2010, December 15). A study sponsored by Johns Hopkins University and the Center on Alcohol Marketing and Youth. Retrieved from http://www.camy.org/research/Youth_Exposure_to_Alcohol_Ads_on_TV_Growing_Faster_Than_Adults/_includes/CAMYReport2001_2009.pdf

Youth exposure to alcohol product advertising on local radio in 75 U.S. markets, 2009. (2011, September 13). A study sponsored by Johns Hopkins University and the Center on Alcohol Marketing and Youth. Retrieved from http://www.camy.org/research/Youth_Exposure_to_Alcohol_Advertising_on_Local_

Radio_2009/_includes/report .pdf

Zakrzewski, P. A., Ho, A. L., & Braga-Mele, R. (2008). Should ophthalmologists receive communication skills training in breaking bad news? *Canadian Journal of Ophthalmology, 43*(4), 419–424.

Zaner, R. M. (2009). Narrative and decision. *Journal of Applied Communication Research, 37,* 174–187.

Zhang, Z. –J. , Chen, H.-Y., Yip, K.-c., Ng, R., & Wong, V. T. (2010). The effectiveness and safety of acupuncture therapy in depressive disorders: Systematic review and meta-analysis. *Journal of Affective Disorders, 124,* 9–21. doi: 10.1016/j.jad.2009.07.005

Zillmann, D., & Vorderer, P. (Eds.) (2000). *Media entertainment: The psychology of its appeal.* Mahwah, NJ: Lawrence Erlbaum.

Zimmerman, F. J. (2008, June). Children's media use and sleep problems: Issues and unanswered questions. Prepaid for the Henry J. Kaiser Family Foundation. Retrieved from http://www.kff.org/entmedia/upload/7674.pdf

Zoller, H. M., & Dutta, M. J. (Eds.) (2008). *Emerging perspectives in health communication: Meaning, culture, and power.* New York: Routledge.

Zook, E. (1993). Diagnosis HIV/AIDS: Caregiver communication in the crisis of terminal illness. In E. B. Ray (Ed.), *Case studies in health communication* (pp. 113–128). Hillsdale, NJ: Lawrence Erlbaum.

Zook, R. (1997, April). Handling in appropriate sexual behavior with confidence: Here are nine tips for keeping the boundaries clear. *Nursing, 27,* 65.

Zoucha, R., & Broome, B. (2008, April). The significance of culture in nursing: Examples from the Mexican-American culture and knowing the unknown. *Urologic Nursing, 28*(2), 140–142.

Zuckerman, M. (1994). *Behavioral expressions and biosocial bases of sensation seeking.* Cambridge: Cambridge University Press.

Author Index

Subject Index